THE ART OF MUSIC LICENSING

THE ART OF MUSIC LICENSING

AL KOHN
BOB KOHN

 PRENTICE HALL LAW & BUSINESS

Permissions, Prentice Hall Law & Business
270 Sylvan Avenue
Englewood Cliffs, NJ 07632

Printed in the United States of America

Library of Congress Cataloging-in-Publication Data

Kohn, Al
    The art of music licensing / Al Kohn, Bob Kohn.
      p. cm.
    Includes index.
    ISBN 0-13-068792-8
    1. Copyright—Music—United States. 2. Copyright
licenses—United States. I. Kohn, Bob. II. Title.
KF3035.K64   1992
346.7304'82—dc20
[347.306482]   92-589
                                   CIP

ISBN: 0-13-0687928

What neat repast shall feast us, light and choice,
Of Attic taste, with wine, whence we may rise
To hear the lute well touched, or artful voice
Warble immortal notes and Tuscan air?
He who of those delights can judge, and spare
To interpose them oft, is not unwise.

— from a sonnet by John Milton (1608-1674)

FOREWORD

L ike a father talking to his son or daughter, in the telling of *The Art of Music Licensing*, Al unfolds an encyclopedia of experience and information, gently and gracefully sharing the wisdom and joy of an art and expertise of which, with all humility, he reveals himself to be a master.

The fascination, affection, and almost reverential respect that Al holds for the songwriters and artists that he represents is an essential guidepost for the reader. I would venture to say that Al's whole being, as it permeates *The Art of Music Licensing*, is as much a model and resource as the technical information and good advice that he shares. As with Al, there is a gentleness to the words of caution about pitfalls and shortsightedness, and because it is Al who advises, there is the implicit instruction that the pursuit of success in the practice of licensing need never be a cutthroat game.

To Al, successful negotiation and guidance of licensing comes from an understanding and respect for the real value of the creative work, the diligent study of the extremely complex issues, precedents and processes surrounding the field of licensing, and a sympathetic view of some of the fears and confusions of those who want to do the best for their clients' work (but are unsure as to how to proceed in the volatile and everchanging world of technology and labyrinthine law); but above all, one gets the message, imbedded in each sentence of his book, that fairness and understanding of both sides of the issues is the only road to ultimate success in the practice of the art of music licensing.

Al has spent a lifetime living his art, and what he shares in this prodigious work is much more than an encyclopedic textbook. Because Al has lived the golden ages of music, has been part of its creation and has represented the titans of music history, he is able to reveal, through loving anecdotes that illustrate the themes and premises of business practice, the real fun and energy, the behind-the-scenes personality, and the understandable artistic compulsivity that is the world of music we inherit.

Al, as much as he is a teacher, is a bard weaving the history of the music business into a work that might well become a model for future attempts to communicate such complexity of information in any field or art form.

This book is a remarkable gift. It's much more than facts and figures. It's even much more than sound advice and a lifetime of wisdom.

It's Al, whom we all admire and love and who has managed, with the extraordinary partnership of a loving and gifted son, to help us remember who we are and might be, as we try to meet the challenges, and share the rewards and joys, of the music business.

Peter Yarrow
September, 1992

Peter Yarrow is a member of Peter, Paul & Mary and has been represented through Warner Bros. Publishing by Al Kohn for over 30 years as the writer and co-writer of such songs as *Puff the Magic Dragon, Weave Me the Sunshine, Light One Candle, Torn Between Two Lovers,* and *Day is Done.*

ABOUT THE AUTHORS

Al Kohn

Al Kohn, a 50-year veteran of the music industry, is Vice President, Licensing for Warner/Chappell Music, Inc. Prior to his 23-year association with Warner Bros., he served for over 11 years as the U.S. representative for the London-based Francis, Day & Hunter music publishing organization, developing acquisition patterns which moved them into the global pop music market. Prior to that, Al was a member of the creative team at Hummert Radio Features and was the key arranger for some of the syndicate's major network radio programs including "Waltz Time" and "Manhattan Merry-Go-Round." During World War II, Irving Berlin tapped Al to orchestrate his all-soldier show, "This is the Army." He also served as an arranger for orchestras, including those of Paul Whiteman, Abe Lyman, Ted Dale, Orrin Tucker and others, and arranged nightclub revues at Lou Walter's Latin Quarter, Billy Rose's Diamond Horseshoe, and the Steel Pier Music Hall. Later, he served as a television arranger for the Milton Berle, Katherine Murray, George Jessel, Martha Raye, and Jane Pickens shows. He has also arranged or conducted for Bob Hope, Billy Rose, Jerry Vale, and many others.

Bob Kohn

Bob Kohn is Vice President, Corporate Affairs and General Counsel of Borland International, Inc., one of the world's leading developers and marketers of personal computer software. Bob previously served as Associate General Counsel for Candle Corporation, a developer of software for IBM mainframe computers, and Corporate Counsel for Ashton-Tate, a microcomputer software company, recently acquired by Borland. Prior to Ashton-Tate, he was an associate attorney at the law offices of Rudin & Richman in Beverly Hills, California, and worked as Associate Editor of the Entertainment Law Reporter. Bob became a member of the California Bar in 1981 after graduating from Loyola Law School, Los Angeles.

THE REASONS FOR THIS BOOK

One need go no further to seek the reasons for this book than to the many friends and colleagues of mine who have urged me over the years to memorialize my thoughts on its subject in writing. Since many of these same people are lawyers, I can only assume they are more interested in the expression of my practical experience as a licensor of music, than my knowledge of the law.

It should be no surprise, therefore, that, though this book is thoroughly intertwined with, and dependent upon, the law of copyright, the primary emphasis of this book is not on the law, but on experience and practice. A book on copyright law would have been easier to write, because, in writing such a book, one can rely on the large body of statutes and legal decisions with which to adorn the pages. In the pages which follow, citations are given for few legal decisions. Presented, instead, is how music publishers and other copyright owners think, or more accurately, should think, in connection with licensing the music in their repertoire.

In contrast to the acquisition side of music publishing, which involves acquiring the publishing rights to new music and established songs, music licensing, the subject of this book, concerns the revenue side of the music publishing business—what you do after you own the song. Of course, what is revenue to the music copyright owner, is cost to the music user. Consequently, this book also addresses the other side of the coin—what you need to do if you want to use the song for commercial purposes.

Music licensing can thus be viewed from two perspectives: (1) the considerations used by music publishers and songwriters in earning a living from their music copyrights, and (2) the clearance of music rights by those who desire to use copyrighted music for commercial purposes.

Because my business career in the music industry has been spent largely in the employ of music publishers, this book will more naturally reflect the perspectives of the copyright owner and songwriter. Yet, my sympathy for those whose job it is to obtain music clearances has concretely found its way into this book. The reader should find no contradiction in the expression of a music publisher's sympathies for the task of rights clearance. If the music publisher is doing its job correctly, the licensing of music rights by those who desire to use music commercially should be a simple, straightforward, and often rewarding effort. The music publisher's reward for facilitating the licensing effort is better representation of the songwriters whose livelihood may often depend on proper representation.

The reader is forewarned that some controversy may attend some of the opinions expressed in this book. Some will resent being shown that their language is confused, inconsistent, and often used unwittingly against their own best interest. At first, I hesitated to speak frankly, but, with a lifetime in this business behind me, I feel I have earned a license to finally declare, *Anything Goes*. Though some will inevitably disagree with the positions taken in this book, it is hoped that they will be viewed, if nothing more, as a call for a common understanding of the terms upon which we do business.

There's no business like show business. That issue was well settled by Ethel Merman. Yet, as Irving Berlin might have agreed, there would be no show business without music. For this reason, I could not begin without first thanking the many songwriters on behalf of whom I've had the great pleasure of working with over the years as a publisher representative and as an arranger and producer of successful radio and television productions.

AL KOHN
October, 1992

ACKNOWLEDGMENTS

We have many people to thank for their assistance in the preparation of this work. We wish to especially express our gratitude to Prof. Lionel S. Sobel, Esq., Ronald H. Gertz, Esq., and Vincent S. Castellucci who made critical readings of parts of the work and provided very helpful suggestions for its improvement. We also wish to thank the following individuals who furnished some of the forms or other information included in this volume: M. William Krasilovsky, Esq., Bernard Korman, Esq., Gary Ford, Marvin L. Berenson, Esq., Lew Bachman, Edward Murphy, Ira B. Selsky, Esq., Martin Cohen, Esq., Don Biederman, Esq., Vincent Chieffo, Esq., Naomi Saltzman, Peter Yarrow, Sid Luft, and Roy Kohn. We give special acknowledgment to Matthew D. Kohn, Esq. for his insight and experience in representing contemporary artists and firms in the entertainment field.

Our sincerest thanks and gratitude are due to those who have contributed to the cumulative experiences that have found their way into this book, including Abe Lyman, Ben Yost, Irving Caesar, Patty Andrews, Wally Weschler, Arthur Hamilton, John Clark, Esq., Edward Slattery, Mrs. Frank Hummert, David Day, Bernard Sorkin, Esq., Louise Dembeck, Esq., Milton A. Rudin, Esq., Ed Perlstein, Esq., Walter Evans, Ed Silvers, Mel Blye, Chuck Kaye, Les Bider, Michael Sandoval, Joe Guardino and Max Berkovitz. It is painful for us to think that while we were carrying on this work, several of those to whom it would have been most interesting have passed away. We therefore wish to add to our acknowledgement the friendship and encouragement of the late Ira Gershwin, Leonore Gershwin, Harry Warren, Jerry Livingston, Herb Magidson, Milton Ager, Ben Oakland, and Sammy Fain.

We thank Philippe Kahn, Chairman and Chief Executive Officer of Borland International, Inc. for having the foresight to provide the company's long-term employees with the sabbatical time required to complete works such as this. We also thank Spencer Leyton, John Hansen, Linda Wallraff, John Smart, Allen Dixon, and other members of the law and corporate affairs department of Borland International, and its outside counsel Peter Astiz, Esq., Gary Reback, Esq., Martin Greenstein, Esq.,

Steven Brower, Esq., Stan Sokoloff, Esq., Peter Gelhaar, Esq., Allen Grogan, Esq., and Samuel Farb, Esq., without whom there would have been no opportunity to take advantage of that sabbatical time. Special thanks to Joan Kanady for her tireless assistance in optically scanning, typing and editing the forms that went into this volume and printing and copying numerous drafts of the manuscript. We also gratefully acknowledge the assistance of Noah J. Gordon, Esq., our editor, and the creative staff at Prentice Hall Law and Business, and Lisa Nielsen of Borland International for a beautiful jacket design.

We also must thank the entire Kohn family, including Ted and Joanne Kohn, and their children Beth and Todd, for their continuous encouragement and, most especially, Lori, Katie and Joey for their patience and unwavering love and support during this prolonged endeavor. Above all, we wish to acknowledge the encouragement, support, and wisdom of the person to whom this book we lovingly dedicate.

Now, let's get on with the show. . . .

AL KOHN
BOB KOHN
October, 1992

To Edna

SUMMARY OF CONTENTS

TABLE OF CONTENTS

CHAPTER 1
THE ART OF MUSIC LICENSING

CHAPTER 2

THE LANGUAGE OF MUSIC LICENSING

CHAPTER 3
FORMALITIES OF LICENSING

CHAPTER 4
DURATION OF COPYRIGHT, ASSIGNMENTS OF COPYRIGHT, AND LICENSES

CHAPTER 5
BASIC CONSIDERATIONS IN MUSIC LICENSING

CHAPTER 6

PRINT LICENSES

CHAPTER 7

MECHANICAL LICENSES

CHAPTER 8
ELECTRICAL TRANSCRIPTION LICENSES

CHAPTER 9
SYNCHRONIZATION LICENSES

Chapter 10
VIDEOGRAM LICENSES

CHAPTER 11
OLD LICENSES AND NEW USES

CHAPTER 12
LICENSES FOR TELEVISION, RADIO, AND PRINT ADVERTISING

CHAPTER 13

LICENSES FOR MUSIC BOXES AND CONSUMER MUSICAL PRODUCTS

CHAPTER 14
LICENSES FOR COMPUTER SOFTWARE, MULTI-MEDIA DISKS, AND NEW MEDIA PRODUCTS

CHAPTER 15
PERFORMANCE LICENSES

CHAPTER 16
THE GRAND RIGHTS CONTROVERSY

CHAPTER 17
THE DIGITAL SAMPLING CONTROVERSY

CHAPTER 18
THE SPLIT COPYRIGHT SYNDROME

CHAPTER 19
TYPICAL LICENSE FEES

THE ART OF MUSIC LICENSING

SUMMARY

THE ART OF GRANTING LICENSES

1. Share in the Economic Success of the Work in Which the Music is Going to be Used
2. Maximize the Long-Term Value of the Work and Avoid Shortsightedness
3. Maintain an Active Relationship Between the Song and the Listening Public

THE ART OF CLEARING LICENSES

1. Understanding the Nature of Rights Involved
2. Know What Music You Wish to License
3. Develop a Licensing Strategy
   A. Approaching the Simple Project
      (a) Find Out Who Owns the Song
      (b) Getting Help From the Harry Fox Agency, ASCAP, BMI and the Copyright Office
      (c) A Last Resort
      (d) Contacting the Music Publisher
   B. Approaching the Complex Project
      (a) Popular Music-Driven Motion Picture Soundtracks, New Media Works
      (b) Music Clearing Houses and Other Professional Assistance
      (c) Finding the Recording or Orchestration
4. Understand the Needs and Fears of the Music Copyright Owner
   A. Fear of Piracy
   B. Fear of Making a Bad Deal
   C. Fear of Getting Sued
5. Spend Time Educating the Copyright Owner About Your Intended Use of the Music
6. Allow Enough Time to Complete the Process

CHAPTER 1

THE ART OF MUSIC LICENSING

This book on music licensing is really about two distinct, yet related, arts: (1) the art of *granting* licenses for the purpose of earning a living from one's music copyrights, and (2) the art of obtaining licenses, or *clearing* permission, to commercially use music owned by another.

The ancient Greeks used the term "art" to refer to the technique, skill, or know-how for making things, such as a chair, a statue, or a house. They also recognized that art refers to the accomplishment of anything that requires human skill or know-how to render well, such as the art of cultivating crops, the art of making wine, and the art of singing a song.

We are living in a world today in which an increasing number of things which individuals desire to consume are not really *things* at all, in a material sense. In the pursuit of the good life, people are desiring the *intangible*—that which they cannot touch, but can feel or experience in an intellectual or emotional sense, such as reading a good story, identifying with a virtuous character, listening to good music, and receiving information (and, with the last-mentioned, one would hope, gaining some knowledge, understanding and, ultimately, some wisdom).

The practice of an art is particularly complex when the product of the activity is diffuse or intangible. This is because the building blocks used to create intangible goods, such as a play or a movie, comprise a vast variety of other intangibles that are easily transportable and combinable. For example, consider a video clip and the intangible nature of the intellectual property of which it can be composed: a few bars of a melody, a few seconds of a sound recording, a short clip from a movie or a television program, a few steps from a choreographed dance routine or ballet, the plot of a novel or short story, the virtue or vice of a lead character, a biographical sketch, a scene from an opera, an animated character, a line of poetry, a still photograph, the cadence of a well-known distinctive voice, the likeness of a rock star. One simple work of art may comprise one or all of these intangible ingredients in some form or to some degree.

3

The complexity of the law governing transactions in intangible works of authorship seems to have inherited the complexity involved in creating these works, and the complexity of the questions concerning their ownership, transfer, use, and distribution are compounded by the fact that any one intangible work may be comprised of a multitude of other works. This makes the distillation, disposition, and exploitation of the ownership rights in intangible products an extremely complex activity. Fortunately, the skill or art of performing this activity may be acquired with cooperative effort and some practical experience.

When an art is performed well, it is the result of something the ancient Greeks called *arete*, which translated into English means having a quality that is something between *virtuous* and *excellent*. To have virtue or excellence in performing an art is to have practical wisdom about the art. The goal of this book, in these noblest of terms, is to impart to the reader some practical wisdom about granting licenses and obtaining clearances for the use of music. We hope this book, together with some practical experience of your own, will help you acquire the art of music licensing.

THE ART OF GRANTING LICENSES

Music has been defined as the art of organizing sounds and silences into meaningful patterns. Music publishing can be similarly defined: the art of organizing sounds and silences into meaningful revenue. Certainly, the goal of the music copyright owner is to maximize the revenues generated by the musical composition. Maximizing revenue, however, involves more than merely how much money you can negotiate in exchange for granting licenses. It involves appraising the value of the song and recognizing that a variety of subtle factors dynamically affect the value of the song over time, including the types of uses, the number of uses, and the scope of uses that you permit over time. Maximizing revenue generated by a musical composition depends more on how you approach the exploitation of your music in the long run than how much money you demand in exchange for each license in the short run.

Arete in granting licenses to use music, accordingly, is achieved by putting the *long term* interests of the song and the songwriter first. Recognizing that maximizing a song's revenue is a dynamic process—

with the earnings potential of the music changing depending upon licensing decisions made over a period of time—is the first step in acquiring excellence in music licensing. With that in mind, we suggest that anyone who is responsible for maximizing the revenues of a song or a song catalog acquire the following three key habits:

1. Share in the economic success of the work in which the music is going to be used;

2. Maximize the long-term value of the work and avoid shortsightedness; and,

3. Maintain an active relationship between the song and the listening public.

1. Share in the Economic Success of the Work in Which the Music is Going to be Used

The compensation one can collect in exchange for granting permission to use copyrighted music in another's work can be structured in a variety of ways. For example, one can receive a one-time flat fee (e.g., $1000 payable upon signing the license) for perpetual use, a flat fee for a limited period of use (e.g., $100 for a 3-year license), or a flat fee for a limited period of use with options to renew the term of use (e.g., $100 for a 3-year license and options to renew for additional one year periods at a rate of $100 per year). However, flat fee arrangements, even if payable over a period of time, do not take into consideration the economic success of the work in which the music is used. Under a flat fee arrangement, whether a record album in which the music is used sells 100 copies or 1 million copies, the fee for the use of the music is the same.

Music copyright owners prefer to share the risk of success or failure of works that embody their music in exchange for receiving the potential rewards of having their music associated with *hit* records, motion pictures and other works. Producers and other users of music will assert that music copyright owners do not deserve to participate in the success of the user's work, because the copyright owner does not bear any of the financial risks associated with the production of the work. In other words, how can the music licensor fail? What does he have at risk that justifies the reward from the success of the work he seeks?

Music copyright owners respond that the producers are undervaluing the importance of their music to the producer's work. For example, a major motion picture may cost $20 million to make and perhaps an equal amount to market. Music is often an extremely important element in these movies, yet the music owners only receive a few thousand dollars at most for the use of the music. An artist performing a song in the movie might command a fee of $1 million for his work in the picture, but only a tiny fraction of that amount is paid to the songwriter who wrote the very song the artist may be performing in the film. From the music copyright owner's perspective, therefore, he *is* taking a risk by accepting a low fee up front in the hope that he can make up for the value the music is adding to the film by sharing in additional revenues from television performances and videocassette sales should the motion picture become successful. Music copyright owners can also point to the profit participation percentages paid to actors, writers, and directors, who are taking no more "risk" in making their contributions than the music copyright owners.

Whatever its justification, this sharing in the economic success (and failure) of works is important and is accomplished by structuring the compensation payable for music licenses in the form of a *royalty*. Royalties are generally calculated on the basis of the number of copies of the work distributed or the revenues received from the sale or performance of the work. For example, one can receive a royalty of 5 cents for each copy of the work distributed or a royalty of 5% of the net revenues derived from the sale or licensing of the work.

Few music licenses do not provide some form of royalty based on the economic success of the work in which the music is included. Where the license does not explicitly provide for royalty payments, some other mechanism usually exists that implicitly provides the music copyright owner with the upside earnings potential that a successful work may provide.

For example, when music licensed for use in a television program is broadcast on television, the music copyright owner will receive payments derived from the collection of performance royalties from the television stations that broadcast the program, through separate fees charged to the stations. The mechanisms involved in the collection of performance royalties are explained in some detail in Chapter 15. Suffice it to say here, that the license granted to the producer of the television program to include the music in the program is, as a matter of practice, granted in exchange for a flat fee. However, the music copyright owner knows that his share in the economic success of the television program is assured from the separate license fees charged for the performance of the television program in which his music is included. If the television program becomes popular and enjoys years of broadcast in syndication, the music copyright owner will similarly enjoy continuing performance royalty credit as long as the television program remains on the air in reruns and is exploited in other markets.

For this reason, music copyright owners should not lose sight of the performance royalty earnings when considering what license fee to charge for the initial inclusion of the song in works such as television programs. If, for example, a television producer is only willing to pay a certain flat fee for permission to use your song and you insist on a fee that is double what the producer is willing to pay, the producer will often find and use a substitute for your song. Ironically, more often than not, the performance royalties earned from the broadcast of the television program would have more than compensated for the difference between the flat fee you were quoting and the fee last offered by the producer. If the television program becomes a hit and enjoys lengthy rerun exhibitions, the music copyright owner will have lost substantial performance revenues. The potential upside from having the song associated with a hit program is substantial, while the downside for accepting a lower up front fee is slight.

Of course, where there is no potential for receiving performance royalties, the music copyright owner should find alternative means of sharing in the economic success in the work. This, for example, is the case with respect to the sale of videocassettes containing copyrighted music; the types of royalty structures used in licenses for videocassette use is discussed at length in Chapter 10.

2. Maximize the Long-Term Value of the Work and Avoid Shortsightedness

We have just seen in the preceding section an example of the folly of placing too much emphasis on the short term in negotiating the compensation of a license fee. In failing to resolve the difference between what the music copyright owner is willing to accept and what the music user is willing to pay in exchange for a license, the music copyright owner often overlooks the additional flow of revenue that could be earned from performance royalties.

The causes of such shortsightedness can be generally identified. It is difficult or perhaps impossible to measure the marginal performance royalties earned in connection with any one license, because performance rights societies do not calculate performance royalties on the basis of every single performance. Further, the increase in performance royalties occurs over time, and usually not in the same quarter in which the license was granted. Thus, it is usually difficult to tie the issuance of one specific license to a specific dollar increase in performance royalties.

Sometimes the shortsightedness is due to inexperience or misunderstanding of the dynamics of music publishing revenues. A songwriter or small music publisher might be represented by a personal manager or attorney who, because he or she may only physically see the checks for the flat fee licenses he or she negotiates and not the performance royalty statements, only appreciates the short term maximization of the size of these flat fee payments. Such representatives often fail to appreciate the dynamic effect that entering into licenses has on performance royalties. In other cases, representatives get mired in the details of the specific language of the license, agonizing over, for example, the inadequacies of a "warranties and representation" clause, losing sight of what's really important to the publishing company or songwriter he or she is representing.

Whatever the reason for this short-term thinking, though the marginal performance royalties earned in connection with any one license may not be measurable, they are real and this additional revenue from the collection of performance royalties is a tangible benefit not to be ignored while negotiating many flat fee licenses. More subtle benefits, such as those discussed in the section which immediately follows, should also encourage the copyright owner to come to resolution on negotiating license fees, even if it means taking less than the going rate on some up front fees.

3. Maintain an Active Relationship Between the Song and the Listening Public

As we have pointed out, maximizing a song's revenue is a dynamic process: the earnings potential of the music changes depending upon licensing decisions made over a period of time. One of the most important, but often ignored, factors that affects the value of the song over the life of the copyright is the *quantity* of licenses issued and the number of uses made of the song. The more often a song is used in other works, the greater the value of the copyright.

The essence of what you are doing when you license the use of the song is helping to maintain the relationship between the song and the listening public. Entering into licenses provides the song with a means of continual exposure to the listening public, including those who select music for use in television programs, motion pictures, commercial advertising and other works that offer alternative licensing revenues. By encouraging use, you therefore increase the likelihood that future requests for licenses of the song will continue. The listening public is surprisingly fickle and will easily forget a tune. You should never let a song fall into a state of such disuse that no one will remember it. Accordingly, the first principal of *arete* in granting music licenses is this: *Encourage as much activity in the song as possible.*

For this reason, a music copyright owner should not allow short term thinking, fear, or uncertainty to creep into the negotiating of fees and get in the way of concluding a license. A music copyright owner should not be afraid to make a decision. Life is decision making, and if you remember that the goal is to encourage as much use of the song as possible, you will inevitably make decisions that are in the long term interest of the song and its songwriter, and *arete* in granting licenses will be achieved.

THE ART OF CLEARING LICENSES

The counterpart to the art of granting licenses is the art of obtaining permission, or "clearing the rights," to commercially use music owned by another. *Arete* in obtaining clearance, or permission, to use music may best be achieved by establishing a good relationship with the music copyright owners from whom you seek to obtain permission. We suggest that the best way to accomplish that is to acquire the following habits:

1. Understand the rights involved;

2. Know what music you wish to license;

3. Develop a licensing strategy;

4. Understand the needs and fears of the copyright owner;

5. Devote some time and effort to educate the copyright owner about your intended use of the music; and,

6. Allow enough time to complete the process.

1. Understanding the Nature of Rights Involved

The importance of understanding the rights involved is best illustrated by a common mistake made by many who are new to the music clearance process: thinking first of a popular recording of the desired song, a person seeking to clear a license to use the recording might overlook the fact that getting permission to do so involves not one, but two copyrights: (1) the copyright in the sound recording and (2) the copyright in the underlying song. While you may properly obtain permission to use the recording, clearance to use the underlying song is sometimes entirely overlooked. (Just as often, persons obtaining clearance to use the music will overlook the need to clear permission to use the recording).

The copyright in a sound recording is completely separate from the copyright in the underlying song featured in the sound recording. For example, there exists a valid copyright in the song *I've Got You Under My Skin* by Cole Porter and the copyright is owned by Warner/Chappell Music, Inc., a music publishing company. At the same time, several records of *I've Got You Under My Skin* have been recorded by numerous recording artists over the years. A completely separate copyright exists for each particular recording—the sequence of sounds that make up the performance of the song by a singer and orchestra. These recordings are owned by the respective record companies that commissioned their creation. For example, Frank Sinatra's recording of *I've Got You Under My Skin*, arranged by Nelson Riddle, is owned by Reprise Records.

Thus, if you wished to obtain permission to use Sinatra's recording of *I've Got You Under My Skin*, you would require the permission of Reprise to use the recording *and* the permission of Warner/Chappell to use the underlying song. You could not use the recording without permission from both companies.

Most record companies have special divisions, often called *special products* departments, dedicated to granting licenses to use sound recordings in their catalog. Licenses for the use of such recordings are sometimes effected by what is called a *master use license*, derived from the term record "master"—a final, mixed recording used in the manufacture of other copies, such as albums, cassette tapes, or compact discs. If you have trouble obtaining approval to use a particular artist's recording of the song, the record company, or other record companies, may have substitute recordings that may meet your needs. You can, of course, always create your own original recording, in which event permission from a record company would not be necessary—the only permission required would be that sought from the copyright owner of the underlying song.

If all you want to do is make and distribute compact discs of a single audio-only recording of a song, the rights that you need to understand are relatively straightforward. The same is true if all you intend to do is quote a song lyric in a book or use a song in a television commercial. In each case, you are dealing with one copyright—the copyright in the song you are seeking permission to use.

Imagine, however, that you wanted to use a short clip from a particular dance scene in the motion picture, *West Side Story*. Not only would you require a license from the studio who owned the film, you would require a license from the record company who owned the sound track recording, a license from the music publisher of the song performed in the scene, and a license from the authors who owned the "grand rights" to the Broadway play of the same name. You may also require permission from the representatives of Jerome Robbins, who reserved by his contract with the producers of the movie the right to approve uses of the film's choreography that were not performed in conjunction with the exhibition of the entire motion picture.

Of course, not all clearances will be so complicated. However, it is good practice to first carefully analyze the work you wish to license and break it down into its component parts. In complex works—i.e., works that contain multiple copyrights and other rights—the breakdown may result in one or more of the following separate rights: a copyright in the underlying song, a copyright in the recording of the song, a copyright in the video aspects of the work (motion picture, television program, etc.), a copyright in any choreography appearing in the work, a copyright in a literary work (where the work is based upon a novel, non-fiction book, newspaper article, biography, autobiography, etc.), a copyright in a theatrical production (such as a musical play, opera, or ballet), a copyright in an animated character, a copyright in a still photograph appearing in the work, a copyright of a translation or arrangement of a work in the public domain, the right of privacy (i.e., the right one has "to be left alone") of one or more individuals, or the right of publicity (i.e., the right an individual has to exclude others from using his or her name, voice, photograph, and likeness) of one or more individuals.

The above list is not exhaustive, and this book does not cover all of the potential rights that must be cleared in connection with the variety of potential uses. It is hoped, however, that the balance of this book will give you a better understanding of each of the music-related rights underlying many of the uses likely to be made of musical compositions, as well as some of the general principles of licensing that may be useful in clearing permission to use some of these other kinds of works.

2. Know What Music You Wish to License

Before approaching a music publisher, it would be helpful if you knew the name of the song for which you are seeking a license. Humming a few bars over the phone might not be adequate or helpful, especially in recent years, as many popular tunes, such as heavy metal and rap songs, are not particularly recognizable when you hum them. Even old standards, many of which have melodies that are quite hummable, might not be recognized by younger staff members of major music publishers who were raised exclusively on popular music of the past ten to twenty years.

It might help to know a few important lines of lyrics, particularly with very old tunes, such as those published by Robbins Music Corp. early in this century. To the great consternation of many a lyrical artist, Jack Robbins insisted that the title of virtually all songs published by his company comprise the first few words of the lyrics. Examples include, *I'm in the Mood for Love, Blue Moon, Don't Blame Me, Sweet and Lovely,* and *You'll Never Know.* As opprobrious as the practice might seem to many songwriters, Jack Robbins knew his business and his idea is one which should be seriously considered today. Many contemporary songwriters attach bizarre titles to their songs which often have no resemblance to any of the lyrics contained in the song. Where the song's title is not readily apparent from reading the lyrics, the clearance of a license for the use of the song can become very difficult. Accordingly, the use of such titles may adversely impact a songwriter's earnings.

If the music was originally featured in a well known motion picture, then knowing the name of the film might help. For example, if you asked for the music in the movie starring Humphrey Bogart, *Casablanca*, or the Woody Allen film, *Play it Again, Sam*, the publisher is likely to know that you are referring to the song, *As Time Goes By*. You might ask for the love theme from the movie, *Superman*, without knowing the title, *Can You Read My Mind*.

If you don't know the name of the song, but somehow know the name of the songwriter, the publisher may be able to look up the name of the song in a biographical index.

If you have heard a recording of the song, and you can locate a copy of an LP or CD album containing the recording, you should have no trouble determining the name of the song, as it should be written on the album cover or in the CD booklet.

If you don't even have a particular song in mind, but are looking for music from a particular era, major publishing firms that have vast music catalogs should be of service in helping you identify songs that meet your requirements. For example, if you were looking for music that was popular during the 1920's, a publisher might recommend, *Baby Face*, *Ain't She Sweet,* and *Ain't We Got Fun*.

Note, however, that many of today's publishing firms are staffed by younger people who are not familiar with many of the older popular tunes. To address this problem, several years ago I helped compile a list of standard songs controlled by Warner Bros. Music, arranged in categories, such as 1920's music, 1930's music, 1940's music, western music, popular music, etc.[1] Warner/Chappell, for example, has prepared a compact disk containing hundreds of short recordings of many of the songs they have available for license.

The bottom line, however, is that unless you know the name of a specific song you are interested in, you might run into some serious problems finding what you are looking for.

---

[1] Throughout this book, references to "I" means co-author, Al Kohn, unless otherwise indicated.

3. Develop a Licensing Strategy

Before making your first phone call, develop a licensing strategy. The basic decision to make at this point is whether you *do it yourself* or whether you *hire a specialist.* The answer will often depend on the complexity of the project involved. Thus, you should, at the outset, get a feel for the complexity of the project.

Music clearance projects can be categorized into the simple and the complex. A simple project would be, for example, obtaining clearance to use one or two songs in a traditional kind of work, such as a novel, record album, or motion picture. A complex project would be obtaining clearance to use many songs for use in a traditional work or in a new form of media, such as a multimedia program distributed on optical disks. The approach you might use in obtaining music licenses for a simple project is likely to be significantly different from that of a complex project.

A. Approaching the Simple Project

You can probably clear licenses for simple projects yourself. If you know you are facing a complex project, or if, after a few attempts, your simple project turns out to be more complex than you originally antici- pated, consider hiring a specialist.

(a) Find Out Who Owns the Song

If you know the name of the song, or you managed to discover it without too much trouble, the next thing you need to know is who controls the rights to the song. In other words, with whom do you need to deal to obtain a license? This is not as easy a question to answer as you might expect. If you already know the answer, you are way ahead of the game. If you don't, you may be in for a rude awakening.

Even if you have a copy of another work in which the music originally appeared, such as a record album or a videocassette of a motion picture, it is not likely that it will contain any useful information about where to find the person who controls the rights to the music. This is because credit in these works is rarely given to the music publishers or even to the songwriters on record albums, motion pictures, and television programs. Few recording artists follow the fine tradition of performers like Frank Sinatra. Mr. Sinatra not only endeavors to give credit to songwriters, but to the arrangers of the particular orchestrations he uses, on records and in public performances.

I often receive calls directly from film companies, television producers, advertising agencies and others who seek permission to use a particular song. When I'm forced to regretfully inform the caller that the song is not among those in the catalog I represent, I am usually asked the next logical question: "Who *does* own the rights?" Quite often, I happen to be familiar with the song in question and would know off the top of my head the name of the music publisher who controlled the rights. Sad to say, the days of music publishers who have staffs familiar with the catalogs of various songs of the major publishers is nearing an end. Yet, even if licensing staffs were to become familiar with the songs contained in the major catalogs, it is becoming more difficult for anyone to know who owns or controls what song, as publishing interests of an increasing number of songs are being retained by songwriters and an increasing number of songs are becoming the subject of *split copyrights*, a problem discussed at length in Chapter 18.

(b) Getting Help from the Harry Fox Agency, ASCAP, BMI and the Copyright Office

If the intended use is merely an audio recording, such as a record album, the best place to start is by calling the Harry Fox Agency in New York City.[2] The Harry Fox Agency represents over 60% of all music publishers in the licensing of mechanical reproduction rights. You might also call the Harry Fox Agency if you are seeking to obtain permission to use a song in a motion picture, because the Harry Fox Agency also grants licenses for the use of music in films on behalf of many music publishers. A more detailed discussion of the Harry Fox Agency and mechanical licenses is set forth in Chapter 7. If the Harry Fox Agency does not represent the copyright owner of the music you require, the agency may be able to tell you who does.

---

[2] Harry Fox Agency, Inc. 205 East 42d Street, New York, New York 10017. Phone: 212-370-5330; Fax: 212-953-2384.

If you do not know who the copyright owner is, the next best place to inquire is with the appropriate performance rights society. If you know the particular performance rights society (such as ASCAP[3] or BMI[4]) with which the writer of the song is affiliated, call the society and ask for the "index" department. The index department maintains a large database which can be accessed by computer and the staff can usually give you over the telephone the names of one or more of the music publishers who own the song. If you don't know the society with which the writer is affiliated, or if you don't know the name of any of the writers of the song, you might take a look at the liner notes on your audiocassette or the little booklet that comes with your CD; nearly all records will list the name of the songs on the album and many records will also list the performance rights society (i.e., ASCAP or BMI) with which the song is registered. If you can't determine which performance rights society to call, you're in luck—the performance rights societies that control performance rights for nearly all the music performed in the United States are only two in number. Flip a coin. (If the coin should land on its edge, you might try calling SESAC,[5] the third, albeit the smallest of the performance rights societies in the United States).[6]

If the performing rights societies are unable to help you, consider commissioning a search of the records of the Copyright Office[7] of the U.S. Library of Congress to find the copyright registration of the song in order to obtain the name and address of the copyright owner appearing on the registration.

(c) A Last Resort

If you cannot find the music publisher, copyright owner, songwriter, heirs of the songwriter, or someone authorized to grant licenses for use

---

[3] ASCAP (American Society of Composers, Authors & Publishers), 1 Lincoln Plaza, New York, New York 10023, Phone: 212-595-3050; Fax: 212-724-9064.

[4] BMI (Broadcast Music, Inc.), 320 West 57th Street, New York, New York 10019, Phone: 212-586-2000; Fax: 212-246-2163.

[5] SESAC, Inc., 156 West 56th St., New York, NY, 10019, Phone: 212-586-3450; Fax: 212-397-4682.

[6] For a discussion of performance rights societies, see Chapter 15.

[7] For information about commissioning a search of the records of the Copyright Office, see the Copyright Office Circular R22 ("How to Investigate the Copyright Status of a Work"), which is set forth at the end of Chapter 18. Further information regarding searches may be obtained by conferring directly with the Copyright Office, Register of Copyrights, Library of Congress, Washington D.C. 20559, Phone: 202-287-8239.

of a song, there is one last resort, if you still want to use the song and are prepared to take some risk. You can attempt to document the fact that you made good faith efforts to locate the licensing source. Perhaps the best way of doing so is to send a registered letter containing your request to clear a license to the name and address found in the Copyright Office files relating to the song you desire to use. If the letter is returned undelivered, you can use it as evidence some later time to show, perhaps to a federal judge if you must, that you used good faith to locate and obtain permission from the copyright owner.

Before relying on this procedure, however, you should be certain that you have used every commercially reasonable effort to discover the identity and location of the copyright owner. This may entail engaging a specialist to make sure that you have exhausted all possibilities.

(d) Contacting the Music Publisher

When, and if, you finally obtain the name of the music publisher who controls the rights to the song, you must speak to the appropriate person at the publisher. When calling a music publisher, ask for the "director of licensing" or "licensing department." Most large music publishing houses have large staffs to handle licensing of their copy-rights, and are able to assign individuals who specialize in granting licenses for the various kinds of uses, such as record albums, motion pictures, and television advertising. Knowing the standard terminology employed for these uses (e.g., mechanical, synchronization, etc.) can help you get to the right person more quickly. So, if you successfully learn the jargon, you should feel free to use it.

B. Approaching the Complex Project

As you can see from the preceding section, even a project that looks simple can turn out to be complex if the search for the music copyright owner becomes problematic. But some projects are complex from the start.

(a) Popular Music-Driven Motion Picture Soundtracks, New Media Works

Many years ago, most music used in motion pictures was acquired by commissioning a composer to write an original score for the film's soundtrack. Obtaining the appropriate license to use the music in the motion picture was merely a matter of entering a standard composer's agreement with the composer.[8] That all changed in the mid-1970's with the release of the movie, *Saturday Night Fever*, the music soundtrack of which was composed of a series of disco tunes that were popular hits at that time. That event spawned a series of song driven motion pictures, such as *Fast Times at Ridgemont High, Footloose, Top Gun*, and others. The process of obtaining clearance to use several popular music songs in a motion picture will always be complex. This is because the producer should be thinking that he needs permission to use the songs not only in the motion picture, but on the soundtrack album for the picture. Once you begin thinking about soundtrack albums, you need to think about resolving any conflicts with exclusive record contracts and songwriter agreements to which the performing artists are likely to be bound. Further, the music publishing interests of songs composed by members of rock groups are often divided among the members of the group and you may find the need to obtain permission from more than one publishing source for each song in the picture.

Clearing music for use in a new media work, such as an electronic multimedia encyclopedia for distribution on optical compact discs, will also be complex. These new media works may contain recordings of hundreds of songs each of which will require separate clearance. The clearance of a few songs for use in a motion picture might look like child's play to one who might wish, for example, to clear several thousand songs for use in an electronic encyclopedia or discography.

Accordingly, for any work that involves the clearance of several songs, particularly recent recordings, you should consider getting professional assistance to clear your licenses.

(b) Music Clearing Houses and Other Professional Assistance

A number of organizations specialize in providing professional assistance for the clearance of music licenses, including the Clearing

---

[8] An example of a standard Composer's Agreement is set forth as Form 3.10 at the end of Chapter 3.

House, Ltd.[9] and BZ Rights and Permissions, Inc.[10] These organizations typically charge a flat fee which varies by project. They cannot promise to actually obtain clearances for all the music you want to license, but because of their long-established relationships with most of the major music publishers and substantial experience in dealing with the problem of split copyrights, they are likely to have a significantly better chance of succeeding than someone approaching the problem of clearance for the first time. You might consider hiring an attorney to clear your rights, but you will find the use of clearance companies less expensive, generally more effective, and often staffed or operated by trained attorneys experienced in the field.

The consulting fees charged by these companies is in addition to the cost of the licenses they may obtain for you. Accordingly, if you're responsible for a budget, don't just budget for the license fee. Be sure to budget for consulting fees for clearing rights and any additional research fees that may be required to obtain copies of the music you need.

(c) Finding the Recording or Orchestration

The right to use all this wonderful music is not worth anything if you can't find the music. Often, your particular use might call for having a copy of a recording of the song, a lead sheet, or a full orchestration. You should be prepared to do your own researching for any tangible copies of the music you seek. Don't expect a music publisher to help you find a recording. Many publishers, especially older and larger firms, might not have files with complete listings of recordings of particular copyrights, such as very old standard songs. The publisher might be able to get you a lead sheet, but don't count on it. The new copyright law that took effect in 1978 allows a publisher or composer to register their song with a tape recording in lieu of creating and filing lead sheets; therefore, if a lead sheet is required for the use intended, the user might have to be satisfied with a lyric sheet and an audio tape of the song.

---

[9]Clearing House, Ltd., 6605 Hollywood Boulevard, Hollywood, California 90028, Phone: 213-469-3186; Fax: 213-469-1213.

[10]BZ Rights and Permissions, Inc., 125 West 72nd Street, New York, New York 10023, Phone: 212-580-0615; Fax: 212-769-9224.

If the music you require originally appeared in a motion picture, and you are seeking a copy of the complete score, you may need to get in touch with the appropriate film music library. A listing of public libraries, motion picture studios, university libraries, libraries of historical societies, art museums, and private collections that contain original film score manuscripts can be obtained by writing for the *Directory of Film Music Collections in the United States* published by the Society for the Preservation of Film Music.[11] You might also try the *Film Composer's Guide,* published by The Lone Eagle Publishing Company.[12]

Even if you find the original orchestrations, you may find the studios who own them highly reluctant to license them. Scores for some film music, however, are available from Warner Bros. through special archive services provided by a major university.[13] Silent film soundtracks were compiled from many separately published pieces (rather than commissioned from one composer). Scores from silent films were compiled in so-called, "conductor books." Even if you are able to find the conductor book you are looking for, the studio that possesses it may not have the right to license it. A studio might issue a *quitclaim* license for the use of the score (a license from them without any warranty or representation that they own the proper rights), but you would still need to obtain licenses from the copyright owners of the underlying music.

4. Understand the Needs and Fears of the Music Copyright Owner

Having gained some understanding of the rights involved, having developed some strategy for obtaining the license you need, and having learned where to contact the music copyright owner, you should be mindful of the basic needs and fears of music copyright owners at the time you approach them for the licenses you require.

---

[11] Society for the Preservation of Film Music, P.O. Box 93536, Hollywood, California 90093-0536.

[12] Lone Eagle Publishing Co., 2337 Roscomare Rd., Suite Nine, Los Angeles, California 90077-1815; Phone: 213-471-8066; Fax: 213-471-4969.

[13] Warner Bros. Archive, USC School of Cinema and Television, University of Southern California, Los Angeles, California 90089.

Music copyright owners have three basic fears:

A. Fear of piracy;

B. Fear of making a bad deal;

C. Fear of getting sued.

Each of these fears is discussed in turn.

A. Fear of Piracy

Copyright means what the word implies—the right to copy. It is the right to exclude others from copying unless they have the right holder's permission to do so. But this right is violated as often as it is respected. Copyright owners lose billions of dollars a year to copyright *piracy*, the unauthorized use of copyrighted works. Ironically, the problem of copyright piracy stems from the very intangibility that gives music its value to mankind: The intangible nature of music renders copying easy to perform and unauthorized copying difficult to discover. Piracy has always been an insidious backdrop to the daily exercise of a music copyright owner's rights. However, recent developments have hurled a new challenge to those who rely on the exercise of copyrights to earn a living: The advent of the new technologies—such as the digital technology that forms the basis of computers, digital tape, and laser discs—have made the process of copying faster, cheaper, easier, and more accurate than ever before. At the same time, few strides have been made to render unauthorized copying less difficult to discover. The recent emergence of these new capabilities has caused music copyright owners to have a heightened perspective on some old fears.

It should therefore be no surprise when you approach a music publisher for a license to use music, especially in new media works, to discover in the copyright owner an immediate resistance to license. The resistance will generally stem from the copyright owner's unwillingness to enter into any arrangement that might have unknown consequences on the value of his work. As far as the copyright owner is concerned, anything that he does not understand may, in fact, result in unforeseen adverse consequences.

The antidote to this fear, of course, is some combination of education and trust. The importance of educating the copyright owner is discussed later in this chapter. Establishing trust is often a function of the relationship between the copyright owner and the licensee or, quite often, the licensee's representative. The use of a reputable music clearing house that has had prior dealings with the music publisher may prove the decisive factor in closing a license to new or esoteric uses.

B. Fear of Making a Bad Deal

One of a copyright owner's worst fears is entering into a deal he will later regret having made. For example, a music copyright owner may regret having quoted too low a fee for the use of his music in a low-budget movie that unexpectedly became a *blockbuster*. Also, if the copyright owner is dealing with a studio, a clearing house, or other person with whom he deals often, the copyright owner will be concerned about setting a precedent of which he will no doubt be reminded in future deals.

More important, because of the nature of copyright (i.e., intangible) and the means by which they may be exploited (i.e., granting permission to use), a bad deal may involve significantly more than failing to obtain a sufficiently high fee. If the copyright owner is not careful, he may find himself on the wrong end of a deal that has serious adverse consequences on the value of his copyright.

For example, a copyright owner may be persuaded to provide a license to use his music in computer software for a flat fee using a written license that grants permission to use the music "in digital form." Notwithstanding the copyright owner's rudimentary understanding of the phrase "in digital form" at the time the license was granted, the license may well have the affect of reducing the value of the copyright to virtually nothing if later virtually all distribution and performance of music is made "in digital form."

The fear of making a bad deal is more pronounced in owners of copyright than in owners of other kinds of assets. The owner of an asset, such as a car, can fairly predict the limited consequences of leasing the asset at an unprofitable rate; the risk of leasing the asset to one who would negligently destroy it may be covered by insurance and, in any event, the loss may be measured precisely and in advance.

The value of a copyright, however, may vary over time and is directly affected by the nature and scope of the licenses granted by its owner. The copyright owner will be very concerned about limiting the scope of the license and to do so, he will be required to understand exactly what the nature of the use is.

Thus, the copyright owner's unwillingness to enter into any arrangement that might have unknown consequences on the value of his work— stemming from a lack of understanding of the use and its consequences —manifests itself in the fear of making a bad deal. Again, the best remedy is education and establishing a relationship with the copyright owner. In the end, you should find that copyright owners are actually quite eager to benefit from the opportunities afforded by the new technologies and most do not wish to be left behind.

C. Fear of Getting Sued

This is of the same genre as making a deal that the copyright owner may regret, but the remorse has another cause. Getting sued is high on the list of a copyright owner's fears. The uncertainty of damage awards, the high costs of litigation, and the immeasurable damage to important long-term contractual relationships and business reputation all tend to make a copyright owner extremely conservative in making decisions that involve any risk that he may become embroiled in a lawsuit.

The latitude a copyright owner has in granting licenses is often limited by the terms of the contracts he may have with the songwriters and co-owners of the copyright. For example, a common provision of many songwriter contracts requires the copyright owner to obtain the permission of the songwriter before authorizing anyone to alter or make any changes to the copyrighted work. Thus, if your use involves changing the lyrics of a song, the copyright owner may require the written consent of the songwriter before issuing the license. Songwriter contracts may also restrict the music publisher's authority to grant licenses for the use of music in radio, television, and print advertising. Some artists are very sensitive about this and will deny consent for all kinds of uses, except recordings (which are subject to the compulsory license provisions of the copyright law, discussed in Chapter 7).

You should not expect that a publisher will be able to give you a definitive answer right away. The publisher may wish to first review a contract to determine whether any consents are required for the use. The publisher might seek a legal opinion on the scope of his ability to grant to you the license you require. All of this will take time, and, where there is a possibility that an ambiguity could be decided against the publisher, there is no assurance that he will want to take any risk to help you.

The fear a publisher has of taking any action that may result in a legal dispute is coupled with a certain amount of frustration; the publisher often desires to issue a license, but may be forced to acquiesce to the shortsightedness of the artist or the artist's representative who insists on arbitrarily invoking a contractual right of approval. Thus, when faced with a situation where the publisher's hands are tied, you should be aware that inability, not unwillingness, is at the root of the matter and you should keep communication with the publisher open in the hope that together you can find an alternative solution to your music clearance problem.

5. Spend Time Educating the Copyright Owner About Your Intended Use of the Music

After you find the person authorized to grant the license you require, you should be prepared to educate that person about precisely how you intend to use the music. Ideally, the person calling a music publisher for a license will know the language of music licensing as described in this book. Understanding the language will go a long way to facilitate the communication between the parties and the result should be a fruitful and efficient experience for all concerned.

In any negotiation, however, there are often hidden assumptions that can be the cause of some misunderstanding. Publishers are likely to test those assumptions, because of the precision they strive to achieve in fashioning the scope of the licenses they grant. You should therefore expect the music publisher to ferret out the precise scope of the permission you need in an effort to limit the scope of the permission to be granted solely to the uses that you intend, and no more. Further, the publisher will also attempt to determine the importance of the song in relation to its intended use or any other information that would be helpful in establishing the appropriate licensee fee structure and license fee. In this regard, you should be prepared to answer some or all of the following questions:

- What is the nature of the work in which the music will appear?
- How will the music be rendered in the work?
- Will the music be featured prominently or used only in the background?
- Will the music comprise all or any part of the work?
- Do you intend to use other songs in the work?
- Will you use non-music components, such as motion pictures, animation, text, photographs, dialogue, or other visual or audio elements?
- Will the music or lyrics be changed or edited?
- Will the title of the song be used in a special way?
- Will the work be a dramatic adaptation of the song's lyrics?
- Will the song be performed dramatically?
- In what markets will the work be distributed?
- Will the song be used to promote a product?
- Will the song be made part of a product?

In inquiring about the use of a song, be prepared to specify the type of use you seek. If the use is in a recording, you should specify whether the recording will be audio-only, or combined with motion pictures or other audiovisual materials. If the use is for television, you should distinguish between *free* television and *pay/cable* television. If the use is in a motion picture, you should specify if it will be in a film for normal theatrical release or whether it will be in a non-theatrical motion picture, such as a corporate training film or student documentary. Presenting this information correctly will assist the publisher in quoting the proper fees.

Some works may defy description. Perhaps the producer of the work can describe the work using the special jargon of a particular field, such as computers, but he should not assume that music publishers are even remotely familiar with the latest developments in technology. For example, if you require a license to use a song in "an MPC-formatted CD-ROM running under on 386-based machines using the MS-DOS operating system with multimedia extensions," you might need to spend a little time explaining just what that means.

Even if the music copyright owner begins to understand the work in which you intend to use the song, he may be entirely unprepared to determine just what kind of license would be appropriate for the use. The fear of making a bad deal suddenly takes center stage, and your project gets delayed while the publisher takes the matter to his lawyers, who are likely to know little more than the publisher about the media for which a license is sought.

Upon the advent of the home videocassette tape market for motion pictures, it took years for standard business practices to evolve that addressed how music copyright owners would be compensated for the use of their music in these tapes. It may not take as long for practices to emerge which resolve issues in licensing music for use in computer, multimedia, and other new media software, but producers of these new media programs will find that they will not be able to ignore the established business practices of the music publishing business when negotiating the appropriate licenses for these uses.

If you have a work that is unusual or complex, such as a multimedia product, you might be asked to send copies of similar products that you developed or copies of any marketing materials that would help the publisher understand how the music will be used in the context of the work.

Many songwriter contracts restrict the publisher's ability to permit others to make changes to lyrics of a song or make fundamental changes to the character of the music. For example, while Ira Gershwin was alive, he would never permit the rendition of his brother George's composition, *Rhapsody in Blue* unless it was performed in its entirety. (He made the first exception when I persuaded him to allow Woody Allen to use a substantial excerpt in the film, *Manhattan*). A user should never consider making any substantial changes to lyrics or the music without first obtaining a license with special provisions permitting such changes.

6. Allow Enough Time to Complete the Process

Licensing music may sound as simple as knowing the name of the song you want, calling the performance rights society to find out who controls the rights, and obtaining the proper license. It sounds easy, but it's rarely that simple in practice.

Any number of things may come up that will delay the completion of a project that contains copyrighted music. For example, music publishers are well aware of the frustrations that producers experience when trying to track down copyright owners. A music publisher on the other side of a phone call will hear a producer express a long sigh of relief when, after 9 or 10 phone calls, he learns that he finally located the publisher. That's the good news. Then the producer learns the bad news, that the song is also controlled by three other publishers. When he finally finds all the publishers, he discovers that he also requires a print license to clear his particular use and then gets hit with the news that none of them control the print rights!

Allow yourself enough time to do the research and complete the negotiations necessary to obtain a license. You should always attempt to obtain your clearance *before* you begin integrating the music into your work. If you use the music before you receive a license and the copyright owner discovers it, you do two things: (i) you create a bad impression that may anger the publisher, who thinks you are trying to pressure him into giving you a license, and, perhaps more important, (ii) you greatly increase the publisher's leverage in the negotiation for the license.

After you've already spent the time and money recording the song or taping the performance, the publisher knows that it will cost you a fortune to find another song and re-record or retape the performance. While most professional publishers would not unreasonably "hold you up," you could find that any persuasive reason you may have had to support a lower fee will fall on deaf ears. Further, remember that these rights are often split up and you just don't know whether you can even obtain the license you require *at all*. If you can't obtain clearance, and you've recorded the song, you are a copyright infringer, subject to civil action and possible criminal penalties. In this situation, impatience can cost you, as the song goes, *More Than You Know*.

The Language of Music Licensing

Summary

Music as Property

Copyright

Right vs. License

Ownership of Music

Works Made for Hire

Joint Ownership of Music

Deriving Income From Music

1. Sale of Copyright
2. Divisibility of Copyright and Sale of Exclusive Rights Under Copyright
3. Deriving Income By Licensing Use on a Non-Exclusive Basis

Types of Licenses for Music

1. Print Licenses
2. Mechanical Licenses
3. Electrical Transcription Licenses
4. Synchronization Licenses
5. Videogram Licenses
6. Commercial Synchronization Licenses
7. Musical Product Licenses
8. Software or New Media Licenses
9. Performance Licenses
10. Dramatic Performance Licenses and Grand Performance Licenses
11. Dramatic Adaptation Licenses

Differences in the Rights and Privileges of Holders of Exclusive Rights and Nonexclusive Licenses

AVOIDING CONFUSION—EXCLUSIVE RIGHT VS. NON-EXCLUSIVE LICENSE

AVOIDING CONFUSION—UNDERSTANDING OWNERSHIP OF THE "UNDIVIDED" COPYRIGHT

AVOIDING CONFUSION—SELLING, ASSIGNING, GRANTING, LICENSING

THE LANGUAGE OF THE ART

CHAPTER 2

THE LANGUAGE OF MUSIC LICENSING

The rules and symbols of musical notation are the language with which composers and arrangers communicate with musicians and singers. The language is precise and the better the writer and the reader understand the common rules of the language the better the performance is likely to be. The same is true with music licensing. The better the owners of music and users of music each understand the basic language of music licensing, the better the chances that they will each get what they expected out of a licensing arrangement. Though this chapter is technical, a better understanding of the language of music licensing will form the basis of successful music licensing.

MUSIC AS PROPERTY

The term *property* should not be confused with the term *property right*. A *property right* represents a relationship among people, recognized and defined by law, with respect to a certain thing or *object*. *Property* is the object over which the *right of property* is exercised. An acre of land, a diamond ring, or a song about a diamond ring lost on an acre of land are all objects which may be the subject of property rights. The property right with respect to a particular diamond ring is a relationship among people, enforceable by law, that dictates that a particular person, for example, has the privilege of possessing, using, and disposing of the diamond ring as that person sees fit and, more important, the right to exclude all others from possessing, using, or even looking at it.

Though there are some obvious differences between them, it should be clear that a song is just as much an object as a diamond ring. Like a diamond ring, a song is an object of perception, the former perceivable by the sense of sight and touch and the latter perceivable by the sense of hearing. As one music industry professional observed, a piece of sheet music is not a song; it only becomes a song when the music is sung.[1] Unlike a diamond ring, however, music is more than an object of perception. It is also an object of conceptual, or intellectual, thought—a song's organized patterns of sounds and silences, whether written in musical notation or performed live, can only be understood by man. While many animals have the sensory perceptions necessary to hear the sounds of music, only man has the intellect necessary to understand and appreciate its beauty. It is, perhaps, for this reason, that music is often referred to as a subject of *intellectual* property.

The property right—or relationship among people—established by law to which an acre of land is the object is called the law of *real property*. The property right to which a diamond ring is the object is called the law of *personal property*. Although a right in music is a form of personal property right, the specific form of personal property right to which music is the object is called *copyright*. The set of laws defining property rights in music is known as the *copyright law*, or *law of copyright*. When used in this book, the term *copyright law* shall refer to the law of copyright as enacted by the Congress of the United States and which took effect in 1978, with all subsequent amendments,[2] and the term *law of copyright* shall refer to general principles of copyright as agreed upon by international treaty.

COPYRIGHT

Copyright has been defined as, quite simply, *the exclusive right to copy*. More specifically, the law of copyright provides the owner of copyright in a musical work with the exclusive right to make and publish

---

[1] Leonard Feist, An Introduction to Popular Music Publishing in America, (National Music Publisher's Association, Inc., N.Y., New York 1980).

[2] 17 U.S.C. Sec. 101, et seq. Act of Oct. 19, 1976, Pub. L. 94-553, 90 Stat. 2541 (the "1976 Act"). An extensive treatment of the law of copyright is beyond the scope of this book. For comprehensive coverage, the reader is referred to the following legal treatises: Nimmer On Copyright (Matthew Bender 1991); Goldstein, Copyright Principals, Law & Practice (Little, Brown & Co. 1991).

copies of the musical work, to make other versions of the work, to make recordings of the work, and to perform the work in public.[3] The concept of *exclusivity* signifies that it is illegal for anyone other than the copyright owner of the work to perform any of the foregoing activities. It is this power to *exclude* others from using the music that forms the basis of one's *claim* to ownership in the music.

When someone makes a copy of or performs a song without the copyright owner's permission, he is said to *infringe upon* the copyright in the song.[4] The copyright owner may file a lawsuit against an infringer to collect damages arising from the infringement and to stop the further infringement of the copyright owner's rights.

This ability to take legal action to exclude others from doing the things that the copyright owner has the exclusive right to do empowers the copyright owner with the ability to grant others the privilege to make copies or render performances of a copyrighted musical composition and to require the payment of compensation in exchange for that privilege. The income that the copyright owner can collect in exchange for granting permission to do such acts is precisely the reward the law of copyright seeks to provide to creators of copyrightable works. Without such a reward, anyone would be free to use an author's works without payment. If authors were not compensated for the use by others of the works they create, few authors could afford to devote sufficient efforts to fully exercise their talents. By providing a means by which talented authors can earn a living by creating works of authorship, more works of authorship by a greater number of people, regardless of their economic background, will be created. The assumption is that society benefits when more original works of authorship are created by a greater number of talented individuals from a wide variety of backgrounds. Few would argue with that assumption.

RIGHT VS. LICENSE

The terms *right* and *license* are often used interchangeably, but they refer to two entirely different concepts and much confusion can be avoided by using these terms with all the precision the law demands.

---

[3] 17 U.S.C. Sec. 106.
[4] 17 U.S.C. Sec. 501.

As we have said, although music is property, the property right in music properly refers to the *legal relation* that the law recognizes between one person and all other persons. The legal relation of one who has a property right in an object is an ownership *claim* to the object. It is a claim to a certain object in relation to all other persons. That claim allows him to exclude all others from making copies of the work. A *right*, properly defined, is a claim in the sense just used. When one is said to have a *right*, one has the ability, enforceable by law, to exclude others from exercising the *privilege* of possessing, using or disposing of the object. And therein lies a most important point: The term *right* should not be used to describe what is really a *privilege*.

A *right*, as we have said, is a claim to property that enables the owner of the right to exclude others from doing some act. A *license* is a permission to exercise a privilege. A *privilege* is a freedom from the claim of another, allowing you to do an act regardless of someone else's claim. A license, therefore, is not a right (i.e., claim of ownership), but merely a *permission* to do something you would not otherwise have the *privilege* to do. For example, if you have a right, or claim of ownership, in a song, it means that you have the right to exclude, or prevent, all others from publicly performing the song. While your *right* affords you the *privilege* to perform the song yourself, others have a duty not to perform the song, unless you give them permission to do so. When you grant to me a license, or permission, to perform a song publicly, I do not acquire any right in, or claim to, the song; I acquire only a limited privilege to perform it. My privilege, or license, is limited by the scope of the permission, or license, which you gave to me.

It should thus be apparent that the term *right* and *license* refer to two completely different concepts—the former a claim to ownership and the latter a permission or privilege to act. Unfortunately, the term *right* is too often confounded with the term *license*.[5] Some examples of these errors, as well as their consequences, will be called to the reader's attention at later points in this book. Although we have no expectation that these errors will be rectified by practitioners overnight,

---

[5] This imprecision in language extends even to many of the major treatises on copyright law. In the social sphere, it leads to some pretty astounding errors in thinking about such fundamental concepts as "property rights," "civil rights," "human rights," and "individual liberty."

we do hope that a recognition of the issue will aid the reader in understanding and finding solutions to practical problems in the licensing and administration of copyrights.

OWNERSHIP OF MUSIC

When a composer writes a song, a copyright is said to *subsist* in the composer the moment he fixes the song in tangible form (for example, on paper or recording tape). Because the copyright automatically "subsists" at that moment, the composer does not need to do anything else to "secure" protection[6]; copyright protection is automatically secured at the moment the work is fixed in some tangible medium of expression.[7] From that moment, the composer is the copyright owner and is considered to *own* a 100% "undivided" interest in the copyright of the song.

WORKS MADE FOR HIRE

The one exception to this principle—that the copyright in the work subsists initially in the person who created it—is where the work was *made for hire*. In the case of a work made for hire, the employer or other person for whom the work was prepared, not the actual creator of the work, is considered to be the *author* of the work and becomes the owner of the 100% undivided interest in the copyright the moment the work is fixed in tangible form.

A *work made for hire* is (i) a work prepared by an employee within the scope of his employment or (ii) a work which is specially ordered or commissioned in a writing that says the work is made for hire and which falls within one of several categories enumerated in the copyright law, such as a language translation, a musical arrangement, a contribution to

---

[6] Prior to 1978, copyright under the U.S. copyright law was secured by publication of the work with a proper copyright notice. 17 U.S.C. Sec. 10 (1909 Act).

[7] 17 U.S.C. Sec. 102(a).

a collective work, a compilation, or a work created for use as part of a motion picture or other audiovisual work.[8]

In 1989, the U.S. Supreme Court ruled that whether a creator of a work is an "employee" under the "scope of employment" clause (i.e., clause (i) above) is to be determined by applying the general rules of agency.[9] Among the criteria to be considered in making such a determination are the hiring party's right to control the manner and means by which the work is accomplished, the skill required, the source of the work tools, the location of the work, the duration of the relationship between the parties, the method of payment, and similar factors. If the creator of the work is not found to be "an employee acting within the scope of employment," then the work product can be considered a work for hire only if the specific criteria set forth in the "specially ordered or commissioned" works clause of the work for hire definition are met—namely, that the work falls within one of the categories specified in clause (ii) and the parties expressly agree in a written instrument signed by them that the work shall be considered a work made for hire.

JOINT OWNERSHIP OF MUSIC

Like any other piece of property, a copyright can be *co-owned*. In other words, a copyright may be owned by more than one person, each of whom is called a *co-owner* of the copyright. In the music business, co-ownership most likely arises from the fact that two or more authors collaborated in the creation of the musical composition—commonly, a composer and a lyricist. Such a work is known as a *joint work*. In the case of a joint work, the co-authors of the work are likewise co-owners of the copyright.

A work is joint if the authors collaborated with each other in the creation of the work, or if each of the authors prepared his or her contribution with the knowledge and intention that it would be merged

---

[8] 17 U.S.C. Sec. 101.

[9] Community for Creative Non-Violence v. Reid, 490 U.S. 730 (1989).

with the contributions of other authors as "inseparable or interdependent parts of a unitary whole."[10] The key fact is the intention of the collaborators. The parts themselves may be either "inseparable" (as in the case of a novel or painting) or "interdependent" (as in the case of a motion picture, opera, or the words and music of a song). If it were the authors' intention at the time the writing was done that the parts be absorbed or combined into an integrated unit, then the work is considered a "joint work."

The contributions of words and music are usually intended by their authors to be merged to form a joint work. The authors of a joint work are co-owners of copyright in the work,[11] and each author automatically acquires an *undivided* ownership interest in the entire work. Unless otherwise agreed among the co-authors, the authors of a joint work usually share equally in the revenues generated by the work. Thus, where two authors collaborate in the creation of a work, each will have a 50% undivided interest in the entire work; where there are three authors, each will have a 33 1/3% undivided interest in the entire work, etc. The authors may, however, agree to another division. For example, where one author contributed words and music and the other worked only on the words, the two may agree to a 75/25% division. Composer George Gershwin always insisted upon receiving a full 50% interest in a composition, even when two lyric writers contributed to the song, each lyric writer in such an instance sharing the other 50% interest equally.

Because each has an interest in the "entire work," each author will benefit to the extent of his or her percentage share in the licensing or exploitation of all or any portion of the joint work. For example, where two authors collaborate in the writing of a song, one writing the words and the other the music, royalties generated by the sale or performance of any instrumental version of the composition will go to both of the authors—equally, or according to percentages otherwise agreed upon—not just the composer of the music. Likewise, royalties from the licensing of any printed edition containing only the lyrics will go to both authors, not just the writer of the words.

---

[10] 17 U.S.C. Sec. 101.
[11] 17 U.S.C. Sec. 201(a).

Co-owners of copyright are generally treated as *tenants-in-common,* with each co-owner having, unless otherwise agreed, an independent right to use, or issue non-exclusive licenses for use of the work, subject to the duty of accounting to the other co-owners for any profits. Co-owners may not grant exclusive rights without the consent of the other co-owners, and a co-owner may transfer or assign only that portion of the copyright which he or she owns. More will be said about co-owners in Chapter 18 on the subject of *split copyrights.*

DERIVING INCOME FROM MUSIC

The law provides three basic ways for you to derive income from your musical copyright:

1. You may *sell* your copyright or portions of it (i.e., assign all or a portion of your interest in the "undivided copyright");

2. You may carve up your copyright and sell to others one or more *exclusive rights under the copyright*; and

3. You may *license* (i.e., permit) others to use your music on a *non-exclusive* basis.

This book primarily concerns this third and most common means of exploiting music copyrights: giving others permission to use the music on a non-exclusive basis, commonly known as *licensing.* Nevertheless, it is essential to understand the meaning of the first and second means of deriving income from music copyrights before delving into the concept of licensing.

1. Sale of Copyright

Copyright, like other property rights, may be bought and sold, given away, taken away, bequeathed, or otherwise transferred. The transfer of copyright may occur in three basic ways: (1) upon the copyright owner's death by his will or, where no will is left, by the operation of state law (i.e., intestate succession), (2) by voluntary transfer, or assignment, and (3) by involuntary transfer, as in the course of a bankruptcy proceeding. By far the most important of these means of copyright transfer is by *assignment*. As has been noted above, assignment is the first basic means by which an owner of a copyright can exploit his property—he can sell it.

A copyright may be assigned, or sold, in exchange for legal *consideration*, meaning something of value—for example, money or a promise to pay money or to perform certain obligations. An unusual story of consideration paid for an undivided interest in a song involved the famous big band orchestra leader, Abe Lyman, who collaborated as a writer of such famous songs as, *Mary Lou* and *After I Say I'm Sorry*. The story goes that Abe was waving his baton on the bandstand of the Cocoanut Grove in Los Angeles in his usual fashion—with his back to the band and his face grinning at the couples on the dance floor—when suddenly he motioned to his pianist to carry on while he stepped off the platform. With typical Lyman brashness, he tapped one of the dancing patrons on the shoulder and explained he had a problem: he had recently purchased a luxury car and needed a few quick bucks to make his payment the next day or lose the car. "If you give me the necessary three C-notes and fifty," he said, "I'll give you a piece of my share of the profits on a song I just wrote with Arthur Freed." The stranger took the proposition in stride and asked to hear the song. Lyman jumped back on the bandstand, played the song, and a few minutes later completed the deal. The impromptu investor was later to be astounded with his first royalty check in the amount of $7,000. The song turned out to be *I Cried For You*, one of the great torch tunes[12] of all time.

Money is not the only thing of value that may be given in exchange for a copyright. Copyrights have been known to be assigned in exchange for physical objects of either economic or sentimental value. For example, Judy Garland's Transcona Company, producers of the Warner Bros. Pictures release, *A Star is Born*, employed Rodger Eden and Leonard Gersh to write the *Born in a Trunk* sequence used in the film. As the story goes, Gersh admired a certain chest of drawers that had been moved from Judy Garland's bedroom to her hallway. He asked

---

[12] The term *torch song*, adapted from the colloquial expression, "to carry a torch for" a loved one, became the phrase for a slow, sad, melancholy ballad.

for the chest in exchange for the copyright and in lieu of any future royalties, and Judy gave it to him.

If money or furniture will not do, then promises to pay or do something will be sufficient. When a songwriter signs a standard music publishing agreement, the publisher is promising to pay to the songwriter the royalties set forth in the contract based upon the publishing revenues from the song. The publisher's obligations under the agreement, together with an implied obligation to use good faith efforts to promote the song, is considered sufficient legal consideration.

Where a copyright is assigned in exchange for a promise, the assignment is said to be made *by contract*, which is the most common way copyrights are assigned or transferred. An assignment of copyright, however, does not require that legal consideration be given in exchange for it; a copyright may be given away as a gift.

As mentioned above, when a composer writes a song, a single copyright is said to *subsist* in the composer the moment he fixes the song in tangible form, such as on paper or recording tape. From that moment, the composer is the copyright owner and is considered to own a 100% *undivided* interest in the copyright of the song. The composer may transfer to another his 100% undivided interest in the copyright. If he does, he will then retain no part of the copyright and his *assignee* (i.e., the recipient in the assignment) will become the owner of the entire 100% interest in the copyright.

The composer is not limited to assigning 100% of his undivided interest in the copyright; he may assign a lesser percentage, such as 50%, or 33 1/3% of his undivided interest. Upon assigning his 50% interest, for example, the composer, and the assignee, will then both own a 50% undivided interest in the copyright.

When a songwriter signs a standard music publishing contract, he is generally assigning to the music publisher all of his 100% undivided interest in his songs. Where a songwriter signs a *co-publishing* agreement or *participation* deal, he is generally agreeing to assign only 75% or 50% of his undivided interest in the songs, reserving the remaining percentage to himself, which in turn the publisher may agree to *administer* on his or her behalf for a standard or negotiated administration fee. Examples of co-publishing and adminstration agreements are set forth as Forms 18.1, 18.2, and 18.3 at the end of Chapter 18.

2. Divisibility of Copyright and Sale of Exclusive Rights Under Copyright

Any or all of the exclusive rights under copyright, or any subdivision of those rights, may be assigned. This concept is known as the *divisibility* of copyright, and is one of the more important, but frequently misunderstood features of the copyright law.

Because copyright is "divisible," a copyright owner is not limited to assigning just some percentage of his undivided interest in his copyright. He may also transfer any of an endless number of exclusive rights which comprise the copyright. Under section 106 of the copyright law,[13] the owner of copyright has the exclusive rights to do and to authorize any of the following:

1. to reproduce the copyrighted work in copies or phonorecords;

2. to prepare derivative works based upon the copyrighted work;

3. to distribute copies or phonorecords of the copyrighted work to the public by sale or other transfer of ownership, or by rental, lease, or lending;

4. in the case of literary, musical, dramatic, and choreographic works, pantomimes, and motion pictures and other audiovisual works, to perform the copyrighted work publicly; and

5. in the case of literary, musical, dramatic, and choreographic works, pantomimes, and pictorial, graphic, or sculptural works, including the individual images of a motion picture or other audiovisual work, to display the copyrighted work publicly.

Thus, for example, a copyright owner may assign to another the exclusive right to perform the work publicly, reserving all other exclusive rights, such as the right to reproduce the copyrighted work in copies or phonorecords and the right to prepare derivative works. This was at

---

[13] 17 U.S.C. Sec. 106.

one time what songwriters and music publishers did when they became members of performing rights societies, such as ASCAP or BMI. In exchange for the copyright owner's assignment of performing rights from the songwriters and publishers, the performing rights society agreed to perform certain tasks, such as surveying performances, collecting performance fees, and distributing royalties to the songwriter and publisher members.[14]

The type of exclusive right which may be assigned, however, is not limited to the several listed in the copyright law. The copyright law provides that any subdivision of any of the rights specified in Section 106, may be transferred and owned separately.[15] Thus, a work may be exclusively licensed in particular markets, in particular forms, in particular territories, and over particular periods of time.

For example, the owner of a copyright in a song may assign any or all of the following exclusive rights: the exclusive right to print sheet music throughout the world; the exclusive right to publish the song in songbooks in the United States and Canada; the exclusive right to publish the song in songbooks in all countries except the United States and Canada; the exclusive right to record the song and distribute phonorecords throughout the world for a period of five years; the exclusive right to record the song and distribute phonorecords in the United States only beginning in five years; the exclusive right to perform the song throughout the world; the exclusive right to record the song in synchronization with audiovisual images for theatrical distribution in the European Common Market countries for three years, and in all other countries for ten years, etc. As the foregoing may suggest, the potential number of exclusive rights comprised in copyright would appear to be, if not unlimited, then limited only by the business practices and imaginations of the buyers and sellers of exclusive rights under copyright.

---

[14] Under certain consent decrees negotiated with the U.S. government, the performing rights societies were required to convert the agreements with their writer and publisher members from an exclusive to a non-exclusive basis, but as a practical matter the societies today exercise their licenses to sublicense music performances virtually on an exclusive basis.

[15] 17 U.S.C. Sec. 201(d)(2).

When a copyright owner assigns any of the many possible exclusive rights under the copyright, he reserves to himself all other rights that comprise and remain with the copyright. Using any or all of the examples mentioned above, the owner of the full *undivided* copyright, after having assigned the several exclusive rights mentioned, would still remain the owner of the undivided copyright, which would, of course, become subject to the rights of the new owners of the exclusive rights. That is, the copyright owner would be able to exercise all of his rights and privileges as owner of the copyright in the song except that he cannot do or authorize any of the things in which he has assigned to others the exclusive rights to do or authorized others to do.

It is important to note that the interest in the copyright remaining with the owner would still be considered "undivided," even though certain exclusive rights have been carved or "divided" out and separately assigned to others, because the interest in all of the unassigned exclusive rights remaining under the copyright (infinite in number) is still undivided.

As we have seen, the copyright owner may then transfer 100%, or any lesser percentage, of that "undivided" copyright interest in what remains of the copyright. His assignee would become the owner of all or a lesser percentage of the "undivided" copyright, subject, of course, to the rights of the owners of any exclusive rights previously assigned to others.

A songwriter signing a standard music publishing agreement should be aware that he is promising (i.e., look for the words, "warranting and representing") to the publisher that he has not previously assigned to anyone else any of the exclusive rights under the copyrights he is transferring to the music publisher (with the exception of the writer's share in performance rights, which are routinely licensed to the writer's performing rights society, such as ASCAP or BMI). Publishers may sometimes refuse to take anything less than full rights, particularly in the case of new, previously unpublished material, for which the publisher may be taking a measure of financial risk to promote. Songwriters should therefore consider carefully any decision to transfer any of the exclusive rights under copyrights, giving particular attention to the potential effect such a decision may have on the value of the copyright. The value of the whole copyright may be greater than the value of the sum of its parts.

3. Deriving Income by Licensing Use on a Non-exclusive Basis

The most common means of deriving income from music copy-rights arises from granting to others permission to use the music on a non-exclusive basis. This is commonly known as *issuing* or *granting* licenses, or merely, *licensing*. Nearly all licenses for the use of music involve the exercise of one of the three following exclusive rights under copyright:

1. the exclusive right to make copies: the *reproduction right*;

2. the exclusive right to perform: the *performance right*; and

3. the exclusive right to prepare derivative works: the *adaptation right*.

TYPES OF LICENSES FOR MUSIC

The copyright law gives the owner of copyright the exclusive rights to make and publish copies of the copyrighted work, to make other versions of the work, to make recordings of the work, and to perform the work in public.[16] As we have said, these exclusive rights involve, by definition, the rights to exclude others, through the power of the legal system, from performing those acts. It is this *right to exclude* that forms the basis of the *right to license*, or, in other words, *right to give permission*. The various types of licenses that a copyright owner may grant are defined by *the use* for which permission is sought.

The following are the primary forms of licenses customarily used in the music industry:

---

[16] 17 U.S.C. Sec. 106.

1. Print Licenses

A *print license* is a permission that authorizes one to make printed copies of music, such as sheet music and printed music folios, and reprints of lyrics in books, magazines, and print advertising. Print licenses are discussed in Chapter 6.

2. Mechanical Licenses

A *mechanical license* is the form of permission that authorizes one to make mechanical reproductions of a musical composition, that are not accompanied by a motion picture or other audiovisual work, and which are made for the purpose of distributing them to the public for private use. Examples of such mechanical reproductions include music embodied in piano rolls, record albums, audiocassettes, digital audio tapes, compact optical discs, and computer chips. Motion picture films, videotapes, and audiovisual laser discs that contain music accompanied by motion pictures or other audiovisual works are never the subject of mechanical licenses. Mechanical licenses are discussed at length in Chapter 7.

3. Electrical Transcription Licenses

An *electrical transcription license* is the form of permission that authorizes one to make mechanical reproductions of a musical composition, that are not accompanied by a motion picture or other audiovisual work, and which are made for radio broadcast or for purposes other than distribution to the public for private use. Mechanical reproductions of music for radio broadcast are called, "electrical transcriptions," or simply, "transcriptions," the term "electrical" being a holdover from the days before magnetic tape. Examples of transcriptions include recordings of radio theme music, musical introductions, and background music for commercial advertising made specifically for radio broadcast, as well as recordings compiled for use in syndicated radio programs. Electrical Transcription licenses are discussed at length in Chapter 8.

4. Synchronization Licenses

A *synchronization license* is the form of permission that authorizes one to make mechanical reproductions of a musical composition, that are accompanied by a motion picture or other audiovisual work, for use in connection with a motion picture theatrical performance and television broadcast. Examples of such reproductions include motion pictures, television programs, and music videos, embodied in any form, such as film, tape, and optical laser disk. Technically, the music is not always "synchronized" or recorded, as some licenses say, "in timed-relation with" the motion picture, but these terms convey the notion that the permission to make reproductions of the music is strictly limited to copies embodying the specified motion picture together with the music. Most synchronization licenses contain a further restriction relating to how the copies of a motion picture which embodies a recording of the licensed music may be distributed: these licenses limit the distribution of the motion picture to only those copies that are directly related to effecting the performance of the picture in motion picture theaters and on television. These licenses may impliedly or explicitly restrict any other form of distribution, including distribution on videocassette laser discs for the home video market. Synchronization licenses are discussed at length in Chapter 9.

5. Videogram Licenses

A *videogram license* is the form of permission that authorizes one to make mechanical reproductions of a musical composition, that are accompanied by a motion picture or other audiovisual work, and which may be distributed on videocassette, optical laser disk, or other home video device for distribution into the home video market. Videogram licenses are discussed at length in Chapter 10.

6. Commercial Synchronization Licenses

A *commercial synchronization license* is the form of synchronization license that authorizes one to make reproductions of and broadcast performances of a musical composition in connection with the promotion or advertising of a commercial product. See Chapter 12 for a more detailed discussion of licenses for the use of music in commercial advertising.

7. Musical Product Licenses

A *musical product license* is the form of permission that authorizes one to make mechanical reproductions of a musical composition in connection with the distribution of a commercial product, such as wind-up music boxes, singing dolls, and musical greeting cards.

This form of license may resemble either a mechanical license or a videogram license, depending on whether the use of music in the product is accompanied by audiovisual images. See Chapter 13 for a more detailed discussion of musical product licenses.

8. Software or New Media Licenses

A *new media license* is a "catch-all" term for the form of permission that authorizes one to make reproductions of a musical composition in connection with the distribution of computer software, karaoke, and other new media devices. See Chapter 14 for a more detailed discussion of this type of license.

9. Performance Licenses

A *performance license* is a permission that authorizes one to perform a work publicly. Performance licenses are discussed in Chapter 15.

10. Dramatic Performance Licenses and Grand Performance Licenses

A *dramatic performance license* is a permission that authorizes the performance of a song dramatically—that is, when the song is used to carry forward the plot or story of a dramatic work, such as a motion picture, television program, or theatrical play. A *grand performance license* is a not a license in music at all—it is a license to perform a grand opera or grand musical play, or portion thereof. The rights that form the basis of these types of licenses are discussed at length in Chapter 16.

11. Dramatic Adaptation Licenses

A *dramatic adaptation license* is a permission that authorizes one to make a dramatization of a musical composition, or more accurately, its lyrics. Just as a motion picture can be a dramatic adaptation of a novel, a motion picture or television program may be a dramatic adaptation of the lyrics of a song. Although a motion picture adaptation of a song may include a performance of the song, a dramatic adaptation license does not authorize one to render a dramatic performance of the song, a license for which must be acquired separately. This type of license is discussed in Chapter 16.

DIFFERENCES IN THE RIGHTS AND PRIVILEGES OF HOLDERS OF EXCLUSIVE RIGHTS AND NON-EXCLUSIVE LICENSES

The copyright law entitles the owner of any exclusive right, to the extent of that right, "all of the protection and remedies accorded to the copyright owner."[17] This means, for example, that a person holding an exclusive right to do something, such as perform a particular composition on television may sue in his own name anyone who infringes that particular right, even though the undivided copyright remains in the hands of someone else. By contrast, a non-exclusive licensee of a similar right of performance would not be able to sue in his own name to stop others who perform the song without permission.

Similarly, an owner of exclusive rights under copyright, unlike a licensee, may file an application for copyright registration for his exclusive claim. (Though the exclusive rights owner may file the application, he must still identify the owner of the "undivided" copyright as the "claimant" on the copyright application.)

As will be noted in Chapter 3, the formalities required to effectuate an assignment of exclusive rights and a grant of non-exclusive licenses differ significantly. An assignment of exclusive rights must be in writing; a non-exclusive license may be effected orally.

Thus, the owner of an exclusive right, to the extent of his exclusive right, is treated much the same as the owner of the "undivided" copyright. By contrast, the non-exclusive licensee of a right under the copyright is not treated at all like an "owner"—he merely has permission to do an act which without such permission would constitute copyright infringement.

As we have pointed out, the potential number and variety of exclusive rights comprised in copyright, and the potential number and variety

---

[17] 17 U.S.C. Sec. 201(d)(2).

of non-exclusive licenses, would appear to be limited only by the imaginations of the owners and users of music. Interestingly enough, as the precision with which exclusive rights are defined increases, the distinction between exclusive rights and non-exclusive rights becomes rather nebulous.

Consider, for example, the "exclusive right to perform a song on a certain television program to be broadcast in the United States next Tuesday evening between the hours of 7:00 and 9:00 PM EST." Would the owner of such an exclusive right have fewer privileges if the equivalent grant were made instead on a non-exclusive basis? The exclusivity being rather ephemeral, it becomes difficult to distinguish such an exclusive right from a non-exclusive license covering the same use.

We have listed above several differences between the rights of owners of exclusive rights and the privileges of non-exclusive licensees. An owner of an exclusive right under copyright, unlike a non-exclusive licensee, may sue in his own name anyone who infringes his exclusive right; an owner of exclusive rights under copyright, unlike a licensee, may file an application for copyright registration; and an assignment of exclusive rights must be in writing, while a non-exclusive license may be effected orally.

Though the foregoing suggests that there are some legal differences between transferring a narrowly defined exclusive license and granting an equivalent license on a non-exclusive basis, it is likely that the differences will have little or no practical significance, if for no other reason than virtually all narrowly defined licenses are formulated on a non-exclusive basis.

AVOIDING CONFUSION
—EXCLUSIVE RIGHT VS. NON-EXCLUSIVE LICENSE

At the outset of this chapter, we explained the difference between a right and a license, saying that a right is a *claim*—the ability, enforceable by law, to exclude others from exercising the privilege of possessing, using or disposing of an object—and a license is a *permission* to do something with the object which, by reason of another's claim in it, one would not otherwise have the privilege to do.

Because the terms *right* and *license* refer to two completely different concepts, they should not be used interchangeably. For example, you should never see the term, "exclusive license," a term which at best contradicts itself. The proper term is "exclusive right." If the "right" is not exclusive (i.e., no intent is present to give the licensee the legal authority to exclude others from doing the same thing), then it probably is a license (i.e., merely permission). If a license purports to be exclusive, then it is actually a right.

A phrase that is commonly used in contracts regarding intellectual property is "exclusive right and license." The use of this phrase may be proper depending upon the context. The only context in which such a use would be proper is if you consider the terms "exclusive right" and "license" separately. When you grant a license, you are granting a permission to another to exercise a privilege to do something. In addition to granting to another a license to do something, you may grant an exclusive right—that is, the right to exclude others from doing the same thing. Correctly construed, the phrase "A hereby grants to B the exclusive right and license to" do something means that (i) A grants to B the privilege to do something that otherwise B would not be able to do, and (ii) A grants to B the right to exclude others from doing the same thing.

It might therefore be helpful if practitioners replaced the phrase, "exclusive right and license" (which may be improperly construed as, "exclusive right and exclusive license") with "license and exclusive right."

As noted in greater detail in Chapters 3 and 4, the distinction between a grant of an "exclusive right" and a grant of a "non-exclusive license" is significant in at least two respects: (1) the formalities necessary to effectuate assignments and licenses, and (2) the duration of assignments and licenses.

AVOIDING CONFUSION—UNDERSTANDING OWNERSHIP OF THE "UNDIVIDED" COPYRIGHT

The understanding of the foregoing definitions and principles, and the solving of many day-to-day copyright problems, can be facilitated by considering one point: there is always just one copyright for each work—we call this the *undivided* copyright.

The undivided copyright may be owned by one or more individuals each with equal or varying shares of a 100% total. Even though the copyright may be "divided" into numerous exclusive rights, and even though some of those rights may be transferred away and owned by others, remember that each separately assigned exclusive right always relates back to that "undivided" copyright.

When this is understood, common legal questions relating to copyright, such as determining the proper copyright "claimant" in an application for copyright registration or the proper name to include in the "copyright notice" becomes simple: in each case it is always the owner or owners of the "undivided" copyright.

AVOIDING CONFUSION
—SELLING, ASSIGNING, GRANTING, LICENSING

Many of the formal terms used in copyright transfers and licenses are also misunderstood and may become the source of some confusion.

When you transfer (e.g., sell or give away) an interest in your undivided copyright, or in any exclusive rights under the copyright, the document effecting the transfer will typically state that you *grant, transfer, sell*, or *assign* such interest to the person receiving the interest. Any one of these words, alone or in combination, will be sufficient. If you are the buyer or assignee of a copyright or exclusive right, you would be advised to use the words, "sells and assigns," which should make it absolutely certain that you are receiving an ownership claim, rather than merely a license.

If the instrument is intended to effect a non-exclusive license, then it would be improper for the instrument to use the words "assign," "transfer," or "sell." Non-exclusive licenses, unlike interests in the undivided copyright or exclusive rights under it, are not "rights." As we have pointed out, a right is a *claim* to ownership. A license is not a claim to ownership; it is merely a *permission* to do something which you would not otherwise have the privilege to do. People *grant* permission; they do not *transfer* or *assign* permission. Likewise, you do not transfer or assign a license, you *grant* a license. (Arguably, you can "sell" your permission, and, accordingly, sell a license, but it is recommended that the word sell be used solely in the context of an actual transfer of rights).

By the same token, to say "Publisher grants a non-exclusive right to . . ." is incorrect, because only a permission is being conferred, not a claim to ownership, or *right*, in any portion of either the undivided copyright or in any of the exclusive rights under the copyright. It is better, therefore, to say "Publisher grants a non-exclusive license to . . .," in the sense that a permission or privilege to do something (i.e., to use the music in a certain way) is being allowed or granted, but not a claim of ownership (i.e., the legal ability to exclude others from doing the same thing).

Finally, the phrase, "Publisher grants the right and license to . . . " is redundant in the context of a non-exclusive license, because only a permission is being conferred, not a claim to ownership, or *right*, and, in that context, the word "right" can only have been meant to be synonymous with "license."

THE LANGUAGE OF THE ART

The language of music licensing is the lifeblood of the music business. The business of music, more than any other, is inextricably intertwined with the laws and contracts that define the legal relationships among owners and the users of the "objects" produced. These laws and contracts are comprised of words that express important concepts relating to the structure of legal relationships—but merely words, nothing more.

An art that is so reliant upon the use of words requires precision in the use of those words to perform the art well. For this reason, words that refer to completely different concepts should not be confounded or used indiscriminately. On the contrary, terms of art should be treated as such. When so much rests upon how and when these words are used, it behooves those who wish to succeed to use them well.

We mean no pedantry. On the contrary, it is fervently hoped that this be genuinely viewed as an aid to understanding. Clarity of thought about an art should increase one's understanding and appreciation of it and should make one's reaction to it more certain. If the precision suggested in this book aids the reader in understanding and finding solutions to practical problems in the business of music licensing, then it has served its purpose.

FORMALITIES OF LICENSING

SUMMARY

FORMALITIES OF ASSIGNMENT

1. Assignment Must Be In Writing
2. Recordation of Assignments
3. Short Form Assignment Document

FORMALITIES OF LICENSING

1. Written Licenses
2. Oral Licenses
3. Implied Licenses
4. Operation of Law

GET IT IN WRITING

LETTER FORM VS. CONTRACT FORM

REFERENCE TO THE PARTIES

STANDARD TERMS AND CONDITIONS

FORMS USED IN THIS BOOK

FORMS

FORM 3.9   1978 Songwriter's Guild of America
                 Popular Songwriter's Contract

FORM 3.10   Standard Studio Film Music
                 Composer/Arranger/Conductor
                 Employment Agreement; Exhibit A,
                 Exhibit B

CHAPTER **3**

FORMALITIES OF
LICENSING

This chapter reviews the formalities necessary to effectuate grants of copyright, exclusive rights under copyright, and licenses.

As noted in the preceding chapter, only interests in undivided *copyrights* and *exclusive rights under copyright* may be *assigned* (i.e., sold, or otherwise transferred from one person to another). Permission to use music on a non-exclusive basis is the subject of a *license*, and licenses are not proper subjects for "assignments," "transfers," or "sales" of rights.[1] A grant of license, or permission, does not require that any particular formalities be followed, but there are good reasons to comply with certain formalities when granting or clearing licenses, and these are discussed later in this chapter.

Certain formalities, however, are necessary conditions for effecting assignments of copyright, and exclusive rights under copyright, and these will be discussed in the following section.

FORMALITIES OF ASSIGNMENT

To *assign* a copyright means to transfer ownership of that copyright from one person to another. The ownership of copyright may be transferred in whole or in part by any means of conveyance or by operation of law, and may be bequeathed by will or pass as personal property by the applicable laws of intestate succession.[2] In recognition of the divisi-

---

[1] "A 'transfer of copyright ownership' is an assignment, mortgage, exclusive license, or any other conveyance, alienation, or hypothecation of a copyright or any of the exclusive rights under copyright, whether or not it is limited in time or in place of effect, *but not including a nonexclusive license.* " 17 U.S.C. Sec. 101 (emphasis added).

[2] 17 U.S.C. Sec. 201(d)(1).

bility of copyright, the law provides that any of the exclusive rights comprised in a copyright may be transferred and owned separately.[3]

1.   Assignment Must Be in Writing

A transfer of copyright, or any exclusive rights under copyright, other than by operation of law, is not valid unless an instrument of conveyance, or a note or memorandum of the transfer, is in writing and signed by the owner of the rights or such owner's duly authorized agent.[4]

Legal *consideration* is not required for an assignment to be valid. This means the *assignee* (i.e., person receiving the assignment of rights) does not need to give something of value (e.g., money, promise to pay royalties, etc.) in return for the rights, unless, of course, the assignment was conditioned upon the receipt of such consideration. Thus, an assignment of rights may be a gift.

An assignment of copyright in a composition may be executed even when the song is not yet in existence; in such cases, the assignment will be deemed effective upon the song's creation. An example of such an assignment appears in any exclusive music publishing contract under which the songwriter promises to assign to the music publisher the copyrights in all of the songs which the songwriter creates during the term of the contract.

The assignment form need not be notarized or witnessed to be valid. Nevertheless, a procedural advantage, though slight, in possible future court actions may be gained by a notarial acknowledgment.[5]

It is important to note that ownership of copyright in a work, or any of the exclusive rights under the copyright, is distinct from ownership of any material object in which the work may be embodied.[6] Accordingly, transfer of ownership of any material object, including the copy or phonorecord in which the work is first fixed (e.g., the original lead sheet or audiocassette recording), does not of itself convey any rights in the copyrighted work embodied in the object.[7] Nor, for that matter, does an

---

[3] 17 U.S.C. Sec. 201(d)(2).

[4] 17 U.S.C. Sec. 204(a).

[5] A properly executed certificate of acknowledgment is prima facie evidence of the execution of the transfer. 17 U.S.C. Sec. 204(b).

[6] 17 U.S.C. Sec. 202.

[7] *Id.*

assignment of the copyright convey property rights in any material object, even if that object contains the only existing copy or recording of the work. Further, the physical transfer of a certificate of copyright registration will not constitute an assignment of copyright. Transfer of ownership in copyrights and exclusive rights under copyright may be effected only by the express terms of written legal instruments, such as contracts, assignment forms, and the like.

2. Recordation of Assignments

Although the Copyright Office does not supply any forms for transfers of copyright, the law does provide for the recordation in the Copyright Office of transfers of copyright.[8] Although recordation is not required to make a valid transfer as between parties, it does provide certain legal advantages and may be required to validate the transfer against third parties. For example, as between two conflicting transfers of the same copyright, the one executed first will be recognized and given legal effect if it is recorded in the Copyright Office within one month after its execution or at any time before the recordation of the later transfer. (Otherwise the later transfer prevails if it is recorded and was received in good faith, for consideration, and without notice of the earlier transfer.) It is therefore good practice for assignees to record all assignments within thirty days after the execution of the assignment.

In addition to resolving conflicting assignments, another good practical reason for promptly recording all assignments is to maintain a complete and independent record of the copyright's *chain of title*. Maintaining a record of the important documents pertaining to a copyright in a safe, central location, such as the Copyright Office of the Library of Congress, will enable the copyright owner to reconstruct his copyright records in the event of a natural disaster or fire.

3. Short Form Assignment Document

Most assignments of copyrights in musical compositions are effected by contract, usually a music publishing contract. Several forms of agreements containing assignments of copyright, portions of copy-

---

[8] 17 U.S.C. Sec. 205.

right, and exclusive rights under copyright are included in this book. For example, a standard form single song music publishing agreement assigning the entire undivided copyright in an individual composition is set forth as Form 3.5 at the end of this chapter. Examples of co-publishing agreements that assign an undivided 50% interest in a copyright are set forth as Forms 18.1 and 18.2 at the end of Chapter 18 on split copyrights. An exclusive print agreement, assigning certain exclusive rights under copyright, is set forth as Form 6.1 at the end of Chapter 6 on print licenses.

Each of these agreements involves an assignment of copyright, portion of copyright, or exclusive right under copyright, and each may be recorded in the Copyright Office. As previously discussed, there are a number of good reasons for recording assignments of copyrights. Nevertheless, there is good reason not to record these or any other kind of detailed music publishing agreement: it may be undesirable for the parties to allow the terms of their contract to become a matter of public knowledge. The problem is that a publishing agreement may contain (i) the detailed terms of the relationship which the parties desire to maintain in confidence, but, at the same time, (ii) a clear assignment of rights, the existence of which the parties desire to disclose to the world.

The industry, however, has provided a solution that apprises the public of the existence of the assignment without disclosing the terms of the contract. When a songwriter, or other assignor of copyright, signs a contract setting forth the full terms of the assignment of copyright (e.g., royalty rates, advances, etc.), he will usually be asked to simultaneously sign a second, often one-page, document, which describes the rights assigned, but omits all other information about what the assignee may have paid for, or agreed to perform, in exchange for the rights assigned. This document is known as a *short-form copyright assignment.*

The assignee records with the Copyright Office only the short-form, and the parties maintain in confidence the details of the agreement contained in their *long-form* contract. The short-form assignment should not refer by its terms to any long-form contract covering the relationship between the parties, because the Copyright Office has been known to require that a copy of any document referred to in the assignment form also be recorded, which would defeat the purpose of using the short form. If the assignee is uncomfortable having a document that does not state the consideration being given in exchange for the assignment, he can include a provision in the short-form that the assignment was made "for good and valuable consideration" or "for and in consideration of One Dollar ($1)." A sample "short-form" copyright assignment is set forth as Form 3.1 at the end of this chapter.

FORMALITIES OF LICENSING

In contrast to what is required to effect an assignment of copyright, or exclusive rights under copyright, the grant of a license on a non-exclusive basis is not required to be in writing. Licenses can be conferred in a number of ways: (1) in writing, (2) orally, (3) implied from the acts of the parties, or (4) created by operation of law.

1. Written Licenses

The most common form of license is a formal written document setting forth precisely the scope of the permission. A *written license* may be in the form of a contract signed by the licensor and the licensee, or merely by a letter granting permission signed by the licensor.

2. Oral Licenses

Oral licenses are licenses spoken in person or over the telephone. Oral licenses are sometimes referred to as *verbal licenses*, even though such use of the word verbal is poor diction—the word "verbal" refers to that which contains or concerns words, and certainly both oral and written licenses fit comfortably within that definition.

Oral licenses are uncommon for a variety of reasons which are discussed below. An apt observation that has been ascribed to movie producer, Samuel Goldwyn of Metro-Goldwyn-Mayer, is that "Oral agreements are not worth the paper they're written on."

3. Implied Licenses

An *implied license* is a license that is not expressed in verbal (i.e., oral or written) form. A license may be *implied* where a person could reasonably infer from the conduct of the copyright owner that permission was granted.[9]

For example, a record company could be deemed to have an implied license to distribute an album containing a song written by the album's recording artist who, by recording the song under the terms of a separate agreement for purposes of putting it on the album, led the record company to reasonably believe it had permission to distribute copies of the song on that album, notwithstanding the absence of a written mechanical license to do so. The scope of the permission would be determined by the conduct of the parties. In the above example, the record company's license would probably be limited to distribution of the song on the album, but would not include a synchronization license in the absence of evidence showing the uses implied from the circumstances would go beyond that of use in the form of mechanical reproductions of the album (e.g., circumstances may also imply that the song was also to be used by the record company in connection with some audiovisual work, such as a music video, but not in a motion picture unrelated to the artist's obligations or performance under his recording agreement).

Licenses that are implied may be revoked at any time, but, in certain instances, the copyright owner's right to revoke may be limited or *estopped*, particularly where the licensee can show he acted in justifiable reliance upon the owner's conduct and would be damaged by an unreasonable or untimely revocation of the license.

4. Operation of Law

Licenses can also be created by *operation of law*. For example, licenses may be bequeathed by will or pass as personal property by the applicable laws of intestate succession. Licenses may also be conferred by operation of the compulsory license provision of the copyright law.[10]

---

[9] See, *Effects Associates, Inc. v. Cohen*, 908 F.2d 555 (9th Cir. 1990) (Expressing its dismay at the parties' failing to memorialize a license in writing—"Movie-makers do lunch, not contracts"—the court nevertheless found a license was implied by the conduct of the parties).

[10] 17 U.S.C. Sec. 115.

GET IT IN WRITING

All transactions discussed in this book should be reduced to writing. It is not a matter of having or showing a trust or distrust in another, or even trust in an otherwise honest person's memory.

Having a license in writing may protect you from a conflicting license or transfer of the copyright. A non-exclusive license, whether recorded with the Copyright Office or not, will be effective even if there exists a transfer of copyright ownership in conflict with it, as long as the license was *in writing* and was either granted before the transfer of copyright was executed or was received in good faith before the recordation of the transfer of copyright and taken without notice of the transfer.

A producer of a work that contains copyrighted works of others would be prudent to maintain a written record showing the contractual basis demonstrating that the producer has all the rights and licenses necessary to effect the intended use of the work. Having a good record of rights and licenses will become useful, and often essential, at the time the producer considers signing an important agreement for the distribution of the work or selling the work to another. Upon a sale of copyright, or important exclusive rights under copyright, the buyer is likely to perform an extensive *due diligence* investigation to confirm whether the seller, indeed, has all of the rights and licenses necessary to support the warranties and representations he is making in the sale contract. Keeping good files of contracts with, and licenses from, all the contributors of intellectual property to the final work will avoid unnecessary delay and unanticipated costs when it comes time to exploit or dispose of the work.

Even licensors are advised to memorialize all licenses in writing. If a copyright owner takes action leading a producer to believe he had a license to synchronize music in a motion picture, a license may be *implied* from the circumstances. In any dispute with the producer regarding the scope of the license, the terms of the implied license would become a matter for the courts to decide. Because of the high costs of litigation, it may be uneconomical to file a lawsuit to have the courts circumscribe the scope of the license, thereby making it difficult to assert the right to collect additional fees for other uses, such as, for example, a royalty on the distribution of videogram copies of the work.

Letter Form vs. Contract Form

A common question in music licensing is what's the difference between a license in *letter* form and a license in standard *contract* form, or long-form, and under what circumstances should one form be used over the other? An example of a "letter agreement" is set forth as Form 6.4 and an example of a "long-form contract" is set forth as Form 6.2 at the end of Chapter 6.

Letter agreements are generally shorter, omitting much of the usual boilerplate contained in longer form contracts. Used for simpler licenses, such as letters permitting the reprint of a song lyric, the letter form is clearly a more informal way of reducing an agreement to writing. Letter agreements are also used, however, to memorialize longer, more sophisticated agreements. Sometimes it is felt that, because of the long standing relationship and previous dealings between the parties, the informality of the letter agreement is more appropriate. Some feel that letter forms should always be used in lieu of long-form contracts, because, if the agreement ever became the subject of litigation, the letter form would be more approachable[11] by the courts and juries.

In answer to the question when to use a letter agreement or long-form contract, we offer the following suggestion: all licenses should be issued using an informal letter agreement; all grant of copyrights, or exclusive rights under copyright, should be effected by the more formal standard contract form. Following this procedure would properly reflect the fundamental difference between granting permission to exercise a privilege, which is the subject of a *license*, and granting a property right, which is the subject of an *assignment* of copyright or exclusive rights under copyright. Granting permission, or license, is a less formal event than assigning a property right, and the form used to effect each should reflect their relative formality. Accordingly, the license form that is most appropriate to the circumstances of the deal will always be used.

A common observation about contracts in the entertainment industry is that the more money that is involved in a transaction, the longer the contract. Motion picture distribution contracts, often involving hundreds of millions of dollars tend to be longer and more complex

---

[11] In computer parlance, more "user-friendly."

than contracts used in the music recording industry which usually involve only millions of dollars, which in turn tend to be longer and more complex than contracts used in the relatively smaller music publishing industry. Mere licenses for the use of music should be placed at the appropriate point along the scale of complexity. In today's world of word processing machines, it is a wonder how even the simplest permission letters have not become the subject of multiple page tomes that can now be generated at the touch of a button. It is hoped that people responsible for drafting or generating licenses from word processing software will continue to use the license form that is most appropriate to the circumstances of the deal.

REFERENCE TO THE PARTIES

Sometimes the letter form goes one step further to become informal, more readable, or user-friendly: discarding terms such as "licensor" and "publisher," and "licensee," and "producer," the letter refers to the parties as "we" and "us," and "you" and "your." Though this approach can be confusing when used in longer agreements, it is often quite appropriate and welcome in short letter agreements of one or two pages. An example of a letter agreement that uses this approach is set forth as Form 6.6 at the end of Chapter 6.

By contrast, the use of the formal terms, "Licensor" and "Licensee," "Grantor" and "Grantee," or "Assignee" and "Assignor," in longer contracts, each of which pair differ only by two letters, can make longer agreements quite tedious to read, and can even create some confusion in shorter contracts or letter agreements. It is therefore recommended that when selecting terms with which to refer to the parties, the draftor should choose a pair of words that are dissimilar and less likely to cause confusion. For example, the music copyright owner, the party granting the license or transferring the rights, may be referred to as, the "Owner." The licensee may be referred to as "Licensee," "Producer," or some other term that best describes the party requiring the clearance.

If, in addition to the privilege to do something with respect to the music, the contract grants an assignment of exclusive rights (i.e., the right to exclude others from doing the same thing), then neither "Licensor" nor "Licensee" may be the most appropriate means of referring to a party. The

"Licensor" is doing more than granting a license and, therefore, should be called something else, such as "Owner." Because the grantee is receiving more than a mere permission to do something, he should be called something other than "Licensee," such as "Producer."

STANDARD TERMS AND CONDITIONS

An increasingly popular compromise between the informality of the letter agreement and the benefits of long-form license agreements is the use of a letter agreement that incorporates by reference a standard set of terms and conditions that is often applicable to several kinds of licenses. An example of such an agreement is set forth as Form 3.10 at the end of this chapter.

FORMS USED IN THIS BOOK

The forms used in this book do not consistently reflect the principles discussed above. They certainly do not always reflect the best principles of drafting and their inclusion here should *not* be construed as their representing some form of ideal. On the contrary, the forms selected are representative of those customarily used in the music publishing industry today and are included primarily for the purpose of illustrating the practical guidance outlined in this book for both copyright owners and persons seeking to clear licenses. Accordingly, the forms should be used primarily to improve the reader's understanding and appreciation of that guidance. They should not be used without further consideration about how they should be applied to the transaction at hand, and should not be used by laymen without seeking the advice of an attorney experienced in the field of licensing or music publishing.

APPENDIX TO CHAPTER 3
FORMALITIES OF LICENSING

FORMS

FORM 3.1

SHORT-FORM COPYRIGHT ASSIGNMENT

ASSIGNMENT

DATED: January 1, 1993

ASSIGNOR (S):   John Doe (Music)
                          Jane Doe (Words)

ASSIGNEE(S):   BIG MUSIC PUBLISHING CORP.

PORTION CONVEYED: One Hundred Percent (100%)

For valuable consideration, ASSIGNOR hereby assigns, transfers, sets over and conveys to ASSIGNEE that proportion of all rights, title and interest set forth in and to the musical composition(s):

I LOVE YOU, BABY

including the copyrights and proprietary rights therein and in any and all versions of said musical composition(s), and any renewals and extensions thereof (whether presently available or sub-sequently available as a result of intervening legislation) in the United States of America and elsewhere throughout the world, and further including any and all causes of action for infringement of the same, past, present and future, all of the proceeds from the foregoing accrued and unpaid hereafter accruing.

ASSIGNOR agrees to sign any and all other papers which may be required to effectuate the purpose and intent of this Assignment, and hereby irrevocably authorizes and appoints ASSIGNEE his attorney and representative in its name or in his name as his true and lawful attorney-in-fact to take such action and make, sign, execute, acknowledge and deliver all such documents as may from time to time be necessary to convey to ASSIGNEE, its successors and assigns, all rights herein granted.

IN WITNESS WHEREOF, the undersigned has executed this Assignment as of the date above written.

Signed:_____

Signed:_____

FORM 3.2

MULTI-PURPOSE WORK FOR HIRE AGREEMENT

WORK FOR HIRE

THIS AGREEMENT MADE THIS_____ day of _____ ,
19_____ , by and between _____
_____(hereinafter referred to as
"Employee") and _____
hereinafter referred to as "Employer")

This agreement is made with reference to the following facts:

    A. Definition: A "work made for hire" is:

        1.   A work prepared by an employee within the scope of his or her employment; or

        2.   A work specially ordered or commissioned for use by employer or other person for whom the work was prepared where the parties expressly agree in a written instrument signed by them that the work shall be considered a work made for hire. For purposes of this agreement, employer is synonymous with any such person for whom the work was prepared.

        3.   Any other work that is within the definition of work made for hire within 17 U.S.C. Sec. 101.

        B.   Employer is engaged in the business of _____ .
Employer desires to acquire the exclusive services of Employee for the purpose of _____ .

        C.   Employee desires to make his services available exclusively for Employer in accordance with the terms and conditions hereinafter stated.

The parties agree as follows:

1. Employee acknowledges and expressly agrees that each _____ work prepared hereunder embodying the results and proceeds of Employee's services

    (a)   is prepared within the scope of Employer's engagement of Employee's personal services and is a work made for hire, or

    (b)   as part of a work specially ordered by Employer or commissioned for use by Employer as a contribution to a collective work shall be considered a work made for hire, or

    (c)   as part of a motion picture or other audiovisual work, as a translation, as a supplementary work, as a compilation, or as an instructional text shall be considered a work made for hire.

2. Employee further acknowledges that Employer is considered the author of the work and Employer is the exclusive owner of copyright in each work made for hire, and of all rights comprised in copyright, and that Employer shall have the right to exercise all rights of copyright owner with respect thereto, including but not limited to: all exclusive rights specified in 17 U.S.C Sec. 106.

Employer shall register for copyright in the name of Employer.

EMPLOYEE

By _____

EMPLOYER

By _____

FORM 3.3

MUSICAL ARRANGEMENT
WORK FOR HIRE AGREEMENT

MUSICAL ARRANGER AGREEMENT

WHEREAS, the undersigned, _____
an employee for hire of_____
("Employer") will at Employer's request and direction make an
arrangement of the music of a composition ("composition")
entitled _____

_____

_____

NOW, THEREFORE, in consideration of the sum of _____
and other good and valuable considerations, the receipt of which
is hereby duly acknowledged, the undersigned hereby confirms said
employment and agrees that such arrangement shall be a work
made for hire of Employer. In the event such arrangement shall be
deemed not to be a work made for hire, then the undersigned
hereby sells, assigns, and transfers over to Employer, and releases
and quitclaims unto Employer, its successors and assigns, all right,
title and interest in and to the Composition and all rights therein
and thereto, for the United States and throughout the world, forever,
including any and all copyright terms, and all extension terms of
copyright, for all uses and purposes whether now known or hereafter
created, free from payment of any royalty or further compensation.
Credit may be given for said arrangement to the undersigned or
not at all. The undersigned warrants and represents that he has
not sold, transferred, assigned or otherwise disposed of any right,
title or interest in or to any of the rights, referred to in this
agreement; and that except insofar as the work is based on material
hereinabove described the same is original with him.

IN WITNESS WHEREOF, the undersigned has hereunto set his hand
and seal this _____ day of_____ ,19 _____

FORM 3.4

LYRIC TRANSLATION WORK FOR HIRE AGREEMENT

LYRIC TRANSLATION

I, _____ ,hereby certify that as an employee-for-hire of _____ ,I have been engaged to create a [French/Spanish/Italian/German/Other] lyric, per copy attached ("Translation"), under the title _____ for the musical composition _____ by, with the consent and permission of_____,the copyright owner of said musical composition, and that the Translation shall be a work made for hire of _____, who, as proprietor of copyright in a work made for hire is the author and owner of the copyright including all renewals and extensions thereof and all other rights of every kind and character in and to said Translation free from the payment of any royalty, or further compensation whatsoever and without participation in any earnings or credits therefrom including public performances, credits and fees. It is understood that on all uses of and references to said lyric, including record labels and record album liners, I am not to receive writer credit.

Dated:_____

By _____

FORM 3.5

STANDARD MUSIC PUBLISHING AGREEMENT
FOR A SINGLE SONG

SINGLE SONG MUSIC PUBLISHING AGREEMENT

AGREEMENT entered into this _____ nd day of _____, 199____, by and between _____ (hereinafter referred to as "Composer") and BIG MUSIC PUBLISH-ING CORP. (ASCAP) (hereinafter referred to as "Publisher").

1.   Composer hereby sells, assigns and delivers to Publisher, its successors and assigns, the original musical compositions written and composed by Composer (words of which were written by _____ and music by_____), presently entitled " _____ " (the "Composition"), including the title, words and music thereof, all worldwide rights therein, all copyrights therein and thereto, all registrations with respect thereto, and the exclusive right to secure copyrights and any extensions of copyrights in the same and in any arrangements and adaptations thereof, all throughout the world, and any and all other rights, claims and demands that Composer now has or to which he might be entitled or that he hereafter could or might secure throughout the world with respect thereto if these presents had not been made, and to have and to hold the same absolutely and forever unto Publisher, its successors and assigns, subject only to any existing agreements between Composer and Publisher and the Performing Rights Society (with which they are affiliated).

2.   Composer hereby warrants and represents that the Composition is an original work, that neither the Composition nor any part thereof infringes upon the title, literary or musical property or copyright of any other work nor the statutory, common law or other rights (including rights of privacy or publicity) of any person, firm or corporation or violates any applicable criminal statute, that

he is the sole writer and composer and the sole owner of the Composition and of all the rights therein, that he has not sold, assigned, transferred, hypothecated or mortgaged any right, title or interest in or to the Composition or any part thereof or any of the rights herein conveyed, that he has not made or entered into any agreement with any other person, firm or corporation affecting the Composition or any right, title or interest therein or in the copyright thereof, that no person, firm or corporation other than Composer has or has had claims or has claimed any right, title or interest in or to the Composition or any part thereof, any use thereof or any copyright therein, that the Composition has never been published, and that Composer has full right, power and authority to make this present instrument of sale and transfer.

3.   In consideration of this agreement and of the rights and interests hereby conveyed and granted, Publisher agrees to pay to Composer the following royalties in respect of the Composition:

(a)   Seven cents ($.07) per copy for each copy of sheet music in standard piano-vocal notation of the Composition printed, published and sold in the United States and Canada by Publisher or its affiliates, for which payment has been received by Publisher, or been finally credited to Publisher's account in reduction of an advance after deduction of reasonable returns. (Wherever the terms "paid," "received," or the equivalent appear in this agreement, they shall be deemed to include such final credit.)

(b)   (i)   If the Composition is included in any folio, songbook or similar publication ("mixed folio"), a proportionate share of a royalty of twelve and one-half percent (12 1/2%) of the net wholesale selling price of such publication for all copies sold by Publisher or its affiliates and paid for in the United States and Canada. Said proportionate share shall be equal to the percentage computed by dividing the number "one" by the total number of all copyrighted musical compositions contained therein.

(ii)   If the Composition is included in a "fake book", "educational edition" or an instrumental, orchestral, choral or band arrangement or other arrangement intended for pedagogical purposes, a royalty of ten percent (10%), or a proportionate share thereof (calculated in the manner prescribed above in the case of a mixed folio) of the net wholesale selling price for all copies of such work sold by Publisher or its affiliates and paid for in the United States and Canada.

(iii)   If, pursuant to a license granted by Publisher to a licensee not controlled by or affiliated with it, the Composition is included in any mixed folio in the United States and/or Canada, a pro rata share of fifty percent (50%) of the gross amount received by Publisher from the licensee as the number of uses of the Composition under the license and during the license period bears to the total number of uses of Publisher's copyrighted musical compositions (including the Composition) under the license and during the license period.

(c)   Fifty percent (50%) of any and all net sums actually received (less any cost for collection) by Publisher or credited to Publisher's account in the United States from the exploitation in the United States and Canada by licensees of Publisher of mechanical rights, electrical transcription and reproducing rights, motion picture and television synchronization rights, and all other rights in the Composition (except print rights which are covered in paragraphs 3(a) and 3(b) above and public performance rights which are covered in (d) below) , whether or not such licensees are affiliated with, owned in whole or in part by, or controlled by Publisher.

(d)   (i)   Composer shall receive his public performance royalties throughout the world directly from his own affiliated performing rights society and shall have no claim whatsoever against Publisher for any royalties received by Publisher from any performing rights society which makes payment directly (or indirectly other than through Publisher) to writers, authors and composers.

(ii)   If, however, (and to the extent that) Publisher shall collect both the Composer's and Publisher's share of performance income directly and such income shall not be collected by Composer's public performance society, Publisher shall pay to Composer fifty percent (50%) of all such net sums which are received by Publisher in the United States from the exploitation of such rights in the Composition, throughout the world.

(e)   Fifty percent (50%) of any and all net sums, after deduction of foreign taxes, actually received (less any reasonable costs for collection) by Publisher in the United States from sales, licenses and other uses of the Composition in countries outside of the United States and Canada (other than public performance royalties described in subparagraph 3(d)(i)) from collection agents, licensees, subpublishers or others, whether or not same are affiliated with, owned in whole or in part by, or controlled by Publisher. This provision shall not apply to copies of printed music shipped from the United States to such countries, to which the rates set forth in paragraphs 3(a) and 3(b) above shall apply.

(f)   Publisher shall not be required to pay any royalties on reasonable numbers of professional or complimentary printed copies of the Composition or copies of mechanical derivatives of the Composition which are distributed gratuitously to performing artists, orchestra leaders and disc jockeys or for advertising, promotional or exploitation purposes for which Publisher receives no payment. Furthermore, no royalties shall be payable to Composer on consigned copies of the Composition unless paid for, and not until the accounting statement for the accounting period within which such payment is received.

(g)   If the Composition does not now have lyrics, and lyrics shall hereafter be added by Publisher, the above royalties shall be divided equally between Composer on the one hand and the writer or writers of the lyrics on the other hand.

(h)   To the extent approved by Publisher in writing in advance, Publisher shall pay the cost of making demonstration records of the Composition. One-half (1/2) of a pro rata share corresponding to Composer's percentage of the Composition as set forth in paragraph 1 above, of such total costs shall be deemed additional advances to Composer hereunder.

(i)   Except as herein expressly provided, no other royalties or moneys shall be paid to Composer. In no event shall Composer be entitled to share in any advance payments, guarantee payments or minimum royalty payments which Publisher may receive in connection with any subpublishing agreement, collection agreement, licensing agreement or other agreement covering the Composition, unless such payment shall be solely related to the Composition; in which event Publisher shall credit Composer's royalty account with fifty percent (50%) of all such sums received by Publisher.

4.   (a)   (i) Publisher shall compute the royalties earned by Composer pursuant to this agreement within sixty (60) days following the end of each semiannual calendar period during which moneys are received (or finally credited) with respect to the Composition, and shall thereupon submit to Composer the royalty statement for each such period together with the net amount of royalties, if any, which shall be payable after deducting any and all unrecouped advances and chargeable costs under this agreement. However, if a particular statement indicates a balance due of less than Fifty Dollars ($50.), Publisher shall not be required to make payment, and the balance due shall be carried forward until the end of the next subsequent accounting period during which the balance due exceeds Fifty Dollars ($50.), at which time such balance due shall be paid. Upon the submission of each statement, Publisher shall have the right to retain, as a reserve against subsequent charges, credits or returns, such portion of payable moneys hereunder (not exceeding 25%) with respect solely to print sales by Publisher or its affiliates as shall be necessary and appropriate in its best business judgment, but each such reserve shall be liquidated within two (2) quarter annual calendar periods following the period in respect of which such reserve is established. The payments to Composer provided for

under this agreement shall be computed as of the date each such statement is due and shall be paid for in United States currency by Publisher to Composer. The rate(s) of exchange utilized by third parties in accounting to Publisher shall also apply as between Publisher and Participant in accounting for the same moneys.

(ii)   If Publisher shall be unable to receive payment in United States dollars in the United States in respect of any exploitation of the Composition due to currency control laws or regulations, royalties in respect thereof shall not be credited to Composer's royalty account hereunder. Publisher shall, however, use its best efforts to accept such payments in foreign currency and deposit in a foreign bank or other depository, at Composer's expense, in such foreign currency such portion thereof, if any, as shall equal the royalties which would have actually been payable to Composer hereunder in respect of such exploitation had such payments been made to Publisher in United States dollars in the United States, and Publisher shall notify Composer thereof promptly. Deposit as aforesaid shall fulfill Publisher's royalty obligations hereunder as to such exploitation.

(b)   Each statement submitted by Publisher to Composer shall be binding upon Composer and not subject to any objection by Composer for any reason unless specific written objection, stating the basis thereof, is sent by Composer to Publisher within two (2) years after the date said statement is received (or deemed received as provided below). Composer or a certified public accountant in Composer's behalf may, at Composer's expense, at reasonable intervals (but not more frequently than once each year), examine Publisher's books insofar as same contain data of concern to Composer, during Publisher's usual business hours and upon thirty (30) days' notice, for the purpose of verifying the accuracy of any statement submitted to Composer hereunder. Publisher's books relating to activities during any accounting period may only be examined as aforesaid during the two (2) year period following receipt by Composer of the statement for said accounting period.

(c)   Notwithstanding any provision to the contrary herein contained, moneys hereunder shall only be payable by Publisher to Composer with respect to moneys actually received by Publisher in the United States or amounts finally credited to Publisher's account in reduction of a previous advance.

(d)   Legal action by Composer with respect to a specific accounting statement or the accounting statement to which the same relates shall be forever barred if not commenced in a court of competent jurisdiction within three (3) years after such statement is received (or deemed received as provided below).

(e)   For the purpose of calculating the time period for audits and legal action by Composer, a statement shall be deemed to have been received thirty (30) days after the same is due unless, within such period, Publisher shall receive notice of nonreceipt of such statement from Composer. However, Composer's failure to give such notice shall not affect Composer's right to receive such statement (and any accompanying payment) thereafter.

5.   Composer hereby grants to Publisher, its associates, affiliates, subsidiaries and licensees the perpetual, nonexclusive right to use and publish and to permit others to use and publish Composer's name (including any professional name heretofore or hereafter adopted by Composer), likeness and biographical material, or any reproduction or simulation thereof and the title of the Composition in connection with the exploitation of the Composition.

6.   Composer hereby acknowledges that Publisher has the right hereunder, in its sole discretion, to substitute a new title or titles for the Composition, to make changes, arrangements, adaptations, translations, dramatizations and transpositions of the Composition, in whole or in part, and in connection with any other musical, literary or dramatic material, and to add new lyrics to the music of the Composition or new music to the lyrics of the Composition. Composer hereby waives any and all claims which he

has or may have against Publisher, its associates, affiliates and subsidiaries and licensees by reason of the fact that the title of the Composition may be the same as or similar to that of any other musical compositions heretofore acquired by Publisher.

7.   Composer agrees to execute and deliver to Publisher all documents which may be required to effectuate the intent of this agreement, including, without limitation, a short-form copyright assignment in the form attached hereto as Exhibit "A," and, in the event that Composer fails to do so within ten (10) days following Composer's receipt of notice requesting same, Composer does hereby irrevocably empower and appoint Publisher, or any of its officers, Composer's true and lawful attorney (with full power of substitution and delegation) in Composer's name, and in Composer's place and stead, or in Publisher's name, to take and do such action, and to make, sign, execute, acknowledge, deliver, and record any and all instruments or documents which Publisher, from time to time, may deem desirable or necessary to vest in Publisher, its successors, assigns and licensees, any of the rights granted by Composer hereunder, including, without limitation, such instruments or documents required to secure to Publisher copyright registration and protection for the Composition for the full term of copyright and for any extensions thereof.

8.   Composer shall not transfer nor assign this agreement nor any interest therein nor any sums that may be or become due hereunder without the prior written consent of Publisher, which shall not be unreasonably withheld. Publisher shall not be deemed unreasonable for withholding its consent to a proposed assignment of Composer's right to receive royalties hereunder to more than one person. No purported assignment or transfer in violation of this restriction shall be valid to pass any interest to the assignee or transferee.

9.   (a)   Publisher may take such action as it deems necessary, either in Composer's name or in its own name, against any person to protect the rights and interest acquired by Publisher

hereunder. Publisher will promptly notify Composer of any claims, action, demand or proceeding which may affect Publisher or Composer's interest in the Composition and Composer shall have the right to participate therein by counsel of Composer's choice, at Composer's sole cost and expense. Composer will, at Publisher's request, cooperate fully with Publisher (but at no material expense to Composer), in any controversy which may arise or litigation which may be brought concerning Publisher's rights and interests acquired hereunder.

(b)   Publisher shall have the right, in its absolute discretion, to employ attorneys and to institute or defend any action or proceeding and to take any other proper steps to protect the right, title and interest of Publisher in and to the Composition and every portion thereof and in that connection, to settle, compromise or in any other manner dispose of any matter, claim, action or proceeding and to satisfy any judgment that may be rendered, in any manner as Publisher in its sole discretion may determine, provided that Composer's written consent shall be required to settle any claims and such consent shall not be unreasonably withheld. If Composer shall not give written consent to a proposed settlement of a claim which Publisher believes is reasonable within five (5) days after Composer's receipt of notice of such settlement offer, then on Publisher's request Composer shall promptly undertake any further action in regard to the claim at Composer's sole cost and expense, and Composer shall thereafter be fully and totally responsible and liable for any damages or costs in excess of the amount set forth in the proposed settlement offer.

(c)   Any legal action brought by Publisher against any alleged infringer of the Composition shall be initiated and prosecuted by Publisher, and if there is any recovery made by Publisher as a result thereof, the expenses of litigation, including but not limited to attorney's fees and court costs, shall be deducted therefrom and Composer shall be paid one-half (1/2) of a pro rata share of the net proceeds corresponding to Composer's percentage of the Composition as set forth in paragraph 1 above.

(d) Composer hereby indemnifies, saves and holds Publisher, its assigns, licensees and its and their directors, officers, shareholders, agents and employees harmless from any and all liability, claims, demands, loss and damage (including reasonable counsel fees and court costs) arising out of or connected with or resulting from any breach of any of the warranties, representations or agreements made by Composer in this agreement which results in an adverse judgment or a settlement entered into with Composer's prior written consent. Notwithstanding the foregoing, such indemnity shall also extend to the deductible under Publisher's errors-and-omissions policy without regard to judgment or settlement. In the event that Composer refuses to consent to a proposed settlement which Publisher considers reasonable, Composer shall assume the defense of the subject claim, action or proceeding, at Composer's expense. Such indemnity shall also extend to reasonable counsel fees and court costs incurred in connection with any claim, action or proceeding brought at Composer's written request. Publisher shall give Composer prompt written notice of any claim, action or proceeding covered by said indemnity, and the notified party shall have the right to participate by counsel of Composer's choice, at Composer's sole cost and expense. Pending the disposition of any adverse claim or action, Publisher shall have the right to withhold payment of such portion of moneys hereunder as shall be reasonably related to the amount of the claim and estimated legal expenses; provided, that any amount so withheld shall be released if (and to the extent that) legal action shall not have been commenced with respect thereto in a court of competent jurisdiction within one (1) year following such withholding; and provided, further, that Publisher shall not withhold moneys otherwise due to Composer if Composer shall deliver to Publisher an indemnity or surety bond, in form satisfactory to Publisher, which shall cover the amount of the claim and estimated legal costs.

10. The term "Composer" shall be understood to include all the writers and composers of the Composition. If there be more than one, the covenants herein contained shall be deemed to be both joint and several, subject to the terms of paragraph 2,

above, on the part of the writers and composers and the royalties hereinabove specified to be paid to Composer shall, unless a different division of royalties be specified in paragraph 16 below, be due to all the writers and composers collectively, to be paid by Publisher in equal shares to each.

11.   (a)   Publisher shall have the right to assign this agreement and any of its rights hereunder to any parent, subsidiary or affiliated person, firm or corporation, any entity into which or with which Publisher may merge or consolidate, or any purchaser of substantially all of Publisher's stock or assets.

(b)   Publisher shall also have the right to enter into sub-publishing, collection, print or other agreements with respect to the Composition with any person, firm or corporation for any one or more countries of the world.

12.   This agreement contains the entire understanding between the parties, and all of its terms, conditions and covenants shall be binding upon and shall inure to the benefit of the respective parties and their heirs, successors and assigns. No modification or waiver hereunder shall be valid unless the same is in writing and is signed by the party sought to be bound.

13.   This agreement has been entered into in, and is to be interpreted in accordance with the Laws of, the State of California. All actions or proceedings seeking the interpretation and/or enforcement of this agreement shall be brought only in the State or Federal Courts located in Los Angeles County, both parties hereby submitting themselves to the jurisdiction of such courts for such purpose.

14.   (a)   All notices, statements and payments required or desired to be given hereunder shall be given by addressing same to the addresses of the respective parties hereinbelow set forth, or to such other address as either party may hereafter designate, by writing and shall be delivered by the United States mails, certified or registered, postage prepaid, or in a telegraph or

cable office (except for royalty statements and payments which shall be sent by regular mail). If the party's consent is required, it shall not be unreasonably withheld (unless expressly provided otherwise herein) and shall be deemed denied unless the notified party gives notice of consent within 15 days after receipt of notice requesting consent. All notices to Publisher shall be sent to the attention of Publisher's Legal Department.

(b)   Publisher shall not be deemed to be in default hereunder unless Composer shall notify Publisher thereof and Publisher shall fail to remedy the same within thirty (30) days thereafter (or, if the alleged default is of such a nature that it cannot be completely remedied within such thirty-day period, Publisher shall fail to commence the remedying of such alleged default within such thirty-day period and to proceed to complete the same within a reasonable time thereafter).

15.   The use of the singular in this agreement shall apply to and mean the plural where appropriate.

16.   Composer hereby acknowledges that presently he is not affiliated as a writer with any Performing Rights Society and will do so as soon as he qualifies as a member. Composer agrees that he will promptly advise Publisher of such affiliation and Publisher shall, if necessary, have the right to assign this Agreement and all of Publisher's interest in the Composition to an affiliated publishing company which is a member of the Society which Composer joins.

IN WITNESS WHEREOF, the parties hereto have executed this agreement as of the date hereinabove set forth.

IMPORTANT

This is a legal document,
and you should review it with
an experienced attorney
before you sign it.

BIG MUSIC PUBLISHING CORP.

By: _____
Vice President
1000 Sunset Boulevard
Hollywood, CA 90069

_____
MR. JOHN DOE (MUSIC)
Address:
S.S.#:
Date of Birth:

_____
MS. JANE DOE (LYRICS)
Address:
S.S.#:
Date of Birth:

FORM 3.6

1939 SONGWRITER'S PROTECTIVE ASSOCIATION UNIFORM POPULAR SONGWRITER'S CONTRACT

Form No. 2
Approved by

1939

For use by_____
Publisher

UNIFORM POPULAR SONGWRITERS CONTRACT

AGREEMENT made this   day of   , 19   , between

(hereinafter called "Publisher") and

jointly and/or severally, (hereinafter called ("Writer(s)");

WITNESSETH:

1. The Writer(s) hereby sells, assigns, transfers and delivers to the Publisher, its successors and assigns, a certain heretofore unpublished original musical composition written and/or composed by the above named Writer(s) now entitled

including the title, words and music thereof, and the right to secure copyright therein throughout the entire world, and to have and to hold the said copyright and all rights of whatsoever nature thereunder existing (herein referred to as "said composition"), upon the terms and conditions hereinafter set forth.

2. In all respects this contract shall be subject to any existing agreements between all of the parties hereto and the American Society of Composers, Authors and Publishers.

3. The Writer(s) hereby warrants that the said composition is his sole, exclusive and original work, and that he has full right and power to make the within agreement, and that there exists no adverse claim to or in the said composition, and that there is no outstanding claim to any moneys to accrue to the Writer(s) therefrom, except as aforesaid in Clause 2 hereof, and except such rights as are specifically set forth in Paragraph 17 hereof.

4. In consideration of this agreement, the Publisher agrees to pay the Writer(s) jointly, in respect of said composition the following:

   (a) An advance of $ in hand paid, receipt of which is hereby acknowledged, which sums shall be deductible from any payments hereafter becoming due the Writer(s) under this agreement.

   (b) In respect of regular piano copies sold and paid for at wholesale in the United States of America, royalties per copy as follows:

Wholesale price	cents — — — royalty	cents per copy.
Wholesale price	cents — — — royalty	cents per copy.
Wholesale price	cents — — — royalty	cents per copy.
Wholesale price	cents (or less) — royalty	cents per copy.

   (c) A royalty of   % (in no case however less than 50% jointly) of all net sums received by the Publisher in respect of regular piano copies and/or orchestrations thereof and in respect of the use of said composition in any folio or composite work, sold and paid for in any foreign country.

(d) A royalty of _____ cents per copy of orchestrations thereof in any form sold and paid for in the United States of America.

(e) Said composition shall not be published in any folio or composite work until after publication thereof in regular piano copies. Subsequent to said date said composition may be published in the United States and Canada in such form, only upon such terms and conditions as may hereafter be agreed to in writing by the parties hereto.

(f) Folios and/or composite works as referred to in the next preceding paragraph shall be deemed to include any publication of ten or more compositions within the same volume and/or binding.

(g) For purposes of royalty statements, if a composition is printed and published in the United States of America, as to copies and rights sold in the Dominion of Canada, revenue herefrom shall be considered as of domestic origin.

If, however, the composition is printed by a party other than the Publisher in the Dominion of Canada, revenue from sales of copies and rights in Canada shall be considered as originated in a foreign country.

(h) As to "professional material"—not sold or resold, no royalty shall be payable.

(i) An amount equal to _____ % (in no case, however, less than 50% jointly) of:

All receipts of the Publisher in respect of any licenses issued authorizing the manufacture of parts of instruments serving to mechanically reproduce said composition, or to use said composition in synchronization with sound motion pictures, or to reproduce it upon so-called electrical transcription for broadcasting purposes; and of any and all receipts of the Publisher from any other source or right now known or which may hereafter come into existence (except for which specific royalty provision is otherwise made or which are specifically excepted under this agreement), all such sums to be divided amongst the Writer(s) of said composition as provided in Paragraph 5 hereof; provided, however, that if the Publisher administers the said licenses, or any of them, through the agent, trustee or other administrator acting for a substantial part of the industry and not in the exclusive employ of the Publisher, the Publisher, in determining his receipts, shall be entitled to deduct from gross license fees paid by the licensees a sum equal to the charges paid by the said Publisher to said agent, trustee or administrator, said deduction in no event, however, to exceed 10% of the license fee.

The percentage of the Writer(s) on moneys received from foreign sources shall be computed on the Publisher's net receipts.

The Writer(s) shall not be entitled to any share of the moneys distributed to the Publisher by the American Society of Composers, Authors and Publishers, or by or through any other performing rights society or agency throughout the world if writers receive through the same source an amount which, in the aggregate, is at least equal to the aggregate amount distributed to publishers.

(j) Upon the use of said composition in synchronization with motion pictures under any bulk or block license made before June 1, 1939, the Writer(s) shall be entitled to receive an amount equal to _____ % (in no case less than 50% jointly) of the license fee for each synchronization by the licensee, but in no event less than the following:

FOR WORLD-WIDE USE

For Entire Uses

In Shorts	In Features
$25 for each background instrumental or background vocal use.	$25 for each background instrumental or background vocal use.
$37.50 for each visual instrumental use.	$50 for each visual instrumental use.
$50 for each visual vocal use.	$75 for each visual vocal use.

For Partial Uses—One-half of foregoing rates.

(k) The Publisher agrees that the use of said composition will not be included in any bulk or block license and that it will not grant any bulk or block license to include the same, without the written consent of Song Writers' Protective Association on behalf of the Writer(s) in each instance, except: (1) That the Publisher may permit the use of the said composition in accordance with and subject to the provisions of Subdivision (j) hereof; (2) In connection with the making of records for electrical transcription for broadcasting purposes, the Publisher may grant licenses for specific medleys or selections.

A license or transaction in bulk or block shall be deemed to mean the licensing of two or more compositions where the currently prevailing license fees are not charged specifically for each separate use of each composition.

(l) Except to the extent that the Publisher and Writer(s) may hereafter assign to or vest in the American Society of Composers, Authors and Publishers the said rights or the right to grant licenses therefor, it is agreed that no licenses shall be granted without the written consent of Song Writers' Protective Association on behalf of the Writer(s) in each instance, for the use of the said composition by means of television, or by any means or for any purpose not commercially established, or for which licenses were not granted by the Publisher on musical compositions prior to June 1, 1937.

(m) The Publisher shall not, without the written consent of the Writer(s) in each case, give or grant any right or license (a) to use the title of the musical composition, or (b) for the exclusive use of said composition in any form or for any purpose, or for any period of time, or for any territory, or (c) to give a dramatic representation of the said musical composition or to dramatize the plot or story thereof, or (d) for a vocal visual rendition of said composition in synchronization with a motion picture. If, however, the Publisher shall give to the Writer(s) written notice, by registered mail or telegram, specifying the right or license to be given or granted, the name of the licensee and the terms and conditions thereof, including the price or other compensation to be received therefor, then, unless the Writer(s) (or any one or more of them, or anyone acting on their behalf) shall, within seventy-two hours (exclusive of Saturdays, Sundays and holidays) after the sending of such notice, if sent by telegram, or within one hundred and forty-four hours (exclusive of Saturdays, Sundays and holidays) after the sending of such notice by registered mail, notify the Publisher of his or its objection thereto, either by registered mail or telegram, the Publisher may grant such right or license, in accordance with such notice without first obtaining the consent of the Writer(s). Such notice shall be deemed sufficient notice to the Writer(s) (whether one or more) if sent to

at

(or at the address of such party last furnished to the Publisher in writing by the Writer(s), or any of them).

(n) Any portion of the receipts which may become due to the Writer(s) from license fees (in excess of off-sets), whether received directly from the licensee or from the agent, administrator and trustee, shall, if not paid immediately on the receipt thereof by the Publisher, belong to the Writer(s) and shall be held in trust for such Writer(s) until payment is made; the ownership of said trust fund by the Writer(s) shall not be questioned whether the moneys are physically segregated or not.

(o) The Publisher shall not, without the written consent of Song Writers' Protective Association on behalf of the Writer(s) in each instance, authorize the use of said composition upon the parts of instruments serving to reproduce said composition on commercial phonograph records for a royalty of less than the statutory fee on each such part manufactured.

5. It is understood and agreed by and between all of the parties hereto that all sums hereunder payable jointly to the Writer(s) shall be divided amongst them respectively as follows:

Name	Share

6. The Publisher shall render the Writer(s), as above, on or before each May 15th covering the three months ending March 31st; each August 15th covering the three months ending June 30th; each November 15th covering the three months ending September 30th; each February 15th covering the three months ending December 31st; hereafter, so long as it shall continue publication or the licensing of any rights in the said composition, royalty statements accompanied by remittance of the amount due, provided, however, that if it shall have heretofore been the custom of the Publisher to render royalty statements accompanied by remittance semi-annually, such custom may be continued.

7. The Publisher agrees to publish in salable form the said musical composition within from the date hereof. Should he fail so to do the Writer(s) shall have the right in writing to demand the return of said composition, whereupon the Publisher must within one (1) month after receipt of such notice either publish the said composition, in which event this agreement remains in full force and effect, or upon failure so to publish, all rights of any and every nature, and the right to secure copyright and/or any copyright secured by the Publisher before publication, in and to the said composition, shall revert to and become the property of the Writer(s) and shall be reassigned to him.

8. Anything to the contrary notwithstanding, nothing in this agreement contained shall prevent the Publisher from authorizing publishers, agents and representatives in countries outside of the United States and Canada (and in Canada if said composition is printed by a party other than the publisher in Canada) from exercising exclusive publication and all other rights in said foreign countries in said composition on the customary royalty basis. If foreign publication or other rights in said composition are separately conveyed, otherwise than as a part of the Publisher's current and/or future catalog, then, but not otherwise, any advance received in respect thereof shall be divided in accordance with paragraph 4, subdivision (i) hereof, and credited to the accounts of the respective Writer(s).

9. The Writer(s) or his representative may appoint a certified public accountant who shall at any time during usual business hours have access to all records of the Publisher relating to said composition for the purpose of verifying royalty statements rendered or which are delinquent under the terms hereof.

10. (a) The Publisher shall, upon written demand of the Writer(s) or his (their) representative, cause the agent, trustee or administrator referred to above, to furnish to the Writer(s) or his (their) representative, statements showing in detail all licenses granted, uses had and payments made in connection with said composition, which licenses or permits were granted, or payments were received, by or through said agent, trustee or administrator, and to permit the Writer(s), or his (their) representative to inspect at the place of business of such agent, trustee or administrator all books, records and documents of the agent, trustee or administrator relating thereto.

(b) The Publisher shall from time to time, upon written demand of the Writer(s) or his (their) representative, furnish to the Writer(s) or his (their) representative, statements showing in detail all licenses granted, uses had and payments made therefor in connection with said composition (other than licenses, uses and payments for commercial phonograph records and music rolls) for which licenses or permits were granted or payments received by the Publisher without the intervention of said agent, trustee or administrator, and to permit the Writer(s) or his (their) representative to inspect at the place of business of the Publisher, all books, records and documents relating to said composition and all licenses granted, uses had and payments made therefor, such right of inspection to include, but not by way of limitation, the right to examine all original accountings and records relating to uses and payments by manufacturers of commercial phonograph records and music rolls. Nothing in this paragraph contained, furthermore, shall be deemed or construed to relieve the Publisher of its obligation to pay royalties on the use of said composition on commercial phonograph records and music rolls or the obligation to include a statement of such royalties in the periodical royalty statements to be rendered to the Writer(s) in accordance with Paragraph 6 of this agreement.

(c) Any and all agreements made by the Publisher with the said agent, trustee or administrator shall provide that said agent, trustee or administrator will comply with the terms and provisions hereof. In the event that the Publisher shall instruct the said agent, trustee or administrator referred to above, to furnish to the Writer or his representative the statements as provided for in paragraph 10 (a) hereof, and to permit the inspection of the books, records and documents as therein provided, and if the said agent, trustee or administrator should refuse to comply with the said instructions, or any of them, then the Publisher agrees to institute and prosecute diligently and in good faith such action or proceedings as may be necessary to compel compliance with the said instructions.

11. In the event that the Publisher shall fail or refuse, within sixty days after written demand, to furnish said statements, or cause the same to be furnished, or to make available or cause to be made available to the Writer(s) or his (their) representative all of such books, records or documents as provided in subdivision (b) of paragraph 10, or to cause the agent or trustee to furnish the same as provided in subdivision (a) of paragraph 10 and the agent or trustee shall refuse to comply with the instructions of the Publisher, then to take such steps as provided in subdivision (c) of paragraph 10, or in the event that the Publisher shall fail to make the payment of any royalties due within thirty days after written demand therefor, then the Writer(s) shall have the option, to be exercised upon ten days' written notice to cancel this agreement.

Upon such cancellation, all rights of the Publisher, of any and every nature, in and to said compositions, shall cease and come to an end and the same rights, including but not limited to the right to secure copyright and/or any copyright theretofore secured by the Publisher, shall revert to and become the property of the Writer(s) and shall be assigned to him (them). The Publisher agrees that it will thereupon execute any and all assignment or other documents which may be necessary or proper to vest the said rights in the Writer(s).

12. Written demands and notices provided for in Paragraphs 10 and 11 hereof shall be sent to the Publisher by registered mail.

13. Any legal action brought by the Publisher against any alleged infringer of said composition shall be initiated and prosecuted at his sole expense, and of any recovery made by him as a result thereof, after deduction of the expense of the litigation, a sum equal to fifty per cent shall be divided as agreed among the Writer(s) of the said composition.

(a) If a claim is presented against the Publisher alleging that the said composition is an infringement upon some other, and because thereof the Publisher is jeopardized, he shall thereupon serve written notice upon the Writer(s), containing the full details of such claim and thereafter until the claim has been adjudicated or settled shall pay any moneys coming due the Writer(s) hereunder in escrow to any bank or trust company to be held pending the outcome of such claim; provided however, if no suit be filed within twelve months, after written notice to the Writer(s) by the Publisher of the adverse claim, the said bank or trust company shall release and pay to the Writer(s) all sums held in escrow, plus any interest which may have been earned thereupon. Such payment shall be without prejudice to the rights of the Publisher in event of a subsequent adverse adjudication.

(b) From and after the service of summons in a suit for infringement filed against the Publisher in respect of the said composition, any and all payments hereunder thereafter coming due the Writer(s) shall be paid by the Publisher in trust to any bank or trust company until the suit has been finally adjudicated and then be disbursed accordingly, unless the Writer(s) shall elect to file an acceptable bond in the sum of such payments, in which event the sums due shall be paid to him.

14. The parties hereto hereby agree to submit to arbitration under the rules of the American Arbitration Association, and pursuant to the New York Arbitration Law any differences arising under this agreement, and hereby agree individually and jointly to abide by and perform any award rendered by the Arbitration and that a judgment of the Supreme Court of the State of New York may be entered upon such award.

15. This agreement is binding upon the parties hereto and their respective sucessors in interest.

16. Three identical copies hereof are executed by the parties, the original copy of which shall remain in the possession of the Publisher, the duplicate in possession of the Writer(s), and the triplicate thereof be forwarded by mail by the Publisher to the Song Writers' Protective Association.

17. The rights specifically excepted, as provided in Paragraph 3 hereof, are as follows:

Witness:

Witness:

Witness:

Witness:

Publisher:

By ....(L.S.)

Address ....   LS

Writer ....(L.S.)

Address ....   LS

Writer ....(L.S.)

Address ....   LS

Writer ....(L.S.)

Address:

FORM 3.7

1969 AMERICAN GUILD OF AUTHORS AND COMPOSERS UNIFORM POPULAR SONGWRITER'S CONTRACT

AMERICAN GUILD OF AUTHORS & COMPOSERS

Authorized for use by..

....

under agreement dated.......................19............ and **Not Valid**

Unless Countersigned by AGAC

UNIFORM POPULAR SONGWRITERS CONTRACT
Copyright ©1948 Songwriters Protective Ass'n.
Copyright ©1969 AGAC.

AGREEMENT made this   day of   , 19   , between

....

(hereinafter called "Publisher") and..

....

Jointly and/or severally hereinafter collectively called "Writer");

WITNESSETH:

Composition

1. The Writer hereby sells, assigns, transfers and delivers to the Publisher a certain heretofore unpublished original musical composition, written and/or composed by the above-named Writer now entitled

(hereinafter referred to as "the composition"), including the title, words and music thereof, and the right to secure copyright therein throughout the entire world, and to have and to hold the said copyright and all rights of whatsoever nature thereunder existing, for the original term of the United States copyright or for the period of twenty-eight years from the date of publication in the United States, whichever may be shorter, and subject to the terms of this contract.

Performing Rights Affiliation

2. In all respects this contract shall be subject to any existing agreements between any of the parties hereto and the small performing rights licensing organization of which Writer is a member or an affiliate.

Warranty

3. The Writer hereby warrants that the composition is his sole, exclusive and original work, that he has full right and power to make the within contract, and that there exists no adverse claim to or in the composition, except as aforesaid in Paragraph 2 hereof and except such rights as are specifically set forth in Paragraph 23 hereof.

Royalties

4. In consideration of this contract, the Publisher agrees to pay the Writer as follows:

Advance

(a) $......................as an advance against royalties, receipt of which is hereby acknowledged, which sum shall remain the property of the Writer and shall be deductible only from payments hereafter becoming due the Writer under this contract.

Piano Copies

(b) In respect of regular piano copies sold and paid for in the United States and Canada, a royalty per copy according to whichever one of the following provisions is checked:

Fixed Royalty ☐   (i) ....¢ (in no case less than 3¢ per copy.)

Sliding Scale ☐   (ii) ....% (in no case, however, less than 11½%) of the wholesale selling price of the first 100,000 copies or less, but in no event less than 2¼¢ per copy; plus

........% (in no case, however, less than 14%) of the wholesale selling price of copies in excess of 100,000 and not exceeding 200,000, but in no event less than 3¢ per copy; plus

........% (in no case, however, less than 16%) of the wholesale selling price of copies in excess of 200,000 and not exceeding 300,000, but in no event less than 3½¢ per copy; plus

........% (in no case, however, less than 18%) of the wholesale selling price of copies in excess of 300,000 and not exceeding 400,000, but in no event less than 4¢ per copy; plus

........% (in no case, however, less than 20½%) of the wholesale selling price of copies in excess of 400,000 and not exceeding 500,000, but in no event less than 4½¢ per copy; plus

........% (in no case, however, less than 23%) of the wholesale selling price of all copies in excess of 500,000, but in no event less than 5¢ per copy.

Foreign Royalties

(c) ....% (in no case, however, less than 50%) of all net sums received by the Publisher in respect of regular piano copies, orchestrations, band arrangements, octavos, quartets, arrangements for combinations of voices and/or instruments, and/or other copies of the composition sold in any country other than the United States and Canada, provided, however, that if the Publisher should sell such copies through, or cause them to be sold by, a subsidiary or affiliate which is actually doing business in a foreign country, then in respect of such sales, the Publisher shall pay to the Writer not less than 5% of the marked retail selling price in respect of each such copy sold and paid for.

Orchestrations and Other Arrangements, etc.

(d) ....% (in no case, however, less than 10%) of the wholesale selling price (after trade discounts if any) of each copy sold and paid for in the United States and Canada, or for export from the United States, of orchestrations, band arrangements, octavos, quartets, arrangements for combinations of voices and/or instruments, and/or other copies of the composition (other than regular piano copies).

Publisher's Song Book, Song Sheet, Folio, etc.

(e) (i) If the composition, or any part thereof, is included in any song book, song sheet, folio or similar publication issued by the Publisher containing at least four, but not more than twenty-five musical compositions, the royalty to be paid by the Publisher to the Writer shall be an amount determined by dividing 10% of the wholesale selling price (after trade discounts, if any) of the copies sold, among the total number of the Publisher's copyrighted musical compositions included in such publication. If such publication contains more than twenty-five musical compositions, the said 10% shall be increased by an additional ½% for each additional musical composition. The composition shall not, however, be included in any such publication earlier than six months after the date on which regular piano copies of the composition shall have been published, except that said six months period may be reduced to three months with the Writer's written consent given at any time after the expiration of three months.

**Licensee's
Song Book,
Song Sheet,
Folio, etc.**

(ii) If, pursuant to a license granted by the Publisher to a licensee not controlled by or affiliated with it, the composition, or any part thereof, is included in any song book, song sheet, folio or similar publication, containing at least four musical compositions, the royalty to be paid by the Publisher to the Writer shall be that proportion of 50% of the gross amount received by it from the licensee, as the number of uses of the composition under the license and during the license period, bears to the total number of uses of the Publisher's copyrighted musical compositions under the license and during the license period. The lyrics alone of the composition may be included in such a publication at any time, but the lyrics and music thereof, in combination, shall not be included earlier than two years after the date on which regular piano copies of the composition shall have been published. Such royalties shall be computed and paid within 30 days after the expiration of the term of each license, but if any such license term is in excess of one year, such royalties shall be computed and paid annually.

(iii) In computing the number of the Publisher's copyrighted musical compositions under subdivisions (i) and (ii) hereof, there shall be excluded musical compositions in the public domain and arrangements thereof and those with respect to which the Publisher does not currently publish and offer for sale regular piano copies.

(iv) Royalties on publications containing less than four musical compositions shall be payable at regular piano copy rates.

**Professional
Material and
Free Copies**

(f) As to "professional material" not sold or resold, no royalty shall be payable. Free copies of the lyrics of the composition shall not be distributed except under the following conditions: (i) with the Writer's written consent; or (ii) when printed without music in limited numbers for charitable, religious or governmental purposes, or for similar public purposes, if no profit is derived, directly or indirectly; or (iii) when authorized for printing in a book, magazine or periodical, where such use is incidental to a novel or story (as distinguished from use in a book of lyrics or a lyric magazine or folio), provided that any such use shall bear the Writer's name and the proper copyright notice; or (iv) when distributed solely for the purpose of exploiting the composition, provided, that such exploitation is restricted to the distribution of limited numbers of such copies for the purpose of influencing the sale of the composition, that the distribution is independent of the sale of any other musical compositions, services, goods, wares or merchandise, and that no profit is made, directly or indirectly, in connection therewith.

**Mechanicals,
Electrical
Transcription,
Synchronization,
All Other
Rights**

(g) ....% (in no case, however, less than 50%) of:

All gross receipts of the Publisher in respect of any licenses (including statutory royalties) authorizing the manufacture of parts of instruments serving to mechanically reproduce the composition, or to use the composition in synchronization with sound motion pictures, or to reproduce it upon electrical transcription for broadcasting purposes; and of any and all gross receipts of the Publisher from any other source or right now known or which may hereafter come into existence, except as provided in subdivision (i) of this paragraph 4.

**Licensing
Agent's
Charges**

(h) If the Publisher administers licenses authorizing the manufacture of parts of instruments serving to mechanically reproduce said composition, or the use of said composition in synchronization or in timed relation with sound motion pictures or its reproduction upon electrical transcriptions, or any of them, through an agent, trustee or other administrator acting for a substantial part of the industry and not under the exclusive control of the Publisher (hereinafter sometimes referred to as licensing agent), the Publisher, in determining his receipts, shall be entitled to deduct from gross license fees paid by the Licensees, a sum equal to the charges paid by the Publisher to said licensing agent, provided, however, that in respect to synchronization or timed relation with sound motion pictures, said deduction shall in no event exceed $150.00 or 10% of said gross license fee, whichever is less; in connection with the manufacture of parts of instruments serving to mechanically reproduce said composition, said deductions shall not exceed 2½% of said gross license fee; and in connection with electrical transcriptions, said deductions shall not exceed 10% of said gross license fee.

**Small
Performing
Royalties**

(i) Nothing contained in this agreement shall alter, vary or modify the rights of Writer and Publisher to share in, receive and retain the proceeds distributed to them by the small performing rights licensing organization (i.e., ...
of which both Writer and Publisher are members or affiliated pursuant to their respective agreements with such small performing rights licensing organization.

Block Licenses

(j) The Publisher agrees that the use of the composition will not be included in any bulk or block license heretofore or hereafter granted, and that it will not grant any bulk or block license to include the same, without the written consent of American Guild of Authors and Composers on behalf of the Writer in each instance, except (i) that the Publisher may grant such licenses with respect to electrical transcription for broadcasting purposes, but in such event, the Publisher shall pay to the Writer that proportion of 50% of the gross amount received by it under each such license as the number of uses of the composition under each such license during each such license period bears to the total number of uses of the Publisher's copyrighted musical compositions under each such license during each such license period; in computing the number of the Publisher's copyrighted musical compositions for this purpose, there shall be excluded musical compositions in the public domain and arrangements thereof and those with respect to which the Publisher does not currently publish and offer for sale regular piano copies; and with respect to such licenses, the Publisher shall account to the Writer annually; (ii) that the Publisher may appoint agents or representatives in countries outside of the United States and Canada to use and to grant licenses for the use of the composition on the customary royalty fee basis under which the Publisher shall receive not less than 10% of the marked retail selling price in respect of regular piano copies, and 50% of all other revenue; if, in connection with any such bulk or block license, the Publisher shall have received any advance, the Writer shall not be entitled to share therein, but no part of said advance shall be deducted in computing the composition's earnings under said bulk or block license. A bulk or block license shall be deemed to mean any license or agreement, domestic or foreign, whereby rights are granted in respect of two or more musical compositions.

**Television
and New Uses**

(k) Except to the extent that the Publisher and Writer have heretofore or may hereafter assign to or vest in the small performing rights licensing organization of which Writer is a member or an affiliate, the said rights or the right to grant licenses therefor, it is agreed that no licenses shall be granted without the written consent, in each instance, of the Writer for the use of the composition by means of television, or by any means, or for any purposes not commercially established, or for which licenses were not granted by the Publisher on musical compositions prior to June 1, 1937.

**Writer's
Consent to
Licenses**

(l) The Publisher shall not, without the written consent of the Writer in each case, give or grant any right or license (i) to use the title of the composition, or (ii) for the exclusive use of the composition in any form or for any purpose, or for any period of time, or for any territory, other than its customary arrangements with foreign publishers, or (iii) to give a dramatic representation of the composition or to dramatize the plot or story thereof, or (iv) for a vocal rendition of the composition in synchronization with sound motion pictures, or (v) for any synchronization use thereof after the expiration of ten years from the date on which regular piano copies of the composition shall have been first published, or (vi) for the use of the composition or a quotation or excerpt therefrom in any article, book, periodical, advertisement or other similar publication. If, however, the Publisher shall give to the Writer written notice, by registered mail or telegram, specifying the right or license to be given or granted, the name of the licensee and the terms and conditions thereof, including the price or other compensation to be received therefor, then, unless the Writer (or any one or more of them) shall, within seventy-two hours (exclusive of Saturdays, Sundays and holidays) after the delivery of such notice to the address of the Writer hereinafter designated, object thereto, the Publisher may grant such right or license in accordance with the said notice without first obtaining the consent of the Writer. Such notice shall be deemed sufficient if sent to the Writer at the address or addresses hereinafter designated or at the address or addresses last furnished to the Publisher in writing by the Writer.

Trust for Writer

(m) Any portion of the receipts which may become due to the Writer from license fees (in excess of offsets), whether received directly from the licensee or from any licensing agent of the Publisher, shall, if not paid immediately on the receipt thereof by the Publisher, belong to the Writer and shall be held in trust for the Writer until payment is made; the ownership of said trust fund by the Writer shall not be questioned whether the monies are physically segregated or not.

Writer Participation

(n) The Publisher agrees that it will not issue any license as a result of which it will receive any financial benefit in which the Writer does not participate.

Writer Credit

(o) Every license or authorization issued by the Publisher authorizing the publication of the composition or any part thereof shall contain a provision requiring the user thereof to print, in addition to the copyright notice, the name of the Writer as the author thereof.

Change in Piano Copy Royalty

(p) If a fixed royalty is designated to be payable with respect to regular piano copies of the composition (as provided in paragraph 4 (b) (i), then, if at any time, the Publisher shall increase or decrease the wholesale selling price which it charged on January 1, 1947 to regular music jobbers for regular piano copies of musical compositions of the same class or category as the composition, then the said fixed royalty shall be increased or decreased in proportion to the change in said wholesale selling price.

Writers' Respective Shares

5. Whenever the term "Writer" is used herein, it shall be deemed to mean all of the persons named herein below, and any and all royalties herein provided to be paid to the Writer shall be paid jointly to the following persons if there be more than one, and shall be divided among them as follows:

Name   Share

....

....

....

....

Publication

6. (a) The Publisher shall, within one year from the date hereof, make, publish and offer for sale regular piano copies of the composition in the form and through the channels customarily employed by it for that purpose, and in addition, either (i) cause a commercial phonograph recording to be made and distributed in the customary form and through the customary commercial channels, or (ii) make, publish and offer for sale a dance orchestra arrangement. As an alternative to compliance with (i) or (ii), the Publisher shall pay to the Writer the sum of $250.00 less the aggregate of any advances paid, as stated in Paragraph 4 (a) hereof, and any royalties paid to the Writer within said one-year period. If, in the statement of "Special Exceptions" hereinafter set forth, the composition shall have been designated as one which is not intended for publication in regular piano copies, the Publisher shall be deemed to have complied with this paragraph by the making and distribution of a commercial phonograph recording and either the publication of a dance orchestra arrangement or the payment of the $250.00, all as aforesaid.

Failure to Publish

(b) Should the Publisher fail to comply with the provisions of subdivision (a) hereof, the Writer shall be entitled to demand in writing the return of the composition at any time after the expiration of said year, whereupon the Publisher must, within one month after the receipt of such notice, either comply with the provisions of subdivision (a) hereof, in which event this contract will remain in full force and effect, or upon its failure so to comply, this contract shall terminate and all rights of any and every nature in and to the composition and in and to any and all copyrights secured thereon in the United States and throughout the world, shall re-vest in and become the property of the Writer and shall be reassigned to him by the Publisher; the Writer shall not be obligated to return or pay to the Publisher any advance or indebtedness as a condition of such re-assignment; the said re-assignment shall be in accordance with and subject to the provisions of Paragraph 13 hereof, and in addition, the Publisher shall pay to the Writer all gross sums which it has theretofore or may thereafter receive in respect of the composition.

Writer's Copies

(c) The Publisher shall furnish the Writer copies of the composition which it publishes and shall use its best efforts to furnish or cause to be furnished to the Writer copies published by others.

Foreign Copyright

7. (a) Each copyright on the composition in countries other than the United States shall be secured only in the name of the Publisher, and the Publisher shall not at any time divest itself of said foreign copyright directly or indirectly, except to the extent that it may be obligated to do so by virtue of an agreement entered into by the Publisher with a foreign publisher prior to January 1, 1947, and then only for the term of said agreement

Foreign Publication

(b) Except to the extent that the Publisher is obligated to a foreign publisher or licensee by written agreement made prior to January 1, 1947, and then only for the term of said agreement, no rights shall be granted by the Publisher in the composition to any foreign publisher or licensee inconsistent with the terms hereof, nor shall any foreign publication rights in the composition be given to a foreign publisher or licensee unless and until the Publisher shall have complied with the provisions of Paragraph 6 hereof.

Foreign Advance

(c) If foreign rights in the composition are separately conveyed, otherwise than as a part of the Publisher's current and/or future catalog, not less than 50% of any advance received in respect thereof shall be credited to the account of and paid to the Writer.

Foreign Percentage

(d) The percentage of the Writer on monies received from foreign sources shall be computed on the Publisher's net receipts, provided, however, that no deductions shall be made for offsets of monies due from the Publisher to said foreign sources; or for advances made by such foreign sources to the Publisher, unless the Writer shall have received at least 50% of said advances.

No Foreign Allocations

(e) In computing the receipts of the Publisher from licenses granted in respect of synchronization with sound motion pictures, or in respect of any world-wide licenses, or in respect of licenses granted by the Publisher for use of the composition in countries other than the United States, no amount shall be deducted for payments or allocations to publishers or licensees in such countries.

Terms of Contract

8. All rights in and to the composition and any copyrights secured thereon throughout the world, shall revert to the Writer upon expiration of the original term of the United States copyright or at the end of twenty-eight (28) years from the date of publication in the United States, whichever period shall be shorter. The Publisher shall, at the expiration of said period, execute any and all documents which may be necessary or proper to re-vest in the Writer any and all rights in and to the composition and in and to any copyright in the United States or any other countries throughout the world; provided, however, that if the Writer shall sell or assign to some person other than the Publisher, his rights in the United States renewal copyright in the composition, or any of his rights in the composition in the United States or elsewhere, for the period beyond said original term or twenty-eight years, as the case may be, then, unless there shall have been given to the Publisher at least six months' written notice of an intention to offer said rights for sale, the Publisher

shall not be obligated to assign to the Writer said rights in countries other than the United States and Canada, and this contract, and the assignment under Paragraph 1 hereof, shall all continue in respect of such rights in countries other than the United States and Canada.

Negotiations for New or Unspecified Uses

9. If the Publisher desires to exercise a right in and to the composition now known or which may hereafter become known, but for which no specific provision has been made herein, the Publisher shall give written notice to the Writer thereof. Negotiations respecting all the terms and conditions of any such disposition shall thereupon be entered into between the Publisher (and/or the National Music Publishers' Association, Inc.) and the American Guild of Authors & Composers; and no such right shall be exercised until specific agreement has been made.

Royalty Statements and Payments

10. The Publisher shall render to the Writer, hereafter, royalty statements accompanied by remittance of the amount due on or before, each May 15th covering the 3 months ending March 31st; each August 15th covering the 3 months ending June 30th; each November 15th covering the 3 months ending September 30th; each February 15th covering the 3 months ending December 31st; provided, however, that if it shall have heretofore been the custom of the Publisher to render royalty statements accompanied by remittance of the amount due semi-annually, or quarterly at the end of different quarterly periods, such custom may be continued. The Writer may at any time, or from time to time, make written request for a detailed royalty statement, and the Publisher shall, within sixty days, comply therewith. Such royalty statements shall set forth in detail the various items, foreign and domestic, for which royalties are payable thereunder and the amounts thereof, including, but not limited to, the number of copies sold and the number of uses made in each royalty category. If a use is made in a publication of the character provided in Paragraph 4, subdivision (e) hereof, there shall be included in said royalty statement the title of said publication, the publisher or issuer thereof, the date of and number of uses, the gross license fee received in connection with each publication, the share thereto of all the writers under contract with the Publisher, and the Writer's share thereof. There shall likewise be included in said statement a description of every other use of the composition, and if by a licensee or licensees their name or names, and if said use is upon a part of an instrument serving to reproduce the composition mechanically, the type of mechanical reproduction, the title of the label thereon, the name or names of the artists performing the same, together with the gross license fees received, and the Writer's share thereof.

Examination of Books

11. (a) The Publisher shall from time to time, upon written demand of the Writer or his representative, permit the Writer or his representative to inspect at the place of business of the Publisher, all books, records and documents relating to the composition and all licenses granted, uses had and payments made therefor, such right of inspection to include, but not by way of limitation, the right to examine all original accountings and records relating to uses and payments by manufacturers of commercial phonograph records and music rolls; and the Writer or his representative may appoint a certified public accountant who shall at any time during usual business hours have access to all records of the Publisher relating to the composition for the purpose of verifying royalty statements rendered or which are delinquent under the terms hereof.

(b) The Publisher shall, upon written demand of the Writer or his representative, cause any licensing agent in the United States and Canada to furnish to the Writer or his representative, statements showing in detail all licenses granted, uses had and payments made in connection with the composition, which licenses or permits were granted, or payments were received, by or through said licensing agent, and to permit the Writer or his representative to inspect at the place of business of such licensing agent, all books, records and documents of such licensing agent, relating thereto. Any and all agreements made by the Publisher with any such licensing agent shall provide that any such licensing agent will comply with the terms and provisions hereof. In the event that the Publisher shall instruct such licensing agent to furnish to the Writer or his representative statements as provided for herein, and to permit the inspection of the books, records and documents as herein provided, then if such licensing agent should refuse to comply with the said instructions, or any of them, the Publisher agrees to institute and prosecute diligently and in good faith such action or proceedings as may be necessary to compel compliance with the said instructions.

(c) With respect to foreign licensing agents, the Publisher shall make available the books or records of said licensing agents in countries outside of the United States and Canada to the extent such books or records are available to the Publisher, except that the Publisher may in lieu thereof make available any accountants' reports and audits which the Publisher is able to obtain.

Default in Payment or Prevention of Examination

12. If the Publisher shall fail or refuse, within sixty days after written demand, to furnish or cause to be furnished, such statements, books, records or documents, or to permit inspection thereof, as provided for in Paragraphs 10 and 11 hereof, or within thirty days after written demand, to make the payment of any royalties due under this contract, then the Writer shall have the option, to be exercised upon ten days' written notice, to terminate this contract. However, if the Publisher shall:

(a) Within the said ten-day period:

(i) serve upon the Writer a written notice demanding arbitration; and

(ii) if the demand be for statements, books, records or documents, or to permit inspection thereof, deposit with National Music Publishers' Association, Inc. a re-assignment to the Writer of the copyright and all other rights in and to the composition, to be held in escrow pending the determination of the arbitration, or if the demand be for royalties, then deposit in escrow with National Music Publishers' Association, Inc., the amount shown by its books to be due the Writer under the provisions of this contract; and,

(b) Submit to arbitration its claim that it has complied with its obligation to furnish statements, books, records or documents, or permitted inspection thereof, or to pay royalties, as the case may be, or both, and thereafter comply with any award of the arbitrators within ten days after such award or within such time as the arbitrators may specify;

then this contract shall continue in full force and effect as if the Writer's option had not been exercised. But if the Publisher shall fail to comply with the foregoing provisions, then this contract shall be deemed to have been terminated as of the date of the Writer's exercise of his option to terminate this contract.

Termination of Contract

13. Upon the termination of this contract, all rights of any and every nature in and to the composition and in and to any and all copyrights secured thereon in the United States and throughout the world, shall re-vest in and become the property of the Writer, and shall be re-assigned to the Writer by the Publisher free of any and all encumbrances of any nature whatsoever, provided that:

(a) The said re-assignment by the Publisher may, however, be subject to such rights, if any, as may have been vested in a foreign publisher respecting the use of the composition in countries other than the United States and Canada under any agreement made prior to January 1, 1947.

(b) If the Publisher, prior to such termination, shall have granted a domestic license for the use of the composition, not inconsistent with the terms and provisions of this contract, the re-assignment may be subject to the terms of such license.

(c) In either of the events mentioned in subdivisions (a) and (b) of this paragraph, however, the Publisher shall assign to the Writer all rights which it may have under any such agreement or license in respect of the composition, including, but not limited to, the right to receive all royalties or other monies earned by the composition thereunder after the date of termination of this contract. Should the Publisher thereafter receive or be credited with any royalties or other monies so earned, it shall pay the same to the Writer.

(d) The Writer shall not be obligated to return or pay to the Publisher any advance or indebtedness as a condition of the re-assignment provided for in this Paragraph 13, and shall be entitled to receive the plates and copies of the composition in the possession of the Publisher.

(e) The termination of this contract shall not relieve the Publisher of his obligation to pay any and all royalties which may have accrued to the Writer prior to such termination.

(f) The Publisher shall execute any and all documents and do any and all acts or things necessary to effect any and all re-assignments to the Writer herein provided for.

Notices 14. All written demands and notices provided for herein shall be sent by registered mail.

Suits for Infringement 15. Any legal action brought by the Publisher against any alleged infringer of the composition shall be initiated and prosecuted at its sole cost and expense, but if the Publisher should fail, within thirty days after written demand, to institute such action, the Writer shall be entitled to institute such suit at his cost and expense. All sums recovered as a result of any such action shall, after the deduction of the reasonable expense thereof, be divided equally between the Publisher and the Writer. No settlement of any such action may be made by either party without first notifying the other; in the event that either party should object to such settlement, then such settlement shall not be made if the party objecting assumes the prosecution of the action and all expenses thereof, except that any sums thereafter recovered shall be divided equally between the Publisher and the Writer after the deduction of the reasonable expenses thereof.

Infringement Claims 16. (a) If a claim is presented against the Publisher alleging that the composition is an infringement upon some other work or a violation of any other right of another, and because thereof the Publisher is jeopardized, it shall forthwith serve a written notice upon the Writer setting forth the full details of such claim. The pendency of said claim shall not relieve the Publisher of the obligation to make payment of the royalties to the Writer hereunder, unless the Publisher shall deposit said royalties as and when they would otherwise be payable, in an account in a bank or trust company in the City of New York in the joint names of the Publisher and the Writer. If no suit be filed within nine months after said written notice from the Publisher to the Writer, all monies deposited in said joint account shall be paid over to the Writer plus any interest which may have been earned thereon.

(b) Should an action be instituted against the Publisher claiming that the composition is an infringement upon some other work or a violation of any other right of another, the Publisher shall forthwith serve written notice upon the Writer containing the full details of such claim. Notwithstanding the commencement of such action, the Publisher shall continue to pay the royalties hereunder to the Writer unless it shall, from and after the date of the service of the summons, deposit said royalties as and when they would otherwise be payable, in an account in a bank or trust company in the City of New York in the joint names of the Publisher and the Writer. If the said suit shall be finally adjudicated in favor of the Publisher or shall be settled, there shall be released and paid to the Writer all of such sums held in escrow less any amount paid out of the Writer's share with the Writer's written consent in settlement of said action. Should the said suit finally result adversely to the Publisher, the said amount on deposit shall be released to the Publisher to the extent of any expense or damage it incurs and the balance shall be paid over to the Writer.

(c) In any of the foregoing events, however, the Writer shall be entitled to payment of said royalties or the money so deposited at and after such time as he files with the Publisher a surety company bond, or a bond in other form acceptable to the Publisher, in the sum of such payments to secure the return thereof to the extent that the Publisher may be entitled to such return. The foregoing payments or deposits or the filing of a bond shall be without prejudice to the rights of the Publisher or Writer in the premises.

Arbitration 17. Any and all differences, disputes or controversies arising out of this contract shall be submitted to arbitration under the laws of the State of New York, and the parties hereby individually and jointly agree to abide by and perform any award rendered in such arbitration, and agree that a judgment of the Supreme Court of the State of New York may be entered upon such award. Together with the demand for arbitration, the party making said demand shall designate an arbitrator and the adverse party shall, within ten days thereafter, likewise designate an arbitrator. The two arbitrators so chosen shall promptly appoint a third arbitrator who shall act as Chairman and any award concurred in by a majority of the arbitrators shall be binding upon the parties. Should the party against whom arbitration is demanded fail to select an arbitrator, or should the arbitrators selected by the parties be unable to agree upon a third arbitrator, then said arbitrator or arbitrators, as the case may be, shall be designated and appointed in the manner provided by the Arbitration Law of the State of New York.

Assignment 18. Except to the extent herein otherwise expressly provided, the Publisher shall not sell, transfer, assign, convey, encumber or otherwise dispose of the composition or the copyright or copyrights secured thereon without the prior written consent of the Writer. The Writer has been induced to enter into this contract in reliance upon the value to him of the personal service and ability of the Publisher in the exploitation of the composition, and by reason thereof it is the intention of the parties and the essence of the relationship between them that the rights herein granted to the Publisher shall remain with the Publisher and that the same shall not pass to any other person, including, without limitations, successors to or receivers or trustees of the property of the Publisher, either by act or deed of the Publisher or by operation of law, and in the event of the voluntary or involuntary bankruptcy of the Publisher, this contract shall terminate, provided, however, that the composition may be included by the Publisher in a bona fide voluntary sale of its music business or its entire catalog of musical compositions, or in a merger or consolidation of the Publisher with another corporation; and provided further that the composition and the copyright therein may be assigned by the Publisher to a subsidiary or affiliated company generally engaged in the music publishing business. If the Publisher is an individual, the composition may pass to a legatee or distributee as part of the inheritance of the Publisher's music business and entire catalog of musical compositions. Any such transfer or assignment shall, however, be conditioned upon the execution and delivery by the transferee or assignee to the Writer of an agreement to be bound by and to perform all of the terms and conditions of this contract to be performed on the part of the Publisher.

Subsidiary Defined 19. A subsidiary, affiliate, or any person, firm or corporation controlled by the Publisher or by such subsidiary or affiliate, as used in this contract, shall be deemed to include any person, firm or corporation, under common control with, or the majority of whose stock or capital contribution is owned or controlled by the Publisher or by any of its officers, directors, partners or associates, or whose policies and actions are subject to domination or control by the Publisher or any of its officers, directors, partners or associates.

Minimums 20. The minimum amounts and percentages specified in this contract shall be deemed to be the amounts and percentages agreed upon by the parties hereto, unless greater amounts or percentages are inserted in the blank spaces provided therefor.

Countersignature and Modifications 21. This contract is binding upon and shall enure to the benefit of the parties hereto and their respective successors in interest (as hereinbefore limited), but shall be effective only when countersigned by the American Guild of Authors & Composers. If the Writer (or one or more of them) shall not be living, any notices may be given to, or consents given by, his or their successors in interest. No change or modification of this contract shall be effective unless reduced to writing, signed by the parties hereto, and countersigned by the American Guild of Authors & Composers.

Marginal Notes 22. The marginal notes are inserted only as a matter of convenience and for reference, and in no way define, limit or describe the scope or intent of this contract nor in any way affect this contract.

Exceptions to Warranties 23. The rights specifically excepted, as provided in Paragraph 3 hereof are as follows:

FORM 3.8

1978 AMERICAN GUILD OF AUTHORS & COMPOSERS POPULAR SONGWRITER'S RENEWAL CONTRACT

AMERICAN GUILD OF
AUTHORS & COMPOSERS

NOTE TO SONGWRITERS: (A) DO NOT SIGN THIS CONTRACT IF IT HAS ANY CHANGES UNLESS YOU HAVE FIRST DISCUSSED SUCH CHANGES WITH AGAC; (B) FOR YOUR PROTECTION PLEASE SEND A FULLY EXECUTED COPY OF THIS CONTRACT TO AGAC.

POPULAR SONGWRITERS RENEWAL CONTRACT
Copyright 1978 AGAC

AGREEMENT made this   day of   , 19   , between

_____

(hereinafter called "Publisher") and _____

_____

jointly and/or severally hereinafter collectively called "Writer"):

WITNESSETH:

Compositions   1.   The Writer hereby sells, assigns, transfers and delivers to the Publisher any and all rights and interests whatsoever now or at any time or times hereafter known or in existence which he now possesses or which he may at any time or times hereafter acquire or possess in or to the following described musical compositions:

Title	Original Publisher	Date of Copyright Registration	Copyright Registration Number

(hereinafter referred to as "the composition"), including the title, words and music thereof and any and all adaptations, arrangements and versions thereof respecting which he is entitled to obtain renewal copyright, for and during the second or renewal period of the United States copyright or for the period of twenty-eight years from the date of expiration of the first original term of the United States copyright, whichever may be shorter, and subject to the terms of this contract.

Performing Rights   2.   In all respects this contract shall be subject to any existing agreements between the parties hereto and the following small
Affiliation   performing rights licensing organization with which Writer and Publisher are affiliated:

(Delete Two) ——▶ (ASCAP, BMI, SESAC). Nothing contained herein shall, or shall be deemed to, alter, vary or modify the rights of Writer and Publisher to share in, receive and retain the proceeds distributed to them by such small performing rights licensing organization pursuant to their respective agreement with it.

Warranty   3.   The Writer, individually and not jointly, warrants and represents that the following are the only co-writers and composers of said composition:

that he has the right to renew and extend the copyright of the said composition; that he has not bargained, sold, assigned, transferred, hypothecated, pledged or encumbered any of his right, title or interest in or to the renewal copyright in said composition, except as aforesaid in paragraph 2 hereof, but nothing herein contained shall be construed as a warranty or representation by any individual Writer-signatory hereof, as to the rights of any other Writer or composer of said composition, it being understood that the warranties by the Writer are individual and not joint.

Royalties

4. In consideration of this contract, the Publisher agrees to pay the Writer as follows:

(Insert amount of Payment and Advance here)

(a) (i) $_____ receipt of which is hereby acknowledged; said sum shall constitute an outright payment, shall remain the property of the Writer and shall not be deductible from any payments heretofore or hereafter due the Writer.

(ii) $_____ as an advance against royalties, receipt of which is hereby acknowledged, which sum shall remain the property of the Writer and shall be deductible only from payments hereafter becoming due the Writer under this Contract.

Piano Copies

Sliding Scale

(Insert percentage here)

(b) In respect of regular piano copies sold and paid for in the United States and Canada, the following royalties per copy:

..........% (in no case, however, less than 10%) of the wholesale selling price of the first 200,000 copies or less; plus

..........% (in no case, however, less than 12%) of the wholesale selling price of copies in excess of 200,000 and not exceeding 500,000; plus

..........% (in no case, however, less than 15%) of the wholesale selling price of copies in excess of 500,000.

Foreign Royalties

(c) ....% (in no case, however, less than 50%) of all net sums received by the Publisher in respect of regular piano copies, orchestrations, band arrangements, octavos, quartets, arrangements for combinations of voices and/or instruments, and/or other copies of the composition sold in any other country other than the United States and Canada, provided, however, that if the Publisher should sell such copies through, or cause them to be sold by, a subsidiary or affiliate which is actually doing business in a foreign country, then in respect of such sales, the Publisher shall pay to the Writer not less than 5% of the marked retail selling price in respect of each such copy sold and paid for.

Orchestrations and Other Arrangements, etc.

(d) In respect of each copy sold and paid for in the United States and Canada, or for export from the United States, of orchestrations, band arrangements, octavos, quartets, arrangements for combinations of voices and/or instruments, and/or other copies of the composition (other than regular piano copies) the following royalties on the wholesale selling price (after trade discounts, if any):

(Insert percentage here)

..........% (in no case, however, less than 10%) on the first 200,000 copies or less; plus

..........% (in no case, however, less than 12%) on all copies in excess of 200,000 and not exceeding 500,000; plus

..........% (in no case, however, less than 15%) on all copies in excess of 500,000.

Publisher's Song Book, Folio, etc.

(e) (i) If the composition, or any part thereof, is included in any song book, folio or similar publication issued by the Publisher containing at least four, but not more than twenty-five musical compositions, the royalty to be paid by the Publisher to the Writer shall be an amount determined by dividing 10% of the wholesale selling price (after trade discounts, if any) of the copies sold, among the total number of the Publisher's copyrighted musical compositions included in such publication. If such publication contains more than twenty-five musical compositions, the said 10% shall be increased by an additional ½% for each additional musical composition.

Licensee's Song Book, Folio, etc.

(ii) If, pursuant to a license granted by the Publisher to a licensee not controlled by or affiliated with it, the composition, or any part thereof, is included in any song book, folio or similar publication, containing at least four musical compositions, the royalty to be paid by the Publisher to the Writer shall be that proportion of 50% of the gross amount received by it from the licensee, as the number of uses of the composition under the license and during the license period, bears to the total number of uses of the Publisher's copyrighted musical compositions under the license and during the license period.

(iii) In computing the number of the Publisher's copyrighted musical compositions under subdivisions (i) and (ii) hereof, there shall be excluded musical compositions in the public domain and arrangements thereof and those with respect to which the Publisher does not currently publish and offer for sale regular piano copies.

(iv) Royalties on publications containing less than four musical compositions shall be payable at regular piano copy rates.

Professional Material and Free Copies

(f) As to "professional material" not sold or resold, no royalty shall be payable. Free copies of the lyrics of the composition shall not be distributed except under the following conditions: (i) with the Writer's written consent; or (ii) when printed without music in limited numbers for charitable, religious or governmental purposes, or for similar public purposes, if no profit is derived, directly or indirectly; or (iii) when authorized for printing in a book, magazine or periodical, where such use is incidental to a novel or story (as distinguished from use in a book of lyrics or a lyric magazine or folio), provided that any such use shall bear the Writer's name and the proper copyright notice; or (iv) when distributed solely for the purpose of exploiting the composition, provided, that such exploitation is restricted to the distribution of limited numbers of such copies for the purpose of influencing the sale of the composition, that the distribution is independent of the sale of any other musical compositions, services, goods, wares or merchandise, and that no profit is made, directly or indirectly, in connection therewith.

Mechanicals, Electrical Transcription, Synchronization, All Other Rights

(Insert percentage here)

(g) ....% (in no case, however, less than 50%) of:

All gross receipts of the Publisher in respect of any licenses (including statutory royalties) authorizing the manufacture of parts of instruments serving to mechanically reproduce the composition, or to use the composition in synchronization with sound motion pictures, or to reproduce it upon electrical transcription for broadcasting purposes; and of any and all gross receipts of the Publisher from any other source or right now known or which may hereafter come into existence, except as provided in paragraph 2.

Licensing Agent's Charges

(h) If the Publisher administers licenses authorizing the manufacture of parts of instruments serving to mechanically reproduce said composition, or the use of said composition in synchronization or in timed relation with sound motion pictures or its reproduction upon electrical transcriptions, or any of them, through an agent, trustee or other administrator acting for a substantial part of the industry and not under the exclusive control of the Publisher (hereinafter sometimes referred to as licensing agent), the Publisher, in determining his receipts, shall be entitled to deduct from gross license fees paid by the Licensees, a sum equal to the charges paid by the Publisher to said licensing agent, provided, however, that in respect to synchronization or timed relation with sound motion pictures, said deduction shall in no event exceed $150.00 or 10% of said gross license fee, whichever is less; in connection with the manufacture of parts of instruments serving to mechanically reproduce said composition, said deductions shall not exceed 5% of said gross license fee; and in connection with electrical transcriptions, said deduction shall not exceed 10% of said gross license fee.

Block Licenses

(i) The Publisher agrees that the use of the composition will not be included in any bulk or block license heretofore or hereafter granted, and that it will not grant any bulk or block license to include the same, without the written consent of the Writer in each instance, except (i) that the Publisher may grant such licenses with respect to electrical transcription for broadcasting purposes, but in such event, the Publisher shall pay to the Writer that proportion of 50% of the gross amount received by it under each such license as the number of uses of the composition under each such license during each such license period bears to the total number of uses of the Publisher's copyrighted musical compositions under each such license during each such license period; in computing the number of the Publisher's copyrighted musical compositions for this purpose, there shall be excluded musical compositions in the public domain and arrangements thereof and those with respect to which the Publisher does not currently publish and offer for sale regular piano copies; (ii) that the Publisher may appoint agents or representatives in countries outside of the United States and Canada to use and to grant licenses for the use of the composition on the customary royalty fee basis under which the Publisher shall receive not less than 10% of the marked retail selling price in respect of regular piano copies, and 50% of all other revenue; if, in connection with any such bulk or block license, the Publisher shall have received any advance, the Writer shall not be entitled to share therein, but no part of said advance shall be deducted in computing the composition's earnings under said bulk or block license. A bulk or block license shall be deemed to mean any license or agreement, domestic or foreign, whereby rights are granted in respect of two or more musical compositions.

Television and New Uses   (j) Except to the extent that the Publisher and Writer have heretofore or may hereafter assign to or vest in the small performing rights licensing organization with which Writer and Publisher are affiliated, the said rights or the right to grant licenses therefor, it is agreed that no licenses shall be granted without the written consent, in each instance, of the Writer for the use of the composition by means of television, or by any means, or for any purposes not commercially established, or for which licenses were not granted by the Publisher on musical compositions prior to June 1, 1937.

Writer's Consent to Licenses   (k) The Publisher shall not, without the written consent of the Writer in each case, give or grant any right or license (i) to use the title of the composition, or (ii) for the exclusive use of the composition in any form or for any purpose, or for any period of time, or for any territory, other than its customary arrangements with foreign publishers, or (iii) to give a dramatic representation of the composition or to dramatize the plot or story thereof, or (iv) for a vocal rendition of the composition in synchronization with sound motion pictures, or (v) for any synchronization use thereof, or (vi) for the use of the composition or a quotation or excerpt therefrom in any article, book, periodical, advertisement or other similar publication. If, however, the Publisher shall give to the Writer written notice by certified mail, return receipt requested, or telegram, specifying the right or license to be given or granted, the name of the licensee and the terms and conditions thereof, including the price or other compensation to be received therefor, then, unless the Writer (or any one or more of them) shall, within five business days after the delivery of such notice to the address of the Writer hereinafter designated, object thereto, the Publisher may grant such right or license in accordance with the said notice without first obtaining the consent of the Writer. Such notice shall be deemed sufficient if sent to the Writer at the address or addresses hereinafter designated or at the address or addresses last furnished to the Publisher in writing by the Writer.

Trust for Writer   (l) Any portion of the receipts which may become due to the Writer from license fees (in excess of offsets), whether received directly from the licensee or from any licensing agent of the Publisher, shall, if not paid immediately on the receipt thereof by the Publisher, belong to the Writer and shall be held in trust for the Writer until payment is made; the ownership of said trust fund by the Writer shall not be questioned whether the monies are physically segregated or not.

Writer Participation   (m) The Publisher agrees that it will not issue any license as a result of which it will receive any financial benefit in which the Writer does not participate.

Writer Credit   (n) On all regular piano copies, orchestrations, band or other arrangements, octavos, quartets, commercial sound recordings and other reproductions of the composition or parts thereof, in whatever form and however produced, Publisher shall include or cause to be included, in addition to the copyright notice, the name of the Writer, and Publisher shall include a similar requirement in every license or authorization issued by it with respect to the composition.

Power of Attorney   5.   The Writer covenants and agrees to make, execute and deliver any and all further instruments, documents and writings that may be requested by the Publisher for the purpose of perfecting and confirming in the Publisher the rights and interests in the renewal(s) of the copyright(s) in the composition herein granted, and the Writer hereby nominates and appoints the Publisher his true and lawful attorney to make, execute and deliver any and all such instruments, documents and writings in the name of the Writer and to renew and extend the copyright in the composition and to make applications therefor in the name of the Writer, subject to the terms of this contract.

Exploitation   6. (a) The Publisher agrees that it shall (i) at all times maintain a stock of regular piano copies of the composition in the form customarily published by it, (ii) include and retain at all times the title of the composition in its catalog of compositions, and (iii) use every reasonable effort and means to exploit and promote the sale of the various uses of the composition. Unless the aggregate amount of any advances (as provided in paragraph 4 (a) (ii)) and the royalties paid to the Writer within two years from the date hereof, shall equal or exceed the sum of $250.00, the Publisher shall pay to the Writer the difference between said aggregate amount and said sum of $250.00.

Failure to Exploit   (b) Should the Publisher fail to comply with the provisions of subdivision (a) hereof, the Writer shall be entitled to demand in writing the return of the composition at any time after the expiration of said two-year period, whereupon the Publisher must within one month after the receipt of such notice either comply with the provisions of subdivision (a) hereof, in which event this contract will remain in full force and effect, or upon its failure so to comply, this contract shall terminate and all rights of any and every nature in and to the composition and in and to any and all copyrights and renewal copyrights secured thereon in the United States and throughout the world (subject, however, to the terms of paragraph 7 hereof), shall re-vest in and become the property of the Writer and shall be reassigned to him by the Publisher; the Writer shall not be obligated to return or pay to the Publisher any outright payment, advance or indebtedness as a condition of such reassignment; the said reassignment shall be in accordance with and subject to the provisions of paragraph 8 hereof, and in addition, the Publisher shall pay to the Writer all gross sums which it has theretofore or may thereafter receive in respect of the composition.

Foreign Copyright   7. (a) Each copyright on the composition in countries other than the United States shall be secured only in the name of the Publisher, and the Publisher shall not at any time divest itself of said foreign copyright directly or indirectly.

Foreign Publication   (b) No rights shall be granted by the Publisher in the composition to any foreign publisher or licensee inconsistent with the terms hereof.

Foreign Advance   (c) If foreign rights in the composition are separately conveyed, otherwise than as a part of the Publisher's current and/or future catalog, not less than 50% of any advance received in respect thereof shall be credited to the account of and paid to the Writer.

Foreign Percentage	(d) The percentage of the Writer on monies received from foreign sources shall be computed on the Publisher's net receipts, provided, however, that no deductions shall be made for offsets of monies due from the Publisher to said foreign sources; or for advances made by such foreign sources to the Publisher, unless the Writer shall have received at least 50% of said advances.
No Foreign Allocations	(e) In computing the receipts of the Publisher from licenses granted in respect of synchronization with sound motion pictures, or in respect of any world-wide licenses, or in respect of licenses granted by the Publisher for use of the composition in countries other than the United States, no amount shall be deducted for payments or allocations to publishers or licensees in such countries.
Termination or Expiration of Contract	8. Upon the termination or expiration of this contract, all rights of any and every nature in and to the composition and in and to any and all copyrights secured thereon in the United States and throughout the world, shall re-vest in and become the property of the Writer, and shall be re-assigned to the Writer by the Publisher free of any and all encumbrances of any nature whatsoever, provided that:

    (a) If the Publisher, prior to such termination or expiration, shall have granted a domestic license for the use of the composition, not inconsistent with the terms and provisions of this contract, the re-assignment may be subject to the terms of such license.

    (b) Publisher shall assign to the Writer all rights which it may have under any such agreement or license referred to in subdivision (a) in respect of the composition, including, but not limited to, the right to receive all royalties or other monies earned by the composition thereunder after the date of termination or expiration of this contract. Should the Publisher thereafter receive or be credited with any royalties or other monies so earned, it shall pay the same to the Writer.

    (c) The Writer shall not be obligated to return or pay to the Publisher any advance or indebtedness as a condition of the re-assignment provided for in this Paragraph 8, and shall be entitled to receive the plates and copies of the composition in the possession of the Publisher.

    (d) Publisher shall pay any and all royalties which may have accrued to the Writer prior to such termination or expiration.

    (e) The Publisher shall execute any and all documents and do any and all acts or things necessary to effect any and all re-assignments to the Writer herein provided for.

Negotiations for New or Unspecified Uses	9. If the Publisher desires to exercise a right in and to the composition now known or which may hereafter become known, but for which no specific provision has been made herein, the Publisher shall give written notice to the Writer thereof. Negotiations respecting all the terms and conditions of any such disposition shall thereupon be entered into between the Publisher and the Writer and no such right shall be exercised until specific agreement has been made.
Royalty Statements and Payments	10. The Publisher shall render to the Writer, hereafter, royalty statements accompanied by remittance of the amount due at the times such statements and remittances are customarily rendered by the Publisher, provided, however, that such statements and remittances shall be rendered either semi-annually or quarterly and not more than forty-five days after the end of each such semi-annual or quarterly period, as the case may be. The Writer may at any time, or from time to time, make written request for a detailed royalty statement, and the Publisher shall, within sixty days, comply therewith. Such royalty statements shall set forth in detail the various items, foreign and domestic, for which royalties are payable thereunder and the amounts thereof, including, but not limited to, the number of copies sold and the number of uses made in each royalty category. If a use is made in a publication of the character provided in Paragraph 4, subdivision (e) hereof, there shall be included in said royalty statement the title of said publication, the publisher or issuer thereof, the date of and number of uses, the gross license fee received in connection with each publication, the share thereto of all the writers under contract with the Publisher, and the Writer's share thereof. There shall likewise be included in said statement a description of every other use of the composition, and if by a licensee or licensees their name or names, and if said use is upon a part of an instrument serving to reproduce the composition mechanically, the type of mechanical reproduction, the title of the label thereon, the name or names of the artists performing the same, together with the gross license fees received, and the Writer's share thereof.
Examination of Books	11. (a) The Publisher shall from time to time, upon written demand of the Writer or his representative, permit the Writer or his representative to inspect at the place of business of the Publisher, all books, records and documents relating to the composition and all licenses granted, uses had and payments made therefor, such right of inspection to include, but not by way of limitation, the right to examine all original accountings and records relating to uses and payments by manufacturers of commercial sound recordings and music rolls; and the Writer or his representative may appoint an accountant who shall at any time during usual business hours have access to all records of the Publisher relating to the composition for the purpose of verifying royalty statements rendered or which are delinquent under the terms hereof.

    (b) The Publisher shall, upon written demand of the Writer or his representative, cause any licensing agent in the United States and Canada to furnish to the Writer or his representative, statements showing in detail all licenses granted, uses had and payments made in connection with the composition, which licenses or permits were granted, or payments were received, by or through said licensing agent, and to permit the Writer or his representative to inspect at the place of business of such licensing agent, all books, records and documents of such licensing agent, relating thereto. Any and all agreements made by the Publisher with any licensing agent shall provide that any such licensing agent will comply with the terms and provisions hereof. In the event that the Publisher shall instruct such licensing agent to furnish to the Writer or his representative statements as provided for herein, and to permit the inspection of the books, records and documents as herein provided, then if such licensing agent should refuse to comply with the said instructions, or any of them, the Publisher agrees to institute and prosecute diligently and in good faith such action or proceedings as may be necessary to compel compliance with the said instructions.

    (c) With respect to foreign licensing agents, the Publisher shall make available the books or records of said licensing agents in countries outside of the United States and Canada to the extent such books or records are available to the Publisher, except that the Publisher may in lieu thereof make available any accountants' reports and audits which the Publisher is able to obtain.

    (d) If as a result of any examination of books, records or documents pursuant to Paragraphs 11(a), 11(b) or 11(c) hereof, it is determined that, with respect to any royalty statement rendered by or on behalf of the Publisher to the Writer, the Writer is owed a sum equal to or greater than five percent of the sum shown on that royalty statement as being due to the Writer, then the Publisher shall pay to the Writer the entire cost of such examination, not to exceed 50% of the amount shown to be due the Writer.

    (e) (i) In the event the Publisher administers its own licenses for the manufacture of parts of instruments serving to mechanically reproduce the composition rather than employing a licensing agent for that purpose, the Publisher shall include in each license agreement a provision permitting the Publisher, the Writer or their respective representatives to inspect, at the place of business of such licensee, all books, records and documents of such licensee relating to such license. Within 30 days after written demand by the Writer, the Publisher shall commence to inspect such licensee's books, records and documents and shall furnish a written report of such inspection to the Writer within 90 days following such demand. If the Publisher fails, after written demand by the Writer, to so inspect the licensee's books, records and documents, or fails to furnish such report, the Writer or his representative may inspect such licensee's books, records and documents at his own expense.

(ii) In the further event that the Publisher and the licensee referred to in subdivision (i) above are subsidiaries or affiliates of the same entity or one is a subsidiary or affiliate of the other, then, unless the Publisher employs a licensing agent to administer the licenses referred to in subdivision (i) above, the Writer shall have the right to make the inspection referred to in subdivision (i) above without the necessity of making written demand on the Publisher as provided in subdivision (i) above.

(iii) If as a result of any inspection by the Writer pursuant to subdivisions (i) and (ii) of this subparagraph (e) the Writer recovers additional monies from the licensee, the Publisher and the Writer shall share equally in the cost of such inspection.

Default in Payment or Prevention of Examination

12. If the Publisher shall fail or refuse, within sixty days after written demand, to furnish or cause to be furnished, such statements, books, records or documents, or to permit inspection thereof, as provided for in Paragraphs 10 and 11 hereof, or within thirty days after written demand, to make the payment of any royalties due under this contract, then the Writer shall be entitled, upon ten days' written notice, to terminate this contract. However if the Publisher shall:

(a) Within the said ten-day period serve upon the Writer a written notice demanding arbitration; and

(b) Submit to arbitration its claim that it has complied with its obligation to furnish statements, books, records or documents, or permitted inspection thereof or to pay royalties, as the case may be, or both, and thereafter comply with any award of the arbitrator within ten days after such award or within such time as the arbitrator may specify;

then this contract shall continue in full force and effect as if the Writer had not sent such notice of termination. If the Publisher shall fail to comply with the foregoing provisions, then this contract shall be deemed to have been terminated as of the date of the Writer's written notice of termination.

Derivative Works

13. No derivative work prepared under authority of Publisher during the term of this contract may be utilized by Publisher or any other party after termination or expiration of this contract.

Notices

14. All written demands and notices provided for herein shall be sent by certified mail, return receipt requested.

Suits for Infringement

15. Any legal action brought by the Publisher against any alleged infringer of the composition shall be initiated and prose-cuted at its sole cost and expense, but if the Publisher should fail, within thirty days after written demand, to institute such action, the Writer shall be entitled to institute such suit at his cost and expense. All sums recovered as a result of any such action shall, after the deduction of the reasonable expense thereof, be divided equally between the Publisher and the Writer. No settlement of any such action may be made by either party without first notifying the other; in the event that either party should object to such settlement, then such settlement shall not be made if the party objecting assumes the prosecution of the action and all expenses thereof, except that any sums thereafter recovered shall be divided equally between the Publisher and the Writer after the deduction of the reasonable expenses thereof.

Infringement Claims

16. (a) If a claim is presented against the Publisher alleging that the composition is an infringement upon some other work or a violation of any other right of another, and because thereof the Publisher is jeopardized, it shall forthwith serve a written notice upon the Writer setting forth the full details of such claim. The pendency of said claim shall not relieve the Publisher of the obligation to make payment of the royalties to the Writer hereunder, unless the Publisher shall deposit said royalties as and when they would otherwise be payable, in an account in the joint names of the Publisher and the Writer in a bank or trust company in New York, New York, if the Writer on the date of execution of this contract resides East of the Mississippi River, or in Los Angeles, California, if the Writer on the date of execution of this contract resides West of the Mississippi River. If no suit be filed within nine months after said written notice from the Publisher to the Writer, all monies deposited in said joint account shall be paid over to the Writer plus any interest which may have been earned thereon.

(b) Should an action be instituted against the Publisher claiming that the composition is an infringement upon some other work or a violation of any other right of another, the Publisher shall forthwith serve written notice upon the Writer containing the full details of such claim. Notwithstanding the commencement of such action, the Publisher shall continue to pay the royalties hereunder to the Writer unless it shall, from and after the date of the service of the summons, deposit said royalties as and when they would otherwise be payable, in an account in the joint names of the Publisher and the Writer in a bank or trust company in New York, New York, if the Writer on the date of execution of this contract resides East of the Mississippi River, or in Los Angeles, California, if the Writer on the date of execution of this contract resides West of the Mississippi River. If the said suit shall be finally adjudicated in favor of the Publisher or shall be settled, there shall be released and paid to the Writer all of such sums held in escrow less any amount paid out of the Writer's share with the Writer's written consent in settlement of said action. Should the said suit finally result adversely to the Publisher, the said amount on deposit shall be released to the Publisher to the extent of any expense or damage it incurs and the balance shall be paid over to the Writer.

(c) In any of the foregoing events, however, the Writer shall be entitled to payment of said royalties or the money so deposited at and after such time as he files with the Publisher a surety company bond, or a bond in other form acceptable to the Publisher, in the sum of such payments to secure the return thereof to the extent that the Publisher may be entitled to such return. The foregoing payments or deposits or the filing of a bond shall be without prejudice to the rights of the Publisher or Writer in the premises.

Arbitration

17. Any and all differences, disputes or controversies arising out of or in connection with this contract shall be submitted to arbitration before a sole arbitrator under the then prevailing rules of the American Arbitration Association. The location of the arbitration shall be New York, New York, if the Writer on the date of execution of this contract resides East of the Mississippi River, or Los Angeles, California, if the Writer on the date of execution of this contract resides West of the Mississippi River. The parties hereby individually and jointly agree to abide by and perform any award rendered in such arbitration. Judgment upon any such award rendered may be entered in any court having jurisdiction thereof.

Assignment

18. Except to the extent herein otherwise expressly provided, the Publisher shall not sell, transfer, assign, convey, encumber or otherwise dispose of the composition or the copyright or copyrights secured thereon without the prior written consent of the Writer. The Writer has been induced to enter into this contract in reliance upon the value to him of the personal service and ability of the Publisher in the exploitation of the composition, and by reason thereof it is the intention of the parties and the essence of the relationship between them that the rights herein granted to the Publisher shall remain with the Publisher and that the same shall

not pass to any other person, including, without limitations, successors to or receivers or trustees of the property of the Publisher, either by act or deed of the Publisher by operation of law, and in the event of the voluntary or involuntary bankruptcy of the Publisher, this contract shall terminate, provided, however, that the composition may be included by the Publisher in a bona fide voluntary sale of its music business or its entire catalog of musical compositions, or in a merger or consolidation of the Publisher with another corporation, in which event the Publisher shall immediately give written notice thereof to the Writer; and provided further that the composition and the copyright therein may be assigned by the Publisher to a subsidiary or affiliated company generally engaged in the music publishing business. If the Publisher is an individual, the composition may pass to a legatee or distributee as part of the inheritance of the Publisher's music business and entire catalog of musical compositions. Any such transfer or assignment shall, however, be conditioned upon the execution and delivery by the transferee or assignee to the Writer of an agreement to be bound by and to perform all of the terms and conditions of this contract to be performed on the part of the Publisher.

Subsidiary Defined 19. A subsidiary, affiliate, or any person, firm or corporation controlled by the Publisher or by such subsidiary or affiliate, as used in this contract, shall be deemed to include any person, firm or corporation, under common control with, or the majority of whose stock or capital contribution is owned or controlled by the Publisher or by any of its officers, directors, partners or associates, or whose policies and actions are subject to domination or control by the Publisher or any of its officers, directors, partners or associates.

Amounts 20. The amounts and percentages specified in this contract shall be deemed to be the amounts and percentages agreed upon by the parties hereto, unless other amounts or percentages are inserted in the blank spaces provided therefor.

Modifications 21. This contract is binding upon and shall enure to the benefit of the parties hereto and their respective successors in interest (as hereinbefore limited). If the Writer (or one or more of them) shall not be living, any notices may be given to, or consents given by, his or their successors in interest. No change or modification of this contract shall be effective unless reduced to writing and signed by the parties hereto.

The words in this contract shall be so construed that the singular shall include the plural and the plural shall include the singular where the context so requires and the masculine shall include the feminine and the feminine shall include the masculine where the context so requires.

Paragraph Headings 22. The paragraph headings are inserted only as a matter of convenience and for reference, and in no way define, limit or describe the scope or intent of this contract nor in any way affect this contract.

Special Provisions 23.

Writers Respective Shares 24. Whenever the term "Writer" is used herein (except as provided in Paragraph 3 hereof), it shall be deemed to mean all of the persons executing this agreement below, (the same being the authors and composers of said compositions or their respective lawful successors), and any and all royalties herein provided to be paid to the Writer shall be paid jointly to the following persons executing this agreement if there be more than one, and shall be divided among them as follows:

Name and Soc. Sec. #	Address	Share	Signature

Witness: Publisher _____

_____   By _____

                                                      Address _____

FOR YOUR PROTECTION,
SEND A COPY OF THE FULLY SIGNED CONTRACT TO AGAC.

FORM 3.9

1978 SONGWRITER'S GUILD OF AMERICA POPULAR SONGWRITER'S CONTRACT

The Songwriters Guild of America

NOTE TO SONGWRITERS: (A) DO NOT SIGN THIS CONTRACT IF IT HAS ANY CHANGES UNLESS YOU HAVE FIRST DISCUSSED SUCH CHANGES WITH THE GUILD; (B) FOR YOUR PROTECTION PLEASE SEND A FULLY EXECUTED COPY OF THIS CONTRACT TO THE GUILD.

POPULAR SONGWRITERS CONTRACT
*Copyright 1978 AGAC

AGREEMENT made this   day of   , 19   , between

....

(hereinafter called "Publisher") and ....

....

(Jointly and/or severally hereinafter collectively called "Writer");

WITNESSETH:

Composition
(Insert title of composition here)

1. The Writer hereby assigns, transfers and delivers to the Publisher a certain heretofore unpublished original musical composition, written and/or composed by the above-named Writer now entitled ....

.... (hereinafter referred to as "the composition"), including the title, words and music thereof, and the right to secure copyright therein throughout the entire world, and to have and to hold the said copyright and all rights of whatsoever nature thereunder existing, for

(Insert number of years here)

.... years from the date of this contract or 35 years from the date of the first release of a

not more than 40

commercial sound recording of the composition, whichever term ends earlier, unless this contract is sooner terminated in accordance with the provisions hereof.

Performing Rights Affiliation
(Delete Two) ⟶

2. In all respects this contract shall be subject to any existing agreements between the parties hereto and the following small performing rights licensing organization with which Writer and Publisher are affiliated: (ASCAP, BMI, SESAC). Nothing contained herein shall, or shall be deemed to, alter, vary or modify the rights of Writer and Publisher to share in, receive and retain the proceeds distributed to them by such small performing rights licensing organization pursuant to their respective agreement with it.

Warranty

3. The Writer hereby warrants that the composition is his sole, exclusive and original work, that he has full right and power to make this contract, and that there exists no adverse claim to or in the composition, except as aforesaid in Paragraph 2 hereof and except such rights as are specifically set forth in Paragraph 23 hereof.

Royalties
(Insert amount of advance here)

4. In consideration of this contract, the Publisher agrees to pay the Writer as follows:

(a) $.....................as an advance against royalties, receipt of which is hereby acknowledged, which sum shall remain the property of the Writer and shall be deductible only from payments hereafter becoming due the Writer under this contract.

Piano Copies

(b) In respect of regular piano copies sold and paid for in the United States and Canada, the following royalties per copy:

Sliding Scale
(Insert percentage here)

..........% (in no case, however, less than 10%) of the wholesale selling price of the first 200,000 copies or less; plus

..........% (in no case, however, less than 12%) of the wholesale selling price of copies in excess of 200,000 and not exceeding 500,000; plus

..........% (in no case, however, less than 15%) of the wholesale selling price of copies in excess of 500,000.

Foreign Royalties
(Insert percentage here)

(c) ....% (in no case, however, less than 50%) of all net sums received by the Publisher in respect of regular piano copies, orchestrations, band arrangements, octavos, quartets, arrangements for combinations of voices and/or instruments, and/or other copies of the composition sold in any country other than the United States and Canada, provided, however, that if the Publisher should sell such copies through, or cause them to be sold by, a subsidiary or affiliate which is actually doing business in a foreign country, then in respect of such sales, the Publisher shall pay to the Writer not less than 5% of the marked retail selling price in respect of each such copy sold and paid for.

Orchestrations and Other Arrangements, etc.

(d) In respect of each copy sold and paid for in the United States and Canada, of orchestrations, band arrangements, octavos, quartets, arrangements for combinations of voices and/or instruments, and/or other copies of the composition (other than regular piano copies) the following royalties on the wholesale selling price (after trade discounts, if any):

(Insert percentage here)

..........% (in no case, however, less than 10%) on the first 200,000 copies or less; plus

..........% (in no case, however, less than 12%) on all copies in excess of 200,000 and not exceeding 500,000; plus

..........% (in no case, however, less than 15%) on all copies in excess of 500,000.

Publisher's Song Book, Folio, etc.

(e) (i) If the composition, or any part thereof, is included in any song book, folio or similar publication issued by the Publisher containing at least four, but not more than twenty-five musical compositions, the royalty to be paid by the Publisher to the Writer shall be an amount determined by dividing 10% of the wholesale selling price (after trade discounts, if any) of the copies sold, among the total number of the Publisher's copyrighted musical compositions included in such publication. If such publication contains more than twenty-five musical compositions, the said 10% shall be increased by an additional ½% for each additional musical composition.

Licensee's Song Book, Folio, etc.

(ii) If, pursuant to a license granted by the Publisher to a licensee not controlled by or affiliated with it, the composition, or any part thereof, is included in any song book, folio or similar publication, containing at least four musical compositions, the royalty to be paid by the Publisher to the Writer shall be that proportion of 50% of the gross amount received by it from the licensee, as the number of uses of the composition under the license and during the license period, bears to the total number of uses of the Publisher's copyrighted musical compositions under the license and during the license period.

(iii) In computing the number of the Publisher's copyrighted musical compositions under subdivisions (i) and (ii) hereof, there shall be excluded musical compositions in the public domain and arrangements thereof and those with respect to which the Publisher does not currently publish and offer for sale regular piano copies.

(iv) Royalties on publications containing less than four musical compositions shall be payable at regular piano copy rates.

Professional Material and Free Copies

(f) As to "professional material" not sold or resold, no royalty shall be payable. Free copies of the lyrics of the composition shall not be distributed except under the following conditions: (i) with the Writer's written consent; or (ii) when printed without music in limited numbers for charitable, religious or governmental purposes, or for similar public purposes, if no profit is derived, directly or indirectly; or (iii) when authorized for printing in a book, magazine or periodical, where such use is incidental to a novel or story (as distinguished from use in a book of lyrics or a lyric magazine or folio), provided that any such use shall bear the Writer's name and the proper copyright notice; or (iv) when distributed solely for the purpose of exploiting the composition, provided, that such exploitation is restricted to the distribution of limited numbers of such copies for the purpose of influencing the sale of the composition, that the distribution is independent of the sale of any other musical compositions, services, goods, wares or merchandise, and that no profit is made, directly or indirectly, in connection therewith.

Mechanicals, Electrical Transcription, Synchronization, All Other Rights

(g) **(Insert percentage here)** ....% (in no case, however, less than 50%) of:

All gross receipts of the Publisher in respect of any licenses (including statutory royalties) authorizing the manufacture of parts of instruments serving to mechanically reproduce the composition, or to use the composition in synchronization with sound motion pictures, or to reproduce it upon electrical transcription for broadcasting purposes; and of any and all gross receipts of the Publisher from any other source or right now known or which may hereafter come into existence, except as provided in paragraph 2.

Licensing Agent's Charges

(h) If the Publisher administers licenses authorizing the manufacture of parts of instruments serving to mechanically reproduce said composition, or the use of said composition in synchronization or in timed relation with sound motion pictures or its reproduction upon electrical transcriptions, or any of them, through an agent, trustee or other administrator acting for a substantial part of the industry and not under the exclusive control of the Publisher (hereinafter sometimes referred to as licensing agent), the Publisher, in determining his receipts, shall be entitled to deduct from gross license fees paid by the Licensees, a sum equal to the charges paid by the Publisher to said licensing agent, provided, however, that in respect to synchronization or timed relation with sound motion pictures, said deduction shall in no event exceed $150.00 or 10% of said gross license fee, whichever is less; in connection with the manufacture of parts of instruments serving to mechanically reproduce said composition, said deductions shall not exceed 5% of said gross license fee; and in connection with electrical transcriptions, said deduction shall not exceed 10% of said gross license fee.

Block Licenses

(i) The Publisher agrees that the use of the composition will not be included in any bulk or block license heretofore or hereafter granted, and that it will not grant any bulk or block license to include the same, without the written consent of the Writer in each instance, except (i) that the Publisher may grant such licenses with respect to electrical transcription for broadcasting purposes, but in such event, the Publisher shall pay to the Writer that proportion of 50% of the gross amount received by it under each such license as the number of uses of the composition under each such license during each such license period bears to the total number of uses of the Publisher's copyrighted musical compositions under each such license during each such license period; in computing the number of the Publisher's copyrighted musical compositions for this purpose, there shall be excluded musical compositions in the public domain and arrangements thereof and those with respect to which the Publisher does not currently publish and offer for sale regular piano copies; (ii) that the Publisher may appoint agents or representatives in countries outside of the United States and Canada to use and to grant licenses for the use of the composition on the customary royalty fee basis under which the Publisher shall receive not less than 10% of the marked retail selling price in respect of regular piano copies, and 50% of all other revenue; if, in connection with any such bulk or block license, the Publisher shall have received any advance, the Writer shall not be entitled to share therein, but no part of said advance shall be deducted in computing the composition's earnings under said bulk or block license. A bulk or block license shall be deemed to mean any license or agreement, domestic or foreign, whereby rights are granted in respect of two or more musical compositions.

Television and New Uses

(j) Except to the extent that the Publisher and Writer have heretofore or may hereafter assign to or vest in the small performing rights licensing organization with which Writer and Publisher are affiliated, the said rights or the right to grant licenses therefor, it is agreed that no licenses shall be granted without the written consent, in each instance, of the Writer for the use of the composition by means of television, or by any means, or for any purposes not commercially established, or for which licenses were not granted by the Publisher on musical compositions prior to June 1, 1937.

Writer's Consent to Licenses

(k) The Publisher shall not, without the written consent of the Writer in each case, give or grant any right or license (i) to use the title of the composition, or (ii) for the exclusive use of the composition in any form or for any purpose, or for any period of time, or for any territory, other than its customary arrangements with foreign publishers, or (iii) to give a dramatic representation of the composition or to dramatize the plot or story thereof, or (iv) for a vocal rendition of the composition in synchronization with sound motion pictures, or (v) for any synchronization use thereof, or (vi) for the use of the composition or a quotation or excerpt therefrom in any article, book, periodical, advertisement or other similar publication. If, however, the Publisher shall give to the Writer written notice by certified mail, return receipt requested, or telegram, specifying the right or license to be given or granted, the name of the licensee and the terms and conditions thereof, including the price or other compensation to be received therefor, then, unless the Writer (or any one or more of them) shall, within five business days after the delivery of such notice to the address of the Writer hereinafter designated, object thereto, the Publisher may grant such right or license in accordance with the said notice without first obtaining the consent of the Writer. Such notice shall be deemed sufficient if sent to the Writer at the address or addresses hereinafter designated or at the address or addresses last furnished to the Publisher in writing by the Writer.

Trust for Writer

(l) Any portion of the receipts which may become due to the Writer from license fees (in excess of offsets), whether received directly from the licensee or from any licensing agent of the Publisher, shall, if not paid immediately on the receipt thereof by the Publisher, belong to the Writer and shall be held in trust for the Writer until payment is made; the ownership of said trust fund by the Writer shall not be questioned whether the monies are physically segregated or not.

Writer Participation

(m) The Publisher agrees that it will not issue any license as a result of which it will receive any financial benefit in which the Writer does not participate.

Writer Credit

(n) On all regular piano copies, orchestrations, band or other arrangements, octavos, quartets, commercial sound recordings and other reproductions of the composition or parts thereof, in whatever form and however produced, Publisher shall include or cause to be included, in addition to the copyright notice, the name of the Writer, and Publisher shall include a similar requirement in every license or authorization issued by it with respect to the composition.

Writers'   5. Whenever the term "Writer" is used herein, it shall be deemed to mean all of the persons herein defined as "Writer" and any
Respective   and all royalties herein provided to be paid to the Writer shall be paid equally to such persons if there be more than one, unless
Shares   otherwise provided in Paragraph 23.

Release of   6. (a) (i) The Publisher shall, within.....................months from the date of this contract (the "initial period"), cause a
Commercial Sound   commercial sound recording of the composition to be made and released in the customary form and through the customary commercial
Recording   channels. If at the end of such initial period a sound recording has not been made and released, as above provided, then, subject to the
(Insert period not provisions of the next succeeding subdivision, this contract shall terminate.
exceeding 12 months)

(Insert amount to be not   (ii) If, prior to the expiration of the initial period, Publisher pays the Writer the sum of $........(which shall not be charged
less than $250) against or recoupable out of any advances, royalties or other monies theretofor paid, then due, or which thereafter may become due the
(Insert period not Writer from the Publisher pursuant to this contract or otherwise), Publisher shall have an additional............months (the "additional
exceeding six months) period") commencing with the end of the initial period, within which to cause such commercial sound recording to be made and
released as provided in subdivision (i) above. If at the end of the additional period a commercial sound recording has not been made and
released, as above provided, then this contract shall terminate.

    (iii) Upon termination pursuant to this Paragraph 6(a), all rights of any and every nature in and to the composition and in
and to any and all copyrights secured thereon in the United States and throughout the world shall automatically re-vest in and become
the property of the Writer and shall be reassigned to him by the Publisher. The Writer shall not be obligated to return or pay to the
Publisher any advance or indebtedness as a condition of such re-assignment; the said re-assignment shall be in accordance with and
subject to the provisions of Paragraph 8 hereof, and, in addition, the Publisher shall pay to the Writer all gross sums which it has
theretofore or may thereafter receive in respect of the composition.

Writer's   (b) The Publisher shall furnish, or cause to be furnished, to the Writer six copies of the commercial sound recording referred to in
Copies   Paragraph 6(a).

Piano Copies,   (c) The Publisher shall
Piano Arrange- ☐ (i) within 30 days after the initial release of a commercial sound recording of the composition, make, publish and offer for sale
ment or Lead Sheet regular piano copies of the composition in the form and through the channels customarily employed by it for that purpose;
(Select (i) ☐ (ii) within 30 days after execution of this contract make a piano arrangement or lead sheet of the composition and furnish six
or (ii) copies thereof to the Writer.

    In the event neither subdivision (i) nor (ii) of this subparagraph (c) is selected, the provisions of subdivision (ii) shall be
automatically deemed to have been selected by the parties.

Foreign   7. (a) Each copyright on the composition in countries other than the United States shall be secured only in the name of the
Copyright   Publisher, and the Publisher shall not at any time divest itself of said foreign copyright directly or indirectly.

Foreign   (b) No rights shall be granted by the Publisher in the composition to any foreign publisher or licensee inconsistent with the terms
Publication   hereof, nor shall any foreign publication rights in the composition be given to a foreign publisher or licensee unless and until the
Publisher shall have complied with the provisions of Paragraph 6 hereof.

Foreign   (c) If foreign rights in the composition are separately conveyed, otherwise than as a part of the Publisher's current and/or future
Advance   catalog, not less than 50% of any advance received in respect thereof shall be credited to the account of and paid to the Writer.

Foreign   (d) The percentage of the Writer on monies received from foreign sources shall be computed on the Publisher's net receipts,
Percentage   provided, however, that no deductions shall be made for offsets of monies due from the Publisher to said foreign sources; or for
advances made by such foreign sources to the Publisher, unless the Writer shall have received at least 50% of said advances.

No Foreign   (e) In computing the receipts of the Publisher from licenses granted in respect of synchronization with sound motion pictures, or
Allocations   in respect of any world-wide licenses, or in respect of licenses granted by the Publisher for use of the composition in countries other
than the United States, no amount shall be deducted for payments or allocations to publishers or licensees in such countries.

Termination   8. Upon the termination or expiration of this contract, all rights of any and every nature in and to the composition and in and to
or Expiration   any and all copyrights secured thereon in the United States and throughout the world, shall re-vest in and become the property of the
of Contract   Writer, and shall be re-assigned to the Writer by the Publisher free of any and all encumbrances of any nature whatsoever, provided
that:

    (a) If the Publisher, prior to such termination or expiration, shall have granted a domestic license for the use of the composition,
not inconsistent with the terms and provisions of this contract, the re-assignment may be subject to the terms of such license.

    (b) Publisher shall assign to the Writer all rights which it may have under any such agreement or license referred to in subdivision
(a) in respect of the composition, including, but not limited to, the right to receive all royalties or other monies earned by the
composition thereunder after the date of termination or expiration of this contract. Should the Publisher thereafter receive or
be credited with any royalties or other monies so earned, it shall pay the same to the Writer.

    (c) The Writer shall not be obligated to return or pay to the Publisher any advance or indebtedness as a condition of the
re-assignment provided for in this Paragraph 8, and shall be entitled to receive the plates and copies of the composition in the
possession of the Publisher.

    (d) Publisher shall pay any and all royalties which may have accrued to the Writer prior to such termination or expiration.

    (e) The Publisher shall execute any and all documents and do any and all acts or things necessary to effect any and all
re-assignments to the Writer herein provided for.

Negotiations   9. If the Publisher desires to exercise a right in and to the composition now known or which may hereafter become known, but for
for New or   which no specific provision has been made herein, the Publisher shall give written notice to the Writer thereof. Negotiations respecting
Unspecified   all the terms and conditions of any such disposition shall thereupon be entered into between the Publisher and the Writer and no such
Uses   right shall be exercised until specific agreement has been made.

Royalty   10. The Publisher shall render to the Writer, hereafter, royalty statements accompanied by remittance of the amount due at the
Statements   times such statements and remittances are customarily rendered by the Publisher, provided, however, that such statements and
and Payments remittances shall be rendered either semi-annually or quarterly and not more than forty-five days after the end of each such semi-annual

or quarterly period, as the case may be. The Writer may at any time, or from time to time, make written request for a detailed royalty statement, and the Publisher shall, within sixty days, comply therewith. Such royalty statements shall set forth in detail the various items, foreign and domestic, for which royalties are payable thereunder and the amounts thereof, including, but not limited to, the number of copies sold and the number of uses made in each royalty category. If a use is made in a publication of the character provided in Paragraph 4, subdivision (e) hereof, there shall be included in said royalty statement the title of said publication, the publisher or issuer thereof, the date of and number of uses, the gross license fee received in connection with each publication, the share thereto of all the writers under contract with the Publisher, and the Writer's share thereof. There shall likewise be included in said statement a description of every other use of the composition, and if by a licensee or licensees their name or names, and if said use is upon a part of an instrument serving to reproduce the composition mechanically, the type of mechanical reproduction, the title of the label thereon, the name or names of the artists performing the same, together with the gross license fees received, and the Writer's share thereof.

Examination of Books

11. (a) The Publisher shall from time to time, upon written demand of the Writer or his representative, permit the Writer or his representative to inspect at the place of business of the Publisher, all books, records and documents relating to the composition and all licenses granted, uses had and payments made therefor, such right of inspection to include, but not by way of limitation, the right to examine all original accountings and records relating to uses and payments by manufacturers of commercial sound recordings and music rolls; and the Writer or his representative may appoint an accountant who shall at any time during usual business hours have access to all records of the Publisher relating to the composition for the purpose of verifying royalty statements rendered or which are delinquent under the terms hereof.

(b) The Publisher shall, upon written demand of the Writer or his representative, cause any licensing agent in the United States and Canada to furnish to the Writer or his representative, statements showing in detail all licenses granted, uses had and payments made in connection with the composition, which licenses or permits were granted, or payments were received, by or through said licensing agent, and to permit the Writer or his representative to inspect at the place of business of such licensing agent, all books, records and documents of such licensing agent, relating thereto. Any and all agreements made by the Publisher with any such licensing agent shall provide that any such licensing agent will comply with the terms and provisions hereof. In the event that the Publisher shall instruct such licensing agent to furnish to the Writer or his representative statements as provided for herein, and to permit the inspection of the books, records and documents as herein provided, then if such licensing agent should refuse to comply with the said instructions, or any of them, the Publisher agrees to institute and prosecute diligently and in good faith such action or proceedings as may be necessary to compel compliance with the said instructions.

(c) With respect to foreign licensing agents, the Publisher shall make available the books or records of said licensing agents in countries outside of the United States and Canada to the extent such books or records are available to the Publisher, except that the Publisher may in lieu thereof make available any accountants' reports and audits which the Publisher is able to obtain.

(d) If as a result of any examination of books, records or documents pursuant to Paragraphs 11(a), 11(b) or 11(c) hereof, it is determined that, with respect to any royalty statement rendered by or on behalf of the Publisher to the Writer, the Writer is owed a sum equal to or greater than five percent of the sum shown on that royalty statement as being due to the Writer, then the Publisher shall pay to the Writer the entire cost of such examination, not to exceed 50% of the amount shown to be due the Writer.

(e) (i) In the event the Publisher administers its own licenses for the manufacture of parts of instruments serving to mechanically reproduce the composition rather than employing a licensing agent for that purpose, the Publisher shall include in each license agreement a provision permitting the Publisher, the Writer or their respective representatives to inspect, at the place of business of such licensee, all books, records and documents of such licensee relating to such license. Within 30 days after written demand by the Writer, the Publisher shall commence to inspect such licensee's books, records and documents and shall furnish a written report of such inspection to the Writer within 90 days following such demand. If the Publisher fails, after written demand by the Writer, to so inspect the licensee's books, records and documents, or fails to furnish such report, the Writer or his representative may inspect such licensee's books, records and documents at his own expense.

(ii) In the further event that the Publisher and the licensee referred to in subdivision (i) above are subsidiaries or affiliates of the same entity or one is a subsidiary or affiliate of the other, then, unless the Publisher employs a licensing agent to administer the licenses referred to in subdivision (i) above, the Writer shall have the right to make the inspection referred to in subdivision (i) above without the necessity of making written demand on the Publisher as provided in subdivision (i) above.

(iii) If as a result of any inspection by the Writer pursuant to subdivisions (i) and (ii) of this subparagraph (e) the Writer recovers additional monies from the licensee, the Publisher and the Writer shall share equally in the cost of such inspection.

Default in Payment or Prevention of Examination

12. If the Publisher shall fail or refuse, within sixty days after written demand, to furnish or cause to be furnished, such statements, books, records or documents, or to permit inspection thereof, as provided for in Paragraphs 10 and 11 hereof, or within thirty days after written demand, to make the payment of any royalties due under this contract, then the Writer shall be entitled, upon ten days' written notice, to terminate this contract. However if the Publisher shall:

(a) Within the said ten-day period serve upon the Writer a written notice demanding arbitration; and

(b) Submit to arbitration its claim that it has complied with its obligation to furnish statements, books, records or documents, or permitted inspection thereof or to pay royalties, as the case may be, or both, and thereafter comply with any award of the arbitrator within ten days after such award or within such time as the arbitrator may specify;

then this contract shall continue in full force and effect as if the Writer had not sent such notice of termination. If the Publisher shall fail to comply with the foregoing provisions, then this contract shall be deemed to have been terminated as of the date of the Writer's written notice of termination.

Derivative Works

13. No derivative work prepared under authority of Publisher during the term of this contract may be utilized by Publisher or any other party after termination or expiration of this contract.

Notices

14. All written demands and notices provided for herein shall be sent by certified mail, return receipt requested.

Suits for Infringement

15. Any legal action brought by the Publisher against any alleged infringer of the composition shall be initiated and prosecuted at its sole cost and expense, but if the Publisher should fail, within thirty days after written demand, to institute such action, the Writer shall be entitled to institute such suit at his cost and expense. All sums recovered as a result of any such action shall, after the deduction of the reasonable expense thereof, be divided equally between the Publisher and the Writer. No settlement of any such action may be made by either party without first notifying the other; in the event that either party should object to such settlement, then such settlement shall not be made if the party objecting assumes the prosecution of the action and all expenses thereof, except that any sums thereafter recovered shall be divided equally between the Publisher and the Writer after the deduction of the reasonable expenses thereof.

Infringement Claims

16. (a) If a claim is presented against the Publisher alleging that the composition is an infringement upon some other work or a violation of any other right of another, and because therof the Publisher is jeopardized, it shall forthwith serve a written notice upon the Writer setting forth the full details of such claim. The pendency of said claim shall not relieve the Publisher of the obligation to make payment of the royalties to the Writer hereunder, unless the Publisher shall deposit said royalties as and when they would otherwise be payable, in an account in the joint names of the Publisher and the Writer in a bank or trust company in New York, New York, if the Writer on the date of execution of this contract resides East of the Mississippi River, or in Los Angeles, California, if the Writer on the date of execution of this contract resides West of the Mississippi River. If no suit be filed within nine months after said written notice from the Publisher to the Writer, all monies deposited in said joint account shall be paid over to the Writer plus any interest which may have been earned thereon.

(b) Should an action be instituted against the Publisher claiming that the composition is an infringement upon some other work or a violation of any other right of another, the Publisher shall forthwith serve notice upon the Writer containing the full details of such claim. Notwithstanding the commencement of such action, the Publisher shall continue to pay the royalties hereunder to the Writer unless it shall, from and after the date of the service of the summons, deposit said royalties as and when they would otherwise be payable, in an account in the joint names of the Publisher and the Writer in a bank or trust company in New York, New York, if the Writer on the date of execution of this contract resides East of the Mississippi River, or in Los Angeles, California, if the Writer on the date of execution of this contract resides West of the Mississippi River. If the said suit shall be finally adjudicated in favor of the Publisher or shall be settled, there shall be released and paid to the Writer all of such sums held in escrow less any amount paid out of the Writer's share with the Writer's written consent in settlement of said action. Should the said suit finally result adversely to the Publisher, the said amount on deposit shall be released to the Publisher to the extent of any expense or damage it incurs and the balance shall be paid over to the Writer.

(c) In any of the foregoing events, however, the Writer shall be entitled to payment of said royalties or the money so deposited at and after such time as he files with the Publisher a surety company bond, or a bond in other form acceptable to the Publisher, in the sum of such payments to secure the return thereof to the extent that the Publisher may be entitled to such return. The foregoing payments or deposits or the filing of a bond shall be without prejudice to the rights of the Publisher or Writer in the premises.

Arbitration

17. Any and all differences, disputes or controversies arising out of or in connection with this contract shall be submitted to arbitration before a sole arbitrator under the then prevailing rules of the American Arbitration Association. The location of the arbitration shall be New York, New York, if the Writer on the date of execution of this contract resides East of the Mississippi River, or Los Angeles, California, if the Writer on the date of execution of this contract resides West of the Mississippi River. The parties hereby individually and jointly agree to abide by and perform any award rendered in such arbitration. Judgment upon any such award rendered may be entered in any court having jurisdiction thereof.

Assignment

18. Except to the extent herein otherwise expressly provided, the Publisher shall not sell, transfer, assign, convey, encumber or otherwise dispose of the composition or the copyright or copyrights secured thereon without the prior written consent of the Writer. The Writer has been induced to enter into this contract in reliance upon the value to him of the personal service and ability of the Publisher in the exploitation of the composition, and by reason thereof it is the intention of the parties and the essence of the relationship between them that the rights herein granted to the Publisher shall remain with the Publisher and that the same shall not pass to any other person, including, without limitations, successors to or receivers or trustees of the property of the Publisher, either by act or deed of the Publisher or by operation of law, and in the event of the voluntary or involuntary bankruptcy of the Publisher, this contract shall terminate, provided, however, that the composition may be included by the Publisher in a bona fide voluntary sale of its music business or its entire catalog of musical compositions, or in a merger or consolidation of the Publisher with another corporation, in which event the Publisher shall immediately give written notice thereof to the Writer; and provided further that the composition and the copyright therein may be assigned by the Publisher to a subsidiary or affiliated company generally engaged in the music publishing business. If the Publisher is an individual, the composition may pass to a legatee or distributee as part of the inheritance of the Publisher's music business and entire catalog of musical compositions. Any such transfer or assignment shall, however, be conditioned upon the execution and delivery by the transferee or assignee to the Writer of an agreement to be bound by and to perform all of the terms and conditions of this contract to be performed on the part of the Publisher.

Subsidiary Defined

19. A subsidiary, affiliate, or any person, firm or corporation controlled by the Publisher or by such subsidiary or affiliate, as used in this contract, shall be deemed to include any person, firm or corporation, under common control with, or the majority of whose stock or capital contribution is owned or controlled by the Publisher or by any of its officers, directors, partners or associates, or whose policies and actions are subject to domination or control by the Publisher or any of its officers, directors, partners or associates.

Amounts

20. The amounts and percentages specified in this contract shall be deemed to be the amounts and percentages agreed upon by the parties hereto, unless other amounts or percentages are inserted in the blank spaces provided therefor.

Modifications

21. This contract is binding upon and shall enure to the benefit of the parties hereto and their respective successors in interest (as hereinbefore limited). If the Writer (or one or more of them) shall not be living, any notices may be given to, or consents given by, his or their successors in interest. No change or modification of this contract shall be effective unless reduced to writing and signed by the parties hereto.

The words in this contract shall be so construed that the singular shall include the plural and the plural shall include the singular where the context so requires and the masculine shall include the feminine and the feminine shall include the masculine where context so requires.

Paragraph Headings

22. The paragraph headings are inserted only as a matter of convenience and for reference, and in no way define, limit or describe the scope or intent of this contract nor in any way affect this contract.

Special Provisions

23.

Witness:	Publisher ....
....	By ....
Witness:	Address ....
....	Writer ....(L.S.)
Witness:	Address ....
....	Soc. Sec. # ....
Witness:	Writer ....(L.S.)
....	Address ....
	Soc. Sec. # ....
	Writer ....(L.S.)
	Address ....
	Soc. Sec. # ....

FOR YOUR PROTECTION,
SEND A COPY OF THE FULLY SIGNED CONTRACT TO THE GUILD.
* * * * *

Special Exceptions to apply only if filled in and initialed by the parties.

☐ The composition is part of an original score (not an interpolation) of

☐ Living Stage Production   ☐ Motion Picture   ☐ Night Club Revue
☐ Televised Musical Production

which is the subject of an agreement between the parties dated _____ , a copy of which is hereto annexed. Unless said agreement requires compliance with Paragraph 6 in respect of a greater number of musical compositions, the Publisher shall be deemed to have complied with said Paragraph 6 with respect to the composition if it fully performs the terms of said Paragraph 6 in respect of any one musical composition included in said score.

FORM 3.10

STANDARD STUDIO FILM MUSIC
COMPOSER/ARRANGER/CONDUCTOR
EMPLOYMENT AGREEMENT

January 1, 1995

Mr. Cameron Composer
c/o John Lawyer, Esq.
1880 Century Park East, Suite 100
Los Angeles, California 90067

Dear Mr. Composer:

The following, when signed by you ("Artist") and by us ("Producer"),
will constitute our agreement.

1.   <u>EMPLOYMENT OF ARTIST</u>: Producer hereby employs Artist
to compose original music and to arrange and conduct all of the
music Producer may require for a sixty minute videotaped television program intended primarily for pay television exhibition (the
"Program") entitled _____ .

2.   <u>TERM</u>: Artist's services shall start on January 1, 1995 and
shall be completed in sufficient time to permit Producer to score
the music to meet delivery requirements.

3.   <u>DELIVERY</u>: Artist will deliver the score and the arrangements to Producer for all the music for the Program in sufficient
time to permit Producer to make the preparations necessary to
score the music in the Program.

4.   <u>PAYMENT</u>: In full consideration for this Agreement, Producer will pay Artist:

(a)   Upon completion of all services referred to in Paragraph 1. and compliance with Paragraph 3., the sum of
_____ .

(b)   Royalties for any publication and other use of music composed by Artist, in accordance with Exhibit "B" (Schedule of Music Royalties) attached hereto.

(c)   Upon initial theatrical exhibition of the Motion Pictures, 50% of the sum set forth in subparagraph (a) hereof.

5.   SCREEN CREDIT: Provided that Artist is not in default, Artist shall be accorded substantially the following screen credit on the Motion Picture:

       MUSIC BY

6.   ASCAP, BMI OR OTHER: Artist represents that Artist is a member of:

       ASCAP (X)   BMI ( )   _____ ( )

7.   STANDARD TERMS: The Standard Terms for Employment of Services and the Schedule of Music Royalties, attached hereto as Exhibit "A" and "B" respectively, are hereby incorporated in and made a part of this Agreement.

If the foregoing correctly sets forth the agreement between Producer and Artist please sign in the place indicated below.

Very truly yours,

THEATRICAL FILM CORPORATION

By _____

AGREED:

_____

EXHIBIT "A"

STANDARD TERMS FOR EMPLOYMENT OF SERVICES

COMPOSER/ARRANGER/CONDUCTOR

Exhibit to Agreement ("Main Agreement") dated January 1, 1995 between THEATRICAL FILM CORPORATION ("Producer") and _____("Artist").

1.   STANDARD TERMS FOR EMPLOYMENT OF SERVICES: These Standard Terms for Employment of Services are hereby incorporated in and made a part of the Main Agreement. The Main Agreement and these Standard Terms for Employment of Services are together referred to as "this Agreement."

2.   ACCEPTANCE: Artist hereby accepts employment hereunder and will comply with Producer's directions, requests, rules and regulations and perform services to the full limit of Artist's capabilities as, when and where, in the United States or any other place, designated by Producer. The judgment of Producer shall be final in all matters, including, but not limited to, matters of artistic taste and the importance and manner of performance of Artist's services.

3.   EXCLUSIVITY: During the Term, Artist will not render any services which would interfere with the services to be rendered by Artist hereunder.

4.   PAYMENT: As full compensation for all services rendered hereunder, the rights granted and warranties, representations and agreements made, and provided that Artist is not in default, Producer shall pay Artist, less applicable withholdings, the applicable sums set forth in this Agreement. Producer shall have the right to apply any portion of Artist's salary as a musician which is in excess of the minimum salary rate to any of the minimum pay-

ments, premiums, allowances, doubling, penalties, overtime or any other minimum requirements of the A.F. of M. Agreement.

5.   START DATE: Unless a start date for Artist's services is set forth in the Main Agreement, Producer will give Artist reasonable notice of such start date, and Artist agrees to be available for services hereunder during schedules established by Producer.

6.   RESULTS AND PRODUCT: Producer shall be the sole owner of all of the results and product ("Work") of all services rendered by Artist hereunder. As the employer for whom the Work is being prepared as a work made for hire by Artist as an employee of Producer within the scope of Artist's employment, Producer shall be the author and copyright owner of the Work.

7.   NAME AND LIKENESS: Producer and its licensees shall have the exclusive and perpetual right, but not the obligation, to use and license the use of Artist's name, photograph, likeness and biographical data ("Name and Likeness") for the following: (a) in billing and credits with respect to the motion pictures produced hereunder, (b) in publicizing Artist's services hereunder and/or the results and proceeds of all Artist's services hereunder, any motion pictures produced hereunder, any television series of which the motion pictures may be a part and in connection therewith and any distributor, network, sponsor, advertising agency or licensee of exhibition rights in the motion pictures produced hereunder or other parties and its or their products and services, (c) in connection with the publication and exploitation of books based on the motion pictures produced hereunder and music and sound recordings of music written for or performed in the motion pictures produced hereunder. Any breach by Artist of the exclusivity provisions of this Paragraph shall be deemed a Default and Producer shall have the right to terminate this Agreement by notice to Artist and/or to withhold any screen and advertising credit provided for hereunder. Producer may not use or license use of Artist's Name and Likeness as a direct endorsement of any sponsor's product or service.

8.   PAY OR PLAY: Nothing in this Agreement shall obligate Producer actually to utilize Artist's services or to exploit the results and proceeds of Artist's services hereunder. If Producer elects not to utilize Artist's services, payment to Artist of the applicable sums set forth in this Agreement constitutes discharge in full of all of Producer's obligations to Artist hereunder.

9.   FEDERAL COMMUNICATIONS ACT: Artist warrants and represents that Artist will neither pay nor agree to pay any money, service or other valuable consideration as defined in Section 508 of the Federal Communications Act of 1934 as amended, for the inclusion of any matter in any motion picture, and that Artist has not accepted nor will accept nor agree to accept any money, service or other valuable consideration (other than payment to Artist hereunder) for the inclusion of any matter in any motion picture. Artist will, during or after the Term, promptly on request, complete Producer's standard Section 508 report forms.

10.   DEFAULT; INCAPACITY; FORCE MAJEURE: In the event of default, incapacity of Artist, or event of force majeure any interference with or suspension or postponement of production by reason of any cause or occurrence beyond the control of Producer, including labor dispute, strikes, any acts of God, war, riot, governmental action, regulations or decrees, casualties, accidents, illness or incapacity of the director or of a member of the cast or other person in connection with any motion pictures produced hereunder, or similar or dissimilar causes which prevent rendition of services), Producer may, at its election, terminate this Agreement by notice to Artist without payment after termination or suspend services without payment during suspension for such period of time, or any part thereof, as such default, incapacity of Artist or event of force majeure shall continue. Producer may, at its election, add to the Term a period of time equal to the period of any such suspension.

11.   ORIGINALITY; INDEMNIFICATION: Artist warrants and represents that all material, if any, written by Artist for Producer will be wholly original with Artist, or in the public domain, and was not

and will not be copied in whole or in part from any other work except for material furnished by Producer for use by Artist hereunder, and does not and will not knowingly invade the right of privacy of any person. Artist further warrants and represents that any material furnished or written by Artist does not and will not constitute a defamation of any person, firm or corporation, or violate or infringe upon any copyright, common law or statutory, or any other right of any person, firm or corporation. Artist hereby agrees to indemnify and hold Producer and its successors, licensees and assigns harmless from and against any claim, loss, damage, liability, judgment, cost or expense of any kind and character, including attorneys' fees, suffered or incurred by Producer resulting from or arising out of any breach or alleged breach of any of the foregoing warranties by Artist, and Producer similarly indemnifies and holds Artist harmless as to material furnished by Producer for use by Artist hereunder.

12.   UNIQUE SERVICES: Artist acknowledges that Artist's services hereunder are of a special, unique, unusual, extraordinary and intellectual character, giving them a peculiar value, the loss of which cannot be reasonably or adequately compensated in damages in an action at law, and in the event of the breach or threatened breach of this Agreement by Artist, and without limiting any other rights or remedies, Producer shall be entitled to equitable relief by way of injunction or otherwise.

13.   SERVICES AS MUSICIAN: Artist's services if any as a musician shall be subject to the applicable collective bargaining agreement between Producer and the American Federation of Musicians.

14.   CREDIT: No casual or inadvertent failure to accord Artist any credits that may be required under this Agreement, or under any applicable collective bargaining agreement, shall constitute a breach of this Agreement. The failure to accord Artist any required credits shall not entitle Artist to injunctive relief or to terminate this Agreement.

15.   MOTION PICTURE RELIEF FUND: Artist hereby authorizes Producer on Artist's behalf to pay to Motion Picture Relief Fund of America, Inc. one percent (1%) of all compensation accruing under this Agreement.

16.   DISTANT LOCATION: If, at Producer's request, Artist is required to remain at a distant location overnight, Artist will be furnished first class round trip transportation (if available and if used), meals and, for each such day, first class accommodations (if available). ‾

17.   ASSIGNMENT; LOANOUT: Producer may assign this Agreement and any of Producer's rights hereunder or lend Artist's services to any third party and this Agreement shall inure to the benefit of Producer, its successors and assigns. No assignment shall relieve Producer of its obligations. Artist may not assign this Agreement.

18.   NOTICES: A notice to Artist may be given orally to Artist or to Artist's agent, if any, set forth on the first page of the Main Agreement, or to any substitute agent designated in writing by Artist or by mailing or telegraphing the notice to Artist at Artist's address set forth on the first page of the Main Agreement. A notice to Producer shall be given by mailing or telegraphing it to Producer addressed to Box 1, Beverly Hills, California 90210, marked Attention: Studio Legal Affairs Department. Producer or Artist may designate a substitute address by written notice to the other. A notice given by mail, postage prepaid, or telegram thereof shall be deemed received on the date mailed or telegraphed. Any notice from Artist to Producer must be in writing.

19.   ARTIST'S WARRANTIES AND REPRESENTATIONS: Artist warrants and represents that Artist has no commitments which will or might conflict or interfere with Artist's ability fully to comply with this Agreement, and that Artist has no outstanding agreement or arrangement for use of Artist's Name and Likeness to advertise any product or service, whether by way of endorsements, testimonials, merchandising, commercial tie-ups, television or radio commer-

cials, or otherwise. No warranties have been made other than those expressly set forth in this Agreement.

20.   COMPLETE UNDERSTANDING; GOVERNING LAW: This Agreement sets forth the complete understanding between Artist and Producer with respect to the subject matter, and all prior agreements have been merged herein, whether written or oral, and may not be modified except by a written instrument signed by the party to be charged. Artist acknowledges that no representation or promise not expressly contained in this Agreement has been made by Producer or any of its agents, employees or representatives. The laws of the State of California applicable to contracts signed and to be fully performed within the State of California shall apply to this Agreement.

EXHIBIT "B"

SCHEDULE OF MUSIC ROYALTIES

EMPLOYMENT AGREEMENT

Exhibit to Agreement ("Main Agreement") dated January 1, 1995 between THEATRICAL FILM CORPORATION ("Producer") and _____("Artist").

All music, including lyrics, arrangements and orchestrations composed and created by Artist under the Main Agreement are hereinafter referred to as "Musical Compositions". Pursuant to 114 (b) of the Main Agreement, Producer will pay Artist or cause Artist to be paid, semi-annually, within ninety (90) days after June 30 and December 31 of each year after the signing of the Main Agreement, the applicable royalties listed below. Producer makes no warranty or representation that the Musical Compositions will be utilized or that any royalties will become payable to Artist.

1.   Eight cents (8 cents) per copy for each regular piano copy of the Musical Compositions, if any, sold and paid for, to Producer or to the publisher designated by Producer ("Publisher") in the United States and Canada.

2.   Ten percent (10%) of the wholesale selling price (after trade discounts, if any) of each copy sold, if any, and paid for, to Publisher in the United States and Canada of orchestrations, band arrangements, octavos, quartets, arrangements for combinations of voices and instruments, and other copies of the Musical Compositions (other than regular piano copies).

3.   Fifty percent (50%) of all Net Receipts, if any, received by Publisher for regular piano copies, orchestrations, band arrangements, octaves, quartets, arrangements for combinations of voices and instruments, and other copies of

the Musical Compositions sold in any country, other than the United States and Canada.

4.   With respect to mechanical reproduction (other than in synchronization with motion pictures including television programs) of the Musical Compositions, a royalty equal to fifty percent (50%) of Net Receipts, if any, attributable to such uses of the Musical Compositions, received by Publisher from licenses, if any, authorizing the manufacture of parts of instruments serving to mechanically reproduce the Musical Compositions.

5.   With respect to synchronization in motion pictures including television programs of the Musical Compositions, a royalty of fifty percent (50%) of all Net Receipts, if any, received by Publisher from said uses of the Musical Compositions except as excluded in the next sentence. Artist shall not be entitled to receive from Producer or Publisher any royalties or payments for the use by Producer, its parent, subsidiaries, successors or assigns, or by third parties producing motion pictures or television programs for or in association with Producer, of the Musical Compositions in synchronization with motion pictures or television programs produced by or for Producer.

6.   Publisher's "Net Receipts" means gross moneys actually received by Publisher in the United States less: (i) taxes other than income taxes thereon, (ii) fifteen percent (15%) of said gross and (iii) Publisher's actual direct costs and expenses, if any.

The above royalties shall cover entire Musical Compositions, including lyrics, if any. If, in addition to the material or any part thereof written by Artist, any such Musical Compositions shall, with Producer's prior written consent, contain the work of other composers, such royalties shall be paid jointly to Artist and to such other composers; and if any such Musical Compositions contain both music and lyrics, such royalties shall be paid one-half jointly to all composers of the music and one-half jointly to all authors of the lyrics.

Notwithstanding anything to the contrary herein contained, if Producer provides for payment to Artist of the aforesaid royalties in a contract with any third party covering publication of the Musical Compositions, which third parties assume Producer's obligations hereunder, Artist will look solely to such third party for payment, and will release Producer from any and all liability or obligation in connection with payment if Producer gives Artist notice of Producer's contract with such third party.

Artist will not be entitled to share in any sum received by Publisher from any performing rights society and Artist will look solely to the performing rights society of which Artist is or becomes a member for any share of performance royalties paid by such societies to composers and authors. Publisher will not be entitled to share in any sum received by Artist from any performing rights society and Publisher will look solely to the performing rights society of which Publisher is or becomes a member for any share of performance royalties paid by such societies to publishers.

Payments to Artist hereunder shall be accompanied by statements in reasonable detail reflecting all receipts from use of the Musical Compositions for each period for which there are receipts. Publisher shall maintain accurate books and records with respect to receipts hereunder and sums payable to Artist. Artist shall have the right, at Artist's expense, to have Artist's representative examine said books and records during reasonable business hours and to make copies and extracts therefrom. Such inspections and audits may not be made more than once each calendar year, and may not be made with respect to any period of time occurring prior to two (2) years before the date of such audit or with respect to any period of time covered by a previous audit, and provided further that each such audit shall be completed within a reasonable period of time after it is commenced.

Any objection to any statement of accounting is to be made to Publisher within eighteen (18) months after the submission of such statement and, failing any such objection, such statement shall be deemed accepted and shall be final and binding upon Artist. Except for any books and records relating to any such objection, Publisher shall not be required to retain any records for more than four (4) years after the date of the incorporation of the information in such records into a statement.

CHAPTER 4

DURATION OF COPYRIGHT, ASSIGNMENTS OF COPYRIGHT, AND LICENSES

SUMMARY

INTRODUCTION

DURATION OF COPYRIGHT

1. Life
2. Creation
3. History
4. The Appropriate Duration of Copyright Protection
5. Duration of Copyright in Works Created After January 1, 1978
6. Duration of Copyright in Works Created Before January 1, 1978

RENEWAL OF COPYRIGHT

1. Permissive Registration
2. When May Renewal Registration Be Submitted
3. Renewal Copyright Claimants
4. Proper Claimants For Renewal of Arrangements, Translations, Compilations, and Other Collective Works, and Derivative Works
5. Renewal Copyright Owners

DURATION OF ASSIGNMENTS OF COPYRIGHT

1. Duration Limited By the Terms of the Assignment
2. Duration Limited By the Terms of the Copyright Law
    A. Grants Executed By the Author After January 1, 1978
    B. Grants Covering the Initial Term of Copyright
    C. Grants Covering the Renewal Term of Copyright
    D. Grants Covering the Extended (19-year) Term of Copyright

DURATION OF AN ASSIGNMENT OF RENEWAL COPYRIGHT

1. Limited Relevancy
2. Renewal Copyright v. Renewal Expectancy
3. Transfer of Renewal Expectancy
4. Operation of the Rule of Renewal Expectancy
5. Formalities of Assigning Renewal Expectancies
6. Renewal Copyright Vesting
7. Renewal Vesting Under Copyright Renewal Act of 1992
8. Effect of 1992 Act on Assignments of Renewal Expectancies
9. Persons Entitled to Submit Renewal Applications
10. Advice for Music Publishers
11. Advice for Songwriters

DURATION OF LICENSES

1. By Terms of the License
2. By Terms of the Copyright Law
   A. Termination of Licenses Granted By Authors After January 1, 1978
   B. Licenses Covering the Initial Term of Copyright
   C. Licenses Purporting to Cover the Renewal Term of Copyright
   D. Effects of Rear Window on Music Licensing
      (a) Effect on Which Songs Will Be Used In New Derivative Works
      (b) Effect on the Terms, if any, Upon Which Previously Produced Derivative Works May Continue to Be Exploited
         (1) Licenses Granted To Music Publishers
         (2) Mechanical Licenses Granted To Record Companies
         (3) Synchronization Licenses Granted To Producers
         (4) Master Licenses Granted To Producers To Use Sound Recordings

(5) Owners of Copies or Phonorecords
Containing Affected Works

E. Effect of 1992 Act

F. Advice for Derivative Licensees

G. Advice for Music Publishers

H. Advice for Songwriters

I. Licenses Covering the Extended (19-year)
Term of Copyright

AFTER LIFE

LISTS

CHAPTER **4**

DURATION OF COPYRIGHT, ASSIGNMENTS OF COPYRIGHT, AND LICENSES

This chapter is about the life of copyrights, including their creation, their expiration, and their renewal. This chapter will also outline the duration of transfers of copyright, transfers of renewal copyrights, and grants of licenses under copyright, and their termination.

Each of these subjects will be discussed in the sections which follow. The reader should be forewarned, however, that topics such as the *duration of copyright*, *renewal of copyright*, and *termination of grants* are among the most complex provisions of the copyright law. Although a great deal of thought has been devoted to organizing these materials in a way that should be understandable to anyone willing to invest in them a thoughtful reading, intricate materials such as these, like good poetry, should not be expected to blossom forth enlightenment in the reader's mind upon a first reading.

A thorough understanding of these subjects is *not*, however, a requisite to understanding the practical licensing guidance and other advice offered in this book. Nevertheless, certain licensing problems cannot be resolved without some understanding of one or more of the topics covered in this chapter.

INTRODUCTION

The duration of copyright protection is prescribed by law. The duration of assignments and licenses are governed by the applicable *term* provisions of agreements that affect the assignments and licenses, but may also be subject to certain provisions of the copyright law that allow previously granted assignments and licenses to be terminated.

125

The discussion which follows is divided into five primary sections:

1. Duration of Copyright;

2. Renewal of Copyright;

3. Duration of Assignments of Copyright, and Exclusive Rights Under Copyright;

4. Duration of Assignments of Interests in Renewal Copy- rights; and,

5. Duration of Licenses

It should be noted that readers using the following materials to help analyze a particular duration of copyright, assignment of copyright, or termination of grant problem should bear in mind that there is a signifi- cant difference in the way the problem is approached depending upon whether the work was created before or after January 1, 1978. Accord- ingly, the reader should try to determine the applicable category in which the work falls before attempting to analyze the impact of any circum- stances that may affect ownership questions.

DURATION OF COPYRIGHT

1. Life

Like life itself, copyright protection does not last forever. In fact, the limitation on the duration of copyright protection is a restriction that is prescribed by *the people* under the U.S. Constitution, which states:

> Congress shall have the power . . . To promote the progress of science
> and useful arts, by securing *for limited times* to authors and inventors
> the exclusive right to their respective writings and discoveries.[1]

The *duration* of copyright (i.e., how long the copyright protection lasts) is often referred to as the *life of the copyright*. When the life of a

---

[1] U.S. Const. Art. I, Sec. 8.

copyright expires, the work is said to fall into the public domain. Works in the *public domain* are works for which copyright protection was never secured or works that were protected by a copyright which has expired.

2. Creation

And, as in life, according to certain philosophers, the duration of copyright begins upon *creation*. Copyright is secured automatically when the work is created, and a work is *created* when it is fixed in a tangible medium of expression for the first time.

The copyright law recognizes two types of *tangible media of expression*: copies and phonorecords. A *copy* is a material object from which a work can be read or visually perceived either directly or with the aid of a machine or device, such as a book, manuscript, piece of sheet music, film, videotape, or microfilm. A *phonorecord* is a material object that embodies fixations of sounds (other than those sounds that are accompanied by a motion picture or other audiovisual work), such as audio tapes, phonograph records, and compact audio disks. Thus, for example, a song (i.e., a *work*) can be fixed in sheet music (i.e., a *copy*) or a compact audio disk (i.e., a *phonorecord*), or both.[2]

A work is *fixed* in a tangible medium of expression when its embodiment in a copy or a phonorecord is "sufficiently permanent or stable to permit it to be perceived, reproduced, or otherwise communicated for a period of more than transitory duration."[3] A work consisting of sounds, images, or both, that are being transmitted, is fixed if a fixation of the work is being made simultaneously with its transmission.[4] If a work is prepared over a period of time, the part of the work existing in fixed form on a particular date constitutes the created work as of that date.

While a work may be fixed in a copy or a phonorecord, the ownership of copyright in the work, or any of the exclusive rights under the copyright, is distinct from ownership of any material object in which the work is embodied.[5]

---

[2] 17 U.S.C. Sec. 101.
[3] Id.
[4] Id.
[5] 17 U.S.C. Sec. 202.

3. History

Anglo-American copyright legislation began in England with the Statute of Anne, enacted in 1709. The Statute gave authors the protection of copyright for 14 years from publication, and at the expiration of the 14 years, if the author was living, the copyright could be renewed for another 14 years. The statute stated in part:

> Whereas *printers, booksellers, and other persons have of late frequently taken the liberty of printing, reprinting and publishing, or causing to be printed, reprinted, and published, books and other writings, without the consent of the authors or proprietors of such books and writings, to their very great detriment, and too often to the ruin of them and their families*: for preventing therefor such practices for the future and for the encouragement of learned men to compose and write useful books; may it please your Majesty, that it may be enacted, and be it enacted by the Queen's most excellent majesty, by and with the advice and consent of the lords spiritual and temporal, and commons, in this present parliament assembled, and by the authority of the same, . . . that the author of any book or books already composed, and not printed and published, or that shall hereafter be composed, and his assignee or assigns, shall have the sole liberty of printing and reprinting such book and books for the term of fourteen years, to commence from the day of the first publishing the same, and no longer; . . . Provided, always, That after the expiration of the said term of fourteen years, the sole right of printing or disposing of copies shall return to the authors thereof, if they are then living, for another term of fourteen years.

In this country, the copyright laws governing the original thirteen states were based largely upon the Statute of Anne. On May 31, 1790, the Congress of the United States enacted this nation's first copyright statute, which reflected its historical antecedents. Under the Copyright Act of 1790, the author was afforded copyright protection for 14 years and "if, at the expiration of said term, the author or authors, or any of them, be living, and a citizen or citizens of these United States, or resident therein, the same exclusive right shall be continued to him or them, his or their executors, administrators or assigns, for the further term of fourteen years."

The copyright law has undergone three major changes since 1790. The Copyright Act of 1831 amended the 1790 Act in two respects: the original term was increased to 28 years, and the renewal term, though still only 14 years long, could pass to the author's widow or widower or children if he did not survive the original term. The Copyright Act of 1909 maintained the original term of 28 years, but extended the length of the renewal term from 14 years to 28 years, and provided additional changes as to who may apply for renewal.[6] Finally, the copyright law underwent a complete overhaul with the Copyright Act of 1976, which took effect on January 1, 1978. Provisions of the law regarding the duration of certain copyrights created prior to January 1, 1978, were amended in 1992. The provisions of the 1976 Act and its recent changes are discussed below.

4. The Appropriate Duration of Copyright Protection

Before moving on to answering the question of how long *do* copyrights last under the law, it may be interesting to first take a moment to ask the question: how long *should* copyright protection last? While the question is interesting to ask, it is not one that can easily be answered, if it can be answered at all.

The purpose of copyright is to secure the general benefits derived by the public from the labors of authors. To this end, the copyright law seeks "to motivate the creative activity of authors . . . by the provision of a special reward."[7] That special reward is the recognition of the exclusive right of copyright—a limited *monopoly* on the exercise of privileges that others would otherwise have but for the author's exclusive rights.

It is generally agreed that, for the most part, monopolies are bad. The owner of a monopoly has the ability to charge monopoly pricing, and economists call the resulting loss to society a loss of economic welfare. If the market economy were a *static* place, there could be no justification for the monopoly of copyright. But the market economy is not static —it is quite, to the contrary, *dynamic*. The special incentive provided to authors serves to motivate the creative activity of authors *over time*. Thus, in contrast to the negative effects of monopolies under a static

---

[6] Act of March 4, 1909, chap. 320, 35 Stat. 1075 (the "1909 Act").

[7] *Sony Corp. v. Universal City Studios, Inc.*, 464 U.S. 417 (1984).

analysis, the monopoly of copyright under in a dynamic world provides positive benefits to society.

The question, then, is whether and to what extent do the *dynamic benefits* to society of copyright outweigh the *static losses* to society resulting from the exercise of that monopoly by authors. Only to the extent that such benefits outweigh such losses should copyright be enforced. This principal of modern economic analysis was recognized over a century and a half ago by Lord Macaulay in a speech delivered to the British House of Commons:

> It is good that authors should be remunerated; and the least exception-able way of remunerating them is by a monopoly. Yet monopoly is evil. For the sake of good we must submit to evil; but the evil ought not to last a day longer than is necessary for the purpose of securing the good.[8]

If the net effect of copyright protection is good for society, then why shouldn't copyright protection last forever? In 1908, Justice Oliver Wendell Holmes suggested one reason:

> The notion of property starts, I suppose, from confirmed possession of a tangible object and consists in the right to exclude others from interference with the more or less free doing with it as one wills. But in copyright property has reached a more abstract expression. The right to exclude is not directed to an object in possession or owned, but is *in vacuo*, so to speak. It restrains the spontaneity of men where but for it there would be nothing of any kind to hinder their doing as they saw fit. It is a prohibition of conduct remote from the persons or tangibles of the party having the right. It may be infringed a thousand miles from the owner and without his ever becoming aware of the wrong. It is a right which could not be recognized or endured for more than a limited time.[9]

Modern scholars have pointed to more specific grounds. As Professor Nimmer instructs:

---

[8] Speech by Lord Macaulay in the British House of Commons, *The Works of Lord Macaulay* (1866).

[9] *White-Smith Music Publishing Co. v. Apollo Co.*, 209 U.S. 1, 19 (1907).

It may be questioned why literary property should be treated differently from other forms of property? If I may own Blackacre in perpetuity, why not also *Black Beauty*? The answer lies in the First Amendment. There is no countervailing speech interest which must be balanced against perpetual ownership of tangible real and personal property. There is such a speech interest with respect to literary property, or copyright.[10]

The issues regarding the appropriate duration of copyright protection were framed long ago by legal jurists, well before they were even taken up in the United States. For example, in 1785, Lord Mansfield said,

> [W]e must take care to guard against two extremes equally prejudicial; the one, that men of ability, who have employed their time for the service of the community, may not be deprived of their just merits, and the reward of their ingenuity, and labour; the other, that the world may not be deprived of improvements, nor the progress of the arts be retarded.[11]

No doubt Lord Mansfield was familiar with the works of Aristotle,[12] who advocated temperance as a moral virtue.

With that, and without answering the question precisely how long is enough protection, we shall proceed by answering the question we began with: how long *do* copyrights last under the law.

5. Duration of Copyright in Works Created After January 1, 1978

Under the new copyright law, the term of copyright protection of works created (i.e., fixed in tangible form for the first time) after January 1, 1978 starts at the moment of creation and lasts for the author's life, plus an additional fifty years after the author's death. In the case of a *joint work* prepared by two or more authors, the term of protection lasts for 50 years after the last surviving author's death.

The above terms will not apply if the work was a work for hire, an anonymous work, or a pseudonymous work. A *work for hire* is (i) a work

---

[10] 1 Nimmer *On Copyright*, Sec. 1.10 [C][1] (1991).

[11] *Sayre v. Moore*, 1 East 361, 362, 102 Eng. Rep. 139, 140 (K.B. 1785).

[12] See, generally, Aristotle, *The Nicomachean Ethics*.

prepared by an employee within the scope of his employment or (ii) a work which is specially ordered or commissioned in a writing that says the work is made for hire and which falls within one of several categories enumerated in the copyright law.[13] (See Chapter 2.) An *anonymous work* is a work on copies or phonorecords of which no natural person is identified as author. A *pseudonymous work* is a work on copies or phonorecords of which the author is identified under a fictitious name. The term of protection for works made for hire, and for anonymous and pseudonymous works (unless the author's identity is revealed in Copyright Office records) is 75 years from publication or 100 years from creation, whichever is shorter.

6. Duration of Copyright in Works Created Before January 1, 1978

Under the copyright law in effect before 1978, copyright was secured either on the date a work was published, or on the date of registration if the work was registered in unpublished form.

Works that had been created before the new law came into effect but had neither been published nor registered for copyright before January 1, 1978, have been automatically brought under the new law and are now given federal copyright protection. The duration of copyright in these works is generally computed in the same way as the duration of copyright for new works: the life-plus-50 or 75/100-year terms. However, all works in this category are guaranteed at least 25 years of statutory protection; the law specifies that in no case will copyright in a work of this sort expire before December 31, 2002, and if the work is published before that date the term may be extended by another 25 years, through the end of 2027.

For works in which statutory copyright protection had been secured before January 1, 1978, the new law retains the old system for computing the duration of protection, but with some changes. The law provides for a first term of 28 years, measured from the date protection was originally secured by publication or registration, with a right to

---

[13] 17 U.S.C. Sec. 101.

a renewal term of 47 years. Renewal of copyright is discussed at length in the next section.

Copyrights that were in their renewal terms (i.e., second 28 year term) during the time spanning December 31, 1965 to December 31, 1977, were automatically extended an additional 19 years (thereby extending the total copyright duration for such works up to a maximum of 75 years), without the need for further renewal. This is referred to as the *19-year extended term.*[14]

Until 1992, copyrights that were in their first term during the time spanning December 31, 1965 to December 31, 1977 were still required to be renewed to receive the full new maximum term of 75 years. After the Copyright Renewal Act of 1992 was signed into law, copyrights first published in 1964 or later are considered automatically renewed. The 1992 Act only applies to copyrights which still had to be renewed in the calendar year 1992 or later. Copyrights that have previously fallen into the public domain as a result of failure to file a renewal registration are not affected (i.e., they remain in the public domain).

The copyright law also provides that all terms of copyright will run through the end of the calendar year in which they would otherwise expire. This not only affects the duration of copyrights, but also the time limits for renewal registrations, discussed below.

RENEWAL OF COPYRIGHT

As may be evident from the historical background noted above, the concept of renewal dates back to the earliest legislative enactments on copyright law. Under a renewal system, the duration of copyright is divided into two consecutive terms. The second term is normally conditioned upon the copyright owner filing a registration, within strict time limits, to secure copyright protection for the second term. However, under a recent amendment to the U.S. copyright law, registration is no longer a condition for renewal of copyright under the copyright law.

---

[14] 17 U.S.C. Sec. 304 (b).

1. Permissive Registration

As noted, registration of renewal is no longer a condition for extending copyright protection through the renewal term (i.e., an additional 47 years beyond the original 28 year term) under U.S. copyright law. By the amendment to the copyright law signed into law on June 26, 1992, renewal is now automatic. Nevertheless, the law retains a permissive procedure of renewal registration which (i) provides a slight procedural incentive for claimants who file a renewal registration and (ii) has a potential impact upon determining who primarily benefits from the renewal.

If the application for renewal is filed within one year of expiration of the original term of copyright, the registration certificate would constitute *prima facie* evidence of validity of the copyright during its renewed and extended term and of the facts stated in the certificate of renewal registration.[15] It has always been the case that an original copyright registration, if filed within certain time limits, would constitute *prima facie* evidence of validity of the copyright and of the facts stated in the certificate of registration,[16] but, until the Copyright Renewal Act of 1992, renewal certificates never enjoyed the same recognition. The advantage is a slight one, but it does afford some convenience to copyright owners seeking to enforce their copyrights; in lawsuits for copyright infringement, the copyright owner with a certificate that constitutes evidence of validity of the copyright and of the facts stated in the certificate may avoid having to call to the stand witnesses to prove all of the facts in the certificate. This is a useful convenience in copyright piracy cases filed in jurisdictions that are a great distance away from the witnesses who could testify as to these facts.

Renewal registration may have an enormous, though hidden, impact on the determination of who primarily benefits from the renewal term. If the author of the work had previously granted his expectancy interest in the renewal copyright to his music publisher, then under certain circumstances, renewal registration may affect whether the renewal copyright will vest in the author's music publisher or the heirs to the

---

[15] 17 U.S.C. Sec. 304(a)(4)(A).
[16] 17 U.S.C. Sec. 410(c).

author's estate. This important subject will be discussed further below with respect to assignments of renewal interests.

2. When May Renewal Registration Be Submitted

In accordance with the Copyright Renewal Act of 1992, an application to register a claim to the renewed and extended term of copyright in a work created during the time spanning the calendar years 1964 through 1977, inclusive, may be made to the Copyright Office (i) within 1 year before the expiration of the original term of copyright and (ii) at any time during the renewed and extended term.[17] For all works created prior to 1964, the renewal application and fee must have been received in the Copyright Office within one year prior to the expiration of the original term; otherwise, the duration of the copyright expired at the end of the 28th year, and the work fell into the public domain.

Note, all terms of copyright run through the end of the year in which they would otherwise expire. Thus, all copyright terms will expire on December 31st of their year of expiration. Accordingly, all periods for renewal registration will run from January 1 of the 28th year of the original term of the copyright and will end on December 31st of the 28th year.

To determine the proper year in which to file a renewal application, follow these steps:

(1) Find out the date of original copyright for the work.

In the case of works originally registered in unpublished form prior to publication, the date of copyright is the date of its registration in the Copyright Office. Otherwise, the date of copyright is the date of first publication of a copy or phonorecord of a work bearing a valid copyright notice. *Publication* is the distribution of copies or phonorecords of a work to the public by sale or other transfer of ownership, or by rental, lease

---

[17] 17 U.S.C. Sec. 304 (a)(3)(A).

or lending.[18] In one limited exception, the date of copyright may be other than above: In any case where the year date in the copyright notice on copies distributed by authority of the copyright owner is earlier than the year of first publication, the date of copyright is considered to be the year contained in the notice.

(2) Add 28 years to the date of copyright.

The answer will be in the calendar year during which the copyright will be eligible for renewal registration, and December 31st of that year will be the renewal deadline.

The following table may be used to determine the time limits for filing a renewal application:

Original Copyright	Must Be Renewed On or After	But By*	Expiration If Renewed
Mandatory Renewal			
1950	1-1-78	12-31-78	12-31-2025
1951	1-1-79	12-31-79	12-31-2026
1952	1-1-80	12-31-80	12-31-2027
1953	1-1-81	12-31-81	12-31-2028
1954	1-1-82	12-31-82	12-31-2029
1955	1-1-83	12-31-83	12-31-2030
1956	1-1-84	12-31-84	12-31-2031
1957	1-1-85	12-31-85	12-31-2032
1958	1-1-86	12-31-86	12-31-2033
1959	1-1-87	12-31-87	12-31-2034
1960	1-1-88	12-31-88	12-31-2035
1961	1-1-89	12-31-89	12-31-2036
1962	1-1-90	12-31-90	12-31-2037
1963	1-1-91	12-31-91	12-31-2038

---

[18] 17 U.S.C. Sec. 101.

| | Original | Must Be Renewed | | Expiration |
	Copyright	On or After	But By*	If Renewed
Permissive Renewal				
	1964	1-1-92	12-31-92	12-31-2039
	1965	1-1-93	12-31-93	12-31-2040
	1966	1-1-94	12-31-94	12-31-2041
	1967	1-1-95	12-31-95	12-31-2042
	1968	1-1-96	12-31-96	12-31-2043
	1969	1-1-97	12-31-97	12-31-2044
	1970	1-1-98	12-31-98	12-31-2045
	1971	1-1-99	12-31-99	12-31-2046
	1972	1-1-00	12-31-00	12-31-2047
	1973	1-1-01	12-31-01	12-31-2048
	1974	1-1-02	12-31-02	12-31-2049
	1975	1-1-03	12-31-03	12-31-2050
	1976	1-1-04	12-31-04	12-31-2051
	1977	1-1-05	12-31-05	12-31-2052

* If the application for renewal for a work created prior to January 1, 1964 was not filed by the deadline, then the work fell into the public domain. This would not be the result for works created on or after January 1, 1964; renewal for such works is now automatic and the only consequence of failing to file a renewal application during the 28th year is the loss of certain procedural advantages in litigation and possibly an effect on who will own the renewal copyright upon its vesting.

Renewal registration is effective upon the Copyright Office's receipt of a completed application and the appropriate fee. Being unable to supply all of the information requested in the form should not deter the applicant from submitting the application, even if it is incomplete. The Copyright Office will consider a renewal application to be "acceptable" if it identifies the work by title and contains a correct statement of either the claimant or basis of claim. All other information supplied in the form will be considered minor and may by supplied later, even after the deadline for renewal, by a supplementary registration on Form CA. Whenever an applicant has cause to believe a formal application for renewal (Form RE), if sent by mail, might not be received in the Copyright Office before the renewal deadline, the application for renewal may be made by telephone, telegram or other method of communication. However, the renewal fee was also required to be received by the Copyright Office by the deadline. Fortunately, as a result of the Copyright Renewal Act of 1992, the practice of getting a friend who lives in the vicinity of Washington, D.C. to brave the cold on New Year's Eve to run down to the Copyright Office with your check or money order is now history.

Note, in the event the last day for filing the renewal falls on a Saturday, Sunday, holiday or other non-business day within the District of Columbia or the Federal Government, the application may be filed on the next succeeding business day, and is effective as of the date when the period expired. Further, in any case in which the Register of Copyrights determines the application, fee or any other material to be delivered to the Copyright Office by the renewal deadline, would have been received in the Copyright Office in due time except for a general disruption or suspension of postal or other transportation or communications services, the actual receipt of such material in the Copyright Office within one month after the date on which the Register makes such determination, shall be considered timely.

The Copyright Office has no discretion to extend the renewal time limits. If an acceptable application and fee for works created prior to 1964 were not received within the strict time limits, copyright protection is lost permanently and the work fell into the public domain. Should that have happened, the copyright cannot be revived.

3. Renewal Copyright Claimants

This section will summarize who under the law is entitled to claim a renewal copyright. Crucial to the understanding of renewal registration is the understanding of the difference between who may *claim* a renewal, who may *submit* an application for renewal, and who ultimately gets to *own* the renewal copyright. The answer is not necessarily the same for each, depending upon the circumstances.

Renewal copyright may be *claimed* only by those persons specified in the copyright law. (The statutory provisions on this point are essentially the same in the 1992 Act as those contained in the 1976 Act and 1909 Act.) Under the Copyright Renewal Act of 1992, an application to register a claim for renewal of copyright may be made (i) within one year before the expiration of the original term by any person entitled to claim the renewal (see below) or (ii) at any time after expiration of the original term by any person in whom such further term vested, or by any successor or assign of such person, if the application is made in the name of such person.

In general, the law gives the right to *claim* renewal to the individual author of the work, regardless of who owned the copyright during the original term. If the author is deceased at the time for renewal, the statute gives the right to claim renewal to certain of the author's heirs in a particular order of preference, listed below.

In the case of the following three types of works, however, the person or entity entitled to claim renewal is not necessarily the individual creator of the work (or his heirs), but the copyright proprietor (i.e., owner of the copyright at the time application is made for renewal):

1. *Posthumous Work.* The owner of a posthumous work may claim renewal in such work. A *posthumous* work is a work as to which no copyright assignment or other contract for exploitation has occurred during the author's lifetime.

2. *Collective Work.* The owner of a collective work (e.g., periodical, encyclopedia, anthology, etc.) may claim renewal in all material in which he originally secured copyright, including the collective work as a whole, as well as any contributions to the collective work in which the owner originally claimed copyright. The author of any contribution to a collective work may claim renewal in his own name with respect to his contribution, if he originally secured a separate copyright in the contribution (i.e., he separately registered the contribution in unpublished form, or, upon publication, copies of the work contained a separate copyright notice in the name of the author).

3. *Works Made For Hire.* The owner of a work-made-for-hire may claim renewal in such work. Renewal rights may not be claimed by an employee-for-hire. To determine whether the relationship between the individual who actually created the work and the person for whom the work was created was a work-for-hire, see Chapter 2.

The persons in the following order of preference may claim renewal in all types of works except those three enumerated above:

1.   The author, if living.

2.   The widow (or widower) and children of the author.

> If the author is not living, the author's widow (or widower) and children are entitled to claim renewal. All members of this class share the renewal interest equally. For example, if the deceased author leaves a widow and two children, the widow and each child shall receive a one-third interest in the right to claim renewal copyright.

> An author's "children" are his or her immediate offspring, whether legitimate or not, and any children legally adopted by the author. The author's widow (or widower) is the author's surviving spouse, as determined under the law of the author's domicile at the time of his or her death, whether or not the spouse has later remarried. Where the author and spouse were divorced, the former spouse does not constitute a "widow" upon the author's death.

3.   The executor(s) named in the author's will.

> If there is no surviving widow (or widower) or children, then the executor(s) named in the author's will are entitled to claim the renewal copyright. This will be the case even if the author leaves surviving grandchildren.

> An *executor* is one who has been designated in a will as the person to carry out the directions and provisions designated in the will by the deceased author. When the renewal rights are claimed by the executors, they are not claimed for their personal benefit, but rather in trust for the benefit of those named in the will to receive the renewals or the residuary assets of the estate of the author. When the author dies leaving a will, but an executor is not named in the will, the courts will appoint an "administrator" to perform the duties of an executor. For renewal purposes, an administrator is the equivalent of an executor.

4.   The next of kin of the deceased author.

If there is no surviving widow (or widower) or children, and the author left no will, then the next of kin of the deceased author are entitled to claim the renewal copyright. Who comprises *next of kin* is determined by the intestate succession laws of the state of the author's domicile at the time of his or her death.

In summary, a person may not be a renewal *claimant* unless he is a member of the appropriate class set forth in the copyright law: a proprietor of the copyright (in the case of a posthumous work, collective work, or work made for hire); the author of the work; the widow (or widower) of the author; a child of the deceased author; or, where none of the foregoing are living, the executor under the author's will; or then, in the event no will is left, the next of kin of the deceased author.

One need not, however, be a member of one of the above classes to be entitled to *submit* an application for renewal on behalf of a proper renewal claimant. A discussion of who is entitled to submit an application for renewal is the subject of a section set forth below.

4. Proper Claimants for Renewal of Arrangements, Translations, Compilations, and Other Collective Works, and Derivative Works

In the case of the renewal of copyright in a new version of a previous work, such as an arrangement, translation, dramatization, compilation or work published with new material, a further consideration must be made in determining the proper claimant.

Generally, the copyright secured in a new version of a work is independent of any protection in the material published earlier. In other words, the copyright in the new version covers only the additions, changes or other new material appearing for the first time in that version, and not to the underlying preexisting material. Thus, for renewal purposes, the "authors" of the new version are only those persons who contributed the new copyrightable matter to it; the person who wrote the original version on which the new work is based cannot be regarded as an "author" of the new version, unless that person also contributed to the new matter.

In the context of music publishing, arrangements, translations, and compilations are usually prepared by employees-for-hire of the publishing company. Therefore, the proper renewal claimant for such works will usually be the music publishing company, claiming as "proprietor of the copyright," not the composer of the song (or his statutory heirs).

Music publishers may ask whether it is desirable to file renewal registrations for their copyrighted arrangements, particularly where a renewal copyright has already been claimed in the underlying composition. The best policy is to file renewal registrations for all copyrighted arrangements of musical compositions. Some arrangements may continue to have sale and performance value well after the copyright in the underlying song has expired. In many instances, arrangements originally prepared for publication in the form of sheet music that was once discontinued were later reprinted, either as part of a folio, or because no replacement for the discontinued arrangement was readily available. Renewal should certainly be claimed if the arrangement was of a work in the public domain to begin with or where the arranger is entitled to a royalty on sales of the arrangement.

5. Renewal Copyright Owners

Determining who is the proper *claimant* of the renewal copyright does not definitively lead to the determination of who will become the *owner* of the renewal copyright upon the expiration of the initial term of copyright. If the author never assigned to another his or her rights in his renewal copyright during the original term, then the claimant(s) will become the owner(s) of the renewal copyright upon the expiration of the initial term.

If the author did assign to another his or her rights in his renewal copyright during the original term, then the claimant(s) will not necessarily become the owner(s) of the renewal copyright. The effect of an assignment of a renewal prior to the expiration of the original copyright term on the claimant's potential right to own the renewal copyright is discussed below.

DURATION OF ASSIGNMENTS OF COPYRIGHT

An assignment of copyright, or assignment of any of the exclusive rights under copyright, may be limited in duration. The duration of an assignment may be limited (1) by the assignment itself, or (2) by the terms of the copyright law.

1. Duration Limited By the Terms of the Assignment

The duration of an assignment may be limited by the terms of the assignment or contract relating to the assignment. For example, a songwriter may assign to a music publisher his copyright in a song for a period of 10 years; at the expiration of the 10 years, the copyright reverts to the songwriter. Such reversion may or may not be automatic, depending on the terms of the assignment. For example, the copyright may revert only if the publisher fails to have a commercial recording of the song distributed or if certain income levels are not achieved.

Sometimes, some specific action is required on the part of the songwriter to effect reversion. For example, under the terms of the AGAC Uniform Popular Songwriter's Contract of 1948 (Paragraph 8) (See Chapter 3), the writer is entitled to be re-vested with all rights and copyrights outside of the United States and Canada. To cause such re-vesting of foreign rights, the writer must send a notice to the publisher within 6 months of the writer's grant of such rights to another music publisher.

2. Duration Limited By The Terms of The Copyright Law

In the event the assignment document does not expressly indicate the term of its duration, it will be deemed effective for the remainder of the copyright term existing at that time. However, certain provisions of the new copyright law, which went into effect on January 1, 1978, affect the duration of certain assignments.

A. Grants Executed by the Author After January 1, 1978

The congressional purpose, in enacting the 1909 Act, in granting an author two consecutive 28-year terms, was to guarantee him the enjoyment of the fruits of his creation after the initial 28-year term during which his work was exploited by his assignee. Under the 1909 Act, after the first term of 28 years, the renewal copyright was supposed to revert to the author or other specified beneficiaries. In the words of the Register of Copyrights, the renewal term was intended to remedy the situation "where the author actually turns out to have sold his birthright for a mess of pottage."[19] To a certain extent, however, this remedy was thwarted by a ruling of the Supreme Court in 1943, discussed below.[20] In enacting the 1976 Act, Congress dropped the renewal feature, except for works already in their first term of statutory protection when the new law took effect, but included several new provisions clearly intended to reinstate the right of the author to enjoy the fruits of his authorship years after his initial assignment of the copyright.

An assignment of copyright subject to the 1976 Act, or exclusive rights under such copyright, which is silent about its *term* (i.e., how long it will remain in effect) or *reversion* (i.e., circumstances under which rights will revert to the assignor), will endure for the life of the copyright. Under the 1976 Act, however, any assignment by an author after January 1, 1978, regardless of the term stated in the agreement effecting the transfer, is subject to being terminated 35 years after the date of the grant.[21] This power to terminate a transfer of copyright or exclusive rights under copyright (and, for that matter, non-exclusive licenses, discussed below) is sometimes referred to as the *35-year termination rule.*

Specifically, for transfers of rights made by an author on or after January 1, 1978, the copyright law permits the author or certain heirs of the author (of a work other than a work made for hire) to terminate a transfer during a 5-year period beginning at the end of 35 years from the date of the grant, or if the grant covers the right of publication, 35 years from the date of publication or 40 years from the date of the grant, whichever is shorter. To terminate a grant, a written notice must be served on the transferee within the time limits specified by the copyright law.[22]

---

[19] Register of Copyrights, *Copyright Law Revision Pt. 3, Preliminary Draft for Revised U.S. Copyright Law and Discussions and Comments on the Draft*, 88th Cong., 2d Sess. (Comm. Print 1964).

[20] See discussion below concerning *Fred Fisher Co. v. M. Witmark & Sons*, 318 U.S. 643 (1943).

[21] 17 U.S.C. Sec. 203.

[22] 17 U.S.C. Sec. 203 (a)(3),(4).

To effect the congressional purpose of the rule, certain key pro-visions were included to prevent the author from prematurely waiving or contracting away his right of termination. For example, termination of the grant may be effected notwithstanding any agreement to the contrary, including an agreement to make a will or to make any further grant.[23] Also, the rule provides that a re-grant of rights that revert after termination is valid only if it is executed after the effective date of termination.[24] An exception, however, was provided in favor of the current grantee: A further grant of a reverted right may be made to the original grantee or his successor in title after the service of notice has been made.[25] Thus, for example, an author who serves notice of termination on his current music publisher may enter into a contract granting rights covering the remainder of the life of the copyright with that music publisher beginning the date the publisher is served with the notice. This, in effect, gives the current publisher a right of first refusal, affording him a two to ten year lead time over other publishers in dealing for the reverted rights.

An author may overcome the competitive advantage of his current publisher by merely waiting until the termination actually takes effect before accepting any offer from the publisher. Some clever publishers have conceived interesting ways of increasing their leverage in the negotiation for these reverted rights. The following is a rather innovative provision that may be found in some music publishing contracts drafted since the passage of the 1976 Act:

> Writer and Publisher hereby acknowledge that the copyrights and certain other rights in the Compositions granted to Publisher hereun-der may be terminated by Writer or his successors (hereinafter, indi-vidually and collectively, "Writer") in accordance with the provisions of the Copyright Act. Writer and Publisher further acknowledge that it is their intention that, in the event that any such grants of copyright or

---

[23] 17 U.S.C. Sec. 203 (a)(5).

[24] 17 U.S.C. Sec. 203 (b)(4).

[25] Id.

other rights are terminated by Writer, Publisher shall have the exclusive right of first refusal with respect thereto, which right of first refusal shall be exercised as follows:

Until the expiration of a period of sixty (60) days following the Publisher's receipt of a valid notice of termination with respect to any such copyrights and other rights, Writer shall not negotiate with any third party with respect to the grant, sale, assignment, license, or other transfer thereof. During said sixty (60) day period, Writer agrees to negotiate in good faith and to exert best efforts to reach an agreement with Publisher for Publisher's acquisition of such copyrights and other rights. In the event that Publisher and Writer fail to reach agreement by the end of said sixty (60) day period, Writer shall be free to negotiate with third parties for the grant, sale, assignment license or other transfer of such copyrights and other rights, only for terms and conditions more favorable to Writer than those last offered by Publisher. If Writer receives such an offer from a bona fide third party, which offer Writer wishes to accept, Writer shall notify Publisher of the terms thereof in writing and Publisher shall have ten (10) days from its receipt thereof to notify Writer in writing that it desires to acquire the copyrights and other rights subject to the terms of such offer on the terms and conditions contained therein. In the event that Publisher so notifies Writer, said copyrights and other rights shall automatically vest in Publisher, and Writer shall enter into a written agreement with Publisher reflecting such terms and conditions promptly after Writer's receipt of such notice. In the event that Publisher does not so notify Writer and Writer does not accept such third party offer, the foregoing procedures shall apply to any future offers which Writer receives and wishes to accept, including any offer containing identical terms and conditions previously rejected by Writer, whether received by Writer from the same or from a different third party.

It is not clear whether such a provision will be enforceable. Arguably, it may be enforceable because it does not preclude the grant from being terminated. On the other hand, although the clause will not directly affect the right of termination, it does interfere with the free exploitation or re-sale of the copyright after termination becomes effective, and, on that ground, may be held unenforceable. Because the rights of termination for songs created under the 1976 Act will not begin to be exercised until 35 years have passed after the execution of the applicable grants, it will be a long time before the enforceability of such a provision is tested in court.

B. Grants Covering the Initial Term of Copyright

An assignment of a copyright in a song created before January 1, 1978 in its original (i.e., first 28 year) term of copyright, which does not provide for any term or reversion, and *did not* provide for an assignment of renewal rights, will endure until the expiration of the original term of copyright only.

C. Grants Covering the Renewal Term of Copyright

The duration of assignment of a copyright in a song created before January 1, 1978 in its original (i.e., first 28 year) term of copyright, which does not provide for any term or reversion, but *did* provide for an assignment of the author's interest in renewal rights, will depend upon the circumstances discussed in the section below on Duration of Assignment of Renewal Copyright.

D. Grants Covering the Extended (19-Year) Term of Copyright

For works created before January 1, 1978, and in their first term of copyright as of December 31, 1977, a right of termination, similar to the 35-year termination rule, is provided with respect to transfers covering the newly added years extending the maximum term of copyright by 19 years, from 56 to 75 years.[26]

The assignment of a copyright in a song created before January 1, 1978 in its original term or its renewal term of copyright, will endure until the expiration of the copyright (i.e., the 75th, and final year of the life of the copyright), unless otherwise provided by the terms of the assignment agreement or unless the author (or certain statutory beneficiaries) exercises a statutory right of termination which may be effective as early as 19 years prior to the final year of the copyright. Within certain time limits, an author or specified heirs of the author, are generally entitled to file a notice terminating the author's transfers covering any

---

[26] 17 U.S.C. Sec. 304 (c).

part of the 19-year period that has now been added to the end of the second term of copyright in a work.

The same procedures provided for regarding the 35-year termination rule discussed above are applicable to terminations of grants covering the 19-year extended term. A termination of the grant may be effected notwithstanding any agreement to the contrary, including an agreement to make a will or to make any further grant.[27] Further, a re-grant of rights that revert after termination is valid only if it is executed after the effective date of termination, and an exception was provided in favor of the current grantee.[28] While the procedures for such termination resemble those for termination under the 35-year termination rule, there are important differences. For example, while the 35-year termination rule provides for the recapture of only those rights that the *author* has transferred after January 1, 1978, grants by *either the author or his statutory successors* covering the 19-year extended term may be terminated, which effectively allows successors to terminate transfers of renewal expectancies, discussed below, and benefit fully from the 19-year extended term of copyright.

DURATION OF AN ASSIGNMENT OF RENEWAL COPYRIGHT

As noted above, an author's assignment of his renewal interest to another prior to the expiration of the original copyright term may affect a renewal claimant's potential right to own the renewal copyright. The person to whom the author assigned his renewal interest (or that person's successors or assigns) may become the owner of the renewal copyright under certain circumstances. Those circumstances— which involve the unfortunate subject of death—are discussed in this section.

1. Limited Relevancy

Before proceeding into this gravely important topic, it will be useful to note what this discussion does and does not concern. This discussion

---

[27] 17 U.S.C. Sec. 304 (c)(5)
[28] 17 U.S.C. Sec. 304 (c)(6)(D)

only concerns those works that were created before January 1, 1978 *and* that were in their original term of copyright as of January 1, 1978. Thus, this discussion concerns primarily the generation of musical composi- tions written and published during the mid-1950's to the end of 1977. Further, this discussion only concerns those compositions in which the author assigned to another during the original term of copyright his or her interest in the renewal copyright. If the author never assigned his or her rights in his renewal copyright or assigned such interest during the renewal term, then this discussion is not relevant to the ownership interests in the copyright.

If the author did assign to another his or her rights in his interest in the renewal copyright during the original term, then, under certain circumstances, the claimant(s) will not become the owner(s) of the renewal copyright.

2. Renewal Copyright v. Renewal Expectancy

Under the 1909 Act, a copyright was secured by publication of the work with the proper copyright notice. The initial 28-year term was said to have *vested* immediately upon such securing. Though the law provided that the author of the work had the right, upon the expiration of the initial term, to *renew* the copyright for an additional 28-year term, the author's right to renew was not considered *vested* until the renewal period. Until then, the author had a mere *expectancy* in the renewal copyright.

In other words, upon the securing of copyright protection in a work created before January 1, 1978, a copyright owner possesses two things: (1) a right in the initial 28-year term of copyright, and (2) an expectancy interest in the 28-year (now, 47-year) renewal. A *right* is not the same as an *expectancy interest*, and the difference may have an impact upon who is entitled to *own* the renewal copyright.

3. Transfer of Renewal Expectancy

The assignment of the *right* in the initial 28-year term of copyright operates the same as the assignment of any other type of property right: the assignee becomes the owner of the right, and may immediately exercise any or all of the incidents of ownership. The assignment of the *expectancy* in the renewal term before the actual commencement of the renewal term (i.e., before the renewal *vests*), does not operate to convey any legal *right* (over which the assignee may exercise as an owner), only the mere *expectancy* in the renewal copyright.

The distinction between *rights* and *expectancies* formed the basis of the following fundamental rule of copyright law concerning claims in renewal copyright announced by the U.S. Supreme Court:

An assignment of a renewal expectancy will, upon its vesting, be binding upon the author so that if the author is living at the time of renewal, the assignee, not the author, will be entitled to own such renewal; if the author is not living at the time of renewal, then those persons who, as specified in the copyright law, are entitled to claim the renewal copyright (i.e., the statutory renewal claimants) are not bound by any assignment executed by the author, so that the assignee of the renewal expectancy takes nothing and the statutory renewal claimants take legal title to the renewal.[29]

4. Operation of the Rule of Renewal Expectancy

In other words, an assignment by an author of his or her interest in the renewal copyright before the initial copyright term expires is valid against the world, if the author lives until the commencement of the renewal period. For convenience, this rule will be called the *rule of renewal expectancy*.

Suppose, for example, a songwriter composed a song and assigned his copyright, including the renewal copyright, to his music publisher in 1967 and the original 28-year term of copyright in the song is expected to expire on December 31, 1995. Even though the music publishing contract may have included an assignment of "any and all renewal copyrights," the law only recognizes an assignment of the author's renewal "expectancy," which will not *vest* (i.e., become a renewal "right") until the renewal period. Accordingly, the rule of renewal expectancy will operate as follows: If the songwriter is living at the time the

---

[29] *Fred Fisher Co. v. M. Witmark & Sons,* 318 U.S. 643 (1943); *Miller Music Corp. v. Charles N. Daniels, Inc.,* 362 U.S. 373 (1960); *Stewart v. Abend,* 495 U.S. 207 (1990), hereinafter called, the *Rear Window* decision. The subject of the case was the 1954 film, "Rear Window," starring Grace Kelly and James Stewart, and directed by Alfred Hitchcock.

renewal copyright vests, then the legal title in the renewal right will automatically become the property of the music publisher. If the songwriter is not living when the renewal copyright vests, then the legal title will become the property of the author's beneficiaries (in a particular order of preference as specified in the copyright law).

The result in the foregoing example may differ if the author's statutory beneficiaries have previously transferred their own renewal expectancies. Suppose, for example, at the time the songwriter assigned his copyright and renewal expectancy in 1967, the songwriter's wife and children (as statutory beneficiaries) also signed documents assigning to the music publisher their own renewal expectancies in the song. In that event, even where the author is not living at the time the renewal vests, the music publisher would still take legal title to the renewal copyright. This, of course, assumes the author's wife and children or other statutory beneficiaries were living at the time the renewal copyright vested, because the renewal expectancies assigned by them to the music publisher are also subject to the rule of renewal expectancies. Thus, if the wife and children were not living when the renewal copyright vested, then the legal title in the renewal copyrights would become the property of the next order of beneficiaries under the statute, not the music publisher.

A music publisher's attempt to secure renewal rights by obtaining assignments of expectancies from as many potential beneficiaries as possible is not foolproof. The effort may be defeated by the songwriter's divorce and subsequent remarriage before death. In that case, his second wife, and widow, assuming she did not subsequently assign to the publisher her expectancy, will take title to her share of the renewal copyright at the commencement of the renewal term. A similar result would occur in the event the songwriter, subsequent to his wife's and children's assignment of their renewal expectancies, has additional children, by either birth or adoption; in that case, the children who did not join in the assignment of renewal expectancies will share in the renewal copyright upon its vesting if the songwriter is not living at the time the renewal copyright vests.

It appears a music publisher may never be absolutely certain about whether it will acquire the entire renewal copyright at the time it receives an assignment of copyright and renewal expectancies. The publisher can only attempt to obtain as many assignments of renewal expectancies as possible from every known member of the class of possible successors to the renewal copyright. For example, the songwriter, his spouse, all of his children, and all known next of kin of the songwriter. The music publisher may also seek agreement from the songwriter to write a will bequeathing to the publisher renewal rights. These attempts are often impractical and not worth the expense, but remain standard in the contracts of some music publishers.

The rule of renewal expectancy will only apply to works created before January 1, 1978 currently in their initial 28-year term of copyright. Works created before that date, but which are already in their renewal term are, of course, not subject to the rule, as the renewal copyrights in those works have vested in their owners. Works created after January 1, 1978 are also not subject to the rule, because under the new copyright law there will never be a renewal term of copyright (or renewal expectancies) in these works.

5. Formalities of Assigning Renewal Expectancies

Virtually all of the normal formalities and other aspects of assigning copyrights discussed earlier in Chapter 3 apply equally to the assignment of renewal expectancies. Note, however, that it appears assignments of renewal expectancies will be binding against their assignors only if the assignment was supported by sufficient legal consideration[30] (e.g., something of value). Note, further, that renewal expectancies may not pass as personal property under a will or by the operation of state law in the absence of a will, because the federal copyright law, by specifying the particular classes of individuals entitled to claim renewal upon the author's death, preempts any state law regarding wills and inheritances.

The courts have ruled on the contractual language necessary to effect an assignment of a renewal expectancy. Briefly, an assignment of "renewal copyright" or just "renewals" will be sufficient to effect an assignment of renewal expectancies. Also, "extensions of copyright" will suffice. In the absence of such relatively express language, the courts are hesitant to construe an assignment of "copyright" to include renewal copyright, without some other evidence the parties intended an assignment of renewal. A transfer of "all, right, title and

---

[30] *Fisher v. Morris & Co.,* 113 U.S.P.Q. 251 (S.D.N.Y. 1957).

interest" has been held not sufficient to cover renewals, but an assign-
.ment of rights "forever" has.

6. Renewal Copyright Vesting

As indicated above, the copyright law gives the author the right
to claim renewal if he is living at the time the renewal copyright vests.
Gone unanswered throughout the discussion has been the question,
at what time must one be living for a renewal claimed in his name
to be effective? In other words, when do rights in the renewal
copyright *vest*?

Prior to the Copyright Renewal Act of 1992, there were two
possibilities: (1) the date on which the renewal application was filed
or duly registered with the Copyright Office, or (2) the commencement
of the renewal term. Until as recently as 1991, the question was the
subject of a split of authority, with a court in the Southern District of
New York holding that rights in a renewal copyright vested on the
date on which the renewal application was filed with the Copyright
Office[31] and the 9th Circuit Court of Appeals in California holding
that rights in a renewal copyright do not vest until the actual commencement of the renewal term.[32]

The consequence of the rule suggested by the 9th Circuit is that it
may become impossible to determine with any degree of certainty who
will be the proper copyright claimant until it becomes too late to file the
claim. For example, the author is alive at the beginning of the 28th year
of the original term and shortly thereafter files an application for renewal
naming himself as renewal claimant. Shortly before the end of the same
year, before the actual commencement of the renewal term, the author
dies. Upon the author's death, the proper renewal claimants would be
those in the appropriate successor class as listed above. Unless one of the
members of the successor class is able to file a timely application for
renewal, the renewal claim would fail, resulting in the work's falling into
the public domain. Requiring members of the successor renewal class to
file renewal claims in their name as an act of insurance against the

---

[31] *Frederick Music Company v. Sickler*, 708 F.Supp. 587 (S.D.N.Y. 1989).

[32] *Marascalco v. Fantasy, Inc.*, 953 F.2d 469 (9th Cir. 1991).

possibility of the author's dying before the year is up would often result in redundant applications, and it is not clear whether the Copyright Office will even accept this practice.

Further, if you are an assignee of a renewal expectancy, you will want to know upon the commencement of the renewal term of copyright whether the copyright is vested in you or in the author or his heirs. The best way to determine this would be to perform a search of the records of the Copyright Office (see Circular R22 set forth at the end of Chapter 18) to discover whether the author was alive at the time of renewal. If the rule announced by the 9th Circuit were followed, then an author could file a renewal application during the 28th year, die subsequent to the filing, but before the end of the year, and the records of the Copyright Office would not reflect the true ownership status of the renewal copyright. Unless the holder of the renewal expectancy had some separate way of confirming whether the author survived the expiration of the original term of copyright, it might take some investigation to determine, in fact, whether the holder is actually the owner of the copyright or whether, if he continues to exploit the work, he is guilty of copyright infringement. Similarly, as will be discussed at length later in this chapter, if you are a *derivative work licensee* (i.e., owner of a derivative work based upon an underlying work of another under license from the author of the underlying work), you will want to know if, under the ruling in the *Rear Window* decision, you have the right to continue distributing your derivative work without further license from the author or his heirs.

7. Renewal Vesting Under Copyright Renewal Act of 1992

It is the better view that, as long as the author survives until the date the renewal application is registered in the Copyright Office, a renewal claimed in the name of an author will be effective, even if he should die subsequent to the registration but before the end of the 28th year. This is in fact the rule adopted by Congress in the 1992 Act:

> (B) At the expiration of the original copyright term of copyright in a work specified in paragraph (1)(C) of this subsection, the copyright shall endure for a renewed and extended further term of 47 years, which—
>
> > (i) if an application to register a claim to such further term has been made to the Copyright Office within 1 year before the

expiration of the original term of copyright and the claim is registered, shall vest, upon the beginning of such further term, in any person who is entitled under paragraph (1)(C) [i.e., the statutory beneficiaries, such as author, widow, widower, children, etc.] to the renewal and extension of the copyright at the time the application is made; or

(ii) if no such application is made or the claim pursuant to such application is not registered, shall vest, upon the beginning of such further term, in any person entitled under paragraph (1)(C), as of the last day of the original term of copyright, to the renewal and extension of the copyright.

The new law clearly indicates that the renewal copyright always *vests* upon the commencement date of the renewal term (i.e., "the copyright shall endure for a renewed and extended further term . . . *which . . . shall vest . . . upon the beginning of such further term . . .* "). However, it is also clear that the person or persons in whom the renewal copyright will actually vest may directly depend upon whether a permissive renewal application is filed with the Copyright Office and when during the 28th year of the original term that application was filed.

If an application to register the renewal is filed within 1 year before the expiration of the original term of copyright, then the renewal copyright will vest in the person(s) entitled to claim the renewal *living at the time the application is made*. If, however, an application to register the renewal was not filed within 1 year before the expiration of the original term, then the renewal copyright will vest in the person(s) entitled to claim the renewal *living as of the last day of the original term of the copyright*.

8. Effect of 1992 Act on Assignments of Renewal Expectancies

The 1992 Act has no effect on the rule of renewal expectancies itself, which remains the law of the land. Depending upon the circumstances, however, the new law may have important consequences on the application of the rule in particular cases.

Taking a previous example, suppose a songwriter composed a song and assigned his copyright, including the renewal copyright, to his music publisher in 1967 and the original 28-year term of copyright in the song is expected to expire on December 31, 1995. Suppose further that the publisher did not receive any assignments of renewal expectancies from the songwriter's family, other than the songwriter's own renewal expectancy granted in 1967 under the terms of the music publishing agreement with the songwriter.

If an application to register the renewal is filed on December 1, 1995 (i.e., within 1 year before the expiration of the original term of copyright), then the renewal copyright will vest in the person entitled to claim the renewal living on December 1, 1995 (i.e., living at the time the application is made). If the songwriter is alive as of December 1, 1995, and the renewal application was filed in the name of the songwriter, then the songwriter's assignee (i.e., music publisher) will own the renewal copyright when it vests on January 1, 1996. If the songwriter died before December 1, 1995, and the renewal application was filed in the name of the songwriter's widow, then the widow will own the renewal copyright when it vests on January 1, 1996.

If no application to register the renewal is made during the calendar year 1995, then the renewal copyright will vest in the person entitled to claim the renewal living on December 31, 1995 (i.e., living as of the last day of the original term of copyright). If the songwriter is alive as of December 31, 1995, then the songwriter's assignee (i.e., music publisher) will own the renewal copyright when it vests on January 1, 1996. If the songwriter had died in a car accident driving home from a Christmas party on December 26, 1995, then the songwriter's widow will own the renewal copyright when it vests on January 1, 1996.

Accordingly, it appears that the determination of who will *own* the renewal copyright may depend on whether a renewal application has been filed and the timing of the author's death in relation to the time the renewal application is filed. This suggests that, even though registration is no longer a condition to claiming renewal copyrights, music publishers and songwriters should give serious consideration as to whether and when to file applications for renewal registration. Some of the issues to be considered by songwriters and publishers in this regard will be discussed below in the context of advice for music publishers and songwriters.

9. Persons Entitled to Submit Renewal Applications

As noted, a registration for renewal of copyright will be valid only if it is claimed in the name of the person or persons who are among the statutory class of individuals entitled to such renewal. This does not mean, however, the person entitled to *claim* renewal must himself *submit* the application for renewal registration.

Generally, as long as the renewal application is filed in the name of the persons entitled to claim renewal, the application may be filed by any person authorized by the proper claimant to do so. A person is considered authorized to file a renewal claim when (1) he is expressly authorized by a proper renewal claimant to do so, or (2) he has an express power of attorney to act generally, or with respect to copyright and renewal copyright matters, on behalf of the renewal claimant.

Of course, anyone who is specifically requested by a claimant to file a renewal application may do so. To remove any doubt about his agent's authority to file renewal applications on his behalf, the claimant should execute a power of attorney. A *power of attorney* is simply a written instrument authorizing another to act as one's agent or "attorney-in-fact." An attorney-in-fact, under a written power of attorney, need only have general powers to act on a person's behalf to be authorized to file renewal applications. Usually, however, copyright owners grant powers of attorney that are limited to the specific actions required by the attorney-in-fact to handle the copyright affairs of the copyright owner. For example, a copyright owner may grant a power of attorney to another for the purpose of filing renewal applications and notices of termination with respect to the 19-year extended term. An example of a power of attorney relating to an assignment of copyrights, including any renewals and extensions, is set forth as part of Form 3.1 at the end of Chapter 3. An attorney licensed to practice law ("attorney-at-law") will always be considered authorized to file renewal applications on behalf of his clients whether or not expressed in writing.

It has also been commonly understood that a person is authorized to file a renewal claim when (1) he himself has a beneficial interest in the renewal copyright; or (2) by virtue of special circumstances, he is considered to have an implied power of attorney to file the renewal application on behalf of the claimant.

Because the failure to file a timely application for renewal registration for pre-1964 works had such drastic consequences, wide latitude was given to allowing persons filing renewal applications in the names of others. For example, it has been thought that, even in the absence of a specific request, anyone who is generally entrusted to conduct the music or copyright affairs of the renewal claimant may probably file an application on the claimant's behalf. Similarly, one who has a beneficial interest in the renewal copyright may file an application for renewal on behalf of the renewal claimants. For example, in the case of a deceased author who has no living widow or children, a person who is named in the will to receive the renewal rights will have a beneficial interest in the renewal copyright. (Recall, however, that under these circumstances, the renewal must be claimed in the name of the executor of the will, who will hold legal title in the renewal in trust for the beneficiaries named in the will. Though the renewal must be filed *in the name of* the executor, a beneficiary may nevertheless *submit* the renewal application, by virtue of his beneficial interest in the renewal copyright).

One who has been granted a renewal expectancy interest (i.e., one who will be entitled to own the renewal once it vests) has also been entitled to submit applications for renewal on behalf of claimants. As previously noted, if the author had assigned his interest in the renewal copyright to a music publisher, then, depending on the circumstances, the ownership of the renewal copyright may vest in the music publisher, not in the author or his heirs, in accordance with the rule of expectancies. Though the renewal application must still be filed in the name of the author, not the publisher, the publisher may nevertheless file the application for renewal. He does so either by virtue of a power of attorney granted to him in the original music publishing contract with the author, or, in the absence of such a power, by virtue of the publisher's beneficial interest in the renewal (obtaining ownership upon its vesting).

However, because of the 1992 Act, the publisher's privilege to submit a renewal application may be subject to challenge if the publisher does not have a written power of attorney authorizing him to submit the application. This will be discussed further below.

10. Advice for Music Publishers

As noted above, the determination of who will *own* the renewal copyright may depend on whether a renewal application has been filed and the timing of the author's death in relation to the time the renewal application is filed. This suggests that, to the extent music publishers have a right to file renewal applications in the name of songwriters, a strategy may be available for increasing the likelihood that a publisher's renewal expectancy will mature into a renewal copyright vested in the music publisher, rather than in the songwriter or the songwriter's heirs.

The strategy would be as follows: Music publishers who hold assignments of renewal expectancies, should attempt to file renewal claims (on behalf of and in the name of each of the authors), as soon into the beginning of the final (i.e., 28th) year of the original term of copyright as possible. The following should illuminate the benefits of this strategy.

Using the previous example, should a music publisher file a renewal application on January 2, 1995 (i.e., the first business day of the 28th and final year of the original term of copyright of a song created in 1967), then the renewal copyright will vest in the person entitled to claim the renewal living on January 2, 1995 (i.e., living at the time the application is made). If the songwriter dies any time during the year 1995 after January 2, then the music publisher (i.e., the assignee of the songwriter's renewal expectancy) will own the renewal copyright when it vests on January 1, 1996. If the publisher waits until December 1, 1995 to file the renewal application, and the songwriter dies prior to that date, then the songwriter's statutory beneficiaries at the time the application was filed will own the renewal copyright when it vests on January 1, 1996. If the music publisher and the songwriter's statutory beneficiaries fail to file the renewal application at all during the calendar year 1995, and the songwriter dies at any time during the year prior to December 31, 1995, then the songwriter's statutory beneficiaries as of December 31, 1995 will own the renewal copyright when it vests on January 1, 1996.

If the music publisher did not have a power of attorney from the songwriter to file renewal applications, can the music publisher nevertheless file the application in connection with implementing the strategy above suggested? As noted, even in the absence of a specific request, anyone who has been generally entrusted to conduct the music or copyright affairs of the renewal claimant has been allowed to file an application on the claimant's behalf. The Copyright Office has liberally allowed persons other than the claimant to file renewal applications, because failing to file had such drastic consequences (i.e., the work falling into the public domain). However, a question arises as to the effect of the Copyright Renewal Act of 1992, which has made renewal automatic, on the scope of the class of persons permitted to *submit* a renewal application to the Copyright Office.

The Act clearly does not affect the ability of the claimant's agent or one with a valid power of attorney to file renewal applications in the name of renewal claimants. Thus, if a music publisher had a power of attorney covering the filing of renewal applications, it could probably implement such a strategy without serious challenge. Suppose, however, the music publisher does not have a power of attorney or some other express authorization by the claimants to file the renewal application. Absent a power of attorney or some agency relationship between the claimant and the person submitting the application, may a music publisher who desires to submit the application do so solely on the basis of his beneficial interest in the renewal expectancy?

Under the law prior to 1992, the answer would clearly have been yes, because it was in both the claimant's interest and the claimant's music publisher's interest that the renewal application be filed (otherwise the term of copyright would expire at the end of the 28th year). Under the 1992 Act, however, the interests of the music publisher and those of the claimants may be in conflict and such a conflict may suggest another conclusion. In fact, the music publisher's authority to file an application on the claimant's behalf may be subject to some doubt if the claimant specifically asked the publisher not to file a renewal application.

11. Advice for Songwriters

Just as there is a strategy for music publishers, there is a strategy for songwriters and their heirs for increasing the likelihood that ownership in the renewal copyright will vest in them over a publisher's renewal expectancy.

The songwriter's strategy might be as follows: If you previously assigned your interest in the renewal copyright and there is a chance you might not live through the end of the original term, don't file an application for renewal registration. If you file and you should then die before the expiration of the original term of copyright, then, while you will be entitled to *claim* the renewal, the person who will be entitled to *own* the renewal is the person to whom you previously assigned your expectancy interest (e.g., the music publisher).

If you have retained (e.g., never assigned to another) your renewal expectancy interest, then your decision whether to file a renewal registration will depend on the chances of your not surviving the expiration of the original term of copyright, and whether you wish your renewal copyright to pass to your beneficiaries either (i) as defined under the copyright law or (ii) as specified in your will. Assuming you wish the copyright to be bequeathed in accordance with your will, then you should file the renewal registration as soon as possible into the final year of the original copyright term. Remember, too, the slight legal advantages of filing a renewal application within one year prior to the expiration of the original term of copyright (i.e., renewal certificate becomes prima facie evidence of validity of the renewal copyright in infringement actions).

Each person who is entitled to claim renewal may file or cause to be filed a renewal application in his or her own name. This may be the case, for example, where a song was written by the collaboration of a composer and a lyricist. Though several persons may be entitled to file a renewal application, the filing of only one application, even if it is submitted in the name of only one of several proper renewal claimants, is required to effect renewal registration. The filing co-claimant and any non-filing co-claimants are considered to be in precisely the same position as though they had all properly filed applications. It would therefore appear that as long as one co-claimant files an application for renewal, it is not necessary for the other co-claimants to file separate, additional renewal applications. Though more than one renewal claimant may wish to file claims, it may be more economical for them to do so on the same form, rather than in separate applications. A renewal application contains room for three claimants, yet the same renewal registration fee will cover all three claims. In the event a question arises as to who will prove to be the proper claimant(s), the registration of competing renewal applications should be made. The Copyright Office will issue competing renewal certificates if, for example, it is not known whether an author, who has been missing for some time, is living or deceased, or there is a question as to the status of an illegitimate child. However, before filing an application for renewal registration, the songwriters or their survivors should carefully consider the potential effects on the vesting of the ultimate ownership interest in the renewal copyright.

Should the author specifically decide not to file an application for renewal registration, and it is thought that a music publisher who was previously assigned a renewal expectancy might file an application as a precaution against the author dying during the 28th year of the initial term of copyright, the author should send a letter to the publisher advising that he does not wish the publisher to file the application. If the author should die during the 28th year, this action may provide his heirs with some grounds for claiming the renewal copyright should vest in their name and not in the name of the music publisher.

DURATION OF LICENSES

1. By Terms of the License

A license normally lasts for as long as it says it lasts, usually in a provision called the *term* of license. For example, a license having a term of "five (5) years" will last five years. If the license does not state any limit on its term and if there is no evidence the parties intended the term to be limited, it will normally be deemed to continue effective for the life of the copyright. Non-exclusive licenses for which there is no stated term and for which there was no legal consideration (e.g., payment in exchange for the license) are revocable by the licensor at any time, unless circumstances are present that would make it unreasonable to allow the licensor to revoke permission.

A music copyright owner may grant licenses only for a term covering the time during which it has a right to grant licenses. For example, if a music publisher were only granted rights with respect to the original term of copyright, he could not grant licenses that purport to extend beyond the original term. An example of contracts containing such a songwriter provision are those that were entered using the form Uniform Popular Song-writer's Contract published in 1947 by the American Guild of Authors & Composers (formerly known as "AGAC" and now known as The Song-writer's Guild) (See Chapter 3). Paragraph 8 of that form provides in part:

> 8. Terms of Contract. All rights in and to the composition and any copyrights thereon throughout the world, shall revert to the Writer upon the expiration of the original term of the United States copyright or at the end of twenty-eight (28) years from the date of publication in the United States, which ever period shall be shorter.

The AGAC contract provided, however, that if the songwriter failed to give to the publisher at least six months' notice of any sale of the writer's United States renewal copyright to anyone other than the publisher, then the publisher shall be entitled to retain its rights under the contract for the renewal term in all countries outside the United States and Canada.

Further, paragraph 13 of the AGAC contract provided:

> 13. Termination of Contract. Upon the termination of this contract, all rights of any and every nature in and to the composition and in and to any and all copyrights secured thereon in the United States and throughout the world, shall re-vest in and become the property of the Writer, and shall be re-assigned to the Writer by the Publisher free of any and all encumbrances of any nature whatsoever, provided that: . . . (b) If the Publisher, prior to such termination, shall have granted a domestic license for the use of the composition, not inconsistent with the terms and provisions of this contract, the re-assignment may be subject to the terms of such license.

Accordingly, licenses issued by publishers during the original term of copyright and providing for a term that extended into the renewal term remain effective into the renewal term to the extent their territory is limited to the United States. As a practical matter, many licenses typically granted by music publishers have been made on a worldwide basis (see Chapter 9). Accordingly, if producers and other users of music cannot acquire from the music publisher a license of sufficient duration to meet their requirements, or at least options to extend the term for additional periods of time, then producers will choose to use substitute songs for which such terms are available. Accordingly, the parties to an AGAC form contract have an incentive to alleviate any impediments to producers' licensing songs that revert to writers under the AGAC form.

Music publisher and songwriters can alleviate the problem by entering into an agreement allowing the music publisher to continue actively issuing licenses that go beyond the original term of copyright, such as will be required for the issuance of synchronization licenses to exploit the songwriter's compositions in motion pictures, television productions, commercials and videograms. An example of such an agreement is set forth as Form 9.6 at the end of Chapter 9 on synchronization licenses. Arrangements such as these should improve the licensing prospects of songs covered by these agreements.

However, the problem is only partially alleviated with respect to certain songs. It was once thought that licenses granted during the original term of copyright purporting to cover the renewal term would continue in effect through the renewal term even though the renewal copyright reverted to a deceased author's survivors.[33] However, under the *Rear Window* decision, discussed below, it is now the law that such licenses may expire at the end of the original term if the renewal copyright reverted to the author's beneficiaries.

2. By Terms of the Copyright Law

Certain provisions of the copyright law affect the duration of certain licenses.

A. Termination of Licenses Granted by Authors After January 1, 1978

Any license which is silent about its *term* (i.e., how long it will remain in effect), will endure for the life of the copyright. However, any license granted by an author after January 1, 1978, regardless of the term stated in the license agreement, is subject to being terminated 35 years after the date of the grant of license.[34] This power to terminate a license is sometimes referred to as the *35-year termination rule* (which is also applicable to the termination of assignment of copyright or exclusive right under copyright made by an author after January 1, 1978).

Specifically, licenses made by an author (of a work other than a work made for hire) on or after January 1, 1978, may be terminated by the author or certain heirs during a 5-year period beginning at the end of 35 years from the date of the grant, or if the grant covers the right of publication, 35 years from the date of publication or 40 years from the date of the grant, whichever is shorter. To terminate a grant, a written notice must be served on the transferee within the time limits specified by the copyright law.[35]

---

[33] *Rohauer v. Killiam Shows, Inc.,* 551 F.2d 484 (2d Cir. 1977); overturned by the U.S. Supreme Court in *Stewart v. Abend,* 495 U.S. 207 (1990) (the *Rear Window* decision).

[34] 17 U.S.C. Sec. 203.

[35] 17 U.S.C. Sec. 203 (a)(3),(4).

If termination is not effected under the terms of the rule, then the grant of license will continue in effect for the life of the copyright or will expire sooner in accordance with any applicable provisions of the agreement effecting the grant. If the termination is properly effected under the rule, then the grant of license terminates, provided that:

> A derivative work prepared under the authority of the grant before its termination may continue to be utilized under the terms of the grant after its termination, but this privilege does not extend to the preparation after the termination of other derivative works based upon the copyrighted work covered by the terminated grant.[36]

This is an important limitation on the rights of a copyright owner of a terminated grant. For example, a synchronization license to use music in a motion picture granted before termination would continue in effect for as long as provided in the license, but the licensee would not be able to use the music in other derivative works without a new license from the terminated rights owner. In other words, a motion picture producer could continue to distribute the motion picture without requiring a further license from the owner of the terminated rights, but, unless the terms of the original license permitted it, he could not use the music in a "remake" of the motion picture (i.e., "preparation after termination of other derivative works") without a new license.

Where a music publisher created derivative works under the terms of its music publishing agreement with a songwriter who has terminated the grant of rights under that agreement, the terminated rights will be subject to the music publisher's right to continue to exploit any derivative works. Such derivative works may include arrangements, translations, compilations, and sound recordings created during the term of agreement.

B. Licenses Covering the Initial Term of Copyright

A license to use a work created before January 1, 1978, in its original (i.e., first 28 year) term of copyright, which does not purport to cover the renewal term of copyright, will endure until the expiration of the original

---

[36] 17 U.S.C. Sec. 203 (b)(1).

term of copyright only. As a practical matter, very few licenses, other than those that contain a fixed limitation on its term (e.g., five years), would fall into this category. A license "under the copyright" would probably expire at the end of the first term. A license granted during the first term of copyright, however, whose term is "in perpetuity" would be construed as covering the renewal term.

C. Licenses Purporting to Cover the Renewal Term of Copyright

Under a decision handed down by the U.S. Supreme Court in 1990 that has been described as "macabre," the duration of license, for the use of a song created before January 1, 1978, in its original (i.e., first 28 year) term of copyright, purporting to cover the renewal term would remain effective during the renewal term only if the author was living at the time of commencement of the renewal term.[37] Thus, it is an infringement of copyright to distribute a derivative work that is based on or incorporates a pre-1978 underlying work to which a license was obtained during its initial term if the author dies before the commencement of the renewal term, even though the author granted the producer of the derivative work a license to use the underlying work for its full term of copyright "including renewals and extensions."

The *Rear Window* decision does not affect (1) derivative works that were based on underlying works that were created or published for the first time since January 1, 1978, (2) derivative works that were based on underlying works that were in their renewal terms of copyright when the license to use the underlying work was granted, (3) derivative works that were based on underlying works that were works-made-for-hire of the owner of the derivative work, (4) derivative works that were based on underlying works that were in their initial term of copyright when the license to use the underlying work was granted, provided that the author of the underlying work lives until the time the renewal copyright may be claimed (i.e., 28th year of the original term of copyright) and an application to register the renewal copyright is actually filed while the author

---

[37] *Stewart v. Abend,* 110 S. Ct. 1750 (1990); *see, generally,* Lionel S. Sobel, *View from the "Rear Window": A Practical Look at the Consequences of the Supreme Court's Decision in Stewart vs. Abend,* 12/1 Entertainment Law Reporter 3 (June, 1990).

is alive,[38] and (5) derivative works that were based on underlying works created prior to 1964 that fell into the public domain because a claim for renewal was not filed by the applicable deadline.

The rule only affects derivative works created before January 1, 1978, that were based on underlying works of others that were in their initial terms of copyright when the license to use the underlying work was granted, provided that the author of the underlying work died prior to when the renewal copyright could be claimed in his name and the derivative licensee did not receive licenses from the author's statutory beneficiaries under their renewal expectancy interests. Nevertheless, because of the number of works that it does affect, the *Rear Window* decision has had far reaching consequences.

D. Effects of Rear Window *on Music Licensing*

(a) Effect on Which Songs Will Be Used in New Derivative Works

As noted in Chapters 5 and 9, producers of derivative works, such as motion pictures, television programs, and other audiovisual works, generally desire to obtain licenses that last as long as possible. Because of the possibility that a license subject to the *Rear Window* rule may have its term prematurely terminated by the untimely death of the songwriter, *derivative works licensees* (i.e., producers of derivative works obtaining licenses to use underlying works, such as music, in their productions) might wish to avoid using music that may be subject to a *Rear Window* termination.

Producers desiring to obtain licenses for the use of songs should ask the music copyright owner whether the song sought to be licensed is *safe* from the *Rear Window* decision or *tainted* by it. For example, works created or first published since 1978 are "safe" from the effects of the *Rear Window* decision. Also safe are works in their renewal terms (e.g., songs first published prior to 1964 that are in their renewal term as of

---

[38] Except in the 9th Circuit: Under *Marascalco v. Fantasy, Inc.,* 953 F.2d 469 (9th Cir. 1991), the rule as stated in this clause should read, "provided that the author of the underlying work lives until the commencement of the renewal term."

1992). Works potentially "tainted" by the *Rear Window* decision, as of 1992, are works published between 1964 and 1977. The initial year of the tainted period will become 1965 in 1993, 1966 in 1994, 1967 in 1995, and so on, but 1977 will always remain the final year of this period.

A song that would otherwise be tainted because it falls inside the tainted period, may have become safe if the songwriters have already died before an application for renewal registration could be filed, because a license for the renewal term can then be obtained directly from the surviving spouses and children. However, there remain many unanswered legal questions that may affect whether or not a particular song is safe from the effects of the *Rear Window* decision. If the work falls within the tainted period, the producer may wish to consider a substitute song that is safe, such as songs falling in the safe periods or songs commissioned on a works-for-hire basis.

Music publishers and songwriters controlling rights in songs affected by the *Rear Window* decision may actually begin to find their licensing revenue from these songs decrease as expiration of the original term of copyright approaches. With respect to songs still in their original term, where it is clear the publisher will not have the right to issue licenses covering the renewal term, music publishers find themselves unable to issue licenses that have terms that go beyond the expiration of the original copyright term. As discussed in Chapter 9, many producers are now requiring licenses that have a term of perpetuity, or at least include options to extend the term by providing notice and additional payment. If the publisher is unable to provide these terms, producers will choose to use substitutes for which such terms are available. Accordingly, music publishers and songwriters have an incentive to alleviate any impediments to producers' licensing their songs affected by the *Rear Window* decision.

As noted above, where renewal copyrights revert to songwriters under the provisions of a music publishing agreement, such as under the AGAC form contract, unless the writer and the publisher enter into an arrangement allowing the publisher to issue licenses during the original term whose term may extend into the renewal term, publishing income for songs whose protection is nearing the end of the original term may decline, because producers will avoid licensing compositions for which long-term licenses are not available. It is interesting to note that, under *Rear Window*, songwriters and music publishers have no similar ability to avoid a similar decline in their publishing income arising from producers' choosing to avoid licensing songs tainted by the *Rear Window* problem, because, under *Rear Window*, any such agreement would be unenforceable against the beneficiaries of the renewal copyright in the event the author should die prior to the commencement of the renewal term. Accordingly, there is some reason to doubt whether the intent of the ruling in *Rear Window* actually serves to further its purported purpose.

(b) *Effect on the Terms, If Any, Upon Which Previously Produced Derivative Works May Continue to Be Exploited*

Not all is doom and gloom for producers and other owners of derivative works containing songs whose licenses are affected by the *Rear Window* decision. It appears that the distribution of such derivative works during the renewal term will probably not be subject to court injunction. The 9th Circuit in deciding the *Rear Window* case specifically refused to grant an injunction and the Supreme Court did not upset the lower court's ruling in that regard.[39] The issue, then, will probably be limited to how much of the proceeds from the exploitation of the derivative work will have to be paid to the author's heirs during the term of the renewal copyright.

Discussion of the variety of works affected by the *Rear Window* decision is beyond the scope of this book. Indeed, some of the most dramatic effects caused by the *Rear Window* decision have been on agreements between producers of motion pictures and television programs and the authors of the literary works that underlie them, and on agreements involving mainframe and minicomputer computer software not created on a work-for-hire basis that has become contributed to other computer programs. The following sub-section sketches some of the effects of the *Rear Window* decision on existing music licenses.

(1) Licenses Granted to Music Publishers

Music publishers create a variety of derivative works during the term of music publishing contracts. Such derivative works may include arrangements, translations, compilations, and sound recordings. Under

---

[39] See, 110 S.Ct. at 1757, 1768.

the *Rear Window* decision, the use of music in all such derivative works will require new licenses from the renewal copyright owner.

(2) Mechanical Licenses Granted to Record Companies

Rights reverting to renewal copyright claimants under *Rear Window* also have the effect of terminating all mechanical licenses issued during the original term of copyright. This should have no practical effect however, to the extent the original mechanical license provided that mechanical fees were payable at the statutory rate in effect at the time phonorecords were made and distributed. If the renewal copyright owner decided to terminate the mechanical license, the derivative licensee would simply enter into a new one under the same statutory terms, or if the copyright owner refused, the derivative licensee could compel the renewal owner to issue a mechanical license at the statutory rate. However, if the mechanical license was originally issued at a *rate* (see Chapter 7) or otherwise provided that the fee be set at the statutory rate in effect at the time the license was entered (i.e., without the benefit of subsequent increases), then the renewal owner could obtain more favorable terms by terminating the license and renegotiating the new license at the more favorable statutory rate.

(3) Synchronization Licenses Granted to Producers

To the extent producers of motion pictures and television programs have used in the soundtracks of their derivative works music that is tainted by the *Rear Window* decision, new licenses for the use of such music will be required from the renewal copyright owners. To the extent the music is replaceable (e.g., recorded on a separate track or not materially featured in the picture), the producer has increased leverage in the negotiations over obtaining the license required.

(4) Master Licenses Granted to Producers to Use Sound Recordings

Producers of motion pictures and television programs who have licensed sound recordings from record companies for use in their derivative works, probably do not have much to be concerned about with respect to the continued use of those recordings. This is because virtually all sound recordings are produced under work-for-hire contracts. Because the recording company is considered the *author* of works it commissioned on a work for hire basis, the recording company's license to the producer for the full term of copyright "including any renewals and extensions" will remain in full force and effect.

(5) Owners of Copies or Phonorecords Containing Affected Works

If a licensee whose license has been terminated upon the expiration of the original term of copyright is the lawful owner of copies (or phonorecords) of works affected by *Rear Window*, then he may still distribute or otherwise dispose of such copies. Of course, he may not produce any new copies without a license covering the renewal term.

E. *Effect of 1992 Act*

For works created on or after January 1, 1964, the rule of the *Rear Window* case will not apply if a renewal application is not made within 1 year before the expiration of the original term of copyright in such works. The Copyright Renewal Act of 1992 states:

> If an application to register a claim to the renewed and extended term of copyright in a work is not made within 1 year before the expiration of the original term of copyright in a work, or if the claim pursuant to such application is not registered, then a derivative work prepared under the authority of a grant of a transfer or license of the copyright that is made before the expiration of the original term of copyright may continue to be used under the terms of the grant during the renewed and extended term of copyright without infringing the copyright, except that such use does not extend to the preparation during such renewed and extended term of other derivative works based upon the copyrighted work covered by such grant.[40]

Thus, if the songwriter or his survivors fail to file within one year before the expiration of the original term of copyright for a work created

---

[40] 17 U.S.C. Sec. 304 (a)(4)(B).

between January 1, 1964 and December 31, 1977, then a producer's previous license covering the term of copyright "including any renewals or extensions thereof" will be effective during the renewal term.

F. Advice for Derivative Licensees

The cost of identifying the thousands of songs tainted with the *Rear Window* problem that may be contained in previously produced motion pictures and television programs may be exorbitant. Accordingly, the producer's only practical alternative may be to simply continue distributing the pictures until a demand letter is received from a songwriter or his estate.

Leaving that alternative aside, a producer who has identified a song affected by *Rear Window* has to choose another path, such as developing a strategy for negotiating with the songwriters, or their applicable statutory beneficiaries or survivors. If the song's copyright is already in its renewal term, the producer can withdraw the picture from distribution and begin negotiating with the songwriter's survivors or executor. If the author died before his statutory beneficiaries are entitled to file a claim for renewal (i.e., before the beginning of the 28th year of the original copyright term), the producer may continue distributing the motion picture under his license for the original term while commencing negotiations with the writer's survivors or executor for a license covering the renewal term. If the author has not died yet, the producer may seek to obtain licenses covering the renewal term from the songwriter's current spouse, children or other beneficiaries; this strategy will only be effective if the author does not subsequently remarry or have any more children before dying.

The problem with the strategies in the foregoing paragraph is that they alert the author's beneficiaries of their rights concerning renewal. As noted above, under the 1992 Act, if a renewal application is not timely made (i.e., within one year before the expiration of the original term of copyright) for a work created between January 1, 1964 and December 31, 1977, then a derivative work prepared under the authority of a grant of a license made before the expiration of the original term of copyright may continue to be used under the terms of the grant during the renewed and extended term of copyright without infringing the copyright. If the songwriter or his survivors fail to file a renewal application, then a producer's previous license covering the term of copyright "including any renewals or extensions thereof" will be effective during the renewal term.

However, if the author has not died yet, and the original license agreement gives the producer the authority to renew the author's underlying copyright, the producer should file a renewal application as soon as possible after January 1st of the 28th year of the initial term. If the author is alive when the renewal application is registered, the renewal application is effective (under the 1992 Act), even if the author dies before the 29th year of copyright protection begins.

G. Advice for Music Publishers

Because licensing music is the life blood of a music publisher's business, music publishers should take whatever measures available to facilitate the licensing of music in their catalogs. Music publishers should try to identify those songs in its catalog that have been affected by the *Rear Window* decision and that were previously licensed in derivative works, such as motion pictures and television programs. If it appears that the song may revert to the author or his survivors, the publisher should attempt to attain the renewal copyright from the estate of the author, entering into contracts giving the publisher renewal expectancy interests if necessary, or obtaining exclusive administration rights to the music for the renewal term. With control of the renewal rights, the publisher can then issue the necessary licenses for the use of music in derivative works that cover the renewal term.

Barring the ability to control the renewal copyright, there is not much else the music publisher can do to alleviate the problems caused by *Rear Window*.

H. Advice for Songwriters

Nor is there much songwriters can do to alleviate the adverse effect *Rear Window* may have on pre-renewal licensing revenue for songs tainted by the decision.

With respect to filing renewal applications, it has been noted that under the Renewal Copyright Act of 1992, if a renewal application is not made within one year before the expiration of the original term of copyright, then "a derivative work prepared under the authority of a grant of a transfer or license of the copyright that is made before the expiration of the original term of copyright may continue to be used under the terms of the grant during the renewed and extended term of copyright without infringing the copyright, except that such use does not extend to the preparation during such renewed and extended term of other derivative works based upon the copyrighted work covered by such grant."[41] This might lead a songwriter to file a registration within the prescribed time period. However, as noted above, if filing the renewal application could cause the renewal copyright to vest in the music publisher, rather than the heirs of the songwriter, it might be best not to file the application within one year before the expiration of the original term. However, should the songwriter die during the 28th year, then his beneficiaries should strongly consider filing a renewal application subsequent to his death in order to avoid the effect of Section 304(a)(4)(B) and preserve the ability to renegotiate licenses for the use of the song in derivative works during the renewal term.

When the songwriter or his beneficiaries are in a position to renegotiate licenses for use of music in derivative works during the renewal term, they should not overlook the importance of coming to an agreement to license the song in derivative works. Remember, that it is unlikely that you will be able to obtain an injunction stopping the exploitation of the derivative work during the renewal term and any litigation will boil down to just determining what a reasonable license fee ought to be. Under these circumstances, litigation will rarely be worth the costs. Further, regardless of how unreasonably low the fee being offered may seem to be in relation to what the producer may stand to gain by exploiting the derivative work (or stand to cost him if you proceed to litigation), in the long run, you will tend to make up more than the difference between what is being offered and what you think you deserve by collecting important performance royalties from exhibition on television or otherwise from maintaining an active relationship between the song and the listening public.

---

[41] 17 U.S.C. Sec. 304 (a)(4)(B).

I. Licenses Covering the Extended (19-Year) Term of Copyright

For works created before January 1, 1978 and in their first term of copyright as of December 31, 1977, a right of termination, similar to that provided to authors of works created after January 1, 1978 (discussed above), is provided with respect to transfers covering the newly added years extending the maximum term of copyright by 19 years, from 56 to 75 years.[42]

The assignment of a copyright in a song created before January 1, 1978 in its original term or its renewal term of copyright, will endure until the expiration of the copyright (i.e., the 75th, and final year of the life of the copyright), unless otherwise provided by the terms of the assignment agreement or unless the author (or certain statutory beneficiaries) exercises a statutory right of termination which may be effective as early as 19 years prior to the final year of the copyright. Within certain time limits, an author or specified heirs of the author, are generally entitled to file a notice terminating the author's transfers covering any part of the 19 year period that has now been added to the end of the second term of copyright in a work.

If termination is not effected under the terms of the rule, then the grant of license will continue in effect for the life of the copyright or will expire sooner in accordance with any applicable provisions of the agreement effecting the grant. If the termination is properly effected, then the grant of license terminates, provided that:

> A derivative work prepared under the authority of the grant before its termination may continue to be utilized under the terms of the grant after its termination, but this privilege does not extend to the preparation after the termination of other derivative works based upon the copyrighted work covered by the terminated grant.[43]

This provision is worded identically to the similar provision concerning termination of terminated grants by authors made after January 1, 1978, and has the same legal and practical effects.

---

[42] 17 U.S.C. Sec. 304 (c).

[43] 17 U.S.C. Sec. 304 (c)(6)(A).

AFTER LIFE

By the end of 1993, all songs published during the year 1918 will have fallen into the public domain. By the end of 1994, all songs published during the year 1919 will have fallen into the public domain. During the next twenty years, a staggering number of popular, standard tunes will fall into the public domain. To give the reader some idea of what is happening, the appendix to this chapter includes a short list of songs compiled by ASCAP that are now in the public domain in the United States, followed by a list of songs in the ASCAP repertoire that will enter the public domain in the United States during the next several years. Persons involved in music licensing, whether granting licenses or clearing them, should take note that an ever increasing number of songs will be available free of charge as substitutes to be used for those purposes for which music is used.

Yes, there is life after copyright. The continuing popularity of songs that will soon enter the public domain will demonstrate that musical works are destined to maintain an active relationship with the listening public, long after the life of their copyright has expired.

APPENDIX TO CHAPTER 4
DURATION OF COPYRIGHTS, ASSIGNMENTS
OF COPYRIGHTS, AND LICENSES

LISTS

LIST 4.1

SOME POPULAR SONGS IN THE
PUBLIC DOMAIN IN THE UNITED STATES

1892
AFTER THE BALL
Charles K. Harris
DAISY BELL
Harry Dacre

1894
SIDEWALKS OF
NEW YORK
James W. Blake
& Charles B. Lawlor

1896
SWEET ROSIE O'GRADY
Maude Nugent Jerome

1898
GYPSY LOVE SONG
Victor Herbert
& Harry B. Smith
ROSARY, THE
Ethelbert Nevin
& Robert Cameron Rodgers

1899
MY WILD IRISH ROSE
Chauncey Olcott

1900
BIRD IN A GILDED
CAGE, A
Arthur J. Lamb
& Harry Von Tilzer

1901
I LOVE YOU TRULY
Carrie Jacobs Bond
JUST A-WEARYIN' FOR YOU
Carrie Jacobs Bond
& Frank Stanton
MIGHTY LAK' A ROSE
Ethelbert Nevin
& Frank Stanton

1902
BECAUSE
Guy D'Hardelot
& Edward Teschemacher
BILL BAILEY WON'T YOU
PLEASE COME HOME
Hughie Cannon

1903
BEDELIA
William Jerome
& Jean Schwartz
KASHMIRI SONG
Lawrence Hope
& Amy Woodforde-Finden
MARCH OF THE TOYS
Victor Herbert
TOYLAND
Victor Herbert
& Glen MacDonough
YOU'RE THE FLOWER OF MY
HEART, SWEET ADELINE
Harry Armstrong
& Richard H. Gerard

**List 4.1 Some Popular Songs in the Public Domain
in the United States (*cont'd*)**

1904

GIVE MY REGARDS TO
BROADWAY
  George M. Cohan
MEET ME IN ST. LOUIS, LOUIS
Kerry Mills
  & Andrew B. Sterling
YANKEE DOODLE BOY
  George M. Cohan

1905

IN MY MERRY OLDSMOBILE
Vincent Bryan
  & Gus Edwards
IN THE SHADE OF THE OLD
APPLE TREE
  Egbert Van Alstyne
  & Harry Williams
KISS ME AGAIN
  Harry Blossom
  & Victor Herbert
MARY'S A GRAND OLD NAME
  George M. Cohan
WAIT TILL THE SUN
SHINES NELLIE
  Andrew B. Sterling
  & Harry Von Tilzer
WHERE THE RIVER
SHANNON FLOWS
  James I. Russell
WHISTLER AND HIS DOG, THE
  Arthur Pryor

1906

EVERY DAY IS LADIES'
DAY WITH ME
  Henry Blossom
  & Victor Herbert
LOVE ME AND THE
WORLD IS MINE
  Ernest R. Ball
  & David Reed, Jr.

MOONBEAMS
  Henry Blossom
  & Victor Herbert
NATIONAL ANTHEM
  E. E. Bagley
SCHOOL DAYS
  Will D. Cobb
  & Gus Edwards
WAITING AT THE CHURCH
  F. W. Leigh
  & Henry E. Pether
YOU'RE A GRAND OLD FLAG
  George M. Cohan

1907

ANCHORS AWEIGH
George D. Lottman,
  A. H. Milies,
  Domenico Savino
  & Charles A. Zimmerman
HARRIGAN
  George M. Cohan
ON THE ROAD TO
MANDALAY
  Rudyard Kipling
  & Oley Speaks
RED WING
  Thurland Chattaway
  & Kerry Mills

1908

CUDDLE UP A LITTLE
CLOSER, LOVEY MINE
  Otto Harbach
  & Karl Hoschna
I WISH I HAD A GIRL
  Grace LeBoy Kahn
  & Gus Kahn
SHINE ON HARVEST MOON
  Nora Bayes
  & Jack Norworth

SUNBONNET SUE
Will D. Cobb
& Gus Edwards
TAKE ME OUT TO THE BALL
GAME
Jack Norworth
& Albert Von Tilzer

1909
BY THE LIGHT OF THE
SILVERY MOON
Gus Edwards
& Edward Madden
FROM THE LAND OF THE SKY
BLUE WATER
Charles Wakefield Cadman
& Nelle Richmond Eberhart
I WONDER WHO'S KISSING
HER NOW
Frank R. Adams,
Will M. Hough
& Joseph E. Howard
I'VE GOT RINGS ON MY
FINGERS
F. P. Barnes,
Maurice Scott
& R. P. Weston
MEET ME TONIGHT IN
DREAMLAND
Leo Friedman
& Beth Slater Whitson
MY HERO
Stanislaus Stange
& Oscar Straus
ON WISCONSIN
Carl Beck
& W. T. Purdy
PUT ON YOUR OLD GREY
BONNET
Stanley Murphy
& Percy Wenrich

1910
AH! SWEET MYSTERY OF LIFE
Victor Herbert
& Rida Johnson Young
CAPRICE VIENNOIS
Fritz Kreisler
CHINATOWN MY CHINATOWN
William Jerome
& Jean Schwartz
DOWN BY THE OLD MILL
STREAM
Tell Taylor
EVERY LITTLE MOVEMENT
Otto Harbach
& Karl Hoschna
I'D LOVE TO LIVE IN
LOVELAND (WITH A GIRL
LIKE YOU)
W. R. Williams
I'M FALLING IN LOVE WITH
SOMEONE
Victor Herbert
& Rida Johnson Young
ITALIAN STREET SONG
Victor Herbert
& Rida Johnson Young
LET ME CALL YOU
SWEETHEART
Leo Friedman
& Beth Slater Whitson
LIEBESFREUD
Fritz Kreisler
LIEBESLIED
Fritz Kreisler
MOTHER MACHREE
Ernest R. Ball,
Chauncey Olcott
& Rida Johnson Young
PERFECT DAY, A
Carrie Jacobs Bond
PUT YOUR ARMS AROUND
ME, HONEY
Junie McCree
& Albert Von Tilzer

List 4.1 Some Popular Songs in the Public Domain in the United States (*cont'd*)

SOME OF THESE DAYS
Shelton Brooks
STEIN SONG
Lincoln Colcord
& E. A. Fenstad

1911
ALEXANDER'S RAGTIME
BAND
Irving Berlin
EVERYBODY'S DOIN' IT NOW
Irving Berlin
I WANT A GIRL (JUST LIKE
THE GIRL THAT MARRIED
DEAR OLD DAD)
William Dilton
& Harry Von Tilzer
LITTLE GREY HOME IN THE
WEST
Hermann Lohr
& D. Eardley Wilmot
LITTLE LOVE,
A LITTLE KISS, A
A. Nilson Fysher,
Adrian Ross
& Lao Silesu
OH YOU BEAUTIFUL DOLL
Nat D. Ayer
& A. Seymour Brown
SOMEWHERE A VOICE IS
CALLING
Eileen Newton
& Arthur P. Tate

1912
BE MY LITTLE BABY
BUMBLE BEE
Henry Marshall
& Stanley Murphy
GIANNINA MIA
Rudolf Friml
& Otto Harbach

IT'S A LONG, LONG WAY
TO TIPPERARY
Jack Judge
& Harry Williams
MOONLIGHT BAY
Edward Madden
& Percy Wenrich
MY MELANCHOLY BABY
Ernie Burnett
& George A. Norton
RAGTIME COWBOY JOE
Maurice Abrahams,
Grant Clarke
& Lewis F. Muir
ROW, ROW, ROW
William Jerome
& James V. Monaco
SWEETHEART OF
SIGMA CHI
Byron D. Stokes
& F. Dudleigh Vernor
SYMPATHY
Rudolf Friml
& Otto Harbach
WAITING FOR THE
ROBERT E. LEE
L. Wolfe Gilbert
& Lewis F. Muir
WHEN IRISH EYES
ARE SMILING
Ernest R. Ball,
George Graff, Jr.
& Chauncey Olcott
WHEN THE MIDNIGHT
CHOO CHOO LEAVES
FOR ALABAM'
Irving Berlin

1913
DANNY BOY
Fred E. Weatherly
(old Irish Air)

IF I HAD MY WAY
James Kendis
& Lou Klein
PEG O' MY HEART
Alfred Bryan
& Fred Fisher
SWEETHEARTS
Victor Herbert
& Robert B. Smith
TOO-RA-LOO-RA-LOO-RAL,
THAT'S AN IRISH LULLABY
James Royce Shannon
TRAIL OF THE LONESOME
PINE, THE
Harry Carroll
& Ballard MacDonald
YOU MADE ME LOVE YOU, I
DIDN'T WANT TO DO IT
Joseph McCarthy
& James V. Monaco

1914
ABA DABA
HONEYMOON, THE
Walter Donovan
& Arthur Fields
BY THE BEAUTIFUL SEA
Harold Atteridge
& Harry Carroll
BY THE WATERS OF
MINNETONKA
Thurlow Lieurance
CAN'T YOU HEAR ME
CALLIN' CAROLINE
William H. Gardner
& Caro Roma
DOWN AMONG THE
SHELTERING PALMS
James Brockman
& Abe Olman
GOOD-BYE, GIRLS, I'M
THROUGH
Ivan Caryll
& John Golden

HE'S A DEVIL IN HIS OWN
HOME TOWN
Irving Berlin
& Grant Clarke
I WANT TO GO BACK TO
MICHIGAN, DOWN ON THE
FARM
Irving Berlin
IF YOU DON'T WANT MY
PEACHES, YOU'D BETTER
STOP SHAKING MY TREE
Irving Berlin
KEEP THE HOME-FIRES
BURNING, TILL THE BOYS
COME HOME
Lena G. Ford
& Ivor Novello
LITTLE BIT OF HEAVEN,
SHURE THEY CALL IT
IRELAND, A
Ernest R. Ball
& J. Keirn Brennan
MISSOURI WALTZ
Frederick Knight Logan
& James R. Shannon
ON THE 5:15
Henry I. Marshall
& Stanley Murphy
ST. LOUIS BLUES
W. C. Handy
SIMPLE MELODY
Irving Berlin
SISTER SUSIE'S SEWING
SHIRTS FOR SOLDIERS
Hermann E. Darewski
& R. P. Weston
SYLVIA
Clinton Scollard
& Oley Speaks
THAT'S A PLENTY
Lew Pollack
THERE'S A LONG,
LONG TRAIL
Zo Elliott
& Stoddard King

**List 4.1 Some Popular Songs in the Public Domain
in the United States** (*cont'd*)

THEY DIDN'T BELIEVE ME
*Jerome Kern
& M. E. Rourke*
TWELFTH STREET RAG
Euday L. Bowman
WHEN YOU WORE A
TULIP AND I WORE
A BIG RED ROSE
*Jack Mahoney
& Percy Wenrich*
WHEN YOU'RE AWAY
*Henry Blossom
& Victor Herbert*
WHEN YOU'RE A LONG, LONG
WAY FROM HOME
*Sam M. Lewis
& George W. Meyer*
YOU PLANTED A ROSE
IN THE GARDEN OF LOVE
*Ernest R. Ball
& J. Will Callahan*

1915
ALABAMA JUBILEE
*George L. Cobb
& Jack Yellen*
ALONG THE ROCKY ROAD
TO DUBLIN
*Bert Grant
& Joe Young*
AUF WIEDERSEHN
*Herbert Reynolds
& Sigmund Romberg*
BABES IN THE WOOD
*Schuyler Greene
& Jerome Kern*
BEATRICE FAIRFAX,
TELL ME WHAT TO DO
*Grant Clarke,
Joe McCarthy
& James V. Monaco*

CANADIAN CAPERS
*Earl Burtnett,
Gus Chandler,
Henry Cohen
& Bert White*
FASCINATION
*Harold Atteridge
& Sigmund Romberg*
GIRL ON THE MAGAZINE
COVER
Irving Berlin
HELLO, FRISCO!
*Gene Buck
& Louis A. Hirsch*
HELLO, HAWAII, HOW ARE
YOU
*Bert Kalmar,
Edgar Leslie
& Jean Schwartz*
I DIDN'T RAISE MY BOY TO
BE A SOLDIER
*Alfred Bryan
& Al Piantadosi*
IF WE CAN'T BE THE SAME
OLD SWEETHEARTS, WE'LL
JUST BE THE SAME OLD
FRIENDS
*Joe McCarthy
& James V. Monaco*
I LOVE A PIANO
Irving Berlin
IN A MONASTERY GARDEN
Albert W. Ketelbey
IRELAND IS IRELAND TO ME
*Ernest R. Ball,
J. Keirn Brennan
& Fiske O'Hara*
IT'S TULIP TIME IN HOLLAND
*Dave Bedford
& Richard A. Whiting*
JELLY ROLL BLUES
Fred Morton

JUST TRY TO PICTURE ME
DOWN HOME IN TENNESSEE
Walter Donaldson
& William Jerome
LOVE IS THE BEST OF ALL
Henry Blossom
& Victor Herbert
MEMORIES
Egbert Van Alstyne
& Gus Kahn
M-O-T-H-E-R, A WORD THAT
MEANS THE WORLD TO ME
Howard Johnson
& Theodore Morse
MY LITTLE GIRL
Will Dillon,
Sam M. Lewis
& Albert Von Tilzer
MY MOTHER'S ROSARY
Sam M. Lewis
& George W. Meyer
NEAPOLITAN LOVE SONG
Henry Blossom
& Victor Herbert
PACK UP YOUR TROUBLES IN
YOUR OLD KIT-BAG
George Asaf
& Feliz Powell
PUT ME TO SLEEP WITH AN
OLD-FASHIONED MELODY
Dick Howard,
Harry Jentes
& Sam M. Lewis
RAGGING THE SCALE
Edward B. Claypoole
SIAM
Fred Fisher
& Howard Johnson
SO LONG LETTY
Earl Carroll
SOME LITLE BUG IS GOING
TO FIND YOU
Bert & Roy Atwell,
Benjamin Hapgood,
& Silvio Hein

SUNSHINE OF YOUR
SMILE, THE
Leonard Cooke
& Lillian Ray
THERE'S A BROKEN HEART
FOR EVERY LIGHT ON
BROADWAY
Fred Fisher
& Howard Johnson
THERE'S A LITTLE LANE
WITHOUT A TURNING ON THE
WAY TO HOME SWEET HOME
Sam M. Lewis
& George W. Meyer
UNDERNEATH THE STARS
Fleta Jan Brown
& Herbert Spencer
WE'LL HAVE A JUBILEE IN MY
OLD KENTUCKY HOME
Walter Donaldson
& Coleman Goetz
WHEN THE BOYS COME HOME
John Hays
& Oley Speaks
WHEN I LEAVE THE WORLD
BEHIND
Irving Berlin
WHEN YOU'RE IN LOVE WITH
SOMEONE WHO IS NOT IN
LOVE WITH YOU
Grant Clarke
& Al Piantadosi
YOU KNOW AND I KNOW AND
WE BOTH UNDERSTAND
Schuyler Greene
& Jerome Kern
YOU'LL ALWAYS BE THE
SAME SWEET GIRL
Andrew B. Sterling
& Harry Von Tilzer

1916
ALLAH'S HOLIDAY
Rudolf Friml
& Otto Harbach

List 4.1 Some Popular Songs in the Public Domain in the United States (*cont'd*)

ARRAH GO ON, I'M GONA GO
BACK TO OREGON
  Bert Grant,
  Sam M. Lewis
  & Joe Young
BABY SHOES
  Joe Goodwin,
  Al Piantadosi
  & Ed Rose
BOY SCOUTS OF AMERICA
  John Philip Sousa
DOWN IN HONKY TONKY
TOWN
  Charles McCarran
  & Chris Smith
GIVE A LITTLE CREDIT TO
YOUR DAD
  William Tracey
  & Nat Vincent
GOOD-BYE, GOOD LUCK,
GOD BLESS YOU
  Ernest R. Ball
  & J. Keirn Brennan
HAVE A HEART
  Jerome Kern
  & P. G. Wodehouse
HOW'S EVERY LITTLE THING
IN DIXIE
  Albert Gumble
  & Jack Yellen
I AIN'T GOT NOBODY
  Rogert Graham
  & Spencer Williams
I CAN DANCE WITH
EVERYBODY BUT MY WIFE
  Joseph Cawthorn
  & John L. Golden
IF I KNOCK THE "L" OUT OF
KELLY
  Bert Grant,
  Sam M. Lewis
  & Joe Young

IF YOU HAD ALL THE WORLD
AND ITS GOLD
  Bartley Costello,
  Harry Edlheit
  & Al Piantadosi
IF YOU WERE THE ONLY GIRL
IN THE WORLD
  Nat D. Ayer
  & Clifford Grey
I'M SORRY I MADE
YOU CRY
  N. J. Clesi
IRELAND MUST BE HEAVEN,
FOR MY MOTHER CAME
FROM THERE
  Fred Fisher,
  Howard Johnson
  & Joe McCarthy
KATINKA
  Rudolf Friml
  & Otto Harbach
LI'L LIZA JANE
  Ada De Lachau
MAMMY'S LITTLE COAL
BLACK ROSE
  Raymond Egan
  & Richard A. Whiting
M-I-S-S-I-S-S-I-P-P-I
  Bert Hanlon,
  Benny Ryan
  & Harry Tierney
NAT'AN, NAT'AN, NAT'AN,
TELL ME FOR WHAT ARE YOU
WAITIN', NAT' AN
  James Kendis
NOLA
  Feliz Arndt
OH! HOW SHE COULD YACKI,
HACKI, WICKI, WACKI, WOO
  Charlene McCarron,
  Stanley Murphy
  & Albert Von Tilzer

POOR BUTTERFLY
  Raymond Hubbell
  & John L. Golden
PRETTY BABY
  Egbert Van Alstyne,
  Tony Jackson
  & Gus Kahn
ROSES OF PICARDY
  Frederick E. Weatherly
  & Haydn Wood
SINCE MAGGIE DOOLEY
LEARNED THE HOOLEY
HOOLEY
  Bert Kalmar,
  Edgar Leslie
  & George W. Meyer
THERE'S A LITTLE BIT OF
BAD IN EVERY GOOD
LITTLE GIRL
  Grant Clarke
  & Fred Fisher
THERE'S A QUAKER DOWN
IN QUAKER TOWN
  David Berg
  & Alfred Solman
THEY MADE IT TWICE AS
NICE AS PARADISE (AND
THEY CALLED IT DIXIELAND)
  Raymond Egan
  & Richard A. Whiting

THEY'RE WEARING 'EM
HIGHER IN HAWAII
  Joe Goodwin
  & Halsey K. Mohr
THROW ME A ROSE
  Emmerich Kalman,
  Herbert Reynolds
  & P. G. Wodehouse
TURN BACK THE UNIVERSE
AND GIVE ME YESTERDAY
  Ernest R. Ball
  & J. Keirn Brennan
WAY DOWN IN IOWA I'M
GOING TO HIDE AWAY
  Sam M. Lewis,
  George W. Meyers
  & Joe Young
WHAT DO YOU WANT TO
MAKE THOSE EYES AT ME FOR
  Howard Johnson,
  Joe McCarthy
  & James V. Monaco
YAAKA HULA HICKEY DULA
  E. Ray Goetz,
  Joe Young
  & Pete Wendling
YOU CAN'T GET ALONG WITH
'EM OR WITHOUT 'EM
  Grant Clarke
  & Fred Fisher

LIST 4.2

POPULAR SONGS TO FALL INTO THE PUBLIC DOMAIN IN THE UNITED STATES BETWEEN NOW AND THE YEAR 2000

1917 (Public Domain in the United States on January 1, 1993)

ALL THE WORLD WILL BE JEALOUS OF ME
Ernest R. Ball
& Al Dubin

BEALE STREET BLUES
W. C. Handy

BELLS OF ST. MARY'S, THE
Emmett Adams
& Douglas Furber

BRING BACK MY DADDY TO ME
Howard Johnson,
George Meyer
& William Tracey

DARKTOWN STRUTTER'S BALL
Shelton Brooks

EILEEN (ALLANINA ASTHORE)
Henry Blossom
& Victor Herbert

EVERYBODY OUGHT TO KNOW HOW TO DO THE TICKLE TOE
Otto Harbach
& Louis A. Hirsch

FOR ME AND MY GAL
E. Ray Goetz,
Edgar Leslie
& George W. Meyer

GIVE A MAN A HORSE HE CAN RIDE
Geoffrey O'Hara
& James Thomson

GIVE ME THE MOONLIGHT, GIVE ME THE GIRL
Lew Brown
& Albert Von Tilzer

GOING UP
Otto Harbach
& Louis A. Hirsch

GOOD-BYE BROADWAY, HELLO FRANCE
Billy Baskette,
Benny Davis
& C. Francis Riesner

HOMING
Teresa Del Riego
& Arthur L. Salmon

I'D LOVE TO BE A MONKEY IN THE ZOO
Bert Hanlon
& Willie White

I DON'T KNOW WHERE I'M GOING BUT I'M ON MY WAY
George Fairman

I DON'T WANT TO GET WELL
Harry Jentes,
Howard Johnson
& Harry Pease

I'M ALL BOUND 'ROUND WITH THE MASON DIXON LINE
Sam M. Lewis,
Jean Schwartz
& Joe Young

INDIANA
James F. Hanely
& Ballard MacDonald

IRISH HAVE A GREAT DAY
TONIGHT, THE
Henry Blossom
& Victor Herbert
JOAN OF ARC, THEY ARE
CALLING YOU
Alfred Bryan,
Willie Weston
& Jack Wells
JOHNSON RAG
Henry Kleinkauf
& Guy Hall
JUMP JIM CROW
Sigmund Romberg
& Rida Johnson Young
LEAVE IT TO JANE
Jerome Kern
& P. G. Wodehouse
LITTLE MOTHER OF MINE
Walter H. Brown
& Harry T. Burleigh
LORRAINE, MY BEAUTIFUL
ALSACE LORRAINE
Alfred Bryan
& Fred Fisher
LOVE WILL FIND A WAY
Harry Graham
& Harold Fraser-Simson
NEAPOLITAN NIGHTS
Harry D. Kerr
& J. S. Zamecnik
OH JOHNNY,
OH JOHNNY, OH!
Abe Olman
& Ed Rose
OUT WHERE THE
WEST BEGINS
Arthur Chapman
& Estelle Philleo
OVER THERE
George M. Cohan
SAILIN' AWAY ON THE
HENRY CLAY
Egbert Van Alstyne
& Gus Kahn

SEND ME AWAY WITH A SMILE
Al Piantadosi
& Louis Weslyn
SMILES
J. Will Callahan
& Lee S. Roberts
SOME SUNDAY MORNING
Raymond Egan,
Gus Kahn
& Richard A. Whiting
THEY GO WILD, SIMPLY
WILD OVER ME
Fred Fisher
& Joe McCarthy
THINE ALONE
Henry Blossom
& Victor Herbert
TIGER RAG
Harry DeCosta
& The Original
Dixieland Jazz Band
TILL THE CLOUDS ROLL BY
Jerome Kern
& P. G. Wodehouse
WAIT TILL THE COWS
COME HOME
Anne Caldwell
& Ivan Caryll
WHEN YANKEE DOODLE
LEARNS TO PARLEZ VOUS
FRANCAIS
William Hart
& Ed Nelson
WHERE DO WE GO FROM HERE?
Howard Johnson
& Percy Wenrich
WHERE THE BLACK-EYED
SUSANS GROW
Dave Radford
& Richard A. Whiting
WHERE THE MORNING
GLORIES GROW
Raymond Egan,
Gus Kahn
& Richard A. Whiting

List 4.2 Popular Songs to Fall into the Public Domain in the United States Between Now and the Year 2000 (*cont'd*)

WILL YOU REMEMBER
Sigmund Romberg
& Rida Johnson Young

1918
AFTER YOU'VE GONE
Henry Creamer
& Turner Layton
BEAUTIFUL OHIO
Mary Earl
& Ballard MacDonald
CHONG
Harold Weeks
DAUGHTER OF ROSIE
O'GRADY, THE
Monty C. Brice
& Walter Donaldson
DEAR LITTLE BOY OF MINE
Ernest R. Ball
& J. Keirn Brennan
DEAR OLD PAL
OF MINE
Gitz Rice
& Harold Robe
EVERYTHING IS PEACHES
DOWN IN GEORGIA
Milton Ager,
Grant Clarke,
& George W. Meyer
GARDEN OF MY DREAMS
Gene Buck
& Dave Stamper
GOOD MAN IS HARD TO FIND, A
Eddie Green
GOOD-MORNING,
MR. ZIP-ZIP-ZIP
Robert Lloyd
HAVE A SMILE (FOR
EVERYONE YOU MEET)
J. Keirn Brennan,
Paul Cunningham
& Bert Rule

HELLO, CENTRAL, GIVE ME
NO MAN'S LAND
Sam M. Levin,
Jean Schwartz
& Joe Young
HINDUSTAN
Oliver G. Wallace
& Harold Weeks
I FOUND THE END OF
THE RAINBOW
Joseph McCarthy,
John Mears
& Harry Tierney
I HATE TO LOSE YOU
Grant Clarke
& Archie Gottler
I'M ALWAYS CHASING
RAINBOWS
Harry Carroll
& Joseph McCarthy
JA-DA
Bob Carleton
JUST A BABY'S PRAYER
AT TWILIGHT
M. K. Jerome,
Sam Lewis
& Joe Young
K-K-K-KATY
Geoffrey O'Hara
MADELON
L. Bousquet,
Alfred Bryan
& Camille Robert
MICKEY
Neil Moret
& Harry Williams
OH! FRENCHY
Con Conrad
& Sam Ehrlich
OH! HOW I HATE TO GET UP
IN THE MORNING
Irving Berlin

OUI, OUI, MARIE
Alfred Bryan,
Fred Fisher
& Joe McCarthy
ROCK-A-BYE YOUR BABY
WITH A DIXIE MELODY
Sam M. Lewis,
Jean Schwartz
& Joe Young
ROSE OF NO MAN'S LAND
James A. Brennan
& Jack Caddigan
SMILIN' THROUGH
Arthur Penn
SOMEBODY STOLE
MY GAL
Leo Wood
SUNRISE AND YOU
Arthur Penn
THAT TUMBLE-DOWN
SHACK IN ATHLONE
Monte Carlo,
Richard W. Pascoe
& Alma Sanders
THAT WONDERFUL
MOTHER OF MINE
Walter Goodwin
& Clyde Hager
THEY WERE ALL OUT
OF STEP BUT JIM
Irving Berlin
TILL WE MEET AGAIN
Raymond B. Egan
& Richard A. Whiting
WHEN YOU LOOK IN THE
HEART OF A ROSE
Marian Gillespie
& Florence Methven
WOULD YOU RATHER BE
A COLONEL WITH AN EAGLE
ON YOUR SHOULDER,
OR A PRIVATE WITH A
CHICKEN ON YOUR KNEE?
Archie Gottler
& Sidney D. Mitchell

1919
ALICE BLUE GOWN
Joseph McCarthy
& Harry Tierney
ALL THE QUAKERS ARE
SHOULDER SHAKERS, DOWN
IN QUAKER TOWN
Bert Kalmar,
Edgar Leslie
& Pete Wendling
AND HE'D SAY OO-LA LA!
WEE WEE
George Jessel
& Harry Ruby
BABY WON'T YOU PLEASE
COME HOME
Charles Warfield
& Clarence Williams
CHINESE LULLABY
Robert Hood Bowers
DADDY LONG LEGS
Sam M. Lewis,
Harry Ruby
& Joe Young
DARDANELLA
Felix Bernard,
Johnny S. Black
& Fred Fisher
HOW YA GONNA KEEP 'EM
DOWN ON THE FARM AFTER
THEY'VE SEEN PAREE?
Walter Donaldson,
Sam M. Lewis
& Joe Young
I MIGHT BE YOUR
"ONCE-IN-A-WHILE"
Victor Herbert
& Robert B. Smith
I WISH I COULD SHIMMY
LIKE MY SISTER KATE
Armand J. Piron
I'M FOREVER BLOWING
BUBBLES
John W. Kellette
& Jean Kenbrovin

**List 4.2 Popular Songs to Fall into the Public Domain in the
United States Between Now and the Year 2000** (*cont'd*)

INDIAN SUMMER
Al Dubin
& Victor Herbert
JUST LIKE A GYPSY
Nora Bayes
& Seymour B. Simons
LET THE REST OF THE
WORLD GO BY
Ernest R. Ball
& J. Keirn Brennan
LOVE SENDS A LITTLE
GIFT OF ROSES
Leslie Cooke
& John Openshaw
MAMMY O'MINE
Maceo Pinkard
& William Tracey
MANDY
Irving Berlin
MY HOME TOWN IS A ONE
HORSE TOWN, BUT IT'S BIG
ENOUGH FOR ME
Alex Gerber
& Abner Silver
MY ISLE OF
GOLDEN DREAMS
Walter Blaufuss
& Gus Kahn
NOBODY KNOWS AND
NOBODY SEEMS TO CARE
Irving Berlin
OH BY JINGO, OH BY GEE,
YOU'RE THE ONLY
GIRL FOR ME
Lew Brown
& Albert Von Tilzer
OH HOW I LAUGH WHEN I
THINK HOW I CRIED
ABOUT YOU
George Jessel,
Roy Turk
& Willy White

OH! WHAT A PAL WAS MARY
Bert Kalmar,
Edgar Leslie
& Pete Wendling
OLD FASHION GARDEN
Cole Porter
ON MIAMI SHORE
Victor Jacobi
& William LeBaron
PEGGY
Neil Moret
& Harry Williams
PRETTY GIRL IS LIKE A
MELODY, A
Irving Berlin
ROSE OF WASHINGTON SQUARE
James F. Hanley
& Ballard MacDonald
SUGAR BLUES
Lucy Fletcher
& Clarance Williams
SWANEE
Irving Caesar
& George Gershwin
TAKE YOUR GIRLIE TO THE
MOVIES IF YOU CAN'T MAKE
LOVE AT HOME
Bert Kalmar,
Edgar Leslie
& Peter Wendling
TELL ME
J. Will Callahan
& Max Kortlander
THAT NAUGHTY WALTZ
Sol P. Levy
& Edwin Stanley
TULIP TIME
Gene Buck
& Dave Stamper
WAIT TILL YOU GET THEM UP
IN THE AIR, BOYS
Lew Brown
& Albert Von Tilzer

WHAT WE DO ON A
SATURDAY NIGHT, WHEN THE
TOWN GOES DRY
  Harry Ruby
WHIP-POOR-WILL
  Bud DeSylva
  & Jerome Kern
WORLD IS WAITING FOR THE
SUNRISE, THE
  Eugene Lockhart
  & Ernest Seitz
YOU ARE FREE
  Victor Jacobi
  & William LeBaron
YOUR EYES HAVE TOLD ME SO
  Egbert Van Alstyne,
  Walter Blaufuss
  & Gus Kahn
YOU'RE A MILLION MILES
FROM NOWHERE WHEN
YOU'RE ONE LITTLE MILE
FROM HOME
  Walter Donaldson,
  Sam M. Lewis
  & Joe Young

1920
ALL SHE'D SAY WAS UMH HUM
  Mac Emery,
  Van & Schenck,
  King Zany
ALT-WEIN
  Leopold Godowsky
AVALON
  B. G. DeSylva,
  Al Jolson
  & Vincent Rose
BEAUTIFUL ANNA BELL LEE
  Alfred Bryan,
  Artie Mehlinger
  & George W. Meyer
BRIGHT EYES
  M. K. Jerome,
  Otto Motzan
  & Harry B. Smith

BROADWAY ROSE
  Martin Fried,
  Otis Spencer
  & Eugene West
CHILE BEAN
  Lew Brown
  & Albert Von Tilzer
DADDY, YOU'VE BEEN A
MOTHER TO ME
  Fred Fisher
DOWN BY THE O-HI-O
  Abe Olman
  & Jack Yellen
FEATHER YOUR NEST
  James Brockman,
  James Kendis
  & Howard Johnson
I LOST THE BEST PAL THAT I HAD
  Dick Thomas
I NEVER KNEW I COULD
LOVE ANYBODY LIKE I'M
LOVING YOU
  Ray Egan,
  Roy K. Marsh
  & Tom Pitts
I USED TO LOVE YOU BUT
IT'S ALL OVER NOW
  Lew Brown
  & Albert Von Tilzer
I'D LOVE TO FALL ASLEEP
AND WAKE UP IN MY
MAMMY'S ARMS
  Fred E. Ahlert,
  Sam M. Lewis
  & Joe Young
IF YOU COULD CARE
  Herman Darewski
  & Arthur Wimperis
I'LL BE WITH YOU IN APPLE
BLOSSOM TIME
  Neville Fleeson
  & Albert Von Tilzer
JAPANESE SANDMAN, THE
  Raymond B. Egan
  & Richard A. Whiting

List 4.2 Popular Songs to Fall into the Public Domain in the United States Between Now and the Year 2000 (*cont'd*)

LEFT ALL ALONE
AGAIN BLUES
  Anne Caldwell
  & Jerome Kern
LILAC TREE (Perspicacity)
  George H. Gartlan
LITTLE TOWN IN THE OULD
COUNTY DOWN
  Monte Carlo,
  Richard W. Pascoe
  & Alma Sanders
LOOK FOR THE
SILVER LINING
  Bud DeSylva
  & Jerome Kern
LOVE NEST
  Otto Harbach
  & Louis A. Hirsch
MAH LINDY LOU
  Lily Strickland
MARGIE
  Con Conrad,
  Benny Davis
  & J. Russel Robinson
MY MAMMY
  Walter Donaldson,
  Sam Lewis
  & Joe Young
OLD PAL WHY DON'T YOU
ANSWER ME
  M. K. Jerome,
  Sam M. Lewis
  & Joe Young
PALE MOON
  Jesse G. M. Glick
  & Frederick Knight Logan
PRETTY KITTY KELLY
  Edward G. Nelson
  & Harry Pease
SAN
  Lindsay McPhail
  & Walter Michels

SO LONG OO-LONG, HOW
LONG YOU GONNA BE GONE
  Bert Kalmar
  & Harry Ruby
TELL ME LITTLE GYPSY
  Irving Berlin
THAT OLD IRISH MOTHER
OF MINE
  William Jerome
  & Harry Von Tilzer
TRIPOLI (On the Shores of Tripoli)
  Paul Cunningham,
  Al Dubin
  & Irving Weill
WHEN BIG PROFUNDO
SANG LOW C
  Marion T. Bohannon
  & George Botsford
WHEN MY BABY SMILES AT ME
  Ted Lewis,
  Billy Munro,
  Andrew B. Sterling
  & Harry Von Tilzer
WHISPERING
  Richard Coburn,
  John Schonberger
  & Vincent Rose
WHOSE BABY ARE YOU
  Anne Caldwell
  & Jerome Kern
WILD ROSE
  Clifford Grey
  & Jerome Kern
YOUNG MAN'S FANCY, A
  Milton Ager,
  John Murray Anderson
  & Jack Yellen

1921
AIN'T WE GOT FUN
  Raymond B. Egan,
  Gus Kahn
  & Richard A. Whiting

ALL BY MYSELF
Irving Berlin
APRIL SHOWERS
B. G. DeSylva
& Louis Silvers
BANDANA DAYS
Eubie Blake
& Noble Sissle
BIMINI BAY
Raymond B. Egan,
Gus Kahn
& Richard Whiting
DAPPER DAN
Lew Brown
& Albert Von Tilzer
DEAR OLD SOUTHLAND
Henry Creamer
& Turner Layton
I AIN'T NOBODY'S DARLING
Elmer Hughes
& Robert A. King
I FOUND A ROSE IN THE
DEVIL'S GARDEN
Fred Fisher
& Willie Raskin
I'LL FORGET YOU
Ernest R. Ball
& Annelu Burns
I'M JUST WILD
ABOUT HARRY
Eubie Blake
& Noble Sissle
KA-LU-A
Anne Caldwell
& Jerome Kern
KITTEN ON THE KEYS
Zez Confrey
& Sam Coslow
LEARN TO SMILE
Otto Harbach
& Louis A. Hirsch
LEAVE ME WITH A SMILE
Earl Burtnett
& Charles Koehler

LOVE WILL FIND A WAY
Eubie Blake
& Noble Sissle
MA, HE'S MAKING EYES AT ME
Sidney Clare
& Con Conrad
MAKE BELIEVE
Bennie Davis
& Jack Shilkret
MY MAN
Jacques Charles,
Channing Pollack,
Albert Willemetz
& Maurice Yvain
PEGGY O'NEIL
Gilbert Dodge,
Ed G. Nelson
& Harry Pease
SALLY
Clifford Grey
& Jerome Kern
SAY IT WITH MUSIC
Irving Berlin
SECOND HAND ROSE
Grant Clarke
& James F. Hanley
SHEIK OF ARABY, THE
Harry B. Smith,
Ted Snyder
& Francis Wheeler
SHE'S MINE, ALL MINE
Bert Kalmar
& Harry Ruby
SHUFFLE ALONG
Eubie Blake
& Noble Sissle
SONG OF LOVE
Dorothy Donnelly,
adapted from melodies
of H. Berte
& F. Schubert
by Sigmund Romberg
SWANEE RIVER MOON
H. Pitman Clarke

List 4.2 Popular Songs to Fall into the Public Domain in the United States Between Now and the Year 2000 (*cont'd*)

SWEET LADY
Frank Crumit,
Howard Johnson
& Dave Zoob
TEN LITTLE FINGERS AND TEN
LITTLE TOES, DOWN
IN TENNESSEE
Ed. G. Nelson,
Harry Pease,
Ira Schuster
& Johnny White
THREE O'CLOCK
IN THE MORNING
Julian Robledo
& Dorothy Terriss
TUCK ME TO SLEEP IN MY
OLD 'TUCKY HOME
Sam Lewis,
George W. Meyer
& Joe Young
WABASH BLUES
Fred Meinken
& Dave Ringle
WANG-WANG BLUES
Henry Busse,
Buster Johnson,
Gus Mueller
& Leo Wood
WHEN BUDDHA
SMILES
Nacio Herb Brown,
Arthur Freed
& King Zany
WHEN FRANCIS DANCES
WITH ME
Benny Ryan
& Violinsky
WYOMING
Gene Williams
YOO-HOO
B. G. DeSylva
& Al Jolson

1922
AGGRAVATIN' PAPA DON'T
YOU TRY TO TWO-TIME ME
Addy Britt,
J. Russel Robinson
& Roy Turk
ALL OVER NOTHING AT ALL
J. Keirn Brennan,
Paul Cunningham
& James S. Rule
ANGEL CHILD
Benny Davis,
George E. Price
& Abner Silver
CAROLINA IN THE
MORNING
Walter Donaldson
& Gus Kahn
CHICAGO, THAT TODDLING TOWN
Fred Fisher
CHINA BOY
Phil Boutelje
& Dick Winfree
CRINOLINE DAYS
Irving Berlin
DANCING FOOL
Harry B. Smith,
Ted Snyder
& Francis Wheeler
DO IT AGAIN
B. G. DeSylva
& George Gershwin
GEORGIA
Walter Donaldson
& Howard Johnson
HOT LIPS
Henry Busse,
Lou Davis
& Henry Lange
I'LL BUILD A STAIRWAY
TO PARADISE
B. G. DeSylva,

George Gershwin
& Ira Gershwin
KISS IN THE DARK, A
B. G. DeSylva
& Victor Herbert
LADY OF THE EVENING
Irving Berlin
L'AMOUR TOUJOUR
L'AMOUR
Catherine C. Cushing
& Rudolf Friml
LIMEHOUSE BLUES
Philip Braham
& Doulgas Furber
LOVESICK BLUES
Cliff Friend
& Irving Mills
LOVIN' SAM, THE SHEIK
OF ALABAMA
Milton Ager
& Jack Yellen
MARY, DEAR, SOME DAY WE
WILL MEET AGAIN
Harry De Costa
& M. K. Jerome
MY BUDDY
Walter Donaldson
& Gus Kahn
MY HONEY'S
LOVING' ARMS
Joseph Meyer
& Herman Ruby
'NEATH THE SOUTH SEA MOON
Gene Buck,
Louis A. Hirsch
& Dave Stamper
NOBODY LIED (When They Said
That I Cried Over You)
Hyatt Berry,
Karyl Norman
& Edwin J. Weber
ON THE ALAMO
Isham Jones,
Gilbert Keyes
& Joe Lyons

O-OO ERNEST, ARE YOU
EARNEST WITH ME
Sidney Clare,
Cliff Friend
& Harry Tobias
ROSE OF THE RIO GRANDE
Ross Gorman,
Edgar Leslie
& Harry Warren
RUNNIN' WILD
A. Harrington Gibbs,
Joe Grey
& Leo Wood
SAY IT WHILE
DANCING
Benny Davis
& Abner Silver
STUMBLING
Zez Confrey
TOOT, TOOT, TOOTSIE
(Goo'Bye)
Ernie Erdman,
Ted Fiorito,
Gus Kahn
& Robert A. King
TREES
Joyce Kilmer
& Oscar Rasbach
'WAY DOWN YONDER
IN NEW ORLEANS
Henry Creamer
& J. Turner Layton
WHEN HEARTS
ARE YOUNG
Alfred Goodman,
Sigmund Romberg
& Cyrus Wood
WONDERFUL ONE
Ferde Grofe,
Dorothy Terriss
& Paul Whiteman
YOU TELL HER
I STUTTER
Cliff Friend
& Billy Rose

**List 4.2 Popular Songs to Fall into the Public Domain in the
United States Between Now and the Year 2000** (*cont'd*)

1923

ANNABELLE
*Lew Brown
& Ray Henderson*
ANNABEL LEE
*John Murray Anderson,
Irving Caesar
& Louis A. Hirsch*
BAMBALINA
*Oscar Hammerstein, 2nd,
Otto Harbach,
Herbert Stothart
& Vincent Youmans*
BARNEY GOOGLE
*Con Conrad
& Billy Rose*
BESIDE A BABBLING
BROOK
*Walter Donaldson
& Gus Kahn*
BUGLE CALL RAG
*Bill Meyers,
Jack Pettis
& Elmer Schoebel*
CHANSONETTE
*Irving Caesar,
Rudolf Friml,
Dailey Paskman
& Sigmund Spaeth*
CHARLESTON
*Jimmy Johnson
& Cecil Mack*
COME ON,
SPARK PLUG!
*Con Conrad
& Billy Rose*
DEAREST YOU'RE THE
NEAREST TO MY HEART
*Harry Akst
& Benny Davis*
DIZZY FINGERS
Zez Confrey

I CRIED FOR YOU (Now It's
Your Turn To Cry Over Me)
*Gus Arnheim,
Arthur Freed
& Abe Lyman*
I LOVE LIFE
*Irwin M. Cassel
& Mana-Zucca*
I LOVE YOU (from "Little
Jessie James")
*Harry Archer
& Harlan Thompson*
I'M SITTING PRETTY IN A
PRETTY LITTLE CITY
*Abel Baer,
Lou Davis
& Henry Santly*
I WON'T SAY I WILL, BUT I
WON'T SAY I WON'T
*Buddy DeSylva,
George Gershwin
& Arthur Francis*
I'M GOIN' SOUTH
*Abner Silver
& Harry Woods*
IT AIN'T GONNA
RAIN NO MO'
Wendell Hall
JUST A GIRL THAT
MEN FORGET
*Al Dubin,
Joe Garren
& Fred Rath*
LAST NIGHT ON THE BACK
PORCH, I LOVED HER
BEST OF ALL
*Lew Brown
& Carl Schraubstader*
LINGER AWHILE
*Harry Owens
& Vincent Rose*

MY SWEETIE WENT AWAY,
SHE DIDN'T SAY WHERE,
WHEN OR WHY
  Lou Handman
  & Roy Turk
NO, NO, NORA
  Ernie Erdman,
  Ted Fiorito
  & Gus Kahn
O, GEE, OH GOSH, OH GOLLY
I'M IN LOVE
  Ernest Breuer,
  Olson & Johnson
ON THE MALL
  Edwin Franko Goldman
RAGGEDY MAN
  Anne Caldwell
  & Jerome Kern
REMEMB'RING
  Vivian
  & Rosetta Duncan
SITTIN' IN A CORNER
  Gus Kahn
  & George W. Meyer
SLEEP (based on "Visions of
Sleep")
  Earl Lebier
SMILE WILL GO A LONG,
LONG WAY, A
  Harry Akst
  & Benny Davis
SWINGIN' DOWN
THE LANE
  Gus Kahn
  & Isham Jones
THAT OLD GANG
OF MINE
  Mort Dixon,
  Ray Henderson
  & Billy Rose
WESTWARD HO! (The Covered
Wagon March)
  R. A. Barnet
  & Hugo Riesenfeld

WHEN IT'S NIGHT-TIME IN
ITALY, IT'S WEDNESDAY
OVER HERE
  Lew Brown
  & James Kendis
WHEN YOU WALKED OUT
SOMEONE ELSE WALKED
RIGHT IN
  Irving Berlin
WHO'LL BUY MY VIOLETS
  E. Ray Goetz
  & Jose Padilla
WHO'S SORRY NOW
  Bert Kalmar,
  Harry Ruby
  & Ted Snyder
WILD FLOWER
  Otto Harbach.
  Oscar Hammerstein, 2nd,
  Herbert Stothart
  & Vincent Youmans
YES! WE HAVE
NO BANANAS
  Irving Cohn
  & Frank Silver
YOU'VE GOTTA SEE MAMMA
EV'RY NIGHT OR YOU CAN'T
SEE MAMMA AT ALL
  Con Conrad
  & Billy Rose

1924
ALL ALONE
  Irving Berlin
CALIFORNIA, HERE I COME
  Bud DeSylva,
  Al Jolson
  & Joseph Meyer
CHARLEY, MY BOY
  Ted Fiorito
  & Gus Kahn
COPENHAGEN
  Charlie Davis
  & Walter Melrose

List 4.2 Popular Songs to Fall into the Public Domain in the United States Between Now and the Year 2000 (*cont'd*)

DEEP IN MY HEART, DEAR
  Dorothy Donnelly
  & Sigmund Romberg
DOES THE SPEARMINT LOSE
ITS FLAVOR ON THE BEDPOST
OVER NIGHT
  Marty Bloom,
  Ernest Breuer
  & Billy Rose
EVERYBODY LOVES MY
BABY, BUT MY BABY DON'T
LOVE NOBODY BUT ME
  Jack Palmer
  & Spencer Williams
FASCINATING RHYTHM
  George Gershwin
  & Ira Gershwin
FOLLOW THE SWALLOW
  Mort Dixon,
  Ray Henderson
  & Billy Rose
GOLDEN DAYS
  Dorothy Donnelly
  & Sigmund Romberg
HARD HEARTED HANNAH
  Milton Ager,
  Charles Bates,
  Bob Bigelow
  & Jack Yellen
HOW COME YOU DO ME
LIKE YOU DO
  Gene Austin
  & Roy Bergere
I WANT TO BE HAPPY
  Irving Caesar
  & Vincent Youmans
I WONDER WHAT'S BECOME
OF SALLY
  Milton Ager
  & Jack Yellen
I'LL SEE YOU IN MY DREAMS
  Isham Jones

  & Gus Kahn
INDIAN LOVE CALL
  Rudolf Friml,
  Otto Harbach
  & Oscar Hammerstein, 2nd
IT HAD TO BE YOU
  Isham Jones
  & Gus Kahn
JEALOUS
  Dick Finch,
  Jack Little
  & Tommie Malie
JUNE NIGHT
  Abel Baer
  & Cliff Friend
KING PORTER STOMP
  Fred (Jelly Roll) Morton
MAN I LOVE, THE
  George Gershwin
  & Ira Gershwin
MEMORY LANE
  Con Conrad,
  B. G. DeSylva
  & Larry Spier
MOUNTIES, THE
  Rudolf Friml,
  Otto Harbach,
  Oscar Hammerstein, 2nd
  & Herbert Stothart
MY DREAM GIRL, I LOVED
YOU LONG AGO
  Victor Herbert
  & Rida Johnson Young
MY TIME IS YOUR TIME
  Leo Dance
  & Eric Little
NOBODY'S SWEETHEART
  Ernie Erdman,
  Gus Kahn,
  Billy Meyers
  & Elmer Schoebel

OH KATHERINA!
Richard Fall
& L. Wolfe Gilbert
OH, LADY BE GOOD
George Gershwin
& Ira Gershwin
ONE I LOVE BELONGS TO
SOMEBODY ELSE, THE
Isham Jones
& Gus Kahn
PRISONER'S SONG, THE
Gus Massey
RHAPSODY IN BLUE
George Gershwin
ROSE MARIE
Rudolf Friml,
Otto Harbach,
Oscar Hammerstein, 2nd
& Herbert Stothart
SERENADE
Dorothy Donnelly
& Sigmund Romberg
S-H-I-N-E
Lew Brown,
Ford Dabney
& Cecil Mack
SOMEBODY LOVES ME
B. G. DeSylva,
George Gershwin
& Ballard MacDonald
TEA FOR TWO
Irving Caesar
& Vincent Youmans
THERE'S YES, YES, IN
YOUR EYES
Cliff Friend
& Joseph H. Santly
TOTEM-TOM-TOM
Rudolf Friml,
Otto Harbach,
Oscar Hammerstein, 2nd
& Herbert Stothart
WEST OF THE GREAT DIVIDE
Ernest R. Ball
& George Whiting

WHAT'LL I DO
Irving Berlin
WHEN MY SUGAR WALKS
DOWN THE STREET, ALL
THE BIRDIES GO
TWEET-TWEET-TWEET
Gene Austin,
Jimmy McHugh
& Irving Mills
WHY DID I KISS THAT GIRL?
Lew Brown,
Robert King
& Ray Henderson

1925
ALABAMY BOUND
Bud DeSylva,
Bud Green
& Ray Henderson
ALWAYS
Irving Berlin
BAM, BAM, BAMY SHORE
Mort Dixon
& Ray Henderson
BROWN EYES-WHY
ARE YOU BLUE?
Alfred Bryan
& George W. Meyer
BYE AND BYE
Lorenz Hart
& Richard Rodgers
CECILIA (Does Your Mother
Know You're Out, Cecilia?)
Dave Dreyer
& Herman Ruby
CHEATIN' ON ME
Lew Pollack
& Jack Yellen
COLLEGIATE
Moe Jaffe,
Nat Bonx
& Lew Brown
CUP OF COFFEE, A SANDWICH
AND YOU, A
Al Dubin,

List 4.2 Popular Songs to Fall into the Public Domain in the United States Between Now and the Year 2000 (*cont'd*)

Joseph Meyer
& Billy Rose
DINAH
Harry Akst,
Sam M. Lewis
& Joe Young
DON'T BRING LULU
Lew Brown,
Ray Henderson
& Billy Rose
DON'T WAKE ME UP,
LET ME DREAM
Abel Baer,
L. Wolfe Gilbert
& Mabel Wayne
DOWN BY THE
WINEGAR WOIKS
Don Bester,
Walter Donovan
& Roger Lewis
DRIFTING AND DREAMING
Egbert VanAlstyne,
Loyal Curtis,
Haven Gillespie
& Erwin R. Schmidt
DRINKING SONG
Dorothy Donnelly
& Sigmund Romberg
D'YE LOVE ME?
Jerome Kern,
Otto Harbach
& Oscar Hammerstein, 2nd
FIVE FOOT TWO, EYES OF BLUE
Ray Henderson,
Sam M. Lewis
& Joe Young
HERE IN MY ARMS
Lorenz Hart
& Richard Rodgers
HILLS OF HOME, THE
Floride Calhoun
& Oscar J. Fox

I LOVE MY BABY,
MY BABY LOVES ME
Bud Green
& Harry Warren
I MISS MY SWISS, MY SWISS
MISS MISSES ME
Abel Baer
& L. Wolfe Gilbert
I NEVER KNEW
Ted Fiorito
& Gus Kahn
I WANNA GO WHERE YOU GO,
DO WHAT YOU DO, THEN I'LL
BE HAPPY
Lew Brown, Sidney Clare
& Cliff Friend
IF YOU KNEW SUSIE, LIKE I
KNOW SUSIE
Bud DeSylva
& Joseph Meyer
I'M IN LOVE AGAIN
Cole Porter
I'M SITTING ON TOP
OF THE WORLD
Ray Henderson,
Sam M. Lewis
& Joe Young
IN THE LUXEMBOURG
GARDENS
Kathleen Lockhart Manning
JALOUSIE
Vera Bloom
& Jacob Gade
JUST A COTTAGE SMALL-BY A
WATERFALL
B. G. DeSylva
& James F. Hanley
MILENBERG JOYS
Paul Mares,
Walter Melrose,
Jelly Roll Morton
& Leon Roppolo

MOONLIGHT & ROSES
Ben Black,
Edwin H Lemare
& Neil Moret
MY YIDDISHE
MOMME
Lew Pollack
& Jack Yellen
OH, HOW I MISS
YOU TONIGHT
Benny Davis,
Joe Burke
& Mark Fisher
ONLY A ROSE
Rudolf Friml
& Brian Hooker
PADDLIN' MADELIN' HOME
Harry Woods
PAL OF MY CRADLE DAYS
Marshall Montgomery
& Al Piantadosi
REMEMBER
Irving Berlin
RIVERBOAT SHUFFLE
Hoagy Carmichael,
Irving Mills,
Dick Volynow
& additional material:
Mitchell Parish
SAVE YOUR SORROW FOR
TOMORROW
B. G. DeSylva
& Al Sherman
SHOW ME THE WAY
TO GO HOME
Irving King
SLEEPY TIME GAL
Joseph R. Alden,
Raymond B. Egan,
Ange Lorenzo
& Richard A. Whiting
SOME DAY
Rudolf Friml
& Brian Hooker

SOMETIMES I'M HAPPY
Irving Caesar,
Clifford Grey
& Vincent Youmans
SONG OF THE VAGABONDS
Rudolf Friml
& Brian Hooker
SUNNY
Jerome Kern,
Otto Harbach
& Oscar Hammerstein, 2nd
SWEET AND LOW-DOWN
George Gershwin
& Ira Gershwin
SWEET GEORGIA BROWN
Ben Bernie,
Kenneth Casey
& Maceo Pinkard
THAT CERTAIN FEELING
George Gershwin
& Ira Gershwin
THAT CERTAIN PARTY
Walter Donaldson
& Gus Kahn
UKELELE LADY
Gus Kahn
& Richard A. Whiting
WHERE THE LAZY DAISIES
GROW
Cliff Friend
WHO
Jerome Kern,
Otto Harbach
& Oscar Hammerstein, 2nd
WHY DO I LOVE YOU
Bud G. DeSylva,
George Gershwin
& Ira Gershwin
YEARNING JUST FOR YOU
Joe Burke
& Benny Davis
YES SIR, THAT'S MY BABY
Walter Donaldson
& Gus Kahn

BASIC CONSIDERATIONS
IN MUSIC LICENSING

SUMMARY

FEE STRUCTURE

VALUE OF THE SONG

**THE IMPORTANCE OF THE SONG IN RELATION
TO ITS INTENDED USE**

1. Why Is the Song Being Used?

2. How Will the Song Be Rendered?

3. Will Any Changes Be Made?

4. Will the Song's Title Be Used for a Special Purpose?

THE SCOPE OF THE INTENDED USE

1. What Media Will the License Cover?

2. Through What Distribution Channels Will the
   Media Be Distributed?

3. How Long Will the Use Be Permitted By the License?

4. Where Will the Use Be Permitted?

5. Who Else May Exercise a Similar Privilege to Use the Work?

**COMMON TERMS AND CONDITIONS REGARDING
FEES AND PAYMENT**

1. Advances

2. Cross-Collateralization

3. Bonus

4. Payment and Accounting

5. Audit Privileges

6. Reserves Against Returns

7. Most Favored Nations

COMMONLY USED BOILERPLATE TERMS AND CONDITIONS

1. Representations and Warranties

2. Indemnification

3. Assignment Clauses

4. Benefit of Successors and Assigns

5. Exclusion of All Other Express or Implied Warranties

6. Exclusion of Consequential Damages

7. Limitation of Liability

8. Severability

9. Cure Period

10 Entire Agreement or Integration Provision

11. Modifications and Amendments

12. Waiver

13. No Partnership or Agency

14. No Third Party Beneficiaries

15. Choice of Law

16. Choice of Forum

17. Confidentiality of Agreement

18. Notice

19. Advice of Legal Counsel

20. Attorneys Fees

21. Recitals

22. Counterparts

23. Captions

24. Gender

25. Effective Date

AFFILIATED COMPANY PROBLEM

GENERAL ADVICE TO MUSIC COPYRIGHT OWNERS — ALWAYS ENCOURAGE ACTIVITY IN THE SONG

GENERAL ADVICE TO PERSONS SEEKING TO CLEAR LICENSES — FULLY DISCLOSE ALL THE USES YOU MIGHT CONCEIVABLY MAKE OF THE MUSIC

CHAPTER 5

BASIC CONSIDERATIONS
IN MUSIC LICENSING

This chapter provides an outline of the basic considerations that are common among the considerations relevant in granting and clearing the several forms of licenses discussed in this book. The basic considerations or factors in determining the provisions of most music licenses are:

1. The fee structure, whether it is established by custom, negotiation, or statute;

2. The value of the song, taking into consideration its popularity, historical significance, and overall quality;

3. The importance of the song in relation to its intended use; and,

4. The scope of the intended use.

Each of these factors will be discussed generally in this chapter and then in more detail, and as they relate specifically to the various forms of licenses discussed, in the chapters which follow.

FEE STRUCTURE

License fees are structured in various ways. Ideally, copyright owners would like to negotiate a fee each time their music is played, taking into consideration all of the factors relevant to determining the fee structure and the appropriate fee to be charged, but certain practical and legal circumstances require that certain customary or compulsory fee structures be employed.

For certain kinds of uses, such as the public performance of music in restaurants, theaters, concert halls, and nightclubs, and broadcast on radio and television, it would be impractical for music publishers to negotiate a separate license for each and every performance that occurs every day throughout the year. The arrangement that has evolved for structuring and collecting fees for public performances is the *blanket license,* discussed more fully in Chapter 15. Once a year, the performance rights societies issue a blanket license to each concert hall, restaurant, and other venue where the music in their repertoires is likely to be played, whether live or by use of a recording, and to every radio and television station that broadcasts programs containing their copyrighted music. The fees collected under blanket licenses are then divided up by the performance rights societies and distributed to their music publisher and songwriter members in accordance with a formula that attempts to allocate the funds on the basis of how much each song was performed during the year. Though they have the opportunity, owners of restaurants and nightclubs rarely negotiate the fees established by the performing rights societies for public performance licenses, but, considering the blanket nature of the license—permitting the performance of one or more of any of the hundreds of thousands of compositions in a performance rights society's repertoire as often as the user desires to perform them during the year—the fees charged are reasonable and it is generally not worth the effort to negotiate them.

In addition to practical constraints, various legal constraints dictate the types of fees and fee structures that are employed in licensing music. For example, a section of the U.S. copyright law commonly called the compulsory license provision,[1] which is more fully described in Chapter 7, compels a music copyright owner to license his music for use in certain audio recordings at a specific per copy fee that is set forth in the copyright law, as revised from time to time by the Copyright Royalty Tribunal. Where the law establishes a maximum fee, as it does here, there is little room for creativity and negotiation in granting and clearing licenses.

Also, certain court judgments, called *consent decrees,* agreed upon between performance rights societies and the U.S. government, require

---

[1] 17 U.S.C. Sec. 115.

that permission to perform music in U.S. movie theatres be granted to film producers at the time the producers receive authorization to record the music in the film. This effectively requires licenses that would otherwise be negotiated by performance rights societies on a blanket basis with motion picture theaters to be licensed to the motion picture producers directly by the music copyright owners on a one time flat fee basis.

In some cases, copyright owners simply do not have the *right* upon which a license may be based. For example, though the copyright law confers upon the copyright owner an exclusive right of *public* performance, it does not confer an exclusive right of *private* performance. Accordingly, the copyright owner cannot require that a fee be paid every time you play a compact disk in your home or insert an audiocassette of copyrighted music in your car stereo. Instead, the fees derived from the use of music in recordings are based on the number of copies of the recording that are made and distributed and the fees are charged to the record manufacturers at the time the recordings are made, rather than when the music is played by the customer.

Thus, the particular structure used for a particular form of license can be influenced by one or more legal or practical considerations. In certain cases, the fee structure is determined merely by industry custom, which can be varied by negotiation. Fees are customarily structured on a flat fee, per copy fee, percentage of revenue, or blanket fee basis. Each of these fee structures will be discussed in the context in which they arise under the several forms of licenses discussed in the following chapters.

VALUE OF THE SONG

Whatever the fee structure, songs with higher inherent values can generally command higher fees for their use. A music copyright owner's ability to determine the value of a particular song will vary depending on his experience and access to information about the value of other musical compositions. The value of a song has both quantitative and qualitative factors, both adding up to the present value of the licensing revenue the song is expected to generate during the remainder of the life of the copyright.

The quantitative factors include how much the song has earned in licensing revenues in the past and how much others might be presently willing to pay for the copyright. It also includes the earnings potential of the song in relation to the earnings potential of other songs, particularly those in its genre. A music publisher with thousands of songs in its catalog and with years of experience in licensing music is likely to have access to much of the information necessary to adequately evaluate these factors. Because of its access to such information, a large music publisher is in a much better position than a typical licensee, songwriter, practicing lawyer, or small-scale music publisher to determine the quantitative value of a song for purposes of determining the appropriate license fee for a given use.

The qualitative factors include the popularity of the song, the demographics of the listeners who are responsible for the song's popularity, the historical significance of the song, and overall quality of the song. Characteristics that help one understand these qualitative factors include, (1) a sound knowledge of music, whether in its writing, arranging or recording, (2) a person's experience with the song, either as having been "on the scene," either as a listener or as one working directly in the music business, when the song first became popular, and (3) a person's experience in having seen numerous examples of music of the same genre applied to a variety of uses. An appreciation of these qualitative factors is significant in determining the importance of the song in relation to its intended use. A large music publisher may have no special advantages over persons seeking to clear a license or others in evaluating these qualitative factors.

THE IMPORTANCE OF THE SONG IN RELATION TO ITS INTENDED USE

The more important the song is in relation to its intended use, the more money the copyright owner can charge in exchange for the license. Determining the importance of the song in relation to its intended use, depends on variety of facts. Before quoting a license fee, the music copyright owner should ask many questions of the potential licensee about the intended use of the song, and the person seeking to clear the license should be prepared with as many answers as possible.

1. Why Is the Song Being Used?

One question is whether the use will be primarily for a theatrical purpose or a promotional purpose. The purpose of the use may be purely to enhance the entertainment values of another work, such as when the use is in a motion picture, television program, television series, or musical play. By contrast, the purpose may be promotional in the sense of promoting some product, service, or the image of a particular company. There are special cases where the purpose of the audiovisual work is to feature the whole song itself, as is the case of a music video, in which case the purpose may be both theatrical (i.e., to entertain) and promotional, in the sense of promoting the recording artist or the song.

2. How Will the Song Be Rendered?

Another issue is whether the use will include a vocal rendition or whether the use will be merely instrumental. Other questions include whether the music will be used as background music, foreground music, or music to help tell a story.

3. Will Any Changes Be Made?

Still another question is whether the user intends to make any changes in the musical work. A licensee might ask for several kinds of changes, including:

1. A change in lyrics, for either purposes of parody, drama, or product endorsement.

2. A change in the fundamental character of the music, such as when a full-length version is edited down to suit special needs.

3. A translation of the lyrics into a foreign language.

Under most standard songwriter music publishing contracts, the songwriter grants to the publisher the right to change the lyrics and to authorize others to do so. However, some songwriters have negotiated provisions that give the songwriter the right to approve any changes to the work. Even if the contract does not contain such a provision, it is still good practice for the music publisher to consult with the songwriter before authorizing any changes in lyrics, particularly when the changes may be in the nature of a product endorsement or have some political significance, such as use in a political campaign. The publisher and the songwriter should weigh the advantages of the license fee, performance credits, and general activity the use provides for the song against the possible damage to the long term value of the song from an unsavory use. If changes to lyrics are approved, the exact nature of the new lyrics should be specified in the license; otherwise final approval should be withheld until the exact lyrics are determined.

4. Will the Song's Title Be Used for a Special Purpose?

Another question may be whether the song's title will be used for any special purpose. For example, the licensee may be intending to use the title as the title of his motion picture, television show, or product, such as a new brand of perfume. Note that song titles are not copyrightable; nor are they protectable as trademarks. However, there are some court decisions that indicate some recognition of rights in song titles akin to trademark protection, where the courts are trying to prevent unfair competition or someone from "palming off" their movie or product as somehow being associated with or endorsed by the writers or owners of the musical composition.[2] Use of the title should be indicative of the importance of the song in relation to its intended use and some consideration should be given to charging an additional fee for its use.

Specific examples of each of the foregoing considerations will be explored in the chapters which follow.

THE SCOPE OF THE INTENDED USE

Music copyright owners should avoid issuing a license which allows the licensee to do more with the song than the licensee originally intends. It is therefore important for the copyright owner to determine, before

---

[2] *Tomlin v. Walt Disney Productions,* 18 Cal.App.3d 226, 235, 96 Cal.Rptr. 118 (1971).

terms are quoted, just what the licensee intends to do with the song, where he intends to do it, and for how long. The license should be limited appropriately in all these respects.

Persons seeking to clear a license should attempt to obtain a license having as broad a scope as possible. Where this is not possible, the licensee should attempt to negotiate up front a series of options for additional uses that would otherwise require an additional license at a later time. It is therefore important for the licensee to tell the copyright owner up front everything he intends to do with the song.

Factors which comprise the scope of a music license include:

- the media in which the music will be embodied

- the term of the license

- the territory in which the use will be exercised

- the exclusivity required, if any

- other terms and conditions

Each of these factors will be discussed in general terms below and at greater length in succeeding chapters.

1. What Media Will the License Cover?

The form of license (e.g., mechanical license, synchronization license, print license, etc.) that is appropriate for the requested use will depend upon the *media* for which the use is intended.

The media is often described with reference to the particular kind of physical copy in which the music is embodied and the compilation of materials with which the music is included. Examples of media include sheet music, songbooks or music folios, phonograph recordings, such as audiocassettes, long-playing albums and compact discs, motion pictures, television programs, videocassettes, laser video discs, music videos, television commercials, radio commercials, syndicated radio programs, published books, consumer products, such as music boxes, dolls, and other items, computer programs, audiovisual educational programs, and other media "now known or hereafter devised."

2. Through What Distribution Channels Will the Media Be Distributed?

Determining the media to be covered by the license involves a consideration of not only the physical media in which the music is to be embodied and any accompanying materials, but also the means by which the music is distributed, exhibited, or communicated to the public. For example, the media may be broadly defined as "motion pictures." But motion pictures may be distributed through exhibition in movie theatres, broadcast on television, and on videocassettes and laser discs intended for home distribution. Television programs may be broadcast on local television stations, over television networks, by cable, by direct broadcast satellite, or by other forms of televised or broadcast distribution. Distribution may also be categorized by the manner in which television station operators are compensated—e.g., free TV, subscription channels, or pay-per-view channels. Music, of course, may also be the subject of live performances, such as those rendered in a nightclub, Broadway, or other stage production, or live performance that is broadcast on radio or television. As we shall see in Chapters 9 (Synchronization Licenses) and Chapter 10 (Videogram Licenses), the terms of the licenses for the same motion picture or television production will vary considerably, depending upon the means of distribution.

3. How Long Will the Use Be Permitted By the License?

How long a use is permitted by the license is referred to as the *term*, or duration, of the license. The term of the license will often depend upon the type of license being granted. The music copyright owner should almost always prefer to restrict the license's duration to the shortest possible time, although the term of the license will normally be dictated by the custom and practice normally associated with similar licenses. Restricting the term of the license will allow the copyright owner to collect an additional fee upon its expiration if renewal of the license is desired by the licensee.

Persons seeking to clear a license should attempt to obtain a license having as long a duration as possible. Where the copyright owner insists upon limiting the term, the licensee should attempt to negotiate, up front, a series of options to renew the term of the license, offering an additional fee payable upon the exercise of each renewal period. Even if the renewal fees, considered at the time the license is entered into, appear unreasonably high, by obtaining options to renew, the licensee will at least be assured that a license to extend the term will be readily available.

4. Where Will the Use Be Permitted?

Music licenses typically contain a restriction on countries, or regions within countries, in which the licensee may perform, exhibit, broadcast or distribute copies of the music. This restriction is referred to as the *territory* of the license.

The territory in which the licensee may exercise his privileges under the license is normally something less than *worldwide*. As with restricting how long the license lasts, the music copyright owner will generally prefer to restrict the territory of the license to the smallest geographic area consistent with the licensee's actual needs. Each additional territory will command an additional fee. Restricting the territory of the license will allow the music copyright owner to collect an additional fee if the licensee later determines that he would like to extend his use to other territories. The music copyright owner's leverage to charge a premium fee increases after the licensee has gone to great expense to incorporate his music into a work, particularly where it would be expensive, inconvenient, or impossible to replace the music with a less expensive alternative.

In many cases, the licensee will not require a license for other territories, such as, for example, where a license to use music in a radio advertisement for a local drugstore limits the territory to the region in which the drugstore finds all its customers. However, a licensee may wish to negotiate options to expand the territory to those areas in which it is likely the work will be used. For example, where a company desires to test a commercial advertisement for one of its national brands in a limited region of the country, the company may wish to pay only for the use of the music in the test region, while at the same time negotiate an option to expand the territory to the rest of the country for eventual network broadcast. The licensee's leverage is at its height before he commits to use the music or makes any substantial expenditures toward that end. A licensee, therefore, is advised to obtain options for additional territories wherever it is known that such licenses might be required. It is probably a good idea to obtain such options even when the likelihood of expanding the territory is remote.

The territory may be restricted to specific countries, such as "the United States," and "the United States and Canada." Licenses may be unrestricted in territory, as what is intended by the use of the term "worldwide," although it has been suggested the word "worldwide" would not cover use on space stations. With this in mind, a licensee might consider whether the term "universe" should be used in its place, or whether—with tongue in cheek —the term, "solar system" would be sufficient for most licenses. (We have seen licenses that employ the terms "universe" and "universe-wide" in place of "worldwide," so the reader should not think this idea is far fetched). To avoid ambiguities, names of actual countries should be used—Africa, Asia, and the Caribbean are not countries.

Certain contractual and organizational considerations may affect how a music publisher determines the territory of the license. Large music publishers may have policies with respect to the ability of its U.S. headquarters to negotiate on behalf of its international affiliates and subsidiaries for the licensing of use in territories outside of the United States. These policies may actually be formally governed by the terms and conditions of the sub-publication agreements between a United States publisher and its international affiliates or subsidiaries. Such policies and contractual terms may vary depending on the type of license. For example, motion picture synchronization licenses are generally negotiated centrally for worldwide use, but licenses for use in connection with product advertising may require negotiation on a country by country basis with local publishing affiliates.

Certain legal considerations may also affect how you define the territory. For example, European Community (EC) regulations that prohibit contracts that restrict the free flow of goods among member countries may invalidate licenses that attempt to provide exclusivity with respect to specified countries within the EC. The solution may be to simply define the territory as "member countries of the European Community." (A publisher might consider problems arising with respect to existing licenses and exclusive publishing arrangements as the membership in the EC changes over time.)

The license may also be limited to certain areas within the United States, such as "the State of New York." This, however, might not be acceptable to a licensee who intends to use the song in television or radio broadcasts. Radio waves don't normally respect state lines. Accordingly, the territory can be defined by some regional designation, such as "the greater New York City area," "Southern California," or "the mid-Atlantic states."

5. Who Else May Exercise a Similar Privilege to Use the Work?

Exclusivity, as we have seen, is a right to exclude or prevent others from doing some act. Granting exclusivity, therefore, is something more than merely granting permission, or a license, to another to do something he or she would not otherwise have the privilege of doing without your permission; it involves granting to another a claim or right under the copyright, an actual piece of property, which is a form of subdivision of the copyright.

Exclusive rights are, of course, granted in connection with a grant of an entire copyright (in which case all exclusive rights under the copyright are granted at one time, less any exclusive rights that are reserved to the original owner). Leaving aside that special circumstance, exclusivity is rarely granted in music revenue transactions, except in connection with the grant of exclusive print rights for printed sheet music or in certain cases where the publisher agrees, in connection with a license to use the music in commercial advertising, to a restriction on licensing the song for limited periods of time in connection with products that compete with the products of the licensee. For example, a music publisher may license the use of the song, *Hooray for Hollywood* for a one year period in connection with television advertising of the Bank of Hollywood and may agree not to license the same song to another bank for advertising banking services in the Los Angeles area for the one year period of the license.

Other than for such limited commercial uses, or other extraordinary uses, such as use of the song's title or story line, music publishers should generally avoid granting exclusivity, because earnings from other sources can be significantly curtailed by broadly applied exclusivity provisions. If exclusivity is granted in the appropriate cases, the operative language should be very carefully defined.

COMMON TERMS AND CONDITIONS
REGARDING FEES AND PAYMENT

Each particular kind of license will often require special provisions depending upon the nature of the distribution involved, the type of payment method agreed upon, or other provisions negotiated by the parties.

1. Advances

An *advance* is a lump-sum payment received in consideration for a grant of rights or license that is *recoupable* (i.e., deductible), by the person who paid the advance, from future royalties that would otherwise be payable to the person who received the advance. Advances are often paid *up front*, such as upon signing of the agreement, but also may be paid on a periodic basis, regardless of whether sufficient royalties have been earned during the period in which the advance is paid.

Advances may be paid for a variety of reasons. A publisher often pays an advance to make sure the person receiving it, such as a songwriter, does not "starve" while he is performing services for the publisher. A songwriter may insist upon receiving an advance to make sure the publisher is making an investment sufficient to provide an incentive for the publisher to recoup that investment by making the proper efforts to promote the songwriter's works.

Advances are usually not *returnable*, meaning that if the advances turn out to be greater than the amount of royalties ever earned from sales, the person who received the advance never has to pay the unearned balance of the advance back to the person who paid it; in other words, an advance is not like a loan. Such advances are generally referred to as, "non-returnable, recoupable advances." However, advances may be returnable if the person who receives the advance fails to perform material provisions of the agreement under which he has received the advance.

2. Cross-Collateralization

Music publishers, recording companies, and other types of publishers who customarily have royalty obligations to artists and writers will nearly always be certain to *cross-collateralize* all contracts under which they pay advances to a particular artist. Contracts that are cross-collateralized are those under which royalties earned under one contract are used to recoup advances earned under another contract. You can spot cross-collateralization by looking for the following *Three Little Words*: "or any other." For example, the concept of cross-collateralization is contained in the following provision:

> Advances paid hereunder may be recouped from royalties earned under this *or any other* agreement between the parties.

Under certain circumstances, cross-collateralization will defeat one of the primary reasons artists seek advances. If the purpose of the advance is to give the person paying the advance the proper incentive to promote a particular song, allowing the cross-collateralization of that advance against royalties payable under a contract for another song, which by reason of its popularity might sell itself, will defeat the purpose of the original advance. Accordingly, a party might reasonably insist that the cross-collateralization provision be stricken from the agreement.

3. Bonus

A *bonus* is a lump-sum payment that is not recoupable from royalties or any other payments earned under an agreement or other agreements. Bonuses are rare, with publishers almost always insisting on recouping lump sum payments from royalties, even where the potential recoupment is remote. However, a publisher may offer a "signing" bonus to an artist whose business he is trying to attract.

4. Payment and Accounting

Licenses that call for a flat fee payable by the licensee upon signing of the license will not require extensive provisions regarding the means of payment and accounting procedures. However, the person clearing a license requiring payment *upon signing* or *upon execution*, should negotiate a change to the payment provision to allow the licensee a reasonable period of time, such as 7 days after execution, to remit payment.

Licenses that contain provisions for the payment of a royalty, such as a percentage of net revenues from sales of copies of the music, will contain sophisticated provisions relating to how and when the copyright owner will be paid the royalties. For example, payments are usually expected on a quarterly basis, within some reasonable period after the end of each calendar quarter in which there are revenues derived from the work. A written royalty statement detailing the sources of the revenues upon which the royalty is based commonly accompanies the payment.

A payment provision drafted in favor of a licensee required to pay royalties might be drafted as follows:

> Licensee will compute the total composite royalties earned by Owner pursuant to this agreement quarterly within forty-five (45) days after the end of each quarter, and will deliver to Owner a royalty statement for each such period together with the net amount of royalties computed in accordance with this section, if any, which shall be payable after deducting any and all unrecouped advances and chargeable costs under this agreement or any other agreement between Owner and Licensee. No statement will be rendered to Owner for any quarterly period for which the cumulative balance due Owner is less than $10.00.

5. Audit Privileges

In any contract providing for the payment of royalties based upon the number of units of a work sold or the gross or net revenues derived from sales of a work, the copyright owner will typically require an *audit privilege*, which is the privilege to inspect the books and records of the licensee relating to the revenues derived from the licensed work. A licensee should negotiate some reasonable limitations on these privileges, such as a provision requiring advance notice of an audit, and requiring that the audit be conducted during normal business hours, only once a year, and at the expense of the copyright owner. The copyright owner will normally insist that if the audit reveals that the licensee underpaid the required license fee by more than 5-10%, then the licensee will pay for the costs of the audit. All licenses that contain audit provisions should also contain a provision that obligates the licensee to maintain accurate books and records in the first place. A number of accounting firms specialize in performing audits of such records, and a publisher should consider having its licensees audited on a periodic basis to, as the saying goes, "keep them honest."

An audit provision drafted in favor of a licensee whose books and records may potentially be made subject to inspection might be drafted as follows:

> Upon at least fifteen (15) days prior written notice to Licensee and at Owner's sole cost and expense, Owner, or a nationally recognized certified public accountant on Owner's behalf, shall have the right once each year to inspect and audit such of Licensee's business books and records as may reasonably be necessary for Owner to verify the accuracy of any royalty statement rendered by Licensee within the twelve (12) month period immediately preceding the date of the inspection. The information contained in a royalty statement shall be conclusively deemed correct and binding upon Owner, resulting in the loss of all further audit privileges with respect to such statement, unless specifically challenged by written notice from Owner within twelve (12) months from the date such royalty statement was delivered by Licensee. Any inspection of Licensee's books and records pursuant to this section shall be conducted by Owner at Licensee's premises, only during Licensee's normal business hours, under Licensee's supervision and in a manner which does not interfere with Licensee's business operations. Owner shall specify, at least fifteen (15) days in advance of any inspection, the list of items that Owner desires to inspect. Owner shall keep all information learned as a result of such inspection in strict confidence.

6. Reserves Against Returns

A licensee obligated to pay royalties should attempt to negotiate the ability to hold a *reserve against returns*. When a licensee makes sales of copies of a work containing licensed music, such as a recording or a videogram, the licensee may expect that some of the sales during a quarter will be returned during a subsequent quarter. (Alluding to the customary designation of *gold*, as a record which sells a million copies, and *platinum,* as a record which sells two million, there circulates an old joke in the record business that a certain artist's album shipped gold and returned platinum!) When a licensee holds a reserve against returns, he deducts a certain percentage (e.g., 10%) from the royalties he would otherwise be required to pay for sales of the work for a particular quarter, and holds on to that deduction in anticipation that there might later be a return of 10% of the records sold during that quarter.

A provision permitting a licensee to hold a reserve against returns might look like this:

> Licensee may retain as a reserve against subsequent charges, credits or returns, a reasonable portion of payable royalties.

The importance of holding a reserve may depend on the licensee's feeling about the copyright owner's willingness and ability to reimburse the licensee in the event of an overpayment due to a subsequent return of sales. The copyright owner, if he is willing to accept this provision at all, would be wise to negotiate a limitation on the provision, requiring that any such reserve will be liquidated within some reasonable period of time after the quarter in which it is withheld. For example, a licensee might be required to liquidate, or pay reserves previously held, to the copyright owner in the quarter immediately following the quarter in which they were held. The copyright owner would also be advised to limit the percentage of the amount to be reserved to an amount that is reasonably related to the amount of sales returns the licensee actually tends to experience for similar kinds of works. For example, the amount of reserves against returns withheld in any one quarter could be limited to 10 or 15%.

Limitations on a licensee's right to hold a reserve against returns might be drafted as follows:

> Licensee may retain as a reserve against subsequent charges, credits or returns, a reasonable portion of payable royalties; provided, however, that such reserve shall be limited to 10% of royalties payable during a quarter and shall be liquidated in the quarterly accounting period immediately following that in which it was retained.

7. Most Favored Nations

A copyright owner who is unsure of what fee to charge, or even how to structure the fee, will sometimes ask that he be paid a license fee that is no less favorable than the fee received for the use of any other song featured in the licensee's work. Such a provision is commonly called a *most favored nations* clause. Most favored nations clauses are often used as a crutch by those who don't know how to analyze a use, don't have any experience with licensing for the particular use (and therefore have a fear of making a bad deal), or don't want to make the effort to analyze the particular use.

A person seeking to clear the license who is reluctant to agree to such a provision should be prepared to argue that the song for which he seeks a license has significantly less importance than other songs in the work. In other words, it makes no sense to compare *apples* and *oranges* when setting the terms of the license. If a licensee does agree to a most favored nations clause, a favorite negotiating technique may present itself to the licensee when clearing permission to use other songs in the same work: "I can't give you a higher fee, Mr. Copyright Owner, because giving you a higher fee would require me, under the most favored nations clauses that I've signed with other copyright owners, to raise all the other fees, and that I just cannot afford to do!"

COMMONLY USED BOILERPLATE TERMS AND CONDITIONS

This section will summarize some of the standard provisions, sometimes referred to as *legal boilerplate* provisions, contained in many long form license agreements.

1. Representations and Warranties

Most long-form license agreements will contain a series of representations or warranties intended to give the licensee some comfort that he will be able to exercise without hindrance the privilege for which he is receiving permission.

A *representation* is a statement as to the existence or nonexistence of a fact or a state of mind which another relies upon in entering into a contract. For example, a copyright owner may represent "that it has the right to grant this license" and "that the work does not infringe any copyrights of another." A copyright owner may also make a representation as to his state of mind, such as when he represents "that, to the best of my knowledge, the work does not infringe any copyrights of another." A *best of knowledge* representation is significantly less meaningful than a representation as to the existence of a fact and will not always be acceptable to assignees or licensees.

A *warranty* is an assurance that certain facts or conditions exist and will continue to exist during the term of the license. A person negotiating a license on behalf of a licensee should request that the term "warrant" be added to provisions containing representations of the licensor. For example, the copyright owner should "represent *and warrant* that the work does not infringe any copyrights of another." The addition of the word "warrant" would enable the licensee to add, in an action for a breach of contract arising from a misrepresentation, a cause of action for *breach of warranty*, which could provide the licensee with some additional remedies and advantages in any litigation arising out of the licensor's breach of the agreement.

Note, however, music licensors are generally reluctant to modify their boilerplate language without legal advice, and where the cost of such legal advice may approach or exceed the license fee being charged for the license, it is unlikely that any change would even be considered. Should a licensee find some resistance in making changes, the licensee should weigh the business risks involved. Normally, it is not worth expending much time or expense to negotiate for these changes and being unable to negotiate such a change is certainly not worth walking away from a license unless you are aware of some specific facts that may justify having a strong set of warranties and representations.

Music licensors typically want to give as few warranties and representations as possible. Warranty provisions providing only minimal comfort are quite common and the following is a good example:

> Publisher warrants only that it has the right to grant this license and this license is given and accepted without any other representations, warranty or recourse, express or implied, except for Publisher's agreement to repay the consideration for this license if said warranty shall be breached with respect thereto. In no event shall the total liability of Publisher in any case exceed the amount of consideration received by it hereunder.

Licensees typically desire a little more than that and typically request warranties and representations sufficient to assure that the work does not infringe copyrights or other rights of another. Those who are receiving a full transfer of copyright might desire certain additional warranties, such as those contained in the following provision:

Owner hereby warrants and represents to Company that Owner has the right to enter into this agreement and to grant to Company all of the rights granted herein, and that the exercise by Company of any and all of the rights granted to Company in this agreement will not violate or infringe upon any common law or statutory rights of any person, firm or corporation including, without limitation, contractual rights, copyrights, and rights of privacy. Owner further warrants that the rights granted herein are free and clear of any claims, demands, liens or encumbrances.

When the person who is transferring a copyright in a newly created work was the one who authored the work, the following set of warranties and representations may be required:

Composer hereby warrants and represents that the Composition is an original work, that neither the Composition nor any part thereof infringes upon the title, literary or musical property or copyright of any other work nor the statutory, common law or other rights (including rights of privacy or publicity) of any person, firm or corporation or violates any applicable criminal statute, that he is the sole writer and composer and the sole owner of the Composition and of all the rights therein, that he has not sold, assigned, transferred, hypothecated or mortgaged any right, title or interest in or to the Composition or any part thereof or any of the rights herein conveyed, that he has not made or entered into any agreement with any other person, firm or corporation affecting the Composition or any right, title or interest therein or in the copyright thereof, that no person, firm or corporation other than Composer has or has had claims or has claimed any right, title or interest in or to the Composition or any part thereof, any use thereof or any copyright therein, that the Composition has never been published, and that Composer has full right, power and authority to make this present instrument of sale and transfer.

Music publishing agreements will also require the songwriter to warrant that he or she is the "sole author," providing an assurance that no one will come forth to claim to be the author or co-author of the work, and that the work was "original," meaning it was original with the songwriter and not copied from the work of another or from a work in the public domain.

If the copyright owner is assigning an exclusive right under the copyright, the assignee will want additional warranties such as the following:

> Owner shall not during the term of this Agreement do any act or authorize, license or knowingly permit any third party (other than a party authorized or licensed by Company) to do any act which would in any way derogate from or violate the exclusive right, license and privilege granted to Company by this Agreement. The parties expressly acknowledge that the Compositions and all rights granted and to be granted to Company hereunder are of a special, unique and intellectual character which gives them peculiar value, and that in the event of a breach by Owner of any term, condition, warranty, representation or agreement hereunder, Company will be caused irreparable injury. Owner expressly agrees that in the event of any such breach, Company shall be entitled to injunctive and other equitable relief or damages, in addition to any other rights and remedies available to it, and Company shall have the right to recoup any damages from any sums which may thereafter become due and payable to Owner hereunder.

2. Indemnification

Representations and warranties are generally given additional force by an indemnification provision. The indemnification provision makes it clear that the entire financial burden incurred as a result of a breach of any representation or warranty set forth in the agreement will fall on the person making those representations and warranties. The following is an example of a short, but comprehensive indemnification provision:

> Owner agrees to indemnify and hold Licensee harmless from any claim, demand, suit, action, proceeding, prosecution, damage, expense (including reasonable attorneys' fees), liability or loss of any kind or nature arising from or out of any claim asserted against Licensee which is inconsistent with any of the warranties, covenants or representations made by Owner herein.

A promise to *hold harmless* another against claims made and actions filed by third parties means that the person making the promise will bear all the expenses of defending the claim or lawsuit, but will also mean he or she will control the defense of the matter, unless contrary terms are specifically provided. Often, an assignee or licensee will not feel comfortable with the assignor or licensor maintaining control over the handling of the claim or lawsuit, particularly where the assignor or licensor is not wealthy or financially stable. Accordingly, publishing and licensing agreements will often clarify the rights and obligations of the parties with respect to any lawsuits filed concerning those matters covered by representations and warranties. For example, a standard publishing agreement between a songwriter and a music publisher may provide that the music publisher has (i) the privilege to defend itself against any claim or lawsuit, (ii) the privilege to choose its own legal counsel to do so, (iii) the privilege to settle any such claim or lawsuit on such terms as it deems appropriate, (iv) the right to reimbursement from the songwriter for any payments made as a result of a settlement or final judgment entered against the publisher, (v) the right to reimbursement of attorneys fees and litigation costs incurred to defend the matter, whether or not such defense is successful, and (vi) the privilege to withhold any royalties and apply them to cover any obligations of the writer with respect to the claim or lawsuit.

A songwriter who has the bargaining leverage to vary such terms should attempt to eliminate any responsibility for mere "claims" and limit the indemnity to "final judgments." Because of their size, music publishers often attract lawsuits merely because of their "deep pockets," and songwriters should not be responsible for nuisance suits. If the publisher has a license from the writer to make derivative works, as they often do, the indemnity should not apply to the extent publisher added material or edited the work. In fact, the songwriter should require the publisher to provide an indemnity regarding any materials supplied to the writer or any materials added over which the writer had no control. For example, the following might be added to the writer's indemnification provision:

> Publisher similarly indemnifies and holds Writer harmless as to material furnished by Publisher for use by Writer hereunder or material added or changes made by Publisher.

A songwriter with great bargaining leverage may request that he be given the option to defend any lawsuits with counsel of his own choosing, at his own expense, provided that if he does, the publisher may participate in the defense with counsel of its choosing and at its expense. The contours of "participating in the defense" can be problematic; generally, it is the person who "controls" the defense who makes the decisions in litigation.

Because any settlement will eventually come out of the songwriter's pocket a songwriter may request that any settlements be made only with his consent, to make sure the publisher does not settle upon unreasonable terms. Publishers will not normally permit this, because it has the deep pockets and may not be able to collect from the songwriter for many years, if at all. A possible compromise to make sure the publisher has a good incentive to settle upon reasonable terms is to concede that the publisher has the sole right to settle, but require that the publisher be responsible for paying some percentage, perhaps 50%, of any settlement.

Publishers will want to withhold any payments due to the writer during the pendancy of any claim or litigation. The writer should seek to curtail the amount that may be withheld to a percentage, place a dollar ceiling on the amount, or limit length of time during which moneys may be withheld with respect to any particular claim. If the publisher withholds any money, the money should go into escrow; this is to protect the writer's money in the event the publisher goes bankrupt.

3. Assignment Clauses

A copyright owner will generally require that any assignment of the license be subject to the copyright owner's consent. The following is a typical provision governing restricting the assignment of a license:

> This license is personal to Licensee and may not be assigned or transferred without Owner's prior written consent. No such transfer or assignment shall become effective unless and until the transferee or assignee shall deliver to Owner a written agreement assuming the further performance of Licensee's obligations hereunder, and no such transfer or assignment shall relieve Licensee of any obligation hereunder. However, Licensee may enter into sublicenses within the Territory to the extent necessary to permit the uses authorized by this license.

The following provision is a stronger, more complete restriction on a party's ability to assign its rights or delegate its obligations under an agreement:

> Licensee may not assign this Agreement or any of its rights or obligations hereunder (including without limitation rights and duties of performance) to any third party or entity, and this Agreement may not be involuntarily assigned or assigned by operation of law, without the prior written consent of Owner, which consent shall be given or withheld by Owner in the sole exercise of its discretion.

The restriction on assignments *by operation of law* is intended to require permission even when two corporations combine by *merger*—a circumstance which does not necessarily involve the transfer of an agreement from one party to another. In a merger, the parties combine to form one entity.[3]

A music publisher engaged in the merger or acquisition of another publisher should, in connection with its due diligence investigation prior to the closing of the transaction, consider the assignment provisions of all material songwriter agreements of the publisher being acquired. For example, the acquiring publisher may come across an assignment provision such as the following, which was excerpted from the 1978 version of the standard Songwriter's Guild Agreement (formerly, AGAC) between songwriters and publishers:

> 18. Except to the extent herein otherwise expressly provided, the Publisher shall not sell, transfer, assign, convey, encumber or otherwise dispose of the composition or the copyright or copyrights secured thereon without the prior written consent of the Writer. The Writer has been induced to enter into this contract in reliance upon the value to him of the personal service and ability of the Publisher in the exploitation of the composition, and by reason thereof it is the intention of the parties and the essence of the relationship between them that the rights herein granted to the Publisher shall remain with the Publisher and that the same shall not pass to any other person including, without limitations, successors to or

---

[3] Despite our experience with mergers and an apparently sound etymological basis to support the suggestion, the word *merger,* as a friend of ours has suggested, was not formed from a combination of the words *marriage* and *murder.*

receivers or trustees of the property of the Publisher, either by act or deed of the Publisher or by operation of law, and in the event of the voluntary or involuntary bankruptcy of the Publisher, this contract shall terminate, provided, however, that the composition may be included by the Publisher in a bona fide voluntary sale of its music business or its entire catalog of musical compositions, or in a merger or consolidation of the Publisher with another corporation, in which event the Publisher shall immediately give written notice thereof to the Writer, and provided further that the composition and the copyright therein may be assigned by the Publisher to a subsidiary or affiliated company generally engaged in the music publishing business. If the Publisher is an individual, the composition may pass to a legatee or distributee as part of the inheritance of the Publisher's music business and entire catalog of musical compositions. Any such transfer or assignment, shall, however, be conditioned upon the execution and delivery by the transferee or assignee to the Writer of an agreement to be bound by and to perform all of the terms and conditions of this contract to be performed on the part of the Publisher.

While the foregoing assignment provision should not normally impose an obstacle to an acquisition or merger, the last sentence of the provision does impose the requirement that the publisher give immediate written notice of the acquisition to the writer and deliver an agreement to be bound by the terms of the writer's contract. The assignment provision of the standard AGAC Songwriter's Agreement varies slightly depending upon the year the form was printed. Where the question of assignment is relevant the applicable form should be consulted.

4.   Benefit of Successors and Assigns

If an agreement contains a restriction on the right of one party or other to assign the agreement to others, then the following provision, which is typically found in many license agreements, should have the word "permitted" included as the penultimate word as follows:

This Agreement shall be binding upon and inure to the benefit of each of the parties hereto, and except as otherwise provided herein, their respective legal successors and permitted assigns.

5. Exclusion of All Other Express or Implied Warranties

If a license agreement provides that any physical materials be transferred or loaned to a licensee in connection with the licensee's exercise
of the license, the license agreement may exclude, for the protection of
the copyright owner, all warranties that are not expressly set forth in the
license agreement, including certain warranties that may be implied by
the law in the absence of such an exclusion.

The following is an example of such a provision:

OTHER THAN THE REPRESENTATIONS AND WARRANTIES
SPECIFICALLY SET FORTH IN THIS AGREEMENT, OWNER
DOES NOT MAKE TO LICENSEE BY VIRTUE OF THIS AGREE-
MENT ANY REPRESENTATION OR WARRANTY, EXPRESS OR
IMPLIED, AND HEREBY EXPRESSLY DISCLAIMS, ANY REP-
RESENTATION OR WARRANTY OF ANY KIND WITH RESPECT
TO THE LICENSED WORK, INCLUDING WITHOUT LIMITA-
TION ANY IMPLIED WARRANTIES OF MERCHANTABILITY
AND FITNESS FOR A PARTICULAR PURPOSE. LICENSEE
SHALL NOT MAKE OR PASS ON TO ITS CUSTOMERS OR
LICENSEES ON BEHALF OF OWNER ANY WARRANTIES EX-
CLUDED HEREUNDER.

A copyright owner may desire such a provision if the physical
materials being supplied with the license may cause damage to any
property of the licensee. For example, music licensed in conjunction
with MIDI software embodying the music may cause damage to other
computer software or work product of the licensee's to the extent the
MIDI software contains "bugs" (i.e., programming errors).

Clauses providing for the exclusion of warranties and other limitations on liability are required, under the Uniform Commercial Code, and
under the Restatement of Contracts, to be *conspicuous*. It has been
common practice to place all provisions that legally require conspicuity
in all capital letters. It may be asked whether language in all capital
letters is really more conspicuous than text printed in standard upper and
lower case. Many people would agree that text printed in all caps can be
most difficult to read. Being that we are on the verge of the release of
low cost color laser printers and photocopy machines (and, soon to
follow, color-capable fax machines), perhaps a better solution would be

to print provisions that are required to be conspicuous in some conspicuous color, such as red.

6. Exclusion of Consequential Damages

Consequential damages are damages incurred by a licensee for lost profits, lost data, lost time, or lost opportunities. A copyright owner may feel that the licensee is in a better position to assume the risk or obtain insurance to cover the risk of lost business income for losses resulting from breaches of the agreement or warranties by the copyright owner. The parties would transfer the risk of such losses to the licensee with the following provision:

> NOTWITHSTANDING ANYTHING TO THE CONTRARY CONTAINED HEREIN, OWNER SHALL NOT, UNDER ANY CIRCUMSTANCES, BE LIABLE TO LICENSEE FOR CONSEQUENTIAL, INCIDENTAL OR SPECIAL DAMAGES, EVEN IF OWNER HAS BEEN APPRISED OF THE LIKELIHOOD OF SUCH DAMAGES OCCURRING.

An alert licensee would quickly realize that such a provision would render meaningless any warranties by the copyright owner that the latter has the right to enter into the agreement and that the licensed work docs not infringe upon the rights of others. Accordingly, a licensee who comes across such a provision, if he is unable to have it stricken from the agreement altogether, would be reasonable in demanding that the express warranties contained in the agreement be excluded from the applicability of this provision.

7. Limitation of Liability

For the same reason a copyright owner would wish to limit consequential damages, the copyright owner would wish to limit all other damages to the price paid for the license, and such a provision may be effected as follows:

> IN NO EVENT SHALL OWNER'S LIABILITY (WHETHER BASED ON AN ACTION OR CLAIM IN CONTRACT, TORT OR OTHERWISE) TO LICENSEE ARISING OUT OF OR RELATED TO THIS AGREEMENT OR THE TRANSACTIONS CONTEM-

PLATED HEREUNDER AND NOT WITH THE SCOPE OF THE SECTION ABOVE ENTITLED "EXCLUSION OF CONSEQUENTIAL DAMAGES" EXCEED THE LICENSE FEE PAID BY LICENSEE HEREUNDER.

Again, a licensee should be able to have all express warranties contained in the agreement excluded from the applicability of this provision, as well.

8. Severability

Agreements that contain provisions for the exclusive services of an individual have come under close scrutiny by the courts. Examples include exclusive songwriter agreements typically entered into between music publishers and their "staff" songwriters, which affords the publisher the right to exclude the songwriter from providing his songwriting services to another. Often these agreements combine a right for the exclusive services of the songwriter with provisions for the assignment of copyrights in compositions developed by the songwriter during the term of the agreement. Should a court hold that a music publisher is unable to enforce the exclusivity provision, the publisher would not wish to risk losing all the copyrights acquired under an exclusive publishing agreement. Accordingly, where there is a possibility that one part of an agreement may be held unenforceable, a copyright owner may wish to make sure that other portions of the agreement are not affected. Such a provision is called a severability clause, which might take the following form:

> In the event that any provision hereof is found invalid or unenforceable pursuant to judicial decree or decision, the remainder of this Agreement shall remain valid and enforceable according to its terms.

If the agreement contains a provision excluding warranties or otherwise limiting the liability of the copyright owner, the copyright owner might add the following sentence to the severability provision:

WITHOUT LIMITING THE FOREGOING, IT IS EXPRESSLY UNDERSTOOD AND AGREED THAT EACH AND EVERY PROVISION OF THIS AGREEMENT WHICH PROVIDES FOR A LIMITATION OF LIABILITY, DISCLAIMER OR WARRAN-

TIES OR EXCLUSION OF DAMAGES IS INTENDED BY
THE PARTIES TO BE SEVERABLE AND INDEPENDENT OF
ANY OTHER PROVISION AND TO BE ENFORCED AS
SUCH. FURTHER, IT IS EXPRESSLY UNDERSTOOD AND
AGREED THAT IN THE EVENT ANY REMEDY HEREUN-
DER IS DETERMINED TO HAVE FAILED OF ITS ESSEN-
TIAL PURPOSE, ALL LIMITATIONS OF LIABILITY AND
EXCLUSION OF DAMAGES SET FORTH HEREIN SHALL
REMAIN IN FULL FORCE AND EFFECT.

9. Cure Period

Copyright owners granting rights or licenses should always include,
at least in long-form licenses, a provision that affords a period within
which to cure any breach of contract alleged by the licensee.

Owner shall not be deemed to be in breach of any of its obligations
hereunder unless and until you shall have given Owner written notice
by certified or registered mail, return receipt requested, specifying the
nature of such breach and Owner shall have failed to cure such breach
within thirty (30) days after Owner's receipt of such written notice.

Licensees should request to make this provision mutual:

Neither party shall be deemed to be in breach of any of its obligations
hereunder unless and until the party claiming a breach shall have given
the other written notice by certified or registered mail, return receipt
requested, specifying the nature of such breach and such other party
shall have failed to cure such breach within thirty (30) days after
receipt of such written notice.

10. Entire Agreement or Integration Provision

When the parties have reduced their agreement to writing, and it is
clear the parties intended that the agreement reflect their entire understanding and agreement or that all understandings and agreements regarding the subject matter were intended to be "integrated" or "merged"
into the written agreement, then evidence of any other agreements,
discussions, representations, or warranties may not be admissible as
evidence to contradict or modify the terms of the agreement. In other
words, unless there is some ambiguity in the terms of the agreement, the

courts will look only to the "four corners" of the written contract to determine the scope of the agreement and the intent of the parties. Accordingly, the parties will often reflect their intent that a written agreement reflects their entire agreement or that all agreements are merged into the written agreement in a clause such as the following:

> This Agreement constitutes the entire understanding and contract between the parties and supersedes any and all prior and contemporaneous, oral or written representations, communications, understandings and agreements between the parties with respect to the subject matter hereof, all of which representations, communications, understandings and agreements are hereby canceled to the extent they are not specifically merged herein. The parties acknowledge and agree that neither of the parties is entering into this Agreement on the basis of any representations or promises not expressly contained herein. This is an integrated agreement.

11. Modifications and Amendments

To avoid disputes about whether or how the terms of a written agreement were subsequently modified, the parties will often agree as follows:

> This Agreement shall not be modified, amended, canceled or in any way altered, nor may it be modified by custom and usage of trade or course of dealing, except by an instrument in writing and signed by both of the parties hereto. All amendments or modifications of this Agreement shall be binding upon the parties despite any lack of consideration so long as the same shall be in writing and executed by the parties hereto.

12. Waiver

To avoid disputes about whether or under what terms a party's duty to perform an obligation of the contract was waived by the other party, the parties may agree as follows:

> Performance of any obligation required of a party hereunder may be waived only by a written waiver signed by the other party, which waiver shall be effective only with respect to the specific obligation described therein. The waiver by either party hereto of a breach of any

provision of this Agreement by the other shall not operate or be construed as a waiver of any subsequent breach of the same provision or any other provision of this Agreement.

13. No Partnership or Agency

An agreement between a buyer and seller or a licensor and licensee should make it clear that no other relationship between the parties is established unless otherwise specifically agreed:

Nothing in this Agreement shall be construed as creating a joint venture, partnership, agency, employment relationship, franchise relationship or taxable entity between the parties, nor shall either party have the right, power or authority to create any obligations or duty, express or implied, on behalf of the other party hereto, it being understood that the parties are independent contractors vis-a-vis one another.

14. No Third Party Beneficiaries

An agreement intended solely to affect the rights and privileges of the parties signing the agreement might state that no rights or privileges are meant to be conferred on any third parties unless specifically provided:

Nothing contained in this Agreement, express or implied, shall be deemed to confer any rights or remedies upon, nor obligate any of the parties hereto, to any person or entity other than such parties, unless so stated to the contrary.

15. Choice of Law

The person drafting the license will generally try to insist that if any disputes arise under the agreement, the law of the state where that party is located should apply to the transaction.

This Agreement shall be construed and enforced in accordance with the laws of the State of California applicable to agreements between residents of California wholly executed and wholly performed therein.

Where the parties reside in the same state, there should be little debate about the laws of which state should govern the agreement. Where the parties cannot agree upon whether to use the laws of the state of one party or the other, the parties should consider including either the state of New York or the state of California, because each of these states has developed a substantial body of case law concerning contracts in the entertainment industry.

16. Choice of Forum

Perhaps more significant than the choice of law provision is the provision that dictates the forum in which a lawsuit arising out of any dispute concerning the agreement must be filed. Unless otherwise agreed, a lawsuit may be brought in any state where the court has jurisdiction over the defendant, such as a state where the defendant is doing business. The costs of a party's litigating an action in a state other than where his principal place of business, and that of his normal legal counsel, is located can be significantly more expensive than litigating in the courts of the party's home state. Further, litigating in an unfamiliar state may induce, whether justified or not, a fear of the unknown or fear of a "home court" advantage.

To alleviate these fears and to minimize the potential costs of litigation, a party may negotiate a provision that identifies the state and county in which lawsuits arising under the agreement are to be brought. The courts will usually respect the agreement of the parties on the matter. Of course, where both parties are located in the same state and county, there is little reason to negotiate the issue of forum, unless one of the parties expects to move its operations to another state or county. Similarly, when both parties are major multi-national corporations who do business in nearly all the states, this provision may not become an issue, unless a party can identify specific laws in a particular state that favor or disfavor one of the parties to the transaction.

While many license agreements contain a choice of law provision, the same agreements often neglect to include a choice of forum provision. Including a choice of law provision, but leaving the choice of forum silent may produce the anomalous result of a court in one state having to apply the laws of another state to resolve the dispute. It will therefore serve to remember that a choice of law provision is not the same as a choice of forum provision, and if the intent is to require that lawsuits be brought in a particular state, the agreement should contain, in addition to a choice of law provision, a provision such as the following:

> Any action or proceeding brought by either party against the other arising out of or related to this Agreement shall be brought only in a state or federal court of competent jurisdiction located in the County of Los Angeles, California, and the parties hereby consent to the *in personam* jurisdiction of said courts.

17. Confidentiality of Agreement

A party may desire, for one reason or another, to maintain the confidentiality of the terms of the agreement. The following provision effects such confidentiality, recognizing the need for certain standard exceptions:

> Each of the parties to this Agreement warrants and agrees that neither it nor its counsel will disclose, disseminate, or cause to be disclosed the terms of this Agreement, except: (a) Insofar as disclosure is reasonably necessary to carry out and effectuate the terms of this Agreement; (b) Insofar as a party hereto is required by law to respond to any demand for information from any court, governmental entity, or governmental agency; (c) Insofar as disclosure is necessary to be made to a party's independent accountants for tax or audit purposes; and (d) Insofar as the parties may mutually agree in writing upon language to be contained in one or more press release.

18. Notice

Notices that may be required or permitted under license agreements, such as for example, notices of exercise of any option provisions in the agreement, should always be in writing. Further, every long form contract should have a provision clarifying just how such notices must be effected. This is to avoid any misunderstanding about whether notice was timely made and to make sure the notice actually gets to the appropriate person or department within each firm responsible for effecting or enforcing the performance of the agreement.

The following notice provision recognizes the global nature of modern business and the new media of business communications that have become common during the past several years.

> Unless otherwise specifically provided, all notices required or permitted by this Agreement shall be in writing and in English and may be delivered personally, or may be sent by cable, telex, facsimile or certified mail, return receipt requested, to the following, unless the parties are subsequently notified of any change of address in accordance with this section:

> If to Owner: Big Music Publishing Corp.
> 1000 Sunset Boulevard
> Hollywood, California 90000
> Attention: Legal Department
> Telex: 123456 BIGPUB
> Facsimile: (213) 555-1212

> If to Licensee: _____
> _____
> _____
> Attention:_____
> Telex: _____
> Facsimile: _____

> Any notice shall be deemed to have been received as follows: (i) personal delivery, upon receipt; (ii) telex, cable or facsimile, twenty-four (24) hours after transmission or dispatch; (iii) certified mail, three (3) business days after delivery to the United States postal authorities by the party serving notice. If notice is sent by telex, facsimile or cable, a confirming copy of the same shall be sent by mail to the same address.

It is not uncommon for agreements to provide that copies of any notices to be provided under the agreement be sent to the outside counsel of the party upon which notice is to be served. This could help bring to the attention of the party entitled to the notice an important notice that might have otherwise gone unnoticed.

19. Advice of Legal Counsel

When one of the parties is known to be unsophisticated in the ways of business, or is among a class of persons considered stereotypically to be "exploited"—such as artists and songwriters—the more sophisticated party should include the following provision in the agreement:

> Each party acknowledges and represents that, in executing this Agreement, it has received advice as to its legal rights from legal counsel and that the person signing on its behalf has read and understood all of the terms and provisions of this Agreement. Further, each party and their counsel have cooperated in the drafting and preparation of this Agreement. It shall be deemed their joint work product and may not be construed against any party by reason of its preparation or word processing.

20. Attorneys Fees

Under the American rule of law, unless an award of attorneys fees is provided by statute or by the express terms of a written agreement between the parties, a court will not award attorneys fees to the prevailing party in litigation. To deter frivolous litigation, the parties may wish to include a specific provision in the agreement providing the prevailing party in any litigation over the agreement with an opportunity to collect its reasonable attorney fees and costs incurred during the course of the litigation.

> In any litigation between the parties regarding the terms or performance of this agreement, the prevailing party shall be entitled to recover its reasonable attorneys' fees and court costs.

21. Recitals

Many agreements contain recitals of fact intended to provide the reader with some background information about the parties or the transaction. Recitals of fact may sometimes be identified by their being preceded by the word, *Whereas*. The parties to an agreement should be certain that the recitals accurately reflect the facts they purport to recite. California Evidence Code Section 622 states that facts recited in a written instrument (other than recitals of consideration) are conclusively presumed true as between the parties. Recitals, therefore, can serve to reduce the number of facts that can be placed into dispute in any litigation relating to the agreement.

If California Law does not govern the agreement, or the law of the state which governs the agreement does not have a law similar to the California provision concerning recitals, the parties may wish to give strong legal effect to the recitals by including the following provision:

> The recitals above set forth are incorporated into this agreement by reference. Each recital of fact concerning a party shall be conclusive as between the parties hereto. Such fact shall be incontestable in the event of any dispute between the parties regarding such fact and each party agrees not to introduce any evidence which would in any way serve to dispute such recited fact.

22. Counterparts

It is our practice to always have one "original" copy signed for each party to the contract. For example, where there are two parties to the contract, each party will sign two agreements, with each receiving a fully executed original bearing the original signatures of both parties. Where the parties are signing an agreement in different locations or at different times, circumstances will require that each sign separate signature pages which will later be attached to the original agreement. Though not necessary, agreements executed in such fashion should contain a provision such as the following:

> This Agreement may be executed in one or more counterparts, each of which shall be deemed an original, but all of which together shall constitute one and the same instrument.

23. Captions

To prevent an unintended result caused by a poorly worded section heading or caption:

> The section headings and captions contained herein are for reference purposes and convenience only and shall not in any way affect the meaning or interpretation of this Agreement.

24. Gender

A favorite provision of ours which never fails to evoke reaction in negotiators who bother to explore the depths of the legal boilerplate typically found in many licenses:

> Where the context so requires, the masculine gender shall include the feminine or neuter, and the singular shall include the plural and the plural the singular.

25. Effective Date

When you send an agreement to another for signature, it could be construed as an "offer" for a contract, which the other party may "accept" by returning the agreement signed.

Most simple permission letters are sent with the understanding that they may be accepted by the licensee's signing and returning the letter to the music copyright owner. As a precaution, and as an incentive for the licensee to pay promptly, the copyright owner should specify that the license does not take effect until the owner receives payment of the license fee.

More formal license agreements will contain signature lines for both parties to sign and are not intended to be binding until the copyright owner counter-signs the agreement. A copyright owner would be prudent to first obtain the signature of the licensee before signing the contract himself. If there is a significant delay between the time you send an agreement and receive it signed, circumstances may change significantly during that time. For example, you may send a license to an advertising agency for the non-exclusive use of a musical composition in a television commercial, and while you are waiting for the license to be reviewed and returned, another advertiser offers a significantly higher license fee for the exclusive use of the song. In such circumstances, you would ideally want to be in a position to cease the negotiations with the first advertiser and accept the terms offered by the new advertiser. To have that ability, you would need to be certain that the first advertiser does not consider the license you sent to him binding upon you. If you had not signed the agreements before you sent them, then it should be an easy matter to be certain that no binding agreement was consummated. If you had signed the agreements before having sent them, then you would have no assurance that the first advertiser considers that agreement not to have been entered until you actually receive written confirmation to that effect from the first advertiser, which may not always be easy.

Accordingly, other than the case of a simple permission letter for minor non-exclusive licenses where some risk can be assumed for the sake of administrative convenience, a copyright owner is advised to always counter-sign agreements after they have first been signed by the licensee. Further, the license agreement should contain the following provision:

> This Agreement shall become effective only after it has been signed by Licensee and has been accepted by Owner at its principal place of business, and its effective date shall be the date on which it is signed by Owner.

Finally, to avoid any misunderstanding as to the Effective Date of the agreement, which is often the start date of licenses whose term is based on loosely specified time periods (e.g., ". . . a term of one year commencing the Effective Date hereof"), the agreement should indicate the Effective Date directly below the signature block of the copyright owner, as follows:

LICENSEE	OWNER
Signature: _____	Signature: _____
Printed Name: _____	Printed Name:_____
Title: _____	Title: _____
Dated: _____	Dated: _____
	(This is the effective date of the Agreement)

AFFILIATED COMPANY PROBLEM

Certain problems arise when a music publisher is affiliated with a motion picture studio, which is the case when both entities are subsidiaries of a parent entertainment company or other conglomerate. Under standard music publishing agreements, the songwriter is generally entitled to receive 50% of any and all sums actually received by the music publisher from the licensing uses of the music in motion pictures, television programs, videograms, and other media. Where the music publisher is affiliated with the entertainment company who desires to license the music in such works, a conflict of interest arises which may influence the publisher to enter into a deal that does not serve the best interests of the songwriter.

Because an obligation of good faith is implied by the relationship between the songwriter and publisher, the music publisher, in considering the terms of a license with an affiliated company, is required to negotiate "at arms length." This means that publisher must treat the affiliated company as it would any other third party in similar circumstances in establishing the terms and conditions of the license. In the case of synchronization licenses, where synchronization fees have become relatively standardized, this is a fairly simple matter. However, in the area of home video licenses, where there are still few standards,[4] and often heated disputes as to whether original synchronization licenses covered home video uses of music,[5] the resolution of conflicts of interest is more difficult.

How a music publisher resolves this conflict will have an impact upon the publisher's legal relationships with its songwriters, the publisher's ability to acquire additional song catalogues, and the publisher's ability to recruit and contract with new songwriters. The senior management of the entertainment company or the conglomerate is not generally in the best position to resolve such conflicts, and the music publisher faced with this situation should come to grips with the question well before disputes arise with the songwriters they represent.

GENERAL ADVICE TO MUSIC COPYRIGHT OWNERS—ALWAYS ENCOURAGE ACTIVITY IN THE SONG

Before exploring the foregoing factors in relation to the various customary forms of music licenses, we would like to admonish music copyright owners against making the fundamental errors that can lead a great song to obscurity. Do not get too mired in the details. For example, do not let a negotiation over the wording of legal boilerplate obscure

---

[4] See the discussion of videogram licensing in Chapter 10.

[5] See the discussion of the extent to which old synchronization licenses apply to new uses in Chapter 11.

your vision of the forest through the trees. Do not let your perception of the value of the copyright go to your head. Remember that no matter how small the license fee you receive, in the long run, you will tend to make up more than the difference from maintaining a continuing active relationship between the song and the listening public. Do not let fear and uncertainty rule the day. Recognize that life is decision making, and don't be afraid to make a decision. A good rule to follow is, when in doubt, license. The music copyright owner's primary interest should always be to encourage as much activity in the song as possible.

GENERAL ADVICE TO PERSONS SEEKING TO CLEAR LICENSES—FULLY DISCLOSE ALL THE USES YOU MIGHT CONCEIVABLY MAKE OF THE MUSIC

There is nothing worse in business than a surprise. Too often, persons seeking to clear licenses think they are being clever by understating the nature or scope of the intended use in an effort to minimize the fee quoted by the copyright owner. This kind of attitude is inimical to the licensee's best interests. If, as a result of understating the nature of your use, you receive a license that does not adequately cover your requirements, you may find yourself being accused of infringement of copyright, subject to a serious threat of injunction at an inopportune time. You should not have to experience the high cost and ugly embarrassment of a lawsuit to learn the lesson that intentionally understating the nature and scope of your intended use for the purpose of minimizing your costs makes no business sense.

Music copyright owners will require a lot of information about your potential use of the music before quoting a license fee. While the copyright owner uses this information to quote a fee that reflects the importance of the use, it is also to your benefit to fully disclose all the uses you might conceivably make of the music. Usually, the music copyright owner will be more than happy to quote you a fee for all the uses that you can foresee. If the fees are reasonable, you would be advised to pick up as much scope and duration as offered to you. If you are on a tight budget, you should ask for options which will give you important flexibility later on and may save you money in the long run.

PRINT LICENSES

SUMMARY

HISTORICAL BACKGROUND

1. Origins of Musical Notation
2. The Art of Printing
3. Printed Music Publishing in America
4. Print Music Publishing Today

TYPES OF PRINTED MUSIC

1. Sheet Music
2. Folio
3. Personality Folio
4. Instrument Folio
5. Music Instruction Books
6. Concert and Educational Editions
7. Fakebooks

PREPARATION AND DISTRIBUTION OF PRINTED MUSIC

1. Independent Print Distributors

PRINT RIGHTS

1. Granting and Acquiring Exclusive Print Rights
   A. Grants By Songwriters to Music Publishers
   B. Grants By Music Publishers to Print
       Music Distributors

PRINT LICENSES

1. Granting and Clearing Non-Exclusive Licenses to Print
   Music in Folios
2. Granting and Clearing Licenses to Print Lyrics
   A. Books
   B. Record Albums
   C. Lyric Magazines
   D. Print Advertising

FORMS

CHAPTER 6

PRINT LICENSES

A *print license* is a form of permission that authorizes one to make printed copies of music, such as sheet music, printed music folios, concert arrangements, and reprints of lyrics in books, magazines, and print advertising. The print license is derived from one of the most basic rights of a copyright owner: the exclusive right to make copies. This chapter sketches the historical and legal background of printed music and provides an outline of some of the common terms and conditions contained in customary print licenses.

HISTORICAL BACKGROUND

1. Origins of Musical Notation

Music would seem to be a part of human nature. What man fails to express through gesturing, speaking, writing, painting, and sculpting, he expresses through making music. If music can be defined as the art of organizing sounds and silences into meaningful patterns, then it clearly had very early origins. Early songs probably developed from hunting calls and other vocal signals. As soon as these calls were used for the pleasure expressed or emotions evoked, apart from any useful purpose, they became music. Archeologists have unearthed evidence dating back to the dawn of antiquity of man's creating music throughout Asia, Europe, Africa, the Americas, and other parts of the globe. The ancient Egyptians, Persians, Africans, and Chinese all used musical instruments of one kind or another.

It was, however, the ancient Greeks, who laid the foundations of modern music. In ancient Greece, poetry and music were treated as one art, and music became an integral part of Greek drama, including the theatrical works of Aeschylus, Sophocles, Euripides, and Aristophanes.

Most common among the Greek instruments was the lyre, a u-shaped instrument with a cross bar that supported 4 strings. The invention of the lyre, according to Greek mythology, occurred when Herme's foot came in contact with the tendons of a dead tortoise, which had dried and tightened on the animal's shell. The philosopher, Terpander, born about 676 B.C., is said to have added three strings to the lyre, and later, Pythagoras, born about 582 B.C., is said to have added the eighth string. Pythagoras, who was the first to give music a scientific basis, also invented the system of four tones known as the *tetrachord*, which later evolved into the first scale of one *octave*.

Early in the 4th century A.D., a school of *chant* was established in Rome. For generations the melodies were handed down aurally from master to pupil. The learning of the growing repertory of melodies by heart was arduous and there eventually evolved a form of musical notation. This notation was called *neumes* from the Greek word *neuma* meaning nod or sign. While the system gradually included combinations of dashes, curves and dots, the neumes notation did not indicate musical pitch. Although there is no official accounts of neume notation before the 8th century, it has been said that Pope Gregory the Great, in the 6th century, collected the sacred music of the Church. *Gregorian* music is the name given to a collection of over 600 songs connected with the Roman Catholic services of that age. By the 8th Century, Charlemagne was sending emissaries to Rome to get full and accurate details on the methods of Gregorian singing.

During the 10th century, an anonymous theorist brought order and progress to musical notation with a single stroke of his pen. With some red ink and a ruler, he drew a line across the page and marked it "F." This was the beginning of the musical staff and clef. The nuemes were now written on the line and higher and lower pitch was indicated above or below the line. They served as a guide to memory and indicated whether the voice should go up or down, but not how far up or down it should go. The idea worked so well that soon another line was added; later, two more lines were added until, finally, another line was added, giving us the five line staff we use today. There soon came a need for the notation to indicate an exact time value, and, in the 13th century, three devices were invented: the dot, the coloration of notes, and time signatures. Circles, broken circles, and circles with dots in them corresponded to beats and rhythms of varying length. These later evolved to form the notes, bars, measures, and the other features of musical notation with which we are familiar today.

Throughout this period, music remained closely associated with the Roman Catholic Church. The seat of the Church was first located in Rome, then in Constantinople, later returning to Rome. With the fall of Constantinople in 1204, its scholars, with their knowledge of Greek and Latin classics, traveled to Rome and Western Europe bringing with them the Hellenic alliance between music and drama. The Italian influence has left its mark on many of the musical terms we use today, including *allegro, andante,* and *legato.*

2. The Art of Printing

Prior to the 16th century, musical manuscripts were arduously drafted and illuminated by hand, usually in monasteries and other places of learning. The diffusion of music received great aid from the art of printing, which commenced upon Gutenberg's invention of the printing press in 1451. About a quarter of a century after the first bible came off Gutenberg's printing press, Ulrich Hahn, a German working in Rome at the time, became the first to print music. But it wasn't until 1501 that a serious business of printing music began in earnest when Ottavanio Petrucci, working in Venice, secured a monopoly for printing music in that city and became the first to print and distribute music on a full time basis. Other music printing concerns were soon established throughout Europe.

In the early 16th century, Winking de Worde published the first English songbook. In the mid-17th century, John Playford, a London publisher of several important books on musical theory, began to specialize in compiling, publishing, promoting and distributing nearly all the important songs composed in England during his time, and in doing so, became the forerunner to modern music publishing businesses.

In 1745, Johann Gottlob Immanuel Breitkopf labored to improve the methods of printing music. By introducing separate movable music type, he brought about a revolution in music printing by 1750. Johann Breitkopf's son, Christoph Gottlob, eventually inherited the publishing house, and transferred the business to his friend Gottfried Christoph Hartel. Hartel worked the business under the name Breitkopf and Hartel, publishing the works of Bach, Hayden, Mozart, Beethoven,

Chopin and others, becoming the world's largest publisher of orchestral music. Years later, Breitkopf and Hartel employed a French music publisher, Paul Heineke, sending him to the United States in 1917 to establish a New York office. As will be noted in Chapter 15, Paul Heineke later established SESAC, the second performance rights society in the United States.

3. Printed Music Publishing in America

During most of the colonial era in America after 1607, the music used by colonists was imported from England. For many years, music was forbidden as a trade altogether in New England. The first book printed in the United States that contained musical notation was the ninth edition of *The Bay Psalm Book*, which contained thirteen songs borrowed from Playford's *Whole Book of Psalms* published in 1677.

In 1712, *The Art of Singing* by John Tufts, the first music instruction book published in America was distributed throughout the colonies. Containing thirty-seven songs, the Tuft's book was printed in many editions from its date of first publication through 1744.

In 1793, Benjamin Carr moved his family from England and established the first music publishing firm in the United States, printing chiefly music that had become popular in England. Other music publishers were established in many of the major cities on the eastern seaboard. With the development and increasing popularity of the piano, singing became a popular form of entertainment, and sales of printed sheet music began to flourish. It is estimated that, during the first 25 years of the 19th century, over 10,000 popular songs were published in the United States. By the end of the century, *After the Ball*, written and published by Charles K. Harris in 1893, became the first song to sell a million copies.

In 1880, after winning a toy printing press from school, Isadore, Julius and J. Witmark opened a printing business in their home on West 40th Street in New York City. They earned a modest living printing Christmas cards. To augment his earnings, Jay became a performer of ballads in minstrel and variety shows. After achieving some success, it suddenly occurred to Jay, if it were possible for him to establish hit songs for others, why couldn't he publish his own music? After all, Isadore could write songs, and they had a printing press on which to print the music. Since the brothers were still minors, they had their father, Marcus become director of the company, and thus, M. Witmark & Sons was established in 1885 as a publisher and printer of sheet music.

Other music publishing firms soon opened their doors, and music publishers quickly developed innovative ways to increase the sale of their sheet music. A part time songwriter, Edward B. Marks established a publishing firm under that name. Marks discovered a way to promote his songs by performing them during the intermissions at variety houses while illustrated slides were flashed onto a white sheet screen. Tom Harms of T. B. Harms Music Publishing Company became the first music publisher to discover the profitability in printing sheet music of songs appearing in successful Broadway shows. M. Witmark and Sons was the first music publisher in America to pay singers to perform their songs. Shapiro-Remick & Company employed Jerome Kern to demonstrate their songs. Kern was soon hired by Max Dreyfus of T.B. Harms as a staff pianist to *plug* (i.e., promote) songs at various department stores.

Sales of sheet music soared. In the days before the advent of sound motion pictures, radio, and television, it was not unusual for a popular song to sell upwards of 2,000,000 copies in sheet music. The sale of sheet music was the primary income of a music publisher, unless the publisher enjoyed other income from operating a musical instrument store, producing musical productions, or managing artists. When sales of single copies of sheet music would slow down, publishers and songwriters looked for successful ways to promote their songs. Sometimes a song would become a hit as a result of a combination of fortuitous circumstances.

In 1919, while dining at Dinty Moore's, a fashionable restaurant on Broadway, Irving Caesar suggested to his dinner partner, George Gershwin, they collaborate on a "two-step" type song that was the trend in dancing at the time. George was enthusiastic and suggested they take a bus to his apartment and try their luck. George played a few notes on the piano and, as Irving told me, "The words rushed out at me with inspired spontaneity." The song was first introduced in a Ned Wayburn revue at the Capitol Theatre in New York. In the lobby of the theatre, George and Irving shouted to the departing audience, "Here it is, '*Swanee*,' get your copies, '*Swanee*.'" They did this night after night, but not one copy was sold. George and Irving having confidence in their creation begged their publisher, Max Dreyfus of T.B. Harms, to promote the song by other means. Max told them he loved the song, but it was not "commercial" enough to sell sheet music. A few weeks later, Buddy DeSylva, a songwriter who had been discovered by Al Jolson, invited George and Irving to a post-midnight party. When George was playing the piano, and Buddy his ukelele, Buddy started to sing *Swanee*. Al Jolson quickly turned to his musical director and told him to arrange the song and put it in his new show. The song became a smash hit. Max Dreyfus finally published the song and orders for sheet music began pouring in. When George and Irving asked Dreyfus how much royalties they had earned, Max told them about $10,000, a huge sum at the time. A little embarrassed, Dreyfus offered the two an advance against prospective royalties from sheet music sales in England. Max bought George the baby grand piano he wanted and Irving settled for cash.

4. Print Music Publishing Today

At the turn of the century, most music publishing revenue was derived from the sale of printed music. With the increasing popularity of the phonograph, the advent of radio, sound motion pictures, or "talkies," and later the introduction of television, recordings of music replaced printed music notation as the primary source of music publishing revenue. Income from licensing the mechanical reproduction of music and performance of the resulting recordings soon eclipsed revenues from printed music to the point that, today, printed music represents only a small portion of a music publisher's income.

Traditionally, most printed music was sold in the form of *sheet* music, which contained the musical notation of a single song, and any accompanying lyrics. As the sales of printed music became a declining portion of music publishing income, modern music publishers continued to seek innovative ways to increase sales of printed music. This led to the development of new forms of "packaging" of sheet music, such as in *personality folios* and *educational editions*, which are described below.

TYPES OF PRINTED MUSIC

Today, printed music is available in various forms, each suited to the particular needs of musical artists.

1. Sheet Music

The traditional form of printed music is *sheet music*. Sheet music is generally one song printed on unbound sheets of paper, containing music and any accompanying lyrics. Sheet music is generally arranged for piano, vocal, and guitar.

2. Folio

A *folio* is a compilation or anthology of sheet music bound into one, usually soft cover, volume. The songs may be written by various writers and recorded by various artists, but they are usually linked by a common theme, such as songs from the roaring twenties, famous movie themes, or songs of romance. Folios, sometimes referred to as *songbooks*, may contain editorial notes regarding the songs in the compilation or the theme of the anthology, related photographs, and similar materials.

3. Personality Folio

A *personality folio* is a folio consisting of songs written, recorded, or performed by the same artist or recording group, or written by the same songwriter. A personality folio may contain biographical material about the featured artist or group, as well as photographs. Such editions make the folio attractive even to fans who do not play an instrument, as many non-performing fans would purchase a personality folio just to obtain the photographs of their favorite artist or group. A personality folio that contains only the songs appearing on a particular record album is called a *companion folio*.

4. Instrument Folio

An *instrument folio* is a folio of compositions specially arranged for a particular musical instrument, such as a cello, harp, clarinet, oboe, recorder, tenor saxophone, alto saxophone, or violin.

5. Music Instruction Books

A *music instruction book*, sometimes called a *method book*, is a book designed to provide instruction on a particular musical instrument. An instruction book may be designed for beginners, intermediate, or advanced players. For example, an instruction book for novices may be used by someone learning to play the clarinet for the first time. Another may be used by an accomplished musician desiring to learn advanced techniques in, or a certain style of, playing the saxophone.

6. Concert and Educational Editions

Sheet music and folios containing special arrangements for professional orchestras and other music groups are published in special editions called *concert editions*. These editions comprise one or more arrangements of popular music, symphonic music, chamber music, and music from Broadway shows, operas, and ballets. With the growth of school orchestras and marching bands, music publishers discovered a ready-made market for their sheet music. Special arrangements, called *educational editions*, were developed to accommodate various grades of young musicians from easy to play arrangements to the professional orchestrations prepared specifically for use by marching bands, jazz bands, and orchestras.

7. Fakebooks

A *fakebook* is a folio containing hundreds of songs presented in very short arrangements. These books enabled a professional musician, who might not be familiar with a particular "request" from his audience, to *fake* the performance (i.e., improvise and render it as though the song were familiar) using merely the melody line presented in the fake book. Early fakebooks were illegal or *bootleg*, meaning they were compiled without the permission of the copyright owners. Fakebooks were compiled by musicians over the years and handed down, copied or sold on an informal basis. In recent years, music publishers, recognizing the demand for fakebooks, compiled and arranged "legal" fakebooks for commercial sale.

PREPARATION AND DISTRIBUTION OF PRINTED MUSIC

In the first half of this century, when a songwriter submitted a tune to his publisher, it was assumed that the composer would prepare his own lead sheet of the music. A *lead sheet* is one or two pages of lined music paper consisting of the notes of the melody on a single staff with chord indications written above and lyrics written below the notes. The music publisher would use the lead sheet to register the copyright in the song with the U.S. Copyright Office. The lead sheet was then used by the music publisher's professional staff as the basis for preparing a piano/vocal arrangement of the song to be used in the printing of sheet music.

In addition to using staff arrangers, publishers frequently engaged freelance arrangers to prepare these arrangements. Staff and freelance arrangers are normally engaged on a *work for hire* basis, meaning they are paid wages on a weekly basis or paid a flat fee per arrangement for their work and do not acquire any ownership interest in their work. Staff and freelance arrangers do not normally participate in any form of royalty payment, unless the arranger is engaged to add some substantial material to the composition or the work performed includes special arrangements of compositions in the public domain, such as the works of Beethoven and Mozart.

At one time, I was one of such freelancers, and had the privilege of creating piano arrangements for the works of artists such as Paul Simon & Art Garfunkel and groups such as Jefferson Airplane. The preparation of piano/vocal arrangements for rock songs is no easy task. I used to call upon my sons when they were young boys to help me discern virtually inaudible lyrics from rock recordings for which I was engaged to prepare piano arrangements. It was Paul Simon's desire that his compositions be arranged for sheet music publication as they were performed on his recordings. This I accomplished to his satisfaction by transposing the "sound" of his guitar to paper. While at that time one would need to play these arrangements on a harpsichord to get the feeling of a guitar sound, today all one would need use is an electronic keyboard.

While sheet music sales have declined over the years, many teachers of music have demanded copies of editions specially arranged for "beginners." The recent work of several talented arrangers, who have become known for their simplified editions, have breathed new life into the market for sheet music. Nevertheless, some rock and contemporary music artists unreasonably insist upon having their sheet music arranged exactly as it was recorded; the resulting arrangements are often difficult for the average home musician to play. These artists forget that, while the professional musician can use any musical notation to fake a performance in his own style, the amateur enthusiast has to play the music as it is printed. Both professional and amateur would be served if all sheet music were arranged in a simplified fashion.

Eminent composers, such as Vincent Youmans, Jerome Kern, and George Gershwin, and master film music composers, such as Max Steiner, Alfred Newman, and Erich Wolfgang Korngold, prepared their own piano arrangements and orchestrations, but it is now extremely rare for a popular song composer to transcribe his music to paper. With the rock era, many artists and groups have emerged from the recording studio with hit records created by improvising the arrangement along the way, without the benefit of written material. Consequently, beginning about the 1950's, nearly all songs were submitted to publishers on records or audiotape and many publishers found it necessary to prepare their own lead sheets just to fulfill the requirements of copyright registration. Through the lobbying efforts of representatives of artists and composers, Congress was made aware that many contemporary artists were not able to write out their compositions in musical notation, and the copyright law they enacted in 1976 finally allowed songwriters to submit audiotape recordings to fulfill copyright deposit requirements.[1]

Not all songs, however, are adaptable to the medium of printed music. Stripped of the production values in the recording, many rock songs simply don't have enough melody to carry a useful piano/vocal arrangement. Even if a song has a melody or lyrics sufficiently meaningful to be rendered in printed form, sheet music would not normally be published unless the song has attained a certain "hit" status or is published with other songs, by the same artist, that have become well known hits.

1. Independent Print Distributors

Today, of the thousands of independent music publishing companies, only a handful engage in the expensive business of printing, selling, and distributing printed music. Even some of the largest music publishers enter into special relationships with print publisher/distributors who specialize in printing and distributing music, such as Plymouth Music Co., Warner Bros. Publications, Inc., Hal Leonard and others. These

---

[1] 17 U.S.C. Sec. 407(a)(2).

print distributors distribute printed music through a network of whole-salers, called *rack jobbers*, retail print music dealers, educational deal-ers, retail stores where musical instruments are sold, booksellers, and other retail establishments.

Some publishers enter into exclusive arrangements with these print distributors for the printed publication of some or all of the songs in the publisher's catalog for a limited time. Under these arrangements, the publisher receives a royalty on the basis of the print distributor's sales. Similar arrangements are also made on a song-by-song basis.

Rather than granting exclusive print rights or a non-exclusive li-cense to print music in return for a royalty, a music publisher may prefer to exercise its print rights through the use of a selling agent. Under this arrangement, the selling agent, usually a print publisher acting in an agency capacity, charges all printing, production, and distribution costs to the copyright owner, and pays over all its sales receipts directly to the copyright owner, deducting only a commission of about 25%.

The consolidation in the business of printed music has resulted from the decline in demand for printed music. But some advantages have resulted from this consolidation. For example, a print publisher who has relationships with several music publishers has the opportunity to cherry pick, from among the several catalogs for which it has print licenses, popular "hit" songs for inclusion in folios designed for maximum appeal.

PRINT RIGHTS

1. Granting and Acquiring Exclusive Print Rights

Exclusive print rights are generally granted in only the following limited contexts: (1) when a songwriter signs a publishing agreement in which he assigns his copyrights, and all rights under copyright, to a music publisher, and (2) when a music publisher grants to a print music distributor the exclusive right to print sheet music.

A. *Grants by Songwriters to Music Publishers*

The terms and conditions under which songwriters contract with music publishers are fairly standard, subject to some negotiation depending upon the leverage or the star status of the writer. Standard songwriter publishing contracts provide that the songwriter assign his copyrights in the music, including exclusive print rights and all other rights under copyright, to the music publisher and sets forth royalty rates for each of the various categories of printed editions. The various techniques of negotiating these songwriter agreements on behalf of the songwriter are well covered in several excellent books on the music industry.[2]

With respect to print rights, writers customarily receive 5 to 7 cents per copy of sheet music sold in the United States and Canada and 50% of the sheet music royalties received by the music publisher for sales in other countries. The royalty for the use of music in folios is generally 10 to 15% of the wholesale selling price, pro rated among the various songs in the folio. Songwriters are advised to make certain that their contract requires that only *copyrighted* works in the folio are used in computing his pro rata share. This is to prevent the royalty from being reduced by the inclusion in the folio of music in the public domain, such as the Star Spangled Banner and classical music from prior centuries. It would be reasonable, however, for a music publisher to insist that copyrighted arrangements of public domain songs upon which it must pay royalties should also be included in computing the writer's pro rata share.

Further, where the music publisher does not engage in the business of printing music and distributing printed music itself, choosing instead to grant rights or licenses to independent print publishers who carry on this business under a royalty arrangement with the publisher, the writer should carefully negotiate provisions that assure that a fair portion of the income derived by the music publisher flows through to the writer.

In general, songwriters should not expect much results from hard line negotiations on terms regarding print rights and royalties. Sales of printed music no longer have the financial significance they once enjoyed, and songwriters, rather than struggle over meaningless royalty percentages, should instead devote their energies toward encouraging the music publisher to effect the printing of at least a sheet music edition of their musical compositions. Leaving aside the sentimental value to the songwriter's posterity, printed music can be quite useful in promoting the song to orchestras, bands, and perhaps other artists who might be

---

[2] *For example, see,* S. Shemel & M. Krasilovsky, *This Business of Music* (Billboard 1985).

persuaded to make further recordings of the song. The late songwriter Ben Oakland (*Java Jive*, *If I Love Again*) once befriended and supplied sheet music to the person who played the organ at a professional ballpark. Sure enough, every once in a while one of Ben's songs could be heard on national television during the broadcast of a baseball game, making the song eligible for important performance credits.

Certain agreements between composers of film music and motion picture companies require that the main theme be printed in order for the elected publisher to claim any publishing rights to the composer's music.

B. Grants by Music Publishers to Print Music Distributors

Music publishers will rarely grant print rights on an exclusive basis. In the few cases that exclusivity is granted, it is normally limited to the printing of sheet music. Permission to print single songs in folios will almost always be on a non-exclusive basis, as publishers desire to remain free to negotiate the use of major songs in folios published by competing print publishers.

Print publishers might require some form of exclusivity in the case of personality folios. For example, a print publisher might acquire a license from a rock star and his publishing company to publish a folio of the star's greatest hits (e.g., "The Elton John Songbook") or may acquire a license to publish a companion folio, a folio of all the songs written and recorded by the artist for a particular album. In such cases, the print publisher would normally insist that the copyright owner not license the same songs for inclusion in a similar songbook or songbook having a confusingly similar title (e.g., "Elton John's Greatest Hits").

Where exclusivity is granted, the music publisher should be certain to reserve (i.e., exclude from the exclusivity) the right to license printed versions of the lyrics, a subject discussed in more detail later in this chapter, and the right to license materials akin to printed music, such as MIDI files, discussed in Chapter 14.

In exchange for granting the exclusive rights to print sheet music, the copyright owner will normally receive from the print publisher a royalty of some fixed number of cents per copy. To participate in price increases, the owner should consider requiring a percentage of the suggested retail or wholesale price in lieu of a fixed amount per copy. The print publisher assumes the costs of production, printing and distribution. The copyright owner usually receives an *advance* against royalties upon the signing of the contract. Should a copyright owner grant prints rights to various songs under separate contracts which each providing for an advance against royalties, the owner should consider making sure that these advances are not *cross-collateralized*.[3]

The territory of exclusive sheet music contracts is generally limited to the United States and Canada. Music copyright owners will enter into separate arrangements with subpublishers overseas for the publication of printed editions. Nevertheless, print deals are beginning to reflect the challenges arising from a changing world marketplace, where printing is being effected in one country in multiple languages for shipment worldwide.

The term of these agreements is generally from 1 to 5 years. With respect to agreements with a term longer than one year, a copyright owner would be prudent to include in the agreement minimum sales or royalty performance levels. If the print publisher does not reach the prescribed level in any given year, the publisher should have the option to convert the agreement to a non-exclusive basis or terminate the agreement altogether.

The copyright owner granting exclusive print rights should require the print publisher to print regular sheet music copies of the composition during the term of the agreement and to pay all cost of preparation, production, art work, arranging and engraving.

PRINT LICENSES

1. Granting and Clearing Non-Exclusive Licenses to Print Music in Folios

As previously noted, print publishers who have relationships with several music copyright owner/publishers have taken the opportunity to cherry pick popular "hit" songs for inclusion in folios designed for maximum appeal. Many print publishers have increased the sale of slow selling or older standard songs by programming material in specialized

---

[3] The concepts of *advances* and *cross-collateralization* are discussed in Chapter 5.

compilations such as, *Music of the Roaring Twenties, Hit Songs of 1950,* and compilations of well-known country and western songs. For this reason, it would be prudent for music copyright owners to reserve to themselves their exclusive rights to authorize the printing of music in folios in order to take advantage of the opportunity to license its compositions in these forms of compilations, on a non-exclusive basis, to as many print publishers and selling agents as possible.

Music copyright owners considering a license to permit the use of a song in a folio or songbook, should attempt to limit the scope of the license to the specific use requested. For example, if a print publisher desires to clear the license to use a single song in a particular folio, the license should identify the folio by name or description and should expressly state that the song may be used solely in the particular folio named or described. Many standard form agreements for the licensing of a single song in folios will contain a broad grant to use the music in any kind of folio during the term of the license. Of course, the licensee would strongly desire the flexibility afforded by this broader form of license.

The royalty for including a song in a folio is customarily 12.5% of the suggested retail selling price of the songbook, pro rated based upon the number of copyrighted songs in the folio. For example, if there are 10 songs in the folio and the suggested retail price of the folio is $10, a publisher that licensed 2 songs for the folio would receive one-fifth of $10 multiplied by 12.5%, or 25 cents per copy sold, less returns. The copyright owner should be certain that the pro rata share is calculated only on the basis of the number of copyrighted songs in the folio, which would prevent the inclusion of public domain works in the folio from reducing the royalty payable. The print publisher should make certain it is clear that copyrighted arrangements of public domain works upon which it must pay royalties should be included in the pro ration.

Personality folios will probably require the permission of the artist featured in the folio, particularly if biographical material or the artist's likeness or photograph are depicted in the folio. Artists typically demand a royalty of an additional 5% of the suggested retail price for such uses. Many contemporary artists refuse to grant permission for the publication of personality folios. Some artists, who have extensive consent provisions in their music publishing contracts, flatly refuse to allow the licensing of their songs in folios of any form. Artists who place such restrictions on the use of their music are being shortsighted and will some day regret making decisions that tend to sever the important relationship between the song and the listening public.

2. Granting and Clearing Licenses to Print Lyrics

A. Books

Quoting a song lyric in a book, such as a novel, biography, or other work, requires permission from the copyright owner of the song. The use of a lyric is not, as some may believe, a *fair use* of copyright, which is a use that would not require permission of the copyright owner. Fair use is limited to some fairly specific circumstances defined in the copyright law,[4] such as criticism, news reporting, teaching, or research. Quotation of a lyric, or a portion of a lyric, in a book or magazine for commercial sale would not qualify for the fair use exception. If you have any doubt whether the fair use exception applies, then you should seek a license.

Music publishers will frequently receive calls for permission to use or quote a song lyric, and, if he controls the rights, will usually have no reluctance to granting such a license. Music publishers should not overlook the earnings potential of licensing lyrics of a song. The fees may be small, but they add up, and more important, it is a good way of keeping the song alive. Requests are often received for permission to use lyrics in text books, particularly History and English books, many of which take the opportunity to print an entire lyric by Bob Dylan or Joni Mitchell to illustrate a modern form of poetry or the mood of the country during the 1960's.

Music publishers generally grant these licenses using a short-form permission letter. An example of such a letter is included as Form 6.4 at the end of this chapter. Book publishers sometimes make release forms available to its authors to facilitate the clearance of permission to use quotes. Whatever the form used to effect them, such licenses are generally not expensive. The copyright owner will normally charge a small flat fee for the use of a lyric in a book and may require two copies of the

---

[4] 17 U.S.C. Sec. 107; *see also,* the discussion of the fair use doctrine in Chapter 16.

book upon publication. For the current fees typically charged for such uses, see Chapter 19.

The license is usually limited to using the lyric in one single hard cover edition of the book and its reprints, with additional payments required for paperback editions, translations, abridgments, and editions published by other firms. Fees are normally a one-time, flat fee, which is sometimes limited to the first 100,000 copies or some such negotiated arrangement. The territory is usually worldwide, but remember, additional permission is required for translated versions.

The privilege to use the lyric in other editions would require additional permission and fees. Persons seeking to clear these licenses who expect that permission for use in paperback editions, translations, abridgments, and other editions will be required should attempt to negotiate, in advance, options to pick up permission for these other editions or otherwise ask whether a license for all editions can be paid in advance. The publisher would be reluctant to issue such a license because of the ambiguity of the term "editions," but language such as "edition in book form" might be suggested to provide the comfort required by both parties.

An option arrangement may be more difficult to attain with respect to foreign language editions. Music publishers generally require that licenses for editions printed overseas be sought directly from its affiliated overseas subpublishing company.

B. Record Albums

Since the turbulent 1960's, with its new forms of rock and psychedelic music, a disturbing number of rock, hard rock, heavy metal and rap songs have been released with lyrics containing offensive, indecent, or violent language. Unsuspecting disc jockeys, after programming and broadcasting these recordings, would became inundated with telephone calls from angry listeners protesting their broadcast. As a result, radio station program directors began requesting that record companies furnish a copy of the lyrics for each new single or album recording submitted for broadcast. Record companies, in turn, began asking music publishers to grant licenses or permission for these lyric reprints.

Many record albums recorded by popular contemporary artists now include a printed set of the lyrics of all the songs on the album, and it has become a standard practice for music publishers to grant permission for this use either for a small royalty or on a *gratis* (i.e., no charge) basis. An example of a permission letter used for this purpose is set forth as Form 6.6 at the end of this chapter.

In cases where the lyrics are not printed on the album, publishers will grant a gratis license to record companies permitting them to distribute printed copies of the lyrics in conjunction with the distribution of promotional copies of the album. An example of a permission letter used for this purpose is set forth as Form 6.7 at the end of this chapter. Many recording companies now request such permission when they submit requests for mechanical licenses (discussed in Chapter 7 below).

C. Lyric Magazines

Permission to print entire lyrics are sought by publishers of magazines specially devoted to printing song lyrics. Examples of licenses permitting such use are set forth as Forms 6.8, 6.9, and 6.10 at the end of this chapter.

D. Print Advertising

Licensing lyrics for use in print advertising involves many of the same considerations in licensing music in connection with advertising in general, which is discussed in great detail in Chapter 12. A form for the license of lyrics for use in print advertising is included as Form 12.2 at the end of Chapter 12.

APPENDIX TO CHAPTER 6
PRINT LICENSES

FORMS

FORM 6.1

EXCLUSIVE PRINT RIGHTS AGREEMENT FOR ALL PRINTED EDITIONS OF A SINGLE SONG

SINGLE SONG PRINTED MUSIC PUBLISHING AGREEMENT

AGREEMENT made effective January 1, 1995 by and between

LITTLE MUSIC PUBLISHING COMPANY
c/o Joseph Schmoe, Esq.
123 West 45th Street
New York, NY 10019

(hereinafter referred to as "Owner") and

OLD MUSIC PRINT PUBLISHER, INC.
1000 Sunset Boulevard
Hollywood, CA 90069

(hereinafter referred to as "Publisher").

THE PARTIES HEREBY AGREE AS FOLLOWS:

1.   Owner hereby grants to Publisher, its successors, assigns, affiliates, subsidiaries and licensees the sole and exclusive right during the term hereof, to print, sell and distribute in bound or unbound editions or forms, singly or together with such other compositions and contents as may be selected by Publisher, at Publisher's sole cost and expense, the copyrighted musical composition entitled:

Title: "I'LL LOVE YOU TILL YOU LEAVE ME"

Composer(s):

Copyright Notice: Copyright © 1980 LITTLE MUSIC PUBLISHING CO.

(which composition is for convenience hereinafter referred to as the "Subject Composition") in any and all arrangements and adaptations thereof as Publisher may elect, throughout the world (hereinafter referred to as the "Licensed Territory"), and to sell the same at such prices and on whatever terms, conditions and discounts as Publisher may in its sole discretion determine from time to time.

2.   In full consideration for all rights, licenses and privileges granted to Publisher hereunder and for all warranties, representations and agreements herein made by Owner, Publisher agrees to pay to Owner the following royalties:

(a)   A sum of seven cents ($.07) per copy in respect of regular sheet music (piano-vocal) sold and paid for. Notwithstanding the foregoing, Publisher shall pay Owner no less than a sum equal to twenty percent (20%) of the marked retail selling price ("MRSP") per copy in respect of net sales of regular sheet music (piano-vocal) editions. (As used in this agreement, "net sales" refers to copies sold and paid for and not returned.)

(b)   In the event the Subject Composition is included in any folio, song book or similar publication containing musical compositions or other musical materials in addition to the Subject Composition, a sum equal to a proportionate part of twelve and one-half percent (12.5%) of the MRSP on net sales of such work.

(c)   In the event the Subject Composition is sold in a pedagogical edition or an instrumental, orchestral, choral, band or other arrangement, a sum equal to ten percent (10%) of the MRSP on net sales of such work, or a proportionate share thereof if included with other copyrighted musical materials that are not subject hereto.

(d)   A sum equal to fifty percent (50%) of sums actually received by Publisher from third party licensees.

3.   (a)   With respect to all sums which may be received by Publisher derived from sales of copies of the Subject composition, Publisher shall, subject to a reasonable reserve against returns (not to exceed forty percent (40%), which reserve shall be liquidated on the accounting statement for the accounting period next following the accounting period in respect of which such reserve is established), within sixty (60) days after the last days of June and December of each year, prepare and furnish statements to Owner, and each such statement shall be accompanied by a check or checks in payment of any and all sums shown to be due thereby. Each such statement shall be binding on Owner and not subject to any objection for any reason, unless specific objection in writing, setting forth the basis thereof, is given to Publisher by Owner within two (2) years from the date rendered.

(b)   To the extent that Owner is paid therefor by Publisher, Owner hereby agrees to pay the writer(s) of the Subject Composition all moneys payable to writer(s) from Owner's receipts hereunder and further agrees to hold Publisher free and harmless from and against any claims of any writer(s) of the Subject Composition.

4.   (a)   Publisher agrees to keep and maintain full and complete books and records concerning the subject matter hereof; and Owner shall have the right to examine Publisher's books and records at Publisher's place of business in Los Angeles, California during its normal business hours and upon reasonable notice to verify the correctness of accounting statements rendered hereunder, within two (2) years, in each instance, after the rendition of the subject accounting statement.

(b)   Legal action with respect to a specific accounting statement or the accounting period to which the same relates shall be forever barred if not commenced in a court of competent jurisdiction within two (2) years following the rendition of such statement.

5.   Owner shall furnish Publisher with all necessary copyright information, an accurate lead sheet and a copy of the original commercial phonograph recording of the Subject Composition. Owner hereby approves Publisher's use of the copyright information as contained on the lead sheet furnished. Owner shall also furnish Publisher with recent photographs of the artists who perform the Subject Composition on such phonograph record and Owner shall use its best efforts to obtain all necessary consents permitting Publisher to use such photographs free of charge in and in connection with the copies of the Subject Composition printed by Publisher.

6.   (a)   Owner warrants and represents that it has the full right, power and authority to enter into and to perform this agreement, and that no part of the Subject Composition infringes upon any rights of any other party.

(b)   Owner shall indemnify Publisher and hold Publisher harmless from and against any and all loss, damage, cost or expense (including court costs and reasonable attorneys' fees) due to a breach of any such warranty or representation and/or Owner's failure to pay royalties to writers, co-publishers or income participants with respect to amounts paid to Owner by Publisher hereunder. Publisher shall give Owner prompt notice of any claim, action or proceeding to which the foregoing indemnity relates, and Owner shall have the right to participate in the defense thereof by counsel of Owner's choice, at Owner's sole cost and expense. In the event of a claim, action or proceeding covered by this indemnity, Publisher shall have the right to withhold from moneys otherwise becoming due to Owner hereunder an amount reasonably related to the scope of Owner's indemnity with respect thereto, unless (and to the extent that) Owner shall provide Publisher with a commercial surety bond issued by a company, and in a form, reasonably satisfactory to Publisher. Any amount so withheld shall be released if (and to the extent that) legal action is not commenced with respect thereto within one (1) year following such withholding.

7.   The term of this Agreement shall commence on the date hereof and continue for a period of five (5) years from and after the date hereof and shall continue thereafter for additional periods of one (1) year, unless and until terminated by either party by giving notice, by registered mail, return receipt requested, not less than ninety (90) days prior to the end of the then current period. Owner agrees that notwithstanding such termination Publisher shall have a non-exclusive license as of the end of the term hereof to market, sell, authorize the continued sale or otherwise dispose of any and all copies (as well as subsequent returns with respect to prior sales) of all editions throughout the Licensed Territory until stocks are exhausted ("sell-off period"). All sales during the sell-off period shall be in the ordinary course of business and shall not be at "close-out", or "distress" prices.

8.   (a)   Any arrangement which Publisher shall cause to be made of the Subject Composition shall be made at Publisher's expense and shall be created only as the result of employment-for-hire, and such arrangement shall be a "Work Made For Hire" as such term is used in the United States Copyright Law, and all copyrights therein and all renewals, extensions and reversions thereof throughout the world shall be owned by the copyright owner of the Subject Composition, subject to Publisher's use under this agreement.

(b)   Publisher agrees to imprint the copyright notice submitted by Owner on each copy of every printed publication of the Subject Composition hereunder, in compliance with the formalities of the United States Copyright Law and of the Universal Copyright Convention as well as imprint under such copyright notice the legend "All Rights Reserved." Any such printed publication not containing such copyright notice shall be deemed to have been published without the permission or authorization of Owner; provided, that in the event of an inadvertent omission of such notice, such omission shall be deemed a breach of contract only and not an infringement of copyright (and Owner's sole remedy therefor shall be in damages).

9.   (a)   Any written notice, statement, payment or matter required or desired to be given to Owner or Publisher pursuant to this agreement shall be given by addressing the same to the addresses of the respective parties referred to above, or to such other address as either party may hereafter designate, in writing, to the other party, and on the date when same shall be sent by registered or certified (return receipt requested) mail, (provided that any royalty statement may be sent by regular mail), or on the date when delivered, so addressed, toll prepaid, to a telegraph or cable company, or on the date when same shall be delivered to the other party personally or to his duly authorized agent (as designated in writing), such notice shall be deemed to have been duly made pursuant hereto.

(b)   Except where expressly provided herein, the consent or approval of a party shall not be unreasonably withheld, and shall be deemed to have been given unless notice of disapproval or nonconsent shall be given by such party within ten (10) days following notice from the other party requesting such consent or approval.

10.   Publisher shall not be deemed to be in breach hereunder unless Owner shall notify Publisher thereof in the manner prescribed herein and Publisher shall fail to remedy such alleged breach within thirty (30) days after receiving such notice (unless the alleged breach is of such a nature that it cannot practicably be completely remedied within such thirty-day period, in which event Publisher shall be deemed to have timely remedied such alleged breach if Publisher commences to do so within such thirty-day period and proceeds to complete the remedying thereof within a reasonable time thereafter).

11.   This agreement constitutes the full and complete understanding and agreement of the parties and it shall not be

amended, modified or altered in any respect, except by an instrument in writing, executed by both parties hereto.

12.   This agreement shall be deemed made in, and is to be construed and interpreted in accordance with the laws of, the State of California.

IN WITNESS WHEREOF, the parties hereto have executed this agreement as of the year and date first above written.

LITTLE MUSIC PUBLISHING COMPANY

By _____
Federal I.D. #:
S.S. #:

OLD PRINT MUSIC PUBLISHER, INC.

By _____

FORM 6.2

NON-EXCLUSIVE PRINT LICENSE AGREEMENT FOR USE OF A SINGLE SONG IN A PARTICULAR FOLIO

SINGLE SONG PRINTED MUSIC LICENSE AGREEMENT

AGREEMENT made effective January 1, 1995 by and between

LITTLE MUSIC PUBLISHING COMPANY
c/o Joseph Schmoe, Esq.
123 West 45th Street
New York, NY 10019

(hereinafter referred to as "Owner") and

OLD MUSIC PRINT PUBLISHER, INC.
1000 Sunset Boulevard
Hollywood, CA 90069

(hereinafter referred to as "Publisher").

THE PARTIES HEREBY AGREE AS FOLLOWS:

1.   Owner hereby grants to Publisher, its successors, assigns, affiliates, subsidiaries and licensees a non-exclusive license during the term hereof, to print, sell and distribute in the bound edition, with such other compositions and contents as may be selected by Publisher, at Publisher's sole cost and expense, the copyrighted musical composition entitled:

Title: "I'LL LOVE YOU TILL YOU LEAVE ME"

Composer(s):

Copyright Notice: Copyright © 1980 LITTLE MUSIC PUBLISHING CO.

(which composition is for convenience hereinafter referred to as the "Subject Composition") in any and all arrangements and adaptations thereof as Publisher may elect, throughout the world (hereinafter referred to as the "Licensed Territory"), for use solely in a music folio entitled:

Folio Title: "LOVE SONGS"

(hereinafter, the "Folio") and to sell the same at such prices and on whatever terms, conditions and discounts as Publisher may in its sole discretion determine from time to time.

2.   In full consideration for all rights, licenses and privileges granted to Publisher hereunder and for all warranties, representations and agreements herein made by Owner, Publisher agrees to pay to Owner a sum equal to a proportionate part of twelve and one-half percent (12.5%) of the marked retail selling price ("MRSP") on net sales of the Folio which the number of compositions bears to the total number of copyrighted compositions, and copyrighted arrangements of public domain works for which royalties are payable, contained in the Folio. (As used in this agreement, "net sales" refers to copies sold and paid for and not returned.) Upon execution hereof, Publisher agrees to pay Owner the sum of $_____ as a non-returnable, recoupable advance against royalties payable hereunder.

3.   (a)   With respect to all sums which may be received by Publisher derived from sales of copies of the Subject Composition, Publisher shall, subject to a reasonable reserve against returns (not to exceed forty percent (40%), which reserve shall be liquidated on the accounting statement for the accounting period next following the accounting period in respect of which such reserve is established), within sixty (60) days after the last days of

June and December of each year, prepare and furnish statements to Owner, and each such statement shall be accompanied by a check or checks in payment of any and all sums shown to be due thereby. Each such statement shall be binding on Owner and not subject to any objection for any reason, unless specific objection in writing, setting forth the basis thereof, is given to Publisher by Owner within two (2) years from the date rendered.

(b)   To the extent that Owner is paid therefor by Publisher, Owner hereby agrees to pay the writer(s) of the Subject Composition all moneys payable to writer(s) from Owner's receipts hereunder and further agrees to hold Publisher free and harmless from and against any claims of any writer(s) of the Subject Composition.

4.   (a)   Publisher agrees to keep and maintain full and complete books and records concerning the subject matter hereof; and Owner shall have the right to examine Publisher's books and records at Publisher's place of business in Los Angeles, California during its normal business hours and upon reasonable notice to verify the correctness of accounting statements rendered hereunder, within two (2) years, in each instance, after the rendition of the subject accounting statement.

(b)   Legal action with respect to a specific accounting statement or the accounting period to which the same relates shall be forever barred if not commenced in a court of competent jurisdiction within two (2) years following the rendition of such statement.

5.   Owner shall furnish Publisher with all necessary copyright information, an accurate lead sheet and a copy of the original commercial phonograph recording of the Subject Composition. Owner hereby approves Publisher's use of the copyright information as contained on the lead sheet furnished. Owner shall also furnish Publisher with recent photographs of the artists who perform the Subject Composition on such phonograph record and Owner shall use its best efforts to obtain all necessary consents

permitting Publisher to use such photographs free of charge in and in connection with the copies of the Subject Composition printed by Publisher.

      6.   (a)   Owner warrants and represents that it has the full right, power and authority to enter into and to perform this agreement, and that no part of the Subject Composition infringes upon any rights of any other party.

      (b)   Owner shall indemnify Publisher and hold Publisher harmless from and against any and all loss, damage, cost or expense (including court costs and reasonable attorneys' fees) due to a breach of any such warranty or representation and/or Owner's failure to pay royalties to writers, co-publishers or income participants with respect to amounts paid to Owner by Publisher hereunder. Publisher shall give Owner prompt notice of any claim, action or proceeding to which the foregoing indemnity relates, and Owner shall have the right to participate in the defense thereof by counsel of Owner's choice, at Owner's sole cost and expense. In the event of a claim, action or proceeding covered by this indemnity, Publisher shall have the right to withhold from moneys otherwise becoming due to Owner hereunder an amount reasonably related to the scope of Owner's indemnity with respect thereto, unless (and to the extent that) Owner shall provide Publisher with a commercial surety bond issued by a company, and in a form, reasonably satisfactory to Publisher. Any amount so withheld shall be released if (and to the extent that) legal action is not commenced with respect thereto within one (1) year following such withholding.

      7.   The term of this Agreement shall commence on the date hereof and continue for a period of three (3) years from and after the date hereof. Owner agrees that notwithstanding such termination Publisher shall have a non-exclusive license as of the end of the term hereof to market, sell, authorize the continued sale or otherwise dispose of any and all copies (as well as subsequent returns with respect to prior sales) of all editions throughout the Licensed Territory until stocks are exhausted ("sell-off period"). All

sales during the sell-off period shall be in the ordinary course of business and shall not be at "close-out", or "distress" prices.

8.   (a)   Any arrangement which Publisher shall cause to be made of the Subject Composition shall be made at Publisher's expense and shall be created only as the result of employment-for-hire, and such arrangement shall be a "Work Made For Hire" as such term is used in the United States Copyright Law, and all copyrights therein and all renewals, extensions and reversions thereof throughout the world shall be owned by the copyright owner of the Subject Composition, subject to Publisher's use under this agreement.

(b)   Publisher agrees to imprint the copyright notice submitted by Owner on each copy of every printed publication of the Subject Composition hereunder, in compliance with the formalities of the United States Copyright Law and of the Universal Copyright Convention as well as imprint under such copyright notice the legend "All Rights Reserved." Any such printed publication not containing such copyright notice shall be deemed to have been published without the permission or authorization of Owner; provided, that in the event of an inadvertent omission of such notice, such omission shall be deemed a breach of contract only and not an infringement of copyright (and Owner's sole remedy therefor shall be in damages).

9.   (a)   Any written notice, statement, payment or matter required or desired to be given to Owner or Publisher pursuant to this agreement shall be given by addressing the same to the addresses of the respective parties referred to above, or to such other address as either party may hereafter designate, in writing, to the other party, and on the date when same shall be sent by registered or certified (return receipt requested) mail, (provided that any royalty statement may be sent by regular mail), or on the date when delivered, so addressed, toll prepaid, to a telegraph or cable company, or on the date when same shall be delivered to the other party personally or to his duly authorized agent (as desig-

nated in writing), such notice shall be deemed to have been duly made pursuant hereto.

(b)   Except where expressly provided herein, the consent or approval of a party shall not be unreasonably withheld, and shall be deemed to have been given unless notice of disapproval or nonconsent shall be given by such party within ten (10) days following notice from the other party requesting such consent or approval.

10.   Publisher shall not be deemed to be in breach hereunder unless Owner shall notify Publisher thereof in the manner prescribed herein and Publisher shall fail to remedy such alleged breach within thirty (30) days after receiving such notice (unless the alleged breach is of such a nature that it cannot practicably be completely remedied within such thirty-day period, in which event Publisher shall be deemed to have timely remedied such alleged breach if Publisher commences to do so within such thirty-day period and proceeds to complete the remedying thereof within a reasonable time thereafter):

11.   This agreement constitutes the full and complete understanding and agreement of the parties and it shall not be amended, modified or altered in any respect, except by an instrument in writing, executed by both parties hereto.

12.   This agreement shall be deemed made in, and is to be construed and interpreted in accordance with the laws of, the State of California.

IN WITNESS WHEREOF, the parties hereto have executed this agreement as of the year and date first above written.

LITTLE MUSIC PUBLISHING COMPANY

By _____
Federal I.D. #:
S.S. #:

OLD PRINT MUSIC PUBLISHER, INC.

By _____

FORM 6.3

EXCLUSIVE PRINT RIGHTS AGREEMENT FOR USE OF ALL COMPOSITIONS OF A MUSICAL GROUP

GROUP PRINT AGREEMENT

AGREEMENT made effective January 1, 1995 by and between

FAMOUS RECORDING GROUP
RIGHTS EXPLOITATION COMPANY, INC.
FAMOUS RECORDING GROUP MUSIC PUBLISHING COMPANY
c/o Joseph Schmoe, Esq.
123 West 45th Street
New York, NY 10019

(hereinafter referred to as "Owner") and

OLD MUSIC PRINT PUBLISHER, INC.
1000 Sunset Boulevard
Hollywood, CA 90069

(hereinafter referred to as "Publisher").

THE PARTIES HEREBY AGREE AS FOLLOWS:

   1.   (a)   Owner hereby grants to Publisher (except as hereinafter provided) the sole and exclusive right, license and privilege to print, publish and sell during the term of this Agreement, or to license to parties in and throughout the territory hereinafter specified, the "Subject Compositions" (as such term is hereinafter defined), in any and all editions as determined by Publisher, including folios, song books, sheet music and other

printed publications of the Subject Compositions, and each of them upon such terms, prices and conditions as Publisher may determine in its sole discretion or to refrain therefrom. Without limiting the generality of the foregoing, Publisher's said rights shall include the right to print, publish, sell and distribute folios and song books containing the Subject Compositions with musical material that is not subject hereto and Publisher's said rights furthermore include the right to print, publish, sell and distribute instrumental versions of the Subject compositions or lyrics of the Subject compositions only, alone or in combination with musical material that is not subject hereto.

(b)   In connection with the foregoing, Owner hereby grants to Publisher a non-exclusive license to use the name of all present and future members of the group known as _____("Artist"), along with photographs, likenesses of and biographical material relating to said Artist, on printed publications hereunder as determined by Publisher and in connection with the advertising, promotion and sale of the same. Publisher shall not use any photographs or likeness of Artist unless same have been submitted to Publisher by Owner or prepared by Publisher, in which event they will require approval by Owner within five (5) working days (which approval shall not be unreasonably withheld).

(c)   Notwithstanding the above, Publisher shall have the right to use the Subject Compositions in a folio containing some or all of the Subject Compositions along with other material performed by Artist, which folio is solely associated with and features only the Artist, along with photographs, likenesses of and biographical material relating to the Artist (any such folio to be called a "Personality Folio"), or to license third parties to use Subject Compositions in "mixed" folios, as that term is generally understood in the music publishing business. The right to issue a "Personality Folio" shall remain exclusive with Publisher during the term of this Agreement, as shall all other rights granted Publisher hereunder.

2.   The term of this Agreement shall be five (5) years from and after the date hereof and shall continue thereafter from year to year until terminated by either party by written notice at least ninety (90) days prior to the end of any such annual period; Publisher's territory hereunder is worldwide.

3.   Subject Compositions shall include each and every musical composition set forth below or on Schedule "A" attached hereto and by this reference made a part hereof. The Subject Compositions hereunder shall furthermore include all musical compositions owned, administered or controlled, directly or indirectly, in whole or in part, by Owner during the term of this agreement, and any and all arrangements and any and all versions of each and every Subject Composition.

4.   Owner represents and warrants that it has the right to enter into this Agreement and to grant all of the rights granted and to be granted to Publisher hereunder and the Publisher's exercise of said rights shall not infringe upon the copyright or other property or contractual or other rights of or constitute unfair competition with or be an invasion of privacy or infringement of the right of publicity of any other person, firm or corporation.

5.   Publisher agrees to pay Owner the following sums in respect of the Subject Compositions, payable as hereinafter provided:

(a)   A sum equal to twelve and one-half (12-1/2%) percent of the suggested retail selling price of folios, song books, legitimate fake books and other publications containing Subject Compositions solely and entirely in respect of all copies of such work sold and paid for.

(b)   In the event any Subject Composition is included in any folio, song book or other publication containing musical compositions or other musical materials that are not subject hereto, then in respect to each such work Publisher shall pay Owner a proportionate share of a royalty of twelve and one-half

(12-1/2%) percent of the suggested retail selling price for all copies of such work sold and paid for. Owner's share of said royalty shall be based on the ratio that Subject Compositions contained in each such work bear to the total number of musical compositions included therein.

(c)   A sum equivalent to $.35 per copy in respect to each copy for regular piano/vocal sheet music sold and paid for in the United States and Canada for which the retail selling price shall be $1.50 or more.

For regular piano/vocal sheet music sold and paid for in the United States and Canada which retails for less than $1.50 per copy, a sum equivalent to 30% of the retail selling price.

For regular piano/vocal sheet music sold and paid for outside the territories of the United States and Canada, a sum equivalent to 50% of the moneys received by us in the United States from the sale of such editions in such territories.

(d)   In the event any Subject Composition is sold in an instrumental, orchestral, choral, band or other arrangement, Publisher shall pay Owner a royalty of ten (10%) percent of the suggested retail selling price for all copies of such work sold and paid for.

(e)   Publisher shall pay to Owner a sum equal to five (5%) percent of the suggested retail selling price of each "Personality Folio" containing Subject Compositions solely and entirely along with the name of the Artist and photographs, likenesses of and biographical material relating to the Artist, said payments to constitute full and complete compensation for the rights granted in Paragraph 1 (b) above, all in respect of copies of such "Personality Folios" sold and paid for. In the event any "Personality Folio" contains compositions other than Subject Compositions, Owner's share of the royalty provided for in this paragraph shall be based upon the ratio that Subject Compositions contained in each such

"Personality Folio" bear to the total number of musical compositions included therein.

      (f)   With respect to any sales to or licenses to musical instrument manufacturers for publications which are not to be sold at retail and bear no retail selling price (i.e., sum of royalties) shall be made at the royalty rate provided for above but shall be based on the price received by us from such manufacturer or our customer for such editions of the Subject Compositions.

      Simultaneously herewith Publisher shall pay to Owner the sum of _____ Dollars, as a non-returnable advance recoupable by Publisher from any and all moneys payable to Owner under this agreement. The parties acknowledge the phrase "non-returnable advance" is to be interpreted as meaning that Publisher shall have no recourse against Owner if Publisher shall be unable to recoup said advance from moneys payable to Owner as above described.

      6.   Publisher agrees that within ninety (90) days after the last days of June and December of each year it will prepare and furnish statements to Owner, and each such statement shall be accompanied by a check or checks in payment of any and all sums shown to be due thereby. Upon submission of each statement, Publisher may maintain reserves against subsequent charges, returns, credits or defective merchandise, such portion of payable moneys as may be reasonably necessary and appropriate in Publisher's best business judgment. Each such statement shall be binding upon Owner and not subject to any objection by them for any reasons, unless specific objection, in writing, setting forth the basis thereof, is given to Publisher by Owner within two (2) years from the date rendered.

      Owner hereby agrees to pay writers of Subject Compositions all moneys payable to writers from Owner's receipts hereunder and further agrees to hold Publisher free and harmless from and against any claims of any writers of any of the Subject Compositions.

7. Publisher agrees to keep and maintain full and complete books and records concerning the subject matter hereof; and Owner shall have the right to examine Publisher's books and records at Publisher's principal place of business during its normal business hours and upon reasonable notice to verify the correctness of accounting statements rendered hereunder.

8. Publisher agrees to imprint a copyright notice on each copy of every printed publication of any of the Subject Compositions hereunder, in compliance with the formalities of the United State Copyright Law of the Universal Copyright Convention as well as the year and date of any prior copyright registration in the United State of America. Owner agrees that Publisher shall be entitled to rely on the accuracy of any such information furnished to Publisher by Owner.

9. Owner hereby agrees to provide Publisher with all necessary original photographs of the Artist and with appropriate biographical material relating to the Artist.

10. Owner agrees that Publisher shall have the non-exclusive right to sell in and throughout the licensed territory all printed copies of Subject Compositions in Publisher's possession or control as of the termination date hereof until Publisher shall have finally disposed of all such inventory, and Owner likewise agrees that the provisions of Paragraph 1 (b) hereby shall apply during said sell-off.

11. All notices, accounting statement, payments, delivery of printed materials and other documents or things required under the terms of this Agreement shall be sent by United States mail, postage prepaid, addressed to the party of whom the same is sent, as set forth on the first page hereof or to such other address or addresses that a party may notify the other from time to time.

12. This Agreement shall be construed and interpreted under the laws of the State of New York relating to agreements

entered into and to be wholly performed in said State, irrespective of the forum or forums to which this Agreement may be presented for construction or interpretation.

13.   This Agreement constitutes the entire agreement between the parties hereto and all prior or contemporaneous agreements of any kind or nature between the parties shall be deemed to be merged herein. This Agreement may be modified or amended only by an instrument in writing duly executed by the parties hereto.

14.   (a)   Owner shall not during the term of this Agreement do any act or authorize, license or knowingly permit any third party (other than a party authorized or licensed by Publisher) to do any act which would in any way derogate from or violate the exclusive right, license and privilege granted to Publisher by this Agreement.

(b)   Owner agrees to indemnify and hold Publisher free and harmless from any and all loss, damages, liability, costs, expenses and reasonable attorneys' fees arising out of any claims, demands or actions against Publisher which are inconsistent with any warranty, representation or agreement made by Owner hereunder. Written notice of any such claim, demand or action shall be promptly given to Owner, and Owner shall have the right to participate, at its own expense, in the defense thereof. Owner shall promptly, upon demand, reimburse Publisher for any payment made by Publisher with respect to any loss, cost, expense, liability or damage to which the foregoing indemnity applies. Pending the determination of any such claim, demand or action, Publisher shall have the right to withhold payment of that portion of moneys hereunder which shall be reasonably related to the size of the claim and estimated expenses.

(c)   Publisher expressly acknowledges that the Subject Compositions and all rights granted and to be granted to Publisher hereunder are of a special, unique and intellectual character which gives them peculiar value, and that in the event of a breach by Owner of any term, condition, warranty, representation or agreement hereunder, Publisher will be caused irreparable injury. Owner expressly agrees that in the event of any such breach, Publisher shall be entitled to injunctive and other equitable relief or damages, in addition to any other rights and remedies available to it, and Publisher shall have the right to recoup any damages from any sums which may thereafter become due and payable to Owner hereunder.

IN WITNESS WHEREOF, the parties hereto have executed this Agreement as of the year and date first above written.

FAMOUS RECORDING GROUP RIGHTS EXPLOITATION COMPANY, INC.

FAMOUS RECORDING GROUP MUSIC PUBLISHING COMPANY

By _____

Federal I.D. #:

OLD PRINT MUSIC PUBLISHER, INC.

By _____

FORM 6.4

LICENSE FOR USE OF LYRICS IN A BOOK

January 1, 1995

BEST SELLER BOOK PUBLISHING COMPANY, INC.
1 Broadway
New York, NY 10017

Gentlemen:

We hereby grant to you permission to reprint portions of the lyric only from our copyrighted musical composition, _____, by _____ in the English language version of your forthcoming book entitled, _____ , subject to the following terms and conditions:

    1. You shall pay us a fee of $ 35.00, check made payable to _____ , and addressed to the attention of the undersigned.

    2. The following copyright notice(s) must appear at the bottom of the page on which the quote appears, suitably asterisked, or as an alternative, we authorize copyright notice to be included on appropriate credit or copyright acknowledgment pages:

            Copyright © _____

            All rights reserved. Used by
            permission.

    3. The territory covered by this permission is worldwide.

    4. You shall furnish us with two (2) copies of the publication for our files.

This permission is for your use only, covering only the English language version of the first single hardcover/softcover edition and its reprints, and does not extend to abridgments, softcover/hardcover or editions published by any other person, firm or corporation, excepting those involved in Braille transcription and/or large type production for the physically handicapped, permission for which is hereby included.

This permission shall be valid upon your signing and returning to us one copy of this letter along with your remittance and upon the performance by you of the other terms and conditions hereof on your part to be performed.

Sincerely yours,

BIG MUSIC PUBLISHING CORP.

By: _____

AGREED & ACCEPTED:

BEST SELLER BOOK PUBLISHING COMPANY, INC.

By: _____

FORM 6.5

LETTER AGREEMENT TO EXTEND PRINT LYRIC LICENSE FOR USE IN NEW EDITION OF A BOOK

January 1, 1995

BEST SELLER BOOK PUBLISHING COMPANY, INC.
1 Broadway
New York, NY 10017

Re: License to Use Lyric Dated _____.

Gentlemen:

Dear _____ :

In consideration of the additional sum of _____
payable within thirty (30) days from the date hereof, our license
to you referenced above permitting you to reprint portions of the
lyric of our musical composition _____
in your book, _____ , is hereby amended to encompass
the release of said book in a [e.g., paperback edition] by Little Paperback Book Publishing Company.

Yours sincerely,

BIG MUSIC PUBLISHING CORP.

By: _____

                              AGREED AND ACCEPTED:

                              By _____

FORM 6.6

PRINT LICENSE FOR USE OF LYRICS IN CONNECTION WITH COMMERCIAL DISTRIBUTION OF A RECORDING

January 1, 1995

VINYL RECORD COMPANY
1 Vince Street
Hollywood, California 90069

RE: Musical Composition:
        Written by:

Gentlemen:

1.   We hereby grant to you a non-exclusive license to print and sell at your sole expense and cost in the United States and Canada printed copies of the lyric of the above-referenced musical composition in and as part of recording packages which contain the recording of said composition covered by a mechanical licensed issued on our behalf by the Harry Fox Agency concurrently herewith.

2.   You agree to pay us the following royalty: $.02 per lyric, per copy, sold with each recording.

3.   You shall account to us quarterly on the basis of music manufactured and sold.

4.   Each copy of each reprint shall contain our copyright notice and credit line:

          Copyright © 1990 BIG MUSIC PUBLISHING CORP.
          All Rights Reserved.

If the foregoing correctly sets forth our understanding, kindly sign and return a copy of this letter.

Yours sincerely,   AGREED TO:

BIG MUSIC PUBLISHING CORP.   LICENSEE

By_____   By_____

FORM 6.7

PRINT LICENSE FOR USE OF LYRICS IN CONNECTION WITH PROMOTIONAL DISTRIBUTION OF A RECORDING

January 1, 1995

VINYL RECORD COMPANY
1 Vince Street
Hollywood, California 90069

RE: Musical Composition:
       Written by:

Gentlemen:

1.   We hereby grant to you for no charge a non-exclusive license to print and distribute at your sole expense and cost in the United States and Canada printed copies of the lyric of the above-referenced musical composition in and as part of, or distributed in conjunction with distribution of, promotional copies of recording packages which contain the recording of said composition covered by a mechanical licensed issued on our behalf by the Harry Fox Agency concurrently herewith.

2.   Each copy of each reprint shall contain our copyright notice and credit line:

               Copyright © 1990 BIG MUSIC PUBLISHING CORP.
               All Rights Reserved.

If the foregoing correctly sets forth our understanding, kindly sign and return a copy of this letter.

Yours sincerely,   AGREED TO:

BIG MUSIC PUBLISHING CORP.   LICENSEE

By _____   By _____

FORM 6.8

EXCLUSIVE RIGHTS TO PRINT LYRICS IN LYRIC MAGAZINE FOR SINGLE SONG(S)

January 1, 1995

Lyric Magazine, Inc.
ADDRESS
CITY, STATE, ZIP

Gentlemen:

We hereby grant to you, your subsidiaries, affiliates and licensees, the exclusive right to print and vend each month in song lyric and fan magazines only, in the United States, its territories and possessions, and Canada only, the lyrics of the following musical composition(s) for a period of one year commencing the date set forth above.

    Musical Composition(s)   Songwriter(s)

You agree to pay us for the rights herein granted, provided the lyrics of said musical composition(s) are available to you during the period of this agreement, the sum of one-hundred ($100.00) Dollars per song listed above, receipt of which is hereby acknowledged.

We agree that during the period of this agreement we will not license or permit any others whatsoever to print or vend the lyrics of the above-named musical composition(s) in song lyric or fan magazines, it being understood that you shall have the exclusive right to use the same in such publications.

We warrant and represent that the lyrics furnished to you are new and original and we agree to indemnify and hold you harmless from any claims whatsoever arising out of the use by you of such lyrics. You agree that all copies of the lyrics of our compositions as printed hereunder shall carry an appropriate copyright notice, furnished by us, showing our ownership of the copyright of the said composition(s).

This agreement shall be binding on the parties hereto, their successors and assigns.

Very truly yours,

BIG MUSIC PUBLISHING CORP.

By _____

ACCEPTED AND AGREED:

LYRIC MAGAZINE, INC.

By _____

FORM 6.9

EXCLUSIVE RIGHTS TO PRINT LYRICS IN LYRIC MAGAZINE FOR ENTIRE CATALOG

Date: January 1, 1995

Lyric Magazine, Inc.
ADDRESS
CITY, STATE, ZIP

Gentlemen:

We hereby grant to you, your subsidiaries, affiliates and licensees, the exclusive right to print and vend each month in song lyric and fan magazines distributed only to customers or sold only on newsstands and similar retail outlets located in the United States, its territories and possessions, and Canada, for a period of one year from the date hereof, the lyrics of all the musical compositions (excluding musical compositions from motion picture, stage and other productions) now and hereafter in our catalog or that of any subsidiaries or affiliates now or hereafter formed to the extent that we do not require permission from third parties to make such grant. If permission is required, we will, upon your request, use our best efforts to obtain such permission. Notwithstanding the foregoing, we shall have the right to exclude from this agreement any musical composition(s) we wish upon written notice to you.

In consideration for the rights granted hereunder, you agree to pay us for the rights herein granted a non-returnable advance of One Thousand Two Hundred Dollars ($1,200) payable in twelve (12) equal monthly installments commencing upon the date hereof, which advance shall be recoupable against the sum of fifty ($50.00) Dollars due and payable for each song printed by you hereunder.

We agree that during the period of this agreement we will not license or permit any others whatsoever to print or vend any of the lyrics of our musical compositions in song lyric publications sold on newsstands and similar retail outlets, it being understood that you shall have the exclusive right to use the same in such publications, except that we reserve the right to use any of our compositions in our publications sold on newsstands and similar retail outlets which publications do not duplicate and are not similar to your song lyric magazines.

We warrant and represent that the lyrics furnished to you are new and original and we agree to indemnify and hold you harmless from any claims whatsoever arising out of the use by you of such lyrics. You agree that all copies of the lyrics of our compositions as printed hereunder shall carry an appropriate copyright notice, furnished by us, showing our ownership of the copyright of the said composition (s).

This agreement shall be binding upon the parties, hereto, their successors and assigns.

Very truly yours,

BIG MUSIC PUBLISHING CORP.

By _____

ACCEPTED AND AGREED:

LYRIC MAGAZINE, INC.

By _____

FORM 6.10

NON-EXCLUSIVE LICENSE TO PRINT LYRICS IN LYRIC MAGAZINE FOR ENTIRE CATALOG WITH SPECIAL PAYMENT PROVISIONS

Date: January 1, 1995

Lyric Magazine, Inc.
ADDRESS
CITY, STATE, ZIP

Gentlemen:

We hereby grant to you, your subsidiaries, affiliates and licensees, the nonexclusive license to print and vend each month in song lyric and fan magazines distributed only to customers and sold only on newsstands and similar retail outlets located in the United States, its territories and possessions, and Canada, for a period of one year from the date hereof, the lyrics of all the musical compositions (excluding musical compositions from motion picture, stage and other productions) now and hereafter in our catalog or that of any subsidiaries or affiliates now or hereafter formed to the extent that we do not require permission from third parties to make such grant. If permission is required, we will, upon your request, use our best efforts to obtain such permission. Notwithstanding the foregoing, we shall have the right to exclude from this agreement any musical composition(s) we wish upon written notice to you.

In consideration for the rights granted hereunder, you agree to pay us for the rights herein granted a non-returnable advance of One Thousand Two Hundred Dollars ($1,200) payable in (12) equal monthly installments commencing upon the date hereof, which advance shall be recoupable against the sums set forth below:

For each song lyric printed under the terms of this agreement, you shall pay us in accordance with the following schedule:

Category	Rate	No. of Uses
"Popular"	$150.00	Unlimited
"Country"	$50.00	Unlimited
"Popular Standard"	$50.00	One
"Country Standard"	$50.00	One

The foregoing terms shall have the meanings defined below:

The term *popular* shall mean the songs listed on the Billboard or Cash Box "Hot 100" singles listing, commonly referred to as the "Pop" charts.

The term *"country"* shall mean the songs listed on the Billboard or Cash Box "Hot Country" singles listing, commonly referred to as the "Country" charts.

The term *"popular standard"* shall mean the songs that appeared on the Billboard or Cash Box "Hot 100" singles listing prior to the start date of this agreement and which do not re-appear on said chart during the term of this agreement.

The term *"country standard"* shall mean the songs that appeared on the Billboard or Cash Box "Hot Country" singles listing prior to the start date of this agreement and which do not re-appear on said chart during the term of this agreement.

In the event that, during the period of this agreement, the lyric of any musical composition that you print during the term hereof is included among the top ten most "Popular" songs in the country on the Billboard or Cash Box "Hot 100" listing, you shall pay us the additional sum of seventy-five ($75.00) dollars. Only one such bonus payment shall be made for any one song no matter how many times the song is listed on the chart.

We warrant and represent that the lyrics furnished to you are new and original and we agree to indemnify and hold you harmless from any claims whatsoever arising out of the use by you of such lyrics. You agree that all copies of the lyrics of our compositions as printed hereunder shall carry an appropriate copyright notice, furnished by us, showing our ownership of the copyright of the said composition (s).

This agreement shall be binding upon the parties hereto, their successors and assigns.

Very truly yours,

BIG MUSIC PUBLISHING CORP.

By_____

ACCEPTED AND AGREED:

LYRIC MAGAZINE, INC.

By _____

MECHANICAL LICENSES

SUMMARY

HISTORICAL BACKGROUND

1. Music Boxes
2. Player Piano Rolls
3. Phonograph Records
4. Compact Discs

LEGAL BACKGROUND

1. Copyright
2. Compulsory Licensing

CONSIDERATIONS IN GRANTING AND CLEARING MECHANICAL LICENSES

1. Fee Structure
   A. Giving or Getting a Rate
   B. Rate Changes
2. Importance of the Song in Relation to its Intended Use
   A. Arrangements and Changes
3. Scope of the License
   A. Record Number v. Master Number
   B. Type of Media
   C. Distribution Channels
   D. Term
   E. Territory
   F. Exclusivity
   G. Credit

MECHANICAL RIGHTS AGENCIES

FORMS

FORM 7.1   Standard Mechanical License Agreement

CHAPTER 7

MECHANICAL
LICENSES

A *mechanical license* is a license which permits the reproduction of music in a form that may be heard with the aid of a "mechanical" device. Like the print license, the mechanical license is derived from the copyright owner's exclusive right to make copies. Today, by far the most common form of mechanical reproduction of music is the laser compact disc (CD). This chapter sketches the historical and legal background of music recorded on mechanical devices and provides an outline of some of the terms and conditions contained in customary mechanical licenses.

HISTORICAL BACKGROUND

1. Music Boxes

The first mechanical device designed to perform music was the *music box*, a mechanical instrument whose sounds are produced by a metal comb, the teeth of which are tuned to specific pitches, plucked by pins protruding from a cylinder that is rotated by a wound spring. Originally placed in snuff boxes, watches, and various ornamental objects and commonly used today in jewel boxes, figurines, and children's toys, the music box was invented in 1796 by Antoine Favre, a Swiss watchmaker. In the 1820s, as they became popular in homes, music boxes were mass produced to fulfill demand. By the mid-19th century, several developments in the technology led to music boxes that could play a wider selection of music for a longer period of time. Sophisticated music boxes, housed in massive pieces of furniture, could provide hours of listening pleasure. In 1885, a box was invented using metal discs instead of cylinders. Costing much less than the earlier box, it sold in vast quantities.

2. Player Piano Rolls

As music boxes gained popularity, a new form of music box, affording a more familiar quality of performed music, emerged: the *player piano*. A player piano is a piano equipped with a mechanical attachment which depresses the piano's keys by air pressure, reproducing notes that are represented by perforations on a paper roll. Player *piano rolls* are special perforated paper rolls manufactured in large quantity for use in player pianos, and represented the second major form of "mechanical" reproduction of music. From the late 1800's to the late 1920's, the popularity of player pianos reached their height, and millions of player piano rolls, embodying the most popular piano music of that time, were sold annually.

3. Phonograph Records

Nevertheless, both the music box and player piano industries were soon dealt a major blow by a new technological development: the record player. In 1877, Thomas Edison first reproduced recorded sound by using cylinders made of tin foil, an invention which he called the *phonograph*. The first phonograph was a hand-turned, metal cylinder covered with tin foil. A stylus resting on the tin foil was attached to a diaphragm which was caused to vibrate as sound was applied. The vibrating diaphragm pressed the stylus onto the surface of the tin foil, embossing it with a groove *analogous* to the sound which produced the vibrations in the diaphragm. (Hence, the name *analog* recording, as contrasted with *digital* recording, discussed below). After the groove was complete, the sounds could be "played back" by applying the stylus to the cylinder and rotating the cylinder at the same speed at which the sounds were originally recorded. Later, other inventors substituted a wax-covered cardboard cylinder for the tinfoil which facilitated the mass production of this new form of mechanical reproduction of music.

The age of cylinders ended in 1912 with the advent of the *78 RPM record*, which was recorded and played back at a speed of 78 *revolutions per minute* (RPM). 78-RPM remained the basic phonograph record speed until 1948, when Columbia Records introduced the *long-playing record (LP)*, which operated at 33 and 1/3 RPM. Shortly thereafter, RCA Victor introduced a smaller 45-RPM record, which eventually became the medium for popular *single* recordings.

For those readers who may be too young to remember, the LP was a vinyl platter, about the same size as a movie laser disc, which was placed onto a *turntable* that rotates at the speed of 33 1/3 revolutions per minute; the tone arm, mounted next to the turntable, which contained a diamond stylus, or record *needle,* would be moved on its pivot so that the stylus would come to gently rest in the *groove* etched into the vinyl record (hence, the 60's slang, *groovy).* As the record revolved, the stylus followed the grooves, spiraling in toward the center of the record, vibrating in response to the variations in the grooves. The vibration was converted into an analogous electrical signal, which, when strengthened by your amplifier, drove your speakers, where the signal was converted back into acoustic vibrations, which could be heard by an ear and understood by the human mind.

4. Compact Discs

For those readers who may be too old to realize, the LP record has become virtually extinct, having been replaced during the past 10 years by the popular optical *compact disc (CD).* Instead of a tone arm, the compact disc player uses a laser beam and a photoelectric cell to read the sound pattern imprinted on the disc as a series of microscopic pits.

During the 1970's, a new recording technique was developed, called *pulse code modulation (PCM),* to reduce the noise and distortion unavoidable in earlier recording methods. In PCM, the frequencies and amplitudes, or *analog* vibrations, of the original sound are analyzed and converted into *digital* pulses by the recording device. These digital pulses share the same basic components of the software that run modern computers: 1's and 0's, representing the *on* and *off* signals of the binary code. These "on" and "off" pulses are then processed and reconverted to ordinary sound signals when the record is cut. Upon the advent of the compact disc in the early 1980's, it was discovered that improved sound reproduction could be obtained by maintaining the digital character of the PCM recording in the process of mastering the CD. Thus, in the production of modern CD's, a digital, rather than analog, tape recorder is used during the sessions in which the sounds are (i) *recorded,* (ii) *mixed* or edited, and (iii) *mastered* for mass production.

LEGAL BACKGROUND

1. Copyright

Even though far removed from the mechanical reproduction of music by piano rolls and music boxes, recordings of music in records, tapes, and compact discs continue to be referred to as *mechanical reproductions*. Likewise, the term used to describe permission to record a copyrighted song on a phonograph record, tape, or compact disc is called a *mechanical license*. Examples of mechanical license agreements are set forth as Forms 7.1, 7.2, and 7.3 at the end of this chapter.

As noted in Chapter 2 above, licenses owe their existence to rights. The right to reproduce copyrighted music in mechanical devices, such as phonograph records, piano rolls, and music boxes, is one of the exclusive rights of reproduction held by the copyright owner. This, however, was not always so. In 1908, the United States Supreme Court startled the music industry by deciding that piano rolls and phonograph records were not "copies" of musical compositions and, therefore, not an infringement of the rights in the compositions, but merely part of the mechanism for their reproduction in sound.[1]

With the Copyright Act of 1909,[2] the U.S. Congress quickly overturned the effect of this decision by specifically recognizing the exclusive right of the copyright owner to make mechanical reproductions of music.

2. Compulsory Licensing

In taking this step, however, Congress had more in mind than merely providing rights to the composer. Congress was concerned about certain developments in the piano roll industry that threatened to create a monopoly in the hands of The Aeolian Co., a leading manufacturer of piano rolls. In anticipation of the legal recognition of mechanical reproduction rights, Aeolian had entered into exclusive contracts with many of the major music publishers of that time for the right to make mechani-

---

[1] *White-Smith Music Pub. Co. v. Apollo Co.*, 209 U.S. 1 (1908).

[2] Act of March 19, 1909, ch. 320, 35 Stat. 1075, as thereafter codified in 17 U.S.C. Sec. 1 et seq., and as amended.

cal reproductions of the works in the repertoires of the publishers. With Aeolian having the exclusive mechanical reproduction rights to a vast majority of popular music, few other manufacturers of piano rolls could acquire the licenses they required to compete in the piano roll business. To thwart this potential monopoly, Congress provided in the 1909 copyright law that if the copyright owner used or permitted the use of a copyrighted song for mechanical reproduction, then anyone else could make mechanical reproductions of that song by payment to the copyright owner of a royalty of two cents per unit. In other words, if the copyright owner licenses the song for mechanical reproduction at least once, then he could be forced to license it for mechanical reproduction to anyone else thereafter for a fee set by the copyright law.

The provision of the copyright statute compelling copyright owners to issue mechanical licenses became known as the *compulsory license* provision, and the prescribed per unit fee set forth in the law is referred to as the *statutory rate*.

The new copyright law enacted by Congress in 1976 maintained the compulsory license concept, with some modification, including the first increase in the statutory rate in nearly 70 years. It is embodied in Section 115 of the copyright law passed in 1976,[3] which is set forth at the end of this chapter. The copyright law also established, for the first time, a Copyright Royalty Tribunal which, among other things, is empowered to review and increase the statutory rate from time to time, as appropriate.[4] The statutory rate, as of January 1, 1992, is the greater of 6.25 cents per unit or 1.2 cents per minute of playing time, or fraction thereof, per unit. This rate will be adjusted every two years through 1996 according to changes in the Consumer Price Index.

Because of the burdensome procedures required by the compulsory license provision—such as the requirement of monthly, rather than quarterly accounting to copyright owners and notice conforming to strict regulation—nearly all mechanical licenses are negotiated directly between the copyright owners and the licensees and do not strictly reflect the terms of the compulsory license provisions of the law. Nevertheless, even though the compulsory license provision is rarely invoked directly,

---

[3] 17 U.S.C. Sec. 115.
[4] 17 U.S.C. Sec. 801-810.

its terms generally provide an outline for those of negotiated licenses and the statutory rate effects a maximum limit on the mechanical license fees charged by copyright owners under negotiated licenses.

Some debate continues over whether it is time for the compulsory license provision to be repealed. Detractors say that the monopoly against which the provision was enacted to combat went out with high button shoes, and there is no reason today why mechanical licenses should not be as freely negotiable as licenses for other kinds of uses. Others say that the compulsory license has served to simplify the process of obtaining mechanical licenses and has reduced a significant amount of unnecessary transaction costs.

Perhaps the best reason for maintaining the compulsory license is that it may be the most effective solution to the problem of split copyrights, discussed in Chapter 18. Split copyright does not become an issue when all the co-owners are required to accept no more than the statutory rate. Further, when the person seeking to clear a mechanical license cannot identify or locate the owner of the copyright, the compulsory license provision provides a safe harbor: if the public records of the Copyright Office do not identify the copyright owner and include an address at which notice under the provision can be served, it is sufficient to file the required notice with the Copyright Office.[5] By properly following the procedure and paying the statutory rate set forth in the compulsory license provision, a person seeking to clear permission will be assured a license without taking any risk of liability for copyright infringement.

CONSIDERATIONS IN GRANTING AND CLEARING MECHANICAL LICENSES

As noted in the preceding section, the compulsory license provision has the effect of limiting the flexibility the copyright owner has in setting the terms of the mechanical license. As a result, two of the four primary factors in considering the terms of most music licenses—the value of the song and the importance of the song in relation to its intended use (see

---

[5] 17 U.S.C. Sec. 115(b)(1).

Chapter 5)—do not come much into play in the negotiation of mechanical licenses (with one notable exception: granting and clearing mechanical licenses for digital samples containing copyrighted music, a topic discussed at length in Chapter 17).

Nevertheless, though the clearance of mechanical licenses is generally an administrative process in which very little negotiation takes place, there remains some degree of flexibility that deserves some discussion.

1. Fee Structure

A. *Giving or Getting a Rate*

A copyright owner will occasionally receive a request that a mechanical license be issued for a fee that is below the statutory rate. This is known as asking for *a rate*. To *give a rate* refers to charging a mechanical license fee that is below the statutory rate set by the compulsory license statute and the Copyright Royalty Tribunal.

When a "rate" is offered, it is usually quoted at either fifty percent or seventy five percent *of statutory*. Thus, assuming, for simplicity, the statutory rate were 8 cents per copy, then a "half of statutory" rate would, of course, be 4 cents per copy.

Under the appropriate circumstances, a person seeking to clear a mechanical license should ask for a rate, and a copyright owner should, when the circumstances are justified, grant a rate. For example, record companies seeking to exploit older recordings will use creative marketing techniques or lower prices, such as the sale of older recordings through record clubs or the packaging of recordings of older artists in an inexpensive album or series of albums, sometimes called a *budget line* record. For budget line and record club releases, most music publishers would consent to a fee of 75% of the statutory rate per song.

B. *Rate Changes*

Many mechanical licenses identify the fee being charged using the words, "statutory rate," rather than using the appropriate denomination of cents per copy in effect. For example, a license may state, "The royalty under this license shall be the statutory rate" or "The royalty under this license shall be one-half the statutory rate." The wording of this provision should be reviewed carefully.

If the license goes no further than to say the royalty shall be the statutory rate, then the license may be construed as meaning the copyright owner is entitled to only receive the statutory rate in effect at the time the license was executed. This would completely deprive the copyright owner of the benefit of any later increases in the statutory rate made by the Copyright Royalty Tribunal.

Accordingly, mechanical licenses which refer to the statutory rate in this way should make it clear that the rate to be applied is the statutory rate "in effect at the time the phonorecords are made."

An alternative means of dealing with rate changes is to draft the license to provide that the initial stated fee shall increase in proportion to increases in the statutory rate made by the Copyright Royalty Tribunal. The mechanical license form set forth as Form 7.2 at the end of this chapter contains an example of this means of reflecting rate increases.

Persons seeking to clear mechanical licenses might attempt to limit the fee to the statutory rate in effect at the time the mechanical license is executed, regardless of when the copies of the licensed recording are made and distributed. The mechanical license form set forth as Form 7.3 at the end of this chapter contains an example of a provision which effects such terms.

2. Importance of the Song in Relation to Its Intended Use

Because of the applicability of the compulsory license provision to mechanical licensing, considerations of the importance of the song in relation to its intended use rarely comes into play in the negotiation of mechanical licenses. Nevertheless, not all uses of music on recordings intended for distribution to the general public will be governed by the compulsory license statute.

A. Arrangements and Changes

In drafting the copyright law of 1976, Congress considered the extent to which someone making a recording under the compulsory license provision may depart from the musical work as originally written or recorded without violating the copyright owner's exclusive right to make an arrangement or other derivative work.

Congress recognized the practical need for a limited privilege to make arrangements of music being used under a compulsory license, but without allowing the music to be "perverted, distorted, or travestied."[6] Accordingly, the compulsory license provision includes the following balance of interests: "A compulsory license includes the privilege of making a musical arrangement of the work to the extent necessary to conform it to the style or manner of interpretation of the performance involved, but the arrangement shall not change the basic melody or fundamental character of the work, and shall not be subject to protection as a derivative work under this title, except with the express consent of the copyright owner."[7]

Nearly all mechanical licenses include a similar limitation or incorporate this provision directly by reference.

Interestingly, this provision would seem to make it clear that a mechanical license under the compulsory license provision of the copyright law would not be available to a person seeking to use a digital sample of another's copyrighted work in a way that would change the basic melody or fundamental character of the song from which the sample was taken. The problem of *digital sampling* is discussed at length in Chapter 17.

Accordingly, if the intended use would depart from the basic melody or change the lyrics, the copyright owner would be free to negotiate the terms of the mechanical license without regard to the restrictions normally imposed by the compulsory license provision.

3. Scope of the License

The form for a mechanical license is usually prepared and completed by the music copyright owner or its agent. Though it is primarily an administrative procedure, care should still be taken to draft the form to suit the intent of the parties.

---

[6] House Report of the Copyright Act of 1976, No. 94-1476, at page 109 (September 3, 1976).

[7] 17 U.S.C. Sec. 115 (a) (2).

A. Record Number v. Master Number

In the mechanical licenses set forth as Forms 7.1 and 7.2 at the end of this chapter, a blank space is provided for the entry of the *number* of the recording (single, album, tape, or CD, as appropriate). If you are representing the music copyright owner, you should complete this space with the *record number*, which is the number that identifies the particular recording made from that master. You should not use the *master number*, which is the number established at the recording studio for identification and filing purposes when the recording master is completed. Thus, when completing a mechanical license on behalf of the music copyright owner, you should ask the licensee for the record number and make sure that what you are being given is not the master number.

By using the record number, rather than the master number, you will have narrowed the scope of the license to permission to make reproductions of the particular album on which the song was intended to initially appear, rather than any record made from recordings appearing in the master. If the master is later used, as, for example, in making a remix of the original recording or in using recordings from the master in other record albums, the recording company would then be required to obtain an additional license from the copyright owner to use the recording for the new use.

This may be quite advantageous, as the terms of the new license will reflect circumstances existing at the time the new use is made, rather than those existing at the time a license was issued for the use of the original master recording. Whenever a copyright owner narrows the scope of the license he is in effect requiring the licensee to ask additional permission for a new use and, by doing so, he is preserving the ability to determine the terms of the license at a time when he can better assess the value of the use for which permission is being sought. For example, if a mechanical license were carefully limited to cover the specific recording originally made from the master (i.e., by use of the record number in identifying the recording licensed rather than the master number), then any new copies made from a remix of the master, or recordings made from the master, placed into other albums, would be subject to a new license, which could then be negotiated to reflect better terms for the copyright owner.

Should the compulsory license provision of the copyright law be repealed after the original mechanical license was granted, then, if the new use were not covered by the old license, the copyright owner would be free to negotiate a new, more favorable license fee for the new use, rather than be limited to the statutory rate set forth in the original mechanical license. More likely than a repeal of the compulsory license provision, the Copyright Royalty Tribunal will have raised the statutory rate after the original mechanical license was issued, and if the mechanical license fee was based upon an old statutory rate, then the new statutory rate may be available to the copyright owner, if the old mechanical license is deemed not to cover the new use.

If you are the person seeking to clear a mechanical license, the advice inherent in the preceding paragraphs should be straightforward: try to obtain a license to use the master by identifying the licensed recording by the master number, instead of the record number.

B. Type of Media

Another technique used to limit the scope of the license is to specify precisely what kind of media configuration the mechanical license covers. If the licensee's intention is simply to release a record album, then there would be no reason to grant a license that permits the use of the song on any other medium unless and until requested. Accordingly, the license should specify whether the use is for LP records, audiocassettes, or compact discs (CDs).

Note, the record number may not necessarily be the same as the *tape number* or the *CD number*—that is, the number identifying audiocassette tape or compact disc versions of the recording. Accordingly, if the form of a previously executed mechanical license did not specify the type of media on which use of the recording is limited, then the use of the record number in the mechanical license may have effectively limited the use to LPs.

Music copyright owners who were careful to limit their mechanical licenses in this way when issuing licenses for the use of music on record albums and audiocassettes may find that they have preserved for themselves the leverage to improve the terms of those licenses when record companies later seek permission to re-release those albums or cassettes in the new CD format. If the copyright owner had, for example, given a *rate* (i.e., charged less than the statutory rate) for the use of a song on an LP, and later became successful enough to warrant its release in the CD format, then, if the license was limited to the record number of the original LP, the recording company might be required to seek a new license to cover the use of the song on CD, and the copyright owner could then require full statutory rate. Had the original mechanical license been defined as including the master number, then the CD use would probably have been covered and the record company could continue licensing the song on the new media configuration at half statutory rate.

Persons seeking to clear mechanical licenses, should try to obtain a license to reproduce the recording in any format, or at least negotiate options to add additional formats at rates and other terms established at the time of the execution of the license.

C. Distribution Channels

The compulsory provision of the copyright law provides that "a person may obtain a compulsory license only if his or her primary purpose in making phonorecords is to distribute them to the public for private use."[8] All mechanical licenses reflect the same limitation. If, for example, the primary purpose of making the recordings is for use in the facilitation of commercial broadcasts of the recording, then a compulsory license is not available and the use is outside the scope of the mechanical license. The type of license required for such use is an *electrical transcription license*, which is discussed in detail in Chapter 8.

D. Term

The term of a mechanical license is often not stated on the face of the license. It is assumed that the term is for the life of the copyright, because the compulsory license provision does not limit the term of mechanical licenses obtained under the statute. The license may be terminated, however, upon 30 days' notice if the licensee fails to pay the mechanical license fee.

E. Territory

The territory of the mechanical license is usually limited. For example, most mechanical licenses issued in the United States limit the territory to the United States, including its territories and possessions.

---

[8] 17 U.S.C. Sec. 115 (a) (1).

F. Exclusivity

A mechanical license is never granted on an exclusive basis. To grant exclusive mechanical rights would be in contradiction to the compulsory license provision which requires that, once recordings of the work have been distributed to the public once, mechanical licenses are available to anyone upon the licensee's fulfillment of certain conditions.

G. Credit

When a recording company asks for a *rate*, the music copyright owner has an opportunity to negotiate terms that he would not otherwise be able to obtain under the compulsory license provision. An example of a condition typically required when a rate is granted is that the songwriters and publishers be given credit on copies of the records distributed under the mechanical license. Such a provision may be added to a standard mechanical license in the following form:

> In regard to all phonorecords manufactured, distributed and/or sold hereunder, you shall include in the label copy of all such phonorecords, or on the permanent containers of all such phonorecords, printed writer/publisher credit in the form of the names of the writer(s) and the publisher(s) of the copyrighted work.

MECHANICAL RIGHTS AGENCIES

Thousands of recording companies seek licenses to record potentially hundreds of thousands of copyrighted compositions. Because it would be economically prohibitive for copyright owners to negotiate with the great number of potential licensees, many copyright owners and music publishers engage the services of a special representative for the purpose of licensing their compositions to be used in sound recordings. In the United States, The Harry Fox Agency, Inc.[9] and The Songwriter's Guild of America (formerly, the American Guild of Authors and Com-

---

[9] The Harry Fox Agency, Inc., 205 East 42d Street, New York, NY 10017, Phone: 212-370-5330, Fax: 212-953-2384.

posers, or AGAC)[10] are among the organizations that issue mechanical licenses in the United States.

The Harry Fox Agency, established in 1927 by the National Music Publisher's Association (NMPA), is by far the largest of these, representing over 10,000 music publishers. In addition to issuing mechanical licenses, the Harry Fox Agency also grants, on behalf of many of its member publishers, licenses for the synchronization of music with motion pictures, television programs, and other audiovisual works, licenses for the creation of electrical transcriptions, and licenses for the use of music in commercial advertising. It also engages in the auditing of books and records of the licensees, such as record companies, using music under licenses issued by the Agency. The NMPA also provides mediation services to those member publishers who require an alternative to litigation as a means of settling a dispute between or among them.

The information required by the Harry Fox Agency for the issuance of a mechanical license includes: (1) the name of the person or company to whom the license is to be issued, (2) the title and writers of the composition, and, if known, the publisher(s), (3) the record number, (4) the performing artist, (5) the playing time in minutes and seconds of the composition, (6) the release date and (7) the configuration or format of the recording (i.e., audiocassette, LP, or CD).

The Harry Fox Agency will not issue a mechanical license for less than the statutory rate without permission from the copyright owner of the song, to whom all such requests are promptly referred. For its services in issuing mechanical licenses, collecting royalties, and distributing to publishers, as well as for the periodic audits of record manufacturers, the Harry Fox Agency charges a small fee based on a percentage of mechanical license fees collected.

Mechanical reproduction rights in music is recognized by law throughout the world. Though mechanical license fees vary from country to country, there is a mechanical rights society in nearly every country that recognizes these rights. Further information on international mechanical rights societies affiliated with the Harry Fox Agency may be obtained from the Harry Fox Agency.

---

[10] The Songwriters Guild of America, 276 Fifth Avenue, New York, NY 10001; Phone: 212-686-6820; Fax: 212-486-3680.

APPENDIX TO CHAPTER 7
MECHANICAL LICENSES

FORMS

FORM 7.1   Standard Mechanical License Agreement

FORM 7.2   Alternative Mechanical License Drafted in Favor
                of Licensor

FORM 7.3   Alternative Mechanical License Drafted in Favor
                of Licensee

LAWS

LAW 7.1   Compulsory License Provision of the Copyright
                Act of 1976 (17 U.S.C. Sec. 115)

FORM 7.1

STANDARD MECHANICAL LICENSE AGREEMENT

<u>MECHANICAL LICENSE AGREEMENT</u>

DATE:

A)   TITLE:

WRITER(S):

B)   PUBLISHER(S):

C)   <u>RECORD #</u>   <u>ARTIST LABEL</u>   <u>TIMING</u>   <u>ROYALTY RATE</u>

<u>RELEASE DATE:</u>

You have advised us as the Publisher(s) referred to in (B) supra, that you wish to obtain a compulsory license to make and distribute phonorecords of the copyrighted work referred to in (A) supra, under the compulsory license provision of Section 115 of the Copyright Act.

Upon doing so, you shall have all rights which are granted to, and all the obligations which are imposed upon, users of said copyrighted work under the compulsory license provision of the Copyright Act, after phonorecords of the copyrighted work have been distributed to the public in the United States under the authority of the copyright owner by another person, except that with respect to phonorecords thereof made and distributed hereunder:

1)   You shall pay royalties and account to us as Publisher(s) quarterly, within forty-five days after the end of each calendar quarter, on the basis of phonorecords made and distributed;

2)   For such phonorecords made and distributed, the royalty shall be the Statutory rate in effect at the time the phonorecord is made, except as otherwise stated in (C) supra;

3)   This compulsory license covers and is limited to one particular recording of said copyrighted work as performed by the artist and on the phonorecord number identified in (C) supra; and this compulsory license does not supersede nor in any way affect any prior agreements now in effect respecting phonorecords of said copyrighted work;

4)   In the event you fail to account to us and pay royalties as herein provided for, said Publisher(s) may give written notice to you that, unless the default is remedied within 30 days of your receipt of the notice, this compulsory license will be automatically terminated. Such termination shall render either the making or the distribution, or both, of all phonorecords for which royalties have not been paid, actionable as acts of infringement under, and fully subject to the remedies provided by, the Copyright Act;

5)   You need not serve or file the notice of intention to obtain a compulsory license required by the Copyright Act;

6)   This agreement is limited to the United States, its territories and possessions.

ACCEPTED AND AGREED: Very truly yours,

By _____   By _____

Date _____

FORM 7.2

ALTERNATIVE MECHANICAL LICENSE DRAFTED IN FAVOR OF THE LICENSOR

<u>MECHANICAL LICENSE</u>

_____(referred to herein as the "Licensor") hereby grants to _____ (referred to herein as the "Licensee") the non-exclusive license to use, in whole or in part, the copyrighted musical composition entitled " _____ " written by_____ (hereinafter referred to as the "Composition") in the recording, making and distribution of:

(Check appropriate lines:)

   A. _____ Single: a non-visual "single" phonorecord in disc form;

   B. _____ Album: a track on non-visual album phonorecord in disc form;

   C. _____ Tape: a segment of a non-visual prerecorded tape phonorecord in reel to reel, cassette or cartridge form;

   D. _____ C.D.: a track on non-visual album phonorecord on compact disc form;

to be made and distributed in the United States, its territories and possessions, in accordance with the provisions of Section 115 of the Copyright Act of the United States of America of October 19, 1976, as amended (the "Act"), except it is agreed that: (1) Licensee need not serve or file the notices required under the Act; (2) the accountings and payment of the royalty herein provided for shall be made quarterly, on the fifteenth day of February, May, August and November for the quarters ending the last day of December, March, June and September, respectively; and (3) a net royalty of

SIX and ONE QUARTER CENT ($.0625) or ONE and TWO HUN-
DREDTHS OF ONE CENT ($.012) per minute of playing time or
fraction thereof, whichever is greater, shall be payable by Licensee
to Licensor on each phonorecord made, distributed and not returned (whether or not sold); provided, however, that no such
royalty shall be payable with respect to promotional phonorecords
sent to disc jockeys, reviewers, and the like, which are clearly
marked "Promotional Records Not For Sale" and which are not
being distributed by Licensee for resale. If the compulsory license
royalty under Section 115 of the Act is hereafter adjusted to
provide for a copyright royalty rate in excess of SIX and ONE
QUARTER CENT ($.0625) and/or ONE and TWO HUNDREDTHS OF
ONE CENT ($.012) per minute of playing time or fraction thereof,
then the rate(s) set forth above shall be deemed automatically
increased (proportionately, if applicable) to conform to such higher
rate(s) for all phonorecords distributed following the effective date
of such adjustment. The term "phonorecord" shall have that meaning set forth in Section 101 of the Copyright Act.

This license is limited to the particular recording and use of the
Composition herein described and shall not include any other
recording or form of recorded sound.

This license includes the privilege of making a musical arrangement of the Composition to the extent necessary to conform it
to the style or manner of interpretation of the performance
involved, but the arrangement made (i) may not change the basic
melody or fundamental character or the lyrics of the Composition, (ii) shall not be subject to protection under the Act by
Licensee as a derivative work, and (iii) may be freely used by
Licensor for any and all purposes.

Failure to render timely accountings or make timely payments to
Licensor shall, if not cured by Licensee within thirty (30) days after
written notice thereof from Licensor, constitute a material breach
of this license entitling Licensor, in addition to its other remedies,
to immediately terminate this license and all rights granted to
Licensee hereunder. Such termination shall render either the mak-

ing or the distribution, or both, of all phonorecords for which royalties have not been paid, actionable as acts of infringement under, and fully subject to, the remedies provided by the Act. A waiver of any breach hereunder shall not constitute a waiver of any succeeding breach, whether similar or dissimilar. Upon written request and during Licensee's regular business hours, Licensee agrees to make its books and records relating to the subject matter hereof available for audit by Licensor and Licensor shall have the right to make copies thereof. Reasonable reserves may be withheld in the same manner as Licensee withholds and liquidates reserves in accordance with its current arrangement with The Harry Fox Agency, Inc.

This license is personal, non-licensable and non-assignable, except by Licensor. This license does not supersede nor affect any prior licenses or agreements now in force respecting recordings of the Composition. This license shall be governed by and construed under the laws of the State of California.

THIS LICENSE IS NOT VALID UNTIL LICENSOR RECEIVES A FREE COPY OF THE SINGLE, ALBUM AND/OR TAPE LICENSED HEREUNDER AND A COUNTERSIGNED COPY OF THIS LICENSE.

Dated:

LICENSEE: LICENSOR:

_____   _____

By: _____   By: _____

Release Date: _____

Timing: _____

Single Number: _____

Album Number: _____

Tape Number: _____

C.D. Number: _____

Recording Artist: _____

All payments to be made to Licensor hereunder shall be made to Licensor in care of:

_____

FORM 7.3

ALTERNATIVE MECHANICAL LICENSE DRAFTED IN FAVOR OF THE LICENSEE

MECHANICAL LICENSE

_____ (referred to herein as the "Licensor") hereby grants to _____ (referred to herein as the "Licensee") the non-exclusive license to use, in whole or in part, the copyrighted musical composition set forth below:

written by_____ (hereinafter referred to as the "Composition") in the recording, making and distribution of phonorecords (as that term is defined in Section 101 of the Copyright Act) to be made and distributed throughout the world in accordance with the provisions of Section 115 of the Copyright Act of the United States of America of October 19, 1976, as amended (the "Act"), except it is agreed that: (1) Licensee need not serve or file the notices required under the Act; (2) the accountings and payment of the royalty herein provided for shall be made quarterly, as set forth below; (3) consideration for such license shall be the statutory rate in effect at the time of execution hereof for each phonorecord made, distributed and not returned (whether or not sold) containing the Composition; provided, however, that no such royalty shall be payable with respect to promotional phonorecords sent to disc jockeys, reviewers, and the like, which are not being distributed by Licensee for resale; and (4) this license shall be worldwide.

This license permits the use of the Compositions, or any of them, in the particular recordings made in connection with the sound recording _____ by _____ , and permits the use of such recording in any phonorecord in which the recording may be embodied in whatever form now known or hereafter devised. This license includes the privilege of making a musical arrangement of the Compositions to the extent necessary to

conform it to the style or manner of interpretation of the performance involved. .

Licensee will compute the royalties earned by Licensor pursuant
to this license within forty-five (45) days after the end of each
calendar quarter (provided that with respect to royalties resulting from non-U.S. transactions such period shall be ninety (90)
days after end of each calendar quarter), and will deliver to
Licensor a quarterly royalty statement for each such period
together with the net amount of royalties computed in accordance with this license, if any.

All payments shall be made to Licensor hereunder shall be made
to Licensor in care of: _____

Upon at least fifteen (15) days' prior written notice to Licensee, a
certified public accountant retained on Licensor's behalf shall have
the right once each year to inspect such of Licensee's business
books and records as may reasonably be necessary for Licensor
to verify the accuracy of any royalty statement rendered by Licensee within the twelve (12) month period immediately preceding the
date of the inspection. The information contained in a royalty
statement shall be conclusively deemed correct and binding upon
Licensor, resulting in the loss of all further audit rights with respect
to such statement, unless specifically challenged by written notice
from Licensor within twelve (12) months from the date such royalty
statement was delivered by Licensee. Any inspection of Licensee's
books and records pursuant to this Section shall be conducted by
Licensor at Licensee's premises, only during Licensee's normal
business hours, under Licensee's supervision and in a manner
which does not interfere with Licensee's business operations.
Licensor shall specify, at least fifteen (15) days in advance of any
inspection, the list of items that Licensor desires to inspect. This
right of audit shall be subject to Licensor's certified public accountant's executing Licensee's standard Nondisclosure Agreement to
maintain all information learned as a result of such inspection in
strict confidence. Licensor's accountants shall be authorized by
Licensee to report to Licensor only the amount of fees due and

payable for the period examined. Licensee may withhold a reasonable reserve for returnable copies. This license may not be terminated for any reason, and Licensor's sole remedy for breach shall be a claim for damages.

This license shall be construed and enforced in accordance with the laws of the State of California applicable to agreements between residents of California wholly executed and wholly performed therein. Any action or proceeding brought by either party against the other arising out of or related to this Agreement shall be brought only in a state or federal court of competent jurisdiction located in the County of Los Angeles, California, and the parties hereby consent to the personal jurisdiction of said courts. The provisions of this paragraph shall survive any termination of the Agreement.

LICENSEE: LICENSOR:

_____   _____

By   By

_____   _____

Name   Name

_____   _____

Date   Date

LAW 7.1

COMPULSORY LICENSE PROVISION OF THE COPYRIGHT ACT OF 1976 (17 U.S.C. SECTION 115)

Section 115. **Scope of exclusive rights in nondramatic musical works: Compulsory license for making and distributing phonorecords**

In the case of nondramatic musical works, the exclusive rights provided by clauses (1) and (3) of section 106, to make and to distribute phonorecords of such works, are subject to compulsory licensing under the conditions specified by this section.

(a)   *Availability and Scope of Compulsory License.* -

(1)   When phonorecords of a nondramatic musical work have been distributed to the public in the United States under the authority of the copyright owner, any other person may, by complying with the provisions of this section, obtain a compulsory license to make and distribute phonorecords of the work. A person may obtain a compulsory license only if his or her primary purpose in making phonorecords is to distribute them to the public for private use. A person may not obtain a compulsory license for use of the work in the making of phonorecords duplicating a sound recording fixed by another, unless: (i) such sound recording was fixed lawfully; and (ii) the making of the phonorecords was authorized by the owner of copyright in the sound recording, or, if the sound recording was fixed before February 15, 1972, by any person who fixed the sound recording pursuant to an express license from the owner of the copyright in the musical work or pursuant to a valid compulsory license for use of such work in a sound recording.

(2)   A compulsory license includes the privilege of making a musical arrangement of the work to the extent necessary

to conform it to the style or manner of interpretation of the performance involved, but the arrangement shall not change the basic melody or fundamental character of the work, and shall not be subject to protection as a derivative work under this title, except with the express consent of the copyright owner.

(b)   *Notice of Intention To Obtain Compulsory License. -*

(1)   Any person who wishes to obtain a compulsory license under this section shall, before or within thirty days after making, and before distributing any phonorecords of the work, serve notice of intention to do so on the copyright owner. If the registration or other public records of the Copyright Office do not identify the copyright owner and include an address at which notice can be served, it shall be sufficient to file the notice of intention in the Copyright Office. The notice shall comply, in form, content and manner of service, with requirements that the Register of Copyrights shall prescribe by regulation.

(2)   Failure to serve or file the notice required by clause (1) forecloses the possibility of a compulsory license and, in the absence of a negotiated license, renders the making and distribution of phonorecords objectionable as acts of infringement under Section 501 and fully subject to the remedies provided by sections 502 through 506 and 509.

(c)   *Royalty Payable Under Compulsory License. -*

(1)   To be entitled to receive royalties under a compulsory license, the copyright owner must be identified in the registration or other public records of the Copyright Office. The owner is entitled to royalties for phonorecords made and distributed after being so identified, but is not entitled to recover for any phonorecords previously made and distributed.

(2)   Except as provided by clause (1), the royalty under a compulsory license shall be payable for every phonorecord made and distributed in accordance with the license. For this purpose, a

phonorecord is considered "distributed" if the person exercising the compulsory license has voluntarily and permanently parted with its possession. With respect to each work embodied in the phonorecord, the royalty shall be either 6.25 cents, or 1.2 cents per minute of playing time or fraction thereof, whichever amount is larger.

(3)   A compulsory license under this section includes the right of the maker of a phonorecord of a nondramatic musical work under subsection (a)(1) to distribute or authorize distribution of such phonorecord by rental, lease, or lending (or by acts or practices in the nature of rental, lease, or lending). In addition to any royalty payable under clause (2) and chapter 8 of this title, a royalty shall be payable by the compulsory licensee for every act of distribution of a phonorecord by or in the nature of rental, lease, or lending, by or under the authority of the compulsory licensee. With respect to each nondramatic musical work embodied in the phonorecord, the royalty shall be a proportion of the revenue received by the compulsory from every such act of distribution of the phonorecord under this clause equal to the proportion of the revenue received by the compulsory licensee from distribution of the phonorecord under clause (2) that is payable by a compulsory licensee under that clause and under Chapter 8. The Register of Copyrights shall issue regulations to carry out the purpose of this clause.

(4)   Royalty payments shall be made on or before the twentieth day of each month and shall include all royalties for the month next preceding. Each monthly payment shall be made under oath and shall comply with requirements that the Register of Copyrights shall prescribe by regulation. The Register shall also prescribe regulations under which detailed cumulative annual statements of account, certified by a certified public accountant, shall be filed for every compulsory license under this section. The regulations covering both the monthly and the annual statements of account shall prescribe the form, content, and manner of certification with respect to the number of records made and the number of records distributed.

(5)   If the copyright owner does not receive the monthly payment and the monthly and annual statements of account when due, the owner may give written notice to the licensee that, unless the default is remedied within thirty days from the date of the notice, the compulsory license will be automatically terminated. Such termination renders either the making or the distribution, or both, of all phonorecords for which the royalty has not been paid, actionable as acts of infringement under section 501 and fully subject to the remedies provided by sections 502 through 506 and 509.

ELECTRICAL TRANSCRIPTION LICENSES

SUMMARY

TYPES OF ELECTRICAL TRANSCRIPTIONS

1. Transcriptions for Radio Broadcast

   A. Themes and Introductions

   B. Syndicated Radio Programs

   C. Commercial Advertisements Prepared
       for Radio Broadcast

2. Transcriptions for Background Music Services

   A. Muzak and 3M

   B. Performance License Aspects

   C. Recent Changes

3. Transcriptions for In-Flight Use on Airlines

CONSIDERATIONS IN GRANTING AND CLEARING ELECTRICAL TRANSCRIPTION LICENSES

1. Fee Structure

2. Value of the Song and its Importance in Relation to
   the Intended Use

   A. Arrangements and Changes

3. Scope of Use

   A. Type of Media

   B. Distribution Channels

   C. Term

   D. Territory

   E. Exclusivity

RIGHTS AGENCIES

FORMS

FORM 8.1   Electrical Transcription License for
              Syndicated Radio Broadcasts Used By
              the Harry Fox Agency

FORM 8.2   Electrical Transcription License for
                  Background Music Services Used By
                  the Harry Fox Agency

FORM 8.3   Electrical Transcription License for
                  Background Music Services Used By
                  3M Company

CHAPTER **8**

ELECTRICAL TRANSCRIPTION LICENSES

An *electrical transcription license* is a license which permits the reproduction of music in recordings that are not accompanied by moving pictures and that are made for the purpose of facilitating radio broadcasts or purposes other than distribution to the public for private use.

The distinction between mechanical recordings and electrical transcriptions inheres in the use for which the recording is intended: copies of *mechanical* recordings, such as record albums, audiocassettes, and compact discs, are primarily intended for distribution to the public for private use; copies of *electrical transcription* recordings are intended for distribution to radio stations, background music services, and special music services for public broadcasting purposes. This distinction is important because only mechanical recordings intended for distribution to the public for private use are subject to the compulsory licensing provision of the copyright law.[1] Accordingly, fees and other terms for licenses to make recordings intended for background music services and radio broadcast may be freely negotiated without regard to the limitations set forth in the compulsory licensing provision.

TYPES OF ELECTRICAL TRANSCRIPTIONS

Electrical transcription licenses are issued in connection with the following kinds of transcription recordings:

---

[1] Section 115 of the copyright law states, "A person may obtain a compulsory license only if his or her primary purpose in making phonorecords is to distribute them to the public *for private use*." 17 U.S.C. Sec. 115 (emphasis added).

339

1. Transcriptions for Radio Broadcast

The making of recordings of introductory musical themes, background music for radio commercials, and compilations of musical compositions distributed as part of syndicated radio shows, all require permission from the copyright owners of the music involved. The permission to make such recordings is entirely distinct from the permission required to perform the recordings. The latter is normally acquired from the performance rights society, such as ASCAP or BMI, but permission to create the recording itself and make copies of it is acquired directly from the copyright owner.

A. Themes and Introductions

Radio programs, such as news programs and talk shows, often use some short familiar theme music as an introduction to the program or as background music for *segues* (i.e., transitions) to and from commercials or other breaks in the program. Music publishers often prepare electrical transcription recordings containing a variety of short themes and introductions for this purpose and distribute them to radio stations free of charge. A music publisher's incentive for providing this service, of course, is the performance fees it will receive from performance rights societies as a result of the airplay of these short pieces of music. Performance licenses are discussed at length in Chapter 15.

B. Syndicated Radio Programs

A *syndicated radio program* is a series of pre-recorded, one or two hour radio programs of music, usually accompanied by introductory and background commentary delivered by an announcer. The pre-recorded tapes of these programs are licensed by their producers on an individual basis to local radio stations around the country. For example, a producer may prepare a series of syndicated radio programs of selected Frank Sinatra recordings, including short commentaries regarding each recording, identifying the songwriters, the arrangers, and any interesting circumstances related to the recording or the time during the artist's life when the recording was made. Short interviews with the artist may also be featured in some of these programs. Series such as these might be attractive to local radio stations that cater to the audience for which the program was designed.

The tapes containing these programs and recordings are not mechanical reproductions, in the strict sense of the term, because they are primarily intended for distribution to broadcast stations for further broadcast —not for distribution to the public for private use. The compulsory license provision would therefore not apply and the music copyright owner is free to negotiate fees for such recordings. The standard form used by the Harry Fox Agency for licensing electrical transcriptions for syndicated radio programs is set forth as Form 8.1 at the end of this chapter.

C. Commercial Advertisements Prepared for Radio Broadcast

Recordings that contain commercial advertising which include licensed music are electrical transcriptions, and the licenses of the use of such music are electrical transcription licenses. Because the use of the music for commercial advertising purposes requires special consideration, the subject of licensing the use of music in radio commercials is discussed in Chapter 12 below.

Licenses to make electrical transcriptions for commercial radio broadcast generally do not contain a license to *perform* the music. The performance license will be covered by the radio station's license from the performance rights societies, such as BMI or ASCAP. Performance licenses are discussed in greater detail in Chapter 15.

2. Transcriptions for Background Music Services

A background music service is the type of music performance described in the BMI public performance license as the "unobtrusive accompaniment to work, shopping, conversation, dining and relaxation," which has been humorously referred to as "elevator" music— the music you hear while standing in an elevator or the mood-setting accompaniment you may or may not notice while waiting in a hotel lobby, standing in line at the bank, or having a meal in a restaurant. It has been said that background music isn't music to listen to; it's music to hear.

A. Muzak and 3M

The two principal organizations that provide background music services are Muzak and 3M. Muzak develops recorded transcription tapes which are sent to their hundreds of franchisees throughout the world who each deliver performances from the recordings to their hotel, restaurant and office clients via FM broadcast, or specially leased phone or cable lines. 3M develops recorded transcription tapes which are sent directly to their hotel, restaurant and office clients.

Electrical transcription licenses that permit the making of such recordings by Muzak and 3M are issued by music publishers, often through their agents, such as the Harry Fox Agency.

Because the terms of electrical transcription licenses are not subject to the compulsory license provisions of the copyright law, terms and conditions of electrical transcription licenses are subject to negotiation. Nevertheless, the fees tend to follow standard patterns and generally do not vary from song to song. Accordingly, many of the basic considerations in granting licenses—determining the value of the song, the importance of the song in relation to its intended use, and the scope of the use (see Chapter 5)—will not in practice apply to granting or clearing electrical transcription licenses for background music services.

Further, the terms and conditions for licensing music for background music services will vary depending upon the delivery method used by the particular background music service. Electrical transcription licenses issued to Muzak are for a fixed term of years, generally 1 or 3 years, with a single payment for all copies of the composition made during the term. A licensee is often given an option to renew for an additional fee payable upon renewal. Electrical transcription licenses issued to 3M work differently. Because 3M sells its tapes to its customers, rather than leasing them, the electrical transcription fee is structured more like a mechanical license fee. A per cent fee is payable per copy of each selection sold.

B. Performance License Aspects

Background music services, whether provided by Muzak or 3M, entail not only the making of recordings of music not intended for distribution to the public for private use, but also the performance of the music to the public. Accordingly, background music services require both an electrical transcription license to make the recording and a performance license to render the performance of the recording to the public.

Electrical transcription licenses for background music services may or may not include the license necessary to perform the music recorded under the authorization of the transcription license. Where a transcription license does not include one, the performance license must be obtained by separate agreement from the applicable performance rights society. Performance licenses are handled differently, depending on the background music service and the performance rights society involved.

With respect to performances of music from recordings made and distributed by Muzak, each franchisee of Muzak obtains a separate performance blanket performing license directly from ASCAP and BMI. This means that the local franchise organization that does the broadcast or electronic transmission to the offices, hotels, and restaurants in which the music is heard pays ASCAP and BMI for the performances, not the offices, hotels or the restaurants. The franchisee pays ASCAP and BMI a percentage of its gross receipts, although with respect to certain kinds of establishments where the music is performed a flat fee is payable instead.

With respect to performances of music from recordings made and distributed by 3M, if the music was from the ASCAP repertoire, the performance license is obtained directly from the publisher at the time the electrical transcription license is issued. The fees paid to the publisher is a number of cents (e.g., three cents) per copy of the song for the three year duration of the license, with a renewal fee of additional cents per year (e.g., one cent). This amount would be in addition to the per copy amount payable for the electrical transcription license. If the music was from the BMI repertoire, the performance license is obtained directly from BMI. BMI would receive a fixed number of cents per copy of a song transcription. Users of the tapes have no license to use the tapes after the performance license expires.

C. Recent Changes

The standard forms of relationship between music publishing companies and some background music services are currently being renegotiated. Future licenses issued to these services may become more akin to the blanket licenses issued by performance rights societies, with organizations such as the Harry Fox Agency distributing collected license fees to music copyright owners in proportion to the number of times each composition is played over the background music system.

3. Transcriptions for In-flight Use on Airlines

Special pre-recorded music programs compiled for use on passenger airlines are akin to both background music services and syndicated radio programs. However, unlike background music services, which are scientifically designed to promote a certain efficiency or relaxation in its listeners, programs designed for in-flight listening are specifically for the active entertainment of its audience. Airline music is programmed to be listened to. These programs, revised on a monthly basis, offer specific categories of music entertainment, such as easy listening, top rock 'n roll hits, country and western, jazz, classical, and international music, from which the passenger may choose. In this respect, they are more like syndicated radio programs, whose "broadcast" is really a "cablecast" distributed to an audience of passengers on board the flights of a particular airline during any given month. Electrical transcription licenses for this purpose are similar to the license set forth as Form 8.1 for syndicated radio programs. Because the performance of music on an airplane or jet liner is a public performance requiring permission of the copyright owner, performance rights societies issue special performance licenses to the airlines for this purpose.

CONSIDERATIONS IN GRANTING AND CLEARING ELECTRICAL TRANSCRIPTION LICENSES

Because it does not apply to recordings made for purposes other than for distribution to the public for private use, the compulsory license provision does not limit the flexibility the copyright owner has in negotiating the terms of electrical transcription licenses.

1. Fee Structure

Although there is room for negotiation in determining the appropriate fee to charge for an electrical transcription license, the fees are generally not high in comparison with other kinds of uses. Fees for making transcriptions for background music used by radio stations, syndicated radio programs are issued on a flat dollar amount per copy made. The same is true for transcriptions made for in-flight use by airlines. Typical fees charged for the making of transcription copies are set forth in Chapter 19.

It is important to remember that licenses for making transcription copies do not normally include the license to perform the music publicly; accordingly, separate fees for music performed publicly by the use of licensed transcriptions are collected on a blanket basis by performance rights societies from the broadcasters or other organizations rendering the performance (see Chapter 15).

2. Value of the Song and Its Importance in Relation to the Intended Use

Because the fees for transcription licenses are generally not high in comparison with other kinds of uses, music copyright owners will not generally engage in the more extensive analysis given to the consideration of other forms of licenses, such as theatrical synchronization, videogram, and commercial advertising licenses. By the same token, copyright owners should not agonize over what fees to charge for these uses, because the ability to share in the economic success of the transcription is available through the collection of performance fees for the public performances of the transcriptions licensed.

A. Arrangements and Changes

Many of the provisions common in electrical transcription licenses are derived from standard mechanical license forms. For example, if new recordings are being made for the transcriptions, the license will provide that the arrangements made shall not change the basic melody or fundamental character of the work. These licenses will also provide that neither the title nor the lyrics of the music shall be changed, added to, or translated, without the further permission of the copyright owner.

3. Scope of Use

A. Type of Media

The electrical transcription license will generally provide the licensee with some flexibility in using the various forms of recording media.

The only important restraint is that the media is limited to audio devices only, and not those that include visual images.

B. Distribution Channels

The transcription license will generally limit the purpose of the recordings and distribution to the purpose stated in the license, such as for syndicated radio broadcasts. Accordingly, a license for syndicated radio broadcasts will not allow copies of the recording to be made for any other purpose, including distribution of copies to the public, distribution of copies for inclusion in juke boxes, distribution of copies for background music services, or distribution of copies for in-flight performance.

Even if the transcription license is limited to a specific use, such as syndicated radio programs, the music copyright owner should try to be as specific as possible, requiring the license to identify by name the specific syndicated radio program, programs, or series of programs for which the music is being licensed. This is particularly important if any form of exclusivity is being considered.

C. Term

The term of an electrical transcription license will generally be from one to three years. Of course, the license may be terminated sooner if the licensee fails to pay the required fee.

D. Territory

The territory of an electrical transcription license is usually limited to the United States and Canada. Most music publishers with overseas affiliates will require licenses for additional territories be negotiated locally on a country-by-country basis.

E. Exclusivity

Transcription licenses are rarely granted on an exclusive basis, but some form of exclusivity could be acceptable for an increased license fee, provided it is narrowly defined. Considerations for granting and clearing exclusivity provisions in connection with the use of music in commercial advertising is discussed more fully in Chapter 12.

RIGHTS AGENCIES

Electrical transcription licenses are generally available directly from music publishers. However, the Harry Fox Agency does issue these licenses on behalf of many of its member publishers. For more information on the Harry Fox Agency, see Chapter 7.

APPENDIX TO CHAPTER 8
ELECTRICAL TRANSCRIPTION
LICENSES

FORMS

FORM 8.1

ELECTRICAL TRANSCRIPTION LICENSE FOR SYNDICATED RADIO BROADCASTS USED BY THE HARRY FOX AGENCY

ELECTRICAL TRANSCRIPTION LICENSE

Agreement made as of _____ by and between _____ (hereinafter referred to as "LICENSEE") and THE HARRY FOX AGENCY, INC., 205 East 42nd Street, New York, New York 10017 (hereinafter referred to as "AGENT").

W I T N E S S E T H:

Whereas, AGENT is the licensing and collecting agent for numerous music publisher-principals (hereinafter individually and collectively referred to as "Publishers") who own or control the rights hereinafter license of their respective musical composition:

Whereas, LICENSEE, is engaged in the business of producing music programming for the purpose of Syndicated Radio Broadcast and furnishing such services to its customers, the Syndicated Radio Broadcast entitled: " _____ ".

Whereas, LICENSEE, in order to record the musical compositions owned by the Publishers and to reproduce and distribute the recordings, is required under copyright law to obtain a license from the Publishers and accordingly desires to obtain such a license from the Publishers for the use of their respective music compositions; and

Whereas, AGENT has been authorized and instructed by its principals, the Publishers, to issue a license to LICENSEE;

NOW, THEREFORE, it is agreed as follows:

1.   This agreement is being entered into by AGENT as the authorized agent, and acting for and on behalf of its principals, the Publishers.

2.   For the purpose hereof the Publishers shall be and be deemed those publishers listed in "THE HARRY FOX MUSIC PUBLISHERS DIRECTORY" as it is from time to time amended and supplemented, excluding therefrom however those publishers who are the subject of notices to LICENSEE from AGENT excluding such publishers from the operation of this agreement. The right to exclude publishers from the operation of this agreement (hereby reserved) may be exercised from time to time by AGENT pursuant to instructions from, and acting on behalf of, such publishers so excluded, provided that any exclusion shall not apply to any compositions licensed and recorded under this agreement prior to the date of the delivery of the notice to LICENSEE relating to their exclusion.

3.   For the purposes of this agreement, a locally-sponsored broadcast shall be deemed to mean a program advertising a business or service that is purely local in character, solely confined within the area of the station's coverage and broadcast over the station's facilities only but shall be deemed to include a program that is purely local in character, solely confined within the area of the stations coverage that is broadcast over the station's facilities only, even though it is paid for in part, not in whole, by a national advertiser, provided that such program is not one, the musical content of which was selected by a national advertiser, and is not a program which was prepared by a national advertiser for national or regional dissemination. All other sponsored commercial broadcasts shall be deemed to be

nationally sponsored broadcasts and not covered by the terms of this license.

4. The term of this Agreement shall be for a period of _____ years commencing _____ and terminating _____ (hereinafter referred to as the "Term").

5. The territory within which the rights hereinafter licensed may be exercised by LICENSEE is limited to the United States of America, its territories and possessions and Puerto Rico (hereinafter referred to as "Territory").

6. For the purposes hereof, the following *non-exclusive* rights are hereby granted to LICENSEE by the Publisher with respect to the "licensed compositions" (as such term is hereinafter defined) during the Term and for use within the Territory:

    a) The rights to mechanically reproduce (i.e. make recordings of) the licensed composition made by the Licensee and transcriptions of previously recorded vocal/instrumental recordings of the licensed musical composition is expressly conditioned upon having valid master recording rights licenses from the respective owner or controller of such rights, in whole or in part for the purposes of using such recordings in and only in connection with the syndicated radio services furnished by LICENSEE to its customers.

    b) The right to make and use copies of such recordings in connection with LICENSEE music program services for Syndicated Radio Broadcast only and the right to make and furnish copies of such recordings to its customers for use in connection with such syndicated radio music services only.

c) The rights herein granted to record and make copies of recordings hereunder embodying performances of the licensed compositions shall include recordings on wire, tape, discs or any other devices now or hereafter known but are limited to audio devices only not accompanied by the recording of visual images.

d) Neither the title nor lyrics of the licensed compositions shall be changed, substituted for, added to or translated without the written consent of its respective Publishers.

e) The pubic performance of the licensed compositions, as embodied in the recordings, by LICENSEE is expressly conditioned upon such performers thereof having valid performing rights licenses from the respective Publishers, the American Society of Composers, Authors and Publishers (ASCAP) or Broadcast Music, Inc. (BMI).

7. For the purposes hereof "licensed compositions" shall be and deemed to mean those musical compositions with respect to which:

a) the rights hereunder licenses are owned or controlled by the Publisher, and

b) AGENT has not indicated a restriction on such use by the respective Publishers within 20 days after the receipt of such notice from LICENSEE, the right to restrict such use hereby being reserved by and on behalf of the Publishers.

8. In consideration of the license hereby granted, LICEN-
    SEE agrees to pay AGENT for and on behalf of its
    principals, the Publishers, for each respective licensed
    composition used by LICENSEE hereunder during the
    Term as follows:

    a) the sum of $15.00 for a one (1) year period for
        each separate recording of a copyrighted mu-
        sical work electrically transcribed on to a mas-
        ter tape thereof in LICENSEE active library
        of _____. In this connection,
        LICENSEE agrees to furnish a list of such licensed
        compositions to AGENT within thirty (30) days from
        the date of the execution of this agreement, which
        list shall be accompanied by payment therefor
        pursuant to this sub-paragraph (a).

    b) Such statements shall identify all of the licensed
        compositions recorded and put into use in Licen-
        see Music service during the applicable period of
        the term, shall identify all publishers grouped in
        alphabetical order, listing each respective li-
        censed composition alphabetically in connection
        to the copyright proprietor, shall show the dates
        of such first use, identify each master tape and
        shall be accompanied by the applicable pay-
        ments hereunder. AGENT shall have the right by
        its authorized representatives to inspect, copy
        and make abstracts of the books and records of
        LICENSEE during reasonable business hours to
        verify the accuracy of LICENSEE statements and
        payments hereunder.

9. This license is non-assignable by LICENSEE except to
    a wholly owned subsidiary or parent or entity which
    purchases all or substantially all of LICENSEE assets or
    the capital stock of LICENSEE or its parent corporation,
    provided, however, that in no event LICENSEE be re-

lieved of its obligations hereunder without the express written consent of AGENT.

10. In the event that LICENSEE shall fail to make any payment or comply with any other provision required to be performed by LICENSEE in this agreement, AGENT shall, without prejudice to any other right of AGENT or its publisher-principals under this Agreement, have the right to revoke this agreement and the rights herein granted by written notice thereof sent to LICENSEE by certified mail. In the event that LICENSEE does not cure such failure within fifteen (15) days from the date of the mailing of such notice, LICENSEE shall be and be deemed to be a willful infringer of copyright with respect to the licensed compositions as to which it has not paid the amounts due hereunder or with respect to which it has otherwise failed to comply with its obligations under this Agreement.

11. This agreement and the license of rights hereunder shall automatically terminate upon the filing by LICENSEE of a petition in bankruptcy, or insolvency, or after any adjudication that LICENSEE is bankrupt or insolvent, which adjudication is not vacated within 60 days, or upon the filing by LICENSEE of any petition or answer seeking reorganization, readjustment or arrangement of LICENSEE business under any federal or state law relating to bankruptcy, or insolvency, or upon the appointment of a receiver for any of the property of LICENSEE, or upon the making by LICENSEE of any assignment for the benefit of creditors or upon the institution of any proceedings for the liquidation of LICENSEE'S business or for the termination of its corporate character. Termination of this agreement shall be without prejudice for monies due to or to become due to AGENT and without prejudice to any other right of AGENT or the PUBLISHER under this agreement.

Termination shall not affect the license for any composition for which the fee has been paid.

12. Nothing herein contained shall constitute a waiver or release of any right, claim or cause of action which AGENT or the Publishers may have at law or in equity against LICENSEE with respect to any act or omission on the part of LICENSEE not expressly licensed hereunder, all being hereby reserved.

13. This agreement sets forth the entire understanding of the parties with respect to the subject matter hereof, may not be altered or amended except in a signed written instrument and shall be governed and construed by and under the laws of the State of New York.

IN WITNESS WHEREOF, the parties hereto have caused this Agreement to be executed as of the____ day of ____ .

_____
(LICENSEE)

By: _____

THE HARRY FOX AGENCY, INC.

(AGENT)

By: _____

FORM 8.2

ELECTRICAL TRANSCRIPTION LICENSE FOR BACKGROUND MUSIC SERVICES USED BY THE HARRY FOX AGENCY

ELECTRICAL TRANSCRIPTION LICENSE

Agreement made as of _____by and between _____ (hereinafter referred to as "LICENSEE") and THE HARRY FOX AGENCY, INC., 205 East 42nd Street, New York, New York 10017 (hereinafter referred to as "AGENT").

W I T N E S S E T H:

Whereas, AGENT is the licensing and collecting agent for numerous music publisher-principals (hereinafter individually and collectively referred to as "Publishers") who own or control the rights hereinafter license of their respective musical compositions:

Whereas, LICENSEE, is engaged in the business of producing background music services and furnishing such services to its customers;

Whereas, LICENSEE, in order to record the musical compositions owned by the Publishers and to reproduce and distribute the recordings, is required under copyright law to obtain a license from the Publishers and accordingly desires to obtain such a license from the Publishers for the use of their respective music compositions; and

Whereas, AGENT has been authorized and instructed by its principals, the Publishers, to issue a license to LICENSEE;

NOW, THEREFORE, it is agreed as follows:

1.	This agreement is being entered into by AGENT as the authorized agent, and acting for and on behalf of its principals, the Publishers.

2.	For the purpose hereof the Publishers shall be and be deemed those publishers listed in "THE HARRY FOX MUSIC PUBLISHERS DIRECTORY" as it is from time to time amended and supplemented, excluding therefrom however those publishers who are the subject of notices to LICENSEE from AGENT excluding such publishers from the operation of this agreement. The right to exclude publishers from the operation of this agreement (hereby reserved) may be exercised from time to time by AGENT pursuant to instructions from, and acting on behalf of, such publishers so excluded, provided that any exclusion shall not apply to any compositions licensed and recorded under this agreement prior to the date of the delivery of the notice to LICENSEE relating to their exclusion.

3.	The term of this Agreement shall be for a period of _____ years commencing _____ and terminating _____ (hereinafter referred to as the "Term").

4.	The territory within which the rights hereinafter licensed may be exercised by LICENSEE is limited to the United States of America, its territories and possessions and Puerto Rico (hereinafter referred to as "Territory").

5.	For the purposes hereof, the following *non-exclusive* rights are hereby granted to LICENSEE by the Publisher with respect to the "licensed compositions" (as such term is hereinafter defined) during the Term and for use within the Territory:

	a)	The rights to mechanically reproduce (i.e., make recordings of) the licensed compositions, in whole or in part for the purposes of using such recordings in and only in connection with the background music services furnished by LICENSEE to its customers.

b)   The right to make and use copies of such recordings in connection with background music services only and the right to make and furnish copies of such recordings to its customers for use in connection with such background music services only.

c)   The rights herein granted to record and make copies of recordings hereunder embodying performances of the licensed compositions shall include recordings on wire, tape, discs or any other devices now or hereafter known but are limited to audio devices only not accompanied by the recording of visual images.

d)   The right granted in paragraph 5(a) to mechanically produce includes the right to record and use the music of a licensed composition without the lyrics thereof (i.e., an instrumental arrangement).

e)   Neither the title nor lyrics of the licensed compositions shall be changed, substituted for, added to or translated without the written consent of its respective Publishers.

f)   The pubic performance of the licensed compositions, as embodied in the recordings, by LICENSEE is expressly conditioned upon such performers thereof having valid performing rights licenses from the respective Publishers, the American Society of Composers, Authors and Publishers (ASCAP) or Broadcast Music, Inc.

(BMI) or any other person authorized to issue such licenses.

6.   For the purposes hereof "licensed compositions" shall be and deemed to mean those musical compositions with respect to which:

   a)   the rights hereunder licenses are owned or controlled by the Publisher, *and*

   b)   AGENT has not indicated a restriction on such use by the respective Publishers within 20 days after the receipt of such notice from LICENSEE, the right to restrict such use hereby being reserved by and on behalf of the Publishers.

7.   In consideration of the license hereby granted, LICENSEE agrees to pay AGENT for and on behalf of its principals, the Publishers, for each respective licensed composition used by LICENSEE hereunder during the Term as follows:

   a)   the sum of $15.00 for a one (1) year period for each separate recording of a copyrighted musical work electrically transcribed on to a master tape thereof in LICENSEE active library as of _____. In this connection, LICENSEE agrees to furnish a list of such licensed compositions to AGENT within thirty (30) days from the date of the execution of this agreement, which list shall be accompanied by payment therefor pursuant to this sub-paragraph (a).

   b)   In connection with its use of the licensed compositions and the payments to be made hereunder by LICENSEE, LICENSEE agrees to render statements to AGENT within thirty (30) days after the end of each six (6) month period of the Term (i.e., the periods ending March 31, and September 30th). Such statements shall identify all of the licensed compositions recorded and put into use in LICENSEE'S music service during the applicable period of the Term, shall show the dates of such use and shall be accompanied by the applicable payments hereunder. AGENT shall have the right by its authorized representatives to inspect, copy and make abstracts of the books and records of LICENSEE during reasonable business hours to verify the accuracy of LICENSEE statements and payments hereunder.

8. This license hereunder is limited to its express terms and all rights in the licensed compositions not expressly licensed hereunder are hereby expressly reserved by and for the Publishers.

9. This license is non-assignable by LICENSEE except to a wholly owned subsidiary or parent or entity which purchases all or substantially all of LICENSEE assets or the capital stock of LICENSEE or its parent corporation, provided, however, that in no event LICENSEE be relieved of its obligations hereunder without the express written consent of AGENT.

10. In the event that LICENSEE shall fail to make any payment or comply with any other provision required to be performed by LICENSEE in this agreement, AGENT shall, without prejudice to any other right of AGENT or its publisher-principals under this Agreement, have the right to revoke this agreement and the rights herein granted by written notice thereof sent to LICENSEE by certified mail. In the event that LICENSEE does not cure such failure within fifteen (15) days from the date of the mailing of such notice, LICENSEE shall be and be deemed to be a willful infringer of copyright with re-

spect to the licensed compositions as to which it has not paid the amounts due hereunder or with respect to which it has otherwise failed to comply with its obligations under this Agreement.

11. This agreement and the license of rights hereunder shall automatically terminate upon the filing by LICEN-SEE of a petition in bankruptcy, or insolvency, or after any adjudication that LICENSEE is bankrupt or insolvent, which adjudication is not vacated within 60 days, or upon the filing by LICENSEE of any petition or answer seeking reorganization, readjustment or arrangement of business under any federal or state law relating to bankruptcy, or insolvency, or upon the appointment of a receiver for any of the property of LICENSEE, or upon the making by LICENSEE of any assignment for the benefit of creditors or upon the institution of any proceedings for the liquidation of LICENSEE'S business or for the termination of its corporate character. Termination of this agreement shall be without prejudice for monies due to or to become due to AGENT and without prejudice to any other right of AGENT or the PUBLISH-ER under this agreement. Termination shall not affect the license for any composition for which the fee has been paid.

12. Nothing herein contained shall constitute a waiver or release of any right, claim or cause of action which AGENT or the Publishers may have at law or in equity against LICENSEE with respect to any act or omission on the part of LICENSEE not expressly licensed hereunder, all being hereby reserved.

13. This agreement sets forth the entire understanding of the parties with respect to the subject matter hereof, may not be altered or amended except in a signed written instrument and shall be governed and construed by and under the laws of the State of New York.

IN WITNESS WHEREOF, the parties hereto have caused this Agreement to be executed as of the ____day of ____.

_____

(LICENSEE)

By: _____

THE HARRY FOX AGENCY, INC.

(AGENT)

By: _____

FORM 8.3

ELECTRICAL TRANSCRIPTION LICENSE FOR
BACKGROUND MUSIC SERVICES
USED BY 3M COMPANY

AGREEMENT made this _____ day of _____ ,
1991 by and between MINNESOTA MINING AND MANUFACTURING
COMPANY, a Delaware Corporation, 3M Center, St. Paul, MN
55144, Attention: Sound Products/3M, Building 551-IW-01 (hereinafter referred to as "3M"), and

(hereinafter referred to as "Licensor", on behalf of itself and all
other music publishing entities controlled and/or administered by
Licensor).

1.   GRANT OF RIGHTS

A.   Mechanical Rights: Licensor hereby grants to 3M the
non-exclusive right to record (and/or use recordings owned by
third parties subject to the clearance of all necessary rights to
use such third party recordings) the musical compositions listed
on Schedule A annexed hereto as well as such additional compositions as 3M may hereafter select from Licensor's catalogs
from time to time subject to Licensor's approval in each instance
(hereinafter individually and jointly referred to as the "Compositions") in whole or in part, as well as the titles thereof, upon
phonorecords embodying the Compositions and the right to
manufacture, sell, rent, lease, advertise, distribute and otherwise exploit such phonorecords throughout the world, provided,
however, that 3M shall obtain licenses to do so from the appropriate mechanical rights agencies and/or publishers outside of
the United States, its territories and possessions (including
Puerto Rico) and Canada. (The aforesaid rights are hereinafter
referred to as "mechanical rights" and the aforesaid phonorecords are hereinafter referred to as "Copies".) 3M shall not be
required to serve or file any notice required to be served or filed

by any copyright act or other law in connection with its exercise of the mechanical rights granted hereunder.

   B.   Public Performance Rights: Licensor hereby grants to 3M the non-exclusive right throughout the United States, its territories and possessions (including Puerto Rico) publicly to perform and to authorize customers publicly to perform the Compositions embodied on the Copies for the period(s) specified in Paragraph 2A. (The aforesaid rights are hereinafter referred to as "public performance rights".)

   C.   Background Music: 3M's exercise of the rights granted hereunder is limited to Background Music (including so-called Foreground Music) as such term is now or may hereafter during the period of 3M's rights hereunder be commonly understood in the music industry.

2.   LIMITATIONS ON MECHANICAL RIGHTS AND PUBLIC PERFORMANCE RIGHTS

   A.   Duration: 3M shall not authorize any customer publicly to perform the Compositions embodied on the Copies for a period in excess of three (3) years after receipt thereof by the customer, unless such customer shall have paid 3M for an extension of his public performance rights and 3M shall have paid to Licensor the additional royalties specified in Paragraph 4B hereof.

   B.   Re-Use: No customer shall be authorized by 3M to rent or lease the Copies to any other person, or to duplicate by any means the Compositions embodied on the Copies.

   C.   Private Use: Nothing herein contained shall be deemed to limit the right of a customer to perform the Compositions embodied on the Copies privately within the home of such customer, and the royalties set forth in Paragraph 4B hereof shall not be payable with respect to Copies delivered to customers exclusively for such use.

D.   Notice to Customers: 3M agrees to advise its distributors and customers of the foregoing limitations.

3.   LICENSOR'S WARRANTIES AND INDEMNITY

A.   Licensor warrants and represents that it owns and/or controls the mechanical and public performance rights granted hereunder; that it has full right, power and authority to enter into this agreement and to grant such rights; and that the exercise of such rights will not constitute a violation or infringement of any right, title or interest, including without limitation copyrights, common law rights and statutory rights, of any person, firm or corporation. Notwithstanding anything contained herein, 3M may at any time exercise any right which 3M now or at any time hereafter may be entitled to as a member of the public as though this agreement were not in existence. Nothing contained herein shall be deemed to constitute a warranty or representation that the mechanical rights specified in Paragraph 1A will be available outside of the United States and Canada or that the performance rights specified in Paragraph 1B will be available outside the United States.

B.   Licensor agrees to indemnify and hold 3M harmless (but only to the extent of the consideration paid to Licensor hereunder) against any loss, damage, cost or expense (including reasonable attorneys' fees) incurred by 3M by reason of any claim, action or proceeding instituted by any person, firm, corporation, mechanical rights society or performing rights society which is inconsistent with any grant by Licensor to 3M or with any of the representations and warranties made by Licensor. 3M agrees to notify Licensor of any claim within the scope of the foregoing indemnity and to afford Licensor an opportunity to participate in the defense thereof, at Licensor's expense, with counsel of Licensor's choice. In such event, 3M may withhold royalties in an amount reasonably related to such claim, until such claim is finally adjudicated or settled with Licensor's consent, which Licensor agrees not to withhold unreasonably. Licensor's liability shall be limited to the amounts payable to Licensor hereunder.

4.   ROYALTIES

A.   For Mechanical Rights: In consideration of the grant of mechanical rights, 3M agrees to pay to Licensor a royalty equivalent to the maximum "statutory" rate in the United States and the "industry" rate in Canada for Compositions not in excess of five (5) minutes in effect when each Copy is initially distributed (presently six and one-quarter cents (U.S. $.0625) in the United States and five and one-quarter cents (Can. $.0525) in Canada) with respect to each Copy delivered to a customer (other than for a limited free trial period) for which 3M receives payment, multiplied by the number of Compositions embodied on each such Copy. The foregoing royalty shall not be payable with respect to any Composition which is in the public domain, or with respect to any Composition for which payment is otherwise made to a mechanical rights society or agency, or with respect to the delivery of "rental rotation" Copies (or replacements of such Copies which are destroyed in the course of rental rotation) to customers other than the first customer to which such Copy is delivered.

B.   For Public Performance Rights: In consideration of the grant of public performance rights during the period set forth in Paragraph 2A hereof, 3M agrees to pay to Licensor a royalty equivalent to three cents (U.S. $.03) with respect to each Copy delivered to a customer (other than for a limited free trial period) for which 3M receives payment, multiplied by the number of Compositions embodied on each such Copy. In addition, 3M agrees to pay to Licensor a royalty equivalent to one cent (U.S. $.01) computed as aforesaid, for each year of public performance rights beyond three (3) years from the date of delivery to a customer, for which such customer pays 3M in accordance with such fee schedule as 3M may establish from time to time in its sole discretion. The foregoing royalties shall not be payable with respect to any Composition which is in the public domain, or with respect to the delivery of "rental rotation" Copies (or replacements of such Copies which are destroyed in the course of rental rotation) during the period set forth in Paragraph 2A to customers other than the first customer to which such Copy is delivered.

C.   Transmission Rights: Notwithstanding the foregoing, if 3M authorizes the transmission of the performances embodied on a Copy, by central studio or otherwise, then in lieu of the royalties set forth in the preceding subdivisions (A) and (B), 3M agrees to pay to Licensor an aggregate royalty of eight and seven-tenths cents (U.S. $.087) per Composition for all necessary mechanical and public performance rights (for a three year period as provided in Paragraph 2A above) multiplied by the number of subscribers for which 3M receives payment and prorated in accordance with the months of actual use thereof by the transmitter. The foregoing royalty shall not be payable with respect to any Composition which is in the public domain or with respect to any Composition for which payment is otherwise paid to a mechanical or public performance society or agency, and shall be increased by the same amount as the maximum "statutory" mechanical royalty hereafter increases from time to time, beginning as of the effective date of each such increase, with respect to Copies thereafter duplicated.

D.   Accountings and Payments: 3M agrees to compute and pay the royalties referred to in subdivisions A, B and C of this paragraph within sixty (60) days after the expiration of each six (6) month period beginning on the June 30 or December 31 following the date of this agreement and continuing for so long as 3M continues to distribute Copies embodying any of the Compositions. Together with each payment, a statement shall be delivered to Licensor showing the number of Copies distributed and the number of Compositions embodied thereon. Each such statement and payment shall be binding upon Licensor unless, within two (2) years after any given statement and payment is delivered, 3M shall have received written notice from Licensor specifying Licensor's objections thereto, in which event such statement and payment shall be binding as to all matters not specifically objected to.

E.   Books and Records: 3M agrees to maintain accurate books and records pertaining to the royalties to be paid to Licensor, which books and records may be inspected by a certified public accountant at 3M's office where such books and records are regularly maintained, during 3M's regular business hours and at Licensor's sole expense. Any information obtained in the course of such inspection shall be held in strict confidence.

5.   TERM

A.   Expiration and Sell-Off: The initial term of this agreement shall commence upon the execution of this agreement and shall terminate   years after the date hereof. Following such termination 3M shall have the exclusive right to continue to distribute its inventory (as of the effective date of such termination) of Copies for not more than twenty-four (24) months thereafter and to authorize customers publicly to perform the Compositions embodied thereon (subject to the payment of royalties and other limitations herein contained).

B.   Rights of Customers Upon Expiration of Term: Notwithstanding the expiration of the term of this agreement pursuant to subdivision A of this paragraph, it is expressly understood and agreed that each customer authorized by 3M during the term of this agreement publicly to perform the Compositions (subject to the limitations herein contained) shall have such public performance rights for a period not less than three (3) years after 3M, its distributors, subdistributors, agents or dealers deliver the Copy embodying such Composition to such customer, and Licensor's warranties in this connection contained in Paragraph 3A hereof shall continue for the benefit of such customer for a concurrent period of time.

6.   USE OF COMPOSITIONS - This agreement is not intended and shall not be construed to obligate 3M to use any or all of the Compositions on any or all of the Copies.

7.   "FAVORED NATION" - 3M agrees that in the event 3M agrees to pay a higher rate of royalty to any third party than is payable hereunder for the use of compositions similar in duration and type to those licensed hereunder, this agreement will be deemed amended to incorporate such higher rate, as of the date when such higher rate is agreed to be paid to such third party and continuing for the duration of the period during which such higher rate is so paid.

IN WITNESS WHEREOF, the parties have caused this agreement to be executed by their duly authorized representatives as of the day and year first indicated above.

MINNESOTA MINING AND
MANUFACTURING COMPANY (3M)

By: _____

SYNCHRONIZATION LICENSES

SUMMARY

CONSIDERATIONS IN GRANTING AND CLEARING SYNCHRONIZATION LICENSES

1. Fee Structure

    A. Performance License Aspects

2. The Value of the Song

3. The Importance of the Song in Relation to Its Intended Use

4. Scope of the Use

    A. Media and Distribution Channels

    B. Term

       (a) Authority to Issue Long-Term Licenses

       (b) Effect of Rear Window Decision

    C. Territory

    D. Exclusivity

    E. Credit

    F. Changes and Translations

    G. Screenings and Free Copies

    H. Most Favored Nations

THEATRICAL MOTION PICTURE TRAILERS

PROMOTIONAL MUSIC VIDEOS

NON-THEATRICAL BUSINESS VIDEO PROGRAMS

FORMS

CHAPTER 9

SYNCHRONIZATION
LICENSES

A *synchronization license* is a form of permission that authorizes another to synchronize music with an audiovisual work, such as a motion picture or television program. More precisely, it is permission to make a recording of a musical composition coupled with the condition that the recording only be used as part of the specified audiovisual work and used (i.e., reproduced or performed) in a particular way. In other words, it is actually a *reproduction license*, but the word, "synchronization" continues to be commonly used, perhaps because, technically, synchronizing involves making a piece of music an integral part of the audiovisual work, and it has always been the intent of licensors of synchronization rights that such licenses be so limited.

The kind of audiovisual work into which music is licensed for synchronization is specified in each synchronization license agreement and is often reflected in the title of the license agreement. For example, permission to synchronize music in a motion picture for theatrical release is usually called a *theatrical* synchronization license; permission to synchronize music in a television program for television broadcast is usually called a *television* synchronization license; and permission to synchronize music in an audiovisual work for promotional music videos is called a *promotional music video* synchronization license. As the need to more precisely specify the uses to which synchronized recordings may be made, new classes of synchronization licenses have also emerged, such as synchronization licenses for cable television, direct satellite broadcast, and other forms of television program exhibition, and for use of motion pictures and television programs containing music in video-grams, such as laser disks and videocassettes.

The discussion of synchronization licenses in this chapter will be limited to the use of music in motion pictures and television programs, including their usual forms of distribution and broadcasting, but excluding other methods of distribution, such as videocassettes, which will be discussed in Chapter 10 on *videogram licenses*. Because the method of distribution often controls the financial terms of the license, these terms are sufficiently different to warrant that they be separately addressed. *Commercial advertising synchronization licenses* will be discussed at length in Chapter 12.

CONSIDERATIONS IN GRANTING AND CLEARING SYNCHRONIZATION LICENSES

What has been said with regard to music licensing in general (see Chapter 5) applies directly with regard to synchronization licensing. The primary factors are:

1. The fee structure;

2. The value of the song, taking into consideration its popularity, historical significance, and overall quality;

3. The importance of the song in relation to its intended use; and,

4. The scope of the intended use.

The following discussion begins where the general discussion in Chapter 5 left off, describing each of the foregoing factors in detail as applied to considerations in granting and clearing synchronization licenses.

1. Fee Structure

The fee structure of nearly all synchronization licenses permitting the exhibition of licensed music in theaters or on television, or both, is a flat fee—the motion picture or television producer will pay a one-time, flat dollar amount for the term of the license, regardless of the number of copies of the film that are made or how many times the film will be exhibited during the term of the license.

Synchronization licenses permit merely the exhibition of the motion picture or audiovisual work in which the music is recorded on television or in theatres. It does not permit the use of the music in videocassettes or laser disks for home distribution; permission for such uses may be provided in a separate videogram license, often included in the same form agreement as the synchronization license. Videogram licenses are discussed in greater detail in Chapter 10.

Further, the synchronization license permits merely the making of a *recording* of music in synchronization with an audiovisual work and the making of copies of that recording; it does not permit the *performance* of music even though the making of recordings was authorized by the synchronization license. Accordingly, if the film is exhibited on television, or in motion picture theatres located outside of the United States (see below), the music copyright owner will still be entitled to collect fees for public performances of the picture from its performance rights society.

The performance fee provides the copyright owner with an opportunity to participate in the economic success of the motion picture in which the music is recorded. Motion picture and television producers will assert that music copyright owners do not deserve to receive a chance to participate in the economic success of their theatrical and television works, because the music copyright owners are not taking any of the risks associated with the financing and development of such works. Nevertheless, it is the broadcasters and distributors of the producer's works who will eventually be responsible for performance and other music license fees associated with the distribution, exhibition and broadcast of their works, and the producers are generally satisfied if they can obtain the necessary synchronization fees they require at a reasonable cost.

A. Performance License Aspects

By court consent decrees entered into between the Department of Justice and the major performance rights societies, music copyright owners are required to issue public performance licenses to movie producers on a per-film basis, if requested. As a result, performance rights societies do not license performance rights in music in theatres located in the U.S., and most synchronization licenses issued today include a provision that provides permission to the producer to publicly perform the music in U.S. theaters. Thus, for a motion picture to be released in theatres located in the United States, a producer obtains from music copyright owners two fundamental licenses in music: (1) a synchronization license to reproduce the music in copies of the motion picture and (2) a performance license to perform the music publicly in movie theaters in the United States.

In determining what to charge for the U.S. theatrical performances of the music, it has long been the custom of music publishers, when determining the total fee, to charge a fee on the same flat fee basis as the synchronization fee, often by merely doubling the synchronization fee. For example, if the synch fee was determined to be $1,000, the total fee for the synch license and the U.S. theatrical performance license would be $2,000. This was done for the sake of simplicity, and not necessarily derived from good music publishing practices. Nevertheless, the practice is likely to continue, because no one has yet scientifically determined the reasonable value of a performance license in the United States for a motion picture playing in several thousand theatres for a normal series of theatrical runs.

Public performances in theaters in countries outside of the United States are subject to local performance fees collected by local performance rights societies.

2. The Value of the Song

The admonition made in Chapter 5 suggesting that copyright owners avoid maintaining inflated perceptions about the value of the musical composition and getting mired in the details of licensing terms is particularly applicable to synchronization licensing. Regardless of the popularity of the song, the scope of the use, or its importance to the licensee, the copyright owner's overall interest should always be getting as much activity in the song as possible.

Often a copyright owner's approach is to attempt to get all the market will bear. Such an attitude should be tempered by several important considerations. First, very few songs have no close substitutes. In other words, there will usually be a song in the same genre owned by someone else which will suit the licensee just as well. A good music licensing executive who knows his catalog will always be able to find a song in the genre for which the licensee is seeking. A person experienced in seeking to obtain clearances for the use of music will always be on the watch for close substitutes for the music he is seeking to clear.

Second, the music performance revenues a copyright owner receives when the audiovisual work is publicly performed (see Chapter 15) acts as a multiplier on the synchronization license fee collected.

The music copyright owner will earn performance credits from its performance rights society (e.g., ASCAP, BMI) on public performances of the song on television worldwide and in theatres overseas, and the income generated by these credits can be substantial when the picture in which the song is licensed becomes a box office success or is broadcast on network television and in television syndication. The fewer licenses you issue, the less performance activity the song receives, and the fewer performance credits and performance income you will receive. Particularly applicable here is the adage, "Penny wise, pound foolish." Accordingly, no music copyright owner, whether he is responsible for a single song or a large catalog of popular songs and standards, can afford to be "too difficult to deal with."

By the same token, if you are seeking to clear a license from a copyright owner who is being difficult, you might persuade him to quote you a more reasonable fee by reminding him of the performance fees he will be forgoing if you choose an alternative song from another publisher that will serve your purposes just as well.

3. The Importance of the Song in Relation to Its Intended Use

Sometimes one song will not serve the purpose just as well as another. Before quoting a synchronization license fee, the copyright owner should ask many questions of the potential licensee about the intended use of the song to find out just how important the song is in relation to its intended use.

To determine the importance of the song in relation to its intended use, it is sometimes useful to inquire in some detail of what the motion picture is about and how the song is going to be used in the picture. For example, the use of the song *Rhapsody in Blue* as purely background music in a comedy is significantly different than the use of the song in a biographical film on the life of George Gershwin; surely, a biography of George Gershwin would not be possible without a license to use several of the composer's most important compositions.

Thus, with respect to motion pictures and television programs, the central questions usually relate to the description of the work in which the music will be used; whether the use is a vocal rendition or merely instrumental; whether the music is used as background music or foreground music; whether the intended use relates to how the composition was originally presented to the public; and whether the music is used to help tell the story.

A *vocal* rendition is when someone is singing, or perhaps humming or whistling, the composition in the motion picture; an *instrumental* rendition is when the composition is played without a rendition of lyrics. Rarely does the fee vary merely because the song is rendered with or without the lyrics; however, information as to whether the lyrics are going to be used may lead to other information that assists a copyright owner in formulating the terms of the license.

If someone is rendering the composition in the motion picture — as, for example, when the protagonist of the picture plays or sings on screen a rendition of Bob Dylan's *Blowin' In the Wind* — it is called a visual or *foreground* use. If the composition is heard in the background and no one is seen performing the song, it is a *background* use. All other things being equal, a foreground use will generally command a higher license fee than a background use.

The extent to which the intended use relates to how the composition was originally presented to the public may also be important. For example, the song *Blowin' In the Wind* was originally presented at a certain time in the 1960's that is usually associated with the "peace" movement or the "new generation" of young people of that time. A background use of the song *Blowin' In the Wind* for a scene in a movie set in the 1990's is different from the use of the same song in a movie about war protesters in the 1960's or otherwise in a movie set in the 1960's to provide the feeling of that decade. Though virtually any song could substitute for a random use of the song in the background of an average, unremarkable scene, a higher fee might be commanded for uses that acutely relate to the setting of the film, as there are few substitutes that convey the particular feeling of the late 1960's that is best conveyed by the song *Blowin' In the Wind.*

Whether the original recording of the song is used in the motion picture or a new recording is made by the producer may also be a factor, though generally most music publishers do not vary the license fee on this basis. If the producer desires to use an original sound recording in the motion picture, he would be required to obtain a separate license to do so from the owner of the recording.

The movie may be a dramatic adaptation of the lyrics of a song, as was the case in the motion picture adaptation of the song, *Ode to Billie Joe* and the 1970's television series adaptation of the song, *Harper Valley PTA*. In each of these cases, the absence of the music from the soundtrack would have been quite unnatural and conspicuous, and, accordingly, the copyright owner should recognize the opportunity to command a higher than average fee for synchronization licenses in these circumstances. In recognition of the copyright owner's separate dramatic adaption rights in the lyric, a separate license and fee would be appropriate for permission to create the dramatic adaptation of the lyrics. *Dramatic adaptations* of song lyrics are discussed in Chapter 16.

The importance of the music to a promotional music video featuring the song is the extreme case of the importance of the song to the audiovisual work, but there are other considerations in setting the terms of music video licenses that tend to reduce the fees typically charged for such uses. These are touched upon in Chapter 10.

If the song's title is used for a special purpose in the motion picture, such as the title of the motion picture, the importance of the song in relation to its intended use becomes obvious. Some additional consideration for the use of the music could be considered, as well as a separate fee for the use of the song's title as the title of the motion picture. In this regard, it might be wise for a copyright owner to make certain that his standard synchronization license agreement states specifically that the license does not include permission to use the title of the song as the title of the audiovisual work in which the music will be synchronized. A producer who intends to use the title of the song for a special purpose should be certain to clear any further permissions that may be required.

4. Scope of the Use

A. *Media and Distribution Channels*

Modern synchronization licenses for motion pictures are carefully drawn to permit only a very narrow set of uses, such as the reproduction of copies for the purpose of normal theatrical exhibition and television broadcast, and even the term "television" is often carefully defined, with distinctions among network, local, syndicated, cable, direct satellite broadcast, etc. being considered. If the motion picture is to be distributed in videograms, such as videocassettes and laser disks, the terms and conditions under which these uses are permitted are separately negotiated, either in a separate license or in special provisions set forth in the synchronization license form.

A person seeking to clear a synchronization license should try to obtain options to distribute the work in all other forms of media and means of distribution at the time the original synchronization license is negotiated, preferably before a final decision to use that piece of music in the work is made—when his or her leverage to obtain the most favorable terms for other uses is best. Considerations for granting and clearing licenses for videograms is covered in Chapter 10.

B. Term

The term of a synchronization license will depend upon the specific use. Though it is preferable to restrict the license's duration to the shortest possible time, the term of synchronization licenses for motion pictures is generally *in perpetuity*. Since the music copyright owner will benefit from the performance of music on the radio, in international theaters and on television, it is generally to his advantage to allow a long term use in motion pictures with hopes that the picture becomes successful and is televised over a period of many years, perhaps in the footsteps of a classic film, such as *Casablanca*. The song, *As Time Goes By*, which was written and published many years before the picture was created, owes its *standard song* status to the synchronization license which permitted its use in the film.

Though motion picture synchronization licenses are commonly granted in perpetuity, such term is generally confined to public performances of the film in theaters and, perhaps, on television; if the same motion picture is to be distributed in videograms (Chapter 10), the duration of such use will normally be stated separately in another license, or in special provisions of the synchronization license, regarding distribution in videogram form.

Synchronization licenses for use of music in television programs are generally shorter in duration, tending normally to be for a five year period, but this is often subject to negotiation. When television synchronization licenses are granted at the same time as a synchronization license for a theatrical motion picture release, the term of the license is normally in perpetuity. But even when the license is only for a program made for television, the recent trend, which has been at the insistence of those seeking to clear these licenses, has been to grant the synchronization licenses for a perpetual term.

(a) Authority to Issue Long-Term Licenses

While producers are increasingly demanding long-term licenses, the music copyright owner may not always have the authority to grant the license desired. A music copyright owner may grant licenses covering only the term for which it has authority to grant licenses; that authority may be limited by the terms of the copyright owner's contract with the songwriter. As noted in Chapter 4 (regarding duration of copyrights, assignments and licenses), certain music publishing agreements between songwriters and publishers only granted rights with respect to the original term of copyright. An example of such a contract is any music publishing agreement based upon the Uniform Popular Songwriter's Contract published in 1947 by the American Guild of Authors & Composers (now known as The Songwriter's Guild). Under that agreement, the renewal copyright for U.S. rights, and under certain circumstances international rights as well, reverted to the songwriter at the expiration of the original term of copyright. If the Publisher granted any licenses for the use of the composition in the United States during the original term, then such licenses will continue in effect under their terms during the renewal term, despite the reversion of rights to the writer. However, this only applies to domestic licenses. In other words, the music publisher in such circumstance does not have the authority to issue licenses for use outside of the United States covering the renewal term, unless it later turned out that the publisher retained international rights (due to the writer's failing to provide the proper notice).

To the extent a publisher cannot issue a worldwide license beyond the initial term of copyright, licensing opportunities will be lost. Virtually all motion picture and television synchronization licenses today are required to be issued on a worldwide basis and most require a term of perpetuity. If a producer cannot obtain a license having a sufficiently broad territory (i.e., worldwide) and a sufficiently long term (i.e., in perpetuity), he is likely to choose a substitute song. Thus, where renewal copyrights revert to songwriters under the provisions of a music publishing agreement, such as under the AGAC form contract, publishing income for songs whose protection is nearing the end of the original term may decline, because producers will avoid licensing compositions for which long-term, worldwide licenses are not available.

A songwriter can alleviate the problem by granting his interest in renewal rights to the song or by entering into an arrangement allowing the publisher during the original term to issue licenses that have terms extending beyond the original term and into the renewal term. An example of such an agreement is set forth as Form 9.7 at the end this chapter.

(b) Effect of Rear Window Decision

As discussed at length in Chapter 4 (regarding duration of copyrights, assignments and licenses), granting renewal interests in copyright will not completely fulfill the need of producers to obtain long-term licenses and there is no agreement that a publisher can reach with a songwriter that would absolutely assure producers that the license will cover the renewal term. Publishers can only assure producers that licenses for songs *tainted* by the *Rear Window* decision will last only until the expiration of the original term of copyright. The producer's options with respect to such songs are limited and are discussed in Chapter 4.

C. Territory

The territory of synchronization licenses for theatrical motion picture releases is generally worldwide. Network television, local television, and syndicated television were at one time granted on a per-country and regional basis, but the recent trend has been to extend the territory to throughout the world. Synchronization licenses are beginning to reflect recent economic changes toward a consolidating global marketplace.

D. Exclusivity

Synchronization licenses for motion pictures and television are nearly always granted on a non-exclusive basis. If the particular use is extraordinary, such as licensing a dramatic use of a song or using the song's title as the title of the motion picture or television program, and a substantial fee is offered, a copyright owner might agree to certain limitations on granting competing licenses for a limited period of time.

E. Credit

Unfortunately, motion picture producers rarely give on screen credit to songs used in motion pictures. This is particularly true for background thematic music. Even more rarely will you find credit given to the artists who performed the material; rarer still is credit to songwriters, and we would offer our gratitude to anyone who can identify a motion picture which gives credit to the music publisher.

It is time that music publishers consider requesting in their synchronization licenses for motion pictures and television programs, that the song, the composers, the music publishing company, and the performance rights society are given credit for the music used in such works. If nothing else, this would facilitate the task of licensing clearance for future uses of the motion picture, such as, perhaps, performance on television under a per program performance license scheme (see Chapter 15).

F. Changes and Translations

The synchronization license should also state that no changes will be made in the lyrics or fundamental character of the music and that no translations will be made of the lyrics without the permission of the copyright owner. Any changes would be subject to additional fee and perhaps approval of the songwriter. If any translations are authorized, ownership in the translations should be retained by the music copyright owner; care should be taken so that the translation made by the licensee is of a good quality and not materially inconsistent with any translations that might have been previously done in international markets.

G. Screenings and Free Copies

Copyright owners should request an invitation to a pre-release screening of the motion picture to examine the use of the music and any credits required under the license. If a videogram of the picture is released, the copyright owner should request two copies for his files.

H. Most Favored Nations

From time to time an artist's representative will ask for a *most favored nations* clause, a provision requiring that the fee to be charged will be on no less favorable terms than those offered for the use of any other song in the motion picture. (See Chapter 5.)

Requests for these clauses are often made by less experienced representatives of copyright owners, who, not knowing what to charge, would offer some guess at an appropriate fee and require favored nations status to make sure his or her client does not receive a lower fee than anyone else who owns music being used in the picture. One problem with this approach, as we have seen, is that each song has a unique inherent value, and may have a different importance in relation to the intended use. Some are standard songs that are irreplaceable in the context of the use; others, like actors playing bit parts in the film, have many substitutes. Another problem is that each song is likely to have a different playing time in the motion picture, and some songs in the picture may be used for foreground music, some as background music. In such cases, how is a producer to determine whether the fee for the use of one song is on "more favorable terms" than the fee for the use of another?

Because of the disputes that may potentially arise from such provisions, a producer would be advised to avoid most favored nations provisions or might consider paying a fee that is slightly higher than warranted rather than get entangled in such an arrangement.

THEATRICAL MOTION PICTURE TRAILERS

A *trailer* is a short film of several minutes length containing a tightly edited compilation or montage of clips from a motion picture created for the purpose of advertising the motion picture (i.e., "coming attraction"). The creation of good trailers is now considered an art form and certain artists specialize in this craft, such as the award winning producer, Lee Stein. Music licensed for use in the motion picture is almost inevitably used in trailers that advertise them, and since the trailer is considered a work separate from the film, a separate synchronization license for the use of the music in the trailer is required. Such licenses are limited to use in the trailer for exhibition in movie theatres, and for additional fees, for inclusion in videocassettes and video discs that contain other motion pictures distributed to the home video market. The license is generally worldwide and limited to one year with options for renewal.

PROMOTIONAL MUSIC VIDEOS

A *promotional music video* is a short audiovisual work customarily created by a record company to promote the recording of a single song. Promotional videos are broadcast on national cable television networks that are devoted to musical entertainment, such as MTV and VH1. The record company who creates a promotional video will be required to obtain a synchronization license to use the music in the video. The license will be limited to one rendition of the licensed song for a length which is not more than the duration of the original recording of the song.

Promotional music video synchronization licenses are generally worldwide and limited to two to five years with options for renewal normally available. The synchronization fee is usually quite nominal, set at an amount intended merely to cover the administrative costs of preparing the paperwork for the license grant. This is because the copyright owner stands to benefit substantially from the performance royalties resulting from the exhibition of the music video on cable television, and from the general benefit the video serves in helping the song become a "hit."

The license is limited to broadcast on television; other uses, such as theatrical exhibition or the making and distribution of videograms containing the video performance, are not permitted unless an additional license, and additional fees, are provided for. The license will not authorize the alteration of the lyric or any change in the fundamental character of the music or the use of the title, or any portion of the lyric of the composition, as the title of the video. Some licenses will prohibit the dramatization of the lyrical content of the licensed composition without further permission from the copyright owner.

NON-THEATRICAL BUSINESS VIDEO PROGRAMS

A publisher will occasionally receive a request from a corporation to use a song in a video program produced for the purpose of training the corporation's employees or customers, or promoting a product or service. For the use of a song in such a work, the publisher will issue a special synchronization license for a flat fee. The term of such a license will be limited to three to five years and the use will generally be limited to the internal exhibition or broadcast of the program by the licensee. Permission may be obtained to make videogram copies of the program for an additional fee (see Chapter 10). Examples of non-theatrical film synchronization licenses are set forth as Forms 9.5 and 9.6 at the end of this chapter.

APPENDIX TO CHAPTER 9
SYNCHRONIZATION LICENSES

FORMS

FORM 9.1

SYNCHRONIZATION LICENSE FOR MOTION PICTURE THEATRICAL AND TELEVISION EXHIBITION (INCLUDES NO LICENSE FOR HOME USE VIDEOGRAM DISTRIBUTION)

MOTION PICTURE AND TELEVISION SYNCHRONIZATION AND THEATRICAL PERFORMANCE LICENSE

FOR AND IN CONSIDERATION OF THE SUM OF
$ for the synchronization rights hereinafter set forth and $ for the performing rights and other rights set forth in Paragraphs 4 and 5 below, and the advance provided in Paragraph 7(d) for the Videogram rights set forth in Paragraph 6(b), said sums payable upon the execution and delivery hereof, and in consideration of all the other promises and agreements contained herein, Publisher listed below, hereby grants to   and its successors and assigns, hereinafter referred to as "Producer" the non-exclusive irrevocable right, license, privilege and authority to record in any manner, medium or form, whether now known or hereafter devised, the music and the words of the musical composition set forth below only in connection with the motion picture entitled below in any language, to make copies of said recording in any and all gauges of film and to import said recording and/or copies of said recording into any country within the territory covered by this license and to perform, as set forth below, said musical composition in said territory, subject to the terms, conditions and limitations set forth below.

1. MUSICAL COMPOSITION.

The musical composition (hereinafter the "Composition"), and the sole use of said musical composition, covered by this license is:

TITLE   WRITER   PUBLISHER   USE

2. MOTION PICTURE TITLE.

The title of the only motion picture (hereinafter the "Motion Picture") with which said recording is to be used is:

3. TERRITORY.

The territory (hereinafter the "Territory") covered by this license is:

4. PERFORMANCE LICENSE—UNITED STATES.

Publisher grants to Producer the non-exclusive right and license in the United States and its possessions to perform publicly, either for profit or non-profit, and to authorize others so to perform, the Composition only in synchronization or timed relationship to the Motion Picture and trailers thereof as follows:

(a)   THEATRICAL PERFORMANCE. In the exhibition of the Motion Picture to audiences in theatres and other public places where motion pictures are customarily exhibited, and where admission fees are charged, including but not limited to, the right to perform the Composition by transmission of the Motion Picture to audiences in theatres and such other public places for the duration of United States copyright of the Composition.

(b)   PUBLIC TELEVISION PERFORMANCE. In the exhibition of the Motion Picture by free television, pay television, networks, local stations, pay cable, closed circuit, satellite transmission, and all other types or methods of television or electronic reproduction and transmissions ("Television Performance") to audiences not included in subparagraph (a) of this Paragraph 4 only by entities having performance licenses therefor from the appropriate performing rights societies. Television Performance of the Motion Picture by anyone not licensed for such performing rights by ASCAP or BMI is subject to clearance of the performing right either from Publisher or ASCAP or BMI or from any other licensor acting for or on behalf of Publisher and to payment of an additional license fee therefor.

5. FOREIGN PERFORMING LICENSE.

It is understood that the performance of the Composition in connection with the exhibition of the Motion Picture in countries or territories within the Territory but outside of the United States and its possessions shall be subject to clearance by performing rights societies in accordance with their customary practice and the payment of their customary fees. Publisher agrees that to the extent it controls said performing rights, it will license an appropriate performing rights society in the respective countries to grant such performing right.

6. LIMITED VIDEOGRAM LICENSE.

Publisher hereby further grants to Producer, in each country of the Territory, the non-exclusive right to cause or authorize the fixing of the Composition in and as part of the Motion Picture on audio-visual contrivances such as video cassettes, video tapes, video discs and similar compact audiovisual devices reproducing the entire motion picture in substantially its original form ("Videogram") only for the purposes, uses, and performances hereinabove set forth.

7. [intentionally omitted]

8. RESTRICTIONS.

This license does not include any right or authority (a) to make any change in the original lyrics or in the fundamental character of the music of the Composition; (b) to use the title, the subtitle or any portion of the lyrics of the Composition as the title or subtitle of the Motion Picture; (c) to dramatize or to use the plot or any dramatic content of the lyrics of the Composition; or (d) to make any other use of the Composition not expressly authorized herein.

9. WARRANTY.

Publisher warrants only that it has the right to grant this license and this license is given and accepted without any other representations, warranty or recourse, express or implied, except for Publisher's agreement to repay the consideration for this license if said warranty shall be breached with respect thereto. In no event shall the total liability of Publisher in any case exceed the amount of consideration received by it hereunder.

10. PUBLISHER'S RESERVATION OF RIGHTS

Subject only to the non-exclusive rights herein above granted to Producer all rights of every kind and nature in the Composition are reserved to said Publisher together with all rights of use thereof.

11. ADVERTISING

The recording and performing rights hereinabove granted include such rights for air, screen and television trailers solely for the advertising and exploitation of the Motion Picture.

12. CUE SHEET

Producer agrees to furnish Publisher a cue sheet of the Motion Picture within thirty (30) days after the first public exhibition of the Motion Picture at which admission is charged (except so-called "sneak" previews).

13. REMEDIES

In the event that Producer, or its assigns, licensees, or sub-licensees, breaches this Agreement by, among other things, failing to pay timely any license fees required hereunder, and fails to cure such breach within thirty (30) days after notice of such breach given by Publisher to Producer, then this license will automatically terminate. Such termination shall render the distribution, licensing, or use of the Composition(s) as unauthorized uses, subject to the rights and remedies provided by the laws, including copyright, and equity of the various countries within the Territory.

14. NOTICES

All notices, demands or requests provided for or desired to be given pursuant to this Agreement must be in writing. All documents shall be deemed to have been given when served by personal delivery or three days following their deposit in the United States mail, postage prepaid, certified or registered, addressed as follows:

(a) To Publisher:

with a courtesy copy to:

and

(b) to Producer:

with a courtesy copy to:

or to such other address in the United States as either party may hereafter designate in writing delivered in the manner aforesaid.

15. ENTIRE AGREEMENT

This license is binding upon and shall inure to the benefit of the respective successors and/or assigns of the parties hereto but in no event shall Producer be relieved of its obligations hereunder without the express written consent of Publisher. This Agreement shall be construed in all respects in accordance with the laws of the State of California applicable to agreements entered into and to be wholly performed therein. The recording and performing and other rights hereinabove granted shall endure for the periods of all copyrights in and to the composition, and any and all renewals or extensions thereof that Publisher may now own or control or hereafter own or control without Producer having to pay any additional consideration therefor.

IN WITNESS WHEREOF, the parties have caused the foregoing to be executed as of the 1st day of January, 1995.

PUBLISHER   PRODUCER

By: _____   By:_____

FORM 9.2

SYNCHRONIZATION LICENSE FOR THEATRICAL TRAILER

THEATRICAL TRAILER SYNCHRONIZATION LICENSE

In consideration of the sum of $ _____ payable on the execution and delivery hereof and upon the agreement hereto and the acceptance hereof as indicated below, the undersigned, for and on behalf of the Publisher(s) referred to herein, does hereby give and grant unto:

the non-exclusive, irrevocable right and license to record the following copyrighted musical composition(s) in synchronism or timed-relation with a trailer made and produced solely for theatrical purposes by the said licensee and now entitled:

SONG TITLE   WRITER(S)   PUBLISHER   USE   TIMING

Subject to the following terms and conditions:

This license is granted upon the express condition that the said recording(s) are to be used solely in synchronism or timed relation with said theatrical trailer, that no sound records produced pursuant to this license are to be manufactured, sold, licensed or used separately or apart from the said theatrical trailer, except as herein provided.

This license is granted for the territory of: THE WORLD.

The term of this license shall be for the period of ONE (1) YEAR from the date hereof and upon such termination any and all rights given and granted hereunder shall forthwith cease and terminate, including the right to make or authorize any use or distribution whatsoever of said recording(s) of said musical composition(s) in said theatrical trailer or otherwise, except as herein provided.

We hereby grant you the option to renew the term of this license for an additional one (1) year period subject to an additional fee of $_____. This option, if exercised, must be exercised by written notice at least thirty (30) days prior to the commencement of the option year.

Licensee has the irrevocable option or right to synchronize the Composition as embodied in the Program and to distribute the Program by means of videocassettes and/or videodiscs and/or other home video devices in the territory ("Video Territory") of the world. Subject to the provisions hereof, for the right to manufacture and duplicate and distribute unlimited Videogram copies of the theatrical trailer during the term, within thirty (30) days of the first distribution Producer shall pay Publisher a Videogram fee of

The option referred to above must be exercised, if at all, by written notice delivered to Publisher within one (1) year from the date hereof and no later than thirty (30) days from the date of first performance or release date of the Program in the specified media embodying the Composition.

This agreement is assignable by you on condition that such assignee shall agree to be bound by all of the terms and conditions hereof, but such assignment shall not relieve you from ultimate liability hereunder.

The undersigned warrants that said publisher(s) are the owners of the recording rights herein licensed, and this license is given without other warranty or recourse, except for their agreement to repay the consideration paid hereunder in respect of any of said musical compositions, if said warranty shall be breached with respect thereto, with the liability for breach of said warranty being limited in any event to the amount of the consideration paid hereunder; with respect to such musical compositions: and the undersigned reserves all rights and uses whatsoever in and to the said musical composition(s) not herein specifically granted.

AIRDATE:

BIG MUSIC PUBLISHING CORP.

By: _____

AGREED TO AND ACCEPTED:

By: _____

FORM 9.3

TELEVISION SYNCHRONIZATION LICENSE

<u>TELEVISION SYNCHRONIZATION LICENSE</u>

In consideration of the sum of $ _____ , payable on the execution and delivery hereof and upon the agreement hereto and the acceptance hereof as indicated below, the undersigned, for and on behalf of the publisher(s) referred to herein, does hereby give and grant unto:

the non-exclusive, irrevocable right and license to record the following copyrighted musical composition(s) in synchronism or timed-relation with a single episode, program or motion picture made and produced solely for television purposes by the said licensee and now entitled:

<u>TITLE</u>	<u>WRITERS</u>	<u>PUBLISHER</u>	<u>USE</u>

Subject to the following terms and conditions:

This license is granted upon the express condition that the said recording(s) are to be used solely in synchronism or timed-relation with said television-film, that no sound records produced pursuant to this license are to be manufactured, sold, licensed or used separately or apart from the said television-film, and upon the further condition that the said television-film shall not be exhibited in or televised in theatres or other public places of amusement where motion pictures are customarily shown or places where an admission is charged.

This is a license to record only, and the exercise of the recording rights herein granted is conditioned upon the perform-ance of said musical composition(s) over television stations having valid licenses from the person, firm, corporation or other entity having the legal right to issue performance rights licenses on behalf of the owner of such rights in the respective territories in which said musical composition(s) shall be performed hereunder, or for the United States from the owner thereof. However, the said recording(s) may not be performed by means of so-called "pay" or "subscription" television, or by means of audio visual devices or contrivances such as "EVR" or any method or devise similar or analogous thereto or otherwise used except in the performance thereof originating from and as actually broadcast by a television station.

This license is granted for the territory of:

The term of this license shall be for the period of _____ years from the date hereof, and upon such termination any and all rights given and granted hereunder shall forthwith cease and terminate, including the right to make or authorize any use or distribution whatsoever of said recording(s) of said musical composition(s) in said television-film or otherwise.

This license cannot be transferred or assigned by affirmative act or by operation of law, without the express consent of the undersigned in writing.

The undersigned warrants that said publisher(s) are the owners of the recording rights herein licensed, and this license is given without other warranty or recourse, except for their agreement to repay the consideration paid hereunder in respect of any of said musical compositions, if said warranty shall be breached with respect thereto, with the liability for breach of said warranty being limited in any event to the amount of the consideration paid hereunder; with respect to such musical compositions: and the undersigned reserves all rights and uses whatsoever in and to the said musical composition(s) not herein specifically granted.

Dated:

                                    BIG MUSIC PUBLISHING CORP.

                                    By: _____

AGREED TO AND ACCEPTED:

By: _____

FORM 9.4

TELEVISION SYNCHRONIZATION LICENSE FOR PROMOTIONAL MUSIC VIDEO

PROMOTIONAL VIDEO SYNCHRONIZATION
LICENSE AGREEMENT

DATED:_____ , 1995

PUBLISHER: BIG MUSIC PUBLISHING CORP.
Address: 1000 Sunset Blvd.
    Hollywood, California 90069

LICENSEE: _____
Address: _____
    _____

COMPOSITION(S): _____
    _____
    _____

AUDIOVISUAL FILM/TAPE:
    ("A/V Film")

For good and valuable consideration, the receipt of which is hereby acknowledged by Publisher, Publisher hereby grants to Licensee, its successors, assigns, licensees and sublicensees, the following rights in and to the Composition(s):

1.   Publisher grants to Licensee the non-exclusive license to record the Composition(s) in synchronism or timed-relation with the visual images contained in the A/V Film, to make copies of such recording of the Composition(s) and to distribute such copies throughout the Territory, subject to the terms and conditions hereinafter set forth.

The use of the Composition(s) is limited to one (1) visual/vocal rendition of the Composition for not more than the duration of the Composition(s) in the original phonograph recording.

2.   The territory covered by this License is the world (hereinafter referred to as the "Territory").

3.   The term of this Agreement shall commence with the date hereof and terminate either two (2) years after release of the A/V Film, or two (2) years after release of the original phonograph recording in the United States, whichever is later (hereinafter referred to as the "Term").

4.   Upon execution hereof, Licensee agrees to pay to Publisher a handling charge of Twenty-Five Dollars ($25.00).

5.   (a)   This Agreement does not grant to Licensee or to its agents, affiliates or subsidiaries the right to perform or to authorize the performance of the Composition(s) in connection with the exhibition of the A/V Film in or by any medium or media.

(b)   The Composition(s) may be performed in connection with exhibition of the A/V Film by cable systems, broadcasters or other entities, or by means of media having valid performance licenses therefor from the American Society of Composers, Authors and Publishers ("ASCAP") or Broadcast Music, Inc. ("BMI"), as the case may be.

(c)   Exhibition of the A/V Film by cable systems, broadcasters or other entities or by means of media not licensed by ASCAP or BMI must be licensed by Publisher or by any other licensing agency acting for or on behalf of Publisher, and payment of additional fees will be required.

6.   It is understood that the performance of the Composition(s) in connection with the exhibition of the A/V Film in countries or territories outside of the United States and its possessions shall be subject to clearance by performing rights societies in accord-

ance with their customary practice and the payment of their customary fees. Publisher agrees that to the extent it controls said performing rights, it will license an appropriate performing rights society in the respective countries to grant such performing right.

7.   (a)   This License does not authorize, permit or license any use of the Composition(s) not expressly granted herein and does not imply or grant the right to alter the lyric or change the fundamental character of the music of the Composition(s). Without limiting the foregoing, Licensee is not authorized (a) to perform or authorize the performance of the Composition in connection with the exhibition of the A/V Film in any theatre, auditorium or other place to which an admission fee is charged, or (b) to record the Composition on a phonograph record other than in the A/V Film, (c) to use the title or any portion of the lyric of the Composition as the title of the A/V Film or otherwise, (d) to dramatize the lyrical content of the Composition, or (e) to reproduce and sell or lease copies of the A/V Film to the public.

8.   Producer warrants and represents that should any other musical composition be licensed in connection with the A/V Film on a more favorable basis to the publisher thereof than is provided to Publisher hereunder, such more favorable basis shall also be extended to the licensing of the Composition(s) hereunder.

9.   Publisher warrants that it has the right to grant this License and no other warranties, express or implied, are granted hereby. Should said warranty be breached, in whole or in part, Licensee shall either repay to Publisher the amount theretofore paid to Publisher for this License, or Publisher shall hold Licensee harmless to the extent of said consideration. In no event shall the total liability of Publisher exceed the consideration received by Publisher hereunder.

10.   Licensee represents and warrants that the A/V Film containing the Composition(s) will be used solely for the purpose of promoting the sale of phonograph records and tapes embodying the featured performances by the Artist.

11.   Upon expiration of the Term hereof, the rights granted herein shall automatically revert to Publisher, and any further use of the Composition(s) hereunder shall be unauthorized.

12.   This License and the rights hereunder are not assignable by Licensee.

13.   Licensee hereby agrees to furnish Publisher with a "cue sheet" of the A/V Film indicating the type and length of usage of the Composition(s) in the A/V Film.

14.   Whenever notice is required, or desired, to be given hereunder such notice shall be in writing addressed to the appropriate party at the address set forth above or at such other address as either party may designate by written notice given hereunder.

15.   This License sets forth the entire agreement between Publisher and Licensee with respect to the subject matter hereof, and may not be modified or amended except by written agreement executed by the parties. This License shall be governed by and subject to the laws of the State of California applicable to agreements made and to be wholly performed within such State. Any controversy arising under this License, if litigated, shall be adjudicated in a court of competent jurisdiction within the County of Los Angeles.

IN WITNESS WHEREOF, the parties hereto have executed this Agreement as of the date first set forth above.

PUBLISHER   LICENSEE

By: _____   By:_____

FORM 9.5

NON-THEATRICAL FILM SYNCHRONIZATION LICENSE

NON-THEATRICAL FILM SYNCHRONIZATION LICENSE

In consideration of the sum of $_____, and upon the payment thereof to the undersigned, the undersigned does hereby give and grant unto:

the non-exclusive, irrevocable right and license to record the following musical composition(s):

in synchronism or timed-relation with a picture made and produced by Licensee tentatively entitled:

and described as

A slide/tape presentation approximately thirty (30) minutes in length for use in non-theatric showings for training purposes to employees of the Licensee.

This license is granted upon condition that the said recording or recordings are not to be used for or in connection with television purposes, including "pay" or "subscription" television, any form of home television exhibition or cable television; that said recording or recordings are not to be employed for any radio or so-called "home-movies" use or other media not specifically set out herein; that no sound records produced pursuant to the said license are to be manufactured, sold, and/or used separately from the said picture; and with the further proviso that the said picture shall not be exhibited in or televised into theatres or other public places of amusement where motion pictures are customarily shown.

The license granted is for the territory of: THE UNITED STATES ONLY.

This license shall terminate on:

and upon such date all rights herein granted shall immediately cease and terminate, and the right derived from this license to make or authorize any further such use of said musical composition in said picture shall also cease and terminate upon such date.

All rights and uses in the said musical composition(s) not herein granted are expressly reserved to the undersigned.

PUBLISHER   LICENSEE

By: _____   By:_____

FORM 9.6

NON-THEATRICAL FILM SYNCHRONIZATION LICENSE WITH OPTIONS TO RENEW TERM

NON-THEATRICAL FILM SYNCHRONIZATION LICENSE

In consideration of the sum of $1,500.00 ($500.00 per composition), and upon the payment thereof to the undersigned, the undersigned does hereby give and grant unto:

("Licensee") the non-exclusive, irrevocable right and license to record the following musical composition(s):

(the "Compositions") in synchronism or timed-relation with a picture made and produced by the said company known as

A slide/tape presentation approximately fifteen (15) minutes in length, for non-theatric showings in 25 small theaters (seating up to 25 persons) to promote Licensee's products.

This license hereinabove set forth is granted under the proviso that the said recording or recordings are not to be used for or in connection with television purposes, including "pay" or "subscription" television, except as noted above or cable television; that said recording or recordings are not to be employed for any radio or so-called "home-movies" use or other media not specifically set out herein; that no sound records produced pursuant to the said license are to be manufactured, sold, and/or used separately from the said picture; and with the further proviso that the said picture shall not be exhibited in or televised into theatres or other public places of amusement where motion pictures are customarily shown.

The license granted is for the territory of: THE UNITED STATES.

The initial period of the Term of this license shall commence on January 1, 1995 and continue for a period of one (1) year.

Licensee is hereby granted two (2) options to renew the term of this license for one (1) year in each instance. An option may be exercised by written notice at least thirty (30) days prior to the commencement of an option year, accompanied by a renewal fee of $1,500.00 ($500.00 per song) for the first renewal and $1,500.00 ($500.00 per song) for the second renewal.

All rights and uses in the said musical composition(s) not herein granted are expressly reserved to the undersigned.

Licensor warrants and represents that it has the legal right and power to grant this license, and makes no other warranty or representation. Licensor agrees to indemnify Licensee and hold Licensee harmless from and against any and all loss, cost, damage or expense (including court costs and reasonable outside attorneys' fees) due to a breach of such warranty and representation resulting in a final, nonappealable adverse judgment or a settlement entered into with Licensor's prior written consent (such consent not to be unreasonably withheld).

Dated:

PUBLISHER   LICENSEE

By: _____   By:_____

FORM 9.7

ARRANGEMENT WITH SONGWRITER THAT PERMITS MUSIC PUBLISHER TO GRANT SYNCHRONIZATION LICENSES COVERING THE RENEWAL TERM

BIG MUSIC PUBLISHING SUBSIDIARY, INC.
c/o Big Music Publishing Corp.
1000 Sunset Boulevard
Hollywood, CA 90069
January 1, 1995

Mr. Songwriter
c/o Psychedelic Music Publishing Corp.
Woodstock, New York 10000

Re: Songwriter - Big Music Subsidiary Compositions
     Synchronization Fees

Dear Mr. Songwriter:

We refer to the January 1, 1967 agreement between our predecessor-in-interest Big Music Publishing Subsidiary, Inc., and you, with the Uniform Popular Songwriter's Agreement (1947 revised) attached as an exhibit thereto, as amended from time to time (hereinafter collectively referred to as the "Songwriter Agreement"). The following, when signed by us and you, confirms our agreement regarding apportionment of "Synchronization Fees" (as defined below) paid for the use of compositions written by you pursuant to the Songwriter Agreement (hereinafter referred to collectively and individually as the "Songwriter Compositions"). As used herein, the term "Synchronization Fees" means the flat fees and/or any royalties payable by a licensee pursuant to a television, motion picture, commercial or home video device license issued by you and us hereunder, which fees or royalties we actually receive during the term of our rights to the Songwriter Composition subject to such license.

1.   This agreement is entered into with reference to the following facts: Our rights to the Songwriter Compositions terminate from time to time during the period of the next several years, on a composition by composition basis. Therefore, we do not have the right to negotiate for or issue licenses for a term exceeding the term of our rights in each Songwriter Composition. You and we enter into this agreement in order to continue actively exploiting the Songwriter Compositions in motion pictures, television productions, commercials and home video devices and to permit us to continue to negotiate and issue licenses and receive payment for such uses during the term of our rights.

2.   Subject to paragraphs 5 and 6, below, with respect to synchronization licenses having a fixed term of years (e.g., a five (5) year term television synchronization license), the Synchronization Fee will be apportioned between you and us on a straight yearly basis. Our share will be a fraction of the Synchronization Fee, the denominator of which will be the number of years in the term of the license and the numerator of which will be the number of years remaining (but the numerator shall in no event be less than one (1)) of our ownership of such Songwriter Composition. You will receive the balance of the Synchronization Fee.

3.   Subject to paragraphs 5 and 6, below, with respect to synchronization licenses that do not have a fixed term of years (e.g., motion picture synchronization licenses with a life-of-copyright term), the Synchronization Fee will be apportioned between you and us based on a seven (7) year life. Our share will be a fraction of the Synchronization Fee, the denominator of which will be seven (7) and the numerator of which will be the number of years remaining (but the numerator shall in no event be less than one (1)) of our ownership of such Songwriter Composition. You will receive the balance of the Synchronization Fee.

4.   We shall pay you your 50% songwriter share of the Synchronization Fee out of our apportioned share of the Synchronization Fee. You shall receive your songwriter share from

us in addition to your apportioned share of the Synchronization Fee payable directly to you by any third party licensee.

5.   We shall not be entitled to receive or retain any moneys paid or payable subsequent to expiration of our rights to a Songwriter Composition which moneys are payable by a licensee pursuant to a license issued hereunder. All such moneys shall be payable to and retainable exclusively by you and each license issued hereunder shall so provide.

6.   Each license issued hereunder shall be of no force or effect until executed both on behalf of us and you. Each license shall provide for direct payment to you and us of your and our proportionate share of each Synchronization Fee. We agree to cause our representatives to obtain your prior written approval for each proposed synchronization use of a Songwriter Composition.

Please confirm your agreement to the foregoing by signing below.

Very truly yours,
BIG MUSIC PUBLISHING CORP.

_____

John Doe
Vice President

AGREED AND ACCEPTED:

_____

Mr. Songwriter

VIDEOGRAM LICENSES

SUMMARY

THE RIGHTS INVOLVED

EMERGING FEE/ROYALTY ISSUES

CONSIDERATIONS IN GRANTING AND CLEARING VIDEOGRAM LICENSES

1. Fee Structure

2. Importance of the Song in Relation to Its Intended Use

3. Scope of the Intended Use

    A. Media

    B. Distribution Channels

    C. Term

    D. Territory

    E. Exclusivity

OTHER TERMS AND CONSIDERATIONS

1. Payment and Accounting

2. Reserves Against Returns

3. Most Favored Nations

4. Free Copies

PROMOTIONAL MUSIC VIDEO VIDEOGRAM LICENSE

NON-THEATRICAL VIDEOGRAM LICENSE

VIDEO YEARBOOKS

FORMS

CHAPTER **10**

VIDEOGRAM
LICENSES

A *videogram* license is a license which permits the reproduction of music in recordings that are accompanied by moving pictures, such as motion pictures, television programs, and other audiovisual works.

As noted in the preceding chapter, when a music copyright owner issues a standard theatrical synchronization license, he is giving permission to the producer to make a recording of a musical composition coupled with the condition that the recording only be used as part of the specified audiovisual work and only be reproduced or performed in a particular way. That particular way is the exhibition of the motion picture in theatres and other public places where motion pictures are customarily exhibited and by television broadcast by entities who are licensed by performing rights societies to publicly perform the music embodied in those works. The license set forth as Form 9.1 at the end of the preceding chapter is limited to theatrical exhibition and television broadcast, and does not include permission to make copies of a motion picture embodying the licensed musical composition in videograms for home video distribution.

This chapter concerns the licensing of music for use in *videograms* —a portmanteau of the words *video* and *program,* used to describe the programs contained in audiovisual devices, such as videocassettes or laser discs, primarily intended for use in the home on a videotape or optical-laser player and a television set. The use of music in other programs, such as videogames, pre-packaged computer software, and multi-media works, such as CD-ROM and other optical disk devices is discussed in Chapter 14.

THE RIGHTS INVOLVED

The essential right involved in the licensing of videograms is the reproduction right. Specifically, it is the exclusive right to record, or *to fix*,[1] a musical composition on an audiovisual device, such as a videocassette or laser disc. The exercise of this right, however, is not subject to the compulsory licensing provision for mechanical reproductions set forth in Section 115 of the copyright law. The compulsory license provision only applies to fixing musical compositions in *phonorecords*, which the law defines as devices in which only sounds are fixed. If the sounds are accompanied by motion pictures or other audiovisual works, then the device is not a phonorecord (it is a *copy*) and the compulsory license provision does not apply. Accordingly, the copyright owner is free to negotiate the fees and other terms of licenses to fix their music in videogram devices, such as videocassettes and videodiscs.

Because these devices are primarily intended for use in the home, the right of *public performance* is not involved. The playing of a videocassette or videodisc of a motion picture, for example, in your home, is merely a *private* performance. The copyright law does not afford copyright owners an exclusive right of private performance, which is why you may play a videocassette in your home as often as you wish without additional payment.

EMERGING FEE/ROYALTY ISSUES

Since the advent of the home video player or video cassette recorder (VCR), in the early 1970s, the terms and conditions of licenses to use musical compositions in videograms for home distribution have evolved slowly. Early on, because of the lack of standards in negotiating license fees for the videogram licenses, music copyright owners approached the licensing of their music for inclusion in videograms with great caution, quoting license fees which motion picture producers viewed

---

[1] The copyright law at 17 U.S.C. Sec. 102(a) notes that a work of authorship is *fixed* in tangible medium of expression. The terms *to fix* and *fixation* are customarily found, in lieu of the terms *to record* and *recording*, in many videogram licenses.

as exorbitant. In many cases, music copyright owners refused to issue licenses altogether until they became further acquainted with all of the economic factors concerning the distribution of their music on videogram devices.

At the heart of the matter was the question whether music copyright owners should receive from the producers of motion pictures some participation in the economic success of home video distribution. Indeed, from the perspective of the music copyright owners the question was not *whether* they would participate in the economic success of home video distribution, but *how* they would do so. Despite the fact that copyright owners charged a flat fee for the synchronization of their music with motion pictures, they had an opportunity to participate in the success of motion pictures, because of the lucrative performance royalties they could receive from performing rights societies, such as ASCAP and BMI, arising from the exhibition of motion pictures on television and from the exhibition of motion pictures overseas in theatres. The more successful the motion picture in which their music was recorded, the greater their share in performance royalties collected in connection with the telecast and exhibition of motion pictures.

The problem with home videocassettes and videodiscs is that once copies are recorded and distributed, no *public* performance is involved in their exhibition. As noted above, the playing of a videocassette or videodisc in your home is merely a *private* performance. Accordingly, no performance royalties arise from the home viewing of videograms, and music copyright owners do not receive any compensation beyond the flat sychronization fee received upon the original recording of the music in the film. The problem is compounded by the fact that home viewing of motion pictures by videocassette and laser disc, resulting in private performances, tends to reduce the audience for public performances of the work on broadcast television and overseas theatrical exhibition, which would generate performance royalties. Accordingly, music copyright owners insisted on a replacement for the participation in the economic success they were beginning to lose as a result of the trend away from broadcast television and theatrical performance to home viewing of videograms.

The solution insisted upon by the music copyright owners was to participate in the economic success of videogram distribution in much the same way as they participate in the success of record albums—by collecting a royalty for each unit sold. The problem they faced in implementing this system, however, was that motion picture producers were not accustomed to paying royalties on a per copy basis. They simply did not have the administrative infrastructure to account for copies sold, and were reluctant to agree upon these terms. For a while, there was a stalemate. Producers, accustomed to paying flat fees for synchronization licenses, refused to accept videogram licenses on terms requiring royalties to be accounted for and paid. Synchronization licenses began to specifically address videograms, but only to expressly provide that separate permission, and some form of additional payment, would be required for the videogram use.

Soon, however, music copyright owners and motion picture producers began to negotiate a variety of interim solutions. For example, some early synchronization licenses provided that the parties should negotiate in good faith to establish an appropriate videogram license fee, and failing an agreement, the parties would agree to submit the question to arbitration. In other cases, the music copyright owner would grant the videogram license for a limited term, such as five years, after which the parties would negotiate a fee or have a permanent fee set by arbitration. The interim fee was sometimes a flat dollar amount and sometimes a fee based upon some multiple (e.g., 200%) of the compulsory mechanical royalties provided for in Section 115 of the copyright law.

Eventually, seeing the writing on the wall, motion picture producers established the administrative capability to compensate copyright owners for videogram licenses on a royalty basis and began accepting videogram licenses containing royalty provisions.

CONSIDERATIONS IN GRANTING AND CLEARING VIDEOGRAM LICENSES

As noted in Chapter 9, modern synchronization licenses for motion pictures are carefully drawn to permit the fixing of music in motion pictures or other audiovisual works solely for the purpose of normal theatrical exhibition and television broadcast. If the motion picture is to be distributed in videogram devices, such as videocassette and laser disc, the terms are separately negotiated, either in a separate license or in special provisions set forth in the synchronization license form.

What has been previously said about the value of the song applies with equal force in considering the terms and fees appropriate in granting videogram licenses. See Chapter 5 for a general discussion, and Chapter 9 for a more specific discussion of that consideration with respect to licensing music in motion pictures and television programs. Considerations regarding the fee structure, the importance of the song in relation to its intended use, and the scope of the intended use are discussed below.

1. Fee Structure

The precise formula used for calculating the royalty may vary. As we have said, early interim licenses simply established some multiple of the compulsory mechanical license provision. Other videogram licenses condition its grant upon the payment of a flat fee for a set number of copies, with an option to make additional blocks of copies for additional flat fee payments. Ideally, from the music copyright owner's perspective, the license would be conditioned upon the payment of an advance against a per unit royalty or percentage of the distributor's revenues derived from the distribution of copies of the videogram. Motion picture producers would prefer a structure that requires the least amount of administration and often insist upon paying a flat fee for each block of copies made and distributed. Several sample videogram license fee provisions illustrating several customary fee structures are set forth as Forms 10.1 through 10.6 at the end of this chapter.

2. Importance of the Song in Relation to its Intended Use

The discussions in Chapters 5 and 9 regarding the importance of the song in relation to its intended use are also applicable in considering the fees and terms of videogram licenses. In addition, however, a music copyright owner should consider the further leverage he may have in considering licenses for the use of musical compositions that were previously recorded in motion pictures and television programs. If the terms of the sycnchronization licenses under which the music was recorded in such programs did not contain provisions permitting the fixation of the compositions in videograms, then the copyright owner is free to negotiate a new license fee in exchange for granting permission for such use. The question whether synchronization licenses granted before the advent of the market for home video devices included a license authorizing the reproduction of the music in videograms is discussed at length in Chapter 11.

Once the music has been used in the soundtrack of a motion picture, television program, or other audiovisual work, the producer of the audiovisual work has virtually no substitute for the music included in that work. To the extent the music has become an integral part of the soundtrack, it cannot be easily isolated and removed from the audiovisual work without affecting its creative or commercial value. In such cases, the bargaining leverage of the copyright owner of the composition increases significantly.

Nevertheless, as noted previously, while the music copyright owner may attempt to charge "what the market will bear" for the use, he should not exercise this leverage to the point where the producer is unwilling to release the picture in the home video market. Regardless of the royalty rate received, the music copyright owner will make up for any perceived shortcoming in the fees received by maintaining an active relationship between the song and the listening public.

3. Scope of the Intended Use

A. Media

A modern synchronization license with videogram provisions will typically authorize the recording of the song as part of a motion picture for the purpose of theatrical and television exhibition and the reproduction of videograms for license or sale to the public for home use.

The licenses do not always expressly define what is meant by the term *videogram*. The terms "video records," "home video devices," and "A/V Film," are sometimes used. A person seeking to clear a videogram license should be certain there is no limitation on the type of format on which the work may be recorded and distributed. A videogram might be defined as "any device or contrivance other than film such as video-discs, videotapes or videocassettes upon which there is fixed an audio-visual performance of a motion picture, which performance is capable of being reproduced by performing equipment." Such a definition would include various formats of videocassettes, such as PAL and SECAM, and VHS and Betamax, and various formats of laser disc video devices. A music copyright owner would normally have no difficulty providing a license that includes use on various formats, but it is always to the copyright owner's advantage to narrow the scope of the license to only those uses actually required by the licensee, and a limitation on the formats permitted could serve that purpose.

B. Distribution Channels

Videogram licenses do not always define what is meant by *home use*, but whether a precise definition is used or not, it is clear that the performance of a videocassette in a small theatre, a nightclub, or a bar would not be considered home use. Inviting several neighbors over to your house to watch a motion picture on videocassette would, however, be a home use, but if you charged a fee, it would probably be considered a public, non-home use performance.

C. Term

The term of the videogram license will depend upon how the compensation provision of the license is structured. If the videogram license is granted in conjunction with a theatrical synchronization license, and the reproduction of videograms is subject to a royalty, then the videogram license will generally have the same term as the theatrical synchronization license. This would typically be in perpetuity or for the life of the copyright in the song.

If the copyright owner and the motion picture producer could not come to terms on a royalty for the videogram license, then the videogram license, if negotiated at all, might have a limited term. For example, the music copyright owner might accept a lower royalty rate, or even a flat fee, provided the term of the videogram license is limited to three to five years, at which time, the producer would require new permission to continue distribution of videogram copies. If by that time the picture has become a perennial favorite, the music copyright owner should have no trouble negotiating an acceptable royalty structure or a higher royalty rate; if by that time the picture has gone into oblivion, a license for further videogram distribution would not be necessary. The motion picture producer thereby reduces his risk of investing too much money to account for music royalties for a flop picture; the music copyright owner thereby reduces his risk of making a bad deal by preserving the right to renegotiate in the event the picture becomes a long-term success.

D. Territory

Many early videogram licenses limited the distribution of videograms to within the United States and Canada, even though the territory of the underlying synchronization license for theatrical and television exhibition was world-wide. In such cases, the exploitation of videogram rights in other territories was made subject to the producer's obtaining licenses from overseas music publishers or the appropriate mechanical or performance rights societies. Even today, the territory of many videogram licenses are limited to the United States and Canada where the publisher does not control the right to administer the song in other countries.

Assuming the music copyright owner does control worldwide administration rights, the territory of the videogram license is usually worldwide. Nevertheless, in some countries, fees for the distribution of videogram licenses are collected by societies of publishers or local governmental authorities established for that purpose. A videogram license, therefore, may provide that where a local agency or authority charges a higher royalty than that provided for in the license, the producer shall pay the publisher the difference.

E. Exclusivity

Videogram licenses, like synchronization licenses for motion pictures and television, are almost always non-exclusive. A music publisher should only guardedly consider a request by a producer for exclusivity, as granting such a request may restrict the publisher's future ability to license the song in many forms of audiovisual works.

OTHER TERMS AND CONSIDERATIONS

1. Payment and Accounting

If the license fee for the videogram license is based on a royalty, such as a percentage of net revenues from sales or licenses of the videograms, the license will normally contain provisions relating to how and when the copyright owner will be paid the fee. These provisions are similar to those commonly found in recording agreements, book publishing agreements, or other licenses under which payments are based on a percentage of revenues or the number of copies distributed.

For example, payments are usually accounted for on a quarterly basis, within some reasonable period after the end of each calendar quarter in which there are revenues derived from the work. A written royalty statement detailing the sources of the revenues upon which the royalty is based will accompany the payment. The music copyright owner will have the privilege to inspect the licensee's books and records relating to the revenues derived from the videogram. In this regard, a number of accounting firms specialize in performing audits of such records, and a music publisher should consider having its licensees audited on a periodic basis to, as the saying goes, "keep them honest."

A discussion of other payment and accounting provisions is set forth in Chapter 5.

2. Reserves Against Returns

A producer might insist upon maintaining a reserve against royalties each quarter in anticipation of a reasonable amount of returns of the videogram (which would represent negative revenue and a credit against royalties), but any such reserve should be liquidated within some reasonable period of time after the quarter in which it is withheld.

3. Most Favored Nations

As has been noted, music copyright owners were reluctant to grant videogram licenses before standards evolved that allowed them to establish a way to participate in the economic success of the videograms in which their musical compositions were embodied. Even as standards eventually began emerging, some music copyright owners continued to feel unable to determine in advance the importance of the song in relation to its intended use or otherwise remained fearful of making a bad deal.

Accordingly, the publisher unsure of what fee to charge, or even how to structure the fee, might ask that he be paid a license fee under terms which are no less favorable than those received for the use of any other song featured in the motion picture, requesting what is called a *most favored nations* provision. The copyright owner would reason that the importance of his song in relation to the intended use would be, at least, no less important than the use of any other song featured in the motion picture; and, as long as he was getting no smaller fee than that being paid to the highest paid music copyright owner, he would avoid making a bad deal.

A producer who is reluctant to agree to such a provision should be prepared to argue that the song for which he seeks a license has significantly less importance than other songs in the motion picture. Nevertheless, if the music has long been included in a previously released motion picture, it would seem that obtaining a license for each song inextricably recorded in the picture is equally important, regardless of the nature or extent of the use.

4. Free Copies

Music copyright owners should request at least two free copies of videocassette or laser disc of the motion picture upon its release in the home video market.

PROMOTIONAL MUSIC VIDEO VIDEOGRAM LICENSE

As discussed in Chapter 9, promotional music videos are customarily produced by record companies to promote the recording of a single song and are broadcast on national cable networks, such as MTV and VH1. From time to time, a music video becomes a successful "hit" in its own right, its success as a video program being independent of the success of the song it promotes. In such a case, a record company may be inclined to release and sell, apart from copies of the audio recording, copies of the video program on videocassette or laser disc. Furthermore, some record albums consist of a recording of a "live" concert performance or recordings of selected live performances from a concert tour. Having recorded these performances on videotape, the record company often considers distributing the video program in the home video market.

As mentioned in Chapter 9, the publishers of the music underlying these programs are usually willing to charge a nominal fee for their exhibition on television, because such performances generate performance income and play an important role in making the song a "hit." However, the distribution of video performances of the music on videocassette or laser disc is akin to, and may be competition for, the distribution of the corresponding audio records of the performances. Accordingly, music publishers normally insist upon a royalty for such use.

Because these recordings are accompanied by moving pictures, the compulsory license provision does not apply and publishers are free to negotiate other fee structures for the use of their music on these videograms. Nevertheless, no standards have yet emerged for structuring fees for the sale of videograms of promotional music videos. Music publishers assert that the fee for the use of their music in such programs should be considerably higher than the use of their music in motion pictures, television programs, and other audiovisual works, because, unlike an incidental use in a motion picture, the music plays a central role in the entertainment value of the music videogram. The royalty provision in Form 10.7 at the end of this chapter contains a formula which attempts to provide the music publisher with a substantial share of the revenues derived from sales of the videogram.

NON-THEATRICAL VIDEOGRAM LICENSE

Non-theatrical synchronization licenses, regarding the use of music in films developed by corporations for internal purposes, such as for employee training or demonstrations of products to customers, are discussed in Chapter 9. Where a corporation desires to make and distribute copies of a video program to employees, retailers, or to end user customers, the copyright owner will usually grant such permission in exchange for an additional fee based on the number of units made and distributed. Corporations which are not set up for, and do not look forward to the prospect of, accounting for the number of videogram copies made, will attempt to negotiate an annual buy-out provision. This allows the corporation to pay a yearly fixed dollar amount in lieu of accounting for royalties. An example of a synchronization license with videogram production privileges is set forth as Form 10.8 at the end of this chapter.

VIDEO YEARBOOKS

In the wake of popular television programs that have introduced the "home video" genre of entertainment, such as *America's Funniest Home Videos* hosted by Bob Saget, high school and college students across America are applying modern technology to update an old tradition: schools are now producing what are being called *video yearbooks*—a videotape of short interviews and scenes encapsulating the senior year in a one hour or 90 minute program for sale in addition to, or in conjunction with, the traditional printed high school or college yearbook.

Music publishers have taken this opportunity to teach young students a valuable lesson in copyright law—that they have to pay for the use of the music they use in such programs—and charge a small flat fee for the use. The license for such use would be quite similar to the non-theatrical videogram license set forth as Form 10.8 at the end of this chapter.

APPENDIX TO CHAPTER 10
VIDEOGRAM LICENSES

FORMS

FORM 10.1

SYNCHRONIZATION LICENSE FOR MOTION PICTURE THEATRICAL AND TELEVISION EXHIBITION WITH VIDEOGRAM LICENSE ON PERCENTAGE ROYALTY BASIS

MOTION PICTURE AND TELEVISION SYNCHRONIZATION, THEATRICAL PERFORMANCE AND VIDEOGRAM LICENSE

FOR AND IN CONSIDERATION OF THE SUM OF $ for the synchronization rights hereinafter set forth and $ for the performing rights and other rights set forth in Paragraphs 4 and 5 below, and the advance provided in Paragraph 7(d) for the Videogram rights set forth in Paragraph 6(b), said sums payable upon the execution and delivery hereof, and in consideration of all the other promises and agreements contained herein, Publisher listed below, hereby grants to and its successors and assigns, hereinafter referred to as "Producer" the non-exclusive irrevocable right, license, privilege and authority to record in any manner, medium or form, whether now known or hereafter devised, the music and the words of the musical composition set forth below only in connection with the motion picture entitled below in any language, to make copies of said recording in any and all gauges of film and to import said recording and/or copies of said recording into any country within the territory covered by this license and to perform, as set forth below, said musical composition in said territory, subject to the terms, conditions and limitations set forth below.

1. MUSICAL COMPOSITION.

The musical composition (hereinafter the "Composition"), and the sole use of said musical composition, covered by this license is:

TITLE   WRITER   PUBLISHER   USE

2. MOTION PICTURE TITLE.

The title of the only motion picture (hereinafter the "Motion Picture") with which said recording is to be used is:

3. TERRITORY.

The territory (hereinafter the Territory) covered by this license is:

4. PERFORMANCE LICENSE—UNITED STATES.

Publisher grants to Producer the non-exclusive right and license in the United States and its possessions to perform publicly, either for profit or non-profit, and to authorize others so to perform, the Composition only in synchronization or timed relationship to the Motion Picture and trailers thereof as follows:

(a)   THEATRICAL PERFORMANCE. In the exhibition of the Motion Picture to audiences in theatres and other public places where motion pictures are customarily exhibited, and where admission fees are charged, including but not limited to, the right to perform the Composition by transmission of the Motion Picture to audiences in theatres and such other public places for the duration of United States copyright of the Composition.

(b)   PUBLIC TELEVISION PERFORMANCE. In the exhibition of the Motion Picture by free television, pay television, networks, local stations, pay cable, closed circuit, satellite transmission, and all other types or methods of television or electronic reproduction and transmissions ("Television Performance") to audiences not included in subparagraph (a) of this Paragraph 4 only by entities having performance licenses therefor from the appropriate performing rights societies. Television Performance of the Motion Picture by anyone not licensed for such performing rights by ASCAP or BMI is subject to clearance of the performing right either from Publisher or ASCAP or BMI or from any other licensor acting for or on behalf of Publisher and to payment of an additional license fee therefor.

5. FOREIGN PERFORMING LICENSE.

It is understood that the performance of the Composition in connection with the exhibition of the motion Picture in countries or territories within the Territory but outside of the United States and its possessions shall be subject to clearance by performing rights societies in accordance with their customary practice and the payment of their customary fees. Publisher agrees that to the extent it controls said performing rights, it will license an appropriate performing rights society in the respective countries to grant such performing right.

6. VIDEOGRAM LICENSE.

Publisher hereby further grants to Producer, in each country of the Territory, the non-exclusive right to cause or authorize the fixing of the Composition in and as part of the Motion Picture on audio-visual contrivances such as video cassettes, video tapes, video discs and similar compact audiovisual devices reproducing the entire motion picture in substantially its original form ("Videogram"), and:

(a)   To utilize such Videogram for any of the purposes, uses and performances hereinabove set forth and,

(b)   To reproduce, and to sell, lease, license, or otherwise distribute and make such Videogram available to the public as a device intended primarily for "home use" (as such term is commonly understood in the phonograph record industry) in the Territory but subject to the provisions of Paragraph 7 hereof.

7. VIDEOGRAM ROYALTY.

Royalties ("the Royalties") with respect to the manufacture and distribution of Videogram copies of the Motion Picture under paragraph 6(b) hereof shall be determined and paid as follows:

(a)   With respect to Videograms sold and not returned pursuant to paragraph 6(b) hereof, an amount equal to the greater
of per Videogram copy of the Motion Picture $ _____,
or that portion of _____percent (%) ("Publisher's pro-rata
portion") of the wholesale distributor selling price (not including
shipping charges or taxes) that the Composition licensed hereunder bears to the total number of Royalty-bearing compositions
contained in the Motion Picture.

(b)   With respect to Videograms manufactured and leased or
rented by Producer to its customers or consumers, an amount
equal to Publisher's pro-rata portion of _____ percent (_____ %)
of Producer's actual net receipts with respect to such lease or
rental.

(c)   With respect to Videograms manufactured and/or rented
by a licensee of Producer, an amount equal to Publisher's pro-rata
portion of _____ percent (_____ %) of Producer's actual net
receipts from such licensee with respect to such lease or rental.

(d)   Producer shall pay upon execution and delivery hereof to
Publisher a non-returnable but recoupable advance ("Advance") in
the sum of _____ against the Royalties provided for in this
Paragraph 7.

(e)   Producer may withhold from royalties otherwise payable with each accounting statement a reasonable and prudent
reserve for anticipated returns, refunds, and exchanges of
Videograms hereunder, and such reserve shall be liquidated in a
reasonable and prudent manner but in no event later than 12
months after the accounting statement with respect to which it
was originally withheld.

(f)   Should a higher royalty, or per-copy rate, than that set
forth in this Paragraph 7 become payable with respect to Videograms manufactured, leased or sold in a particular country or
sub-territory within the Territory either by (i) operation of law
(including, inter alia, by statute, Governmental regulation of final

judicial determination), (ii) agreement between a society or other organization collecting a significant portion of the music publishing revenue of said country or sub-territory and the manufacturers or distributors of Videograms or (iii) the establishment of a higher royalty rate by custom and practice within said country or sub-territory, Producer or its affiliates, agents, licensees or sub-licensees shall either pay such higher royalties to Publisher with respect to said country or sub-territory, or delete the applicable Composition from the Motion Picture with respect to said country or sub-territory.

(g)   Producer hereby warrants and represents that no other musical composition will be licensed for a substantially similar use in connection with the Videogram exploitation of the Motion Picture by or on behalf of a publisher on a more favorable basis to such publisher than is provided to Publisher hereunder. In the event a musical composition is licensed in connection with the Motion Picture on a more favorable basis in any of the areas hereunder, Producer hereby agrees that such more favorable basis shall also be extended to the licensing of the Composition hereunder.

(h)   (i)   Producer shall render to Publisher, on a quarterly basis, within forty-five (45) days after the end of each calendar quarter after the first commercial sale or rental of a Videogram containing the Motion Picture, a detailed written statement of the royalty due to Publisher with respect to the Videograms of the Motion Picture containing the Composition. Such statement shall be accompanied by a remittance of such amount as shown to be due. Any statement remitted by Producer hereunder shall conclusively be deemed true and correct and binding on Publisher unless Publisher submits to Producer in writing within three (3) years after such statement has been remitted to Publisher specific objections to the submitted statement. (ii) Publisher shall have the right to examine and inspect the books and records of Producer which relate to the Motion Picture and Videograms of the Motion Picture containing the Composition, and to make extracts thereof, for the purpose of determining the accuracy of statements rendered by Producer hereunder. Such examination shall be made during reasonable business hours, on reasonable business days, on no less than ten (10) days prior written notice at the regular place of business of Producer where such books and records are maintained. (iii) Each statement and the accompanying remittance will be made in United States currency. If foreign receipts in the Territory are frozen or unremittable, such receipts shall be transferred to Producer's account in such foreign country, and Producer shall notify Publisher to such effect. Upon Publisher's written request and upon condition that the same shall be permitted by the authorities of such foreign country, Producer shall transfer to Publisher in such foreign country and in the currency thereof at Publisher's cost and expense such part of such foreign receipts to which Publisher would be entitled hereunder if the funds were transmitted and paid in the United States in accordance with the terms hereof. Such notice and appropriate transfer shall discharge Producer of its obligation to remit such frozen funds. If the laws of any jurisdiction require that taxes on such remittance be withheld at the source, then remittance hereunder to Publisher shall be reduced accordingly. Producer shall provide Publisher upon request with copies of all applicable documentation with respect to such withholding.

(i)   Nothing herein shall obligate or require Producer to embody the Composition in Videogram copies of the Motion Picture and it is expressly understood and agreed that the Royalties payable to Publisher hereunder in respect of the Videogram and exploitation of the Motion Picture is conditioned upon the embodiment of the Composition therein provided that such royalties shall not be reduced by the use of the Composition that is less than the use specified in paragraph 1 hereof and provided further that in no event shall the Advances provided in paragraph 7(d) hereof be reduced or returned to Producer.

8. RESTRICTIONS.

This license does not include any right or authority (a) to make any change in the original lyrics or in the fundamental character of the music of the Composition; (b) to use the title, the subtitle or any portion of the lyrics of the Composition as the title or subtitle of the Motion Picture; (c) to dramatize or to use the plot or any dramatic content of the lyrics of the Composition; or (d) to make any other use of the Composition not expressly authorized herein.

9. WARRANTY.

Publisher warrants only that it has the right to grant this license and this license is given and accepted without any other representations, warranty or recourse, express or implied, except for Publisher's agreement to repay the consideration for this license if said warranty shall be breached with respect thereto. In no event shall the total liability of Publisher in any case exceed the amount of consideration received by it hereunder.

10. PUBLISHER'S RESERVATION OF RIGHTS

Subject only to the non-exclusive rights herein-above granted to Producer all rights of every kind and nature in the Composition are reserved to said Publisher together with all rights of use thereof.

11. ADVERTISING

The recording and performing rights hereinabove granted include such rights for air, screen and television trailers solely for the advertising and exploitation of the Motion Picture.

12. CUE SHEET

Producer agrees to furnish Publisher a cue sheet of the Motion Picture within thirty (30) days after the first public exhibition of the Motion Picture at which admission is charged (except so-called "sneak" previews).

13. REMEDIES

In the event that Producer, or its assigns, licensees, or sub-licensees, breaches this Agreement by, among other things, failing to pay timely any license fees required hereunder, and fails to cure such breach within thirty (30) days after notice of such breach given by Publisher to Producer, then this license will automatically terminate. Such termination shall render the distribution, licensing, or use of the Composition(s) as unauthorized uses, subject to the rights and remedies provided by the laws, including copyright, and equity of the various countries within the Territory.

14. NOTICES

All notices, demands or requests provided for or desired to be given pursuant to this Agreement must be in writing. All such documents shall be deemed to have been given when served by personal delivery or three days following their deposit in the United States mail, postage prepaid, certified or registered, addressed as follows:

(a) To Publisher:

with a courtesy copy to:

and

(b) to Producer:

with a courtesy copy to:

or to such other address in the United States as either party may hereafter designate in writing delivered in the manner aforesaid.

15. ENTIRE AGREEMENT

This license is binding upon and shall inure to the benefit of the respective successors and/or assigns of the parties hereto but in no event shall Producer be relieved of its obligations hereunder without the express written consent of Publisher. This Agreement shall be construed in all respects in accordance with the laws of the State of California applicable to agreements entered into and to be wholly performed therein. The recording and performing and other rights hereinabove granted shall endure for the periods of all copyrights in and to the composition, and any and all renewals or extensions thereof that Publisher may now own or control or hereafter own or control without Producer having to pay any additional consideration therefor.

IN WITNESS WHEREOF, the parties have caused the foregoing to be executed as of the day of 1995

PUBLISHER   PRODUCER

By: _____   By: _____

FORM 10.2

VIDEOGRAM LICENSE PROVISIONS ON
"BLOCK OF COPIES" BASIS
(REPLACING SECTIONS 6 AND 7 OF FORM 10.1)

6. VIDEOGRAM LICENSE.

Publisher hereby further grants to Producer, in each country of the Territory, the non-exclusive right to cause or authorize the fixing of the Composition in and as part of the Motion Picture on audio-visual contrivances such as video cassettes, video tapes, video discs and similar compact audiovisual devices reproducing the entire motion picture in substantially its original form ("Video-gram"), and:

(a)   To utilize such Videogram for any of the purposes, uses and performances hereinabove set forth and

(b)   To reproduce, and to sell, lease, license, or otherwise distribute and make such Videogram available to the public as a device intended primarily for "home use" (as such term is commonly understood in the phonograph record industry) in the Territory but subject to the provisions of Paragraph 7 hereof.

7. VIDEOGRAM LICENSE FEE

The Videogram License Fee for the rights granted pursuant to paragraph 6(b) hereof shall be paid and determined as follows:

(a)   License Fee. Subject to the provisions in paragraph 7(a), (c) and (d) hereof, for the right to manufacture, duplicate and distribute up to _____ Videogram copies of the Motion Picture pursuant to paragraph 6(b) hereof, Producer shall pay to Publisher a Videogram License Fee of $_____ upon execution hereof. Producer may, from time to time, extend the license of the rights granted pursuant to paragraph 6(b) hereof for additional blocs of up to_____Videogram copies of the Motion Picture provided that Producer pays to Publisher the sum of $_____

for each additional bloc of _____Videogram copies not later than 30 days after the total number of Videogram copies of the Motion Picture previously licensed hereunder have been manufactured or duplicated by Producer, or its assignees or licensees. In the event Producer does not make such license extension payment to Publisher within said 30 day period, then the manufacturing, duplication, and distribution of the Videogram copies of the Motion Picture in excess of the total number of Videogram copies of the Motion Picture with respect to which Producer has already paid a Videogram License Fee shall be unauthorized and without the permission and license of Publisher.

(b)   Accounting of Videogram Copies Distributed. Producer shall render to Publisher, on a quarterly basis, within forty-five (45) days after the end of each calendar quarter after the first commercial sale or rental of a Videogram containing the Motion Picture, a statement of each country within the Territory on a cumulative basis, setting forth the totals (i) of all Videogram copies of the Motion Picture manufactured or duplicated and (ii) of all Videogram copies of the Motion Picture sold, leased, or otherwise distributed in each country within the Territory pursuant to the license of rights granted under paragraph 6(b) hereof.

(c)   Foreign Royalties. Notwithstanding anything to the contrary as may be contained herein, in the event that a per-copy rate for the exercise of the rights granted pursuant to paragraph 6(b) hereof greater than the product of \$_____ divided by _____ shall become payable with respect to Videogram copies manufactured, duplicated, leased or sold in a particular country or sub-territory within the Territory (other than the United States and Canada, and their respective territories and possessions), whether by (i) operation of law (including, inter alia, by statute, Governmental regulation or final judicial determination), (ii) agreement between a society or other organization collecting a significant portion of the music publishing revenue of said country or sub-territory and the manufacturers or distributors of Videograms or (iii) the establishment of a higher royalty rate by custom and practice within said country or sub-territory, Producer or its affiliates, agents, licensees or sub-licensees shall either pay such higher royalties to Publisher with respect to said country or sub-territory, or delete the applicable Composition from the Motion Picture with respect to said country or sub-territory.

(d)   Producer hereby warrants and represents that no other musical composition will be licensed for a substantially similar use in connection with the Videogram exploitation of the Motion Picture by or on behalf of a publisher on a more favorable basis to such publisher than is provided to Publisher hereunder. In the event a musical composition is licensed in connection with the Motion Picture on a more favorable basis in any of the areas hereunder, Producer hereby agrees that such more favorable basis shall also be extended to the licensing of the Composition hereunder.

FORM 10.3

VIDEOGRAM LICENSE PROVISIONS
ON "FLAT FEE" BASIS FOR FIXED TERM
WITH ARBITRATION PROVISION
(REPLACING SECTIONS 6 AND 7 OF FORM 10.1)

6. VIDEOGRAM LICENSE.

Publisher hereby further grants to Producer, in each country of the Territory, the non-exclusive right to cause or authorize the fixing of the Composition in and as part of the Motion Picture on audio-visual contrivances such as video cassettes, video tapes, video discs and similar compact audiovisual devices reproducing the entire motion picture in substantially its original form ("Videogram"), and:

(a)   To utilize such Videogram for any of the purposes, uses and performances hereinabove set forth and

(b)   To reproduce, and to sell, lease, license, or otherwise distribute and make such Videogram available to the public as a device intended primarily for "home use" (as such term is commonly understood in the phonograph record industry) in the Territory but subject to the provisions of Paragraph 7 hereof.

7. VIDEOGRAM LICENSE FEE

The Videogram License Fee for the rights granted pursuant to paragraph 6(b) hereof shall be paid and determined as follows:

(a)   Initial Fee. Subject to the provisions in paragraph 7(a), (c) and (d) hereof, for the rights granted pursuant to Paragraph 6(b) hereof, Producer shall pay to Publisher an initial fee of $ _____ upon execution hereof, of which $_____ shall be allocated as the license fee for the exercise in the United States and Canada, and their respective territories and possessions, of the rights granted pursuant to Paragraph 6(b) hereof ("Domestic Videogram License Fee") and $ _____ shall be allocated as the license fee for the exercise of all countries included within the Territory, other than the United States and Canada and their respective territories and possessions, of the rights granted pursuant to Paragraph 6(b) hereof (the "Foreign Videogram License Fee"). Producer shall give written notice to Publisher no later than 10 days after copies of such Videograms are first offered for distribution to the public for home use. Such written notification shall include the identification of the Motion Picture and the Composition subject to this license and shall specify the date upon which copies of said Videograms will be, or had been, first offered for distribution to the public for home use.

(b)   Additional License Fee. At any time commencing on the date which is _____ years after the date upon which copies of said Videograms had been first offered for distribution to the public for home use, Publisher, by written notice to Producer, may request Producer to pay an additional license fee, whether computed as a flat fee, royalty, or otherwise, for the grant of the rights pursuant to Paragraph 6(b) hereof. Upon receipt of such written notice, Producer shall meet and negotiate in good faith with Publisher to determine such increased license fee, if any, to be paid by Producer to Publisher. Such additional license fee requested by Publisher, and required to be negotiated in good faith by Publisher and Producer, shall be with respect to both domestic and foreign exercise of the rights granted pursuant to Paragraph 6(b) and with respect to both the exercise of such rights by Producer during the _____ years commencing upon the initial exercise of such rights by Publisher and for the remaining balance of the term of this license. If Producer and Publisher cannot agree upon an additional license fee with respect to either the Domestic Videogram License Fee and/or the Foreign Videogram License Fee within thirty (30) days after said written notification by Publisher to Producer, then the additional license fee, if any, for the domestic and/or foreign exercise of the rights granted pursuant to Paragraph 6(b) hereof shall be settled by binding arbitration in Los Angeles, California in accordance with the rules and regulations of the American Arbitration Association then in effect.

FORM 10.4

VIDEOGRAM LICENSE PROVISIONS ON TWICE "STATUTORY RATE" BASIS WITH ARBITRATION PROVISION (REPLACING SECTIONS 6 AND 7 OF FORM 10.1)

6. VIDEOGRAM LICENSE.

Publisher hereby further grants to Producer, in each country of the Territory, the non-exclusive right to cause or authorize the fixing of the Composition in and as part of the Motion Picture on audiovisual contrivances such as video cassettes, video tapes, video discs and similar compact audiovisual devices reproducing the entire motion picture in substantially its original form ("Videogram"), and:

(a)   To utilize such Videogram for any of the purposes, uses and performances hereinabove set forth and

(b)   To reproduce, and to sell, lease, license, or otherwise distribute and make such Videogram available to the public as a device intended primarily for "home use" (as such term is commonly understood in the phonograph record industry) in the Territory but subject to the provisions of Paragraph 7 hereof.

7. VIDEOGRAM LICENSE FEE

The Videogram License Fee for the rights granted pursuant to paragraph 6(b) hereof shall be paid and determined as follows:

If Producer shall exercise the rights granted pursuant to Paragraph 6(b) hereof in the U.S., there shall be payment of an additional fee and/or royalty ("Additional Payment") therefor. In view of the early stage of development of exploitation, it will be difficult to determine the amount and basis of such Additional Payment until such time as the prevailing experience in the entertainment industry provides a better basis for determination of a fair and appropriate Additional Payment. Producer and Publisher each hereby agree to negotiate the basis and amount of Additional Payment in good faith at any time after the exercise of such right upon request of the other and, if they have not agreed upon the basis of computation and amount of Additional Payment within nine (9) months from the exercise of such right, they agree that: upon written notice from one to the other after the expiration of nine (9) months they shall renegotiate in good faith regarding such basis of computation and the amount of Additional Payment; if they are unable to reach agreement within 30 days after the date of such notice, they shall submit to, and be bound by a determination under, arbitration in accordance with the rules and regulations of the American Arbitration Association for the calculation and establishment of such Additional Payment hereunder. During the period between Producer's initial exercise of the right subject to this provision and agreement between the parties for additional payment or a final arbitration determination, Publisher shall be paid a royalty for each Videogram made and distributed. The royalty payable shall be twice the compulsory royalty payable for a phonorecord pursuant to the Copyright Laws of the United States (presently Title 17 U.S.C Sec. 115(c)(2). Said royalty payment shall be in accordance with the same provisions set forth in Title 17 U.S.C. Sec. 115(c)(3), and the Publisher shall enjoy the same rights as the copyright owner pursuant to 17 U.S.C. Sec. 115(c)(3). If such matter becomes the subject of arbitration, among the factors which shall aid in the determination of such Additional Payment shall be:

(a)   the number of copies, if any, of such Videogram then sold, licensed, leased, or otherwise made or to be made available to the public and the wholesale, retail, rental or license fee or price paid for each copy;

(b)   the type and number of uses of the composition hereunder in the Videogram and the types and number of uses of other musical compositions embodied in the Videogram;

(c)   the nature and use of the music in the motion picture (e.g., the subject of the motion picture is a dramatico-musical work or other work)

(d)   the negative cost of the motion picture and the relation of the cost of the music rights and production of music recordings (i.e., recording, musicians, and other performing artists, copying, arranging, and other costs).

Producer may exercise the rights under Paragraph 6(b) hereof in such portion of the territory as is outside the U.S. only pursuant to agreements, licenses or arrangements made with sub-publishers, agents, or other licensees or parties who then control such rights in the compositions in such portion of the territory as is outside the U.S. .

FORM 10.5

AUDIOVISUAL WORK SYNCHRONIZATION
AND VIDEOGRAM LICENSE
(INCLUDES NO THEATRICAL OR TELEVISION
EXHIBITION PROVISIONS)

VIDEOPROGRAM-SYNCHRONIZATION
AND VIDEOGRAM LICENSE AGREEMENT

LICENSE AGREEMENT entered into this _____ day of _____
19 _____ between _____
_____ whose address is _____
_____ hereinafter referred to as ("Producer")
and_____
_____ whose address is _____
_____
(hereinafter referred to as ("Publisher").

    1.   The musical composition(s) ('the Compositions(s)" covered
by this License is (are):

Title   Writer
Publisher

    2.   The only Program ("the Program") covered by this License
is entitled_____

_____

    3.   The type and number of uses ("Uses") in the program of
the Composition(s) is (are)_____

_____

    4.   The "Territory" covered under this License is_____

_____

    5.   Subject to the terms hereof, Publisher hereby grants to
Producer the non-exclusive right, license and authority:

(a)   · to record or re-record within each country of the Territory the Uses of the Composition(s) in synchronism or timed relationship with the Program, but not otherwise, and to make copies of the Program containing the Composition(s), all in accordance with the terms and conditions set forth below;

(b)   to cause or authorize the fixation of the Composition(s) in and as part of the Program on video cassettes, video tapes, video discs and similar compact and audio-visual devices intended primarily for home use ("Videograms"); and

(c)   to sell, rent or otherwise distribute such Videograms to the public within the Territory for use in conjunction with a television-type playback system or mechanism intended for home use only.

6.   The term (hereinafter the "Term") during which the rights licensed hereunder may be exercised shall endure for the worldwide period for all copyrights in and to the Composition(s), and any and all renewals or extensions thereof that Publisher may now own or control or hereafter own or control with Producer having to pay any additional consideration thereafter.

7.   Producer shall pay to publisher or its designee the following sums on the terms and conditions set forth below:

(a)   With respect to Videograms sold and not returned in the Territory, a royalty in an amount equal to the greater of $_____ per Videogram copy of the Program or that portion of _____(____%) percent ("Publishers pro-rata portion") of the wholesale distributor selling price (not including shipping charges or taxes) that the Composition(s) bears to the total number of Royalty-bearing compositions contained in the Program.

(b)   With respect to Videograms manufactured and rented by Producer or by a licensee of Producer, to its customers or consumers, a Royalty in an amount equal to Publishers pro-rata portion of % _____ of Producer's actual net receipts with respect to such rental.

(c)   Producer shall pay upon execution of this Agreement to Publisher, a non-returnable advance recoupable only from the Royalties provided for in this paragraph 7, in the sum of $ _____ for the first _____ units and _____ per disc and cassette unit thereafter.

(d)   Producer may withhold from royalties otherwise payable with each accounting statement a reasonable and prudent reserve for anticipated returns, refunds and exchanges of Videograms hereunder, and such reserves shall be liquidated in a reasonable and prudent manner, but in no event later than 12 months after the accounting statement with respect to which it was originally withheld.

(e)   Should a higher royalty than that provided in Paragraphs 7 (b) or (c) above become payable with respect to Videograms manufactured, leased or sold in a particular country or sub-territory within the Territory, other than the United States and Canada, either by (a) operation of law (including, *inter alia,* by statute, governmental regulation or final judicial determination), (b) agreement between a society or other organization collecting a significant portion of the music publishing revenues in said country or sub-territory and the manufacturers or distributors of Videograms, or (c) by custom and practice within said country or sub-territory, Producer or its affiliates, agents, licensees or sub-licensees, shall either pay such higher royalties to Publisher with respect to said country or its sub-territory, or delete the Composition(s) from the Program with respect to said country or its sub-territory.

8.   Producer hereby warrants and represents that no other musical composition will be licensed for a substantially similar use to the Composition(s) licensed hereunder in connection with the Program by or on behalf of a publisher on a more favorable basis to such publisher than is provided to Publisher hereunder. In the

event a musical composition is to licensed in connection with the Program on a more favorable basis in any of the areas hereunder, Producer hereby agrees that such more favorable basis will also be extended to the licensing of the Composition(s) hereunder. By way of clarification of the foregoing and not in limitation thereof, if another musical composition is licensed in connection with the Program and the publisher thereof is paid amounts for such composition exceeding the sums paid to Publisher hereunder, Producer shall immediately pay to Publisher an amount equal to the difference between the amount paid for such other musical composition and the sums and/or royalties theretofore paid Publisher hereunder.

9.   (a)   Producer shall render to Publisher, on a semiannual basis, as of June 30 and December 31, for the prior six months, a detailed written statement of the royalties due to Publisher with respect to the Videograms of the program containing the Composition(s). Such statement shall be accompanied by a remittance of such amount shown to be due in United States currency. Any statement remitted by Producer hereunder shall be presumed to be true and correct and binding upon Publisher, except in the case of fraud, unless Publisher submits to Producer specific objections to the submitted statement in writing within three (3) years after such statement has been remitted to Publisher.

. (b)   Publisher shall have the right to examine and inspect the books and records of Producer which relate to the Program and Videograms of the Program containing the Composition(s) for the purpose of determining the accuracy of statements rendered by Producer hereunder. Such examination shall be made during reasonable business hours, on reasonable business days, on no less than 10 days prior written notice at the regular place of business of Producer where such books and records are maintained.

10.   In the event that Producer shall fail to pay to Publisher the amounts specified herein on a timely basis or shall fail to

account to Publisher and pay royalties as provided for hereunder, Publisher shall give Producer written notice that unless such default is remedied within thirty (30) days from receipt of the notice, this License will automatically terminate. Such termination shall render the distribution, licensing or use of the Composition(s) as unauthorized uses, subject to the rights and remedies provided by the laws and equity of the Territory.

11.   Nothing herein shall obligate or require Producer to embody the Composition(s) in either the Program or any Videogram of the Program and it is expressly understood and agreed that the compensation, in excess of the advance provided in Paragraph 7 (c) payable to Publisher hereunder in respect of sales of Videogram copies of the Program is conditioned upon the embodiment or fixation of the Composition(s) in such Videograms, but shall not be reduced by a lesser use of the entire Composition(s) than the Use(s) provided herein.

12.   All rights granted hereunder are granted on a nonexclusive basis and Publisher shall have the right to grant similar licenses for the use of the Composition(s) to other licensees. Upon the expiration of the period specified in paragraph 6 hereinabove, the respective rights granted to Producer herein shall automatically revert to Publisher and any further use of the Composition(s) shall be unauthorized.

13.   Producer may use the Composition(s) in the Program for screen and television excerpts and/or trailers only in connection with the advertising and exploitation of Videogram copies of the Program for the period specified in paragraph 6.

14.   This License is limited to those uses of the Composition(s) expressly set forth herein, and Producer hereunder; provided, however, that nothing contained herein shall be deemed to limit or curtail any rights previously granted to and/or hereafter to be granted to Producer under any other Agreement. By way of clarification and not in limitation thereof, this license does not grant the right to: (a) exhibit or authorize the exhibition of the Program in

or by any medium not specified here; (b) record or authorize the recording of the composition(s) in any manner except as specified herein; (c) make, authorize or permit any change in the fundamental character of the music or lyrics of the Composition(s); (d) use the title of the Composition(s) as the title of the Program; or, (e) use the story of the Composition(s) as the story of the Program.

15.   Publisher warrants only that it has the legal right to grant this License and this License is given and accepted without any other warranty or recourse, express or implied. If said warranty shall be breached in whole or in part, Publisher shall either re-pay to Producer the consideration theretofore paid to Publisher by Producer for this License to the extent of the part hereof which is breached or shall hold Producer harmless to the extent of the consideration theretofore paid to Publisher by Producer for this License. In no event shall Publisher's total liability to Producer or to third parties exceed the amounts received by it hereunder.

16.   This Agreement sets forth the entire agreement be-tween Publisher and Producer with respect to the subject matter hereof, and may not be modified or amended except by written agreement executed by the parties. This License shall be governed by and subject to the laws of the State of California, applicable to agreements made and to be wholly performed within such State. Any controversy arising under this Agreement, if litigated, shall be adjudicated in a court of competent jurisdiction within the County of Los Angeles.

17.   Producer shall have the right to assign this License Agreement or any rights granted to Producer hereunder provided no such assignment shall relieve Producer of any liability hereun-der, and no such assignment shall be effective unless Producer or the assignee shall deliver to Publisher a written assumption by the assignee of the further performance by assignee of Producers obligations hereunder.

18.   All notices, demands or requests provided for or de-sired to be given pursuant to this Agreement must be in writing. All

such documents shall be deemed to have been given when served by personal delivery or three (3) days following their deposit in the United States mail, postage prepaid, certified or registered, addressed as follows:

If to Publisher:

with a courtesy copy to

If to Producer:

with a courtesy to

or to such other address as either party may hereafter designate in writing delivered in the manner aforesaid.

IN WITNESS WHEREOF, the parties have caused the foregoing to be executed as of the_____ day of _____

BIG MUSIC PUBLISHING CORP.
("Publisher")

BY: _____

_____
("Producer")

BY: _____

FORM 10.6

FORM OF VIDEOGRAM SYNCHRONIZATION LICENSE USED BY HARRY FOX AGENCY

THE HARRY FOX AGENCY, INC.
205 EAST 42ND STREET, NEW YORK, NY 10017

VIDEOGRAM SYNCHRONIZATION LICENSE

LICENSE NO.:
LICENSE DATE:
LICENSE FEE:

YOU (THE "LICENSEE: REFERRED TO IN (A) HAVE ADVISED US, IN OUR CAPACITY AS AGENT FOR OUR PUBLISHER-PRINCIPAL(S) REFERRED TO IN (C) (HEREIN REFERRED TO AS LICENSOR(S)), THAT YOU WISH TO OBTAIN CERTAIN RIGHTS (HEREIN REFERRED TO AS THE 'LICENSE RIGHTS') TO USE THE MUSICAL COMPOSITION REFERRED TO IN (B) (HEREIN REFERRED TO AS THE 'COMPOSITION') FOR THE PURPOSE OF MANUFACTURING AND DISTRIBUTING TO THE GENERAL PUBLIC FOR HOME USE AUDIO VISUAL DEVICES (HEREIN REFERRED TO AS 'VIDEOGRAMS') EMBODYING A RECORDED PERFORMANCE OF THE COMPOSITION IN SYNCHRONISM WITH CERTAIN VISUAL IMAGES COMPRISING THE WORK REFERRED TO IN (D) (HEREIN REFERRED TO AS 'THE WORK').

(A) LICENSEE:

(B) COMPOSITION: WRITERS:

(C) LICENSOR AND PAYMENT PERCENTAGE:

(D) WORK:

(E) RELEASE DATE:

NOW, THEREFORE, IT IS AGREED AS FOLLOW:

1.   FOR THE PURPOSES OF THIS AGREEMENT, THE TERM 'VIDEOGRAM' SHALL MEAN AND INCLUDE ALL AUDIO VISUAL DEVICES UTILIZED IN HOME USE FOR THE PERFORMANCE VIA APPROPRIATE MACHINES OF AUDIO VISUAL WORKS INCLUDING, BUT NOT LIMITED TO, VIDEO-DISCS AND VIDEO CASSETTES.

2.   FOR THE PURPOSES OF THIS AGREEMENT, THE TERM 'FIXATION' SHALL MEAN THE PROCESS WHEREBY THE PERFORM-ANCE OF A MUSICAL COMPOSITION IS EMBODIED IN AND AS PART OF AN AUDIO VISUAL WORK IN SYNCHRONISM WITH THE VISUAL IMAGES THEREOF FOR OR IN CONNECTION WITH THE PRODUC-TION OF VIDEOGRAMS THEREFROM.

3.   LICENSOR HEREBY GRANTS TO THE LICENSEE THE FOLLOWING NON-EXCLUSIVE RIGHTS WITH RESPECT TO THE WORK, IN ALL RESPECTS SUBJECT TO THE TERMS AND CONDI-TIONS HEREIN PROVIDED:

    (A)   TO RECORD AND/OR RE-RECORD THE COMPOSI-TION FOR USE IN CONNECTION WITH THE WORK AS HEREIN EXPRESSLY PROVIDED;

    (B)   TO CAUSE THE FIXATION OF THE COMPOSITION IN SYNCHRONISM OR TIMED RELATION WITH THE WORK; AND

    (C)   TO MAKE AND DISTRIBUTE VIDEOGRAM COPIES OF THE WORK EMBODYING THE FIXATION OF THE COMPOSITION THROUGHOUT THE TERRITORY ONLY.

4.   THE COMPOSITION SHALL BE USED IN SYNCHRO-NISM WITH THE WORK FOR AN AGGREGATE DURATION WHICH SHALL BE_____ .

5.   THE USE OF THE COMPOSITION HEREUNDER SHALL BE _____ .

6.   THE TERRITORY (HEREIN THE 'TERRITORY') WITHIN WHICH THE RIGHTS LICENSED HEREUNDER MAY BE EXERCISED SHALL BE LIMITED TO:

7.   THE PERIOD (HEREIN THE 'PERIOD') DURING WHICH THE RIGHTS LICENSED HEREUNDER MAY BE EXERCISED SHALL BE _____YEARS FROM THE LICENSE DATE OR THE RELEASE DATE, WHICHEVER IS EARLIER. AT THE EXPIRATION OF THE PERIOD, LICENSEE'S RIGHT TO MAKE VIDEOGRAM COPIES SHALL TERMINATE. LICENSEE SHALL, HOWEVER, HAVE THE RIGHT TO SELL OFF ITS THEN CURRENT INVENTORY OF VIDEO-GRAM COPIES FOR A PERIOD OF ONE (1) YEAR THEREAFTER, SUBJECT TO ITS CONTINUING OBLIGATION TO PAY ROYALTIES THEREFOR AS HEREIN PROVIDED.

8.   UPON EXECUTION OF THIS AGREEMENT, LICENSEE SHALL PAY TO THE HARRY FOX AGENCY, INC., LICENSOR'S AGENT, AFORESAID ROYALTIES (HEREIN THE 'ROYALTY') WITH RESPECT TO THE MANUFACTURE AND SALE OF VIDEOGRAM COPIES HEREUNDER, AS FOLLOWS:

1)   WITHIN FORTY-FIVE (45) DAYS AFTER THE END OF EACH CALENDAR QUARTER DURING WITHIN THE VIDEOGRAM COPIES ARE SOLD HEREUNDER, SUMS EQUAL TO: $ _____ PER VIDEOGRAM COPY OF THE WORK WHICH IS SOLD DURING EACH SUCH RESPECTIVE CALENDAR QUARTER.

2)   LICENSEE SHALL PERMIT LICENSOR'S (OR ITS AGENT'S) AUTHORIZED REPRESENTATIVE TO EXAMINE LICEN-SEE'S BOOKS AND RECORDS FOR THE PURPOSE OF VERIFYING THE ACCURACY OF THE STATEMENT RENDERED BY LICENSEE HEREUNDER.

9.   IN THE EVENT THAT LICENSEE FAILS TO ACCOUNT TO LICENSOR AND PAY ROYALTIES AS HEREIN PROVIDED, LICENSOR SHALL HAVE THE RIGHT TO GIVE WRITTEN NOTICE TO LICENSEE THAT UNLESS THE DEFAULT IS REMEDIED WITHIN THIRTY (30) DAYS FROM THE DATE OF THE NOTICE, THIS LICENSE WILL

AUTOMATICALLY TERMINATE AND LICENSOR SHALL THEREUPON BE ENTITLED TO ALL RIGHTS AND REMEDIES FOR ACTS OF INFRINGEMENT UNDER THE UNITED STATES COPYRIGHT ACT WITH RESPECT TO THOSE VIDEOGRAMS AS TO WHICH PAYMENT WAS NOT MADE BY LICENSEE HEREUNDER, WHICH VIDEOGRAMS SHALL BE DEEMED INFRINGING COPIES.

10.   THIS LICENSE DOES NOT INCLUDE ANY RIGHT OR AUTHORITY TO:

A)   MAKE ANY CHANGE IN THE ORIGINAL LYRICS OR IN THE FUNDAMENTAL CHARACTER OF THE MUSIC OF THE MUSICAL COMPOSITION;

B)   USE THE TITLE OR SUBTITLE OF THE COMPOSITION AS THE TITLE OF THE WORK;

C)   USE THE STORY OF THE COMPOSITION; OR

D)   MAKE ANY OTHER USE OF THE COMPOSITION NOT EXPRESSLY AUTHORIZED HEREIN.

11.   LICENSOR HEREBY RESERVES UNTO ITSELF ALL RIGHTS OF EVERY KIND AND NATURE, EXCEPT THOSE EXPRESSLY GRANTED TO LICENSEE HEREIN.

12.   LICENSOR WARRANTS ONLY THAT IT HAS THE RIGHT TO GRANT THIS LICENSE, AND THIS LICENSE IS GIVEN AND ACCEPTED WITHOUT ANY OTHER REPRESENTATION, WARRANT OR RECOURSE, EXPRESS OR IMPLIED, EXCEPT FOR LICENSOR'S AGREEMENT TO REPAY THE CONSIDERATION PAID FOR THIS LICENSE IF THE AFORESAID WARRANTY SHOULD BE BREACHED. IN NO EVENT SHALL THE TOTAL LIABILITY OF THE LICENSOR EXCEED THE TOTAL AMOUNT OF CONSIDERATION RECEIVED BY IT HEREUNDER.

13.   THIS AGREEMENT SETS FORTH THE ENTIRE UNDERSTANDING OF THE PARTIES HERETO WITH RESPECT TO THE

SUBJECT MATTER THEREOF, MAY NOT BE ALTERED, AMENDED OR ASSIGNED WITHOUT AN EXPRESS WRITTEN INSTRUMENT TO SUCH EFFECT ACCEPTED BY LICENSOR AND SHALL BE GOVERNED AND CONSTRUED BY AND UNDER THE LAWS OF THE STATE OF NEW YORK.

IN WITNESS WHEREOF, LICENSOR, BY ITS AGENT, THE HARRY FOX AGENCY, INC., AND LICENSEE HAVE CAUSED THIS AGREEMENT TO BE EXECUTED AS OF THE DATE FIRST WRITTEN ABOVE.

THE HARRY FOX AGENCY, INC.

By: _____

AGREED AND ACCEPTED:

By: _____

FORM 10.7

SYNCHRONIZATION LICENSE FOR PROMOTIONAL MUSIC VIDEOS WITH VIDEOGRAM PROVISIONS

PROMOTIONAL VIDEO SYNCHRONIZATION LICENSE AGREEMENT

DATED: _____ , 1995

PUBLISHER: BIG MUSIC PUBLISHING CORP.
Address: 1000 Sunset Blvd.
                Hollywood, California 90069

LICENSEE: _____
Address: _____
             _____

COMPOSITION(S):   _____
                   _____
                   _____

AUDIOVISUAL FILM/TAPE:
   ("A/V Film")

For good and valuable consideration, the receipt of which is hereby acknowledged by Publisher, Publisher hereby grants to Licensee, its successors,, assigns, licensees and sublicensees, the following rights in and to the Composition(s):

1.   Publisher grants to Licensee the non-exclusive license to record the Composition(s) in synchronism or timed relation with the visual images contained in the A/V Film, to make copies of such recording of the Composition(s) and to distribute such copies throughout the Territory, subject to the terms and conditions hereinafter set forth.

The use of the Composition(s) is limited to one (1) visual/vocal rendition of the Composition for not more than the duration of the Composition(s) in the original phonograph recording.

2.   The territory covered by this License is the world (hereinafter referred to as the "Territory").

3.   The term of this Agreement shall commence with the date hereof and terminate either two (2) years after release of the A/V Film, or two (2) years after release of the original phonograph recording in the United States, whichever is later (hereinafter referred to as the "Term").

4.   Upon execution hereof, Licensee agrees to pay to Publisher a handling charge of Twenty-Five Dollars ($25.00) for the preparation of this license and related paperwork. In addition, when the production costs of the A/V Film have been recouped (from whatever source), Licensee shall pay Publisher a one-time synchronization fee of $250, if income is received by Licensee from subsequent exhibition thereof.

5.   (a)   This Agreement does not grant to Licensee or to its agents, affiliates or subsidiaries the right to perform or to authorize the performance of the Composition(s) in connection with the exhibition of the A/V Film in or by any medium or media.

(b)   The Composition(s) may be performed in connection with exhibition of the A/V Film by cable systems, broadcasters or other entities, or by means of media having valid performance licenses therefor from the American Society of Composers, Authors and Publishers ("ASCAP") or Broadcast Music, Inc. ("BMI"), as the case may be.

(c)   Exhibition of the A/V Film by cable systems, broadcasters or other entities or by means of media not licensed by ASCAP or BMI must be licensed by Publisher or by any other licensing agency acting for or on behalf of Publisher, and payment of additional fees will be required.

6.   It is understood that the performance of the Composition(s) in connection with the exhibition of the A/V Film in countries or territories outside of the United States and its possessions shall be subject to clearance by performing rights societies in accordance with their customary practice and the payment of their customary fees. Publisher agrees that to the extent it controls said performing rights, it will license an appropriate performing rights society in the respective countries to grant such performing right.

7.   (a)   This License does not authorize, permit or license any use of the Composition(s) not expressly granted herein and does not imply or grant the right to alter the lyric or change the fundamental character of the music of the Composition(s). Without limiting the foregoing, Licensee is not authorized (a) to perform or authorize the performance of the Composition in connection with the exhibition of the A/V Film in any theatre, auditorium or other place to which an admission fee is charged, (b) to record the Composition on a phonograph record on other than in the A/V Film, (c) to use the title or any portion of the lyric of the Composition as the title of the A/V Film or otherwise, or (d) to dramatize the lyrical content of the Composition.

(b)   (i)   In the event that the Composition as embodied in the A/V Film is included in home video devices, Producer shall pay Publisher a pro rata share (based upon comparative running time of the various musical compositions included therein) of 5% of the wholesale price on all units for which Licensee is paid (or in respect of which Licensee receives credit in reduction of an advance). Licensee shall account to and pay Publisher, in each instance, within thirty (30) days after Licensee is accounted to by its home video distributor, and each such accounting shall be accompanied by a photocopy of the relevant portion of the accounting statement furnished to Licensee by its distributor.

(ii)   In the event that Licensee receives income from the lease or rental of home video devices, Publisher shall be entitled to receive a pro rata share thereof, to be determined by multiplying such income by a fraction, the numerator of which is 5 and the denominator of which is the number equal to the number of percentage points of wholesale (or the equivalent) payable to Licensee by its distributor on sales of home video devices.

8.   Producer warrants and represents that should any other musical composition be licensed in connection with the A/V Film on a more favorable basis to the publisher thereof than is provided to Publisher hereunder, such more favorable basis shall also be extended to the licensing of the Composition(s) hereunder.

9.   Publisher warrants that it has the right to grant this License and no other warranties, express or implied, are granted hereby. Should said warranty be breached, in whole or in part, Licensee shall either repay to Publisher the theretofore paid to Publisher for this License, or Publisher shall hold Licensee harmless to the extent of said consideration. In no event shall the total liability of Publisher exceed the consideration received by Publisher hereunder.

10.   Licensee represents and warrants that the A/V Film containing the Composition(s) will be used for the principal purpose of promoting the sale of phonograph records and tapes embodying the featured performances by the Artist.

11.   Upon expiration of the Term hereof, the rights granted herein shall automatically revert to Publisher, and any further use of the Composition(s) hereunder shall be unauthorized.

12.   This License and the rights hereunder are not assignable by Licensee.

13.   Licensee hereby agrees to furnish Publisher with a "cue sheet" of the A/V Film indicating the type and length of usage of the Composition(s) in the A/V Film.

14.   Whenever notice is required, or desired, to be given hereunder such notice shall be in writing addressed to the appro-

priate party at the address set forth above or at such other address as either party may designate by written notice given hereunder.

15. This License sets forth the entire agreement between Publisher and Licensee with respect to the subject matter hereof, and may not be modified or amended except by written agreement executed by the parties. This License shall be governed by and subject to the laws of the State of California applicable to agreements made and to be wholly performed within such State. Any controversy arising under this License, if litigated, shall be adjudicated in a court of competent jurisdiction within the County of Los Angeles.

IN WITNESS WHEREOF, the parties hereto have executed this Agreement as of the date first set forth above.

PUBLISHER   LICENSEE

By: _____   By _____

FORM 10.8

Non-Theatrical Film Synchronization License With Videogram Provisions

NON-THEATRICAL FILM SYNCHRONIZATION AND VIDEOGRAM LICENSE

In consideration of the sum of $ _____ per composition, and upon the payment thereof to the undersigned, the undersigned does hereby give and grant unto:

("Licensee") the non-exclusive, irrevocable right and license to record the following musical composition(s):

(the "Compositions") in synchronism or timed-relation with a picture made and produced by Licensee tentatively entitled:

(the "Program") described as:

[A slide/tape presentation approximately fifteen (15) minutes in length, for non-theatric showings in 25 small theaters (seating up to 25 persons) to promote Licensee's products.]

This license hereinabove set forth is granted under the proviso that the said recording or recordings are not to be used for or in connection with television purposes, including "pay" or "sub-scription" television, except as noted above or cable television; that said recording or recordings are not be employed for any radio or so-called "home-movies" use or other media not specifically set out herein; that no sound records produced pursuant to the said license are to be manufactured, sold, and/or used separately from the said picture; and with the further proviso that the said picture shall not be exhibited in or televised into theatres or other public places of amusement where motion pictures are customarily shown.

The Territory of this license is: THE WORLD.

The Term of this license shall commence on the date hereof and shall continue for a period of five (5) years.

VIDEO BUYOUT OPTION:

Licensee has the irrevocable option to synchronize the composition(s) as embodied in the Program and to distribute the Program by means of Video cassettes and/or video discs and/or other home video devices in the territory ("Video Territory") of the World. Subject to the provisions hereof, for the right to manufacture and duplicate and distribute an unlimited number of Videogram copies of the Program, within thirty (30) days of the first distribution, Producer shall pay Publisher a Videogram fee of $ _____ .

VIDEO ROYALTY OPTION (FIXED TERM):

Licensee has the irrevocable option to synchronize the Composition(s) as embodied in the Program and to distribute the Program by means of Video cassettes and/or video discs and/or other home devices in the territory ("Video Territory") of the World, for a term of _____ years (to the extent we now or hereafter own or control the copyrights in and to the Composition(s) and any renewals or extensions thereof). If Licensee exercises this option, Licensee will pay Publisher an amount equal to ____ cents (___) per song, per home video device embodying the Composition(s) in the Program distributed in the Video Territory and not returned. Within thirty (30) days of the first distribution of such home video devices in the Video Territory, Producer will pay Publisher the sum of _____ for the first _____ ($) per song, for the first _____ units, as an advance against the royalty of $ _____ per song, as set forth above.

U. S. THEATRICAL - OPTION LANGUAGE

Licensee has the irrevocable option to exhibit the Program in Motion Picture theatres and other public places where motion pictures are customarily exhibited, and where admission fees are charged, in the United States, subject to a fee of $_____ , for the worldwide period of all copyrights in and to the Composition that Licensor may now own or control, and any and all renewals or extensions thereof which Licensor may hereafter acquire but, in the latter instance Licensee shall not be required to pay any additional fees of or compensation beyond those prescribed above.

The option(s) referred to above, if exercised, must be exercised within eighteen (18) months following the Program's initial broadcast by written notice delivered to Publisher not later than thirty (30) days from the date of first broadcast.

All rights and uses in the said musical compositions(s) not herein granted are expressly reserved to the undersigned.

Licensor warrants and represents that it has the legal right and power to grant this license, and makes no other warranty or representation. Licensor agrees to indemnify Licensee and hold Licensee harmless from and against any and all loss, cost, damage or expense (including court costs and reasonable outside attorneys' fees) due to a breach of such warranty and representation resulting in a final, nonappealable adverse judgment or a settlement entered into with Licensor's prior written consent (such consent not to be unreasonably withheld).

Dated:

PUBLISHER   LICENSEE

By: _____   By: _____

CHAPTER 11

OLD LICENSES AND NEW USES

SUMMARY

TYPES OF OLD SYNCHRONIZATION LICENSES

1. Old Licenses That Clearly Include Home Video Reproduction Privileges
2. Old Licenses That Clearly Exclude Home Video Reproduction Privileges
3. Old Licenses Whose Scope Is Unclear
   A. Several Old Licenses
   B. Several Court Cases
   C. Recent Court Cases

DETERMINING THE SCOPE OF AMBIGUOUS LICENSES— A SUGGESTED APPROACH

1. Evidence of Intent of the Parties
2. Where No Clear Intent of the Parties Is Evident
   A. Expectations of the Film Producer
   B. Expectations of the Music Copyright Owner

AVOIDING AMBIGUITY

FORMS

469

CHAPTER 11

OLD LICENSES
AND NEW USES

As the local home video rental store was becoming as common-place as the neighborhood bakery, the motion picture studios that produced the movies that made up the bread and butter of these stores found themselves in the middle of quite a fix: they began to realize they were not participating in the increasing amount of rental revenues derived from the rental of their videocassettes by the video rental stores. After receiving only one payment for the sale of a videocassette to a video rental store, the producer would watch that same videocassette be rented to home viewers over and over, as many times as the tape could physically endure being played and rewound, and replayed. In addition, the availability of videocassettes for home viewing would mean a certain decline in the number of people who went out to movie theatres for their motion picture entertainment. Making matters worse, motion picture producers and their distributors began receiving notices from music publishers that their use of music in these videocassettes was not author-ized by their synchronization licenses and required the payment of additional license fees.

For motion pictures made in recent years, after it had become clear that nearly every film would likely be distributed in the lucrative home video market, producers normally have been able to obtain, concurrent with their synchronization licenses, the videogram license necessary to permit them to reproduce their musical works in home video devices. But what about motion pictures that were released many years ago, well before the advent of the videocassette and laser disk players? Did not the old licenses for the use of music in these films cover the new use in the home video market? Music publishers reviewed these old synchroniza-tion licenses and concluded, "no." In many cases, this answer was clearly correct. Some of these old synchronization licenses either spe-cifically identified home video use and expressly excluded it or the license was otherwise clear with respect to what uses were granted, all other uses, including home video use, whether or not anticipated at the time, being reserved by implication.

As noted in the preceding chapter, synchronization licenses for motion pictures grant permission to record a composition as part of a specified motion picture and to reproduce copies of the resulting audiovisual work, but carefully drafted synchronization licenses specify that the copies reproduced may only be used to effect the theatrical release of the motion picture or its television broadcast. Use of copies of the film for distribution to the public for home viewing is neither a "theatrical release" nor "television broadcast." Thus, for many synchronization licenses, an additional license permitting home video distribution is required.

The problem is that not all older synchronization licenses were as clear as they should have been in limiting how copies of the motion picture could be used. The need for precision in drafting perceived at the time did not always adequately anticipate the rapid advances in technology we see today.

Old synchronization licenses fall into three general classes:

1. Licenses that Clearly *Include* Home Video Reproduction Privileges.

2. Licenses that Clearly *Exclude* Home Video Reproduction Privileges.

3. Licenses Whose Scope is *Unclear.*

Each of these will be discussed in turn.

TYPES OF OLD SYNCHRONIZATION LICENSES

1. Old Licenses that Clearly Include Home Video Reproduction Privileges

Before the advent of the home video market, some attorneys representing motion picture producers foresaw the possibility of new forms of distribution of motion pictures and negotiated synchronization licenses which reflected their prescience. Such licenses permitted the recording of the music in synchronism or timed-relation with the specified motion picture,

"for use in any form or medium, and in any manner, now known or hereafter devised."

A license such as this would seem to clearly include the right of reproduction of the motion picture for home video distribution.

More recently, motion picture synchronization licenses have been drafted to specifically include permission to reproduce copies of the motion picture for home video distribution. These license provisions are commonly called *videogram licenses* and have been discussed in detail in the preceding chapter. Early in the history of videogram licensing, when music publishers were reluctant to negotiate specific terms until some standards had begun to emerge, videogram licenses were granted for short duration and called for good faith negotiations and arbitration upon the expiration of their terms. Later, specific royalty provisions became common.

2. Old Licenses that Clearly Exclude Home Video Reproduction Privileges

At the other extreme are those synchronization licenses which clearly exclude home video reproduction. Licenses which specifically refer to home video devices and specifically exclude their use are relatively rare, as they are likely to have been issued during that short few years between the advent of the home video market and the time when provisions for the licensing of music in films for the home video market started to become standard.

The following provision of a typical synchronization license issued in the early to mid-1970's makes it clear that the license does not include the use of copies made for home video distribution:

Cassettes. Notwithstanding anything to the contrary hereinabove contained, this agreement does not grant to Producer the right to manufacture or duplicate said motion picture by means of audio-television devices or contrivances, such as cassettes, discs or other similar configurations (herein called "cassettes"), for the purpose of selling such cassettes to the public. The sale of cassettes of the motion picture to the public shall be governed by the applicable law and/or by future good faith negotiations of the parties with respect to the fees to be paid in connection with such sales to the public, giving due consideration to customary practices which may develop with respect thereto.

Consider a license, in common use about 1927, which would also appear to clearly exclude the making of copies for home video distribution:

You are hereby granted a license to manufacture devices serving to mechanically reproduce the same, in whole or in part, and to use such devices solely in conjunction with and as an integral part of the appliance or mechanism known as THE VITAPHONE, in the United States and Canada, subject to the following conditions:

1. This License is not exclusive, and applies solely to the above described mechanical recording and public reproduction of the above named composition.

2. This License extends to and includes public performances by means of records as aforesaid serving to reproduce mechanically such above described composition in conjunction with THE VITAPHONE.

3. This License is subject to the rights of the American Society of Composers, Authors, and Publishers in the said composition with respect to the public performance thereof for profit; and the public reproductions or performance thereof for profit shall take place only in establishments licensed by the said Society.

The above license appears to have been very narrowly drafted to cover the reproduction of the composition "solely in conjunction with and as an integral part of the appliance or mechanism known as THE VITAPHONE." A little history will make clear the reason for such precision.

Under a patent licensed from Western Electric, Vitaphone Corporation—a joint venture established by Warner Bros. and a talented inventor—developed the first practical synchronized recording system and became the first producer of motion pictures to enter the sound picture (i.e., *talkies*) market. Originally, the Vitaphone process employed separate records for the sound portion of the motion picture. In the case of very early talkies, the records contained only the musical scores. Later, the records contained music, dialogue, and sound effects. Since records containing the musical scores could easily be misused to compete with commercial sound recordings, it was necessary to make it very clear in the license that the use of music was confined to the Vitaphone process, which was a sound process used solely for the theatrical exhibition of motion pictures. This is precisely what was accomplished by the Vitaphone license set forth in part above. It seems clear, therefore, that any other device, such as mechanisms used today to reproduce works in home video devices, for use in the home, would be outside the scope of the old Vitaphone license.

As noted in the preceding chapter, the essential right involved in the licensing of videograms is the reproduction right. Because the sounds reproduced on a videogram are accompanied by moving visual images, the reproduction of videograms does not involve a "mechanical" reproduction right under the United States copyright law and, therefore, is not subject to the copyright law's compulsory licensing provision for mechanical reproductions. Thus, music copyright owners are free to negotiate videogram licenses under a variety of terms.

While the current copyright law is quite clear on this point, it was not always so. At the turn of the century, with the advent of motion pictures, it was thought that the process of integrating music with motion pictures was permissible under the compulsory license provision of the copyright law existing at that time.[1] In fact, because the sounds in the Vitaphone process that accompanied the motion pictures were originally recorded onto phonograph records, Vitaphone took the position that a compulsory license under the law was available to it for this purpose. Vitaphone quickly discovered, however, that a strong combination of music publishers, through an organization called the Music Publishers' Protective Association, would insist otherwise and began a determined and successful effort to require motion picture producers to buy licenses for negotiated fees. Their strategy was simple: By 1926, a movie theatre was required to have an ASCAP license if the theatre wished to perform music in the extensive ASCAP repertoire; the music publishers threat-

---

[1] 17 U.S.C. Sec. 1(e) (1909 Act).

ened to withdraw their performing rights from ASCAP unless Vitaphone agreed to buy special synchronization licenses at rates much higher than the statutory rate, which at that time was two cents per composition per record. In October, 1926, Vitaphone finally capitulated and agreed to pay approximately $100,000.00 per year.

3. Old Licenses Whose Scope Is Unclear

A. Several Old Licenses

During the time that the carefully crafted Vitaphone license set forth above was in use, other licenses that were issued during this period were less sophisticated.

For example, a license issued in 1927 stated simply:

Gentlemen:

We hereby grant you permission to record and reproduce publicly for profit, but only in association with the motion picture, entitled XYZ, the following named musical composition, upon which we own the copyright, to wit: ABC.

Very truly yours, . . .

To argue that such a seemingly broad license did not grant permission for home video use, the music copyright owner would have to take the position that by saying "reproduce publicly . . . with the motion picture" he was intending to refer solely to the means of performing motion pictures (e.g., theatrical exhibition) that existed at that time. Perhaps the phrase "reproduce publicly" would itself indicate that distribution for *private* viewing was not contemplated. The motion picture producer might assert that the license limited distribution of copies "only in association with the motion picture" and that if any other limitation were intended the copyright owner could have expressed it just as easily.

In 1932, a more sophisticated synchronization license began wide circulation and had been used for many years thereafter as the basis for countless synchronization licenses. Its salient provisions were as follows:

In consideration of the sum of $xxx the undersigned does hereby
give XYZ Pictures the non-exclusive, irrevocable right, license, privilege and authority to record in any manner, medium or form, in any
country covered by this license, the musical composition hereinbelow
set out, and to make copies of such recording and to import said copies
of recordings into any country covered by this license, all in accordance with the terms, conditions, and limitations hereinafter set out.

... The license hereinabove set out is limited to the use of the musical
compositions in synchronism or timed-relation with the motion picture hereinabove specified.

... The right to record the musical compositions as covered by this
agreement is conditioned upon the performance of the musical work
in theatres having valid licenses from the American Society of Composers, Authors, and Publishers, or any other performing rights society
having jurisdiction in the territory in which the said musical compositions are performed.

... Licensor reserves to itself all rights and uses in and to said musical
compositions not herein specifically granted.

Was the above license intended to restrict the use of motion pictures
containing the licensed music to exhibition in theatres or did it allow
distribution by another media, such as videograms distributed for home
viewing?

A producer might assert that the broad grant to record "in any
manner, medium, or form" subject only to conditions set forth in the
license should be broadly interpreted in favor of the licensee, and that
the true intent of the agreement is to limit the use "in synchronism or
timed-relation with the motion picture." As long as the recording is used
only in connection with that motion picture or wherever the motion
picture may be exploited, the producer would argue, the use is within the
license. In other words, all uses were licensed, subject to clearing the
performance rights by theatres. No reference to television or videocassettes being made, no restriction was intended.

The music copyright owner would, however, refer our attention to
the provision in the license stating that "the right to record" the songs is
"conditioned upon the performance of the musical work in theatres."
While the intent of the paragraph containing this language appears to be

to assure that performances were made only in theatres having valid performance licenses (e.g., from ASCAP or BMI, etc.), it would also appear to indicate that the performance of the motion picture was contemplated to take place in theatres and not elsewhere, such as in private homes

The language in the above license underwent some modification by the mid-1950's:

In consideration of the sum of $xxx, the receipt of which is hereby acknowledged, the undersigned does hereby give XYZ Pictures, its successors and assigns, the non-exclusive irrevocable right and license, privilege and authority to record, in any manner, medium, form or language, in any country within the territory covered by this license, the words and music of the musical composition hereinbelow set out, and to make copies of said recordings and to import said recordings and/or copies of said recordings into any country within the territory covered by this license, and to perform said musical composition everywhere, all in accordance with the terms, conditions, and limitations hereinafter set out.

. . . The license hereinabove set out is limited to the use of the musical composition in synchronism or timed-relation with the motion picture hereinabove specified, and trailers thereof.

. . . The right to *perform* said musical composition as covered by this agreement is conditioned upon the performance of said musical composition in theatres having valid licenses from any performing rights society having jurisdiction in the territory in which the said musical composition is performed.

. . . Licensor reserves to itself all rights and uses in and to said musical compositions not herein specifically granted.

A producer might take heart in the fact that the third paragraph above was modified by the replacement of the word "record" with the word "perform." It would appear that the license to record was no longer conditioned upon the performance of the song in theatres having valid licenses; only the license to perform was. The music copyright owner would be quick to point out, however, that the first paragraph was modified so that the license was "to make copies of said recordings . . .

and to perform said musical composition everywhere, all in accordance with the terms, conditions, and limitations hereinafter set out." It appears that the words "to perform" were used merely to make it clear at the outset that the license included both a recording license and a public performing license, and was not intended to expand or further restrict the uses permitted under the license. This is confirmed by the fact that the change in language coincided precisely with the entry of the consent decrees between the Department of Justice and the performance rights societies, which, among other things, required music copyright owners to grant performance licenses for U.S. theatrical distribution.[2]

Consider the following television synchronization license issued in the 1970's which attempted to narrowly define what use may be made of the synchronized recording:

> In consideration of the sum of $xxx, and upon agreement hereto and the acceptance hereof as indicated below and the payment of said consideration to the undersigned, the undersigned does hereby give and grant unto, XYZ Pictures, the non-exclusive, irrevocable right and license to record the following copyrighted musical composition in synchronism or timed-relation with a picture made and produced solely for television purposes by the said licensee and known as: The TV Movie.

The license was drafted with a view toward limiting the use to television, intending to exclude exhibition in motion picture theatres and like establishments. It may be questioned, however, whether the above language successfully excluded the privilege of reproducing videocassettes for home video distribution. The first paragraph limits the use "solely for television purposes." Is the making of videocassettes of the picture for home video distribution a "television purpose"? If "television purpose," as used here, is synonymous with "broadcast purpose," the answer to the question would be, "no," and therefore home video use would not be covered by the license.

---

[2] See Chapter 15 on Performance Licenses.

B. Several Court Cases

The general question arising from the applicability of the old synchronization licenses discussed above to the desire of producers to effect a new use of their works is whether the licenses restricted the use to a particular media or did it allow distribution through another media subsequently developed? In other words, is the scope of the license sufficiently broad to cover new uses that became possible only years after the license was issued?

A similar question was asked over a century ago in connection with a license to make a dramatization of a book—that is, a license permitting another to adapt a novel in the creation of a theatrical play or opera. Did a license to permit a dramatization of a book, issued before the advent of motion pictures in 1889, permit the licensee to make a motion picture based upon the book? In 1920, the U.S. Supreme Court held that a license to produce or dramatize a play *did not* include permission to produce a motion picture based on the play.[3]

Not long after that decision, the courts were asked to decide whether a license to make a dramatization or motion picture, issued before the advent of talkies, permitted the licensee to make a sound motion picture. One court held that where the same person holds both the silent picture rights and the dramatic rights, equating the latter with dialogue rights, he owns everything necessary to the making of a talking motion picture.[4] Another court held that a grant of motion picture rights was sufficient to constitute a grant of talkie motion picture rights, stating, "The mere fact that the species 'talkies' may have been unknown and not within the contemplation of the parties in their description of the generic 'moving pictures' does not prevent the latter from comprehending the former."[5]

It should be no surprise that the question whether a license to make and exhibit a motion picture, issued before the advent of television, authorized the exhibition of the motion picture on television, has also been the subject of litigation in the courts. In 1936, a prizefighter permitted the making and exhibition of a motion picture of his prize fight, and the issue before the court was whether the picture could be

---

[3] *Manners v. Morosco*, 252 U.S. 317 (1920).

[4] *Cinema Corporation of America v. De Mille*, 267 N.Y.Supp. 589 (1933).

[5] *L.C. Page & Co. v. Fox Film Corp.*, 83 F.2d 196, at 199 (2d Cir. 1936).

performed both in theatres and on television, or only in theatres.[6] The court held that the picture could only be performed in theatres, basing its decision on the mistaken belief that the televising of motion pictures was a "use not in existence" in 1936. In fact, the feasibility of television was contemplated as early as 1927. By 1929, a provision granting motion picture studios the license to televise motion pictures began appearing in standard motion picture rights acquisition contracts, and by 1932, Warner Bros.'s Brunswick subsidiary was experimenting with color television.

C. Recent Court Cases

The question whether old licenses applied to new uses appeared in a fairly recent class action lawsuit led by the well known entertainer, Mickey Rooney, against nearly all of the major motion picture studios, including Columbia Pictures, Metro-Goldwyn-Mayer, Paramount Pictures, RKO General, Twentieth Century Fox, United Artists, Universal City Studios, and Warner Bros.[7] The case involved the contracts between the studios and all performers appearing in motion pictures produced or distributed by the studios prior to 1960. The court ruled that the contracts between the performers and the studios, which granted rights to exhibit these films, also gave the studios the right to sell videocassettes of the films, without further compensation to the performers. The court's conclusion was based on the sweeping language of the contracts, which included, for example, the right to "record, reproduce, transmit, exhibit, distribute, and exploit" the films "by any present or future methods or means" and by "any other means now known or unknown." The court concluded that the contracts gave the studios extremely broad rights in the distribution and exhibition of the films, "plainly intending that such rights would be without limitation unless otherwise specified and further indicating that future technological advances in methods of reproduction, transmission, and exhibition would inure to the benefit of [the studios]."

Shortly following the decision in the *Rooney* case, a federal district court in New Jersey considered a case filed by a small record company

---

[6] *Ettore v. Philco Television Broadcasting Corp.*, 229 F.2d 481 (3d Cir. 1956).

[7] *Rooney v. Columbia Pictures Industries, Inc.*, 538 F.Supp. 211 (S.D.N.Y. 1982).

against Lucasfilm, Universal City Studios, and MCA, Inc.[8] In 1973, the record company granted to Lucasfilm a license to use the master recordings of four popular songs on the soundtrack of the motion picture, *American Graffiti*. The license granted to Lucasfilm "the right to record, dub and synchronize the . . . master recordings, or portions thereof, into and with [the] motion picture and trailers therefor, and to exhibit, distribute, market and perform said motion picture, its air, screen and television trailers, perpetually throughout the world by any means or methods now or hereafter known." In 1980, Universal released the film for sale and rental to the public on videocassettes. The court ruled in favor of Lucasfilm and the studio, reasoning that the language in the agreement was "extremely broad and completely unambiguous, and precludes any need in the Agreement for an exhaustive list of specific potential uses of the film. . . . It is obvious that the contract in question may 'fairly be read' to be including newly developed media, and the absence of any specific mention in the Agreement of videotapes and videocassettes is thus insignificant."

The question whether a license permitting the use of music in a motion picture or television program, authorized the reproduction of copies of the music in connection with the distribution of videocassettes of the motion picture or television show, finally became the subject of a lawsuit that was concluded in the 9th Circuit Federal Court of Appeals in 1988.[9] Paramount Pictures had just begun the reproduction of videocassettes of the motion picture, *Medium Cool,* when the copyright owner of the song *Merry-Go-Round*, one of the songs contained in the film's soundtrack, filed suit claiming that the old synchronization license to use the song in the motion picture did not grant a license to distribute copies of the song in videocassettes of the motion picture.

The court of appeals considered the scope of a synchronization license, which was not unlike the scope of the licenses described in the preceding section. That license granted to Paramount:

> . . . the authority . . . to record, in any manner, medium, form or language, the words and music of the musical composition . . . with the motion picture . . . to make copies of such recordings and to perform

---

[8] *Platinum Record Company, Inc. v. Lucasfilm, Ltd.*, 566 F.Supp. 226 (D.N.J. 1983).

[9] *Cohen v. Paramount Pictures Corp.*, 845 F.2d 851 (9th Cir. 1988).

said musical composition everywhere, all in accordance with the terms, conditions and limitations hereinafter set forth . . ."

The . . . license herein granted to perform . . . said musical composition is granted for: (a) The exhibition of said motion picture . . . to audiences in motion picture theatres and other places of public entertainment where motion pictures are customarily exhibited . . . (b) The exhibition of said motion picture . . . by means of television . . . , including "pay television," "subscription television," and "closed circuit into homes' television". . . .

It was undisputed that category (a) of the preceding paragraph could not be construed as authorizing the distribution of videocassettes through the sale and rental to the general public for viewing in their homes. Paramount argued, however, that videogram distribution was covered by category (b), in that the distribution of videocassettes for showing in private homes was the equivalent of "exhibition by means of television." The court disagreed and ruled that the license did *not* include the distribution of videocassettes for home viewing.

After going to great lengths to describe the differences between broadcast television and home videocassette viewing,[10] the court stated

---

[10] In reaching its conclusion, the court drew a distinction between the characteristics of broadcast television and home videocassette television:

"The general tenor of the section [b] contemplates some sort of broadcasting or centralized distribution, not distribution by sale or rental of individual copies. Furthermore, the exhibition of the videocassette in the home is not "by means of television." Though videocassettes may be exhibited by using a television monitor, it does not follow that, for copyright purposes, playing videocassettes constitutes "exhibition by television." Exhibition of a film on television differs fundamentally from exhibition by means of a videocassette recorder ("VCR"). Television requires an intermediary network, station, or cable to send the television signals into consumers' homes. The menu of entertainment appearing on television is controlled entirely by the intermediary and, thus the consumer's selection is limited to what is available on various channels. Moreover, equipped merely with a conventional television set, a consumer has no means of capturing any part of the television display; when the program is over it vanishes, and the consumer is powerless to replay it. Because they originate outside the home, television signals are ephemeral and beyond the viewer's grasp.

"Videocassettes, of course, allow viewing of a markedly different nature. Videocassette entertainment is controlled within the home, at the viewer's that the "primary reason" why the words "exhibition by means of television" in the license could not be construed as including the distribution of videocassettes for home viewing was that "VCR's were not invented or known in 1969, when the license was executed."[11]

Because videocassettes did not exist when the license was executed, the court reasoned, the licensor must have assumed television exhibition was to be effected by broadcast and the "licensee could not have bargained for, or paid for, the rights associated with videocassette reproduction." This reasoning, of course, is flawed, because it is simply incorrect to say that the licensee could not have bargained for the rights of use that did not exist or were unknown at the time the license was executed.[12]

---

complete discretion. A consumer may view exactly what he or she chooses. The viewer may even 'fast forward' the tape so as to quickly pass over parts of the program he or she does not wish to view. By their very essence, then videocassettes liberate viewers from the constraints otherwise inherent in television, and eliminate the involvement of an intermediary, such as a network.

"Television and videocassette display thus have very little in common besides the fact that a conventional monitor of a television set may be used both to receive television signals and to exhibit a videocassette. It is in light of this fact that Paramount argues that VCRs are equivalent to "exhibition by means of television." Yet, even that assertion is flawed. Playing a videocassette on a VCR does not require a standard television set capable of receiving television signals by cable or broadcast; it is only necessary to have a monitor capable of displaying the material on the magnetized tape." 845 F.2d at 854

[11] Id.

[12] In fact, at a later point in its opinion, the court suggested that a party could bargain for a use that was not yet known at the time of the license, as long as the license specifically conferred the right to exhibit the films by methods yet to be invented. 845 F.2d at 855. This is precisely what the parties are doing when they enter into licenses that are specifically intended to cover uses unknown or not invented at the time the license is executed (e.g., a license for "use in any form or medium, and in any manner, now known or hereafter devised"). To enforce licenses for only those uses that were either known or invented at the time the license was executed would unduly limit the scope of licenses for which parties are otherwise free to bargain. Second, it is not clear, under the court's reasoning, whether the use must actually be *invented* or merely *known* or conceived at the time the license is entered. If the court would require the use to have been invented at the time the license was executed, then what legal doctrine would support the unenforcability of a bargain over a specific use that parties clearly contemplated? There seems to be no reason why a court should not enforce, for example, a license to use music in a holographic motion picture several years before the practicability of holographic movies. If the court would require the use to be "known" at the time the license was executed, who is to say whether a particular use is "known" generally or to a party at any particular point in time? Science fiction books, television shows, and motion pictures

Although the court disagreed with the *Rooney* and *Platinum* decisions to the extent those decisions equated exhibition by means of television with home video display, the court appeared to merely distinguish their applicability to the *Cohen* synchronization license, because it did not contain the broad, sweeping language contained in the licenses considered in *Rooney* and *Platinum*.

But can the license in the *Cohen* case really be distinguished from that in the *Platinum case*? Paramount may have made a tactical error by asserting that videogram distribution was covered by category (b) of the performance provision of the synchronization license. Home video viewing is a *private*, not public performance. Because private performances are not among the activities over which music copyright owners enjoy exclusive rights under the copyright law, no *performance* license was necessary to engage in home video distribution. All that was necessary was a license to make and distribute copies of the work containing the music without restriction as to their means of use. Would not such a license clearly be included in the rather broad language of the first section of the license?

> . . . the authority . . . *to record, in any manner, medium, form or language*, the words and music of the musical composition . . . with the motion picture . . . *to make copies of such recordings and to perform said musical composition everywhere*, all in accordance with the terms, conditions and limitations hereinafter set forth . . . "

Whether or not the court in the *Cohen* case reached the correct result, it is believed that the decision, and others like it, should rest on a more practical legal basis than merely a listing of the technical and practical differences between the two media in question (here, broadcast television and home videocassette viewing). The following discussion attempts to provide such a basis and may be of value in determining the application of old licenses to new uses, either to the parties negotiating a settlement of their dispute or to a court presiding over its adjudication.

---

present hundreds of examples of uses commonly known long before their actual invention. There appears to be no reason, for example, not to enforce a license for use of a work in an entertainment program for use on a device resembling the "holodeck" of the fictional television series *Star Trek: The Next Generation*. Finally, contracts often try to cover what is not known and it is not unreasonable to enforce bargains struck between parties over the allocation of unknown or unforeseen risks or contingencies, such as the subsequent development of a new use.

DETERMINING THE SCOPE OF
AMBIGUOUS LICENSES
—A SUGGESTED APPROACH

All of the above controversies—whether a dramatic license included a license to make silent motion pictures, whether a motion picture license included a license to make "talkies," whether a motion picture license included a license to broadcast by means of television, whether a motion picture synchronization license included a license for home video distribution, and whether a television synchronization license included a license for home video distribution—have two common basic characteristics: a license to make certain uses and the subsequent development of a new use.

In all of these cases, the court should seek to determine for what would the parties have likely bargained if they had foreseen the subsequent development of the new use at the time the license was entered into? How would they have allocated the risk of an unforeseen use, had they actually foreseen it?

1. Evidence of Intent of the Parties

It is assumed that in determining the scope of an old license a court would first look to the language of the license itself. In interpreting the language, the court would use common legal principles in making that determination. For example, courts will normally permit the parties to a lawsuit to introduce evidence that falls outside the "four corners" of the document to aid in the interpretation of ambiguous provisions. Such evidence might include letters and testimony of the parties reflecting their intent at the time the license was entered into. However, evidence of the intent of the parties to a license entered 50 years ago might prove difficult to find, particularly as many old synchronization licenses were issued on standard forms and signed without negotiation of their terms (with the possible exception of price and territory).

Another principle of contract interpretation is that a document is interpreted against the party who drafted it. This is because the drafter was in a better position to avoid the ambiguity by being more precise in his employment of language in the document, thus providing an incentive for drafters to be precise. Since most of these old synchronization license forms were drafted by music publishers and their representatives, there is an argument that they were in a better position to prevent the ambiguity by being more precise in their use of terms such as "exhibition on television." On the other hand, the music publishers could take the position that the producers of the motion pictures were in a better position to predict what potential forms of distribution could be made of their films and if they could have foreseen these new forms of distribution, they should have informed the music publishers of the potential new use at the time the license was entered into. This could have led to a negotiated allocation based upon a full disclosure of information.

Without concrete evidence of what the intent of the parties was at the time the license was signed, the court in the *Paramount* case, discussed above, compared and contrasted the characteristics of broadcast television and home videocassette viewing in arriving at a meaning and usage of the term, "exhibition by television." Although the court was insightful in pointing to some important differences that would have affected a negotiation had the facts been known, a comparison of the characteristics of these two systems alone does not provide us with the answer to the question, what would the music publishers and producers have actually negotiated had this different use been known to the parties at the time of the license?

2. Where No Clear Intent of the Parties Is Evident

In the absence of clear evidence of intent as to what the parties would have done had they foreseen the new use, it is suggested that the decision as to whether an old license covered a new use should depend upon an analysis of the likely expectations of the parties at the time the license was executed.

A. Expectations of the Film Producer

In determining what the film producer would likely have done at the time the license was entered into had he foreseen the new use (i.e., home video distribution), it may be well to ask whether the copyright owner's exercise of its exclusive right to the new use (i.e., to license to others the recording of his music in home video devices) would impair the expectations of the film producer? If the old synchronization license were non-exclusive, as most of them were, then no action by the copyright owner to grant permission to others to record the same music in other video programs should produce any unexpected or unjust effect on the film producer's original use. In other words, by virtue of the non-exclusive nature of the license, the licensee fully expected that the licensor could and would grant other licenses for similar uses to other potential licensees.

If the new use (i.e., home video distribution) effectively impairs the film producer's expectations with respect to the original use (i.e., theatrical and television performances), and the producer's expectations can only be fulfilled if the old license were construed as covering the new use, could it then be said that the producer would have reasonably expected that the old license, at the time it was granted, would cover the new use? In other words, does the advent of a new use that impairs the film producer's expectations regarding the old use justify construing an old license as covering the new use? No. Even though the exercise of the old use may no longer be lucrative, the producer still has the license to continue using the music for the originally licensed uses, however outmoded they may have become. The unforeseen risk at the time the license was executed was not only that a particular new use may eventually come into existence, but that the new use would change the economics of motion picture distribution. The question here is, who was in a better position to assume the risk that a new distribution media would arise that affects the economics of motion picture distribution? A court could properly place that risk at the foot of the motion picture producers, and not music publishers or songwriters.

B. Expectations of the Music Copyright Owner

In determining what the music copyright owner would likely have done at the time the license was entered into had he foreseen the new use, it may be useful to ask whether the film producer's exercise of the new use (i.e., making and distributing videogram copies for home use) under the old license without paying additional compensation to the copyright owner would impair the expectations of the copyright owner's ability to exercise its exclusive right to the new use (i.e., to license to others the recording of his music in home video devices)? Construing an old synchronization license as granting a license to make videocassette reproductions without further compensation would not impair the copyright owner's ability to exercise his right to license his music for use on other videocassettes. It may impair the copyright owner's ability to grant a license to use the song in videocassettes on an *exclusive* basis, but rarely is a copyright owner inclined to grant such exclusivity.

If the copyright owner did not contemplate the new use at the time the old license was executed, then it could be said he would not have had an expectation of deriving income from the producer for the new use. But this is not universally the case. It is probably true that the motion picture producers who procured synchronization licenses expected to pay a one time flat fee and never expected to have to go back to the licensor again for a license to distribute his film by whatever means. But it is not equally true that the copyright owners had no expectations beyond the one time fees they received.

It appears from the face of the old synchronization licenses that a principal concern of the music copyright owners was that, for whatever use was to be permitted, there be some mechanism in place to collect performance fees (e.g., through ASCAP or BMI) on all exhibitions or broadcasts of the work containing the musical composition. This was the mechanism by which the music copyright owners could participate in the economic success of the works containing their music. The flat fee required under the synchronization license simply could not serve this purpose. The performance fees, collected on performances occurring at the time the film is exhibited in theatres or on television, were expected *in addition* to the flat synchronization fee required for the privilege to make the copies of the motion pictures necessary for distribution.

So important was the requirement that performance fees be collected on performances of works for which the synchronization of their music was licensed, it seems clear that if there were no mechanism for the collection of fees for the performance of the music, music copyright owners would not have granted the license to synchronize the music in copies—at least not without negotiating some mechanism to collect compensation based upon the success of the work in which the music appeared.

Because the distribution of motion pictures in videocassette form deprives the music copyright owner of his expected additional compensation from theatrical and television performances, synchronization licenses that are silent or ambiguous as to their coverage of such distribution should not be construed as including the distribution of the videocassettes and other devices used for home viewing.

The copyright law provides the copyright owner with the exclusive right of *public* performance and it is on *public* performances that performance rights societies collect license fees on behalf of copyright owners. The exhibition of a videocassette at home is a *private* performance. Since neither the distribution, sale, rental, or home performance of videocassettes involve a public performance, there is no public performance upon which a performance fee can be based. When the original synchronization licenses were issued for a flat fee, music copyright owners anticipated that fees to be later collected for the public performances of the works containing their music would afford a means by which the copyright owner could participate in the economic success of the work in which his music was included. The more popular the motion picture, the more it would be exhibited and the more performance royalties would accrue to the copyright owner of the music.

Prior to 1948, when performance rights societies in the United States, such as BMI and ASCAP, began to be made subject to court ordered consent decrees, music copyright owners were entitled to fees from the performance of their music in motion picture theatres located in the United States and overseas. The consent decrees changed this by requiring music copyright owners to issue licenses to permit producers and their distributors to perform their music in motion picture theatres located in the United States. This performance license was required to be issued at the same time the copyright owner issued the license to synchronize their music in copies for theatrical distribution. In practice, the license to perform the music in U.S. theatres was included in the same document as the synchronization license and the copyright owner typically charged the same one-time flat fee, in effect doubling the fee normally charged for the synchronization license. The consent decrees are still in effect today.

Despite the consent decrees' effectively eliminating the music copyright owner's ability to share in the success of U.S. theatrical performances of motion pictures containing their music, music copyright owners still expected the payment of performance fees for performances of music in theatres outside of the United States as well as for performances that occurred on broadcast television. The requirement that copyright owners include a license (for a flat fee) for the public performance of music in U.S. movie theatres did not apply to television exhibition and exhibition in theatres outside of the United States, for which the performing rights societies do collect performance fees to this day.

Not only is the music copyright owner unable to share in the success of motion pictures distributed by videocassette (because virtually all performances of videocassettes are private, not public, performances), but to the extent the home videocassette performances of motion pictures, for which no public performance payment is collected by ASCAP or BMI, replaces broadcast television performances and international theatrical exhibition, for which ASCAP and BMI fees are collected, the performance revenue that the copyright owner anticipated when he granted the old synchronization license actually decreases.

Accordingly, the advent of home video distribution on videocassette and laserdisks of motion pictures containing copyrighted music seriously thwarts the expectations that the copyright owner was likely to have had at the time of entering the old synchronization license. If the music copyright owner had known of this new development at the time the license was executed, an alternative to performance fees would probably have been developed to ensure the music copyright owner with some ability to share in the success of the motion pictures in which their music was used. The kinds of mechanisms that would have evolved would probably have been similar to those that have recently emerged since the advent of the videogram market, and these are illustrated by the provisions described in Chapter 10 on videogram licenses.

The one historical anomaly that producers can point to that would appear to belie the music copyright owners' expectations of a share in the economic success in the exploitation of motion pictures containing their music is that music publishers never objected when producers licensed non-theatrical 16mm film rights to independent distributors. Either publishers expected that these films were primarily intended for performance in establishments licensed by ASCAP and BMI, such as schools and libraries, or that the revenues from the sales of 16mm films to individuals for private performances were just too small to notice.

AVOIDING AMBIGUITY

Music copyright owners should grant only the permission required to meet the known needs of those requesting the permission. The language effecting the owner's permission should be precise, should include clear definitions of all the important terms used, and should always expressly reserve all other privileges not specifically granted.

Producers, and others seeking to clear synchronization licenses, should attempt to obtain licenses that have as broad a scope as possible. Because of the availability of broad language that has been specifically confirmed by the courts, it is easier for a producer to draft language that will provide a license having an expansive scope than it is for music copyright owners to draft language that is tailored to the specific, immediately foreseeable needs of the producer. However, persuading a music copyright owner to accept such broad language may, today, truly be the *Impossible Dream*.

Appendix to Chapter 11
Old Licenses and New Uses

Forms

FORM 11.1   Old Motion Picture Synchronization License

FORM 11.1

OLD MOTION PICTURE SYNCHRONIZATION LICENSE

New York, New York, October 12, 1933

In consideration of the sum of ONE HUNDRED AND FIFTY DOLLARS ($150), the undersigned does hereby give to <u>Columbia Pictures Corporation, 729 Seventh Avenue, New York City</u>, the non-exclusive, irrevocable right, license, privilege and authority to record in any manner, medium or form, in any country covered by this license, the musical compositions hereinbelow set out, and to make copies of such recordings and to import said copies of recordings into any country covered by this license, all in accordance with the terms, conditions and limitations hereinafter set out.

1.   The Compositions covered by this license are:

Prisoner's Song   Massey   Shapiro Bernstein & Co. Inc.

2.   The title of the motion picture with which said musical compositions are to be used is <u>"Lady For a Day"</u> .

3.   The type of use to be made of the musical composition is <u>vocal visual—short whistling</u>, and the amount of uses to be made is <u>two</u> .

4.   The license hereinabove set out is limited to the use of the musical compositions in synchronism or timed-relation with the motion picture hereinabove specified.

5.   The right to record the musical compositions as covered by this agreement is conditioned upon the performance of the musical work in theatres having valid licenses from the American Society of Composers, Authors and Publishers, or any other

performing rights organization having jurisdiction in the territory in which the said musical compositions are performed.

6. The territory covered by this license is the entire world.

7. Except that the undersigned warrants that the principal for whom he is acting is the owner of the said musical compositions, this license is given without warranty or recourse, and the licensor reserves to itself all rights and uses in and to the said musical compositions not herein specifically granted.

Agent and Trustee

LICENSES FOR TELEVISION, RADIO, AND PRINT ADVERTISING

SUMMARY

INDUSTRY BACKGROUND

CONSIDERATIONS IN GRANTING AND CLEARING LICENSES TO USE MUSIC IN ADVERTISING

PRINT ADVERTISING

FORMS

CHAPTER 12

LICENSES FOR TELEVISION, RADIO, AND PRINT ADVERTISING

The convergence of radio and television with the commercial advertising industry has created one of the most lucrative markets for the licensing of music. This chapter will explore the considerations in licensing music in radio, television, and print advertising.

INDUSTRY BACKGROUND

Advertisers and the advertising agencies that represent them both recognize and appreciate the great value that music adds to commercial advertising. Music plays an important role in setting the mood and enhancing the memorability of the commercial message. Advertising experts have shown that with short commercials—in 30-second and 15-second lengths—music becomes even more important, because of the music's ability to quickly set the mood and convey information about the product.

In producing a radio or television commercial, an advertising agency has several alternatives in considering the application of music to its client's commercial message. The agency may hire a composer to write a song specially created for the commercial, called a commercial *jingle*, or it may license an established, popular song. The agency might use music without lyrics, use an instrumental version of a song that originally had lyrics, modify a song's lyrics, or create new lyrics to suit the commercial message.

Increasingly, agencies and advertisers have been deciding to use established, popular songs, rather than having new ones custom made, to sell a product. Popular songs are already known to the audience, so the advertiser does not have to wait for the tunes to catch on with its

499

audience, as he does with music created just for the advertising. Also, advertisers have become increasingly sophisticated in directing their messages to specific target audiences. Hit music of the 1950's and early 1960's, for example, can be quite effective in advertising that is targeted to reach the post World War II baby-boom generation. With an established song, an advertiser can capitalize on the customer's identification with a familiar song to improve the customer's continued recall of the product. Although creating a jingle or a new song tailored to an advertisement provides the advertiser with certain flexibility, it's hard to compete with a great, standard song, especially if the song already says a lot of things that the advertiser wants to say.

CONSIDERATIONS IN GRANTING AND CLEARING LICENSES TO USE MUSIC IN ADVERTISING

1. Fee Structure

The fee structure of the typical commercial synchronization license is a one-time, flat fee for the term of the license, with additional fees payable on any extensions to the term or expansion of the territory. These fees vary greatly and are subject to negotiation. Typical fees charged at the time of this writing for the use of music in commercial advertising are set forth in Chapter 19.

As with synchronization licenses for motion pictures and television programs and electrical transcriptions for radio programs, commercial synchronization licenses do not permit the *performance* of music; accordingly, separate performance fees are payable by radio and television stations that broadcast performances of commercials containing copyrighted music.

2. The Value of the Song

A. *Nature of the Product or Service*

Publishers and writers should consider the possibility that associating a hit song with a commercial product might harm the future earning potential of the song. A song that has become associated with a particular product in the mind of consumers may become less attractive to recording artists considering whether to include a song on a new album, to producers considering the use of the music in a motion picture, or to other advertisers considering the use of the music in connection with another product. For this reason, a publisher will charge a *premium* (i.e., higher than average fee) if he believes that an identification with a specific product might adversely affect the song's future mechanical, synchronization, or commercial advertising revenues. In addition, a publisher would be warranted in demanding a premium if the song has never before been made available for use in commercial advertising.

B. Reluctance to License

Because they understand and appreciate the maturing life of their copyright, older composers, and the surviving family of deceased composers, tend to make no objection to, and often encourage, the exploitation of their musical compositions in commercial advertising. It remains a mystery why many contemporary artists have an aversion to permitting the use of their music in commercial advertising. Where these artists have the right to approve such uses in their music publishing contracts, they tend to deny approval. If an artist's song should fall into disuse, the value of the copyright will decline over time, along with the number of people who may still remember it. Modern artists who find their popularity on the wane will soon regret their decision to withhold their approval of licensing their music for commercial purposes. A more prudent course would be to take the long term view and recognize the importance of licensing music in advertising.

C. Overcoming Reluctance

An advertiser who comes across a copyright owner who is reluctant to license music for commercial advertising should remind the copyright owner of the revenues that would arise from the public performances of the music. The performance royalties earned from performing rights society (e.g., ASCAP, BMI) on public performances of the commercial on radio and television can be substantial and will act as a multiplier on the synchronization license fee. The use of music in commercials will also maintain that special relationship between a song and the listening public. This is particularly important with respect to older songs, such as those songs written in the 1930's and 1940's, as well as songs written more recently, including songs written in the 1950's and 1960's. As the public gets older, unless there is some medium through which the song is continually exposed to the public—such as the classic movie, *Casablanca*, which features the standard song, *As Time Goes By*—there will be, as time goes by, fewer and fewer people who will recognize and appreciate the song. Maintaining continual exposure through commercial advertising will likely lead to other uses of the song by new generations.

If a copyright owner otherwise willing to grant a license for a commercial advertising use informs you that he is unable to obtain the consent of the songwriter for the use you are requesting, (i) you should not blame your troubles on the music publisher (who is probably just as frustrated as you are) and (ii) you should attempt to approach the artist or the artist's representatives directly to determine just what the specific objection is and how you can overcome it. If the objections cannot be overcome, you should ask the publisher to recommend another song in his catalog that would serve as an adequate substitute for your needs.

3. The Importance of the Song in Relation to Its Intended Use

A. Nature of the Product or Service

The central question an advertiser will be asked concerns the nature of the product or service the song will be used to promote. By first asking the reason a particular song was chosen, the music copyright owner may discover the importance of the song in relation to its intended commercial use, and thereby find a reason to ask for a premium for the use.

Sometimes a variety of songs may fit the need of the advertiser. For example, a commercial bank producing a television commercial may desire to use, *We're In the Money*. Should that song not be available, the bank may well use in its place, *Pennies From Heaven*, or *With Plenty of Money and You*. When a variety of substitutes are available, a premium fee will be difficult to obtain.

Every once in a while, however, one, and only one, particular song will best fit the message of the advertiser. That just may have been the case when an advertiser selected the song, *Anticipation* by Carly Simon for television advertisements of Heinz ketchup to help dramatize the "anticipation" on the faces of people as they wait for the thick, tasty

concoction of tomatoes and 57 varieties of spices to slowly come drip-
ping out of the bottle. It would be difficult to imagine a more fitting song
for the commercial.

The more closely a song is related to the message of the advertising
campaign, the less likely it is that close substitutes for the song are available
to the advertiser, and the higher the license fee the publisher can command.
Even when only one song will do, however, an advertiser may consider
using an old negotiating technique when haggling over the license fee: tell
the copyright owner that the music is only one of several, alternative songs
under consideration. It may be an old ploy,[1] but it often works.

B. Nature of the Use

Some of the same questions relevant in granting a synchronization
license for the use of music in motion pictures and television programs
will also apply here. For example, whether the music is to be used in a
vocal rendition or merely instrumental; whether the music is used as
background music or foreground music; whether the intended use relates
to how the composition was originally presented to the public; and
whether the music is used to help tell the story, or in the case with
commercials, directly used to help promote the product or just used to
set the mood. As with synchronization licenses, a foreground use will
generally command a higher license fee than a background use.

Some licenses specify the length and number of the commercials
in which the music is licensed. For example, a license might limit the
use to "a maximum of three thirty-second television commercials" or
"one fifteen second radio commercial." Most advertisers, however,
desire a greater amount of flexibility in producing differing versions
of a commercial, particularly those used in extensive national advertising campaigns. Publishers would generally have no objection to
providing such flexibility, provided the boundaries of the use are
specified in the license. Commercial synchronization licenses generally
have no limitation on the number of times a commercial may be
broadcast during the term of the license. This lack of a limitation is
for good reason: as far as the publisher is concerned, the more times
a commercial is broadcast, the more performance royalties the publisher
is likely to earn. This underscores the role commercial advertising

---

[1] See, for example, Stendhal, *The Red and the Black*, Ch. 5, "Coming to Terms" (1830).

plays in generating and sustaining the performance royalties. Accordingly, license terms should be crafted to recognize this.

C. Use of Original Recordings

If the producer desires to use an original sound recording in the commercial, he would normally be required to obtain a separate license to do so from the owner of the recording, such as a record company. If the original hit version is being licensed, a music publisher, having recognized the advertiser's acute interest in a particular recording, may quote a higher fee.

D. Use of Sound-Alike Recordings

To protect the music copyright owners against claims by recording artists and other entertainers from tortious claims concerning unauthorized use of their "name, voice, or likeness," publishers are advised to include a prohibition in their commercial synchronization licenses against the use of *sound-alike* recordings. These are recordings in which professional singers and studio musicians perform the composition in such a manner as to imitate or simulate an earlier recorded performance of the composition by an artist who may have made a distinctive popular recording of the song. Prohibiting the use of sound-alike recordings is particularly important where the music publisher has, and wants to maintain, a business relationship with the particular artist/songwriter sought to be simulated.

E. Lyric Changes

Generally, music copyright owners are prepared to permit changes or additions to the original lyrics of a composition, as long as such changes or additions are subject to the publisher's final written approval. Lyric changes should be approved only after the publisher has taken care to make certain it has the right to authorize the change. A publisher may be under a contractual obligation to consult with or obtain the approval of the songwriter prior to authorizing any changes to lyrics of the song.

The conditions under which a songwriter would be willing to agree to a modification of lyrics are unpredictable. If changes to lyrics are to be approved, the exact nature of the new lyrics should be specified in the license or final approval should be withheld until the exact lyric is determined. One experience should illustrate the point: Ira Gershwin gave his permission for the use of the song *I Got Rhythm* in a commercial advertisement for a chain of supermarkets in New York. He also permitted the use of a parody lyric in place of the original, but when he learned that the new lyric used the words, "*I've* Got Rhythm, he insisted that it be changed back to "*I* Got Rhythm." Ira said he deliberately chose the phrase "*I* Got Rhythm" instead of "*I've* Got Rhythm" for the title and lyrics of the composition written by his brother George, not because of its colloquial sound, but because it emphasized the powerful rhythmic structure his brother gave the music.

Even when a publisher is under no contractual obligation to obtain the permission of the songwriter, it is good practice to at least consult with the writer on any proposed changes. Changes to any artistic work may evoke some emotional reaction from the artist. Informing the writer in advance of proposed changes, at the very least, may avoid some surprise and embarrassment. Going the extra mile to satisfy any objections of the writer is also a good way to help build a long-term relationship with the writer, which may be important down the road, when it comes time for negotiating with the writer for a further grant of renewal rights or terminated rights under the 19-year extension period or the 35-year termination rule.

Performing rights societies, such as BMI and ASCAP, will pay performance royalties even when a new or parody lyric is used; however, the credits received may be less than if the original lyric is used. Nevertheless, the lower performance credits per use should not deter a decision to grant permission to alter the lyrics.

F. Use of the Song's Title

If the song's title is used for a special purpose, such as the name of the product, the importance of the song in relation to its intended use becomes obvious. Some additional consideration for the use of the music could be considered, as well as a separate fee for the use of the song title as the name of the product.

The ability of the publisher to command a fee for the use of the song's title as the name of the product, whether or not the music is used, will depend upon the distinctiveness of the title. For example, if the name of the song is merely a common word, such as *Misty*, then it might be difficult to command a fee for the use of the word "Misty" as the name of a product. It would, however, be quite reasonable to ask for a premium for the use of the song *Misty* or its lyrics in advertisements of the product. On the other hand, if the title of the song is distinctive, because either it consists of a wholly fictitious word or phrase or it contains some distinctive or recognizable grammatical error or misspelling, a fee for the use of the title may be demanded. For example, the titles "Supercali-fragilisticexpialidocious" and "Ain't Misbehavin" could probably not be used as the name of a product without the permission of the owner of the song's copyright.

4. Scope of the Intended Use

A. Media and Distribution Channels

Generally, commercial synchronization licenses should be narrowly drawn to permit the recording of the music in conjunction with radio or television commercials solely for radio or television broadcast. The license may also be expanded to permit "off-air" or non-broadcast trade uses, such as performance of the commercial at a trade show or for over-the-counter use in retail stores. If the commercial is to be distributed in videogram devices, such as videocassettes and laser discs, special licensing and fee provisions similar to those discussed in connection with videogram licenses may also be negotiated.

Advertisers who conduct a television and radio advertising campaign will usually try to place print ads that *tie in* with the broadcast messages. If such is the case, the advertiser will ask for a license to print any lyrics used in the television or radio commercials in printed advertising published during the term. Music copyright owners will generally grant permission to do so for an additional fee. Occasionally, the only permission that is sought is for the use of the lyrics in a print advertisement. A simplified license for such a use is set forth as Form 12.3 at the end of this chapter.

B. Term

The term of a commercial synchronization license will customarily commence upon the first broadcast of the commercial embodying the licensed musical composition, and will last for one week, one month, thirteen weeks, or other term negotiated between the parties, but will not normally endure for more than one year, unless options are negotiated. Because the success of advertising campaigns are difficult to predict, advertisers should always attempt to negotiate options to extend the term for one or two renewal periods upon payment of additional license fees. An option to renew a one year term usually must be exercised at least 30 days before the expiration of the initial term.

C. Territory

The territory for commercial advertising use varies depending upon the business of the advertiser. The territory of nationally advertised products is generally limited to the United States and Canada, although where a regional test of the advertising is contemplated, the territory may be restricted to a specific region with an option to expand the territory as appropriate, upon the payment of additional license fees.

When issuing a license whose territory is limited to the United States and Canada, keep in mind that certain television networks, such as CNN, are broadcast worldwide via satellite. Accordingly, a music copyright owner should be careful to exclude advertising on CNN if his right to license the use outside of North America is contractually limited or he is otherwise unwilling to permit the use of the music in advertising outside of the United States and Canada. By the same token, when the territory of the license is intended to be restricted to a certain region or city, such as the vicinity of Atlanta, Georgia, the music copyright owner should be careful to exclude advertising on "superstations" such as WTBS, which is a local station in Atlanta that is broadcast nationwide via satellite to local cable television operators. Other superstations include WOR in New York and WGN in Chicago. Where the advertising is specifically intended to be broadcast on superstations, the music publisher should become familiar with the number of markets into which the superstations' broadcasts are retransmitted and price the license accordingly. In other words, license fees for use of compositions on superstations should tend to be nearly the same as fees for use nationwide, because the superstations are usually transmitted to cable stations across the country.

Certain regions, such as New York City and Southern California, are larger, and comprise larger markets, than others, and can therefore command higher license fees. If you are a music copyright owner, keep in mind that if you receive a request for use of music in advertising to be broadcast in, for example, Newark, New Jersey, don't be fooled — such advertising could be received by viewers in the greater New York area, one of the largest television markets in the country.

Advertisers of products that have international appeal may request options for the use of music in additional countries. Consideration should be given to local subpublishing contracts or local publishing affiliate control over the music licensed for commercial advertising that takes place in their local markets.

D. Exclusivity

An advertiser paying a substantial fee for a commercial synchronization license may well request the exclusive right to use the song for commercial purposes during the license term. Music copyright owners are normally willing to agree to some form of limited exclusivity. For example, the music publisher may agree not to license the song in connection with the commercial advertising of products that directly compete with the advertiser's licensed product.

An advertiser would normally find that acceptable, but, in addition, may request that the publisher not license the song in connection with products that not only "compete with" the licensed product or service, but "relate to" the licensed product or service — that is, products that are complementary, not necessarily competing with the licensed products. Thus, for example, a sporting goods manufacturer licensing a song for use in advertising its line of golf clubs may well expect that the publisher would not license the song to another sporting goods manufacturer for use in connection with the advertising of its golf balls.

It should be evident that there is some degree of ambiguity inherent in phrases such as "compete with" or "relate to." To avoid ambiguity, a publisher may phrase the restriction in terms of precisely what kind of product(s) or service(s) in connection with which the publisher will not grant a license to use the song. For example, instead of providing that "The license is exclusive with respect to products that compete with stuffed animals," music copyright owners would be advised to state instead, "During the Term of the license, Publisher will not grant a license to use the Composition in the Territory in connection with the advertising of stuffed animals." While the former provision might be construed as preventing the license of the song in connection with dolls—on the basis that dolls are directly competitive with stuffed animals—the latter provision would be more narrowly construed to prevent the license of the song in connection with only those items that could reasonably be called a "stuffed animal." If the advertiser believes such a restriction is too narrow, the publisher should ask the advertiser to list the kinds of products it believes should be within the scope of the restriction, leaving it to the advertiser, who is in a better position to foresee potential conflicts, to take the risk of leaving a product off the list.

Care should also be taken in choosing the name of the product for which exclusivity is sought. For example, if the advertised product is aspirin, the copyright owner should try to limit the scope of the exclusivity to "aspirin." It might be reasonable for the advertiser to request that the exclusivity cover "pain relievers," which would include non-aspirin pain relievers, but a request for coverage of "pharmacology products," which might include cosmetics, would be too broad. Similarly, if the product advertised is beer, the scope of exclusivity should not be "all beverages," but "alcoholic beverages" or "domestic beer." In some rare cases, the advertiser may be willing to pay the extremely high premium required to obtain a broader scope of exclusivity.

PRINT ADVERTISING

The considerations described above regarding television and radio advertising apply also to print advertising, although the latter generally involves the more limited use of lyrics. Sometimes a television or radio advertising campaign will be supported by print advertising and a commercial synchronization license may include a provision allowing the use of lyrics in print advertising, product brochures and point-of-sale displays.

APPENDIX TO CHAPTER 12
LICENSES FOR TELEVISION, RADIO
AND PRINT ADVERTISING

FORMS

FORM 12.1

LICENSE FOR USE OF MUSIC IN RADIO OR TELEVISION ADVERTISEMENTS

COMMERCIAL SYNCHRONIZATION LICENSE

Date: January 1, 1995

Owner: BIG MUSIC PUBLISHING CORP.
a California Corporation
1000 Sunset Boulevard
Hollywood, California 90069

Licensee: ABC Advertising Agency, Inc.
a New York Corporation
10 Madison Avenue
New York, New York 10017

on behalf of the following Sponsor and Product(s):

Licensed Area:

Composition:

       by:

       Copyright © _____ 19__

1.   (a)   Owner hereby grants to Licensee the right to use the title and music to the Composition in the Licensed Area during the Term for commercial advertising, trade and related purposes without limitation as to frequency in the television and radio media (excluding so-called "pay" and "subscription" television) on behalf of the Sponsor, its subsidiaries and affiliates for the purpose of advertising the Product.

(b)   This license allows Licensee to arrange and adapt all or part of the music of the Composition to utilize a parody lyric (subject to the prior written approval of Owner's Director of Licensing) and to record all or part of the music of the Composition in synchronism or timed relation with television and/or radio commercials, and is granted upon the following express conditions, the violation of any of which shall cause this license to terminate immediately:

(i)   that the recordings produced hereunder shall be used solely for television and/or radio commercials and for off-air trade purposes to promote the Product(s);

(ii)   that neither the sound recordings produced pursuant to this license nor copies thereof shall be sold or licensed apart from said commercials;

(iii)   that said commercials shall not be exhibited in or televised into theatres or other public places of amusement where motion pictures are customarily shown (except in cases of private trade screenings); and

(iv)   that said commercials shall not utilize a "sound-a-like" recording in which an artist (solo or group) performs the Composition in such a way as to imitate an earlier recorded performance of the Composition by a different artist (unless Licensee or Sponsor shall first obtain the express permission of the latter artist or from a person, firm or corporation authorized to grant such permission on behalf of the latter artist).

(c)   Licensee will not make any use of the Composition (or of any arrangement or adaptation thereof) following the end of the Term, but Licensee shall have the right to retain copies of all commercials produced hereunder for file and reference purposes only.

(d)   Upon Owner's written request Licensee shall deliver to Owner an audiotape or videotape copy of each commercial (plus a copy of any parody lyric).

2.   (a)   The initial period of the Term of this license shall be one year, commencing with the first on-air use of a commercial produced hereunder or on _____, whichever occurs first.

(b)   Provided Licensee shall have complied with the terms and conditions of this license during the initial period, Licensee shall have the option to extend the Term for one one-year renewal period, by written notice delivered to Owner at least thirty (30) days prior to the expiration of the initial period.

3.   (a)   Owner shall not authorize any other person, firm or corporation to make commercial, advertising, trade or related use of the Composition in the Licensed Area during the Term in connection with the advertising or publicizing of any product(s) of the following types or descriptions:

(b)   Except as provided in the preceding paragraph, this license shall be non-exclusive.

(c)   Owner agrees to employ its best efforts, consistent with its good-faith business judgment, to prevent and restrain any use of the Composition by any person, firm or corporation contrary to the provisions of paragraph 3(a), above. In the event that Licensee (by written notice delivered to Owner) requests that Owner take action against an allegedly unauthorized use, and Owner declines to proceed because of a good faith belief either that no unauthorized use is involved or that the unauthorized use is too insignificant to warrant the cost of enforcement, Licensee shall have the right (and it shall be Licensee's sole remedy) to proceed against the user(s) in its own behalf (and at Licensee's sole cost and expense) and to retain any amount recovered thereby. Owner's failure to proceed within thirty (30) days after receipt of such a request shall be deemed Owner's decision not to proceed.

4.   (a)   Owner, or an organization such as BMI or ASCAP, to which Owner belongs and which licenses performing rights on Owner's behalf, will license the use of the Composition on radio and television stations and networks throughout the Licensed Area.

(b)   (i)   In the event that Licensee or Sponsor wishes to allow the use of any commercial(s) embodying the Composition in whole or in part on any station(s) and/or network(s) not then holding valid performing rights licenses from Owner or such an organization, Owner agrees to issue a performing rights license for such use at Owner's then-customary rates.

(ii)   In the alternative, or in the event that Licensee or Sponsor wishes to acquire a direct performing rights license from Owner without reference to whether or not such station(s) and/or network(s) possess such performing rights licenses, Licensee may secure such performing rights license by an additional payment to Owner equal to one percent (1%) of the total time buy on the station(s) or network(s) in respect of which Licensee is securing such performing rights license.

(c)   Within a reasonable time following receipt of written request therefor from Owner, Licensee shall deliver to Owner copies of documents setting forth the names and addresses of all stations and networks upon which commercials produced hereunder have been and/or will be broadcast, and, in each instance, the number of times each commercial has been or will be broadcast. Owner understands and agrees that such information is confidential, and such information shall be disclosed only to such stations or networks or to Owner's performing rights society or societies (who shall likewise be instructed to keep such information confidential).

(d)   Owner shall not attempt to enjoin the broadcast or other transmission of commercials produced hereunder by any station or network selected by Licensee, Sponsor (or any person, firm or corporation acting on behalf of either of them), it being understood and agreed that Owner's sole remedy for unlicensed broadcast or other unlicensed transmission or performance shall be an action for money damages in accordance with the Copyright Act.

5.   In consideration of the rights granted herein, Licensee shall make a payment to Owner upon execution of this license in the amount of $ _____ . In the event that Owner exercises its renewal option, an additional fee of $ _____ shall be payable at the time Licensee gives notice of its exercise of such option. Timely payment of these fees shall be of the essence of this agreement.

6.   (a)   Owner warrants and represents that it has the right to enter into and perform this agreement, and that the proper exercise by Licensee of the rights granted hereunder will not violate the rights of any third party. Licensee warrants and represents that it has the right to enter into and perform this agreement, and that the Sponsor has expressly authorized Licensee to agree to the requirements and restrictions set forth above.

       (b)   (i)   Each party agrees to indemnify the other party and hold the other party harmless, from and against any and all loss, cost, damage or expense (including court costs and reasonable outside counsel fees) arising out of a breach of the foregoing warranty and representation by such party and resulting in an adverse judgment or a settlement entered into with the indemnitor's prior written consent (not to be unreasonably withheld).

              (ii)   A party claiming indemnity shall deliver to the other party prompt written notice of any claim, action or proceeding to which such indemnity relates, and the indemnitor shall have the right to participate in the defense thereof by counsel of its choice, at its sole cost and expense. Where required by the terms of the indemnitor's errors-and-omissions insurance policy, the indemnitor's insurance carrier shall be permitted to control the defense of such claim, action or proceeding.

7.   All notices hereunder shall be given by registered or certified (return receipt requested) mail, by telegraph, or by any other

means by which delivery may be verified. Notice shall be given to the above addresses or to such other addresses as the parties may designate from time to time by notice delivered in like manner.

8.   This license is personal to Licensee and may not be assigned or transferred except to the Sponsor without Owner's prior written consent. No such transfer or assignment shall become effective unless and until the transferee or assignee shall deliver to Owner a written agreement assuming the further performance of Licensee's obligations hereunder, and no such transfer or assignment shall relieve Licensee of any obligation hereunder. However, Licensee may enter into sublicenses within the Licensed Area to the extent necessary to permit the exhibition of commercials in accordance with this license.

9.   This agreement has been entered into in, and is to be interpreted in accordance with the laws of, the State of California. This agreement contains the entire agreement between the parties and may not be altered or amended except by a further writing signed by both parties.

OWNER   LICENSEE

By: _____   By: _____

FORM 12.2

ALTERNATIVE LICENSE FOR USE OF MUSIC IN RADIO OR TELEVISION ADVERTISEMENTS

COMMERCIAL SYNCHRONIZATION LICENSE

AGREEMENT made and entered into as of this   day of   by and between having a place of business at   (hereinafter referred to as "Licensee"), on behalf of its client,   (hereinafter referred to as "Sponsor"), and with a place of business at   (hereinafter referred to as "Owner").

W I T N E S S E T H:

1.   Owner hereby grants to Licensee the right to use the music to the composition entitled _____ published by Owner (hereinafter referred to as the "composition") on behalf of Sponsor, its subsidiaries and affiliates for the purpose of advertising of Sponsor's product (hereinafter collectively referred to as the "Product").

2.   (a)   The term of this agreement shall be for one year, commencing with first on-air use on _____ whichever shall come first (hereinafter referred to as the "first Term"). During said First Term, Licensee may use the title and music to the Composition for commercial advertising, trade and related purposes without limitation as to frequency in the television and radio media in the United States, its territories and possessions (hereinafter referred to as the "licensed Area"), excluding so-called "pay" and "subscription" television.

       (b)   Licensee shall have the option to extend the term of the agreement for one additional successive one (1) year period (hereinafter referred to as the "Second Term") to commence on the first day following the termination of the prior term, by giving Owner written notice to such effect no later than thirty (30) days prior to the termination of the then current term. During said Second Term, if any, Licensee may use the Composition in the same manner permitted during the First Term as specified in Paragraph 2(a) above.

3.   While this Agreement is in effect, Licensee may use all, part, and non-consecutive parts, of music of said Composition and arrange and adapt said Composition.

4.   The License issued herein shall be deemed non-exclusive; however, Owner agrees not to authorize any other person, firm or corporation to make commercial, advertising, trade or related use of the Composition in the Licensed Area in connection with either the advertising or giving publicity to any of the following products: _____ Owner agrees to use its best efforts to prevent and restrain any unauthorized use of said Composition by any person, firm or corporation.

5.   Licensee agrees that it will not broadcast all or any part of the original music, of the said Composition following the authorized period of use as elsewhere set forth in the Agreement, except that it may retain copies of the commercials for file and reference purposes only.

6.   Licensee agrees the license granted herein is to record the Composition in synchronism or time-relation with a picture made and produced in connection with television commercials or for radio commercials. Licensee further agrees this license is granted upon the express condition that any and all recording(s) produced hereunder are to be used solely for television or radio and that no sound records produced pursuant to this license are to be sold or licensed apart from said commercials, and upon further condition the said commercials shall not be exhibited in or televised into theatres or other public places of amusement where motion pictures are customarily shown. Notwithstanding the generality of the foregoing, Licensee, Sponsor and its sub-

sidiaries and affiliates shall have the right during the term of this Agreement to use commercials embodying the Composition for off-air trade purposes.

7.   Owner, or an organization such as ASCAP or BMI, to which Owner belongs and which licenses performance rights on Owner's behalf, will license the use of the Composition on radio and television stations and networks throughout the United States. In the event Licensee desires to use the Composition on stations or networks which have not entered into a license agreement with Owner or any organization on Owner's behalf, this agreement shall be deemed to constitute a license for such uses without any limitation or further compensation. Neither Owner nor anyone deriving any rights from Owner shall interfere with or hold up the performance of the Composition pursuant to this Agreement

8.   Owner warrants and represents that Licensee will not be subject to any performance fees or any other fee or tax by another person, firm or corporation or society or other legal entity for using said Composition in accordance with the rights granted Licensee hereunder.

9.   Owner represents and warrants that it has the right and authority to grant the rights given to Licensee herein and that the exercise by Licensee of the rights granted herein will not violate the rights of any third party. Owner agrees to defend, indemnify and hold harmless Sponsor, its subsidiaries and affiliates, the Licensee, and their respective directors, officers, employees and agents from and against any and all claims, damages, liabilities, costs and expenses (including reasonable attorneys' fees), arising out of the permitted use of the Composition by Licensee or Sponsor hereunder. Licensee similarly agrees to indemnify and hold harmless Owner, its affiliated companies, from and against any and all claims, damages, liability, costs and expenses (including reasonable attorneys' fees), arising out of or in any way connected with any advertising materials utilizing the licensed property other than those furnished by Owner. Indemnitee will promptly notify Indemnitor of any claim or litigation to which this indemnity applies.

Indemnitee reserves the right, without being required to do so, to settle any claim or litigation, or defend any claim or suit at his own expense, provided that in the event Indemnitee settles any claim or litigation without prior written consent of the Indemnitor, the Indemnitor shall be released from any and all liabilities under said indemnity.

10.   In consideration for the rights granted Licensee hereunder, and the duties and obligations assumed by Owner, Licensee agrees to pay and Owner agrees to accept the following sums:

a)   For the rights granted during the First Term referred to in paragraph 2(a) above Licensee agrees to pay Owner the sum of   Dollars payable within fifteen (15) working days of the date on which Licensee furnishes Owner with a fully executed copy of this agreement.

b)   In the event Licensee exercises its option for the Second Term referred to in paragraph 2(b) above Licensee shall pay Owner   Dollars within fifteen (15) working days of the date on which Licensee furnishes notice of the exercise of said option.

c)   All payments due or which may become due Owner hereunder shall be made by check to the order of BIG MUSIC PUBLISHING CORP. and delivered to the address set forth on the face page of this Agreement.

11.   Notice to Licensee shall be sufficient if mailed or telegraphed to it all charges prepaid addressed as follows:

or to such other address as may hereafter be designated by Licensee from time to time in writing.

12.   Notice to Owner shall be sufficient if mailed or telegraphed to it, all charges prepaid, addressed as follows:

Attention:

or to such other address as may hereafter be designated by Owner from time to time in writing.

13.   This Agreement constitutes the entire understanding between the parties hereto and cannot be changed orally. No waiver by either party hereto of any breach of any agreement to be performed by the other party hereunder shall be deemed to be a waiver of any preceding or succeeding breach of the same or any other agreement hereunder.

This Agreement shall be interpreted and construed according to the laws of the State of California.

IN WITNESS WHEREOF, this Agreement has been duly executed by the parties hereto, as of the day and year first written.

OWNER   LICENSEE

By: _____   By: _____

FORM 12.3

LICENSE FOR USE OF LYRICS IN A
PRINT ADVERTISEMENT

January 1, 1995

FORTUNE 500 COMPANY, INC.
456 Main Street
San Francisco, California 95000

Gentlemen:

We grant you permission to reprint portions of the lyric only from
our copyright "_____" by _____for
use in print advertising for your product _____,
subject to the following terms and conditions:

1.   You shall pay us a fee of $5000.00, check made payable to
BIG MUSIC PUBLISHING COMPANY, INC. and addressed to the
attention of the undersigned.

2.   The following copyright notice must appear at the bottom of
the page on which the quote appears, suitably asterisked, or as an
alternative, we authorize copyright notice to be included on appropriate credit pages if the complete publication is registered with
the U.S. Copyright Office.

      Copyright © 1965 BIG MUSIC PUBLISHING CORP.
      All Rights Reserved   Used By Permission

3.   The territory covered by this permission is the United States.

4.   The term of this agreement shall expire on December, 1996.

5.   You shall furnish us with two (2) copies of the ad copy for our
files.

This permission shall be valid upon your signing and returning to us one copy of this letter along with your remittance and upon the performance by you of the other terms and conditions hereof on your part to be performed.

All rights not specifically granted herein are reserved to and by us.

Yours sincerely,

BIG MUSIC PUBLISHING CORP.

AGREED AND ACCEPTED:

By: _____

By:_____

LICENSES FOR MUSIC BOXES AND CONSUMER MUSICAL PRODUCTS

SUMMARY

BACKGROUND

CONSIDERATIONS IN GRANTING AND CLEARING MUSICAL PRODUCT LICENSES

1. Fee Structure
   A. Applicability of Compulsory License Provision
2. Value of the Song
3. Importance of the Song in Relation to Its Intended Use
4. Scope of Use
   A. Media
   B. Term
   C. Territory
   D. Exclusivity

PRINTING OF MUSIC OR LYRICS

FORMS

CHAPTER 13

LICENSES FOR MUSIC BOXES AND CONSUMER MUSICAL PRODUCTS

From time to time, a music publisher will receive a request for permission to use a musical composition in a consumer product. The variety of consumer products in which music is being employed is ever increasing and hardly a month goes by without an innovative use of music being brought to the attention of a publisher for licensing consideration. This chapter will explore the considerations in licensing music in music boxes and other consumer musical products.

BACKGROUND

As noted in Chapter 7, a *music box* is a mechanical instrument whose sounds are produced by the spring activated rotation of a cylinder having specially placed protruding pins that pluck the teeth of a metal comb. The music box was the first mechanical device designed to perform music and is used today in jewelry boxes, figurines, novelty items, and children's toys.

Modern technology has spawned new, innovative applications of the music box idea. For example, a toy manufacturer has marketed a musical coin bank, called the *Musical Bogie Bank* which plays the melody of the song *As Time Goes By* whenever a coin is deposited in its slot. A greeting card containing a special sound-capable computer chip may perform, for example, a few bars of *My Funny Valentine* when the card is opened. An exercise machine may play the melody of *Chariots of Fire* while the user is cycling or running in place. A doll bearing the likeness of the movie character, *Mary Poppins* might sing *A Spoonful of Sugar* when the child pulls a string or claps his or her hands.

Other consumer musical products may use music in a way that does not involve a performance of the melody. For example, a tea kettle might bear the imprint of the words and musical notation of the song, *Tea For Two* by Irving Caesar and Vincent Youmans. And a greeting card may contain the printed lyric of the song, *I Love You Truly*.

CONSIDERATIONS IN GRANTING AND CLEARING MUSICAL PRODUCT LICENSES

In granting permission to use a song in connection with a consumer product, a music copyright owner will consider many of the same factors applicable to determining the appropriate rate to charge for use of his music in television, radio, or print advertising (see Chapter 12), including the fee structure, value of the song, the importance of the song in relation to its intended use, and the scope of the use. These factors are discussed below.

1. Fee Structure

Music copyright owners typically charge some percentage of the sales of the consumer music product in exchange for the license. The percentage may be a portion of the suggested retail price, wholesale price, or net revenues (gross revenues less product returns). Because the price charged for the musical product by its manufacturer is completely within the discretion of the manufacturer, the copyright owner may establish some minimum fixed penny or dollar amount per copy. The fixed amount per copy will often serve as a *floor*, or minimum fee, below which the royalty will not fall, regardless of what the manufacturer charges for the product. The copyright owner will also seek an advance against royalties payable upon the execution of the license. See Forms 13.1 and 13.2 at the end of this chapter for model licenses for music boxes and musical product licenses.

A person seeking to clear a license for a musical product might attempt to negotiate a one-time flat fee for the use during the term of the license. However, music copyright owners would be reluctant to grant such licenses on a flat fee basis, because of the absence of any means to share in the economic success of the product in which the music will be included. For example, the television broadcast of a young child playing with a *Mary Poppins* doll that sings *A Spoonful of Sugar* will earn the song's copyright owner performance fees that are in addition to any initial licensee fee charged for the synchronization of the song to the advertisement. By contrast, the child's playing with the doll day after day at home does not earn the music copyright owner any additional fees, no matter how popular the doll becomes with little girls. This is because all performances of the song in the home are *private* performances. These performances are not subject to the permission of the copyright owners, and, because there are no fees collectable for private performances, the music copyright owner will seek alternative means to share in the economic success of the use. It has therefore been the practice of music publishers to charge a royalty for the use based on the number of units of the products sold or the revenues derived from sales of the product.

If, at the same time you are seeking to clear a musical product license, you are seeking to clear a synchronization license for the use of the music in television commercials to advertise the musical product, you may be able to negotiate a flat fee rate, or in any event, better terms for the musical product license, if you can persuade the copyright owner that your use of the song will significantly increase the copyright owner's income during the term of the license. The copyright owner may also accept a flat fee if it is high enough to overcome the copyright owner's fear of making a "bad deal."

A. *Applicability of Compulsory License Provision*

Before a person seeking to clear a license for a musical product accepts any terms offered by a music copyright owner, he should first determine whether the compulsory license provision of the copyright law applies to the particular use intended. If the compulsory license provision does apply, then the licensee would be entitled to limit the fee to the *statutory rate* existing at that time. Currently, the statutory rate is $6\frac{1}{4}$ cents per copy. The music copyright owner is free to negotiate better terms only if the compulsory license statute does not apply.

Technically, when a music box or a musical greeting card *plays* a song, the performance is not accompanied by motion pictures or some other form of audiovisual work. Accordingly, one might assert that the purely mechanical reproduction of the song in the music box or greeting card appears to be subject to the compulsory mechanical licensing provision of the copyright law (see Chapter 7). A music copyright owner might argue that the compulsory license provision only applies to phonorecords, or record albums as they are customarily understood, and does not apply to devices that might technically contain a phonorecord, such as a sound-capable computer chip, but are incorporated into a consumer product. Since the incorporation of music into a consumer product commercially ties the music to the product, the tie in can be considered in the nature of an endorsement of the product. Thus, something more is present than the mere incorporation of the music in a phonorecord for private use. It is not clear how this question would be decided if ever tested in court. It is not likely to be decided as long as the royalty rates customarily charged for the use of music in consumer products remains reasonably consistent with the statutory rate.

Note, however, that the reprinting of lyrics is clearly not a mechanical reproduction and therefore is clearly not subject to the compulsory license provision. Nor is music embodied in a product that contains an audiovisual work a mechanical reproduction of the music subject to compulsory licensing. Accordingly, if the lyrics are used, with or without the music, or the music is used in connection with moving pictures, the compulsory license provision of the copyright law would not apply and the publisher would clearly be free to negotiate more favorable terms.

2. Value of the Song

As in the consideration of licensing music for use in advertising commercial products, discussed in Chapter 12, music copyright owners in considering licensing music for use in the products themselves should consider the possibility that associating a hit song with a commercial product might harm the future earning potential of the song. A song that has become associated with a particular product may become less attractive to recording artists considering whether to make new recordings of the song, to producers considering whether to use the music in motion pictures, or to other advertisers considering whether to use the music in the marketing or advertising of other products. For these reasons, a publisher would consider charging a premium if he believes that an identification with a specific product might adversely affect the song's future revenues from other sources. In addition, a publisher would be warranted in demanding a premium if the song has never before been made available for use in a consumer product.

A person seeking to clear a license for musical products would do well to remind a reluctant copyright owner of the importance of maintaining continual exposure of the song to the listening public, despite the lack of public performances arising from the license. Licensing music for a toy music box or wind-up doll will expose the music to a new generation and will increase the likelihood that licenses for use and performance of the song will continue over the full life of the copyright.

3. Importance of the Song in Relation to Its Intended Use

Again, the music copyright owner should ask himself, or the potential licensee, why *this* particular song? When one, and only one, particular song will best fit the use in the product, the copyright owner may have a good reason to ask for a premium fee. As previously noted, the fewer substitutes that are available for the use, the more the licensee may be willing to pay. For example, there may be only a limited number of songs or themes logically available for a musical doll based on a popular motion picture or television program character. Also, if the song's title will be used as the name of the product, a separate fee for that use should be considered, though the music copyright owner's ability to charge a fee for the use of the song's title will depend upon the distinctiveness of the title.

4. Scope Of Use

A. *Media*

The product in which the music will be embodied should be described with particularity. To this end, the copyright owner should ask for a full description of the product at the time the license is being sought.

B. *Term*

The terms of musical product licenses are, generally, for a period of one to three years, with a provision to allow the manufacturer to sell off his inventory for a period of no more than six months after the expiration of the term. A person seeking to clear such a license should be able to negotiate options to renew the term upon the payment of additional advances against future royalties.

C. Territory

The territory that the licensee is permitted to distribute the licensed product is limited to the local market in which the license is issued, such as the United States and Canada. Options permitting the export of the musical product to other countries may be available, but the music publisher may require that such licenses be sought from the local music publishers in each of the countries in which the licensee intends to market the product.

D. Exclusivity

When requested, product exclusivity is often granted. The discussion of exclusivity set forth in Chapter 12, with respect to commercial advertising, applies equally to consumer product licenses, though exclusivity may not be as important here as it is to the licensee in establishing a product identity in the course of a commercial advertising campaign. An exclusivity provision of a musical product license should, of course, be narrow in scope and worded with great care to assure the license reflects the intent of the parties.

PRINTING OF MUSIC OR LYRICS

Makers of some consumer musical products merely require permission to print the lyrics on or in the product. For example, a tea kettle might bear the imprint of the words and musical notation of the song, *Tea For Two* or a greeting card may contain the printed lyric of the song, *I Love You Truly*. In each instance, the music copyright owner will generally grant permission under terms and conditions similar to those applicable to other musical consumer products.

However, music copyright owners should first reflect upon whether they have the right to grant such a license to begin with. If the copyright owner previously granted to a print music publisher the exclusive rights to make copies of the music in printed form, then, unless the grant of rights in the print music publishing agreement excluded uses for consumer products or reprints of lyrics in books and other products, then the copyright owner may be required to refer the person who is seeking the musical product license to the owner of the exclusive print rights of the music.

APPENDIX TO CHAPTER 13
LICENSES FOR MUSIC BOXES AND
CONSUMER MUSICAL PRODUCTS

FORMS

FORM 13.1

LICENSE FOR USE OF MUSIC
IN MUSIC BOXES

MUSIC BOX LICENSE AGREEMENT

AGREEMENT, dated as of _____ , 1995, between

BIG MUSIC PUBLISHING CORP., with its principal office at 1000 Sunset Boulevard, Hollywood, California 90069 ("Owner") and DELICATE MUSIC BOX MAKER & SONS, with its principal office at P.O. Box 1000 Harmony Lane, Melody, Missouri 50505 ("Maker").

WHEREAS, Owner owns the copyrights in the song "_____" (_____ , _____) (the "Song"), including the exclusive right to license the reproduction of the Song; and

WHEREAS, Maker desires to obtain from Owner a license to use the Song in connection with the manufacture and sale of Music Boxes.

NOW, THEREFORE, in consideration of the mutual agreements contained herein, the parties agree as follows:

1.   Owner grants to Maker, upon the terms and conditions set forth in the Agreement, the right and license to use the Song in connection with the manufacture, distribution, and sale of the Music Box in the United States; provided, however, this license does not permit Maker to use the music and/or lyrics of the Song in connection with any advertising of the Music Box.

2.   The term of this Agreement shall be for the life of the Music Box, but no longer than December 31, 2000. However,

either party may terminate this Agreement upon ninety (90) days' written notice to the other.

3.   (a)   Maker agrees to pay Owner a royalty equal to five percent (5%) of amounts received from the sale in the United States, payable quarterly within thirty (30) days after the end of each quarter. For purposes of this Agreement, the term "amounts received" shall mean the amounts Maker invoices to its customers or distributors for the music boxes.

(b)   Timely and accurate payments shall be of the essence of this Agreement. Owner shall have the right, upon ten (10) days' prior written notice, and during ordinary business hours, to audit Maker's books and records (insofar as they relate to the subject matter of this Agreement), which shall be kept in accordance with generally accepted accounting principles and maintained at Maker's principal place of business.

4.   The following copyright notice must appear on the packaging of the Music Box so long as the Song "_____" is used:

_____

Words by   Music By

Copyright © 19____ BIG MUSIC PUB. CORP.
All Rights Reserved   Used By Permission

5.   Maker's exercise of the license granted by Owner under this Agreement shall constitute Maker's warranty and representation that Maker then has all rights necessary for the manufacture, distribution and sale of the Music Boxes. Maker agrees to indemnify and hold Owner harmless against any loss, damage, or liability, including reasonable attorneys' fees and court costs, arising out of a breach of said representation and warranty. Owner shall similarly indemnify Maker with respect to Owner' rights in and to the Song.

IN WITNESS WHEREOF, the parties have caused their duly authorized officers to execute this Agreement as of the day and year first written above.

BIG MUSIC PUBLISHING CORP.

By_____

DELICATE MUSIC BOX MAKER & SONS

By_____

FORM 13.2

ALTERNATIVE LICENSE FOR USE OF MUSIC IN A CONSUMER MUSICAL PRODUCT

MUSICAL PRODUCT LICENSE

Date: January 1, 1995

Owner: BIG MUSIC PUBLISHING CORP.   Licensee:
                   1000 Sunset Blvd.
                   Hollywood, CA 90069

Composition: By:

Copyright Notice:

Description of Licensed Item:

Licensed Territory:

Term of this Agreement: From   To

Renewal options (exercisable by written notice delivered at least 30 days prior to commencement of renewal period):
_____renewal period(s) of _____ each.

Post-Term Sell-Off Rights:

Product-Line Exclusivity (if in addition to the Licensed Product):

Suggested Retail List Price: $

Licensee's Wholesale Price: $

Advance(s): $. payable on execution

                 $. payable

                 $. payable

Royalty: $_____   per copy, or, if greater,____% of the
_____ price per copy, payable on all copies sold and
not returned.

THIS LICENSE INCLUDES THOSE TERMS AND CONDITIONS SET
FORTH ON THE ANNEXED RIDER.

LICENSEE: OWNER:

By: _____   By: _____

RIDER

Annexed to and made part of the
Musical Product License Agreement
dated January 1, 1995

between _____ ("Owner")

and _____ ("Licensee").

1.   (a)   This license is personal to the Licensee, and may not be sold, assigned, transferred, exchanged or encumbered in any manner. However, in the event of a merger or consolidation, or a sale of substantially all of the Licensee's stock or assets, the Licensee shall have the right to assign this Licensee to the surviving or acquiring entity provided such entity assumes the further performance of this license in accordance with its terms and conditions in a writing delivered to the Owner.

       (b)   (i)   This license is exclusive with respect to the inclusion of the Composition in products directly competitive with the Licensed Product or products which are of the same generic type as the Licensed Product within the Licensed Territory during the Term hereof. (For example, "stuffed animals" would be a generic type, as would be "housewares" or "coin banks".)

               (ii)   However, unless specified otherwise on the first page of this license, this license is nonexclusive with respect to all other uses of the Composition, whether within or outside the Licensed Territory, and whether during or after the Term.

2.   (a)   All merchandise and packaging manufactured pursuant to this license shall be of the highest quality of similar items regularly sold in the Licensed Territory (in each country thereof, if this license covers more than one country).

       (b)   Prior to first shipment, and again in any subsequent instance in which the specifications of the Licensed Product and/or the packaging thereof are altered, the Licensee shall deliver a representative sample thereof to the Owner (to the attention of the Owner's General Counsel) for the Owner's review and approval, which approval shall not be unreasonably withheld (and which shall be deemed to have been granted unless the Owner delivers detailed written notice of disapproval within fifteen (15) days after delivery of the sample to the Owner).

3.   (a)   This license allows the Licensee to manufacture, advertise, distribute and sell the Licensed Product including a device capable of reproducing the Composition, within the Licensed Territory during the Term.

(b)   (i)   In addition, provided the Licensee is not then in breach of any of the terms or conditions of this Agreement, the Licensee shall have the right, for six months following the end of the Term, to sell off its ending inventory of the Licensed Product.

(ii)   All sales during the sell-off period shall be at regular prices, and not at "close-out" or "distress" prices.

(iii)   The Licensee shall provide the Owner with an ending inventory, certified by a responsible corporate officer, within thirty (30) days following the end of the Term. Any copies of the Licensed Product remaining unsold as of the end of the sell-off period (or as of the end of the Term, in the event that the Licensee is not entitled to take advantage of the sell-off period) shall be destroyed within fifteen (15) days thereafter, and an affidavit of such destruction, executed by a responsible corporate officer, shall be delivered to the Owner within ten (10) days following such destruction.

4.   The Licensed Product may only be sold within the Licensed Territory. The Licensed Product shall not be exported to countries outside of the Licensed Territory, nor knowingly sold to buyers who do so.

5.   (a)   The Licensee shall keep true and accurate books and records with respect to all transactions pursuant to this license, in accordance with generally accepted accounting principles.

      (b)   The Licensee shall deliver a true and accurate accounting statement to the Owner (to the attention of Owner's Accounting Department) within forty-five (45) days after the end of each calendar quarter during which copies of the Licensed Product are sold hereunder, or during which moneys are collected by or credited to the Licensee with respect thereto. Such accounting statement shall be accompanied by payment of any amount shown to be due to the Owner thereon.

      (c)   The timely rendition of accounting statements, and the timely payment of any amount(s) due or to become due hereunder (whether by way of fixed payments or by reason of sales of the Licensed Product), shall be of the essence of this agreement.

      (d)   (i)   The Owner shall have the right from time to time, upon at least ten (10) days' prior written notice to the Licensee, to examine and audit the Licensee's books and records relative to this agreement, and to make copies or extracts of relevant portions therefrom. Each statement (and the related accounting period) shall be available for examination and audit for four (4) years after such statement is received by the Owner, or, if later, until two (2) years after the end of the sell-off period (or the end of the Term, if there is no sell-off period).

            (ii)   Such examination and audit shall take place during normal business hours at the Licensee's address as set forth above, or at such other address at which the Licensee's books and records are then regularly kept.

            (iii)   Such examination and audit shall be at the Owner's expense, provided, however, that in the event that any such examination and audit reveals an underpayment of ten percent (10%) or more for the period(s) audited, the Licensee shall pay the reasonable cost of such examination and audit.

6.   (a)   While the Owner shall have the right to refer to the Composition in the packaging for the Licensed Product and/or in advertising or promotional materials related thereto, it is a condition of this license that neither the music nor the lyrics of the Composition are to be used in commercials or in printed form by or under the authority of the Licensee.

(b)   Further, it is also a condition of this license that the copyright notice prescribed above appear on each copy of the Licensed Product, on any package, insert, or liner used in connection therewith, and on any advertising or promotional materials used with respect to the Licensed Product.

7.   (a)   (i)   The Licensee shall at all times pertinent to this license maintain in full force and effect errors and omissions insurance and public liability insurance with $1,000,000/- $3,000,000 limits, issued by a reputable carrier and naming the Owner, its officers, agents, employees and directors as additional insureds, and providing that coverage shall not be terminated without thirty (30) days' prior notice to the Owner.

(ii)   A certificate of such coverage shall be delivered to the Owner prior to the first shipment of copies of the Licensed Product hereunder.

(b)   In addition, the Licensee shall at all times pertinent to this license comply with all applicable federal, state and local statutes, ordinances, and regulations applicable to the manufacture, distribution, advertising or sale of the Licensed Product, including but not limited to, licensing laws, safety regulations, and consumer-protection laws.

8.   Any failure on the part of the Licensee to render accounting statements and/or to make payment when due, or any other breach of this license not cured by the Licensee within thirty (30) days following receipts of written notice from the Owner, shall constitute cause for termination of the Term of this license by the Owner (and shall void the sell-off period).

9.   (a)   Each party warrants and represents to the other that it has the full right, power, and authority to enter into and to perform this agreement and, in the case of the Owner, to grant the rights granted to the Licensee hereunder.

(b)   (i)   Each party hereby indemnifies the other, its officers, directors, agents and employees and agrees to hold it and them harmless from and against any and all loss, damage, cost or expense (including reasonable outside attorneys' fees and court costs) which may be incurred as the result of a breach of this agreement on the part of the indemnitor.

(ii)   Each party shall notify the other party promptly of any claim, action or proceeding to which the foregoing indemnity relates, and the notified party shall have the right to participate in the defense thereof by counsel of its choice, at its sole cost and expense.

(iii)   However, in the event that any claim is made that the Composition infringes any other musical work (or any other third party right), the Owner shall have the right and obligation to assume control of the defense of such claim (and any related action or proceeding).

(c)   (i)   This agreement has been entered into in, and is to be interpreted in accordance with the laws of, the State of California. This license constitutes the entire agreement between the parties, superseding any and all prior oral and/or written agreements, and may not be altered or amended except by a further written agreement signed by both parties.

(ii)   Any and all disputes with respect to the interpretation and/or enforcement of this license shall be resolved in the Federal or State Courts situated in Los Angeles County, and both parties hereby submit to the jurisdiction of such Courts for such purpose.

(iii)   In any litigation between the parties, the prevailing party shall be entitled to recover its reasonable outside attorneys' fees and court costs.

(d)   (i)   Any notice required or permitted to be given pursuant to this agreement shall be given by registered or certified mail (return receipt requested), by telex or other telegraphic means, or by personal delivery under circumstances permitting delivery to be verified (e.g., Federal Express) to the parties at their respective addresses set forth above, or to such address as a party may hereafter designate by notice in like manner.

(ii)   All notices to the Owner shall be directed to the attention of the Vice President, Legal & Business Affairs, with a copy by ordinary mail to the Executive Vice President.

(iii)   Notice shall be deemed given when sent in accordance with this paragraph, except for notice of change of address, which shall only be effective when received.

LICENSES FOR COMPUTER SOFTWARE, MULTI-MEDIA DISKS, AND NEW MEDIA PRODUCTS

SUMMARY

TECHNOLOGICAL DEVELOPMENTS

1. Computer Software
   A. Videogame or Entertainment Software
   B. Educational Software
   C. Music Software
   D. Musical Instrument Digital Interface (MIDI) Software
   E. Business Software
2. Multi-Media Programs
3. New Media Products
   A. Karaoke
   B. Electronic Bulletin Board Services (BBS)
   C. Holographic Motion Pictures

CONSIDERATIONS IN GRANTING AND CLEARING LICENSES FOR COMPUTER SOFTWARE, MULTI-MEDIA PROGRAMS, AND NEW MEDIA PRODUCTS

1. Fee Structure
   A. Flat Fee
   B. Royalty
   C. Pro Rata
   D. Applicability of the Compulsory License Provision
2. Value of the Song
3. Importance of the Song in Relation to Its Intended Use
   A. Special Nature of Interactive Works
   B. Traditional Factors
4. Scope of the Use
   A. Media
   B. Term
   C. Exclusivity

D. Territory

ADDITIONAL CONSIDERATIONS IN CLEARING LICENSES FOR MULTI- MEDIA AND NEW MEDIA PRODUCTS

1. Understanding All the Rights Involved
2. Educate the Music Copyright Owner

FORMS

CHAPTER **14**

LICENSES FOR COMPUTER SOFTWARE, MULTI-MEDIA DISKS, AND NEW MEDIA PRODUCTS

A t the turn of the century, music publishing involved primarily the sale of sheet music and the promotion of live perform-ances. Since then, advances in technology have opened up large, new markets for the promotion of music: beginning with player pianos, which gave rise to the market for mechanical piano rolls; to record players, which gave rise to the long-playing album; to motion pictures, radio, and television by broadcast, cable, and worldwide satellite transmission; and to the technological miracles developed within the current generation, such as videotape players, compact audio laser disks, audiovisual laser discs, video games, karaoke ma-chines, computer software, multi-media programs, sound-capable silicon chips, and on-line information databases and electronic bulletin boards.

The future promises no letup from these relentless advances in technology. The coming revolution in our telephone system, which will allow low-cost, high speed digital transmissions of information and software, should combine with existing technologies to open up vast new markets and means of delivering music and other entertain-ment programming. These technological achievements and develop-ments, together with the industries that support them, are converging to form a highly complex and interlocking system of distribution capable of delivering music to the listening public when and where it wants it.

These technologies will also afford copyright owners of entertain-ment programming new ways to control and enforce their exclusive rights in their works. The trend will be away from flat-fee and blanket license arrangements and toward *pay-per-view*, which allows copyright owners to collect a fee each time their work is performed, publicly or privately. Computer databases and information systems will also enable distributors of entertainment programming to track and analyze the tastes and buying habits of consumers of entertainment works. This will allow a more efficient communication between providers and consumers of these works, giving consumers information about the works available that are likely to interest them, and giving producers information about what kinds of works should be produced and marketed to which consumers.

Future applications of these technologies, and of technologies that have yet to be developed, will challenge the music publisher's ability to understand and exploit these new means of delivery. The challenges which these emerging technologies present can best be approached with a willingness to invest the time to understand them, and such under-standing can best be gained by one's actually becoming a "user" of some of these new technologies. For example, you need only use a personal computer and modem to dial up an electronic bulletin board service to gain insight into what might be in store for the electronic distribution of printed music. By the same token, if one does not understand how a computer and telephone lines could affect the future of printed music publishing, it serves to underscore the point that one must actually use the technology to fully understand its full portent. Copyright owners who fail to understand the new technologies risk being left behind, in much the same way as the silent film maker was left behind upon the advent of "talkies."

This chapter will first sketch some of the recent developments in high technology, such as computer software, videogames, multi-media, karaoke, and other new media products and distribution systems, and will then discuss considerations in granting and clearing licenses for the use of music in these products.

TECHNOLOGICAL DEVELOPMENTS

The advent of the microchip, a device which can pack hundreds of thousands of "transistors" onto a sliver of silicon the size of a thumbnail, has spawned several entirely new categories of commercial and con-sumer products. A greeting card that plays a song when you open it up (see Chapter 13) is just one simple example of a musical application of the computer chip. These chips have become so powerful that computing power previously reserved for the large refrigerated rooms that housed large mainframe computers is now available in personal computers and videogame players that you can buy for a few hundred dollars. The computer chip is, indeed, the electronic "brain" upon which all of these technological developments rely.

1. Computer Software

The term computer program, or *computer software*, refers to the set of instructions given to a machine to bring about a certain result. The copyright law provides the same protection to computer software that is afforded to literary works.[1] It is important not to confuse the computer with the software that instructs the computer what to do. The computer is the physical machine, or *hardware,* that performs certain limited kinds of tasks; the *software* is the copyrighted work that provides the instructions that tell the machine what tasks to perform. An apropos analogy that best illustrates the relationship between computer hardware and computer software is one which suggests that you conceive the software as the *record album* and the hardware as the *record player and stereo system* that plays the music embodied in the record album. Just as the record player cannot play music without the record, a computer cannot perform any meaningful tasks without the computer software that instructs it.

The following outlines the various kinds of computer software being marketed for use on computers in use today, including videogame software (sometimes referred to as entertainment software), educational software, music software for professional and amateur musicians, musical instrument digital interface (MIDI) software, and business software. Other forms of software-related products are discussed under the headings, "Multi-Media Programs" and "New Media Products."

---

[1] 17 U.S.C. Secs. 101, 117.

A. Videogame or Entertainment Software

Increasingly, producers of *videogames*, or *entertainment software* as they prefer to call it, are recognizing the value of music as an integral part of the entertainment mix provided to users of videogames. For example, the enjoyment of a simple electronic table tennis game, such as *Pong*, may be enhanced if the game could be instructed to play a victory jingle, such as the theme from the movie *Rocky*, each time the player succeeds at performing a certain score or level of competence. Certainly, the absence of the music from the movie *Star Wars* would be conspicuous if it were not an element of a videogame based upon the movie.

Initially, videogames were incorporated exclusively in large game machines which contain their own television monitors and control systems (e.g., joy stick, buttons, pedals). These machines are normally distributed to pin-ball arcades, now called *video arcades*. Makers of these machines require synchronization licenses for the incorporation of music in the videogames programmed into these machines. Most video arcades obtain performance licenses from ASCAP or BMI and any music that may emanate from a videogame machine at an arcade would be covered by the arcade's performance license. The vast proportion of videogames sold today, however, are sold in the form of cartridges or computer "floppy" disks designed for use on home videogame machines, such as Nintendo, or personal computers, such as the Apple Macintosh or IBM and IBM-compatible personal computers. A new generation of *portable* videogame machines, such as the *Gameboy* by Nintendo, have become popular, and the importance of the audio aspects of these games is evidenced by the earphone attachments that these game machines now support.

B. Educational Software

We have barely seen the tip of the proverbial iceberg of potential educational applications to which computers can be put to use, and music is expected to play an important role in the development of these applications. We are beginning to see computer software that teaches the alphabet and reading by phonics, electronic books that contain lyrics or play music, software that teaches you how to play the piano, and software that explores the boundaries of music appreciation. The recording of popular music in even non-music specific software, such as the geography program, *Where in the World is Carmen San Diego*, and history program, *Where in Time is Carmen San Diego?* (both published by Broderbund Software) is likely to greatly enhance the educational experience these programs aim to provide.

One of the first products to demonstrate the marvels of applying computer technology in education is a program called *The Magic Flute*, a set of three CD-ROM optical disks for use on an Apple Macintosh personal computer equipped with a CD-ROM drive or player. Published by Warner New Media, a division of Time-Warner, Inc., the program contains a digital recording of Mozart's opera, enhanced by more than one hour of commentary, additional music, and more than 7000 screens of information. While listening to the opera, or any portion of the opera, a user may simultaneously read the English or German libretto, or put the program on hold to read the story, look up a definition in the glossary, explore a character analysis, or view a complete map of the opera, and then, of course, take a final exam.

Beethoven: The Ninth Symphony is an interactive optical disk program that can be played on any IBM-compatible personal computer using the Microsoft Windows operating system. With this program, you can see and hear everything from an overview of the symphonic form to an in-depth analysis of each movement of the *Ninth Symphony*. The program, distributed by Microsoft Corporation, includes biographical material, examples of Beethoven's other works, and an interactive game for one to four players to test your musical knowledge.

More recently, *Luciano Pavarotti: O Sole Mio, Louis Armstrong: An American Songbook,* and *Mozart: A Musical Biography* have been released by the MusicWorks team at Philips Interactive Media of America. These programs may be played on a regular CD player, but if you have a CD-I player, a special interactive media player that works with a television set, you can explore all the interactive features that the CD-I format affords. For example, the Mozart disk contains a full multi-media biography of the composer, features artists performing his works, and allows you to play an interactive version of a musical dice game invented by Mozart. Philips and Sony Corporation, who manufacture these CD-I players, are betting that this technology will become as widely popular as home video tape machines.

C. Music Software

Some personal computer software programs were specifically designed for professional or amateur composing and playback of musical compositions.

For example, MusicWorks, published by Hayden Software, is an inexpensive computer program that operates on the Apple Macintosh computer. MusicWorks presents on the computer screen the five-line musical staff, and gives the user the ability to place on the staff musical notes, including whole, half, quarter, eighth, sixteenth, etc., and all of the customary musical notation terminology. The program allows the user to arrange his own notes on the musical scale or to load into the computer pre-arranged notes. The user can then "play" the notes in sequence, rendering a performance of the song so arranged. The program also has the ability to store the music in the computer's permanent memory, together with any changes made to the music by the user, so that it can later be played back. Any notation of the songs that are presented on the computer screen can be printed out on the user's printer, and, depending on the resolution of the user's computer printer, the print-out may have a quality approaching that of printed sheet music. When played, the music may be heard through the speaker provided with the computer, or an external speaker.

More sophisticated music software programs provide the user with the capability to completely automate the music creation process. Midisoft's STUDIO, which operates on IBM-compatible personal computers using the Microsoft Windows operating system, includes a sequencing program that has to be seen to be believed. While you are playing an electronic keyboard, or any properly equipped musical instrument, the program displays your exact musical performance instantly on the screen as standard musical notation. With powerful editing features, you can rearrange your music, combine parts, change instruments, replay your changes, print it out, or save your performance to a file on your computer disk for later playback.

D. Musical Instrument Digital Interface (MIDI) Software

The magic behind the process in Midisoft's STUDIO is something called the *musical instrument digital interface (MIDI)*. MIDI is the standard computer format or protocol for transmitting music data electronically. Most electronic instruments today, such as electronic piano keyboards and synthesizers, are MIDI equipped. Even sounds from acoustic instruments (including the human voice) can be converted to MIDI with special hardware and software. Compared to digitized audio, MIDI data is significantly more compact and more easily manipulated without loss of sound quality.

The significant aspect of this new technology is that it allows you to store the equivalent of a live performance on a computer disk. Since all of these music computer *files* are stored in digital magnetic form, they can be easily copied from one computer diskette to another, and can even be transmitted over telephone lines.

This is not expensive technology. Midisoft's STUDIO program has a suggested retail price of less than $250. A MIDI interface card can be installed into any IBM-compatible computer for about $100. The latest, powerful IBM-compatible personal computers are available for less than $2000.

Programs such as MusicWorks and STUDIO, and the music files they can produce, raise several interesting music licensing questions with which the music industry is just beginning to grapple.

For example, is a MIDI computer file a phonorecord (i.e., a mechanical reproduction), the distribution of which requires a mechanical license, or is it a copy of an audiovisual work, the distribution of which may be negotiated, through the terms, for example, of a synchronization or videogram license? The Harry Fox Agency has considered the fixation of music in MIDI files and, to deal with the increasing number of requests for this new form of license, has developed a special form MIDI license, a copy which is set forth as Form 14.2 at the end of this chapter. While producers of many forms of MIDI files might legitimately assert that the compulsory license provision (17. U.S.C. 115) applies to their works, MIDI appears to be emerging as a right separate and outside the scope of conventional mechanical and synchronization licenses.

Is a computer file that contains the ability to display music notation on the screen of a personal computer and to print out the notation on a computer printer the equivalent of printed sheet music? Is it a combination of sheet music and mechanical reproduction or audiovisual work? The question becomes significant, because many music copyright owners have granted to print publishers the rights to distribute their music in printed form, such as sheet music and folios, on an exclusive basis. If the music copyright owner grants permission for the reproduction of MIDI files, and those files have the capability of printing out musical notation on laser printers, a print publisher who holds exclusive print rights in the music might take the position that the granting of the license was a breach of its exclusive print rights contract.

The Harry Fox license set forth as Form 14.2 at the end of this chapter states that the license does not grant permission to the licensee "to program into the MIDI sequence [file] the capability of making any other use of the Composition not expressly authorized" by the license. One of the permissions not granted to the licensee is the license to print the licensed composition in sheet music form. Further, the license requires that a warning notice be placed conspicuously on each copy of the MIDI file stating that it is a violation of copyright law to print the file in the form of standard music notation without the permission of the copyright owner. While it is clear that the music copyright owner can limit the scope of the license to prevent the licensee from distributing laser-printed copies of musical notation displayed by a licensed MIDI file, it is not clear how one who distributes files that operate with, for example, Midisoft's STUDIO program, would practically be able to comply with a requirement of making a file that is capable of displaying musical notation on a computer screen incapable of having that notation printed out on a printer.

It would appear that the distribution of MIDI files containing copyrighted music notation capable of being printed out would not be within the scope of the license. If the copyright owner still owned the print rights, the license could be revised to permit the use of any print capabilities inherent in the software. Otherwise, the only way one could clear a license for such use would be to also obtain clearance from the owners of the exclusive print rights. This, obviously, is a burdensome solution, and perhaps one that might not be worth the effort.

It seems that the purpose of the severe scope of the Harry Fox MIDI license is to protect music copyright owners who have granted exclusive print rights from breach of contract claims of holders of exclusive print rights in their music. Should such a breach of contract dispute ever occur, the resolution of the case may well depend upon what was meant by the term "print" or "sheet music" at a time when the only means of distributing copies of music notation were on paper. An analysis of the question would parallel those considered in Chapter 11 on Old Licenses and New Uses. We suspect that, unless there is language in these contracts specifically covering electronic forms of printed music, the courts would narrowly construe "print" and "sheet" music as being limited to distribution on paper form. Perhaps distribution of sheet music via telecopier, or "fax," machines would still be considered a form of distribution on paper, but files that are only usable with the aid of a machine or device (i.e., a computer) take on an entirely different character. If this does, in fact, become the result of these cases, then obtaining clearance of publishers who hold exclusive print rights to music for distribution of MIDI files containing printable music notation would become unnecessary.

Finally, a MIDI file distributor would probably have no need to be concerned with potential violations of exclusive print rights by purchasers and users of MIDI files, because it is not likely that a music copyright owner could legally prevent a purchaser of a licensed MIDI file from printing out a copy of the musical notation for personal use, and not for distribution. The printing out of MIDI files by the end user would be akin to the home taping of sound recordings, a practice which was specifically condoned by Congress when considering the Copyright Act of 1978.

The publisher of MusicWorks has developed a companion program called, VideoWorks. VideoWorks allows you to create animated cartoons that can be performed on your computer screen. The animation produced can, of course, be synchronized with music. The publishers of programs such as MusicWorks and VideoWorks, may well wish to include arrangements of copyrighted musical compositions on the disks distributed with the software. Independent software publishers, sometimes referred to as publishers of "add-on" software, may wish to separately sell diskettes that contain copyrighted music that can be played back by the user of such programs. Users may wish to exchange songs stored on disk with other users. Since computer software files may easily be transferred over telephone lines, such song files may well find themselves on one or more electronic bulletin board services, which allows callers to transfer, or *download,* these files to their own personal computers over the telephone. Music copyright owners are beginning to see more and more requests for these forms of uses, but few standards have yet emerged on how music copyright owners can best respond to these requests.

E. Business Software

The variety of applications to which powerful desktop and home computers can be applied is limited only by the imagination of the people who are writing the software for use on these machines. Today, the largest segment of the market for personal computer software is software designed for business uses, such as word processing, electronic spreadsheets and database management systems.

Few personal computer software programs designed for business, however, require music. Nevertheless, some business programs may lend themselves to the application of music in unexpected ways. For example, business graphics programs, used by executives to make business presentations, have the capability to perform a variety of special effects. One product, *Quattro Pro* from Borland International, an integrated spreadsheet and graphics presentation program for IBM-compatible personal computers, allows the user to place sound effects in business presentations that can best be described as "electronic slide shows." Computer software diskettes containing customized sound effects, including public domain and copyrighted music, may well become an after-market product sold by independent software publishers to users of the *Quattro Pro* product.

If a software publisher wished to distribute a set of "sound files" on diskette which, when combined with a presentation graphics software program, performs copyrighted music, would the use of the music require a mechanical reproduction license or a synchronization license? Under what circumstances would a performance license be required for a business presentation which used such sound files? These are questions that remain without definitive answers.

2. Multi-Media Programs

It has been said that we are now in an "age of information" and nothing could be better evidence of that than the advent of new technologies that are revolutionizing the way we accumulate, store, retrieve, analyze, and interact with the vast amounts of information being generated by modern society. One of the most exciting developments that has emerged in this new era has been the convergence of various audio, visual, and database technologies to form what has been called, appropriately, *multi-media.*

We use the term multi-media here to describe a certain class of products that combine the attributes of several different traditional media, such as motion pictures, still photographs, recorded sounds, printed text, computer generated sounds and graphics, and the like. Most multi-media programs are designed to be used in an *interactive* way, with the user controlling the sequence and organization of the information or entertainment that is to be produced or generated.

In the preceding section concerning educational software, we described several examples of music-related educational applications of interactive multi-media, including *Mozart's The Magic Flute*, a CD-ROM disk for the Apple Macintosh; *Beethoven's Ninth Symphony,* a CD-ROM disk for IBM-compatible computers; and *Louis Armstrong: An American Songbook,* a CD-I disk for Philips or Sony home CD-I players.

Another exciting development in the field of interactive media is the advent of the electronic encyclopedia. Britannica Corporation has released a multi-media version of *Compton's Encyclopedia* for use on Apple Macintosh and IBM-compatible personal computers. Music copyright owners should expect to see in the future the creation of multi-media encyclopedias dedicated to music, such as an encyclopedia of jazz and popular music. The *electronic discography* that might be included in such a work could allow the user to listen to clips from the listed recordings, or read the music notation or lyrics of any particular song, at the mere press of a button.

3. New Media Products

The term new media is used here to encompass a variety of products that are just coming on the market, as well as products that have not yet been invented. Several new technologies are only now converging and the result has been and will continue to be the establishment of new markets for licensing musical works and new means of distributing these works. Consider some existing, and yet to exist, examples:

A. *Karaoke*

In the 1940's, the Ben Yost singers made popular *sing-along* performances in night clubs of that era. Later, Mitch Miller further popularized the idea with a highly successful television program called, *Sing-along with Mitch.* The modern-day equivalent of these sing-along programs is *karaoke* (pronounced "Kara-OK"), which has become quite a phenomenon in Japanese night life. Meaning literally "empty orchestra," karaoke is the sing-along of the 1990's. In Japan, a businessman may take his guests to a small bar, where they may imbibe western spirits and take turns at karaoke singing.

A karaoke system is composed of special hardware, which combines a stereo amplifier with a compact disk player, hooked to a television monitor. Recordings of standard songs are digitally recorded without the lead vocal, often fully orchestrated with back-up singers. The disk also contains the lyrics for the lead vocal. In a typical Japanese karaoke bar, a patron, usually after having imbibed a few drinks to acquire the nerve necessary to volunteer,[2] chooses a song from a list of titles, walks up to a small stage, faces the audience (of other bar patrons), and views a small television monitor facing him on the stage. When the music starts, the lyrics begin to scroll onto the monitor, highlighted, line by line, in tempo with the music to cue the performer when to sing the appropriate line. The karaoke players come equipped with special features, such as echo, reverb and pitch control, which can make even the worst voice seem listenable. The lyrics are usually displayed in the foreground of random motion pictures of popular American scenes, such as surfing, and other amusement scenes. A video camera may be focused on the performer and the performer's image may be displayed on video monitors located throughout the bar. The karaoke bars, where performances of music by karaoke takes place, are licensed by performance rights societies.

This technology has been marketed in several novel ways. Consumers at a shopping mall may now go to what is called a *karaoke booth* where they can render a live karaoke performance and purchase a videotape of their performance to take home. Complete karaoke systems for home use made by companies such as Pioneer and the Daiichi Kosho Co. are now available for less than $1,000. Karaoke disks for playback on these machines are available for under $20.

Being that there are several uses to which the term karaoke has been applied, a license to permit karaoke use of music should carefully define precisely what forms of karaoke use is permitted. See Form 14.3 at the end of this chapter for an example of a karaoke license agreement.

---

[2] Confirmed by personal experience one late night in Tokyo — Bob.

B. Electronic Bulletin Board Services (BBS)

As we have seen, a variety of computer software programs are available which allow users to arrange musical notes on a musical scale, play these notes in sequence, render a performance of the song so arranged, store this music in the computer's permanent memory (e.g., to a computer *file* on a hard disk or a floppy disk), and reload the file from the computer's disk memory back to the computer's main memory to be played again.

Anything that can be presented on the screen of a personal computer, such as musical notation or lyrics, can be printed out on the user's printer. Depending on the resolution of the user's computer printer, the print-out may have a quality approaching that of printed sheet music. Music, when played on a computer, may be heard through the speaker provided with the computer, or an external speaker. More sophisticated programs give the computer the ability to completely control a professional synthesizer system, so that you can actually store on your computer the equivalent of a live performance. Since all of these music computer "files" are stored in digital magnetic form, they can be easily copied from one computer diskette to another, and can even be transmitted over telephone lines.

An *electronic bulletin board service (BBS)* is a service that enables people with personal computers equipped with modems to communicate with each other over the phone lines. A *modem* (a portmanteau comprising the communications terms, *modulate* and *demodulate*) is a device that converts, or modulates, the information in your computer stored in *binary* or *digital* form (i.e., ones and zeros) to a form that can be transmitted over the phone line, or *analog* form. In simple terms, what happens is that the *ones* of the digital format are converted to a high pitch tone and the *zeros* are converted to a low pitch tone; the modem converts the ones and zeros generated by your computer into a series of analogous high pitched and low pitched tones and sends them over the phone lines to another modem at the receiving end of the line, which is connected to another computer. The receiving modem demodulates, or converts, the high and low pitched tones back into the binary ones and zeros and forwards the signals to the computer where they can be stored to disk or sent to your computer screen in the form of text or pictures.

A BBS is simply a computer—either a mainframe, minicomputer or personal computer—equipped with special software that performs the tasks of an electronic bulletin board and modems connected to telephone lines which can receive calls from users of other computers. BBS services may be run by large national or multinational organizations, such as *CompuServe*, a division of H&R Block, *GEnie*, a division of General Electric, and *Prodigy*, a joint venture between IBM and Sears; by small regional services, and even by personal computer users operating a BBS system out of their homes. These home BBS operators, called *sysops* (i.e., system operators), range from professionals, such as doctors and lawyers operating a board as a forum for local colleagues, to teenagers offering electronically stored nude photographs and likenesses of favorite television celebrities.

A BBS is like an electronic meeting place, where anyone, at any time of day or night, from virtually anywhere in the world where adequate telephone service is available, can call up and leave messages to others, receive messages left by others, participate in live, *real-time* or *chat conferences*, or transfer down to their computers (i.e., *download*) virtually any kind of computer file that can be stored on a computer, or transfer to the BBS (i.e., *upload*) any kind of computer file to enable others to download such computer files to their computers. When those computer files contain copyrighted music—whether in a form that can be printed on paper, as sound recordings that can be played on a computer, or in MIDI format that can be played via computer on electronic music equipment—interesting music licensing problems arise.

Is the downloading of these files—the sending and receiving of high pitched tones representing the ones and zeros of the binary format—a "performance" of the music or the making of a copy? How should the music industry address the practical problem of collecting royalties for such uses? What would be the appropriate license fee to charge for such use? If anyone with a personal computer and a copy of BBS software can instantly set up a BBS, how will copyright owners practically enforce their copyrights?

The implications of the transfer of computer files containing music to and from electronic bulletin boards is potentially far reaching. Whole libraries of sheet music stored in electronic form can be made available on a BBS for downloading through the telephone to any computer hooked up to a phone line by modem. Digitized recordings, MIDI files, and any of the files that work with any of the computer software products described in the preceding sections of this chapter can be distributed the same way. It is not surprising that music copyright owners tend to exhibit some concern and fear when approached by persons seeking licenses for new uses such as this.

C. Holographic Motion Pictures

Research scientists in Japan and other countries are developing new forms of audiovisual media. One technology under development is *holographic projection*—the projection of visual images in three dimensions. A potential application of this technology in an entertainment program would be theater productions in which characters and scenery are projected in such a way that they look like live characters walking on a stage. A live stage performance on Broadway in New York could be simultaneously projected to legitimate theatres across the country, or a Shakespearean play recorded on a holographic laser disk could be projected in three dimensions right in front of you in your living room. These works might also have interactive qualities, allowing the audience to participate or affect the denouement of the work presented, or interact with the work as though they were players of a videogame.

Licenses for the use of music in such works would not look much different from the standard synchronization license and videogram license provisions in use today. Nevertheless, unless the licenses issued today are carefully drafted to reflect the intent of the parties (e.g., would any of the uses described in the preceding paragraph be considered a "television exhibition" as that term is used in many synchronization licenses today?), old licenses might be construed as permitting new uses against the better interests of the copyright owners (see Chapter 11).

CONSIDERATIONS IN GRANTING AND CLEARING LICENSES FOR COMPUTER SOFTWARE, MULTI-MEDIA PROGRAMS, AND NEW MEDIA PRODUCTS

Licensing the use of music in such products requires consideration of some of the same basic factors discussed in preceding chapters, including the fee structure, the value of the song, the importance of the song in relation to its intended use, and the scope of the intended use.

1. Fee Structure

A. Flat Fee

In certain limited circumstances, it may be appropriate for a music copyright owner to charge a one-time, flat fee, for the use of music in certain computer software, multi-media, or new media works. Such a fee structure would be appropriate where the software will not be offered for sale. Interactive multi-media is being increasingly used for corporate training purposes, and the use of music in such works, where relatively few copies will be made and none sold, would warrant a flat fee, much like a synchronization fee for nontheatrical motion pictures. However, the music copyright owner should be sure to either (i) define the license narrowly to assure that a subsequent decision by the licensee to distribute copies of the work for commercial sale would require further permission of the copyright owner, or (ii) structure the fee so that if the licensee elects to commercially release the work, royalties will be paid on the basis of each unit distributed or revenues derived from such sales. The form of license for such arrangements would be similar to Forms 9.5 and 9.6 set forth at the end of Chapter 9.

B. Royalty

Like the use of music in consumer products, the performance of music in the course of using computer software, videogames, multi-media programs and new media products will usually be *private*, not public. Because no fees are collectable for private performances of music, the music copyright owner will seek alternative means to share in the economic success of the use. The most common means is collecting a royalty based on the sales of the work embodying the music. The fee structure for most uses of music in computer software, multi-media and new media products is, therefore, much the same as that found in videogram licenses and licenses for consumer musical products. See Forms 10.1 through 10.7 at the end of Chapter 10, and Forms 12.1 and 12.2 at the end of Chapter 12.

C. Pro Rata

Licensing the use of music in certain computer software, multimedia, or new media products poses a special problem that usually does not arise in the case of other consumer products, such as music boxes, exercise machines, and greeting cards. In each of the latter three examples, it is unlikely that more than one song will be required. With respect to computer software, multi-media programs, and new media products, it is likely that several songs, perhaps hundreds of songs, will be used in the work. For example, a single software disk, such as a floppy disk or CD-ROM laser disk may contain hundreds or thousands of files, each containing music in the MIDI format or some similar format capable of being performed with the aid of a computer. Similarly, a multi-media encyclopedia reproduced on laser disks may also contain portions of thousands of songs in mechanical or "electronic print" format.

In instances where there is more than one song involved in the work, music copyright owners will typically request a royalty, using a percentage of net revenues *pro rated* among the number of copyrighted musical compositions in the work. For example, if there are 10 songs in the computer software or new media program, and the royalty percentage charged is 5%, the royalty for the use of one particular song would be 1/10 of 5% of the net revenues that the producer of the computer software program receives on sales of the work. Of course, this does not mean that the owners of the 9 other musical compositions used in the software will receive the same fee. Each owner would negotiate its own pro rata percentage or other license fee for the use of the music.

A copyright owner granting a license containing a provision for the payment of royalties on the basis of a pro rata share in relation to all of the musical compositions in the work should be certain the license provides that only *copyrighted* musical compositions be used in calculating the share. In other words, songs in the public domain, such as *The Star Spangled Banner*, should not be counted in determining the number of songs in the work. This is to prevent the licensee from adding several, or hundreds, of public domain songs to the work at no cost for the purpose of reducing the amount of royalties payable to owners of licensed musical compositions in the work. Nor should sound recordings be included in the calculation of the number of songs used to pro rate the royalties—only musical compositions.

A person seeking to clear a license to use a song in a work containing hundreds or thousands of songs should be prepared to come across one or more music copyright owners unfamiliar with multi-media technologies. A copyright owner inexperienced with licensing music for use in such works may insist upon receiving a royalty rate on par with rates normally obtained when licensing music for works containing one or just a few compositions. For example, if the music copyright owner asks for an un-prorated 5% of net revenues for the use of a song in a work that will contain several hundred songs, you may have to devote some further time educating the copyright owner about the nature of the use.

Pro rating the royalty based upon the number of songs, or copyrighted songs, appearing in the work, may not always be the optimal or fairest method of structuring a fee for a particular use of a composition. Either the music copyright owner or the producer, depending upon the circumstances, could take the position that it would not be fair to pro rate the fee on a straight line basis (i.e., dividing the fee strictly by the number of songs in the work), without accounting for the duration that each song appears in the work or the quality of the use.

But alternative methods of pro rating fees among works are often ineffective or inefficient. Some have suggested that the duration of each song used be a factor, but this would favor long symphonic works over shorter more popular compositions. Others have suggested an allocation on the basis of how much *real estate*, or memory space, each work uses on the disk containing the work, but this poses special problems. The amount of disk space used by a MIDI file that can generate a performance with the aid of a computer is significantly less than the disk space required by an analog or even digital recording of the very same performance. Thus, some recordings would be favored over others on a purely arbitrary basis.

Producers of multi-media works have suggested that music copyright owners should not forget that permission must be cleared to use a multitude of other types of media works in the multi-media program. They have proposed that the disk space used by all the music on the disk should be compared with the disk space used by all other materials, such as text, photographs, moving pictures, dialogue, and other sounds. Under this method, the producer might propose to budget 20% of revenues to royalties and suggest that an allocation be made among the various types of works used on the disk, as for example, 25% to music, 25% to visuals, 25% to text, and 25% to monologue or dialogue. Leaving aside the merits of this proposal, it still leaves open the question of how the percentage paid for music would be allocated among the owners of the music (and sound recording) copyrights used in the multi-media program.

Perhaps the soundest method of allocation, and perhaps the easiest to administer, is the straight-line proration based on the number of copyrighted songs used in the work, and adjusted for the relative importance of the song in relation to its intended use by raising or lowering the percentage charged for the particular song. For example, a valuable song that is used each time the work is accessed might command 7% of the net revenues prorated among the number of copyrighted songs in the work; a less valuable song that plays a minor role in the work would receive 3% of the net revenues prorated among the number of total copyrighted songs in the work.

Perhaps another compromise that preserves the simplicity of the pro rata method, but one which still takes into consideration the particular value of the song and its importance in relation to its intended use, could be to provide that the use of an important song in a substantial way is assigned a value of two songs in calculating the proration and that less valuable songs used in less substantial ways or duration could be assigned a value of a fraction of one song. Of course, multi-media producers tend to avoid any formula that might complicate their business or produce accounting errors. At the same time, copyright owners might acquiesce to using the simple straight-line proration, considering that it is just not worth negotiating what it takes to account for these finer distinctions, and that it is more important to just make sure the song is included in the work and that the copyright owner will be paid some fair amount for its use.

D. *Applicability of the Compulsory License Provision*

Almost all interactive multi-media programs will contain some audiovisual information, with either moving images or a series of related images. The same is true for videogames and is likely to be true for most educational software. Accordingly, licenses for recording music on such works will normally not be subject to the compulsory license statute.

But what if an interactive program consists solely of text and music, with no pictures or other visual images? Would the mere text displayed on a computer screen be considered a visual image for the purpose of determining whether the compulsory license provision applies? For example, would the use of music in a software program that consists of music performances and the display of merely text on a computer screen (with no motion pictures or other visual images) merely require a mechanical license? More specifically, suppose a publisher produces an electronic discography of every popular recording made in the 1960's which allows the user to select any recording on the list and hear several bars of the recording for identification. Would the text appearing on the screen be considered a "motion picture", a "series of related images", or other "audiovisual work" for purposes of determining whether the compulsory license statute is applicable?

The answer remains entirely unclear. Text presented on a computer screen would seem no different from text contained in the package that comes along with a standard compact disk. However, the user interface of computer software has been held to be an audiovisual work.[3] Thus, the user interface of the computer software that permits you to access the textual material may constitute a sufficient audiovisual work that accompanies the recording that would remove the recorded music from the scope of the compulsory license provision.

2. Value of the Song

As with considerations of licensing music for use in consumer products, music copyright owners should consider the potential impact of associating a hit song with computer software or new media products on the future earning potential of the song. However, it should be noted that associating a song with a computer or new media product, unlike with a consumer product or commercial advertising, is more likely to enhance the earnings potential of the song, than to harm it.

Just as one might get a negative impression by associating a song with a personally or politically undesirable consumer product (e.g., milk of magnesia, nuclear energy), one is likely to get a positive impression from the association of a song with a more popular or

---

[3] *Computer Associates v. Altai*, 23 P.Q. 1241 (2d Cir. 1992).

culturally laudable product (e.g., electronic children's book), a product that is conceived as being on the "cutting edge" of high technology (e.g., computer software, electronic encyclopedia), or a product that is clearly making a contribution to scholarship or historical research (e.g., an electronic discography).

A music copyright owner who is offered to have his song placed in a work such as an electronic encyclopedia or discography should seize the opportunity, because the value of the copyright will benefit from merely the exposure provided by inclusion of the song in such a work. In an information explosion, the competition for a share of the mind of the listening public is intense. Licensing the song, even for a momentary use in an encyclopedia or other interactive product, particularly in those products that are likely to be used as a reference work in libraries, in business, and in the home, will help maintain the relationship between the song and the listening public, and increase the likelihood that future requests for licenses of the song will continue.

For these reasons, a music copyright owner should not allow the difficulties and complexities of setting a proper fee for new media works to get in the way of consummating a license and providing the song with a means of continual exposure to the listening public.

3. Importance of the Song in Relation to its Intended Use

Again, why is a license being sought for *this* particular song? The fewer substitutes for the song that are available, the more the licensee is willing to pay. In contrast with the limited number of songs or themes logically available for a musical doll based on a character of a popular motion picture or television program, there is more likely to be a large variety of songs available to provide in an electronic encyclopedia, a demonstration of the kind of music that was popular in the 1930s. Of course, a limited universe of songs will be available for a videogame software program based upon, for example, *Star Wars*. Careful consideration should be given to the particular circumstances in evaluating the importance of the song in relation to its intended use in computers, multi-media programs and new media products.

A. *Special Nature of Interactive Works*

A special problem may arise in using the usual means of structuring the appropriate license fees for use of music in interactive multi-media works, and this involves an important difference between interactive media devices and traditional works: traditional media are *linear*, while interactive media are *non-linear*.

Traditional media, such as record albums and videotapes, are linear in the sense that they are generally listened to or viewed from beginning to end. By contrast, interactive media, such as compact discs and CD-ROMs, are generally non-linear, in the sense that one can gain immediate access to any portion of the work by skipping from any one point in the work to any other point in the work.

In a traditional work, such as a motion picture, the music that the producer chooses to play over the main title and opening credits of the work will remain the same for every performance of the motion picture and the viewer will hear the music every time he watches the movie (unless he intentionally skips over, or *fast forwards* through, the main title). By contrast, in an interactive work, an excerpt of the song may be played back under a variety of different circumstances. For example, the new media work may be set up so that a few bars of the song, *Tea For Two* is rendered only when a picture of Irving Caesar and Vincent Youmans, the song's writer and composer, appear on the screen. If the user never goes to the part of the work that displays the picture of Irving Caesar and Vincent Youmans, the song will never be performed, even though the work as a whole might be used as much as on a daily basis. It may be impossible to gauge just how much one particular song would be performed, or where it will most likely appear, in relation to the balance of the work. On the other hand, the producer of the interactive work can arrange for the song to be played every time the work is started up by the user, no matter what use will be made of the interactive work in any particular session. Further, the producer can allow the user to customize the work, so that any number of songs can be played every time the user starts up the work. They may alternate randomly or the user can choose to hear only one particular song over and over again.

In other words, the importance of the song in relation to its intended use may depend entirely upon the use put to the work *by the user*. This makes it very difficult to determine just how valuable the music is likely to be in relation to the work in which it is to be incorporated.

B. Traditional Factors

As discussed in Chapter 9, a licensor should consider a variety of factors in determining an appropriate fee for a standard synchronization license (for use of a composition in a motion picture or television program). Such factors may include whether the use is a vocal rendition or merely instrumental; whether the use is of the entire song or just a few bars; whether the music is used as background music or foreground music; whether the use is at a prominent point in the motion picture, such as over the main title or credits; whether the intended use relates to how the composition was originally presented to the public; and whether the music is used to help tell the story. These are all factors which help determine the importance of the song in relation to its intended use. If, for example, the song will be played at the beginning of the motion picture over the main titles of the film, or in its entirety at any point in the film, the use would command a premium fee.

A synchronization license for a traditional work, such as a motion picture, will typically limit the number of seconds the licensed song may be used in the picture. This customary restriction generally causes no difficulties in the context of a motion picture or television program, where the performance of the audiovisual work is usually linear— played from one point in time to another, at one or several instances in the picture. In the context of interactive media, however, difficult questions arise from the fact that, depending upon the interaction between the user and the new media work, there may be no one readily identifiable period of time in which the composition is played during the performance of the work.

Under these circumstances, the rules for determining the appropriate fees for use in traditional works do not lend themselves very well to application in this new media. In a synchronization license for a motion picture, a music copyright owner may use as a rule of thumb the number of seconds the music will be performed in the movie, yet there may be no way of determining that number in an interactive work.

With a variety of possibilities such as these, it behooves the music copyright owner who wishes to maximize the value of his property to gain as much understanding as possible about the media and the particular program in which the music will be licensed. Asking for "most favored nations" status will not work in situations where, as here, it would be virtually impossible to determine whether the licensor of some other song appearing in the work received more favorable terms for its use.

The music copyright owner should learn as much about the particular multi-media work as possible and simply do the best he can to determine the value of the song and the importance of the song in relation to its intended use. It should also be remembered that licensing a few bars of a song for use in an electronic encyclopedia is not the equivalent of licensing the entire song in a work in which the song will always be played from beginning to end. A license fee that is significantly less than the statutory rate for a mechanical license could well be appropriate where only enough of the song is used to allow the listener to recognize the melody, as opposed to the rendering of the entire song.

4. Scope of the Use

A. Media

A copyright owner would want the license to fully describe the product in which the music will be embodied. The work should be referenced by title, or tentative title, and any other useful information to describe the work, thereby defining the scope of the license as narrowly as possible. A person seeking to clear a license would want no limitation on the media format or configuration, as technological advances are rapidly changing the standard formats used in the distribution of these works.

B. Term

It is always in the interest of copyright owners to limit the duration of music licenses. Music copyright owners generally try to limit these licenses to five years, sometimes giving an option to extend for an additional three to five years upon the payment of an additional advance against royalties. The term of most karaoke licenses is currently about seven years.

Insisting upon a fixed limited term, however, might not always be practical. The producer of an interactive encyclopedia, for example, might convincingly argue that it cannot predict just how long the edition of the encyclopedia will remain "in print" and to require a new license between publication of editions would not be practical. In that event, the music copyright owner might suggest that the term be limited to the one edition and its reprints (including foreign language versions) however long new printings are made, but that a new license would be required for subsequent editions. But even this would not be a practical solution in some cases. Because of the ease with which these works can be electronically *updated* (i.e., revised), a new "edition" can be published every month or even every week!

C. Exclusivity

The principles of exclusivity discussed in connection with commercial advertising do not apply equally to computer software, educational software, videogames, multi-media and other new media works. Using music to help establish a product identity is no more a factor in the use of music in an electronic encyclopedia or videogame than it is in the use of music in a motion picture or television program. As is true for synchronization licenses for motion pictures, television and video, exclusivity is rarely granted for uses in interactive media and software.

Accordingly, a music copyright owner would be quite reluctant to provide any form of exclusivity in connection with the licensing of music in computer software or multi-media programs. If exclusivity were considered, the scope of the exclusivity should be very narrowly defined. For example, granting "exclusivity for educational software" when the intent is for works to be distributed in the K-12 educational market, might be construed to cover electronic encyclopedias and even adult training programs. The types of educational software could vary to such a degree that it may be impossible to narrowly circumscribe the terms of exclusivity. In any event, software and new media are usually differentiated sufficiently that a licensee would not normally require exclusivity to the music in order to help differentiate his product in the software market.

D. Territory

Copyright owners have tried to restrict the territory of these licenses to the United States and Canada and require that separate licenses be obtained for use in other territories from their affiliated subpublishers around the world. The world, however, has changed dramatically from the days of locally produced sheet music and phonograph records, and music copyright owners are under increasing pressure to grant worldwide licenses.

It has become the practice of computer software and multi-media producers to establish facilities at one or two locations in the world, such as Singapore or Ireland, where virtually all copies of their products, in various language versions, are made and distributed to their subsidiaries and affiliates around the world. This is a much more efficient method of operation than the traditional means of distributing record albums with which music publishers are familiar. The technology itself is facilitating the trend toward a one-world marketplace: the vast amounts of memory capacity of optical laser disks permit the storage of multiple language versions of a single program all on the same disk, vastly facilitating the distribution of such works overseas. Accordingly, music publishers are beginning to accept proposals for licensing on a worldwide basis to reflect these new technologies and business practices.

Music publishers should, of course, first consider whether they are under any contractual restriction with its songwriters or international co-publishers that would preclude them from issuing a worldwide license without special clearance. Where rights are split by territory (see Chapter 18), the co-administrators of the copyright should work out a deal by which royalties from worldwide licenses may be split in some equitable manner.

Music publishers and those with whom they share music rights overseas should work these deals out among themselves and not try to place unreasonable burdens on the prospective licensee, such as requesting the licensee to account for sales on a territory by territory basis. The rights owner in each territory has a great incentive to cooperate in working out such an arrangement. Rather than provide territory-by-territory accounting, a producer will accept licenses for the territories he can get and simply choose not to sell directly into territories for which he cannot obtain a license. In an environment with multiple distribution channels, producers cannot control the territories in which their products will end up. Consequently, the owner of rights for a territory that refuses to license will discover he receives no royalties for products that end up being sold in his territory.

The music publishers have created much of the bind they are in because of the way they structured their subpublishing deals in the past. Now that the world has changed, they should work out administrative solutions to facilitate the efficient licensing of their copyrights. Anything less would be a disservice to the songwriters they are supposed to represent.

ADDITIONAL CONSIDERATIONS IN CLEARING LICENSES FOR MULTI-MEDIA AND NEW MEDIA PRODUCTS

1. Understanding All the Rights Involved

As noted in Chapter 1, persons seeking to clear licenses for multi-media programs or new media products can avoid difficulties by first fully understanding all of the potential rights that may be involved in the use. For example, if you are seeking permission to use a particular recording in your multi-media program, don't overlook the fact that you will require two separate licenses, one under the copyright in the sound recording and another under the copyright in the underlying musical composition. A license to use the underlying composition may be obtained from the music publisher or its agent, such as the Harry Fox Agency; the license to use the sound recording may be sought by conferring with the record company who owns the recording.

In some cases, more than two licenses to use a certain piece of material will need to be cleared. For example, the use of a simple film clip from a motion picture may require separate permission from each of several parties holding various rights underlying the clip. As noted in Chapter 1, any of the following rights may be hidden beneath the surface of an apparently simple clearance problem: a copyright in the underlying song featured in the clip, a copyright in the recording of the song performed in the clip, the copyright in the motion picture from which the clip was excerpted, a copyright in any choreography appearing in the clip, a copyright in a literary work upon which the clip is based (where the film from which the clip was taken is based upon a novel, non-fiction book, newspaper article, biography, autobiography, etc.), a copyright in a theatrical production (such as a musical play, opera, or ballet) performed in the clip, a copyright in an animated character, a copyright in a still photograph appearing in the clip, a copyright of a translation or arrangement of a work in the public domain, a right of privacy (i.e., the right an individual has "to be left alone") of one or more individuals appearing in the clip, or a right of publicity (i.e., the exclusive right an individual has to the use of one's name, voice, photograph, and likeness) of one or more individuals appearing in the clip.

Considerations in granting and clearing rights to use works other than musical compositions is beyond the scope of this book. However, an example of a license to use a film clip is set forth as Form 14.4 at the end of this chapter. Form 14.6, set forth at the end of this chapter, is an example of a license typically used by record companies and motion picture producers for the synchronization of sound recordings in audiovisual works. An example of a license to use a still photograph is set forth as Form 14.5 and a location release is set forth as Form 14.7.

2.   Educate the Music Copyright Owner

Finally, as also noted in Chapter 1, where necessary, persons seeking to clear licenses for complex works, such as multi-media and new media works, should take the time to educate the music copyright owner on just how the music is intended to be used. For at least the next several years, a substantial number of people in society will remain frightened or distrustful of computers and high technology, but a simple live demonstration of a multi-media application could go a long way to promote the understanding and trust required to persuade a music copyright owner, fearful of making a bad deal, to grant the license you desire.

APPENDIX TO CHAPTER 14
LICENSES FOR COMPUTER SOFTWARE, MULTI-MEDIA DISKS, AND NEW MEDIA PRODUCTS

FORMS

FORM 14.1

MULTI-MEDIA LICENSE USED BY HARRY FOX AGENCY

THE HARRY FOX AGENCY, INC.
205 East 42nd Street
New York, New York 10017

MULTI-MEDIA RIGHTS LICENSE (MMERL)

License No.:
Date of Issuance:

The following provisions shall apply as indicated in the body of this License:

(A) Licensee:

(B) Musical Composition:

(C) Licensor(s) and percentage of ownership:

(D) License Date:

(E) Term:

(F) Advance:

(G) Units:

(H) Royalty Per Unit: "Two times the so-called 'statutory royalty rate' (provided pursuant to Section 115 of the United States Copyright Act for the making and distribution of phonorecords) [17 U.S.C. 115]."

<u>OR</u>

(H) Royalty Per Unit: "_____ cents"

(I)   Territory:

(J)   Software Serial Number:

DEFINITIONS

1.   For the purposes hereof, the following terms shall have the following meanings:

a)   **"MULTI-MEDIA"** shall mean the medium in which a musical composition will be utilized in conjunction with, but not limited to, computer monitor visual displays.

b)   **"MULTI-MEDIA DISK"** which shall include, but not be limited to CD Rom or computer assisted laser disks, shall mean those Multimedia disks containing those musical recordings which is the subject of this license.

C)   The term **"MULTI-MEDIA DISK MARKET"** shall refer to the sale, lease, license, use or other distribution of **MULTIMEDIA DISKS** directly or indirectly to individuals for playback through, but not limited to, a personal computer, whether now in existence or hereafter developed.

d)   **"Copy"** or **"copies"** shall mean all **MULTI-MEDIA DISK** copies manufactured and distributed by Licensee.

Now it is therefore agreed as follows:

1.   Licensee is hereby applying to Licensor for a **MULTI-MEDIA** rights license to use the musical composition referred to in (B) (above) for the purposes of manufacturing, distributing and selling to the public throughout the territory [(I)), **MULTI-MEDIA,** embodying the musical composition.

2.   Licensor hereby grants to the Licensee the following non-exclusive rights with respect to **MULTI-MEDIA DISK,** in all respects subject to the terms and conditions herein provided:

a)   To record and re-record in digital, computer readable or other form consistent with the integral requirements of the **MULTI-MEDIA,** the musical composition for use in whole or in part in connection with and with respect to **MULTI-MEDIA DISK;**

b)   To make and distribute copies of the **MULTI-MEDIA DISK** program throughout the territory only ((l)].

c)   Licensee may make arrangements and orchestrations of the Composition for its recording purposes, however, this license does not include the right to alter the fundamental character of the Composition, to print sheet music or to make any other use of the Composition not expressly authorized hereunder, all rights to uses not expressly granted hereunder are hereby expressly reserved by the Licensor.

3.   Licensee covenants that it shall place on the outside of all containers or, where possible, in every **MULTI-MEDIA DISK** copy a conspicuous notice to clearly read as follows:

c   Title of Composition and Names of writers. Copyright © 19_____ (owner of composition). International Rights Secured. Not for broadcast transmission. All rights reserved. **DO NOT DUPLICATE. NOT FOR SEPARATE RENTAL.**

WARNING: "It is a violation of Federal Copyright Law to synchronize this **MULTI-MEDIA DISK** with video tape or film, or to print this **MULTI-MEDIA DISK** in the form of standard music notation without the express written permission of the copyright owner."

4.   The musical composition recorded as a **MULTI-MEDIA DISK** shall not exceed _____ minutes and _____ seconds.

5.   The use of the musical composition hereunder shall be:

6.   The term during which the rights licensed hereunder may be exercised shall be [the number referred to in (E)] years from the License date (D).

7.   a)   Licensee shall make the royalty payments hereunder, which shall be accompanied by a detailed accounting statement listing units distributed within 45 days after the end of each calendar quarter during which the **MULTI-MEDIA DISK** copies are distributed, equal to [the amount referred to in (H)] per **MULTI-MEDIA DISK** copy of the work which is manufactured and distributed during each such respective calendar quarter. Within thirty (30) days after the execution of this license, Licensee shall make such payment and render such statement for all units distributed prior to the execution of this license.

       b)   In the event that Licensee fails to account and pay royalties as herein provided, Licensor shall have the right to give written notice to Licensee that unless the default is remedied within thirty (30) days from the date of the notice, this license shall be deemed terminated. Such failure to pay and cure default in such thirty (30) day period shall render either the making or the distribution, or both, of all **MULTI-MEDIA DISK** copies hereunder for which royalties have not been paid, actionable acts of infringement under, and fully subject to the remedies provided by the U.S. Copyright Act.

8.   Upon ten business days prior written notice, Licensor, by the Harry Fox Agency ("HFA"), shall have the right during reasonable business hours at Licensee's place of business and at HFA's sole expense to examine, and make copies and extracts from the books and records of Licensee relating to its production, making and distribution of **MULTI-MEDIA** copies hereunder for the purpose of verifying the accuracy of statements and payments and the performance of Licensee's obligations hereunder. Licensee shall not be required to submit to such an examination more than once during any twelve (12) month period.

9.   This license does not include the rights to:

a)   Rent separately the musical composition included in the **MULTI-MEDIA** copies or to permit purchasers or others to do so;

b)   Use the story of the musical composition or dramatically depict the musical composition;

c)   Parody the lyrics and/or music of the musical composition in any way;

d)   Publicly perform, Broadcast/cablecast or transmit the work in any manner;

e)   Make, sell or distribute audio phonorecords of the musical composition;

f)   Utilize a sound recording and/or audiovisual master(s) not owned or separately licensed by Licensee.

10.   All rights of every kind and nature with respect to the composition which are not expressly granted to licensee hereunder are expressly reserved by Licensor.

11.   Licensor warrants only that it has the right to grant this license, and this license is given and accepted without any other representation, warrant or recourse, express or implied, except for Licensor's agreement to repay the consideration paid for this license if the aforesaid warranty should be breached. In no event shall the total liability of the Licensor exceed the total amount of consideration received by it hereunder.

12.   Upon the expiration of this license, all rights herein granted shall cease and terminate and the right to make or authorize any further use or distribution of any recordings made hereunder shall also cease and terminate subject to Licensee's right to sell off its inventory of **MULTI-MEDIA DISK** for an additional period of one year subject to the continuing obligation to pay royalties therefor. No right to make, sell, or distribute **MULTI-MEDIA DISK** programs

or copies embodying the composition shall survive the termination of this license pursuant to Paragraph 7 (A) hereof.

13.   This license does not include a grant of performing rights. The public performance of the musical composition as part of the **MULTI-MEDIA DISK** which is the subject of this license, is expressly conditioned upon such performers or places of performance thereof, having valid performing rights licenses from the respective copyright owners or their designated performing rights societies.

14.   This license supersedes and renders null and void any prior agreements otherwise in effect respecting the Composition and those rights which are the subject of this license.

15.   This license is being entered into on an experimental and nonprejudicial basis, shall apply for the term set forth herein only, and shall not be binding upon or prejudicial to any position taken by Licensor or Licensee for any period subsequent to the period of this license.

16.   This license sets forth the entire understanding of the parties hereto with respect to the subject matter thereof, may not be altered, amended or assigned without an express written instrument to such effect accepted by Licensor and shall be governed and construed by and under the laws of the State of New York applicable to contracts wholly to be performed therein.
                    BY:

                    BY: _____
                            (Licensee)

BY: THE HARRY FOX AGENCY, INC. ON
BEHALF OF:

BY: _____
     (Licensor)

FORM 14.2

MIDI LICENSE USED BY HARRY FOX AGENCY

THE HARRY FOX AGENCY, INC.
205 East 42nd Street
New York, New York 10017
Musical Instrument Digital Interface (MIDI)
Rights License

License No.:
Date of Issuance:

The following provisions shall apply as indicated in the body of this license:

(A)　Licensee:

(B)　Musical Composition:

(C)　Licensor(s) and percentage of ownership:

(D)　License date:

(E)　Term:

(F)　Advance:

(G)　Units:

(H)　Royalty Per Unit:

(I)　Territory:

(J)　Software Serial Number:

DEFINITIONS

For purposes hereof, "MIDI" is an acronym for Musical Instrument Digital Interface, which is an accepted international standard for exchanging musical information on a computer.

For purposes hereof, a "MIDI Sequence" is a computer data file embodying one particular MIDI data recording of the musical Composition, capable of playback through a computer.

For purposes hereof. the term "MIDI" Sequence Market" shall refer to the sale, lease, license, use or other distribution of MIDI Sequences directly or indirectly to individuals for playback through a hardware sequencer or a personal computer connected to a MIDI capable synthesizer using MIDI software or any similar devices, whether now in existence or hereafter developed.

For purposes hereof, the words "copy" or "copies" shall mean all MIDI Sequence copies made and/or distributed by Licensee.

For purposes hereof, the word "computer" shall mean an electronic machine with a visual display used to store, display, manipulate, and analyze data or information fed into it, and control peripheral machinery automatically or otherwise.

1.   We [the Licensee referred to in (A)] are hereby applying to you [the Licensor referred to in (C)] for a MIDI rights license to use the musical composition referred to in (B) for the purposes of manufacturing, distributing and selling to the public throughout the territory [(I)] for public and home use, MIDI sequence(s), in the form of computer software copies embodying the musical composition in (i.e. MIDI sequence copies).

2.   Licensor hereby grants to the Licensee the following non-exclusive rights with respect to MIDI sequence(s), in all respects subject to the terms and conditions herein provided:

(A)   To record and re-record the musical composition for use in connection with respect to MIDI sequence(s);

(B)   To make and distribute copies of the MIDI sequence program throughout the territory only [(I)].

(C)   Licensee may make arrangements and orchestrations of the Composition for its recording purposes, however, this license does not include the right to alter the fundamental character of the Composition, to print sheet music or to make, or to program into the MIDI sequence the capability of making, any other use of the Composition not expressly authorized hereunder.

3   Licensee covenants that it shall place on the outside of all containers and, where possible, in every MIDI sequence copy a conspicuous notice to clearly read as follows:

> (Fill In) title of Song and Names of Writers. The word "Copyright" © 19_____ followed by the Names of Licensor. International Rights Secured. All rights reserved. Not for broadcast or transmission of any kind. **DO NOT DUPLICATE. NOT FOR RENTAL.**

WARNING: "It is a violation of Federal Copyright Law to synchronize this MIDI Sequence with video tape or film, or to print this MIDI Sequence in the form of standard music notation without the express written permission of the copyright owner."

4.   The musical composition recorded as a MIDI sequence(s) shall not exceed _____ minutes and _____ seconds.

5.   The use of the musical composition hereunder shall be non-dramatic background, vocal, instrumental.

6.   The term during which the rights licensed hereunder may be exercised shall be [the number referred to in (E)] years from the license date (D).

7.   Licensee shall make the royalty payments hereunder, which shall be accompanied by a detailed accounting statement listing units sold within 45 days after the end of each calendar quarter during which the MIDI Sequence copies are sold, equal to [the amount referred to in (H)) per MIDI Sequence copy of the work which is sold during each such respective calendar quarter. Within thirty (30) days after the execution of this license, Licensee shall make such payment and render such statement for all units sold prior to the execution of this license.

(A)   In the event Licensee fails to account and pay royalties as herein provided, Licensor shall have the right to give written notice to Licensee that unless the default is remedied within thirty (30) days from the date of the notice, this license shall be deemed terminated. Such failure to pay and cure default in such thirty (30) day period shall render either the making or the distribution, or both, of all MIDI sequence copies hereunder for which royalties have not been paid, actionable acts of infringement under, and fully subject to the remedies provided by the U.S. Copyright Act.

(B)   Licensee shall have the right to maintain a reserve for returns in a reasonable amount consistent with Licensee's arrangements with its distributors, but in no event shall such amount exceed 20% of the number of the MIDI Sequences sold in any Accounting Period. This reserve shall be liquidated quarterly, three quarters after the Accounting Period in which the reserve was maintained. Licensee shall account to Licensor within 45 days after the close of any such Accounting Period in which MIDI Sequence copies are finally distributed. Licensee shall have no right to hold reserves with respect to any copies of the MIDI sequence(s) with respect to which Licensee has received payment.

8.   Upon ten business days' written notice to Licensee, for the purpose of verifying the accuracy of statements rendered, an

authorized representative of Licensor may conduct an annual examination of Licensee's books and records pertaining to the sales of MIDI Sequences during normal business hours at the place where Licensee maintains said books and records.

9.   This license does not include the rights to:

    A.   Rent the MIDI sequence copies or to permit purchasers or others to do so;

    B.   Use the story of the musical composition or dramatically depict the musical composition;

    C.   Parody the lyrics and/or music of the musical composition in any way;

    D.   Broadcast/cablecast or transmit the work in any manner;

    E.   Make, sell or distribute audio phonorecords of the musical composition except as demonstration units;

    F.   Utilize a sound recording and/or audiovisual master(s) not owned or separately licensed by Licensee.

10.   Licensor hereby reserves unto itself all rights of every kind and nature not expressly granted to Licensee herein.

11.   Licensor warrants only that it has the right to grant this license, and this license is given and accepted without any other representation, warrant or recourse, express or implied, except for Licensor's agreement to repay the consideration paid for this license if the aforesaid warranty should be breached. In no event shall the total liability of the Licensor exceed the total amount of consideration received by it hereunder.

12.   Upon the expiration of this License, all rights herein granted shall cease and terminate and the right to make or authorize any

further use or distribution of any recordings made hereunder shall also cease and terminate subject to Licensee's right to sell off its inventory of MIDI Sequences for an additional period of one year subject to the continuing obligation to pay royalties therefore. No right to make, sell, or distribute MIDI Sequence programs or copies embodying the composition shall survive the termination of this license pursuant to Paragraph 7 (A) hereof.

13.   This license does not include a grant of performing rights. The public performance of the musical composition as part of the MIDI sequence program which is the subject of this license, is expressly conditioned upon such performers or places of performance thereof, having valid performing rights licenses from the respective copyright owners or their designated performing rights societies.

14.   This License does not supersede nor in any way affect any prior agreements now in effect respecting the musical compositions or the rights which are the subject of this license.

(A)   However, this license does supersede any mechanical license issued to the Licensee, for the subject musical composition, under the compulsory licensing provisions of the U.S. Copyright Act (or any agreement embodying such provisions).

15.   This License is being entered into on an experimental and non-prejudicial basis, shall apply for the term set forth herein only, and shall not be binding upon or prejudicial to any position taken by Licensor or Licensee for any period subsequent to the period of this license.

16.   This license sets forth the entire understanding of the parties hereto with respect to the subject matter thereof, may not be altered, amended or assigned without an express written instrument to such effect accepted by Licensor and shall be governed and construed by and under the laws of the State of New York.

BY:

BY: _____
       (Licensee)

BY:　THE HARRY FOX AGENCY, INC.
      O/B/O

BY: _____
       (Licensor)

FORM 14.3

LICENSE TO USE MUSIC IN KARAOKE RECORDINGS

KARAOKE SYNCHRONIZATION LICENSE

Date:

Publisher: BIG MUSIC PUBLISHING COMPANY INC.
1000 Sunset Boulevard
Hollywood, California 90069

Producer: JAPAN KARAOKE, LTD.
1-1-1, Aoyama Building
Minato-ku, Tokyo
JAPAN

1.   Programs

The programs covered by this Agreement are all edited versions of a videotaped program (the **"Programs"**) for use in **"Karaoke machines."** Karaoke machines are hereby defined as machines (utilizing technologies and media now known or hereafter devised) which play music videos containing musical tracks but no vocal track, which may be utilized by Producer or Producer's sublicensees in commercial establishments and other public places at which members of the public sing along with such music videos and/or which may be distributed by Producer or its sublicensees for home use by members of the public.

2.   Territory:

The **"Territory"** covered under this Agreement is the United States and Canada and their respective territories and possessions.

3.   Grant of Rights/Restrictions:

3.1. Subject to the terms and conditions contained in this Agreement, Publisher hereby grants to Producer, its successors and assigns, the non-exclusive, limited right, license, privilege and authority

3.1.1. to create and use arrangements of, and to record and re-record, compositions controlled by Publisher and approved in writing by Publisher from time to time **("Compositions")** in synchronization or timed relation with Programs;

3.1.2. to use the titles of Compositions and display the original lyrics of Compositions on Programs; and

3.1.3. to manufacture, distribute, advertise, rent and sell copies of Programs containing Compositions, solely for home use in karaoke machines sold to members of the public and for use in commercial establishments within the Territory where members of the public sing along with Programs and/or record their vocal performances of instrumental versions of Compositions embodied in Programs and thereafter purchase copies of all or part of Programs embodying such performances.

3.2   Term/Expiration:

3.2.1. The Term of this Agreement as to each Composition shall be seven (7) years from the date of written approval of the use of such Composition by Publisher, <u>Provided</u>, however, that in the event that any portion of a **"Rollover Advance"** (as defined in 4.3, below) in respect of a specific Composition remains unrecouped as of the date when such Term would otherwise expire, such Term shall continue as to such Composition until the end of the calendar quarter during which such Rollover Advance is fully recouped.

3.2.2. Upon the expiration of the Term as to a specific Composition, all rights granted herein with respect thereto shall revert to Publisher, and Producer shall not thereafter manufacture, advertise, distribute or sell or lease Programs embodying such Composition or copies thereof or authorize others to do so, <u>provided</u>, that if Producer is not then in material, uncured breach of this Agreement, Producer shall have the right for a period of six (6) months following the expiration of the Term **("Sell-Off Period")** to continue to sell off its ending inventory of such Programs (subject to Producer's continuing obligation to account to and pay Publisher pursuant to paragraph 4, below).

     3.2.3. Producer shall not duplicate or authorize others to duplicate excessive numbers of copies of Programs in anticipation of the Sell-Off Period (and in no event shall Producer duplicate or authorize the duplication of a greater number of copies of a specific Program during the final six (6) months of the Term as to the Composition(s) contained in such Program than were duplicated during the immediately preceding six-month period), and all sales during the Sell-Off Period shall be at regular prices (and not at "distress" or "close-out" prices).

3.3.   As to each Composition not 100% owned and controlled by Publisher, this license extends only to that portion of such Composition owned and/or controlled by Publisher.

3.4.   Nothing herein shall obligate or require Producer to embody Compositions either in Programs or in videograms embodying Programs and it is expressly understood and agreed that the compensation payable to Publisher hereunder with respect to each specific Composition is conditioned upon the utilization of such Composition in Programs.

3.5.   Reservation of Rights:

     3.5.1. Publisher reserves all rights not expressly granted to Producer hereunder, including but not limited to public performing rights in Compositions as embodied in Programs.

     3.5.2. Compositions as embodied in Programs may only be performed publicly by a person, firm or other entity holding a valid performing rights license therefor from Publisher, from Publisher's performing rights society, or from another party authorized to grant such license on behalf of Publisher.

3.5.3 Arrangements:

(A)   All arrangements of Compositions shall be created as "works for hire," Publisher (or its designee(s)) shall be deemed the "author" thereof for copyright purposes, and (subject to Producer's right to use such arrangements for the purposes of this Agreement) all rights in such arrangements shall belong to Publisher from inception.

(B)   In each instance, Producer shall obtain and deliver to Publisher a written "work for hire" agreement executed by each arranger of a Composition embodied on a specific Program on or before the first distribution of copies of such Program.

4.   Consideration For Grant:

In consideration of the rights granted herein for the use of each Composition in connection with Programs as described in paragraph 3, Producer shall pay to Publisher the following sums on the terms and conditions hereinafter set forth, timely payment being of the essence of this agreement:

4.1.   A fixing fee in the amount of Two Hundred Dollars ($200.00) per Composition, payable to Publisher to be paid within ten days after the completion of recording of the first Program embodying such Composition;

4.2.   A nonreturnable payment in the amount of Three Hundred Dollars ($300) per Composition, payable to Publisher in each instance within the same ten-day period, as an advance against the following royalties **("Royalties")** with respect to the sale or rental of copies of Programs to commercial establishments and with respect to the sale of copies of Programs for home use:

4.2.1.   Ten Cents ($.10) per Composition for each copy of each Program embodying such Composition distributed during the first three and one-half (3 1/2) years of the applicable Term; and

4.2.2. Twelve and one-Half Cents ($.125) per Composition for each such copy distributed during the remainder of such Term.

4.2.3. In any instance in which only a portion of a Composition is licensed hereunder, the otherwise applicable royalty shall be reduced pro rata.

4.2.4. In the event that during the Term applicable to a specific Composition Producer shall agree to pay any other publisher a higher fixing fee and/or royalty rate than that prescribed above, such higher fee and/or royalty rate shall be deemed applicable hereunder from the commencement of the applicable Term, Producer shall promptly pay Publisher retroactive to the commencement of such Term the difference between the fixing fee prescribed above and such higher fee and/or (as applicable) the difference between the royalty rate prescribed above and such higher rate as to past sales, and Producer shall continue to pay Publisher at such higher royalty rate with respect to copies distributed thereafter.

4.3. In each instance at or prior to the final six months of the Term applicable to a specific Composition in which Publisher's accounting statement indicates that the advance in respect of a specific Composition has been recouped, Producer shall (at the time when such statement is rendered) make a further advance against Royalties in respect of such Composition in the amount of One Hundred Fifty Dollars ($150.) **("Rollover Advance")** .

5.   Royalty Accountings, Payments, and Audits:

5.1.   Producer shall keep accurate books of account and shall render a true, accurate and detailed accounting statement to Publisher, within 45 days following the end of each calendar quarter during which distribution activity occurs in respect of Programs embodying one or more Compositions, commencing with the quarterly period during which the first commercial sale or rental of a videogram containing a Program takes place.

5.2.   Each sale or rental shall be accounted for on the statement for the quarter during which a particular copy of a Program is distributed by Producer or by a sublicensee from Producer, and such statement shall be accompanied by a remittance of such amount as is shown to be due.

5.3.   Each statement and the accompanying remittance will be made in United States currency. If foreign receipts in the Territory are subject to "blocked currency" laws and/or regulations and/or are subject to exchange controls which prevent their remittance to the U.S., Producer shall notify Publisher to such effect. Upon Publisher's written request and upon condition that the same shall be permitted by the authorities of such foreign country, Producer shall deposit Publisher's share of such receipts in a depository in such foreign country at Producer's cost and expense and shall notify Publisher thereof. Such deposit and notice shall discharge Producer of its obligation to remit such frozen funds.

5.4   The exchange rates utilized by third parties in accounting to Producer shall be utilized by Producer in accounting to Publisher, so long as payment is made at or prior to the date when payment is due (or if payment is delayed due to currency and/or exchange control) . However, if payment is late (not due to currency and/or exchange control) Publisher shall be entitled to the most favorable exchange rate between the due date and the date of payment.

5.5   Tax Withholdings:

5.5.1.   If the laws of any jurisdiction require that taxes on such remittance be withheld at the source, then remittance hereunder to Publisher shall be reduced accordingly, provided, that in each instance, Producer shall notify Publisher of the name and address of the withholding jurisdiction, the amount withheld, and the basis for such withholding, and shall upon request provide Publisher with such document(s) as may be required in order to permit Publisher to apply for any available tax credit(s).

5.5.2. Only taxes specifically attributable to Publisher and/or to Publisher's royalties hereunder shall be subject to such withholding. Specifically, and without limiting the generality of the foregoing, moneys which would otherwise be due and payable to Publisher shall not be subject to reduction by reason of any income, corporate franchise, or other tax levied upon Producer and/or any sublicensee or other representative of Producer, or by reason of the transfer of moneys from any sublicensee or other representative to Producer prior to payment to Publisher.

5.6. Audits:

5.6.1. Publisher shall have the right to examine and inspect the books and records of Producer which relate to the manufacture, distribution and sale and/or rental of Programs containing Compositions for the purpose of determining the accuracy of statements rendered by Producer hereunder. Each such statement shall be subject to examination and inspection for four (4) years after such statement has been received by Publisher.

5.6.2. Such examination shall be made during reasonable business hours, on reasonable business days, on no less than ten (10) days' prior written notice at the regular place of business of Producer where such books and records are maintained. Such examination shall not be made more frequently than once in each year, and not more than once with respect to any quarterly period or statement rendered hereunder.

5.6.3. Such examination and inspection shall be conducted on Publisher's behalf by a certified public accountant or other qualified representative and shall be at Publisher's expense, provided, that if any audit reveals an underpayment of 10% or more for the period(s) audited, Producer shall pay Publisher's reasonable audit costs (excluding travel and subsistence costs).

6. Warranties and Representations; Indemnities:

6.1. Each party warrants and represents to the other that such party has full right, power and authority to enter into and perform this Agreement in accordance with its terms.

6.2. Except to the extent provided otherwise herein Publisher warrants and represents as to each Composition that such composition does not infringe upon the rights of any third parties, provided, that if Publisher is the licensor of the lyrics only or the music only, such warranty and representation shall extend only to that element licensed hereunder.

6.3. Indemnities:

6.3.1. Each party ("the Indemnitor") agrees to indemnify the other party ("the Indemnitee") against any and all loss, damage or expense (including court costs and actual and reasonable outside attorneys' fees) which the Indemnitee may incur by reason of a breach by the Indemnitor of its obligations, warranties and/or representations pursuant to this Agreement which results in a final, nonappealable adverse judgment or a settlement entered into with the Indemnitor's prior written consent (not to be unreasonably withheld) .

6.3.2. The Indemnitee shall deliver prompt notice of any claim, action or proceeding in respect of which indemnity is claimed, and the Indemnitor shall have the right to participate in the defense thereof by counsel of the Indemnitor's choice, at the Indemnitor's sole cost and expense. Where Publisher is the Indemnitor, and the provisions of Publisher's errors-and-omissions insurance policy so require, Publisher shall have the right to control the defense of such claim, action or proceeding.

6.3.3. In any instance involving a third party claim, action or proceeding in which a settlement is proposed which the Indemnitor considers reasonable, and the Indemnitee refuses to approve such settlement, the Indemnitee shall defend such claim, action or proceeding thereafter at the Indemnitee's sole cost and expense and payment to such third parties) shall be the Indemnitee's sole responsibility to the extent that such payment is in excess of the amount the Indemnitor considered reasonable.

7.   Notices and Correspondence:

7.1.   All notices shall be sent to the parties by registered or certified mail (return receipt requested) or by any other means by which delivery may be verified, to the parties at their respective addresses set forth or to such other address(es) as a party may designate by notice in the same manner from time to time. All notices from Producer to Publisher shall be sent to Attention: Vice President, Legal & Business Affairs.

7.2.   All statements, payments and requests for approval hereunder from Producer to Publisher shall be sent via the same procedure to Attention: Vice President, Licensing.

8.   Miscellaneous:

8.1.   This Agreement sets forth the entire agreement between Publisher and Producer with respect to the subject matter hereof, superseding any and all prior written and/or oral agreements or understandings, and may not be modified or amended except by written agreement executed by the parties.

8.2.   No breach of this Agreement shall be deemed a material breach until the party against whom such breach is alleged shall have received written notice of same from the party alleging such breach, and the notified party shall have failed to cure such breach within thirty (30) days after the receipt of such notice (ten [10] days, in the case of a payment of money).

8.3.   Governing Law and Forum; Fees and Costs:

8.3.1.   This Agreement shall be governed by and subject to the laws of the State of California, applicable to agreements made and to be wholly performed within such State, and the State and/or Federal Courts in Los Angeles shall be the sole forums for the resolutions of disputes with respect to this agreement. Both parties hereby submit to the jurisdiction of such Courts for such purpose.

8.3.2.   In any legal action between the parties, the prevailing party shall be entitled to recover its court costs and actual and reasonable outside attorneys' fees.

8.4.   Assignment:

8.4.1.   Publisher may assign this agreement or any of the rights, licenses or privileges hereunder to any person, firm, corporation or other entity.

8.4.2.   Producer may not assign its rights, licenses or privileges except to a corporate parent or subsidiary, in a merger or consolidation or to a purchaser of substantially all of Producer's stock or assets.

8.4.3.   No assignment shall relieve the assignor of any liability hereunder, and no such assignment shall become effective unless and until the assignor shall deliver to the other party hereto a written agreement on the part of the assignee assuming the performance of the assignor's obligations hereunder from and after the effective date of such assignment.

IN WITNESS WHEREOF, the parties have caused the foregoing to be executed as of the date set forth above.

Publisher:

By _____

Producer:

By _____

Form 14.4

License to Use Film Footage from a Motion Picture

FILM FOOTAGE LICENSE

Agreement dated _____ between Theatrical Film Corporation ("Owner") and _____ ("Licensee").

1.   SPECIFIED FOOTAGE: Owner hereby grants to Licensee, without any representations or warranties of any kind, expressed or implied, a perpetual non-exclusive and non-transferable license to use the film footage (including the soundtrack thereof) described in Exhibit "A" attached hereto ("Footage").

2.   RESTRICTED USE: The Footage is restricted to use only in and as part of the _____ audiovisual work entitled "_____" ("A/V Work") for exhibition in the "Media" described in Exhibit "A" for the "Territory" described in Exhibit "A". The Footage will not be used for any other purpose or purposes whatsoever. Licensee will not make any reproduction of or from the Footage whatsoever in whole or in part, except for use in and as part of the A/V Work herein specified.

3.   RELEASES: Licensee shall not have the right to use the Footage obtained without obtaining all required individual authorizations, releases, consents, clearances and licenses ("Releases") as may be necessary with respect to the use of the Footage as herein contemplated including without limitation the Releases set forth below. Licensee shall pay any fees and other payments required in connection with the Releases and furnish Owner with copies of all such Releases.

    (a)   Written releases from all individuals appearing recognizably in the scene(s) contained in the Footage and from all stunt persons appearing in any stunt identifiable in the scene(s) contained in the Footage.

(b)   Written releases from any unions or guilds to the extent required under applicable collective bargaining agreements in connection with the use of the Footage.

(c)   If any music is included in the Footage, synchronization and performing licenses from the copyright proprietors of such music and such other persons, firms or associations, societies or corporations as may own or control the performing rights thereto.

4.   COSTS: Licensee will pay all costs arising in any way by reason of the license granted hereunder including screening, processing, laboratory, transfer and shipping charges in connection with the manufacture of any pre-print material and positive prints of the Footage and the costs involved in replacing any lost or damaged materials delivered to Licensee.

5.   NATURE OF A/V WORK: The A/V Work shall not be derogatory to or critical of the entertainment industry or of Owner, or any officer, director, agent, employee, affiliate, parent or subsidiary of Owner or of any motion picture produced or distributed by Owner and none of the Footage will be used in a manner which would be derogatory to or critical of the motion picture from which the Footage was taken or to the persons involved with the making of the motion picture from which the Footage was taken.

6.   RETURN OF MATERIALS: Upon the completion of the use permitted hereunder, Licensee shall return all preprint material and positive prints of the Footage to such location as Owner shall designate.

7.   ADVERTISING: Licensee shall not use the name of Owner for any purposes in connection with the distribution, advertising or publicizing of the A/V Work without the prior written consent of Owner.

8.   WARRANTIES: Licensee represents and warrants that the incorporation of the Footage into the A/V Work shall in no way affect Owner's continued and separate copyright ownership in the

motion picture from which the Footage was taken and that the copyright ownership of Owner will not merge with the A/V Work nor deprive Owner of its copyright ownership. Licensee represents and warrants that it shall be the copyright proprietor of the A/V Work, that the A/V Work shall bear a copyright notice thereon and shall be duly registered for copyright in the United States Copyright Office.

9.   INDEMNITY: Licensee will indemnify, defend and hold Owner and its officers, directors, agents, employees, representatives, associates, affiliates and subsidiary corporations, and each and all of them harmless from and against any and all loss, costs, damage, liability and expense, including reasonable attorneys' fees, arising out of any claim whatsoever, whether or not groundless, which may arise, directly or indirectly, by reason of Licensee's use of the Footage.

10.   REMEDIES: Licensee further acknowledges that a breach by Licensee of any of its representations, warranties or undertakings hereunder will cause Owner irreparable damage, which cannot be readily remedied in damages in an action by law and may, in addition thereto, constitute an infringement of Owner's copyright, thereby entitling Owner to equitable remedies, costs and attorneys' fees.

11.   LICENSE FEE: Licensee agrees to pay Owner upon signature of this Agreement _____Dollars ($_____) for the use of the Footage as herein provided.

12.   ADMINISTRATIVE FEE: Licensee agrees to pay Owner upon signature of this Agreement _____ Dollars ($_____) as an administration fee in connection with the furnishing of the Footage for the use as herein provided.

13.   GOVERNING LAW: This Agreement and all matters or issues material thereto shall be governed by the laws of the State of California applicable to contracts performed entirely therein.

14.   <u>ENTIRE AGREEMENT</u>: This Agreement contains the entire understanding of the parties hereto relating to the subject matter herein contained, and it cannot be changed or terminated orally.

THEATRICAL FILM CORPORATION ("Owner")

By_____   By_____
      Its   Its

Exhibit "A" of Film Footage License Agreement dated _____ between Theatrical Film Corporation ("Owner") and _____ _____ ("Licensee").

1.   <u>FOOTAGE</u>:

2.   <u>MEDIA</u>:

3.   <u>TERRITORY</u>:

FORM 14.5

LICENSE TO USE A STILL PHOTOGRAPH

January 1, 1995

Gentlemen:

You and Twentieth Century-Owner Film Corporation ("Owner") hereby agree as follows:

1.   USE OF STILL: Subject to the terms and conditions hereof, Owner consents, insofar as Owner is concerned, to your nonexclusive utilization of the still photography or photographs ("Still") specified in Paragraph 7. hereof, only for the purpose specified in Paragraph 5. hereof. The Still may not otherwise be reproduced or used.

2.   NO REPRESENTATION OR WARRANTIES: Owner makes no representation or warranty of any kind either with respect to the Still, your use thereof or otherwise.

3.   CREDIT: You agree to give Owner credit in the following form:

COURTESY OF [OWNER]

4.   CONDITIONS OF USE: The consent of Owner is conditioned upon:

(a)   your obtaining all other consents and releases, including but not limited to the consent of any person appearing in the Still;

(b)   your compliance with the provisions of the Universal Copyright Convention and of the laws of the United States to protect the copyright of the Still.

5.   RESTRICTIONS ON USE: The Still shall be used solely in connection with the book entitled " _____ ".

6.   FEE: You agree to pay to Owner the sum of $ _____ upon signature hereof.

7.   DESCRIPTION OF STILL: _____
_____
_____

8.   MATERIALS:

____ Owner is not supplying a copy of the Still or any other
        material to you.

____ Owner has supplied to you the following material:
_____
_____

9.   COPYRIGHT NOTICE: The following copyright notice must appear in connection with your use of the Still:

Copyright ©19__ [OWNER] ALL RIGHTS RESERVED

10.   COPIES FURNISHED: You agree to deliver to Owner at no cost to Owner two (2) free copies of the publication or other work in which the Still is to be used within ten (10) days after the first publication or other use thereof.

11.   INDEMNIFICATION: You shall indemnify, defend and hold harmless Owner, its directors, officers, agents and employees against all costs and expenses (including attorneys' fees), claims, damages, liabilities or losses of whatever kind arising from or relating to (a) the breach or claim or breach by you of any of your statements, representations or warranties made herein, or (b) your use of the Still.

12.   ENTIRE AGREEMENT/APPLICABLE LAW: This Agreement represents the entire understanding of the parties and shall be

construed in accordance with the laws of the State of California applicable to agreements fully executed and performed therein.

If the foregoing is in accordance with your understanding, please so signify by signing where indicated below.

Very truly yours,

OWNER

By_____

ACCEPTED AND AGREED TO:

By _____

FORM 14.6

LICENSE TO USE A SOUND RECORDING

January 1, 1995

VINYL RECORDS, INC.
1 Vine
Hollywood, California

RE: Master Sound Recording Synchronization License

Gentlemen:

The following, when signed by you and us, will constitute our agreement:

      1.   This agreement is made with respect to the master recording of the musical composition entitled " _____ " (the "Master") embodying the performance of _____ . You represent and warrant that you have the right throughout the world to license the Master for purposes of synchronizing the Master with an audio-visual work.

      2.   You hereby license and grant to us the following non-exclusive rights in the Master:

      (a)   The right to synchronize the Master, or a portion thereof, in time-relation with the audiovisual work presently entitled " _____ " as the same may be exploited in any and all media and modes of uses throughout the world (the "A/V Work") and in any and all trailers, radio, television and, other promotions and advertisements of the A/V Work.

      (b)   The right to use the Master as embodied in the A/V Work in any and all media, whether known or hereafter devised, including (but not by way of limitation) the following:

(i)   Television exhibition, whether by network, non-network, local or syndicated broadcast;

(ii)   Pay television, subscription television, CATV, cable television or any and all other closed circuit broadcasts into home or hotel-motel television;

(iii)   Video-cassette, video-disc, CD-ROM or any and all other functionally similar home use or computer device technologies; and

(iv)   any transportation facility.

(c)   The right to use or refer to the artist's name whose performance is embodied on the Master in the credits, and in any promotions, advertisements and publicity of the A/V Work. In this regard, we agree to accord you and the artist appropriate credit on copies of the A/V Work in substantially the same manner as we will accord credit to all of the other artists and record companies whose previously recorded licensed masters (as opposed to material originally commissioned by us and/or originally recorded for the A/V Work and/or previously unreleased material, credits for which may but need not appear in a different portion of the A/V Work) are being embodied in the A/V Work.

3.   In consideration for the license and grant of rights herein made and if we use the Master or any part thereof, in the A/V Work, we shall pay you, within days after the first commercial release of the A/V Work, the sum of

4.   Nothing herein shall obligate or require us to embody the Master in the A/V Work.

5.   You warrant and represent that you have obtained approval from any and all persons or entities whose approval is required for the license and grant of rights made herein other than the appropriate music publishers, and that you shall be solely responsible for (and shall indemnify and hold us harmless from) any

payments to the artists and/or producers of the Master with regard to our use of the Master. Notwithstanding the foregoing, we agree to pay any and all re-use fees that may be required by applicable unions and/or guilds as a result of our use of the Master in the A/V Work, immediately after you have given us notice of what the amount of the applicable re-use fees are.

6.   The license and grant of rights made herein shall subsist, at minimum, for the remainder of the term of all copyrights in and to the Master, and any and all renewals or extensions thereof that you or your successors or assigns may now own or control or hereafter own or control without additional consideration therefor.

7.   You hereby agree to indemnify and hold us harmless from and against any claims, damages, other costs (including reasonable attorneys' fees), actions or other proceedings by any third party arising out of or related to your representations, warranties or covenants hereunder.

8.   This agreement is binding upon and shall inure to the benefit of the respective successors and/or assigns of the parties hereto.

9.   This agreement shall be subject to and construed in accordance with the laws of the State of New York applicable to agreements entered into and to be performed fully therein.

10.   In the event of any breach of any provisions of this agreement by us, you hereby agree that your sole remedy with respect thereto shall be an action at law for damages, if any, and that in no event shall you be entitled to enjoin, interfere or inhibit or seek to enjoin, interfere or inhibit, the distribution, exhibition, exploitation or other turning to account of the A/V Work.

11.   This agreement sets forth the entire agreement and understanding between you and us with respect to the subject matter hereof and supersedes all prior agreements and understandings, if any, whether oral or written pertaining thereto. This

agreement may not be changed or modified, or any covenant, representation, warranty or provision hereof waived, except by an agreement in writing, signed by the party against whom enforcement of the change, modification or waiver is sought, and not otherwise.

Please indicate your acceptance and agreement to the foregoing by signing in the space provided below.

Very truly yours,

A/V WORK PRODUCTION CO., INC.

By: _____

AGREED TO AND ACCEPTED:

VINYL RECORDS, INC.

By: _____

FORM 14.7

LOCATION RELEASE

<u>LOCATION RELEASE</u>

     1.   For good and valuable consideration, receipt of which is hereby acknowledged, the undersigned grants to _____ _____ (the "Producer"), the following:

     (a)   The right to enter upon and use the property located at _____ (the "Location") for the purpose of photographing, recording and otherwise reproducing in any manner the Location and any still photographs, sound recordings, motion pictures or other works of authorship photographed, recorded or created on or around the Location in connection with the production of a work tentatively entitled " _____ " (collectively, the "Location Elements");

     (b)   The right to include or otherwise use any or all of the Location Elements in and in connection with other still or motion pictures, sets or locations so as to represent that the Location, or any portion thereof, includes, is connected with, or is a part or portion of other property or sets, either real or simulated; and

     (c)   The right to exhibit, distribute, use and exploit, by any means, in any media and in any language, throughout the world, the Location Elements or any portions thereof.

     2.   The undersigned hereby waives, and release and discharge Producer from, any and all claims, demands, liabilities, damages, costs, expenses (including attorneys' fees and costs), actions and causes of actions which the undersigned may now or hereafter have against Producer based upon defamation, right of privacy, right of publicity or any other personal or property rights arising from or in connection with Producer's use of any or all of the rights granted herein, and specifically agree that the under-

signed will not at any time claim that any characters in any work picture in which any photographs, recordings or other works of authorship made hereunder are used to represent the undersigned or point to the undersigned, by reason of the use of any such photographs, recordings or works of authorship.

3.   The undersigned hereby warrants and represents that the undersigned is (the owner) (the lessee) (the agent for the owner) of the location and that the undersigned has the right, power and authority to enter into this Location Release and to grant to Producer all of the rights granted herein. The undersigned hereby indemnifies and holds Producer harmless from any and all claims, liabilities, damages, costs, expenses (including attorneys' fees and costs), actions and causes of action arising out of or related to any breach by the undersigned of the foregoing warranty and representation.

4.   Producer shall have the right, but shall not be obligated, to utilize any of the rights granted herein. The rights which the undersigned has granted to Producer herein are irrevocable, and the grant of rights and other terms hereof cannot be modified except by a writing executed by the parties hereto.

5.   This instrument shall be binding upon and inure to the benefit of Producer's successors, assigns, licensees and all other persons, firms and corporations claiming under or through Producer, and shall also be binding upon the undersigned's successors.

DATED: _____

                    Signed _____

                    _____
                    (Name Printed)

                    _____
                    _____
                    _____
                    (Address)

In complete and full consideration of the above release, Producer hereby agrees to pay to the above signed the sum of _____ _____ Dollars ($ _____).

                    PRODUCER

                    By: _____

PERFORMANCE LICENSES

SUMMARY

HISTORICAL BACKGROUND

1. Performance Rights Societies
2. American Society of Composers, Authors & Publishers (ASCAP)
3. Broadcast Music Incorporated (BMI)
4. Society of European State Authors and Composers (SESAC)
5. International Performance Rights Societies

LEGAL BACKGROUND

1. Performances Under the Copyright Law Today
2. Limitations on the Exclusive Right of Public Performance
   A. Non-Profit Performances
   B. Mom & Pop Stores
   C. Record Stores
   D. State Fairs
   E. Public Broadcasting

PERFORMANCE RIGHTS SOCIETIES TODAY

1. ASCAP
2. BMI, Inc.
3. SESAC Inc.
4. International Performance Rights Societies
5. Membership Requirements
6. Choosing the Society With Which to Affiliate
7. Procedures Upon Affiliation

PERFORMANCE LICENSE GRANTS TO PERFORMING RIGHTS SOCIETIES

1. Non-Exclusive
2. Equal Shares
3. Assignability of Writer's Share
4. Nondramatic Performances

CONSIDERATIONS IN GRANTING AND CLEARING PERFORMANCE LICENSES

1. Blanket Licenses

2. Source Licenses and Direct Licenses

3. Per Program Licenses

COLLECTION OF PERFORMANCE ROYALTIES FROM MUSIC USERS

DISTRIBUTION OF PERFORMANCE ROYALTIES TO PUBLISHER AND WRITER MEMBERS

1. Statistical Sampling

2. Credit Systems

3. Grievance Procedures

FORMS

LISTS

CHAPTER 15

PERFORMANCE
LICENSES

This chapter sketches the historical and legal background of performance rights and performance rights societies and provides an outline of the customs and practices in licensing public performances of music.

As previously noted, the most common means of exploiting music copyrights involves giving others permission to use the music on a non-exclusive basis. Of all the forms of using music—making recordings, printing sheet music, synchronizing with motion pictures, etc.—clearly the most common use is its *performance*.

Performance of music has become ubiquitous in our society. You hear performances of music while listening to the radio, dining in a restaurant, shopping at a mall, and standing in an elevator. A casual listener may often wonder, how does the songwriter get paid for this performance? Does the shopping mall send a check to Sammy Cahn every time the song, *My Kind of Town* is performed over its sound system? Does anyone have to get Mr. Cahn's permission before performing the song?

HISTORICAL BACKGROUND

1. Performance Rights Societies

In 1914, at a dinner meeting held at the famous theatrical club, *The Lambs* in New York City, a small group of songwriters was engaged in a serious discussion about these very questions. At that dinner, songwriter Victor Herbert told Irving Berlin, John Philip Sousa ("the march king"), Jay Witmark (successful writer and publisher), Nathan Burkan, Esq. (an attorney), Gene Buck (writer of the many Florenz Ziegfeld Broadway shows and later president of ASCAP) and others at this

623

meeting, of his frustration at hearing a song of his performed at a nearby swank New York restaurant, but having no means of collecting a royalty for the performance.

The problem these songwriters faced was two-fold. First, as Nathan Burkan, Esq. surely must have advised, it wasn't altogether clear whether songwriters had a right to collect for performances of their songs in restaurants, nightclubs, cabarets, and like establishments. Granted, the revision of the United States copyright act in 1897 established for the first time the copyright owner's exclusive right of public performance. The 1909 revision of the United States copyright law, however, placed a restriction on the right of performance, stating that a license from the copyright owner is required only if the performance was rendered "publicly for profit."[1] This provision was generally interpreted to mean that a license was required only if an admission fee was charged to hear the performance. If, for example, no admission fee was charged for entering a restaurant, performances of music at the restaurant would not be considered "for profit."

Indeed, the common wisdom among music publishers at that time was that public performances of music stimulated the sales of sheet music. Accordingly, the publishers did not want to do anything that would discourage public performances, whether authorized or not. In those days, sheet music often bore a printed notice that granted the purchaser of the sheet music the right to perform the composition in public.

The second problem was the very practical problem of policing the performance of compositions in every nightclub, cabaret, music hall, theatre, or any other place where music can be performed in public. It would be financially impractical for every individual songwriter to attempt to enforce his right of exclusive public performance in his work and for every nightclub, cabaret, music hall and theatre owner to clear permission to perform music by obtaining a separate license for each performance of a song from each individual songwriter or publisher.

---

[1] 17 U.S.C. Sec. 1(d) (1909 Act).

2. American Society of Composers, Authors & Publishers (ASCAP)

It was to address these problems that the American Society of Composers, Authors and Publishers (ASCAP) was established by this small group of songwriters and music publishers in 1914.

The group then took the major step of filing a lawsuit against a restaurant located in Times Square in New York called *Shanley's* for the unauthorized public performance of the ASCAP musical composition, *Sweethearts* by Victor Herbert. *Shanley's* argued, predictably, that since no specific charge was made for admission to the premises where the performances occurred, the music was not being performed "for profit." The case went all the way to the U.S. Supreme Court.[2] In rendering the majority decision in 1917, Chief Justice Oliver Wendell Holmes, himself a writer of poetry, said "If music did not pay, it would be given up. If it pays, it pays out of the public's pocket. Whether it pays or not, the purpose of employing it is for profit and that is enough." Thus, the business of a restaurant was to make a profit, and, because the music was part of the service which the restaurant rendered to make a profit, that was enough.

On the heels of this great victory, ASCAP quickly established a nation-wide policing organization and went on a licensing crusade, issuing music performance licenses to hotels, concert halls, cabarets and other similar places where music was performed for profit under the Supreme Court's new interpretation of that term.

The advent of coast-to-coast radio broadcasting in 1926 brightened the economic interests of songwriters on a scale never before conceived. Here was a new opportunity to earn performance royalties from this new medium and ASCAP was quick to recognize it. By that time, the U.S. Supreme Court, in another landmark decision,[3] had held that even though a radio broadcast was disseminated free of charge, performances by radio broadcast were "for profit" and therefore required a license from the copyright owner.

At first, broadcasters resisted paying for performances, but publishers finally overcame their objections after winning several lengthy court

---

[2] *Herbert v. Shanley* 242 U.S. 591 (1917).

[3] *M. Witmark & Sons v. L. Bamberger & Co.*, 291 F. 776 (D.N.J. 1923).

battles. ASCAP was gaining strength and, with the backing of the courts, was able to raise the rates it charged. The broadcasters were becoming concerned that, with ASCAP's virtual monopoly in the field, rates could be increased to unreasonable levels. With each passing year, negotiations between ASCAP and the broadcasters became increasingly difficult.

3. Broadcast Music Incorporated (BMI)

In 1940, in anticipation of a breakdown in negotiations with ASCAP over the rates to be charged for the following year, a group of broadcasters, including the major radio networks and nearly 500 independent radio stations, established an organization called Broadcast Music Incorporated (BMI).

At that time, I was the producer and arranger of the popular national radio show, *Waltz Time*, broadcast over the NBC radio network, featuring Abe Lyman's orchestra with Frank Munn, "The Golden Voice of Radio." We were aware negotiations between ASCAP and the radio networks were not going too well. During the rehearsal of *Waltz Time* on Friday afternoon, December 27, 1940, I received a call from two executives of the newly formed Broadcast Music Incorporated, Robert Burton and Robert Sour, who told me of "problems next week." Sure enough, the following week we were advised that the ASCAP repertoire would not be available for broadcast after Tuesday December 31, 1940 and we were to clear all music prior to our next broadcast with NBC's clearance department. Our next broadcast was scheduled for Friday, January 3, 1941. A new show was prepared overnight.

The first salvo was fired in the war between BMI and ASCAP when I became the first arranger to call upon "public domain" writer, Stephen Foster, in arranging and programming the song, *I Dream of Jeannie With the Light Brown Hair*, together with several waltzes by Waldteufel and Strauss. Our broadcast on the evening of January 3, 1941 had an unexpected "continental" sound. But what about next week? To my surprise, BMI was well prepared. During the previous year, BMI had been acquiring a catalog of popular songs for licensing in competition with ASCAP. That week, the BMI "song pluggers" furnished us with new popular songs from their newly compiled catalogue. Remarkably, BMI had been prepared with full orchestrations that had already been printed. George M. Cohan remarked during this period that of the hundreds of thousands of songs which BMI claimed to control, "Half are called *Turkey in the Straw* and the other half are about a girl named *Jeannie*."

In early January, 1941, BMI become the new self-proclaimed "automatic performance royalty earning machine" for songwriters and publishers. New BMI affiliated publishers were established along with some older ASCAP affiliated firms such as Edward B. Marks Music and the Peer-Southern Music Organization. After having seen its songs off the air for about eight months, ASCAP finally settled with the networks and its repertoire was again available for broadcast. BMI has remained ever since a strong competitive factor in performance rights licensing.

4. Society of European State Authors and Composers (SESAC)

From 1914 to 1931, ASCAP was the sole organization engaged in the licensing of performing rights in the United States. In 1931, Paul Heineke, a European music publisher, established the second oldest music licensing organization in the United States. Originally known as the Society of European State Authors and Composers, it is presently known just as SESAC, Inc.

In the past, SESAC considered itself a publisher-oriented organization noted primarily for its activity in the Gospel and Country music fields. In 1973, SESAC began to affiliate writers directly and has since rapidly expanded its repertory in the areas of pop, rock, rhythm and blues, jazz, latin, and classical music.

5. International Performance Rights Societies

Performance rights societies were operating overseas long before ASCAP was established in the United States. The first European performance rights society, Société des Auteurs, Compositeurs et Editeurs de Musique (SACEM), was formed in France in 1851. ASCAP is said to have been modeled after SACEM. By the end of the 19th century, SACEM had established an office in London for the purpose of collecting fees for the public performance of French compositions in England even before the establishment of a performance rights society for British composers. This left the British in an awkward position: while British compositions could be freely performed without compensation, it was necessary for restaurants and concert halls in England to pay for a license if they wished to perform French compositions. In 1914, after a series of meetings between important British music publishers, authors, and composers, including David Day of Francis, Day and Hunter and William Boosey of Chappell & Co. Ltd., the English Performing Right Society was finally established. Around the turn of the century, other societies had been established in Europe, including the first German society, Genosenschaft Deutscher Tonsetzer (GDT), the predecessor to today's GEMA, which was founded in Berlin in 1903.

LEGAL BACKGROUND

1. Performances Under the Copyright Law Today

To *perform* music means to "recite, render, [or] play . . . it, either directly or by means of a device or process."[4] For example, a singer is performing when he or she sings a song; a broadcaster is performing when it transmits his or her performance (whether simultaneously or from records); a local broadcaster is performing when it transmits the network broadcast; a cable television system is performing when it retransmits the broadcast to its subscribers; and any individual is performing when he or she plays a record album embodying the performance or communicates the performance by turning on a radio.[5]

The *performance right* in music is the exclusive right to perform or authorize the performance of the music publicly.[6] To perform music *publicly* means (1) to "perform . . . it at a place open to the public or at any place where a substantial number of persons outside of a normal circle of a family and its social acquaintances is gathered" or (2) "to transmit or otherwise communicate a performance . . . . of the work to a place specified by clause (1) or to the public, by means of any device or process, whether the members of the public capable of receiving the performance receive it in the same place or in separate places and at the same time or different times."[7] The term "family" in this context would include an individual living alone, so that a gathering confined to the individual's social acquaintances would normally be regarded as private.

---

[4] 17 U.S.C. Sec. 101.

[5] House of Rep. Report No. 94-1476, 94th Cong., 2d Sess. (1976) at p. 63.

[6] 17 U.S.C. Sec. 106(4).

[7] 17 U.S.C. Sec. 101.

Performances of music at routine meetings of business and governmental personnel would not be considered public because they do not represent the gathering of a "substantial number of persons." However, performances in semi-public places, such as clubs, lodges, factories, summer camps, and schools are considered public performances.

The Copyright Act of 1976 specifically eliminated the requirement that performances be "for profit" and gave the owner of copyright the exclusive right to license the performance of a musical composition in public, whether it be for profit or otherwise.[8]

2. Limitations on the Exclusive Right of Public Performance

In eliminating the "for profit" requirement, however, the new copyright law substituted in its place a series of limitations to the exclusive right of public performance.[9]

A. Non-Profit Performances

These limitations include exemptions for four kinds of *nonprofit* performances. The first exempts from the exclusive right of public performance those performances of music that are rendered in the course of the face-to-face teaching activities of nonprofit educational institutions. The second exempts certain governmental and nonprofit educational broadcasts of music where the purpose is to further systematic instructional activities. The third exempts performances of music of a religious nature rendered during the course of religious services; this exemption does not apply, however, to any religious broadcast, even when the broadcast originates at the place of worship. The fourth exempts performances that lack any direct or indirect commercial advantage; for this exemption to apply, no direct or indirect admission may be charged for the performance and no payment of any fee or other compensation for the performance may be made to any of its performers, promoters, or organizers.

---

[8] 17 U.S.C. Sec. 106.
[9] 17 U.S.C. Sec. 110.

B. Mom & Pop Stores

Another exemption from the exclusive right of public performance are certain performances by small public establishments by means of radio broadcasts. The exemption applies to public performances by the reception of a radio transmission "on a single receiving apparatus of a kind commonly used in private homes." This exemption was intended only to apply to small commercial establishments (e.g., "mom & pop" stores) where the performances are made by using a small radio or home stereo receiver, with no more than four ordinary speakers grouped within a relatively narrow circumference from the receiving equipment.[10] The exemption would not apply to broadcasts transmitted by speakers or similar devices in such establishments as bus terminals, supermarkets, factories and commercial offices, department and clothing stores, hotels, restaurants and fast-food or quick-service chain stores, or where the establishment makes use of any commercial sound equipment or converts a home-type receiver into its equivalent.

C. Record Stores

The copyright law also exempts performances of music in record stores where the sole purpose of the performance is to demonstrate, and thereby promote the sales of, the records offered for sale at the store. For the exemption to apply, no charge may be made for admission to the store. Further, the exemption applies only if the performance is not transmitted beyond the place where the store is located and is limited to the immediate area where the sale is occurring. Accordingly, where record sales are made in one part of a large department store, the exemption does not apply to performances transmitted to other parts of the department store.

D. State Fairs

Also exempt are performances of music at state fairs by governmental bodies and nonprofit organizations, and performances of music as part of programs designed for the blind, deaf, or handicapped, provided they are broadcast through the facilities of government,

---

[10] House Report at pp. 86-87

nonprofit organizations, public broadcasting entities, and cable radio or television systems.

E. Public Broadcasting

Fearing the political pressure that the public broadcasting industry could apply to Congress at the time the copyright law of 1976 was being considered, Congress adopted a compulsory license for performances of music broadcast by public broadcasting entities. The provision encourages copyright owners, through their respective performance rights societies, and public broadcasters, to negotiate in good faith and reach agreement on performance license fees. Should they fail to reach agreement, the compulsory fees would be established by the newly created Copyright Royalty Tribunal.

PERFORMANCE RIGHTS SOCIETIES TODAY

Today, nearly all licensing of performances of music in the United States is conducted through the auspices of ASCAP, BMI, and SESAC, and through over forty music license organizations operating throughout the world. Virtually all professional songwriters and music publishers are members of, or are affiliated with, performance rights societies.

1. ASCAP

ASCAP is owned and run by over 30,000 writers and music publishers, who are referred to as *members*.[11] Members have the opportunity to raise questions and express their views at four meetings each year, two in New York and two in Los Angeles. The society also holds meetings in Nashville, Tennessee. The Board of Directors of ASCAP is elected by its membership and is composed of composers, lyricists and music publishers. The Board, which meets once a month to plan, review, set policy, and appoint officers, has twelve writer directors elected by the writer members and twelve publisher directors elected by the publisher members.

---

[11] American Society of Composers, Authors & Publishers, 1 Lincoln Plaza, New York, New York 10023, Phone: 212-595-3050; Fax: 212-724-9064.

2. BMI, Inc.

BMI is owned by about 500 radio and television stations who are successors to the radio stations who established BMI in 1940.[12] No dividends, however, have ever been paid to the shareholders of BMI; after the deduction of operating expenses, all amounts collected have been paid to the over 65,000 writers and publishers affiliated with BMI, called *affiliates.*

3. SESAC Inc.

SESAC, by far the smallest of the U.S. performance rights organizations, is a private company owned by the Heineke family.[13] SESAC represents over 900 writers and 750 publishers with respect to over 150,000 musical compositions. Like ASCAP and BMI, SESAC makes its catalog available to the broadcast industry, airlines, auditoriums, nightclubs, hotels, restaurants. Unlike the other performance rights societies, however, SESAC promotes performance activity of the music in its writers' and publishers' catalogs. SESAC is also unique in that it provides its affiliates with consultation, legal advice on copyrights, and placement assistance with publishers and record labels.

4. International Performance Rights Societies

Performance rights societies similar to ASCAP, BMI, and SESAC operate in many countries around the world. Under reciprocal representation agreements, each society licenses performances and collects royalties in its local country on behalf of songwriter and publisher members of affiliated performance rights societies in other countries. Overseas performance rights societies generally divide performance royalties into equal publisher and writer shares. The writers' shares of performance fees are paid to the respective societies representing the writers; the publishers' shares are paid to the respective societies representing the publishers or, if the publisher instructs, to its local publisher representative located in the country in which the fees are

---

[12] Broadcast Music, Inc., 320 West 57th Street, New York, New York 10019, Phone: 212-586-2000; Fax: 212-246-2163.

[13] SESAC, Inc., 156 West 56th St., New York, NY, 10019, Phone: 212-586-3450, Fax: 212-397-4682.

collected. A list of the major international performance rights societies is set forth at the end of this chapter.

5. Membership Requirements

Membership in the performance rights societies is fairly open. Applications for membership may be obtained by writing to or visiting any of their regional offices.

A songwriter desiring to become a member of ASCAP must show he or she has written a musical composition that has been (a) commercially recorded, (b) made available in the form of sheet music for sale in regular commercial outlets, or (c) performed in a medium licensed by ASCAP, such as radio. To become a publisher member of ASCAP, you must be regularly engaged in the business of music publishing. If you do not meet the requirements for full membership, you may become an associate writer member if you have had at least one work written and registered with the U.S. Copyright Office. It does not cost anything to join ASCAP. Annual dues are only $10 for writers and $50 for publishers.

Similarly, a songwriter is eligible to affiliate with BMI by showing he or she has written a musical composition that has been either commercially published or recorded or otherwise likely to be performed. BMI charges no fees or annual dues to writers. To affiliate with BMI as a publisher member, you must satisfy reasonable standards of literacy and integrity and should have some musical compositions being performed, or likely to be performed, by broadcasting stations or in other public performances. BMI does not charge publisher members any annual fees or dues. Instead, BMI charges publishers an initial charge of $25.00, made only at the time of affiliation, and intended only to help defray the administrative cost involved in affliation. There is no fee for affiliation of either writers or publishers with SESAC.

6. Choosing the Society With Which to Affiliate

A songwriter may only affiliate with one performance rights society, foreign or domestic, at any one time. However, a writer who belongs to one society may collaborate on the writing of a song with a writer who is affiliated with another society.

Songwriters and publishers frequently ask the question, "Which performing rights society should I join?" Large music publishers will belong to both ASCAP and BMI, establishing separate publishing subsidiaries for this purpose, but the question as to which performance society would be best for any particular song or catalog of songs remains.

It was once believed that the decision of which society to join depended on the type of music the songwriter composes or the type of music that comprises the catalog. A composer of rock, jazz, or country and western was said to be better off with BMI, because of the emphasis BMI placed on independent radio stations, rather than radio networks, in making its surveys; composers of music more likely to be performed on networks over a long period of time were advised to join ASCAP. However, these distinctions no longer apply, and songwriters and publishers are advised to meet with representatives of each society to determine which is better for them.

To attract new members and affiliates, ASCAP and BMI will, from time to time, offer certain writers and publishers advances against future performance royalties. The amount of advances offered by a society might seem a good reason to select one society over another, but if you are considering such an offer, you should remember that the advance being offered is really your money to begin with. The basis of your decision about which society to join should be made on longer term considerations as to which society is really best for you.

7. Procedures Upon Affiliation

It is the music publisher's responsibility to provide to the performance rights society the information necessary to collect and pay royalties for performances. After affiliation with a performance rights society, publishers should follow the following procedures:

1.   Register your active musical compositions with your performance rights society immediately. You will not be credited for performances until your songs are registered with the society. Forms for registration are available from the performance rights society.

2.   Register each new work promptly after it is created, preferably before its anticipated first recording or first performance.

3.   When a music publisher in the United States signs a *sub-publishing agreement* with a music publisher in another country, the procedures for the collection of performance royalties should be speci-

fied in the agreement. For example, the agreement should specify to which performance rights society (e.g., ASCAP, BMI, or SESAC) the U.S. publisher has granted performing rights and the percentage of the publisher's share of performance royalties it should receive. The agreement should also specify whether the publisher's share will be collected on its behalf by the foreign publisher or whether it is to be paid by the foreign society to the U.S. performance rights society for its account. The writers' shares of foreign performance fees collected by the overseas societies are transfered to the appropriate U.S. society, which in turn pays these fees directly to writers.

4. Notify your performance rights society whenever you change your address.

PERFORMANCE LICENSE GRANTS TO
PERFORMING RIGHTS SOCIETIES

1. Non-Exclusive

Because of the impracticability of enforcing their exclusive right to public performances of the song, music copyright owners customarily become members of performance right societies. Upon affiliation with a society, songwriters and copyright owners grant to performance rights societies a license to sublicense the rendition of public performances of their musical works. In accordance with the court-ordered consent decrees that govern the agreements between the performance rights societies and their members and affiliates, the licenses granted by writers and publishers to the societies are made strictly on a *nonexclusive* basis.

2. Equal Shares

In return, performance rights societies will pay 50% of the performance royalties earned by any particular composition to the copyright owner of the song—this is known as the *publisher's share* of performance royalties. The other 50% is paid directly to the songwriters, whether or not they own the copyright in the song—this is known as the *writer's share* of performance royalties. Both the songwriters and the publishers will each receive their respective 50% shares of performance royalties directly from the performance rights societies. Guidelines for the allocation of royalties within each of these groups is governed by the amended consent decree.[14]

3. Assignability of Writer's Share

When a songwriter signs a standard music publishing agreement, he assigns to the publisher his copyright in his song, but reserves the rights necessary to grant to his performance rights society his writer's portion of public performance rights. In return for granting these rights to a performance rights society, the writer will receive directly from the society his writer's share of performance royalties. Should a writer assign the right to receive his writer's share of performance royalties to another, the performance rights society will not always recognize the assignment. The societies will do this as a matter of policy to protect writers from entering into unconscionable contracts. However, this policy is not universally applied and may be subject to overruling by a court. Accordingly, a writer should not rely upon it when considering making an assignment he or she is later likely to regret.

4. Nondramatic Performances

Performance rights societies receive from their music publisher and songwriter members the right to license only *nondramatic* performances of their musical compositions, not *dramatic* performances. Accordingly, performance licenses issued by the societies to radio and television stations, nightclubs, concert halls, and like establishments, permit the rendition of performances of music in only a manner that is *nondramatic* in nature. The differences between dramatic and nondramatic performances are discussed at great length in Chapter 16.

---

[14] See *United States v. ASCAP*, 32. C.O. Bull. 601 (S.D.N.Y. 1960) and *United States v. ASCAP*, 442 F.2d 601 (2d Cir. 1971).

CONSIDERATIONS IN GRANTING AND CLEARING PERFORMANCE LICENSES

Performance rights societies control virtually all administration of performance licenses. Accordingly, persons seeking permission to render nondramatic public performances of music usually must seek permission directly from one or more of the performance rights societies.

1. Blanket Licenses

Persons or entities acquiring public performance licenses pay AS-CAP and BMI an annual fee for the privilege to render an unlimited number of nondramatic performances of one or more of any of the hundreds of thousands of songs in their respective catalogs. Because of its extraordinarily broad coverage, this type of licensing arrangement is called a *blanket license*.

The fee charged for a blanket license, in the case of radio and television stations and certain other establishments, is based on the adjusted gross receipts of the station or establishment, approximating 2 percent. For other businesses, such as restaurants, nightclubs, dancing schools, and the like, the fee for the blanket license may be an annual flat fee in accordance with various schedules established by the respective societies. Examples of several forms of blanket licenses are set forth at the end of this chapter.

If any music user believes the fees quoted by a performance rights society are unreasonable, he may apply for a ruling with the federal court under either of the respective consent decrees that govern the dealings of ASCAP and BMI.[15]

2. Source Licenses and Direct Licenses

Under the terms of the consent decrees entered into between ASCAP and the U.S. Department of Justice and between BMI and the U.S. Department of Justice, and the agreements between the societies and their members or affiliates, all members and affiliates of the performance rights societies are free to negotiate nonexclusive

---

[15] *See generally*, Sobel, *The Music Business and the Sherman Act: An Analysis of the 'Economic Realities' of Blanket Licensing*, 3 Loyola of Los Angeles Ent. L.J. 1 (1983).

licenses directly with users, such as radio and television stations, on any mutually agreeable terms.

When members or affiliates negotiate performance licenses directly with users, they do so by entering into either a direct license or a source license. A *direct license* is a license to perform music on television that a television broadcaster obtains directly from the composers and/or publishers of the music it broadcasts. A *source license* is a license to perform music on television that a producer of a television program obtains directly from the composers and/or publishers of the music contained in the program. The difference between a *source license* and a *direct license* is that a source license is one that is obtained by the person who owns the work in which the song is used (e.g., motion picture, television program) and a direct license is a license that is obtained by one who broadcasts (e.g., television network or local television station), but does not necessarily own, the work being broadcast.

Over the years since the entry of the consent decrees, very, very few nondramatic performance licenses have been issued by music copyright owners directly to broadcasters or other users of music. Most users, including the three national television networks, local television stations, local radio stations, have not sought source or direct licenses from copyright owners, but, instead have sought and obtained blanket licenses from the performance rights societies. Under their blanket licenses, these users have been entitled to perform some or all of the music in the repertories of the performance rights societies without the need to seek individual performance licenses from the individual members or affiliates.

From time to time, however, television and radio stations have sought to improve their leverage in bargaining with the performance rights societies by either threatening to cease negotiating for blanket licenses or by filing lawsuits claiming that the arrangements under which performance rights societies operate violate the U.S. antitrust laws. In the early 1980's a group of local television broadcasters filed a lawsuit against ASCAP and BMI charging just such violations.[16] Later, a group of local radio broadcasters filed a similar lawsuit against the societies.[17]

---

[16] *Buffalo Broadcasting Company, Inc. v. ASCAP and BMI, ASCAP*, 223 U.S.P.Q. 478 (2d Cir. 1984).

[17] *Alton Rainbow Corp. v. ASCAP*, 98 F.R.D. 299 (1983).

After these lawsuits were filed, music publishers began receiving requests from broadcasters for direct licenses to perform music in their catalogs, intended, apparently, to elicit responses that could later be used as evidence in the pending litigation.

Even though music copyright owners are entirely free to enter into source or direct licenses under any terms that may be agreeable to them, few have much experience in issuing direct or source performance licenses. In considering the terms upon which to enter into a source or direct license, a music copyright owner should consider that, while a single lump sum payment may be attractive in the short-term, accepting such terms will mean forgoing any compensation from the performance rights society based upon the type and number of performances of the work rendered over time. It will be recalled that the performance revenues of a society are distributed under a system that awards performance fees on the basis of statistical surveys. Surveyed performances upon which these fees are based must necessarily exclude performances that are licensed directly by the member or affiliate; otherwise, the copyright owner would theoretically be paid twice for the same performance. Accordingly, members or affiliates of performance rights societies who enter into direct or source licenses are required to notify their performance rights society that a direct or source license has been issued, the title of the song licensed, the writer or writers of the song, the publisher or publishers of the song, the name of the licensee, and the term of the license.

In other words, unless the source or direct license is structured on some royalty basis, the music copyright owner entering into such licenses is giving up the important ability to benefit from the economic success of the work or broadcast for which the music is being licensed. While there may be economic circumstances under which it would make good business sense to license nondramatic performances of a song or catalog of songs directly, rather than through the performance rights societies, those circumstances should be considered very carefully with the advice of skilled legal counsel and financial analysts.

3. Per Program Licenses

The court's ruling in the *Buffalo Broadcasting* case resulted in a new form of license that is now available to television stations from the performance rights societies. Under the ruling, each television station has a choice between a traditional blanket license and a new *per program license.* A number of television stations are choosing to secure a per program license instead of the traditional blanket license.

A per program license is often considered a modified blanket license, because it operates much the same way as the blanket license. Television stations that desire a per program license may broadcast any and all songs in the ASCAP or BMI catalogs, but instead of paying fees for a license to use all of the music in each society's catalog—whether they use them or not—stations pay each society only for television programs which contain music controlled by that society pursuant to a prescribed formula. Per program fee structures are negotiated between the performance rights societies and various representatives of the television industry, much the same way as blanket licenses are negotiated. As in the case of blanket licenses, if an agreement cannot be reached, a proceeding before the Federal District Court in New York will take place to establish a reasonable rate structure.

Stations electing the per program license option pay fees to ASCAP and BMI on a monthly basis. However, unlike the blanket license, a vast amount of recordkeeping attends the per program licensing scheme. For example, a station must report the episode titles of the television programs it broadcasts, together with records of what music is contained in each program and when each program is broadcast. The key document used to determine which composers and publishers are entitled to receive royalty distributions is the music cue sheet. A *cue sheet* is a document that lists all of the music in a program, the order of performance, the amount of time each performance runs, the names of the song's composers and music publishers, and performance rights society affiliations. The television stations participating in the per program option are using the services of independant database management companies to assimilate all this information and prepare reports based on the cue sheets and the information furnished by the television stations who choose the per program option.

The per program license should not be confused with either the source license or the direct license. While source and direct licenses are issued to producers and broadcasters by music publishers and other music copyright owners, the per program license is issued by the performance rights society much the same as they issue blanket licenses.

COLLECTION OF PERFORMANCE ROYALTIES
FROM MUSIC USERS

A *music user*, for purpose of performance rights collection, is any person, business, or other entity that publicly performs music. A music user may publicly perform music (i) by live performance in concert on stage with or without the aid of a loudspeaker, or (ii) by transmission of a live performance or a recorded performance by radio, television, cable, telephone or other form of broadcast or retransmission. Examples include, local and network radio stations, local and network television stations, cable television operators, theaters, concert halls, nightclubs, restaurants, discos, ballrooms, hotels and motels, sports arenas and stadiums, amusement parks, airlines, jukebox operators, retail stores, corporations who play music over the telephone to callers "on hold" and many others. In general, each society negotiates directly with radio and television networks, independent stations, and all other establishments where their respective music repertoires are performed publicly.

Performing rights societies generally divide their collection operations into two divisions: broadcast licensing and general licensing. The broadcast licensing division engages in complex negotiations with radio and television stations to establish the annual rates and fees due with respect to the use of music in these media. The general licensing division collects fees from all licensees other than radio and television broadcasters, such as nightclubs, restaurants, sports arenas, and the like. The performance rights societies have separate licenses and rate schedules for each major category of general users. Information about current licensing terms and rates may be obtained by calling any of the regional offices of the societies.

DISTRIBUTION OF PERFORMANCE ROYALTIES TO
PUBLISHER AND WRITER MEMBERS

ASCAP, BMI, and SESAC calculate and distribute performance royalties under different systems. These systems are exceedingly complex and, accordingly, no effort is made here to provide a comprehensive description of them. Readers interested in more information on this subject should confer directly with the performance rights societies.

1. Statistical Sampling

ASCAP and BMI both employ elaborate systems of statistical sampling to determine which selections from their respective repertoires have been used and with what frequency. No effort is made to determine exactly the actual number of times each selection is performed during the year in the United States. Because of the vast numbers of musical performances that are rendered each year and locations at which music is performed publicly in this country, such an effort would require an expenditure that would far exceed the aggregate income of all the U.S. performance rights societies. Fortunately, statistical science has rendered such a complete survey unnecessary. By surveying a relatively few number of performances, the societies can establish a surprisingly accurate measurement of what songs are being performed during the year and with what relative frequency.

Most performance data is drawn from broadcast sources, under the assumption that the music being performed over radio and television is roughly the same as the music being performed in cafes, hotels, sports arenas, and restaurants, and nightclubs. ASCAP and BMI have different ways of sampling broadcast performances. ASCAP primarily relies upon tape recordings made by teams of surveyors sent to different parts of the country during the year. BMI primarily relies upon logs of all songs performed during a particular week by statistically selected broadcast stations. These logs are prepared by television and radio stations once every year or so as a condition of their performance license.

While the royalty distribution payments by ASCAP to its affiliated publisher and writer members are primarily based on a survey of users and BMI by a logging system prepared by users, SESAC payments to its affiliates begin when a recording of its product is released for sale to the public or otherwise begins to earn monies. SESAC does not have a formal logging procedure, but relies instead on performance of songs on industry standard "Top 100" charts, combined with spot checking of broadcast stations, to gage the relative performances of songs in its repertoire. Payments are determined by set rates based on industry hit chart activities.

2. Credit Systems

Once the sample is taken, the resulting information is rolled into a complex formula that takes into consideration a number of factors, including the size of the broadcast stations sampled, the time of day of the performance, the type of program on which the music is performed, whether the performance is a feature performance or a background performance, etc. Each performance is assigned one or more credits, or fractions thereof, and the accumulated credits are used to allocate the fees collected from music users among the various writer and publisher members and affiliates of the society. After deductions of operating expenses, the funds collected from all sources are divided equally between writers and publishers in accordance with the credit formula.

3. Grievance Procedures

ASCAP and BMI have each adopted a grievance procedure under which any of its writer or publisher members or affiliates may file formal complaints with the respective society. Complaints filed against ASCAP are reviewed by a special Board of Review. Disputes with BMI may be governed by arbitration under the rules of the American Arbitration Association. Complaints may ultimately be subject to the Federal Courts retaining jurisdiction of the consent decrees to which ASCAP and BMI remain respectively subject. SESAC is not subject to a consent decree.

APPENDIX TO CHAPTER 15
PERFORMANCE LICENSES

FORMS

**FORM 15.20   ASCAP Symphony Orchestras Which Have
                  Annual Total Expenses of $250,000 or More License**

LISTS

LIST 15.1   Major Overseas Performance Rights Societies

FORM 15.1

BMI WRITER AGREEMENT

BMI • 320 West 57th Street, New York, NY 10019 • 212-586-2000 • Telex 127823

Dear

The following shall constitute the agreement between us:

1. As used in this agreement:

(a) The word "period" shall mean the term from   to

, and continuing thereafter for additional terms of two years each unless terminated by either party at the end of said initial term or any additional term, upon notice by registered or certified mail not more than six months or less than sixty (60) days prior to the end of any such term.

(b) The word "works" shall mean:

(i) All musical compositions (including the musical segments and individual compositions written for a dramatic or dramatico-musical work) composed by you alone or with one or more collaborators during the period; and

(ii) All musical compositions (including the musical segments and individual compositions written for a dramatic or dramatico-musical work) composed by you alone or with one or more collaborators prior to the period, except those in which there is an outstanding grant of the right of public performance to a person other than a publisher affiliated with BMI.

2. You agree that:

(a) Within ten (10) days after the execution of this agreement you will furnish to us two copies of a completed clearance sheet in the form supplied by us with respect to each work heretofore composed by you which has been published in printed copies or recorded commercially or which is being currently performed or which you consider as likely to be performed.

(b) In each instance that a work for which clearance sheets have not been submitted to us pursuant to sub-paragraph (a) hereof is published in printed copies or recorded commercially or in synchronization with film or tape or is considered by you as likely to be performed, whether such work is composed prior to the execution of this agreement or hereafter during the period, you will promptly furnish to us two copies of a completed clearance sheet in the form supplied by us with respect to each such work.

(c) If requested by us in writing, you will promptly furnish to us a legible lead sheet or other written or printed copy of a work.

3. The submission of clearance sheets pursuant to paragraph 2 hereof shall constitute a warranty by you that all of the information contained thereon is true and correct and that no performing rights in such work have been granted to or reserved by others except as specifically set forth therein in connection with works heretofore written or co-written by you.

4. Except as otherwise provided herein, you hereby grant to us for the period:

(a) All the rights that you own or acquire publicly to perform, and to license others to perform, anywhere in the world, any part or all of the works.

(b) The non-exclusive right to record, and to license others to record, any part or all of any of the works on electrical transcriptions, wire, tape, film or otherwise, but only for the purpose of performing such work publicly by means of radio and television or for archive or audition purposes and not for sale to the public or for synchronization (i) with motion pictures intended primarily for theatrical exhibition or (ii) with programs distributed by means of syndication to broadcasting stations.

(c) The non-exclusive right to adapt or arrange any part or all of any of the works for performance purposes, and to license others to do so.

5. (a) The rights granted to us by sub-paragraph (a) of paragraph 4 hereof shall not include the right to perform or license the performance of more than one song or aria from a dramatic or dramatico-musical work which is an opera, operetta, or musical show or more than five minutes from a dramatic or dramatico-musical work which is a ballet if such performance is accompanied by the dramatic action, costumes or scenery of that dramatic or dramatico-musical work.

(b) You, together with the publisher and your collaborators, if any, shall have the right jointly, by written notice to us, to exclude from the grant made by sub-paragraph (a) of paragraph 4 hereof performances of works comprising more than thirty minutes of a dramatic or dramatico-musical work, but this right shall not apply to such performances from (i) a score originally written for and performed as part of a theatrical or television film, (ii) a score originally written for and performed as part of a radio or television program, or (iii) the original cast, sound track or similar album of a dramatic or dramatico-musical work.

(c) You retain the right to issue non-exclusive licenses for performances of a work or works (other than to another performing rights licensing organization), provided that within ten (10) days of the issuance of such license we are given written notice of the titles of the works and the nature of the performances so licensed by you.

6. (a) As full consideration for all rights granted to us hereunder and as security therefor, we agree to pay to you, with respect to each of the works in which we obtain and retain performing rights during the period:

(i) For performances of a work on broadcasting stations in the United States, its territories and possessions, amounts calculated pursuant to our then current standard practices upon the basis of the then current performance rates generally paid by us to our affiliated writers for similar performances of similar compositions. The number of performances for which you shall be entitled to payment shall be estimated by us in accordance with our then current system of computing the number of such performances.

It is acknowledged that we license the works of our affiliates for performance by non-broadcasting means, but that unless and until such time as feasible methods can be devised for tabulation of and payment for such performances, payment will be based solely on broadcast performances. In the event that during the period we shall establish a system of separate payment for non-broadcasting performances, we shall pay you upon the basis of the then current performance rates generally paid by us to our other affiliated writers for similar performances of similar compositions.

(ii) In the case of a work composed by you with one or more collaborators, the sum payable to you hereunder shall be a pro rata share, determined on the basis of the number of collaborators, unless you shall have transmitted to us a copy of an agreement between you and your collaborators providing for a different division of payment.

(iii) All monies received by us from any performing rights licensing organization outside of the United States, its territories and possessions, which are designated by such performing rights licensing organization as the author's share of foreign performance royalties earned by your works after the deduction of our then current handling charge applicable to our affiliated writers.

(b) We shall have no obligation to make payment hereunder with respect to (i) any performance of a work which occurs prior to the date on which we have received from you all of the information and material with respect to such work which is referred to in paragraphs 2 and 3 hereof, or (ii) any performance as to which a direct license as described in sub-paragraph (c) of paragraph 5 hereof has been granted by you, your collaborator or publisher.

7. We will furnish statements to you at least twice during each year of the period showing the number of performances as computed pursuant to sub-paragraph (a) (i) of paragraph 6 hereof and at least once during each year of the period showing the monies due pursuant to sub-paragraph (a) (iii) of paragraph 6 hereof. Each statement shall be accompanied by payment to you, subject to all proper deductions for advances, if any, of the sum thereby shown to be due for such performances.

8. (a) Nothing in this agreement requires us to continue to license the works subsequent to the termination of this agreement. In the event that we continue to license any or all of the works, however, we shall continue to make payments to you for so long as you do not make or purport to make directly or indirectly any grant of performing rights in such works to any other licensing organization. The amounts of such payments shall be calculated pursuant to our then current standard practices upon the basis of the then current performance rates generally paid by us to our affiliated writers for similar performances of similar compositions. You agree to notify us by registered or certified mail of any grant or purported grant by you directly or indirectly of performing rights to any other performing rights organization within ten (10) days from the making of such grant or purported grant and if you fail so to inform us thereof and we make payments to you for any period after the making of any such grant or purported grant, you agree to repay to us all amounts so paid by us promptly on demand. In addition, if we inquire of you by registered or certified mail, addressed to your last known address, whether you have made any such grant or purported grant and you fail to confirm to us by registered or certified mail within thirty (30) days of the mailing of such inquiry that you have not made any such grant or purported grant, we may, from and after such date, discontinue making any payments to you.

(b) Our obligation to continue payment to you after the termination of this agreement for performances outside of the United States, its territories and possessions shall be dependent upon our receipt in the United States of payments designated by foreign performing rights organizations as the author's share of foreign performance royalties earned by your works. Payment of such foreign royalties shall be subject to deduction of our then current handling charge applicable to our affiliated writers.

(c) In the event that we have reason to believe that you will receive or are receiving payment from a performing rights licensing organization other than BMI for or based on United States performances of one or more of your works during a period when such works were licensed by us pursuant to this agreement, we shall have the right to withhold payment for such performances from you until receipt of evidence satisfactory to us of the amount so paid to you by such other organization or that you have not been so paid. In the event that you have been so paid, the monies payable by us to you for such performances during such period shall be reduced by the amount of the payment from such other organization. In the event that you do not supply such evidence within eighteen (18) months from the date of our request therefor, we shall be under no obligation to make any payment to you for performances of such works during such period.

9. In the event that this agreement shall terminate at a time when, after crediting all earnings reflected by statements rendered to you prior to the effective date of such termination, there remains an unearned balance of advances paid to you by us, such termination shall not be effective until the close of the calendar quarterly period during which (a) you shall repay such unearned balance of advances, or (b) you shall notify us by registered or certified mail that you have received a statement rendered by us at our normal accounting time showing that such unearned balance of advances has been fully recouped by us.

10. You warrant and represent that you have the right to enter into this agreement; that you are not bound by any prior commitments which conflict with your commitments hereunder; that each of the works, composed by you alone or with one or more collaborators, is original; and that exercise of the rights granted by you herein will not constitute an infringement of copyright or violation of any other right of, or unfair competition with, any person, firm or corporation. You agree to indemnify and hold harmless us and our licensees from and against any and all loss or damage resulting from any claim of whatever nature arising from or in connection with the exercise of any of the rights granted by you in this agreement. Upon notification to us or any of our licensees of a claim with respect to any of the works, we shall have the right to exclude such work from this agreement and/or to withhold payment of all sums which become due pursuant to this agreement or any modification thereof until receipt of satisfactory written evidence that such claim has been withdrawn, settled or adjudicated.

11. (a) We shall have the right, upon written notice to you, to exclude from this agreement, at any time, any work which in our opinion (i) is similar to a previously existing composition and might constitute a copyright infringement, or (ii) has a title or music or lyric similar to that of a previously existing composition and might lead to a claim of unfair competition, or (iii) is offensive, in bad taste or against public morals, or (iv) is not reasonably suitable for performance.

(b) In the case of works which in our opinion are based on compositions in the public domain, we shall have the right, upon written notice to you, either (i) to exclude any such work from this agreement, or (ii) to classify any such work as entitled to receive only a fraction of the full credit that would otherwise be given for performances thereof.

(c) In the event that any work is excluded from this agreement pursuant to paragraph 10 or sub-paragraph (a) or (b) of this paragraph 11, all rights in such work shall automatically revert to you ten (10) days after the date of our notice to you of such exclusion. In the event that a work is classified for less than full credit under sub-paragraph (b) (ii) of this paragraph 11, you shall have the right, by giving notice to us, within ten (10) days after the date of our letter advising you of the credit allocated to the work, to terminate our rights therein, and all rights in such work shall thereupon revert to you.

12. In each instance that you write, or are employed or commissioned by a motion picture producer to write, during the period, all or part of the score of a motion picture intended primarily for exhibition in theaters, or by the producer of a musical show or revue for the legitimate stage to write, during the period, all or part of the musical compositions contained therein, we agree to advise the producer of the film that such part of the score as is written by you may be performed as part of the exhibition of said film in theaters in the United States, its territories and possessions, without compensation to us, or to the producer of the musical show or revue that your compositions embodied therein may be performed on the stage with living artists as part of such musical show or revue, without compensation to us. In the event that we notify you that we have established a system for the collection of royalties for performance of the scores of motion picture films in theaters in the United States, its territories and possessions, we shall no longer be obligated to take such action with respect to motion picture scores.

13. You make, constitute and appoint us, or our nominee, your true and lawful attorney, irrevocably during the term hereof, in our name or that of our nominee, or in your name, or otherwise, to do all acts, take all proceedings, execute, acknowledge and deliver any and all instruments, papers, documents, process or pleadings that may be necessary, proper or expedient to restrain infringement of and/or to enforce and protect the rights granted by you hereunder, and to recover damages in respect to or for the infringement or other violation of the said rights, and in our sole judgment to join you and/or others in whose names the copyrights to any of the works may stand; to discontinue, compromise or refer to arbitration, any such actions or proceedings or to make any other disposition of the disputes in relation to the works, provided that any action or proceeding commenced by us pursuant to the provisions of this paragraph shall be at our sole expense and for our sole benefit.

14. You agree that you, your agents, employees or representatives will not, directly or indirectly, solicit or accept payment from writers for composing music for lyrics or writing lyrics to music or for reviewing, publishing, promoting, recording or rendering other services connected with the exploitation of any composition, or permit use of your name or your affiliation with us in connection with any of the foregoing. In the event of a violation of any of the provisions of this paragraph 14. we shall have the right, in our sole discretion, by giving you at least thirty (30) days' notice by registered or certified mail, to terminate this agreement. In the event of such termination no payments shall be due to you pursuant to paragraph 8 hereof.

15. No monies due or to become due to you shall be assignable, whether by way of assignment, sale or power granted to an attorney-in-fact, without our prior written consent. If any assignment of such monies is made by you without such prior written consent, no rights of any kind against us will be acquired by the assignee, purchaser or attorney-in-fact.

16. In the event that during the period (a) mail addressed to you at the last address furnished by you pursuant to paragraph 19 hereof shall be returned by the post office, or (b) monies shall not have been earned by you pursuant to paragraph 6 hereof for a period of two consecutive years or more, or (c) you shall die, BMI shall have the right to terminate this agreement on at least thirty (30) days' notice by registered or certified mail addressed to the last address furnished by you pursuant to paragraph 19 hereof and, in the case of your death, to the representative of your estate, if known to BMI. In the event of such termination no payments shall be due you pursuant to paragraph 8 hereof.

17. You acknowledge that the rights obtained by you pursuant to this agreement constitute rights to payment of money and that during the period we shall hold absolute title to the performing rights granted to us hereunder. In the event that during the period you shall file a petition in bankruptcy, such a petition shall be filed against you, you shall make an assignment for the benefit of creditors, you shall consent to the appointment of a receiver or trustee for all or part of your property, or you shall institute or shall have instituted against you any other insolvency proceeding under the United States bankruptcy laws or any other applicable law, we shall retain title to the performing rights in all works for which clearance sheets shall have theretofore been submitted to us and shall subrogate your trustee in bankruptcy or receiver and any subsequent purchasers from them to your right to payment of money for said works in accordance with the terms and conditions of this agreement.

18. Any controversy or claim arising out of, or relating to, this agreement or the breach thereof, shall be settled by arbitration in the City of New York, in accordance with the Rules of the American Arbitration Association, and judgment upon the award of the arbitrator may be entered in any Court having jurisdiction thereof. Such award shall include the fixing of the expenses of the arbitration, including reasonable attorney's fees, which shall be borne by the unsuccessful party.

19. You agree to notify our Department of Performing Rights Administration promptly in writing of any change in your address. Any notice sent to you pursuant to the terms of this agreement shall be valid if addressed to you at the last address so furnished by you.

20. This agreement cannot be changed orally and shall be governed and construed pursuant to the laws of the State of New York.

21. In the event that any part or parts of this agreement are found to be void by a court of competent jurisdiction, the remaining part or parts shall nevertheless be binding with the same force and effect as if the void
part or parts were deleted from this agreement.

Very truly yours,

BROADCAST MUSIC, INC.

ACCEPTED AND AGREED TO:

By ....

Vice President

FORM 15.2

BMI PUBLISHER AGREEMENT

BMI
*

AGREEMENT made on .... between BROADCAST MUSIC, INC.
("BMI"), a New York corporation, whose address is 320 West 57th Street, New York, N.Y. 10019 and

....

a .... doing business as ....

.... ("Publisher"), whose address is..

....

WITNESSETH:

FIRST: The term of this agreement shall be the period from ....

to ...., and continuing thereafter for additional periods of five (5) years each unless terminated by either party at the end of such initial period, or any such additional five (5) year period, upon notice by registered or certified mail not more than six (6) months or less than three (3) months prior to the end of any such term.

SECOND: As used in this agreement, the word "works" shall mean:

A. All musical compositions (including the musical segments and individual compositions written for a dramatic or dramatico-musical work) whether published or unpublished, now owned or copyrighted by Publisher or in which Publisher owns or controls performing rights, and

B. All musical compositions (including the musical segments and individual compositions written for a dramatic or dramatico-musical work) whether published or unpublished, in which hereafter during the term Publisher acquires ownership or copyright or ownership or control of the performing rights, from and after the date of the acquisition by Publisher of such ownership or control.

THIRD: Except as otherwise provided herein, Publisher hereby sells, assigns and transfers to BMI, its successors or assigns, for the term of this agreement:

A. All the rights which Publisher owns or acquires publicly to perform, and to license others to perform, anywhere in the world, any part or all of the works.

B. The non-exclusive right to record, and to license others to record, any part or all of any of the works on electrical transcriptions, wire, tape, film or otherwise, but only for the purpose of performing such work publicly by means of radio and television or for archive or audition purposes and not for sale to the public or for synchronization (1) with motion pictures intended primarily for theatrical exhibition or (2) with programs distributed by means of syndication to broadcasting stations.

C. The non-exclusive right to adapt or arrange any part or all of any of the works for performance purposes, and to license others to do so.

FOURTH:

A. The rights granted to BMI by subparagraph A of paragraph THIRD hereof shall not include the right to perform or license the performance of more than one song or aria from a dramatic or dramatico-musical work which is an opera, operetta, or musical show or more than five (5) minutes from a dramatic or dramatico-musical work which is a ballet if such performance is accompanied by the dramatic action, costumes or scenery of that dramatic or dramatico-musical work.

B. Publisher, together with all the writers and co-publishers, if any, shall have the right jointly, by written notice to BMI, to exclude from the grant made by subparagraph A of paragraph THIRD hereof performances of works comprising more than thirty (30) minutes of a dramatic or dramatico-musical work, but this right shall not apply to such performances from (1) a score originally written for and performed as part of a theatrical or television film, (2) a score originally written for and performed as part of a radio or television program, or (3) the original cast, sound track or similar album of a dramatic or dramatico-musical work.

C. Publisher retains the right to issue non-exclusive licenses for performances of a work or works (other than to another performing rights licensing organization), provided that within ten (10) days of the issuance of such license BMI is given written notice of the titles of the works and the nature of the performances so licensed by Publisher.

FIFTH:

A. As full consideration for all rights granted to BMI hereunder and as security therefor, BMI agrees to make the following payments to Publisher with respect to each of the works in which BMI has performing rights:

(1) For performances of works on broadcasting stations in the United States, its territories and possessions BMI will pay amounts calculated pursuant to BMI's then standard practices upon the basis of the then current performance rates generally paid by BMI to its affiliated publishers for similar performances of similar compositions. The number of performances for which Publisher shall be entitled to payment shall be estimated by BMI in accordance with its then current system of computing the number of such performances.

It is acknowledged that BMI licenses the works of its affiliates for performance by non-broadcasting means, but that unless and until such time as feasible methods can be devised for tabulation of and payment for such performances, payment will be based solely on broadcast performances. In the event that during the term of this agreement BMI shall es ablish a system of separate payment for non-broadcasting performances, BMI shall pay Publisher upon the basis of the then current performance rates generally paid by BMI to its other affiliated publishers for similar performances of similar compositions.

(2) For performances of works outside of the United States, its territories and possessions BMI will pay to Publisher all monies received by BMI in the United States from any performing rights licensing organization which are designated by such organization as the publisher's share of foreign performance royalties earned by any of the works after the deduction of BMI's then current handling charge applicable to its affiliated publishers.

(3) In the case of works which, or rights in which, are owned by Publisher jointly with one or more other publishers who have granted performing rights therein to BMI, the sum payable to Publisher under this subparagraph A shall be a pro rata share determined on the basis of the number of publishers, unless BMI shall have received from Publisher a copy of an agreement or other document signed by all of the publishers providing for a different division of payment.

B. Notwithstanding the foregoing provisions of this paragraph FIFTH, BMI shall have no obligation to make payment hereunder with respect to (1) any performance of a work which occurs prior to the date on which BMI shall have received from Publisher all of the material with respect to such work referred to in subparagraph A of paragraph TENTH hereof, and in the case of foreign performances, the information referred to in subparagraph B of paragraph FOURTEENTH hereof, or (2) any performance as to which a direct license as described in subparagraph C of paragraph FOURTH hereof has been granted by Publisher, its co-publisher or the writer.

SIXTH: BMI will furnish statements to Publisher at least twice during each year of the term showing the number of performances of the works as computed pursuant to subparagraph A(1) of paragraph FIFTH hereof, and at least once during each year of the term showing the monies received by BMI referred to in subparagraph A(2) of paragraph FIFTH hereof. Each such statement shall be accompanied by payment of the sum thereby shown to be due to Publisher, subject to all proper deductions, if any, for advances or amounts due to BMI from Publisher.

SEVENTH:

A. Nothing in this agreement requires BMI to continue to license the works subsequent to the termination of this agreement. In the event that BMI continues to license any or all of the works, however, BMI shall continue to make payments to Publisher for so long as Publisher does not make or purport to make directly or indirectly any grant of performing rights in such works to any other licensing organization. The amounts of such payments shall be calculated pursuant to BMI's then current standard practices upon the basis of the then current performance rates generally paid by BMI to its affiliated publishers for similar performances of similar compositions. Publisher agrees to notify BMI by registered or certified mail of any grant or purported grant by Publisher directly or indirectly of performing rights to any other performing rights organization within ten (10) days from the making of such grant or purported grant and if Publisher fails so to inform BMI thereof and BMI makes payments to Publisher for any period after the making of any such grant or purported grant, Publisher agrees to repay to BMI all amounts so paid by BMI promptly on demand. In addition, if BMI inquires of Publisher by registered or certified mail, addressed to Publisher's last known address, whether Publisher has made any such grant or purported grant and Publisher fails to confirm to BMI by registered or certified mail within thirty (30) days of the mailing of such inquiry that Publisher has not made any such grant or purported grant, BMI may, from and after such date, discontinue making any payments to Publisher.

B. BMI's obligation to continue payment to Publisher after the termination of this agreement for performances outside of the United States, its territories and possessions shall be dependent upon BMI's receipt in the United States of payments designated by foreign performing rights licensing organizations as the publisher's share of foreign performance royalties earned by any of the works. Payment of such foreign royalties shall be subject to deduction of BMI's then current handling charge applicable to its affiliated publishers.

C. In the event that BMI has reason to believe that Publisher will receive or is receiving payment from a performing rights licensing organization other than BMI for or based on United States performances of one or more of the works during a period when such works were licensed by BMI pursuant to this agreement, BMI shall have the right to withhold payment for such performances from Publisher until receipt of evidence satisfactory to BMI of the amount so paid to Publisher by such other organization or that Publisher has not been so paid. In the event that Publisher has been so paid, the monies payable by BMI to Publisher for such performances during such period shall be reduced by the amount of the payment from such other organization. In the event that Publisher does not supply such evidence within eighteen (18) months from the date of BMI's request therefor, BMI shall be under no obligation to make any payment to Publisher for performances of such works during such period.

EIGHTH: In the event that this agreement shall terminate at a time when, after crediting all earnings reflected by statements rendered to Publisher prior to the effective date of such termination, there remains an unearned balance of advances paid to Publisher by BMI, such termination shall not be effective until the close of the calendar quarterly period during which (A) Publisher shall repay such unearned balance of advances, or (B) Publisher shall notify BMI by registered or certified mail that Publisher has received a statement rendered by BMI at its normal accounting time showing that such unearned balance of advances has been fully recouped by BMI.

NINTH:

A. BMI shall have the right, upon written notice to Publisher, to exclude from this agreement, at any time, any work which in BMI's opinion (1) is similar to a previously existing composition and might constitute a copyright infringement, or (2) has a title or music or lyric similar to that of a previously existing composition and might lead to a claim of unfair competition, or (3) is offensive, in bad taste or against public morals, or (4) is not reasonably suitable for performance.

B. In the case of works which in the opinion of BMI are based on compositions in the public domain, BMI shall have the right, at any time, upon written notice to Publisher, either (1) to exclude any such work from this agreement, or (2) to classify any such work as entitled to receive only a stated fraction of the full credit that would otherwise be given for performances thereof.

C. In the event that any work is excluded from this agreement pursuant to subparagraph A or B of this paragraph NINTH, or pursuant to subparagraph C of paragraph TWELFTH hereof, all rights of BMI in such work shall automatically revert to Publisher ten (10) days after the date of the notice of such exclusion given by BMI to Publisher. In the event that a work is classified for less than full credit under subparagraph B(2) of this paragraph NINTH, Publisher shall have the right, by giving notice to BMI within ten (10) days after the date of BMI's notice to Publisher of the credit allocated to such work, to terminate all rights in such work granted to BMI herein and all such rights of BMI in such work shall revert to Publisher thirty (30) days after the date of such notice from Publisher to BMI.

TENTH:

A. With respect to each of the works which has been or shall be published or recorded commercially or synchronized with motion picture or television film or tape or which Publisher considers likely to be performed, Publisher agrees to furnish to BMI:

(1) Two copies of a completed clearance sheet in the form supplied by BMI, unless a cue sheet with respect to such work is furnished pursuant to subparagraph A(3) of this paragraph TENTH.

(2) If such work is based on a composition in the public domain, a legible lead sheet or other written or printed copy of such work setting forth the lyrics, if any, and music correctly metered; provided that with respect to all other works, such copy need be furnished only if requested by BMI pursuant to subsection (c) of subparagraph D(2) of this paragraph TENTH.

(3) If such work has been or shall be synchronized with or otherwise used in connection with motion picture or television film or tape, a cue sheet showing the title, composers, publisher and nature and duration of the use of the work in such film or tape.

B. Publisher shall submit the material described in subparagraph A of this paragraph TENTH with respect to works heretofore published, recorded or synchronized within ten (10) days after the execution of this agreement and with respect to any of the works hereafter so published, recorded, synchronized or likely to be performed prior to the date of publication or release of the recording, film or tape or anticipated performance.

C. The submission of each clearance sheet or cue sheet shall constitute a warranty by Publisher that all of the information contained thereon is true and correct and that no performing rights in any of the works listed thereon has been granted to or reserved by others except as specifically set forth therein.

D. Publisher agrees:

(1) To secure and maintain copyright protection of the works pursuant to the Copyright Law of the United States and pursuant to the laws of such other nations of the world where such protection is afforded; and to give BMI prompt written notice of the date and number of copyright registration and/of each work registered in the United States Copyright Office.

(2) At BMI's request:

(a) To register each unpublished and published work in the United States Copyright Office pursuant to the Copyright Law of the United States.

(b) To record in the United States Copyright Office in accordance with the Copyright Law of the United States any agreements, assignments, instruments or documents of any kind by which Publisher obtained the right to publicly perform and/or the right to publish, co-publish or sub-publish any of the works.

(c) To obtain and deliver to BMI copies of: unpublished and published works; copyright registration and/or renewal certificates issued by the United States Copyright Office; any of the documents referred to in sub-section (b) above.

E. Publisher agrees to give BMI prompt notice by registered or certified mail in each instance when, pursuant to the Copyright Law of the United States, (1) the rights granted to BMI by Publisher in any work shall revert to the writer or the writer's representative, or (2) copyright protection of any work shall terminate.

ELEVENTH: Publisher warrants and represents that:

A. Publisher has the right to enter into this agreement; Publisher is not bound by any prior commitments which conflict with its undertakings herein; the rights granted by Publisher to BMI herein are the sole and exclusive property of Publisher and are free from all encumbrances and claims; and exercise of such rights will not constitute infringement of copyright or violation of any right of, or unfair competition with, any person, firm, corporation or association.

B. Except with respect to works in which the possession of performing rights by another person, firm, corporation or association is specifically set forth on a clearance sheet or cue sheet submitted to BMI pursuant to subparagraph A of paragraph TENTH hereof, Publisher has exclusive performing rights in each of the works by virtue of written grants thereof to Publisher signed by all the authors and composers or other owners of such work.

TWELFTH:

A. Publisher agrees to defend, indemnify, save and hold BMI, its licensees, the advertisers of its licensees and their respective agents, servants and employees, free and harmless from and against any and all demands, loss, damage, suits, judgments, recoveries and costs, including counsel fees, resulting from any claim of whatever nature arising from or in connection with the exercise of any of the rights granted by Publisher in this agreement; provided, however, that the obligations of Publisher under this paragraph TWELFTH shall not apply to any matter added to, or changes made in, any work by BMI or its licensees.

B. Upon the receipt by any of the parties herein indemnified of any notice, demand, process, papers, writ or pleading, by which any such claim, demand, suit or proceeding is made or commenced against them, or any of them, which Publisher shall be obliged to defend hereunder, BMI shall, as soon as may be practicable, give Publisher notice thereof and deliver to Publisher such papers or true copies thereof, and BMI shall have the right to participate by counsel of its own choice, at its own expense. Publisher agrees to cooperate with BMI in all such matters.

C. In the event of such notification of claim or service of process on any of the parties herein indemnified, BMI shall have the right, from the date thereof, to exclude the work with respect to which a claim is made from this agreement and/or to withhold payment of all sums which may become due pursuant to this agreement or any modification thereof until receipt of satisfactory written evidence that such claim has been withdrawn, settled or adjudicated.

THIRTEENTH: Publisher makes, constitutes and appoints BMI, or its nominee, Publisher's true and lawful attorney, irrevocably during the term hereof, in the name of BMI or that of its nominee, or in Publisher's name, or otherwise, to do all acts, take all proceedings, and execute, acknowledge and deliver any and all instruments, papers, documents, process or pleadings that may be necessary, proper or expedient to restrain infringement of and/or to enforce and protect the rights granted by Publisher hereunder, and to recover damages in respect of or for the infringement or other violation of the said rights, and in BMI's sole judgment to join Publisher and/or others in whose names the copyrights to any of the works may stand, and to discontinue, compromise or refer to arbitration, any such actions or proceedings or to make any other disposition of the disputes in relation to the works; provided that any action or proceeding commenced by BMI pursuant to the provisions of this paragraph THIRTEENTH shall be at its sole expense and for its sole benefit.

FOURTEENTH:

A. It is acknowledged that BMI has heretofore entered into, and may during the term of this agreement enter into, contracts with performing rights licensing organizations for the licensing of public performing rights controlled by BMI in territories outside of the United States, its territories and possessions (hereinafter called "foreign territories"). Upon Publisher's written request, BMI agrees to permit Publisher to grant performing rights in any or all of the works for any foreign territory for which, at the time such request is received, BMI has not entered into any such contract with a performing rights licensing organization; provided, however, that any such grant of performing rights by Publisher shall terminate at such time when BMI shall have entered into such a contract with a performing rights licensing organization covering such foreign territory and shall have notified Publisher thereof. Nothing herein contained, however, shall be deemed to restrict Publisher from assigning to its foreign publisher or representative the right to collect a part or all of the publishers' performance royalties earned by any or all of the works in any foreign territory as part of an agreement for the publication, exploitation or representation of such works in such territory, whether or not BMI has entered into such a contract with a performing rights licensing organization covering such territory.

B. Publisher agrees to notify BMI promptly in writing in each instance when publication, exploitation or other rights in any or all of the works are granted for any foreign territory. Such notice shall set forth the title of the work, the country or countries involved, the period of such grant, the name of the person, firm, corporation or association entitled to collect performance royalties earned in the foreign territory and the amount of such share. Within ten (10) days after the execution of this agreement Publisher agrees to submit to BMI, in writing, a list of all works as to which Publisher has, prior to the effective date of this agreement, granted to any person, firm, corporation or association performing rights and/or the right to collect publisher performance royalties earned in any foreign territory.

C. In the event that BMI transmits to Publisher performance royalties designated as the writer's share of performance royalties earned by any of the works in any foreign territory, Publisher shall promptly pay such royalties to the writer or writers of the works involved. If Publisher is unable for any reason to locate and make payment to any of the writers involved within six (6) months from the date of receipt, the amounts due such writers shall be returned to BMI.

FIFTEENTH:

A. Publisher agrees that Publisher, its agents, employees, representatives or affiliated companies, will not directly or indirectly during the term of this agreement:

(1) Solicit or accept payment from or on behalf of authors for composing music for lyrics, or from or on behalf of composers for writing lyrics to music.

(2) Solicit or accept manuscripts from composers or authors in consideration of any payments to be made by or on behalf of such composers or authors for reviewing, arranging, promotion, publication, recording or any other services connected with the exploitation of any composition.

(3) Permit Publisher's name, or the fact of its affiliation with BMI, to be used by any other person. firm, corporation or association engaged in any of the practices described in subparagraphs A(1) and A(2) of this paragraph FIFTEENTH.

(4) Submit to BMI, as one of the works to come within this agreement, any musical composition with respect to which any payments described in subparagraphs A(1) and A(2) of this paragraph FIFTEENTH have been made by or on behalf of a composer or author to any person, firm, corporation or association.

B. Publisher agrees that Publisher, its agents, employees or representatives will not directly or indirectly during the term of this agreement make any effort to ascertain from, or offer any inducement or consideration to, anyone, including but not limited to any broadcasting licensee of BMI or to the agents, employees or representatives of BMI or of any such licensee, for information regarding the time or times when any such BMI licensee is to report its performances to BMI, or to attempt in any way to manipulate performances or affect the representative character or accuracy of BMI's system of sampling or logging performances.

C. Publisher agrees to notify BMI promptly in writing (1) of any change of firm name of Publisher, and (2) of any change of twenty percent (20%) or more in the ownership thereof.

D. In the event of the violation of any of the provisions of subparagraphs A, B or C of this paragraph FIFTEENTH, BMI shall have the right, in its sole discretion, to terminate this agreement by giving Publisher at least thirty (30) days' notice by registered or certified mail. In the event of such termination, no payments shall be due to Publisher pursuant to paragraph SEVENTH hereof.

SIXTEENTH: In the event that during the term of this agreement (1) mail addressed to Publisher at the last address furnished by it pursuant to paragraph TWENTIETH hereof shall be returned by the post office, or (2) monies shall not have been earned by Publisher pursuant to paragraph FIFTH hereof for a period of two consecutive years or more, or (3) the proprietor, if Publisher is a sole proprietorship, shall die, BMI shall have the right to terminate this agreement on at least thirty (30) days' notice by registered or certified mail addressed to the last address furnished by Publisher pursuant to paragraph TWENTIETH hereof and, in the case of the death of a sole proprietor, to the representative of said proprietor's estate, if known to BMI. In the event of such termination, no payments shall be due Publisher pursuant to paragraph SEVENTH hereof.

SEVENTEENTH: Publisher acknowledges that the rights obtained by it pursuant to this agreement constitute rights to payment of money and that during the term BMI shall hold absolute title to the performing rights granted to BMI hereunder. In the event that during the term Publisher shall file a petition in bankruptcy, such a petition shall be filed against Publisher, Publisher shall make an assignment for the benefit of creditors, Publisher shall consent to the appointment of a receiver or trustee for all or part of its property, Publisher shall file a petition for corporate reorganization or arrangement under the United States bankruptcy laws, Publisher shall institute or shall have instituted against it any other insolvency proceeding under the United States bankruptcy laws or any other applicable law, or, in the event Publisher is a partnership, all of the general partners of said partnership shall be adjudged bankrupts, BMI shall retain title to the performing rights in all works for which clearance sheets shall have theretofore been submitted to BMI and shall subrogate Publisher's trustee in bankruptcy or receiver and any subsequent purchasers from them to Publisher's right to payment of money for said works in accordance with the terms and conditions of this agreement.

EIGHTEENTH: Any controversy or claim arising out of, or relating to, this agreement or the breach thereof, shall be settled by arbitration in the City of New York, in accordance with the Rules of the American Arbitration Association, and judgment upon the award of the arbitrator may be entered in any court having jurisdiction thereof. Such award shall include the fixing of the expenses of the arbitration, including reasonable attorney's fees, which shall be borne by the unsuccessful party.

NINETEENTH: Publisher agrees that it shall not, without the written consent of BMI, assign any of its rights hereunder. No rights of any kind against BMI will be acquired by the assignee if any such purported assignment is made by Publisher without such written consent.

TWENTIETH: Publisher agrees to notify BMI's Department of Performing Rights Administration promptly in writing of any change in its address. Any notice sent to Publisher pursuant to the terms of this agreement shall be valid if addressed to Publisher at the last address so furnished by Publisher.

TWENTY-FIRST: This agreement cannot be changed orally and shall be governed and construed pursuant to the laws of the State of New York.

TWENTY-SECOND: In the event that any part or parts of this agreement are found to be void by a court of competent jurisdiction, the remaining part or parts shall nevertheless be binding with the same force and effect as if the void part or parts were deleted from this agreement.

IN WITNESS WHEREOF, the parties hereto have caused this agreement to be duly executed as of the day and year first above written.

BROADCAST MUSIC, INC.

By ....
Vice President

....

By ....
(Title of Signer)

FORM 15.3

ASCAP PUBLISHER/WRITER AGREEMENT

1986-1995

No.:

Rec'd:

Agreement Between

AND

American Society
OF
Composers, Authors & Publishers
1 LINCOLN PLAZA
NEW YORK, N.Y. 10023

Dated:

ASCAP THE VOICE OF MUSIC.
AMERICAN
SOCIETY OF
COMPOSERS
AUTHORS &
PUBLISHERS

Agreement made between the Undersigned (for brevity called *"Owner"*) and the AMERICAN SOCIETY OF COMPOSERS, AUTHORS AND PUBLISHERS (for brevity called *"Society"*), in consideration of the premises and of the mutual covenants hereinafter contained, as follows:

1. The *Owner* grants to the *Society* for the term hereof, the right to license non-dramatic public performances (as hereinafter defined), of each musical work:

Of which the *Owner* is a copyright proprietor; or

Which the *Owner*, alone, or jointly, or in collaboration with others, wrote, composed, published, acquired or owned; or

In which the *Owner* now has any right, title, interest or control whatsoever, in whole or in part; or

Which hereafter, during the term hereof, may be written, composed, acquired, owned, published or copyrighted by the *Owner*, alone, jointly or in collaboration with others; or

In which the *Owner* may hereafter, during the term hereof, have any right, title, interest or control, whatsoever, in whole or in part.

The right to license the public performance of every such musical work shall be deemed granted to the *Society* by this instrument for the term hereof, immediately upon the work being written, composed, acquired, owned, published or copyrighted.

The rights hereby granted shall include:

(a) All the rights and remedies for enforcing the copyright or copyrights of such musical works, whether such copyrights are in the name of the *Owner* and/or others, as well as the right to sue under such copyrights in the name of the *Society* and/or in the name of the *Owner* and/or others, to the end that the *Society* may effectively protect and be assured of all the rights hereby granted.

(b) The non-exclusive right of public performance of the separate numbers, songs, fragments or arrangements, melodies or selections forming part or parts of musical plays and dramatico-musical compositions, the *Owner* reserving and excepting from this grant the right of performance of musical plays and dramatico-musical compositions in their entirety, or any part of such plays or dramatico-musical compositions on the legitimate stage.

(c) The non-exclusive right of public performance by means of radio broadcasting, telephony, "wired wireless," all forms of synchronism with motion pictures, and/or any method of transmitting sound other than television broadcasting.

(d) The non-exclusive right of public performance by television broadcasting; provided, however, that:

(i) This grant does not extend to or include the right to license the public performance by television broadcasting or otherwise of any rendition or performance of (a) any opera, operetta, musical comedy, play or like production, as such, in whole or in part, or (b) any composition from any opera, operetta, musical comedy, play or like production (whether or not such opera, operetta, musical comedy, play or like production was presented on the stage or in motion picture form) in a manner which recreates the performance of such composition with substantially such distinctive scenery or costume as was used in the presentation of such opera, operetta, musical comedy, play or like production (whether or not such opera, operetta, musical comedy, play or like production was presented on the stage or in motion picture form); provided, however, that the rights hereby granted shall be deemed to include a grant of the right to license non-dramatic performances of compositions by television broadcasting of a motion picture containing such composition if the rights in such motion picture other than those granted hereby have been obtained from the parties in interest.

(ii) Nothing herein contained shall be deemed to grant the right to license the public performance by television broadcasting of dramatic performances. Any performance of a separate musical composition which is not a dramatic performance, as defined herein, shall be deemed to be a non-dramatic performance. For the purposes of this agreement, a dramatic performance shall mean a performance of a musical composition on a television program in which there is a definite plot depicted by action and where the performance of the musical composition is woven into and carries forward the plot and its accompanying action. The use of dialogue to establish a mere program format or the use of any non-dramatic device merely to introduce a performance of a composition shall not be deemed to make such performance dramatic.

(iii) The definition of the terms "dramatic" and "non-dramatic" performances contained herein are purely for the purposes of this agreement and for the term thereof and shall not be binding upon or prejudicial to any position taken by either of us subsequent to the term hereof or for any purpose other than this agreement.

(e) The *Owner* may at any time and from time to time, in good faith, restrict the radio or television broadcasting of compositions from musical comedies, operas, operettas and motion pictures, or any other composition being excessively broadcast, only for the purpose of preventing harmful effect upon such musical comedies, operas, operetta, motion pictures or compositions, in respect of other interests under the copyrights thereof; provided, however, that the right to grant limited licenses will be given, upon application, as to restricted compositions, if and when the *Owner* is unable to show reasonable hazards to his or its major interests likely to result from such radio or television broadcasting; and provided further that such right to restrict any such composition shall not be exercised for the purpose of permitting the fixing or regulating of fees for the recording or transcribing of such composition, and provided further that in no case shall any charges, "free plugs", or other consideration be required in respect of any permission granted to perform a restricted composition; and provided further that in no event shall any composition, after the initial radio or television broadcast thereof, be restricted for the purpose of confining further radio or television broadcasts thereof to a particular artist, station, network or program. The *Owner* may also at any time and from time to time, in good faith, restrict the radio or television broadcasting of any composition, as to which any suit has been brought or threatened on a claim that such composition infringes a composition not contained in the repertory of *Society* or on a claim by a non-member of *Society* that *Society* does not have the right to license the public performance of such composition by radio or television broadcasting.

2. The term of this agreement shall be for a period commencing on the date hereof and expiring on the 31st day of December, 1995.

3. The *Society* agrees, during the term hereof, in good faith to use its best endeavors to promote and carry out the objects for which it was organized, and to hold and apply all royalties, profits, benefits and advantages arising from the exploitation of the rights assigned to it by its several members, including the *Owner*, to the uses and purposes as provided in its Articles of Association (which are hereby incorporated by reference), as now in force or as hereafter amended.

4. The *Owner* hereby irrevocably, during the term hereof, authorizes, empowers and vests in the *Society* the right to enforce and protect such rights of public performance under any and all copyrights, whether standing in the name of the *Owner* and/or others, in any and all works copyrighted by the *Owner*, and/or by others; to prevent the infringement thereof, to litigate, collect and receipt for damages arising from infringement, and it its sole judgment to join the *Owner* and/or others in whose names the copyright may stand, as parties plaintiff or defendants in suits or proceedings; to bring suit in the name of the *Owner* and/or in the name of the *Society*, or others in whose name the copyright may stand, or otherwise, and to release, compromise, or refer to arbitration any actions, in the same manner and to the same extent and to all intents and purposes as the *Owner* might or could do, had this instrument not been made.

5. The *Owner* hereby makes, constitutes and appoints the *Society*, or its successor, the *Owner's* true and lawful attorney, irrevocably during the term hereof, and in the name of the *Society* or its successor, or in the name of the *Owner*, or otherwise, to do all acts, take all proceedings, execute, acknowledge and deliver any and all instruments, papers, documents, process and pleadings that may be necessary proper or expedient to restrain infringements and recover damages in respect to or for the infringement or other violation of the rights of public performance in such works, and to discontinue, compromise or refer to arbitration any such proceedings or actions, or to make any other disposition of the differences in relation to the premises.

6. The *Owner* agrees from time to time, to execute, acknowledge and deliver to the *Society*, such assurances, powers of attorney or other authorizations or instruments as the *Society* may deem necessary or expedient to enable it to exercise, enjoy and enforce, in its own name or otherwise, all rights and remedies aforesaid.

7. It is mutually agreed that during the term hereof the Board of Directors of the *Society* shall be composed of an equal number of writers and publishers respectively, and that the royalties distributed by the Board of Directors shall be divided into two (2) equal sums, and one (1) each of such sums credited respectively to and for division amongst (a) the writer members, and (b) the publisher members, in accordance with the system of distribution and classification as determined by the Classification Committee of each group, in accordance with the Articles of Association as they may be amended from time to time, except that the classification of the *Owner* within his class may be changed.

8. The *Owner* agrees that his classification in the *Society* as determined from time to time by the Classification Committee of his group and/or The Board of Directors of the *Society*, in case of appeal by him, shall be final, conclusive and binding upon him.

The *Society* shall have the right to transfer the right of review of any classification from the Board of Directors to any other agency or instrumentality that in its discretion and good judgment it deems best adapted to assuring to the *Society's* membership a just, fair, equitable and accurate classification.

The *Society* shall have the right to adopt from time to time such systems, means, methods and formulae for the establishment of a member's status in respect of classification as will assure a fair, just and equitable distribution of royalties among the membership.

9. **"Public Performance" Defined.** The term *"public performance"* shall be construed to mean vocal, instrumental and/or mechanical renditions and representations in any manner or by any method whatsoever, including transmissions by radio and television broadcasting stations, transmission by telephony and/or "wired wireless"; and/or reproductions of performances and renditions by means of devices for reproducing sound recorded in synchronism or timed relation with the taking of motion pictures.

10. **"Musical Works" Defined.** The phrase *"musical works"* shall be construed to mean musical compositions and dramatico-musical compositions, the words and music thereof, and the respective arrangements thereof, and the selections therefrom.

11. The powers, rights, authorities and privileges by this instrument vested in the *Society*, are deemed to include the World, provided, however, that such grant of rights for foreign countries shall be subject to any agreements now in effect, a list of which are noted on the reverse side hereof.

12. The grant made herein by the owner is modified by and subject to the provisions of (a) the Amended Final Judgement (Civil Action No. 13-95) dated March 14, 1950 in U.S.A. v. ASCAP as further amended by Order dated January 7, 1960, (b) the Final Judgment (Civil Action No. 42-245) in U.S.A. v. ASCAP, dated March 14, 1950, and (c) the provisions of the Articles of Association and resolutions of the Board of Directors adopted pursuant to such judgments and order.

SIGNED, SEALED AND DELIVERED, on this................................day of..,19.................

Owner {

Society {

AMERICAN SOCIETY OF COMPOSERS,
AUTHORS AND PUBLISHERS,

By ....
                    President

FOREIGN AGREEMENTS AT THIS DATE IN EFFECT
(See paragraph 11 of within agreement)

COUNTRY	WITH (Name of Firm)	EXPIRES	REMARKS

50M-6/91-CH

FORM 15.4

BMI General License
(FOR RESTAURANTS, BARS, CAFES, DISCOS, ETC.)

MUSIC PERFORMANCE AGREEMENT
GENERAL LICENSE
COMPLETE ALL SHADED AREAS BELOW

BMI

(Date Will Be Entered By BMI Upon Execution)

AGREEMENT, made at New York, N.Y. on _____ between BROADCAST MUSIC, INC., a corporation organized under the laws of the State of New York (hereinafter called BMI) with principal offices at 320 West 57th Street, New York, N.Y. 10019, and

_____
Name of Corporation, Partnership or Individual Owner (Legal Name of Licensee)

CHECK APPROPRIATE BOX AND COMPLETE

☐ If a corporation, indicate state of incorporation _____
                                                    (State)

☐ If a partnership, indicate names of all partners _____
                                                    (Names of Partners)

_____
(Names of Partners)

☐ If an individual owner, indicate residence address below under Mailing Address

(hereinafter called LICENSEE) _____
                                        Doing business under the name of (Trade Name)

PREMISES ADDRESS *(herein called the licensed premises)*	MAILING ADDRESS *(residence address if individual owner)*
(Street Address)	*(Street Address)*
(City)	*(City)*
(State)　　　　*(Zip)*	*(State)*　　　　*(Zip)*
(　　)　　　　　　　　　　*(Telephone No.)* *(Area Code)*	(　　)　　　　　　　　　　*(Telephone No.)* *(Area Code)*

1. BMI hereby grants to LICENSEE a non-exclusive license to perform publicly at the licensed premises all of the musical works the rights to grant public performance licenses of which BMI shall during the term hereof control. Said license shall not include dramatic rights, the right to perform dramatico-musical works in whole or in substantial part, the right to present individual works in a dramatic setting or the right to use the music licensed hereunder in any other context which may constitute an exercise of the "grand rights" therein. Said license also shall not include the right to broadcast, telecast, or otherwise transmit the performances licensed hereunder to persons outside of the licensed premises. This license does not authorize performances of music by means of a coin-operated phonorecord player (juke box) as defined in the Copyright Law (17 U.S.C. §116).

2. As used in this agreement:

    (a) **"Term"** shall mean the period beginning on the first day of _____ and ending on the last day
                                                (Month/Year)

of _____ and continuing thereafter for additional periods of one (1) year each, unless cancelled by either party
   (Month/Year)

at the end of said period or any subsequent period, upon thirty (30) days advance written notice by regular first-class U.S. mail to the other party. Each one (1) year period during the term is referred to herein as a "contract year."

    (b) **"Live music"** shall mean music performed by musicians, singers or other entertainers actually present and performing at the licensed premises.

    (c) **"Live music and entertainment costs"** shall mean all expenditures of every kind and nature (whether in money or any other form of consideration) made by LICENSEE, or on LICENSEE's behalf, for live music. The services of LICENSEE and/or non-compensated musicians or entertainers shall be included in "entertainment costs" at the prevailing rate for such services in the community. Also included in "entertainment costs" are expenditures for room and board where LICENSEE is obligated to provide accommodations to musicians and entertainers as part of the consideration for such entertainment services.

    (d) **"Recorded music"** shall mean the performance of music by means of a mechanical or electronic device or via the reception of broadcast audio transmissions on receiving apparatus and amplification thereof (including audio-visual equipment) for public performance. Such performances may be reproduced only by loudspeakers located on the licensed premises.

(e) **"Dancing"** shall mean that there is dancing to recorded music by patrons or performers anywhere on the licensed premises.

(f) **"Discontinuance"** shall mean the total abandonment, rather than a seasonal or periodic cessation, of the use of both live and recorded music.

3. LICENSEE agrees to pay to BMI for each contract year of the term hereof an **estimated** fee as an advance on account of the **actual** fee. Such **estimated** fee shall then be subject to adjustment in accordance with Paragraph 6 hereof and the resulting **actual** fee shall be determined in the following manner:

(a) **LIVE MUSIC AND ENTERTAINMENT ONLY:** LICENSEE shall pay the applicable amount directly opposite LICENSEE's bracket of live music and entertainment costs indicated on **Schedule A** herein.

(b) **RECORDED AND LIVE MUSIC:** LICENSEE shall pay both (i) the applicable amount indicated on Schedule A herein and (ii) the applicable amount indicated on **Schedule B-Section I** herein.

(c) **RECORDED MUSIC ONLY:** LICENSEE shall pay the applicable amount indicated on **Schedule B-Section II** herein.

4. For the **first contract year** of this agreement, it is agreed that LICENSEE's **estimated** fee shall be the sum of (i) the applicable license fee for the use of **live music and entertainment** in accordance with **Schedule A,** and (ii) the applicable license fee for the use of **recorded music** in accordance with **Schedule B.**

COMPLETE ALL SHADED AREAS BELOW. IF NOT APPLICABLE, WRITE — "N/A"

- If LICENSEE uses live music, LICENSEE estimates that its live music and entertainment costs for the first contract year is .... *(Live music and entertainment costs, see Schedule A)* ...... 1 $ _____

- and the estimated annual license fee for the use of live music and and entertainment as determined from Schedule A is .... *(Estimated Annual Fee from Schedule A)* ...... 2 $ _____

- If LICENSEE uses recorded music (including licensable audio-visual use), LICENSEE warrants and represents that the maximum room occupancy of the licensed premises is *(Maximum Room Occupancy)* ...... 3 _____

- and falls within Class .... *(From Schedule B)* ...... 4 _____

- of Schedule B and the estimated Annual Fee as determined from Schedule B is ... *(From Schedule B)* ...... 5 $ _____

- If licensable audio-visual performances (projection TV, televisions, monitors, video cassettes, etc.) of recorded music are given, LICENSEE shall pay an additional 35% of the annual recorded music fee .... *(Enter 35% (.35) of Line 5)* ...... 6 $ _____

- The total estimated annual recorded music fee is .... *(Add Line 5 and Line 6)* ...... 7 $ _____

- For the first contract year, LICENSEE's total estimated license fee, payable in full upon the signing of this agreement, is .... *(Add Box 2 and Box 7)* ...... 8 $ _____
  TOTAL FEE

5. For each subsequent contract year the estimated license fee shall be due and payable no later than 20 days after each anniversary date during the term of this agreement. Beginning with the second contract year and at the option of LICENSEE, payment of the estimated fee may be made in quarterly installments, provided that said quarterly installments are made no later than twenty (20) days after the start of each quarterly period. If any quarterly payment is not timely received, the option herein granted to LICENSEE to make quarterly payments shall terminate, and the balance of the then-current year's estimate will immediately become due and payable. All subsequent estimates will then become due and payable annually. The estimated fee for each contract year subsequent to the first contract year of the term shall be the actual annual fee payable by LICENSEE for the previous contract year, pursuant to Paragraph 6 hereof.

6. At the same time that the estimated annual fee is paid, LICENSEE shall furnish BMI (on forms available from BMI) with a report, certified either by an officer, owner, operator, or by the auditor of LICENSEE, which shall include the following information for such contract year: if live music was performed, the total live music and entertainment costs for such contract year and if recorded music was performed, the maximum room occupancy of the licensed premises, whether or not there is dancing at the premises, and whether or not licensable audio-visual performances of recorded music were given. Such reports shall continue to be made during any period of discontinuance.

(a) If the actual fee due BMI is less than the estimated fee already paid to BMI for such contract year, BMI agrees to credit the difference to the account of LICENSEE and, if such difference shall occur during the last year of the term, BMI agrees to return same promptly.

(b) If the actual fee due BMI is greater than the estimated fee already paid by LICENSEE to BMI for such contract year, LICENSEE shall pay BMI the difference between the actual and estimated license fee within thirty (30) days of LICENSEE's receipt of the adjusted statement of license fees sent by BMI.

(c) In the event LICENSEE's Class of recorded music use changes in any contract year, there shall be an adjustment in LICENSEE's recorded music fee made for such year and it shall be in an amount equal to the fee for a premises of that Class in which LICENSEE operated for the greatest part of the year in which said change(s) occurred.

(d) In the event that LICENSEE fails to timely submit to BMI an annual report required by this Paragraph 6 (or a resumption of music report as required by Paragraph 10), LICENSEE hereby appoints, authorizes and directs BMI, at BMI's option, to assess a reasonable estimated license fee for such contract year. BMI shall give written notice to LICENSEE of the license fee so calculated by BMI. LICENSEE shall have ninety (90) days after the mailing of such written notice by BMI to submit the required report. If BMI does not receive from LICENSEE the required report after such notice period has expired, BMI and LICENSEE agree that BMI's estimated fee shall then be established as the actual fee for the year unreported by LICENSEE. BMI and LICENSEE further agree that such established actual fee shall also become the basis for the estimated fee for the following contract year. LICENSEE agrees to waive its right to file its report for any contract year in which BMI's estimated fee becomes the actual fee.

7. BMI shall have the right to require such reasonable data or information relating to LICENSEE's annual expenditures for live music and entertainment and the recorded music policy at the premises, in addition to that furnished pursuant to Paragraph 6 hereof, as may be necessary in order to ascertain the actual annual license fee. BMI shall have the right upon reasonable notice to LICENSEE, by its authorized representatives, at any time during customary business hours, to examine the books and records of account of LICENSEE to such extent as may be necessary to verify the statements made hereunder. BMI shall consider all data and information coming to its attention as a result of any such examination of books and records as confidential.

8. In the event that BMI, at any time during the term hereof, shall, for the individual licensing of establishments of the same class and category as that of LICENSEE, issue licenses granting rights similar to those in this agreement on a more favorable basis, BMI shall, for the balance of the term hereof, offer LICENSEE a comparable agreement.

9. If, during the term hereof, LICENSEE shall permanently cease to operate the premises, whether by reason of sale or lease thereof, or otherwise, this agreement and the obligation of LICENSEE to BMI shall thereupon terminate; provided that LICENSEE shall, within ten (10) days thereafter, give written notice of such termination to BMI, setting forth the effective date thereof and the name of the new owner or operator of the premises, as the case may be, and that LICENSEE shall submit all reports and pay to BMI all fees due hereunder until said effective date, in accordance with the adjustments set forth in Paragraph 10 hereof.

SCHEDULE A — LIVE MUSIC AND ENTERTAINMENT

LIVE MUSIC AND ENTERTAINMENT COSTS		ANNUAL FEE FOR CONTRACT YEAR BEGINNING IN		
WEEKLY EXPENDITURE	ANNUAL ENTERTAINMENT COSTS	1990 & 1991	1992 & 1993	1994 AND SUBSEQUENT CONTRACT YEARS
($3,100 or more) ....$160,000 or more		$1,260+ $^4/_{10}$ of 1% (.006) of each dollar of expense thereafter	$1,420+ $^7/_{10}$ of 1% (.007) of each dollar of expense thereafter	$1,530+ $^8/_{10}$ of 1% (.008) of each dollar of expense thereafter
($2,700 — $3,099) ....$140,000 to $159,999.99		$1,260	$1,420	$1,530
(2,100 — 2,699) .... 120,000 to 139,999.99		1,050	1,180	1,275
(1,900 — 2,099) .... 100,000 to 119,999.99		900	1,015	1,095
(1,500 — 1,899) .... 80,000 to 99,999.99		750	845	910
(1,200 — 1,499) .... 65,000 to 79,999.99		630	710	765
(900 — 1,199) .... 50,000 to 64,999.99		570	640	690
(700 — 899) .... 35,000 to 49,999.99		500	565	610
(500 — 699) .... 25,000 to 34,999.99		440	495	535
(300 — 499) .... 15,000 to 24,999.99		360	405	440
(200 — 299) .... 10,000 to 14,999.99		270	305	330
(150 — 199) .... 8,000 to 9,999.99		215	245	260
(100 — 149) .... 5,000 to 7,999.99		180	205	220
(99 or less) .... Less than 5,000.00		145	165	175

SCHEDULE B$^{(*)}$ — SECTION I — RECORDED MUSIC
THIS SECTION TO BE USED WHEN BOTH LIVE AND RECORDED MUSIC UTILIZED

MAXIMUM ROOM OCCUPANCY OF PREMISES (AS DETERMINED BY LOCAL FIRE OR BUILDING AUTHORITY)	WITH DANCING (including Discotheques)					WITHOUT DANCING			
	C L A S S	ANNUAL FEE FOR CONTRACT YEAR BEGINNING IN			C L A S S	ANNUAL FEE FOR CONTRACT YEAR BEGINNING IN		
		1990 & 1991	1992 & 1993	1994 AND SUBSEQUENT CONTRACT YEARS		1990 & 1991	1992 & 1993	1994 AND SUBSEQUENT CONTRACT YEARS
751 & over	11A	$650	$790	$900	11B	$480	$560	$630
676 — 750	10A	600	720	805	10B	440	510	580
601 — 675	9A	550	660	750	9B	400	480	525
526 — 600	8A	490	590	660	8B	360	420	475
451 — 525	7A	455	540	620	7B	320	375	420
376 — 450	6A	390	460	520	6B	280	320	370
301 — 375	5A	340	410	470	5B	210	280	310
226 — 300	4A	300	350	400	4B	200	235	280
151 — 225	3A	240	290	325	3B	160	185	210
76 — 150	2A	190	225	260	2B	120	140	160
1 — 75	1A	140	170	190	1B	80	95	105

SCHEDULE B(*) — SECTION II — RECORDED MUSIC
THIS SECTION TO BE USED WHEN RECORDED MUSIC ONLY UTILIZED BUT NO LIVE MUSIC USED

MAXIMUM ROOM OCCUPANCY OF PREMISES (AS DETERMINED BY LOCAL FIRE OR BUILDING AUTHORITY)	WITH DANCING (including Discotheques)					WITHOUT DANCING		
	C L A S S	ANNUAL FEE FOR CONTRACT YEAR BEGINNING IN			C L A S S	ANNUAL FEE FOR CONTRACT YEAR BEGINNING IN		
		1990 & 1991	1992 & 1993	1994 AND SUBSEQUENT CONTRACT YEARS		1990 & 1991	1992 & 1993	1994 AND SUBSEQUENT CONTRACT YEARS
751 & over	11C	$1275	$1520	$1715	11D	$585	$700	$800
676 — 750	10C	1170	1395	1575	10D	540	640	725
601 — 675	9C	1070	1275	1435	9D	500	590	665
526 — 600	8C	970	1150	1310	8D	450	535	600
451 — 525	7C	860	1025	1155	7D	400	480	540
376 — 450	6C	760	800	1015	6D	360	430	480
301 — 375	5C	650	775	875	5D	320	380	430
226 — 300	4C	550	650	735	4D	270	320	360
151 — 225	3C	445	520	595	3D	220	265	300
76 — 150	2C	340	405	455	2D	180	210	235
1 — 75	1C	235	280	315	1D	150	170	195

AUDIO VISUAL FEE
(*) If audio-visual performances of recorded music (projection TV, televisions, monitors, video cassettes, etc.) are given, add 35% to the applicable Schedule B rate. This charge is not payable, however, for performances for which a license is not required by U.S. Copyright Law.

10. In the event that LICENSEE discontinues the use of *all* music at the premises during the term and so notifies BMI in writing by certified mail, within sixty (60) days after receipt of such notice an adjustment shall be made by BMI for that contract year, provided that LICENSEE has submitted a report as required by Paragraph 6 hereof for all music used up to the date of discontinuance. In no event, however, shall any such adjusted live music fee be less than the lowest fee on Schedule A for that contract year or any such adjusted recorded music fee, which shall be a proration of the full year's fee, be less than the applicable Class 1 fee on Schedule B for that contract year. LICENSEE shall not be obligated to make future payments to BMI for the discontinued music (provided all of any previously due license fees have been paid) until such time as LICENSEE shall resume the use of music. If LICENSEE discontinues the use of either live or recorded music, but not both, this agreement shall continue to be applicable to that music which continues to be used. LICENSEE shall send written notice of any resumption of music to BMI within thirty (30) days thereof and at the same time provide BMI with the information required in Paragraph 4. If LICENSEE fails to notify and/or provide BMI with such information, BMI shall establish, pursuant to the authorization in Paragraph 6(d) hereof, a reasonable estimated fee for the applicable contract year. If discontinuance and resumption occur in the same contract year, license fees shall be payable as if discontinuance never occurred (and LICENSEE's estimated fee immediately prior to discontinuance shall be reinstated). If resumption occurs in a subsequent contract year, license fees shall be payable in accordance with the adjustments set forth in this Paragraph.

11. In the event that subsequent to the date of this agreement LICENSEE shall acquire ownership or commence operation of one or more other premises at which music licensed by BMI is performed, LICENSEE agrees to notify BMI in writing within thirty (30) days thereof, setting forth the name and address of each such new premises and further agrees to execute the appropriate license agreement promptly upon receipt from BMI. No such new premises shall be deemed to be licensed hereunder.

12. BMI agrees to indemnify, save harmless and defend LICENSEE, its officers and employees, from and against any and all claims, demands or suits that may be made or brought against them or any of them with respect to the performance of any material licensed under this agreement. Such indemnity shall be limited to works which are licensed by BMI at the time of LICENSEE's performances. BMI's Clearance Department will, upon request, advise LICENSEE whether particular musical works are available for performance as part of BMI's repertoire. LICENSEE agrees to give BMI immediate notice of any such claim, demand or suit, to deliver to BMI any papers pertaining thereto and to cooperate with BMI with respect thereto, and BMI shall have full charge of the defense of any such claim, demand or suit.

13. BMI reserves the right at its discretion to withdraw from the license granted hereunder any musical work as to which any legal action has been instituted or a claim made that BMI does not have the right to license the performing rights in such work or that such work infringes another composition.

14. All disputes of any kind, nature or description arising in connection with the terms and conditions of this agreement shall be submitted to the American Arbitration Association in New York, New York for arbitration under its then prevailing rules, the arbitrator(s) to be selected as follows: Each of the parties hereto shall, by written notice to the other, have the right to appoint one arbitrator. If, within ten (10) days following the giving of such notice by one party, the other shall not, by written notice, appoint another arbitrator, the first arbitrator shall be the sole arbitrator. If two arbitrators are so appointed, they shall appoint a third arbitrator. If ten (10) days elapse after the appointment of the second arbitrator and the two arbitrators are unable to agree upon the third arbitrator, then either party may, in writing, request the American Arbitration Association to appoint the third arbitrator. The award made in the arbitration shall be binding and conclusive on the parties and judgment may be, but need not be, entered in any court having jurisdiction. Such award shall include the fixing of the costs, expenses and attorney's fees of arbitration, which shall be borne by the unsuccessful party.

15. Upon any breach or default of the terms and conditions contained herein, BMI shall have the right to cancel this agreement if such breach or default continues thirty (30) days after LICENSEE's receipt of written notice thereof. The right to cancel granted to BMI shall be in addition to any and all other remedies which BMI may have. No waiver by BMI of full performance of this agreement by LICENSEE in any one or more instances shall be deemed a waiver of the right to require full and complete performance of this agreement thereafter or of the right to cancel this agreement in accordance with the terms of this Paragraph.

16. Any notice required or permitted to be given under this agreement shall be in writing and shall be deemed duly given when sent by ordinary first-class U.S. mail (unless specifically required elsewhere in this agreement to be sent by certified mail) to the party for whom it is intended, at its indicated mailing address hereinabove stated, or any other address which either party hereto may from time to time designate for such purpose, and when such notice is so mailed, it shall be deemed given upon the mailing thereof. Any such notice sent to BMI shall be to the attention of the Licensing Department. Any such notice sent to LICENSEE shall be to the attention of the person signing this agreement on behalf of LICENSEE or such other person as LICENSEE may advise BMI.

17. This agreement constitutes the entire understanding between the parties, shall not be binding until signed by both parties, and cannot be waived or added to or modified orally, and no waiver, addition or modification shall be valid unless in writing and signed by the parties. The rights of LICENSEE shall not be assignable. This agreement, its validity, construction and effect, shall be governed by the laws of the State of New York. The fact that any provisions herein are found by a court of competent jurisdiction to be void or unenforceable shall not affect the validity or enforceability of any other provision.

IN WITNESS WHEREOF, this agreement has been executed by the duly authorized representatives of BMI and LICENSEE all as of the date first above written.

(To Be Completed by BMI)	(To Be Completed by LICENSEE)

BROADCAST MUSIC, INC.

_____
Name of Corporation, Partnership or Individual Owner
(Legal Name of Licensee)

BY _____   SIGN HERE ▶ BY _____
        (Signature)   *(Signature)*

_____   _____
     (Print name of Signer)   *(Print name of Signer)*

_____   _____
     (Title of Signer)   *(Fill in Title in which Signed)*

(a) If corporation, state corporate office held;
(b) if partnership, write "Partner", (c) if individual owner, write "Individual owner"

PLEASE COMPLETE SHADED AREA ONLY

FORM 15.5

BMI HOTEL/MOTEL LICENSE

MUSIC PERFORMANCE AGREEMENT
HOTEL/MOTEL
COMPLETE ALL SHADED AREAS BELOW

BMI

AGREEMENT, made at New York, N.Y. on *(Date Will Be Entered By BMI Upon Execution)* _____ between BROADCAST MUSIC, INC., a corporation organized under the laws of the State of New York (hereinafter called BMI) with principal offices at 320 West 57th Street, New York, N.Y. 10019, and

_____
Name of Corporation, Partnership or Individual Owner (Legal Name of Licensee)

☐ If a corporation, indicate state of incorporation _____
(State)

CHECK APPROPRIATE BOX AND COMPLETE

☐ If a partnership, indicate names of all partners _____
(Names of Partners)

_____
(Names of Partners)

☐ If an individual owner, indicate residence address below under Mailing Address

(hereinafter called LICENSEE)   *Doing business under the name of (Trade Name)*

PREMISES ADDRESS *(herein called the licensed premises)*	**MAILING ADDRESS** *(residence address if individual owner)*
(Street Address)	*(Street Address)*
(City)	*(City)*
(State) *(Zip)*	*(State)* *(Zip)*
( )	( )
(Area Code) *(Telephone No.)*	*(Area Code)* *(Telephone No.)*

IT IS HEREBY AGREED AS FOLLOWS:

1. As used in this agreement:

(a) **"Term"** shall mean the period commencing on January 1, 1991 and ending on December 31, 1993 and continuing thereafter unless canceled by either party at the end of said period, or at the end of any subsequent one (1) year period, upon thirty (30) days advance written notice to the other party.

(b) **"LICENSEE's activities"** shall mean all activities engaged in by LICENSEE in the public rooms or public areas of the premises. "LICENSEE's activities" shall include the presentation on the premises of any entertainment attraction presented by a person or entity who is in the business of promoting attractions, whether or not such persons or entity is employed by or associated with LICENSEE.

(c) **"Live music and entertainment costs"** (herein sometimes referred to as "Costs") shall mean all expenditures of every kind and nature (whether in money or any other form of consideration) made by LICENSEE or on LICENSEE's behalf, for all live music and entertainment in connection with LICENSEE's activities on the premises. Such Costs shall include the agreed value of room and board and any other accommodations or services which are made available to any person or entity as part of the consideration for their rendering or presenting entertainment services in connection with LICENSEE's activities. For purposes of this agreement, the agreed value of accommodations or services shall be deemed to be one-half of the prevailing rate charged to LICENSEE's guests for similar accommodations or services. The term "live music and entertainment costs" shall not include the cost of the services of a disc jockey, video jockey, or other services in connection with a discotheque or any entertainment services rendered by LICENSEE's regular employees, except to the extent that such employees shall be engaged primarily for the purpose of rendering entertainment services.

(d) **"Recorded music"** shall mean the performance of music by means of a mechanical or electronic device or via the reception of broadcast audio transmissions on receiving apparatus and amplification thereof for public performance. Such performances may not be reproduced other than by loudspeakers located only on the licensed premises. Recorded music does not include performances by means of a coin-operated phonorecord player (juke box) otherwise licensed under 17 U.S.C. Section 116 or performance by means of any device for which a license is not required by law.

2. BMI hereby grants to LICENSEE a non-exclusive license to publicly perform or cause to be performed by any means or method whatsoever in the course of LICENSEE's activities at the licensed premises all the musical works, the right to grant public performance licenses of which BMI shall during the term hereof control. Said license shall not include dramatic rights, the right to perform dramatico-musical works in whole or in substantial part, the right to present individual works in a dramatic setting, which constitute an exercise of "grand rights", or the right to use the music licensed hereunder in any other context which may constitute an exercise of "grand rights" therein. Said license also shall not include the right to broadcast, telecast or otherwise transmit the performances licensed hereunder to persons outside of the licensed premises, the right to authorize performances by means of so-called background music procured from an outside service to the extent that BMI shall not have licensed such service to render performances by such means at the licensed premises, or the right to authorize performances which are telecast or otherwise transmitted to the premises by any cable or television system or to authorize video performances by any other means supplied by an outside service, to the extent that BMI shall not have licensed such service to render performances of BMI music by any such means at the licensed premises. Further, this license shall not include any performances of musical works as part of industrial or trade shows, expositions, or business presentations at the licensed premises.

3. LICENSEE agrees to pay to BMI for each contract year of the term hereof a license fee determined in the following manner:

(a) **LIVE MUSIC ONLY:** LICENSEE shall pay the amount for the applicable year directly opposite LICENSEE's bracket of live music and entertainment costs indicated on Schedule A herein. Fill in amount for first contract year in Paragraph 4(a) using prior year's costs as defined below.

(b) **RECORDED MUSIC ONLY:** LICENSEE shall pay the amount for the applicable year indicated on Schedule B herein under the heading "RECORDED MUSIC ONLY". Fill in amount in Paragraph 4(b).

(c) **RECORDED MUSIC AND LIVE MUSIC:** LICENSEE shall pay both (i) the amount for the applicable bracket and year indicated on Schedule A herein and (ii) the amount for the applicable year indicated on Schedule C herein under the heading "RECORDED MUSIC AND LIVE MUSIC". Fill in amounts in Paragraphs 4(a) and 4(c) and the total in Paragraph 4(d).

(d) If the initial period of the term is a partial calendar year, LICENSEE's Costs for such initial period shall be determined by multiplying its average monthly Costs in such partial calendar year by twelve (12), and the applicable license fee for both live music and entertainment and recorded music shall be prorated on a monthly basis.

(e) The license fee for each calendar year of the term (other than an initial partial calendar year) in which any live music and entertainment are performed in connection with LICENSEE's activities at the premises shall be not less than the lowest fee provided on Schedule A for such year.

Page 1

4. For the first contract year of this agreement, the Schedule A "Bracket of Annual Live Music and Entertainment Costs" to be used to determine the applicable license fee shall be that bracket which would have been applicable for the twelve (12) month period immediately preceding the commencement date of this agreement (herein called the "prior year"). If LICENSEE operated with a policy of live music and entertainment for less than the full prior year, the applicable Schedule A bracket shall be deemed to be that which includes the amount equal to twelve (12) times LICENSEE's average monthly Costs during such partial prior year. If LICENSEE did not offer live music and entertainment during any part of the prior year, the applicable Schedule A bracket shall be that which includes the amount equal to twelve (12) times LICENSEE's actual (or estimated) costs during the first full month live music and entertainment was (or will be) offered during the term hereof.

(COMPLETE IF LICENSEE USES LIVE MUSIC AND ENTERTAINMENT)

(a) LICENSEE's Costs for the prior year were . . . .   **1** $ _____

and the annual license fee (prorated on a monthly basis if the initial term hereof is a partial year) for the use of live music and entertainment during the first contract year as determined from Schedule A is . . . . . . *(Insert Fee From Schedule A)*   **2** $ _____

(COMPLETE IF LICENSEE USES RECORDED MUSIC BUT NO LIVE MUSIC)

(b) If LICENSEE uses Recorded Music *Only*, LICENSEE warrants and represents that the annual license fee (pro-rated on a monthly basis if the initial term hereof is a partial year) as determined from Schedule B and the number of guest rooms on the licensed premises and the music policy is as follows:

Number of guest rooms at the licensed premises _____ ; Dancing _____ ;
                                       No. Guest Rooms   *Yes/No*

Cover, minimum or admission charge _____ ; Shows or acts _____ . . . . *(Insert Fee From Schedule B)*   **3** $ _____
                                     Yes/No   *Yes/No*

Add 45% of above amount for licensable audio-visual performances, as defined in Schedule B sub-paragraph 5: . . . . *(enter 45% (.45) of line 3)*   **4** $ _____

Recorded Music Fee where NO LIVE music is used. . . . . *(Add Line 3 and Line 4)*   **5** $ _____

Insert Box 5 total in Box 9 below

(COMPLETE IF LICENSEE USES BOTH RECORDED AND LIVE MUSIC)

(c) If LICENSEE uses Recorded Music And Live Music, LICENSEE warrants and represents that the annual license fee (pro-rated on a monthly basis if the initial term hereof is a partial year) as determined from Schedule C and the number of guest rooms on the licensed premises and the music policy is as follows:

Number of guest rooms at the licensed premises _____ ; Dancing _____ ;
                                       No. Guest Rooms   *Yes/No*

Cover, minimum or admission charge _____ ; Shows or acts _____ . . . . *(Insert Fee From Schedule C)*   **6** $ _____
                                     Yes/No   *Yes/No*

Add 45% of above amount for licensable audio-visual performances, as defined in Schedule C sub-paragraph 5: . . . . *(enter 45% (.45) of line 6)*   **7** $ _____

Recorded Music Fee where LIVE music is used . . . . *(Add Line 6 and Line 7)*   **8** $ _____

(d) Total estimated fee. . . . . *(Add Box 2 and Box 8 or Enter Total from Box 5)*   **9** $ _____
                                                             TOTAL ESTIMATED FEE

(e) The estimated fee for each contract year subsequent to the first contract year of the term hereof shall be the actual fee reported by LICENSEE for the previous contract year, pursuant to Paragraph 6 hereof.

5. The license fee calculated pursuant to Paragraph 4 hereof is due and payable in full upon the signing of this agreement. The license fee for each subsequent calendar year shall be due and payable on January 20th of each year during the term of this agreement. At the option of LICENSEE, payment of the estimated fee may be made in quarterly installments, provided that said quarterly installments are made no later than twenty (20) days after the start of each quarterly period. If any quarterly payment is not timely received, the option herein granted to LICENSEE to make quarterly payments shall terminate, and the balance of the then-current year's estimate will immediately become due and payable. All subsequent estimates will then become due and payable annually within twenty (20) days of each anniversary date.

6. On or before the 20th day of January following each calendar year of the term, LICENSEE shall furnish BMI (on forms to be supplied by BMI) with a statement, certified either by an officer or by the auditor of LICENSEE, which shall include the following information for such calendar year: (i) the total live music and entertainment costs for the previous calendar year; (ii) if recorded music was performed, the number of guest rooms on the licensed premises, whether dancing is permitted, whether a cover, minimum or admission charge is made, whether shows or acts are presented and whether audio-visual performances take place.

(a) If the actual license fee due BMI is greater than the estimated license fee already paid by LICENSEE to BMI during the previous calendar year (or part thereof), LICENSEE agrees to pay to BMI an amount equal to the difference between the actual and the estimated license fees within thirty (30) days of BMI's billing therefor.

(b) If the actual license fee due BMI is less than the estimated license fee already paid to BMI during the previous calendar year (or part thereof), BMI agrees to credit the difference to the account of LICENSEE, and if such difference shall occur during the last calendar year of the term, BMI agrees to refund the same promptly.

7. (a) BMI shall have the right to require such reasonable data or information relating to (i) the annual expenditures for live music and entertainment costs, (ii) recorded music at the licensed premises as provided by this agreement, in addition to that furnished pursuant to paragraph 6 above, as may, in its discretion, be necessary in order to ascertain the annual license fee.

(b) BMI shall have the right, by its authorized representatives, at any time during customary business hours, to examine the books and records of account of LICENSEE to such extent as may be necessary to verify the statements made hereunder. BMI shall consider all data and information coming to its attention as a result of any such examination of books and records as completely confidential.

(c) BMI may conduct an audit pursuant to this paragraph for a period not to exceed three calendar years preceding the year in which the audit is made. In the event such audit reveals a deficiency, then BMI may conduct an audit for the additional preceding three calendar years. In the event LICENSEE, after written notice from BMI, refuses to permit an audit, or refuses to produce the books and records of account of LICENSEE necessary to verify the statements and reports required hereunder, BMI shall not be restricted to the time limitation set forth herein. BMI shall have the right to audit for periods licensed under previous license agreements between BMI and LICENSEE, provided, however, BMI shall be limited to three years or six years (as the case may be) for all audits under said license agreements.

(d) In the event BMI conducts an audit of LICENSEE, and such audit reveals that LICENSEE underpaid license fees to BMI to the extent of ten (10) percent or more, then LICENSEE shall pay a late payment charge on the additional license fees due as of a result of the audit(s) only of one and a half percent per month, or the maximum rate permitted by law, whichever is less, from the date(s) the license fees should have been paid pursuant to this agreement.

PLEASE COMPLETE SHADED AREAS ONLY

FEE SCHEDULES
IF LIVE MUSIC IS PERFORMED, USE SCHEDULE A
IF RECORDED MUSIC ONLY IS PERFORMED, USE SCHEDULE B
IF BOTH LIVE AND RECORDED MUSIC ARE PERFORMED, USE SCHEDULES A & C

SCHEDULE A
LIVE MUSIC AND ENTERTAINMENT

Bracket of Annual Live Music and Entertainment Costs		Annual License Fee for Calendar Years			
		1990	1991	1992	1993
Less Than	$ 2,000.00	$ 105	$ 105	$ 105	$ 105
$ 2,000.00 to	$ 4,999.99	$ 130	$ 135	$ 140	$ 145
$ 5,000.00 to	$ 9,999.99	$ 170	$ 185	$ 200	$ 215
$ 10,000.00 to	$ 14,999.99	$ 230	$ 250	$ 265	$ 285
$ 15,000.00 to	$ 24,999.99	$ 350	$ 375	$ 405	$ 430
$ 25,000.00 to	$ 34,999.99	$ 460	$ 500	$ 535	$ 570
$ 35,000.00 to	$ 49,999.99	$ 570	$ 615	$ 660	$ 705
$ 50,000.00 to	$ 64,999.99	$ 685	$ 740	$ 790	$ 845
$ 65,000.00 to	$ 79,999.99	$ 870	$ 935	$ 1,005	$ 1,070
$ 80,000.00 to	$ 99,999.99	$ 1,150	$ 1,245	$ 1,335	$ 1,425
$ 100,000.00 to	$ 119,999.99	$ 1,445	$ 1,555	$ 1,670	$ 1,780
$ 120,000.00 to	$ 139,999.99	$ 1,725	$ 1,865	$ 2,000	$ 2,135
$ 140,000.00 to	$ 159,999.99	$ 2,020	$ 2,175	$ 2,335	$ 2,490
$ 160,000.00 to	$ 179,999.99	$ 2,305	$ 2,485	$ 2,665	$ 2,845
$ 180,000.00 to	$ 199,999.99	$ 2,595	$ 2,800	$ 3,000	$ 3,205
$ 200,000.00 to	$ 249,999.99	$ 2,885	$ 3,110	$ 3,335	$ 3,560
$ 250,000.00 to	$ 299,999.99	$ 3,175	$ 3,425	$ 3,670	$ 3,920
$ 300,000.00 to	$ 349,999.99	$ 3,460	$ 3,730	$ 4,000	$ 4,270
$ 350,000.00 to	$ 399,999.99	$ 3,840	$ 4,145	$ 4,445	$ 4,745
$ 400,000.00 to	$ 449,999.99	$ 4,035	$ 4,350	$ 4,665	$ 4,980
$ 450,000.00 to	$ 499,999.99	$ 4,325	$ 4,665	$ 5,000	$ 5,340
$ 500,000.00 to	$ 599,999.99	$ 4,595	$ 4,950	$ 5,310	$ 5,670
$ 600,000.00 to	$ 749,999.99	$ 5,015	$ 5,405	$ 5,800	$ 6,190
$ 750,000.00 to	$ 999,999.99	$ 5,855	$ 6,310	$ 6,765	$ 7,220
$ 1,000,000.00 to	$ 1,499,999.99	$ 6,685	$ 7,205	$ 7,730	$ 8,250
$ 1,500,000.00 to	$ 1,999,999.99	$ 7,520	$ 8,105	$ 8,695	$ 9,280
$ 2,000,000.00 to	$ 2,999,999.99	$ 8,355	$ 9,010	$ 9,660	$ 10,315
$ 3,000,000.00 to	$ 3,999,999.99	$ 9,190	$ 9,910	$ 10,625	$ 11,345
$ 4,000,000.00 to	$ 4,999,999.99	$ 10,855	$ 11,705	$ 12,560	$ 13,410
$ 5,000,000.00 to	$ 5,999,999.99	$ 12,115	$ 13,060	$ 14,010	$ 14,955
$ 6,000,000.00 to	$ 6,999,999.99	$ 15,035	$ 16,215	$ 17,390	$ 18,565
$ 7,000,000.00 and over		$ 15,245	$ 16,625	$ 18,010	$ 19,390

SCHEDULE B
RECORDED MUSIC ONLY (NO LIVE MUSIC USED)

1. (a) No Dancing; (b) No Cover, Minimum or Admission Charge; and (c) No Shows or Acts*

No. of Rooms	Annual License Fee for Calendar Years			
	1990	1991	1992	1993
1-300	$ 145	$ 150	$ 155	$ 165
Over 300	$ 200	$ 205	$ 215	$ 225

2. One of: (a) Dancing; (b) Cover, Minimum or Admission Charge; or (c) Shows or Acts*

No. of Rooms	Annual License Fee for Calendar Years			
	1990	1991	1992	1993
1-100	$ 195	$ 200	$ 210	$ 220
101-300	$ 265	$ 275	$ 285	$ 300
301-500	$ 400	$ 420	$ 435	$ 455
Over 500	$ 530	$ 550	$ 575	$ 600

3. Two of: (a) Dancing; (b) Cover, Minimum or Admission Charge; or (c) Shows or Acts*

No. of Rooms	Annual License Fee for Calendar Years			
	1990	1991	1992	1993
1-100	$ 265	$ 275	$ 285	$ 300
101-300	$ 400	$ 420	$ 435	$ 455
301-500	$ 595	$ 620	$ 645	$ 675
Over 500	$ 795	$ 825	$ 860	$ 905

4. With: (a) Dancing; (b) Cover, Minimum or Admission Charge; and (c) Shows or Acts*

No. of Rooms	Annual License Fee for Calendar Years			
	1990	1991	1992	1993
1-100	$ 440	$ 460	$ 475	$ 500
101-300	$ 680	$ 710	$ 735	$ 775
301-500	$ 915	$ 950	$ 990	$ 1,040
Over 500	$ 1,140	$ 1,185	$ 1,235	$ 1,295

5. AUDIO-VISUAL PERFORMANCES. If audio-visual performances of recorded music (such as a large screen projection television) are given, add 45 percent to the applicable Schedule B rate. This charge is not payable however, for performances for which a license is not required by the US Copyright Law, including those by means of a single receiving apparatus of a kind commonly used in private homes, unless a direct charge is made to see the transmission or the transmission thus received is further transmitted to the public.

*"Shows or Acts" shall include, but not be limited to, use of a disc jockey or video jockey.

SCHEDULE C
RECORDED MUSIC AND LIVE MUSIC

1. (a) No Dancing; (b) No Cover, Minimum or Admission Charge; and (c) No Shows or Acts*

No. of Rooms	Annual License Fee for Calendar Years			
	1990	1991	1992	1993
1-300	$ 85	$ 90	$ 90	$ 95
Over 300	$ 120	$ 125	$ 130	$ 135

2. One of: (a) Dancing; (b) Cover, Minimum or Admission Charge; or (c) Shows or Acts*

No. of Rooms	Annual License Fee for Calendar Years			
	1990	1991	1992	1993
1-100	$ 115	$ 120	$ 125	$ 130
101-300	$ 160	$ 165	$ 175	$ 180
301-500	$ 210	$ 215	$ 225	$ 240
Over 500	$ 275	$ 285	$ 295	$ 310

3. Two of: (a) Dancing; (b) Cover, Minimum or Admission Charge; or (c) Shows or Acts*

No. of Rooms	Annual License Fee for Calendar Years			
	1990	1991	1992	1993
1-100	$ 160	$ 165	$ 175	$ 180
101-300	$ 210	$ 215	$ 225	$ 240
301-500	$ 295	$ 310	$ 320	$ 335
Over 500	$ 435	$ 450	$ 470	$ 495

4. With: (a) Dancing; (b) Cover, Minimum or Admission Charge; and (c) Shows or Acts*

No. of Rooms	Annual License Fee for Calendar Years			
	1990	1991	1992	1993
1-100	$ 440	$ 460	$ 475	$ 500
101-300	$ 680	$ 710	$ 735	$ 775
301-500	$ 915	$ 950	$ 990	$ 1,040
Over 500	$ 1,140	$ 1,185	$ 1,235	$ 1,295

5. AUDIO-VISUAL PERFORMANCES. If audio-visual performances of recorded music (such as a large screen projection television) are given, add 45 percent to the applicable Schedule C rate. This charge is not payable however, for performances for which a license is not required by the US Copyright Law, including those by means of a single receiving apparatus of a kind commonly used in private homes, unless a direct charge is made to see the transmission or the transmission thus received is further transmitted to the public.

*"Shows or Acts" shall include, but not be limited to, use of a disc jockey or video jockey.

(e) In the event BMI conducts an audit of LICENSEE and such audit reveals that LICENSEE underpaid license fees to BMI to the extent of less than ten (10) percent, then LICENSEE shall pay a late payment charge of one and one half percent per month, or the maximum rate permitted by law, whichever is less, if payment is not made to BMI by LICENSEE within sixty (60) days after BMI demands payment of said license fees found due as a result of the audit(s).

8. In the event that LICENSEE discontinues the use of all live and recorded music at the premises during the term of this agreement and so notifies BMI in writing, within sixty (60) days after receipt of such notice an adjustment shall be made by BMI for that partial calendar year, provided that, in the case of live music, LICENSEE has submitted a statement of Costs incurred up to the date of discontinuance. In no event, however, shall any such adjusted live music license fee be less than the lowest listed license fee on Schedule A for the year of discontinuance or any such adjusted recorded music license fee, which shall be a proration of the full year's license fee, be less than the lowest license fee on Schedule B or Schedule C, whichever is applicable to LICENSEE, for the year of discontinuance. LICENSEE shall not be obligated to make future payments to BMI thereafter for the discontinued music (provided the balance of any previously due license fee has been paid) until such time as LICENSEE shall resume the use of such music at the premises, and LICENSEE agrees to send written notice of any resumption to BMI within thirty (30) days thereof. Such resumption shall be treated in all respects as though the term of this agreement had commenced on the date of resumption. If LICENSEE discontinues the use of either live or recorded music, but not both, the provisions of this agreement shall continue to be applicable to that music which continues to be used at the premises. The term "discontinuance" as used herein shall mean the total abandonment, rather then a seasonal or periodic cessation, of the use of music and entertainment. Notwithstanding such discontinuance, LICENSEE agrees to continue to furnish to BMI statements as provided in paragraph 6 hereof unless or until this agreement has been canceled.

9. In the event that BMI, at any time during the term, shall, for the individual licensing of establishments of the same class and category as that of LICENSEE, issues licenses granting rights similar to those conveyed by this agreement at more favorable rates of payment than are set forth herein, BMI shall, for the balance of the term, tender to LICENSEE a contract containing such more favorable rates of payment.

10. BMI agrees to indemnify, save harmless and defend LICENSEE, its officers and employees, from and against any and all claims, demands or suits that may be made or brought against them or any of them with respect to the performance of any material licensed under this agreement. Such indemnity shall be limited to works which are licensed by BMI at the time of LICENSEE's performances. BMI's Clearance Department will, upon request, advise LICENSEE whether particular musical works are available for performance as part of BMI's repertoire. LICENSEE agrees to give BMI immediate notice of any such claim, demand or suit, to deliver to BMI any papers pertaining thereto and to cooperate with BMI with respect thereto, and BMI shall have full charge of the defense of any such claim, demand or suit.

11. If during the term LICENSEE shall cease to operate the premises, whether by reason of sale or lease thereof, or otherwise, this agreement and the obligation of LICENSEE to BMI shall thereupon terminate; provided, however, that LICENSEE shall, within ten (10) days thereafter, give written notice of such termination to BMI, setting forth the effective date thereof and the name of any vendee or lessee of the premises, as the case may be, and that LICENSEE shall pay to BMI all fees due hereunder until said date.

12. BMI reserves the right at its discretion to withdraw from the license granted hereunder any musical work as to which any legal action has been instituted or a claim made that BMI does not have the legal right to license the performing rights in such work or that such work infringes a composition in the BMI repertoire.

13. All disputes of any kind, nature or description arising in connection with the terms and conditions of this agreement shall be submitted to the American Arbitration Association in New York, New York for arbitration under its then prevailing rules, the arbitrator(s) to be selected as follows: Each of the parties hereto shall, by written notice to the other, have the right to appoint one arbitrator. If, within ten (10) days following the giving of such notice by one party, the other shall not, by written notice, appoint another arbitrator, the first arbitrator shall be the sole arbitrator. If two arbitrators are so appointed, they shall appoint a third arbitrator. If ten (10) days elapse after the appointment of the second arbitrator and the two arbitrators are unable to agree upon the third arbitrator, then either party may, in writing, request the American Arbitration Association to appoint the third arbitrator. The award made in the arbitration shall be binding and conclusive on the parties and judgment may be, but need not be, entered is any court having jurisdiction.

14. Upon any breach or default of the terms and conditions contained herein, BMI shall have the right to cancel this agreement if such breach or default continues thirty (30) days after LICENSEE's receipt of written notice thereof. The right to cancel granted to BMI shall be in addition to any and all other remedies which BMI may have. No waiver by BMI of full performance of this agreement by LICENSEE in any one or more instances shall be deemed a waiver of the right to require full and complete performance of this agreement thereafter or of the right to cancel this agreement in accordance with the terms of this Paragraph.

15. BMI may impose a late payment charge of one and one half percent (1 1/2%) per month, or the maximum rate permitted by law, whichever is lesser, from the date payment was due on any payment that is received by BMI more than sixty (60) days after the due date. For the applicable late payment charges which may result from audits, see Paragraph 7 of this Agreement.

16. Any notice required or permitted to be given under this agreement shall be in writing and shall be deemed duly given when sent by ordinary first-class U.S. mail to the party for whom it is intended, at its address hereinabove stated, or any other address which either party hereto may from time to time designate for such purpose, and when such notice is so mailed, it shall be deemed given upon the mailing thereof. Any such notice sent to BMI shall be to the attention of the Licensing Department. Any such notice sent to LICENSEE shall be to the attention of the person signing this agreement on behalf of LICENSEE or such other person as LICENSEE may advise BMI.

17. This agreement shall enure to the benefit of and shall be binding upon the parties hereto and their respective successors and assigns, but no assignment shall relieve the parties hereto of their respective obligations hereunder.

18. This agreement constitutes the entire understanding between the parties and cannot be waived or added to or modified orally and no waiver, addition or modification shall be valid unless in writing and signed by the parties. This agreement, its validity, construction and effect, shall be governed by the laws of the state of New York. The fact that all provisions herein are found by a court of competent jurisdiction to be void or unenforceable shall not affect the validity or enforceability of any other provisions.

IN WITNESS WHEREOF: the parties hereto have duly executed this agreement the day and date hereinbefore set forth.

| (To Be Completed by BMI) | | (To Be Completed by LICENSEE) |

BROADCAST MUSIC, INC.

_____
LICENSEE (Legal Name)

By: _____   Sign Here▶ By: _____
        (Signature)   (Signature)

_____   _____
(Print Name of Signer)   (Print Name of Signer)

_____   _____
(Title of Signer)   (Title of Signer)

FORM 15.6

BMI MUSIC ON HOLD LICENSE

UL (MOH)-88 42

DATE WILL BE ENTERED BY BMI UPON EXECUTION

AGREEMENT, made at New York, N.Y. on _____ , 19 _____ , between BROADCAST MUSIC, INC., a corporation organized under the laws of the State of New York (hereinafter called BMI) with principal offices at 320 West 57th Street, New York, N.Y. 10019, and

_____
Name of Corporation, Partnership or Individual Owner (Legal Name of Owner or Operator)

☐ If a corporation, indicate the state of incorporation _____

CHECK APPROPRIATE BOX AND COMPLETE

☐ If a partnership, indicate the names of all partners _____

_____

☐ If an individual owner, indicate residence address _____
(street address)

City _____ , State _____ Zip _____ ☐

(hereinafter called LICENSEE) with offices located at _____
(street address)

City _____ , State _____ Zip _____ ☐

Premises Telephone No. (____) _____
(Area Code)

Office/Home Telephone No. (____) _____
(Area Code)

doing business under the name of_____
(trade name)

located at _____
(street address)

in the City of_____ in the State of _____ Zip _____ ☐
(herein the "licensed premises").

CHECK ADDRESS TO WHICH MAIL SHOULD BE SENT

GENERAL PROVISIONS

1. BMI hereby grants to LICENSEE a non-exclusive license to cause and permit at the licensed premises the public performance of all musical works of which BMI shall have the right to grant public performance licenses during the term hereof. Said license shall be restricted to performances of music in the manner described herein and is granted in consideration of the payment of the license fees as set forth herein and is subject to all of the terms and conditions hereof. This license does not include:

(a) dramatic rights, the right to perform dramatico-musical works in whole or in substantial part, the right to present individual works in a dramatic setting or the right to use the music licensed hereunder in any other context which may constitute an exercise of the "grand rights" therein; or

(b) the right to broadcast, telecast, or otherwise transmit the performances licensed hereunder to persons outside of the licensed premises.

(c) This license does not authorize performances of music by means of a coin-operated phonorecord player (juke box) as defined in the Copyright Law (17 U.S.C. §116).

2. The term of this agreement shall begin on_____ and end on _____ and shall continue thereafter unless cancelled by either party as of the end of the initial term or any subsequent one (1) year term (herein sometimes referred to as a "contract year") upon thirty (30) days advance written notice to the other party. BMI shall have the right to cancel this agreement along with the simultaneous cancellation of the agreements of all other licensees of the same class and category as LICENSEE, as of the end of any month during the term, upon sixty (60) days advance written notice.

PLEASE COMPLETE ALL WHITE AREAS

3. In the event that BMI, at any time during the term hereof, shall, for the same class and category as that of LICENSEE, issue licenses granting rights similar to those in this agreement on a more favorable basis, BMI shall, for the balance of the term, offer LICENSEE a comparable agreement.

4. BMI agrees to indemnify, save harmless and defend LICENSEE, its officers and employees, from and against any and all claims, demands or suits that may be made or brought against them or any of them with respect to the performance of any material licensed under this agreement. Such indemnity shall be limited to works which are licensed by BMI at the time of LICENSEE's performances. BMI's Clearance Department will, upon request, advise LICENSEE whether particular musical works are available for performance as part of BMI's repertoire. LICENSEE agrees to give BMI immediate notice of any such claim, demand or suit, to deliver to BMI any papers pertaining thereto and to cooperate with BMI with respect thereto, and BMI shall have full charge of the defense of any such claim, demand or suit.

5. If, during the term hereof, LICENSEE shall permanently cease to operate the premises, whether by reason of sale or lease thereof, or otherwise, this agreement and LICENSEE's obligation to BMI shall thereupon terminate; provided, however, that LICENSEE shall, within ten (10) days thereafter, give written notice of such termination to BMI, setting forth the effective date thereof and the name of the new owner or operator of the premises, as the case may be, and that LICENSEE shall pay to BMI all fees due hereunder until said effective date.

6. BMI reserves the right at its discretion to withdraw from the license granted hereunder any musical work as to which any legal action has been instituted or a claim made that BMI does not have the right to license the performing rights in such work or that such work infringes another composition.

7. BMI shall have the right upon reasonable notice to LICENSEE, by its authorized representatives, at any time during customary business hours, to examine the books and records of account of LICENSEE to such extent as may be necessary to verify the statements made hereunder or under any prior agreement with BMI. BMI shall consider all data and information coming to its attention as the result of any such examination as confidential.

8. Upon any breach or default of the terms and conditions of this agreement, BMI shall have the right to cancel this agreement, but any such cancellation shall only become effective if such breach or default continues thirty (30) days after the date of BMI's written notice to LICENSEE thereof. The right to cancel shall be in addition to any and all other remedies which BMI may have. No waiver by BMI of full performance of this agreement by LICENSEE in any one or more instances shall be deemed a waiver of the right to require full and complete performance of this agreement thereafter or of the right to cancel this agreement in accordance with the terms of this Paragraph.

9. Any notice required or permitted to be given under this agreement shall be in writing and shall be deemed duly given when sent by ordinary first-class U.S. mail (unless it is stated elsewhere in this agreement that a notice is to be sent by certified mail) to the party for whom it is intended, at its indicated mailing address hereinabove stated, or any other address which either party hereto may from time to time designate for such purpose, and when such notice is so mailed, it shall be deemed given upon the mailing thereof. Any such notice sent to BMI shall be to the attention of the Licensing Department. Any such notice sent to LICENSEE shall be to the attention of the person signing this agreement on behalf of LICENSEE or such other person as LICENSEE may advise BMI in writing.

10. All disputes of any kind, nature or description arising in connection with the terms and conditions of this agreement shall be submitted to the American Arbitration Association in the City, County and State of New York, for arbitration under its then prevailing rules, the arbitrator(s) to be selected as follows: Each of the parties shall, by written notice to the other, have the right to appoint one arbitrator. If, within ten (10) days following the giving of such notice by one party, the other shall not, by written notice, appoint another arbitrator, the first arbitrator shall be the sole arbitrator. If two arbitrators are so appointed, they shall appoint a third arbitrator. If ten (10) days elapse after the appointment of the second arbitrator and the two arbitrators are unable to agree upon a third arbitrator, then either party may, in writing, request the American Arbitration Association to appoint the third arbitrator. The award made in the arbitration shall be binding and conclusive on the parties and judgment may be, but need not be, entered in any court having jurisdiction. Such award shall include the fixing of the costs, expenses and attorneys' fees of arbitration, which shall be borne by the unsuccessful party.

11. This agreement constitutes the entire understanding between the parties, shall not be binding until signed by both parties, and cannot be waived or added to or modified orally, and no waiver, addition or modification shall be valid unless in writing and signed by the parties. The rights of LICENSEE shall not be assignable. This agreement, its validity, construction and effect, shall be governed by the laws of the State of New York. The fact that any provisions herein are found by a court of competent jurisdiction to be void or unenforceable shall not affect the validity or enforceability of any other provisions.

12. BMI may impose a late payment charge of 1% per month from the date any payment is due hereunder on any payment that is received by BMI more than one month after the due date.

UL (A/DC) -R 89

RIDER

This is a Rider to the UL (A/DC)-88 agreement (the "Agreement") between BMIand LICENSEE dated_____.

It is acknowledged and agreed that the term "FIRST YEAR'S FEE' as used throughout the Agreement, including in the LICENSE FEE SCHEDULE, shall not mean the amounts printed in the Agreement but instead shall mean the following amounts:

CLASS	FIRST YEAR'S FEE
1A	$ 82
2A	$163
3A	$245
4A	$326
5A	$435
1B	$130
2B	$261
3B	$391
4B	$522
5B	$696
1C	$163
2C	$326
3C	$489
4C	$652
5C	$870

All other provisions of the Agreement are hereby ratified and affirmed.

BROADCAST MUSIC, INC.

_____
(Legal Name of LICENSEE)

By _____   By _____

SPECIAL PROVISIONS
MUSIC-ON-HOLD

13. The license granted to LICENSEE pursuant to Paragraph 1 hereof shall extend to performances of recorded music by means of "music-on-hold" (as that term is commonly understood) through LICENSEE's telephone system at the licensed premises and shall authorize LICENSEE to transmit such performances to persons connected to the licensed premises by telephone. In no event shall this license extend to any performances of music audible other than on a telephone or to a service that provides music-on-hold to subscribers. This license also shall not be applicable to more than one premises.

14. LICENSEE warrants and represents that, as of the date of this agreement, LICENSEE provides music-on-hold on the licensed premises through a telephone system using _____ telephone trunk lines, and accordingly on the License Fee Schedule below falls within Class _____ . LICENSEE agrees to pay to BMI for the license granted herein the sum of $ _____ , which constitutes the fee for the first contract year of this agreement (the "first year's fee") for such Class and shall be payable at the time of the signing of this agreement. The fee for each subsequent contract year shall be in the respective amounts determined in accordance with Paragraph 15, subject to any adjustment pursuant to Paragraph 16, and shall be paid no later than ten (10) days following the beginning of each such contract year.

LICENSE FEE SCHEDULE		
(FILL IN APPLICABLE CLASS AND FEE IN PARAGRAPH 14 ABOVE)		
Number of Telephone Trunk Lines Used to Provide Music-On-Hold	Class	First Year's Fee
Under 10	1	$120
10 — 29	2	210
30 — 49	3	315
50 — 74	4	420
75 — 124	5	525
125 — 199	6	630
200 — 349	7	775
350 and over	8	950

15. The amount of the license fee for the second and subsequent contract years of this agreement shall be an adjustment of the first year's fee based upon the percentage increase or decrease in the United States Consumer Price Index (National, All Items) between September, 1987 and September of the year preceding the anniversary date of this agreement, rounded to the nearest dollar. BMI will advise LICENSEE in writing of the amount of each new fee.

16. (a) At the same time that LICENSEE pays its license fee hereunder for the second and subsequent contract years, LICENSEE shall submit a report, on a form available from BMI, certified by LICENSEE or by the auditor of LICENSEE, indicating the number of telephone trunk lines used to provide music-on-hold during the previous contract year on the licensed premises. If any such report causes the licensed premises to fall into a Class other than that for which LICENSEE is then currently paying BMI license fees, BMI shall adjust LICENSEE's fee pursuant to Paragraph 15 and 16 to reflect the new Class in which LICENSEE belongs, effective with the contract year following such change of Class.

(b) If the adjusted fee is greater than the license fee already paid by LICENSEE for the contract year, LICENSEE agrees to pay BMI the difference within thirty (30) days of the mailing by BMI to LICENSEE of the adjusted statement of license fees.

(c) If the adjusted fee is less than the license fee already paid by LICENSEE to BMI for the contract year, BMI agrees to credit the difference to the account of LICENSEE, and if such adjustment occurs in the last contract year of this agreement, BMI shall refund said sum promptly.

(d) In the event that LICENSEE fails to submit a report pursuant to Paragraph 16(a) and BMI subsequently is made aware of a current change of Class, BMI shall have the option, in lieu of its right of cancellation pursuant to Paragraph 8, to notify LICENSEE in writing by certified mail of its knowledge of such change and adjust LICENSEE's fee for the then current contract year in accordance with this Paragraph 16 as if LICENSEE had reported such change for the previous year. LICENSEE shall have thirty (30) days from the date of BMI's notice to submit the missing reports. If such reports are not received by BMI by the end of said 30-day period, LICENSEE agrees to waive its right to submit such past due reports thereafter and authorizes BMI to deem the adjusted fee as being accurate.

PLEASE COMPLETE ALL WHITE AREAS

—3—

17. If Paragraph 5 of this agreement shall become applicable, the fee due BMI by LICENSEE through the effective date of termination shall be a proration of the fee for the contract year of termination, but in no event less than the Class 1 fee indicated on the License Fee Schedule.

IN WITNESS WHEREOF, this agreement has been executed by the duly authorized representatives of BMI and LICENSEE all as of the date first above written.

BROADCAST MUSIC, INC.

_____
Name of Corporation. Partnership or Individual Owner
(Legal Name of Owner or Operator)

By _____   By _____
        (Signature)   *(Signature)*

_____   _____
        (Print name of signer)   *(Print name of signer)*

_____   _____
        (Title of signer)   *(Fill in Title in which signed)*
                                           (a) If corporation, state corporate office held; (b) If partnership, write "partner";
                                                   (c) If individual owner, write "individual owner".

                                           PLEASE COMPLETE WHITE AREA ONLY

—4—

FORM 15.7

BMI ATHLETIC CLUBS/DANCE CLASSES

BMI

MUSIC PERFORMANCE AGREEMENT
Athletic Clubs/Dance Classes

AGREEMENT, made at New York, N.Y. on *(Date Will Be Entered By BMI Upon Execution)*   between BROADCAST MUSIC, INC. (hereinafter BMI), a State of New York corporation with its principal offices at 320 West 57th Street, New York, N.Y. 10019 and the entity described below and referred to thereafter as LICENSEE:

ENTER LEGAL NAME ▶ _____

Name of Corporation, Partnership or Individual Owner

ENTER TRADE NAME▶ _____

(Doing business under the name of)

CHECK APPROPRIATE ▶
BOX AND COMPLETE

☐ Corporation   ☐ Partnership (Enter names of partners)   ☐ Individual Owner *(indicate residence address below under Mailing Address)*

_____
(State of incorporation)

PREMISE ADDRESS	MAILING ADDRESS
(Street Address)	*(Street Address)*
(City) *(State)* *(Zip)*	*(City)* *(State)* *(Zip)*
( ) *(Telephone No.)* *(Contact Name)*	( ) *(Telephone No.)* *(Contact Name)*
(Title)	*(Title)*

1. DEFINITIONS:

(a) "Background music" shall mean recorded music, whether vocal or instrumental, designed to be used as an unobtrusive accompaniment to routine activities, including, but not limited to, conversation and relaxation, as long as such music is not intended to accompany non-instructional dancing or any other type of entertainment.

(b) "Instructional use" shall mean the performance of recorded music in a designated area on the LICENSEE's premise (the "studio") for use during athletic classes and dance instruction including, but not limited to, classes in aerobics, gymnastics, slimnastics, social dancing, ballroom dancing, jazz dancing, tap dancing, square dancing, modern dancing, and ballet, as those terms are commonly understood in the dance profession.

(c) "Background use" shall mean the performance of recorded background music on the licensed premise adjacent to or outside of the studio.

2. BMI GRANT

(a) BMI hereby grants to LICENSEE a non-exclusive license to perform, present, or cause the public performance of, all musical works of which BMI shall have the right to grant public performance licenses during the term hereof. Said license shall be restricted to performance on the licensed premise either by the playing of records, prerecorded tapes, or other mechanical devices or via the reception of broadcast audio transmissions on receiving apparatus and amplifications thereof for public performance, and such performances may be reproduced only through loudspeakers on the licensed premise and is granted in consideration of the payment of the license fees as set forth herein and is subject to all of the terms and conditions hereof. This license does not include: (i) dramatic rights, the right to perform dramatico-musical works in whole or in substantial part, the right to present individual works in a dramatic setting or the right to use the music licensed hereunder in any other context which may constitute an exercise of the "grand rights" therein; (ii) the right to broadcast, cablecast, telecast, or otherwise transmit the performances licensed hereunder to persons outside of the premise; or (iii) performances of music by means of a coin-operated phonorecord player (jukebox) as defined in the Copyright Law (17 U.S.C. §116).

(b) BMI reserves the right at its discretion to withdraw from the license granted hereunder any musical work as to which any legal action has been instituted or a claim made that BMI does not have the right to license the performing rights in such work or that such work infringes another composition.

(c) In no event shall this license authorize performances of music outside the perimeter of LICENSEE's premise into an area not owned and/or controlled by LICENSEE. This license shall also extend to performances of incidental live or recorded music on the licensed premise for promotional social dances and to dance recitals by students and instructors, as long as no admission is charged.

3. TERM OF AGREEMENT

The initial term of this annual agreement shall begin on the first day of _____ and end on the last day of _____
                                                             (Month Year)   *(Month Year)*
and shall continue thereafter unless cancelled by either party as of the end of the initial term or any subsequent one (1) year term (herein sometimes referred to as a "contract year") upon thirty (30) days advance written notice to the other party.

4. FEES

LICENSEE agrees to pay to BMI for each contract year during the term of this agreement a license fee as follows.

(a) (I) INSTRUCTIONAL USE ONLY—If LICENSEE uses recorded music on the premise that is only for athletic classes and dance instruction and the music is not audible other than incidentally outside of the studio when classes are in session and no music is used when classes are not in session then LICENSEE shall pay the appropriate fee on the License Fee Schedule under the category Instructional Use Only.

(II) BACKGROUND AND INSTRUCTIONAL USE—If LICENSEE uses recorded music on the premise both in classes and instruction and the music is also audible other than incidentally anywhere else on the premise outside of the studio while classes are in session or otherwise, then LICENSEE shall pay the appropriate fee on the License Fee Schedule under the category Background and Instructional Use.

(iii) BACKGROUND USE ONLY—If LICENSEE uses music on the premise that is only for "background use" as defined in the license and no music is used at athletic classes or dance instruction (or no such activities take place), then LICENSEE shall pay the appropriate fee on the License Fee Schedule under the category Background Use Only. Each individual floor (level) where music is audible is to be considered a separate premise, but the annual fee for all floors (levels) after the first shall be $60.00 regardless of square footage.

(b) LICENSEE warrants and represents that during the twelve-month period preceding the initial term of this agreement (or if LICENSEE did not operate during that full twelve-month period, LICENSEE shall make a good-faith estimate for the first contract year of this agreement) LICENSEE's number of floors (levels) and students are as set forth in the Music Policy Statement and License Fee Schedule which are part of this agreement.

(c) The first annual fee due hereunder shall be payable upon the signing of this agreement by LICENSEE. The fee for each subsequent contract year shall be in the respective amount determined in accordance with this paragraph, subject to any adjustment pursuant to this paragraph, and shall be paid to BMI no later than ten (10) days following the beginning of each such contract year.

(d) For Instructional Use Only and Background and Instructional Use—The amount of the license fee for the second and subsequent contract years of this agreement shall be an adjustment of the first year's fee based upon the percentage increase or decrease in the United States Consumer Price Index (National, All Items) between September 1989, and September of the year preceding each anniversary date of this agreement, rounded to the nearest dollar. BMI will advise LICENSEE in writing of the amount of each new fee.

5. REPORTING OF ANNUAL FEES

(a) At the same time that LICENSEE pays its license fee hereunder for the second and subsequent contract years, LICENSEE shall submit a report, on a form available from BMI, certified by LICENSEE or by the auditor of LICENSEE, indicating the average number of different students or participants per week during the previous contract year who attended instructional athletic or dance classes using music on the licensed premise (except if background use only), whether LICENSEE's music was instructional only or both background and instructional or background use only, and the number of floors (levels) comprising the licensed premise. If any such report causes the licensed premise to fall into a Category other than that for which LICENSEE is then currently paying BMI license fees. BMI shall adjust LICENSEE's fee pursuant to Paragraph 4 to reflect LICENSEE's new fee, effective with the contract year following such change of Category.

(b) If the adjusted fee is greater than the license fee already paid by LICENSEE for the contract year, LICENSEE agrees to pay BMI the difference within thirty (30) days of the mailing by BMI to LICENSEE of the adjusted statement of license fees.

(c) If the adjusted fee is less than the license fee already paid by LICENSEE to BMI for the contract year, BMI agrees to credit the difference to the account of LICENSEE, and if such adjustment occurs in the last contract year of this agreement, BMI shall refund said sum promptly.

(d) In the event that LICENSEE fails to submit a report pursuant to this Paragraph and BMI subsequently is made aware of a current change of Category, BMI shall have the option, in lieu of its right of cancellation pursuant to this Paragraph, to notify LICENSEE in writing by certified mail of its knowledge of such change and adjust LICENSEE's fee for the then current contract year in accordance with this Paragraph as if LICENSEE had reported such change for the previous year. LICENSEE shall have thirty (30) days from the date of BMI's notice to submit the missing reports. If such reports are not received by BMI by the end of said 30-day period, LICENSEE agrees to waive its right to submit such past due reports thereafter and authorizes BMI to deem the adjusted fee accurate.

6. TERMINATION OF AGREEMENT BY LICENSEE

If, LICENSEE shall permanently cease to operate the premise, whether by reason of sale or lease thereof or otherwise, this agreement and LICENSEE's obligation to BMI shall thereupon terminate, provided that LICENSEE shall, within ten (10) days thereafter, give written notice of such termination to BMI, setting forth the effective date thereof and the name of the new owner or operator of the premise, and that LICENSEE shall pay to BMI all fees due hereunder until said effective date. The fee due BMI by LICENSEE through the effective date of termination shall be a proration of the fee for the contract year of termination, but in no event less than the lowest appropriate fee indicated in the applicable category on the License Fee Schedule.

7. REVIEW OF STATEMENTS AND/OR ACCOUNTINGS

BMI shall have the right, by its authorized representatives, at any time during customary business hours, and upon reasonable notice, to examine those portions of LICENSEE's books and records of account to such extent as may be necessary to verify any and all statements and/or accountings made hereunder or under prior agreement with BMI. BMI shall consider all data and information coming to its attention as the result of any such examination of LICENSEE's books and records as confidential.

8. LATE PAYMENT CHARGE

BMI may impose a late payment charge of 1% per month from the date any payment is due hereunder on any payment that is received by BMI more than one month after the due date.

9. INDEMNITY BY BMI

BMI agrees to indemnify, save harmless and defend LICENSEE, its officers and employees, from and against any and all claims, demands or suits that may be made or brought against them or any of them with respect to the performance of any material licensed under this agreement. Such indemnity shall be limited to works which are licensed by BMI at the time of LICENSEE's performances. BMI's Clearance Department will, upon reasonable written request, advise LICENSEE whether particular musical works are available for performance as part of BMI's repertoire. LICENSEE shall provide the title and the writer/composer of each musical composition requested to be identified. LICENSEE agrees to give BMI immediate notice of any such claim, demand or suit, to deliver to BMI any papers pertaining thereto, and to cooperate with BMI with respect thereto, and BMI shall have full charge of the defense of any such claim, demand or suit.

10. CANCELLATION OF ENTIRE CATEGORY

BMI shall have the right to cancel this agreement along with the simultaneous cancellation of the agreements of all other licensees of the same class and category as LICENSEE, as of the end of any month during the term, upon sixty (60) days advance written notice.

11. OFFER OF COMPARABLE AGREEMENT

In the event that BMI, at any time during the term hereof, shall for the same class and category as that of LICENSEE, issue licenses granting rights similar to those in this agreement on a more favorable basis, BMI shall, for the balance of the term, offer LICENSEE a comparable agreement.

12. BREACH OR DEFAULT/WAIVER

Upon any breach or default of the terms and conditions of this agreement, BMI shall have the right to cancel this agreement, but any such cancellation shall only become effective if such breach or default continues thirty (30) days after the date of BMI's written notice to LICENSEE thereof. The right to cancel shall be in addition to any and all other remedies which BMI may have. No waiver by BMI of full performance of this agreement by LICENSEE in any one or more instances shall be a waiver of the right to require full and complete performance of this agreement thereafter or of the right to cancel this agreement in accordance with the terms of this Paragraph.

13. ARBITRATION

All disputes of any kind, nature or description arising in connection with the terms and conditions of this agreement shall be submitted to the American Arbitration Association in the City, County and State of New York, for arbitration under its then prevailing arbitration rules. The arbitrator(s) to be selected as follows: Each of the parties shall, by written notice to the other, have the right to appoint one arbitrator. If, within ten (10) days following the giving of such notice by one party the other shall not, by written notice, appoint another arbitrator, the first arbitrator shall be the sole arbitrator. If two arbitrators are so appointed, they shall appoint a third arbitrator. If ten (10) days elapse after the appointment of the second arbitrator and the two arbitrators are unable to agree upon a third arbitrator, then either party may, in writing, request the American Arbitration Association to appoint the third arbitrator. The award made in the arbitration shall be binding and conclusive on the parties and judgment may be, but need not be, entered in any court having jurisdiction. Such award shall include the fixing of the costs, expenses and attorneys' fees of arbitration, which shall be borne by the unsuccessful party.

14. NOTICES

Any notice required or permitted to be given under this agreement shall be in writing and deemed given when sent by first-class U.S. mail to the party intended, at its mailing address hereinabove stated, or any other address which either party hereto may designate. Any such notice sent to BMI shall be to the attention of the General Licensing Department. Any such notice sent to LICENSEE shall be to the attention of the person signing this agreement on behalf of LICENSEE or such other person as LICENSEE may advise BMI in writing.

15. MISCELLANEOUS

This agreement constitutes the entire understanding between the parties, shall not be binding until signed by both parties, and cannot be waived or added to or modified orally, and no waiver, addition or modification shall be valid unless in writing and signed by the parties. This agreement is executed by the duly authorized representative of BMI and LICENSEE. The rights of LICENSEE shall not be assignable. This agreement, its validity, construction and effect, shall be governed by the laws of the State of New York. The fact that any provisions herein are found by a court of competent jurisdiction to be void or unenforceable shall not affect the validity or enforceability of any other provisions. All headings in this agreement are for the purpose of convenience and shall not be considered to be part of this agreement.

MUSIC POLICY STATEMENT

Indicate music use by checking **one** appropriate category below.

☐ CATEGORY A—Instructional Use Only

☐ CATEGORY B—Background and Instructional Use

      Indicate number of floors (levels) _____

☐ CATEGORY C—Background Use Only.

      Indicate number of floors (levels) _____

LICENSE FEE SCHEDULE

1) These rates apply when music is utilized for Instructional Use Only, Background and Instructional Use, or Background Use Only. This includes, but is not limited to, records, tapes, CD's, broadcasts, satellite signals, and/or cablecasts.

2) **USING YOUR CATEGORY AS INDICATED ABOVE, CHECK THE APPLICABLE SHADED BOX BELOW.**

Average Number of Different Students or Participants Per Week	CATEGORY A INSTRUCTIONAL USE ONLY		CATEGORY B BACKGROUND AND INSTRUCTIONAL USE		
	CHECK BOX		CHECK BOX	Single Floor (level)	CHECK BOX	Multiple Floor (level)
Under 60 Students		$ 91		$144		$181
60-124		181		289		361
125-249		272		433		542
250-374		361		578		722
375 & over		482		771		963

► LICENSEE's total annual fee within Category A or B is $ _____

Square Footage	CATEGORY C BACKGROUND USE ONLY	
	CHECK BOX	Single Floor (level)
Up to 1500		$ 60.00
1501 to 2500		$120.00
2501 to 5000		$240.00
Over 5000		$480.00

► LICENSEE's total annual fee within Category C, including additional floors (levels) (each at $60), is $ _____

(To Be Completed by BMI)

BROADCAST MUSIC, INC.

By: _____
             (Signature)

_____
      (Print Name of Signer)

_____
      (Title of Signer)

(To Be Completed by LICENSEE)

_____
Name of Corporation, Partnership or Individual Owner
(Same legal name of LICENSEE as on page 1)

Sign here ► By: _____
                        (Signature)

_____
      (Print Name of Signer)

_____
(Fill in Title in which Signed)
(a) If corporation, state corporate office held; (b) If a partnership, write "Partner", (c) If individual owner, write "individual owner"

FORM OF PAYMENT:
(check one)
☐ Check (Make payable to BMI.)
☐ Money Order (Make payable to BMI.)
☐ MasterCard·
☐ VISA·

Card Number

Exp. Date ___/___

Signature

4

FORM 15.8

BMI SUBSCRIPTION MUSIC SERVICE LICENSE

BMI

BMI ···

DATE WILL BE ENTERED BY BMI UPON EXECUTION

AGREEMENT, made at New York, N.Y. on _____ 19____, between BROADCAST MUSIC, INC., a corporation organized under the laws of the State of New York (hereinafter called BMI) with principal offices at 320 West 57th Street, New York, N.Y. 10019, and

_____
Name of Corporation, Partnership or Individual Owner (Legal Name of Licensee)

☐ If a corporation, indicate the State of incorporation _____

☐ If a partnership, indicate names of all partners _____

PLEASE CHECK APPROPRIATE BOX AND COMPLETE

_____

☐ If an individual owner, indicate residence address _____
(Street Address)

City of _____ State _____ Zip _____ ☐

(hereinafter called LICENSEE) with offices located at _____
(street address)

City of _____ State _____ Zip _____ ☐

Telephone No. (____)_____ doing business under the name of _____
      Area Code   (trade name)

located at _____
(street address)

in the City of _____ in the State of _____ Zip _____ ☐

CHECK ADDRESS TO WHICH MAIL SHOULD BE SENT

WHEREAS, BMI is engaged in licensing for public performance non-dramatic renditions of the separate musical compositions of which BMI has the right to license the performing rights, and

WHEREAS, LICENSEE is engaged in the business of operating subscription music or storecast music services primarily to individual places of entertainment, resort, residential common public areas, business, industry and others which are not under LICENSEE's direct or indirect ownership or control (each of which is hereinafter called a "serviced premises"),

IT IS HEREBY AGREED AS FOLLOWS:

1. The initial term of this agreement shall be the period beginning _____ and ending December 31, 1993 and continuing thereafter for additional periods of one (1) year each, unless cancelled by either party at the end of said period or any subsequent period, upon not less than sixty (60) days' advance written notice by regular first-class U.S. mail to the other party.

2. (a) "Subscription music services" as used herein shall mean and be limited to non-dramatic audio-only performances of recorded music (including music-on-hold performances), whether vocal or instrumental, and regardless of the means employed by LICENSEE to provide such music to a serviced premises. It is understood that such "subscription music services" are intended to be used as an accompaniment to routine activites, including, but not limited to, work, shopping, conversation, dining and relaxation, as long as such music is not offered to subscribers as an accompaniment to dancing or to serve as an adjunct to any other physical activity or form of entertainment.

(b) "Serviced Premises" as used herein shall mean a premises which is provided subscription music services by LICENSEE, but shall not under any circumstances extend to (i) a ballroom, discotheque, dance studio or skating rink; or (ii) any premises to which an admission fee is charged (limited to such portion of the premises from which the event or entertainment for which admission is charged is intended to be observed or heard, and provided that any other portion of such premises shall be covered by this license).

(c) "On-Premise Delivery" shall mean that LICENSEE provides subscription music services to its serviced premises by means of an on-premise record, compact disc, tape playback unit and/or any other device for the reproduction of music located at the premise of its subscribers.

(d) "Off-Premises Delivery" shall mean that LICENSEE provides subscription music services to its serviced premises by means of FM radio broadcasts made pursuant to a Subsidiary Communications Authorization, satellite relay, telephone lines, wires or other conductors, or by any other means whatsoever by which music is delivered from the central studio to a serviced premises.

(e) "Sub-distributors" as used herein shall mean only those persons, firms or corporations authorized by LICENSEE to furnish its music service.

(f) "Storecast Music" as used herein shall mean the non-dramatic performances of recorded music interspersed with

PLEASE COMPLETE WHITE AREAS ONLY   (1)

advertising announcements for which consideration is received from the advertisers for the placing of the advertisement; serving as an accompaniment to shopping in a retail store where merchandise is sold or services rendered to the public are audible solely to persons physically on the serviced premises and, by means of loudspeakers, in the immediate vicinity of such serviced premises. It is understood that if no consideration is received from the advertiser for the placing of advertisements, the providing of a music service which includes commercial announcements shall be considered a subscription music service. It is further understood that no storecast music license fee shall be due under this agreement where no compensation (in money or any other form) is paid to LICENSEE directly or indirectly for such announcements.

3. This license shall be deemed to embrace:

    ☐ LICENSEE's owned music service operations only;

PLEASE CHECK

APPROPRIATE BOX

    ☐ LICENSEE's owned music service operations as well as those of its sub-distributors for which LICENSEE assumes the obligations under this agreement. LICENSEE shall annex as Schedule A hereto a list of **all** of its sub-distributors and shall indicate whether each is one for whom LICENSEE is assuming the obligations hereunder or not. LICENSEE shall supply BMI with subsequent additions and deletions to Schedule A hereof at least once in each year of this agreement, within ten (10) days of BMI's request therefor.

4. BMI hereby grants to LICENSEE a non-exclusive license to perform publicly and to cause or permit to be performed publicly, by means of LICENSEE's subscription or storecast music services at one or more serviced premises, all the separate musical compositions of which BMI shall, during the term hereof, own or control the right to grant public performance licenses. Except to the extent that music on telephone hold lines originating at a serviced premises is audible at remote locations on telephone lines as part of "music-on-hold" (as that term is currently understood in the industry). LICENSEE's performances shall be audible only within and immediately adjacent to the serviced premises supplied by LICENSEE. In no event shall this license extend to any other type of performances whatsoever or to any cable television system or cable radio system or to transmission by any radio or television station to a place other than on LICENSEE's serviced premises.

5. LICENSEE agrees to pay BMI for the license granted herein the annual license fee stated on the LICENSE FEE SCHEDULE below for the applicable contract year of this agreement; provided, however, that payment to BMI for all serviced premises to which music service (other than storecast music) is furnished shall not be less than forty-five (45) times the applicable annual on-premise delivery fee for the applicable year.

LICENSE FEE SCHEDULE

	ANNUAL FEE PER SERVICED PREMISES:		
CONTRACT YEAR	**ON-PREMISE DELIVERY**	**OFF-PREMISE DELIVERY**	**STORECAST MUSIC**
1987	$12.50	The greater of $11.50 or (2%) of the gross billings	$1.47 per month
1988	$12.50	The greater of $11.50 or (2%) of the gross billings	$1.47 per month
1989	$13.50	Two percent (2%) of the gross billings	$1.50 per month
1990	$15.00	Two percent (2%) of the gross billings	$1.65 per month
1991	$17.50	Two percent (2%) of the gross billings	$1.95 per month
1992	$18.50	Two and one-quarter percent (2 1/4%) of the gross billings	$2.05 per month
1993	$20.50	Two and one-quarter percent (2 1/4%) of the gross billings	$2.15 per month

6. (a) The fees due BMI under this agreement shall be payable monthly, no later than thirty (30) days following the last day of the month for which said fees are due.

(b) LICENSEE shall submit to BMI a monthly report calculating the license fees due on report forms to be provided by BMI to LICENSEE for such purposes, which report shall be due on the date on which the monthly fees are due and payable pursuant to Sub-paragraph 6(a) above.

(c) BMI may impose an interest charge of one percent (1%) per month from the date payment was due on any payment that is received by BMI more than sixty (60) days after the due date.

7. As used in this agreement, the term "gross billings" shall:

(a) include all sums (including the reasonable value of any merchandise, service, or anything of value in lieu of or in addition to cash consideration) due to LICENSEE from its subscribers in connection with (i) its providing of its subscription music services; and (ii) its lease (including conditional sale) of the SCA receiver, the antenna mast and mounts, up to ten (10) standard speakers per floor and other relevant equipment used primarily for supplying of the subscription music service.

PLEASE COMPLETE WHITE AREA ONLY   (2)

(b) exclude all sums due to LICENSEE from its subscribers only for the following: (i) a bona fide sale (not include conditional sale) of equipment; (ii) the lease of equipment to subscribers which is extraneous and unrelated to LICENSEE subscription music services, but for any such deduction LICENSEE shall supply BMI, simultaneously with its report for the quarter in which such deduction is taken, the name and address of each such lessee; (iii) any sales, use or excise taxes which are collected from subscribers and actually paid to any Federal, State or local taxing authority; (iv) one-time installation charges billed not later than ninety (90) days following completion of the subject installation work; (v) all ad hoc charges (i.e., extraordinary or one-time charges) for service and maintenance work actually performed on subscriber-leased or subscriber-owned equipment provided that said ad hoc charges are separately billed, not later than ninety (90) days following completion of the subject service and maintenance work and provided that under no circumstances, in the case of leased equipment, shall that portion of the monthly fee charged to a serviced premises for music service be less than $40; and further provided that the amount charged for music service and the amount charged for service and maintenance must be clearly stated on the face of any agreement with a serviced premises and a copy of the page of such agreement setting forth such separate charges shall be provided to BMI by LICENSEE simultaneously with its report for the quarter in which such deduction is first taken; (vi) the license fees paid to BMI pursuant to this agreement; (vii) the amount of any billings (previously included as "gross billings") which are written off as uncollectible, provided however, that any amounts written off as uncollectible that are later collected shall be reported as and when collected; (viii) any penalties for late payments or finance or interest charges imposed on subscribers by LICENSEE.

8. Subject to the provisions of Sub-paragraph 8(d) below, LICENSEE agrees to provide BMI with a **quarterly report of musical compositions** as follows:

a) **If LICENSEE uses On-Premise Delivery,** said report shall be provided as follows: No later than twenty (20) days following the end of the first full or partial calendar quarter of this agreement, LICENSEE shall provide BMI with an initial list of all records and tapes which were available to its serviced premises during the previous quarter, indicating such records and tapes by name and/or number, whichever methods are used by LICENSEE to identify such recordings. With respect to each such record and tape, LICENSEE shall list each musical composition contained thereon, giving the title of the composition and the writer and publisher to the extent indicated on the source material (record, tape, sheet music, etc.) of such work. Further quarterly reports required hereunder shall be in the form of updates to said initial list by listing any record or tape added since the last list supplied to BMI, with title, writer and publisher information, as well as an indication of any recordings on a previous list which have been modified (such as compositions added or deleted) or discontinued. Also, LICENSEE shall provide BMI with the average number of serviced premises which were supplied with each record or tape during the previous quarter.

b) **If LICENSEE uses Off-Premise Delivery,** LICENSEE shall provide with respect to *each channel* of off-premise delivery, the name or other legend of the record or tape transmitted, a listing by title, writer and publisher of each musical composition contained on the record or tape and an indication of how often each such tape was transmitted by LICENSEE during the previous quarter, as well as a statement of the average number of serviced premises during the previous quarter of both LICENSEE and LICENSEE's sub-distributors for whom payment is being made under this agreement.

c) If LICENSEE is a sub-distributor, or if LICENSEE receives its music from a subscription music supplier which is itself licensed by BMI under a background music service license agreement, in lieu of the reports required by Sub-paragraphs 8(a) or 8(b) hereof, each such quarterly report shall merely indicate the average number of serviced premises to which LICENSEE has transmitted background music during the previous quarter.

d) If LICENSEE provides a subscription music service to less than 100 serviced premises, LICENSEE shall not be required to submit quarterly reports of musical compositions. If LICENSEE provides a subscription music service to 100 or more serviced premises but its music supplier does not supply the information necessary to prepare said quarterly reports of musical compositions, then LICENSEE shall not be required to submit said quarterly reports, provided that LICENSEE has made a good-faith effort, consistent with reasonable business practices, to obtain the information from its music supplier necessary to prepare said quarterly reports. Upon written demand, LICENSEE shall detail to BMI its good-faith efforts under this Paragraph 8.

9. (a) BMI shall have the right by its authorized representatives, at any time during customary business hours and upon no less than thirty (30) days advance written notice, to examine the books and records of account of LICENSEE to such extent as may be necessary to verify any and all statements rendered and accountings made hereunder and under prior license agreements with BMI to the extent that such audit rights existed under prior license agreements. Nothing herein, however, shall be deemed to extend the statute of limitations on any period sought to be audited if it would have otherwise expired. LICENSEE shall give BMI's auditor full access to all relevant records of LICENSEE, including names and addresses of, and any other pertinent information concerning, the subscribers of LICENSEE. BMI agrees to instruct its auditors not to make any list of names and addresses of subscribers of LICENSEE except insofar as necessary for the verification of LICENSEE's statements and accountings to BMI and not to make any such list available to any third party or to any person within BMI except on a need-to-know basis, and to destroy any such list upon completion of the audit or, if a deficiency be found as to which such data may be relevant, upon the payment or other disposition of such audit deficiency.

(b) BMI shall not audit more than once in any twelve (12) month period unless an audit reveals a deficiency of more than ten percent (10%) between the amount paid by LICENSEE and the amount actually found to be due BMI for the audited period, in which case BMI may conduct an additional audit during the said twelve-month period.

(c) Effective with reporting periods on and after January 1, 1989, if any audit conducted by BMI reveals a deficiency of more than twenty-five percent (25%) between the amount previously reported by LICENSEE and the amount actually found to be due BMI for the audited period, LICENSEE shall pay, in addition to the sum additionally due, a surcharge of fifteen percent (15%) of the total amount remaining due BMI. If LICENSEE does not pay said surcharge and deficiency within thirty (30) days of written notice by BMI, an interest charge of one percent (1%) per month may be imposed by BMI on said surcharge and deficiency from the date of such written notification.

(3)

10. BMI agrees to indemnify, save harmless and defend LICENSEE, its officers and employees, and the proprietors of the serviced premises supplied by it hereunder, from and against any and all claims, demands or suits (and liabilities, expenses and costs associated therewith, including without limitation, except to the extent BMI elects to control the matter and supplies counsel of its own choosing, the reasonable fees of counsel of the indemnified party's choosing) that may be made or brought against them, or any of them, with respect to the performance of any material licensed under this agreement. Such indemnity shall be limited to all works which are licensed under this agreement. Such indemnity shall not apply to performances at the serviced premises of LICENSEE after written request by BMI that they refrain from such performances, unless LICENSEE uses its best efforts to immediately refrain from such performances, it being understood that a determination of willful infringement by an arbitrator or court of competent jurisdiction shall be conclusive proof that LICENSEE did not use its best efforts. BMI's Clearance Department will, upon request, advise LICENSEE whether particular musical works are available for performance as part of BMI's repertoire. LICENSEE agrees to give BMI immediate notice of any such claim, demand or suit, either against it or against any serviced premises supplied by it, to deliver to BMI any papers pertaining thereto and to cooperate and to cause the serviced premises to cooperate with respect thereto, and BMI shall have full charge of the defense of any such claim, demand or suit. LICENSEE, however, shall have the right to engage counsel, at its own expense, who may participate in the defense of any such action or proceeding and with whom counsel for BMI shall cooperate.

11. In the event that BMI, at any time during the term hereof, shall issue licenses to similar subscription music or storecast music licensees on a more favorable basis, BMI shall offer LICENSEE a comparable agreement for the balance of the term of this agreement.

12. BMI reserves the right to withdraw from the license granted hereunder any musical work as to which any legal action has been instituted or a claim made that BMI does not have the right to license the performing rights in such work or that such work infringes another composition.

13. It is agreed that LICENSEE may assign this agreement to any subsidiary, affiliated or associated company of LICENSEE or in connection with any sale, merger, reorganization or consolidation in which LICENSEE is a party.

14. Any notice required or permitted to be given under this agreement shall be in writing and shall be deemed duly given when sent by ordinary first-class U.S. mail to the party for whom it is intended, at its address hereinabove stated, or any other address which either party hereto may from time to time designate for such purpose, and when such notice is so mailed, it shall be deemed given upon the mailing thereof. Any such notice sent to BMI shall be to the attention of the Licensing Department. Any such notice sent to LICENSEE shall be to the attention of the person signing this agreement on behalf of LICENSEE or such other person as LICENSEE may advise BMI in writing.

15. All disputes of any kind, nature or description arising in connection with the terms and conditions of this agreement shall be submitted to the American Arbitration Association in the City, County and State of New York for arbitration under its then prevailing rules, the arbitrator(s) to be selected as follows: Each of the parties shall, by written notice to the other, have the right to appoint one arbitrator. If, within ten (10) days following the giving of such notice by one party, the other shall not, by written notice, appoint another arbitrator, the first arbitrator shall be the sole arbitrator. If two arbitrators are so appointed, they shall appoint a third arbitrator. If ten (10) days elapse after the appointment of the second arbitrator and the two arbitrators are unable to agree upon the third arbitrator, then either party may, in writing, request the American Arbitration Association to appoint the third arbitrator. The award made in the arbitration shall be binding and conclusive on the parties and judgment may be, but need not be, entered into any court having jurisdiction. Such award shall include the fixing of the costs, expenses and attorneys' fees of arbitration, which shall be borne by the unsuccessful party.

16. Upon any material breach or default of the terms and conditions of this agreement by LICENSEE, BMI shall have the right to cancel this agreement, but any such cancellation shall only become effective if such breach or default continues thirty (30) days after the date of LICENSEE's receipt of written notice thereof without LICENSEE having acted to cure such material breach or default. The right to cancel shall be in addition to any and all other remedies which BMI may have. No waiver by BMI of full performance of this agreement by LICENSEE in any one or more instances shall be deemed a waiver of the right to require full and complete performance of this agreement thereafter or of the right to cancel this agreement in accordance with the terms of this Paragraph. For purposes of this Paragraph 16, a "material breach" by LICENSEE shall include, but not be limited to, failure to timely pay any license fee and failure to timely submit full and complete reports of LICENSEE's sub-distributors, musical performances and license fee calculations which are required by this agreement.

17. This agreement constitutes the entire understanding between the parties, shall not be binding until signed by both parties and cannot be waived or added to or modified orally, and no waiver, addition or modification shall be valid unless in writing and signed by the parties. This agreement, its validity, construction and effect shall be governed by the laws of the State of New York. The fact that any provisions herein are found to be void or unenforceable by a court of competent jurisdiction shall in no way affect the validity or enforceability of any other provisions.

IN WITNESS WHEREOF, this agreement has been executed by the duly authorized representatives of BMI and LICENSEE all as of the date above written.

BROADCAST MUSIC, INC.

Name of Corporation Partnership or Individual Owner (Legal Name of Licensee)

By_____   By_____

(Signature)   (Signature)

(Print name of signer)   (Print name of signer)

(Title of signer)   (Title of signer)

(a) If corporation, state corporate office held; (b) If partnership, write "partner"; (c) If individual owner, write "individual owner"

PLEASE COMPLETE WHITE AREA ONLY (4)

FORM 15.9

BMI INFLIGHT/BOARDING LICENSE

INFLIGHT/BOARDING-88
18

DATE WILL BE ENTERED BY BMI UPON EXECUTION

AGREEMENT, made at New York, N.Y. on _____, 19 ____,
between BROADCAST MUSIC, INC., a corporation organized under the laws of the
State of New York (hereinafter called BMI) with principal offices at 320 West
57th Street, New York, N.Y. 10019, and

Name of Corporation, Partnership or Individual Owner (Legal Name of LICENSEE)

|__| If a corporation, indicate the State of incorporation
      _____

|__| If a partnership, indicate names of all partners

PLEASE CHECK   _____
APPROPRIATE BOX
AND COMPLETE   _____

|__| If an individual owner, indicate residence address
      _____
                        (street address)

City of _____ State _____ Zip _____

(hereinafter called LICENSEE) with offices located at _____
                                              (street address)

City of _____ State _____ Zip _____

Telephone No. (   ) _____
            Area Code

W I T N E S S E T H :

WHEREAS, BMI is engaged in licensing music for public performance, and

WHEREAS, LICENSEE is engaged in providing an inflight and/or boarding music
service to one or more airline companies for public performance in serviced
airplanes,

IT IS HEREBY AGREED AS FOLLOWS:

1.   As used in this agreement:

      (a) "Inflight music service" shall mean the supplying and leasing by
LICENSEE of pre-recorded musical tapes or other forms of recordation capable of
aural reproduction only (herein called "tapes") for use while serviced airplanes
are in the air.

(b) "Boarding music service" shall mean a music service providing tapes for use only when passengers are boarding and disembarking from serviced airplanes or seated in serviced airplanes when they are otherwise on the ground.

PLEASE COMPLETE ALL OF THE BOXED AREA

(c) "Airline companies" shall mean airline companies to whom LICENSEE shall provide an inflight or boarding music service.

(d) "Serviced airplanes" shall mean all of each airline company's airplanes or other type of aircraft utilizing LICENSEE"s inflight or boarding music service.

(e) "Seating capacity" shall mean the total number of passenger seats available for sale.

2. (a) Subject to the provisions of Sub-paragraph 2(b) hereof, BMI hereby grants to LICENSEE for the term of this agreement a non-exclusive license to perform publicly in serviced airplanes (and in no other place) as part of its inflight and/or boarding music services to airline companies (and in no other manner whatsoever) all of the musical works, the right to grant public performance licenses of which BMI shall during the term hereof control.

(b) Notwithstanding anything to the contrary contained herein: (i) with respect to inflight music service, said license shall apply only to flights of serviced airplanes over and to and from the United States, its territories and possessions, to the extent that BMI may have the right to license such performances outside of the United States; (ii) said license shall not include dramatic rights, the right to perform dramatico-musical works in whole or in substantial part, the right to present individual works in a dramatic setting or the right to use the music licensed hereunder in any other context which may constitute an exercise of the "grand rights" therein; (iii) said license shall not extend or apply to performances associated with advertising or commercial announcements of any kind or nature, excepting only announcements relating to the air transportation and related services of airline companies and credit announcements given to LICENSEE's music service and to the companies whose recordings are utilized in the music service; (iv) said license shall extend only to the right of public performance (in the manner provided herein) of the musical works specified in Paragraph 2(a) hereof and shall not be construed as authorizing LICENSEE to mechanically reproduce such works by any method or means now or hereafter known; (v) said license shall not extend to performances of music as part of audio-visual presentations or within any airline terminal buildings.

3. The term of this agreement shall begin on January 1, 1988 and end on December 31, 1989 and continue thereafter unless cancelled by either party at the end of said period or at the end of any subsequent one (1) year period, upon thirty (30) days advance written notice to the other party. BMI shall have the right to cancel this agreement along with the simultaneous cancellation of the agreements of all other licensees of the same class and category as LICENSEE, as of the end of any month during the term, upon sixty (60) days advance written notice.

4. (a) LICENSEE agrees to pay BMI for each serviced airplane for each month of the term hereof the applicable license fee(s) computed as follows:

INFLIGHT MUSIC SERVICE

BOARDING MUSIC SERVICE

SEATING
CAPACITY
OF SERVICED
AIRPLANE   MONTHLY LICENSE FEE

For each serviced airplane, a monthly license fee equal to **twenty-five percent (25%)** of the applicable monthly Inflight Music Service license fee for the relevant year.

If LICENSEE offers both an Inflight Music Service and a Boarding Music Service, both license fees shall be payable.

SEATING CAPACITY OF SERVICED AIRPLANE	1988	1989	1990 and all subsequent years of this agreement
Under 150	$17.50	$25	1989 fee as adjusted for the CPI per ¶4(b)
150-249	27.50	35	
250 and over	37.50	50	

(b)   The amount of the Inflight Music Service license fee for 1990 and all subsequent calendar years of this agreement shall be an adjustment of the 1989 fee based upon the percentage increase or decrease in the United States Consumer Price Index (National, All Items) between September, 1988 and September of the preceding calendar year, rounded to the nearest dollar. BMI will advise LICENSEE in writing of the amount of each new fee.

5.   On or before the 10th day of the month following each month of the term hereof, LICENSEE agrees to furnish BMI (on forms available from BMI) with a statement, certified either by an officer or by the auditor of LICENSEE, setting forth any information regarding the subject matter of this agreement which BMI may reasonably require, including, without limitation:

(a)   the total license fee for the month reported;

(b)   the name and address of each airline company to which an inflight and/or boarding music service was provided during any part of the month reported; and

(c)   for each airline company referred to in Paragraph 5(b) hereof, the number of its serviced airplanes and the seating capacity of each as certified by such airline company.

6.   LICENSEE agrees to provide BMI, at the same time that the statement required by Paragraph 5 hereof is due, with a) a report of all musical works utilized in the music service during the month reported, setting forth the title and, to the extent known or reasonably available to LICENSEE, the writer(s) and publisher(s) of each such composition and b) a copy of the printed program form which it supplies to each airline company for the month covered by such statement.

7.   BMI shall have the right, upon reasonable notice to LICENSEE, by its authorized representatives, at any time during customary business hours, to examine the books and records of account of LICENSEE to such extent as may be necessary to verify any and all statements and reports rendered and accountings made hereunder or under any prior agreement with BMI. BMI shall consider all

data and information coming to its attention as the result of any such examination of books and records as confidential. In the preparation and maintenance of its books and records, LICENSEE shall be entitled to rely on written statements from airline companies as to the number of serviced airplanes and seating capacities.

8. In the event that BMI, at any time during the term hereof, shall, for the same class and category as that of LICENSEE, issue licenses granting rights similar to those in this agreement on a more favorable basis, BMI shall, for the balance of the term, offer LICENSEE a comparable agreement.

9. BMI agrees to indemnify, save harmless and defend LICENSEE, its officers and employees, from and against any and all claims, demands or suits that may be made or brought against them or any of them with respect to the performance of any material licensed hereunder. BMI's Clearance Department shall at any time, upon written request, advise LICENSEE whether particular works are available for performance as part of BMI's repertoire. Such indemnity shall be limited to works which are licensed by BMI at the time of LICENSEE's performances. LICENSEE agrees to give BMI immediate notice of any such claim, demand or suit, to deliver to BMI any papers pertaining thereto, and to cooperate with BMI with respect thereto, and BMI shall have full charge of the defense of any such claim, demand or suit.

10. BMI reserves the right to withdraw from the license granted hereunder any musical work as to which any legal action has been instituted or a claim made that BMI does not have the right to license the performing rights in such work or that such work infringes another composition.

11. Upon any breach or default of the terms and conditions of this agreement, BMI shall have the right to cancel this agreement, but any such cancellation shall only become effective if such breach or default continues thirty (30) days after BMI's written notice to LICENSEE thereof. The right to cancel shall be in addition to any and all other remedies which BMI may have. No waiver by BMI of full performance of this agreement by LICENSEE in any one or more instances shall be deemed a waiver of the right to require full and complete performance of this agreement thereafter or of the right to cancel this agreement in accordance with the terms of this Paragraph.

12. All disputes of any kind, nature or description arising in connection with the terms and conditions of this agreement shall be submitted to the American Arbitration Association in the City, County and State of New York for arbitration under its then prevailing rules, the arbitrator(s) to be selected as follows: Each of the parties shall, by written notice to the other, have the right to appoint one arbitrator. If, within ten (10) days following the giving of such notice by one party, the other shall not, by written notice, appoint another arbitrator, the first arbitrator shall be the sole arbitrator. If two arbitrators are so appointed, they shall appoint a third arbitrator. If ten (10) days elapse after the appointment of the second arbitrator and the two arbitrators are unable to agree upon the third arbitrator, then either party may, in writing, request the American Arbitration Association to appoint the third arbitrator. The award made in the arbitration shall be binding and conclusive on the parties and judgment may be, but need not be, entered into any court having jurisdiction. Such award shall include the fixing of the

costs, expenses and attorneys' fees of arbitration, which shall be borne by the unsuccessful party.

13. Any notice required or permitted to be given under this agreement shall be in writing and shall be deemed duly given when sent by ordinary first-class U.S. mail to the party for whom it is intended, at its address hereinabove stated, or any other address which either party hereto may from time to time designate for such purpose, and when such notice is so mailed, it shall be deemed given upon the mailing thereof. Any notice sent to BMI shall be to the attention of the Licensing Department. Any notice sent to LICENSEE shall be to the attention of the person signing this agreement on behalf of LICENSEE or such other person as LICENSEE may advise BMI in writing.

14. This agreement constitutes the entire understanding between the parties and cannot be waived or added to or modified orally, and no waiver, addition or modification shall be valid unless in writing and signed by the parties. This agreement, its validity, construction and effect shall be governed by the laws of the State of New York. The fact that any provisions herein are found to be void or unenforceable by a court of competent jurisdiction shall in no way affect the validity or enforceability of any other provisions.

IN WITNESS WHEREOF, the parties hereto have duly executed this agreement the day and date hereinabove set forth.

BROADCAST MUSIC, INC.

```
                                    _____
                                    Name of Corporation, Partnership or
                                    Individual Owner (Legal Name of
                                    Owner or Operator)

By: _____            By: _____
        (Signature)                         (Signature)


_____                _____
(Print Name Of Signer)              (Print Name Of Signer)


_____                _____
(Title of Signer)                   (Title of Signer)
                                    (a) If corporation, state corporate
                                    office held; (b) If partnership, write
                                    "partner"; (c) If individual owner,
                                    write "individual owner".
```

PLEASE COMPLETE BOXED AREA ONLY

FORM 15.10

BMI EDUCATIONAL INSTITUTION LICENSE (ONE TIER)

C/U—One Tier-88
58

DATE WILL BE ENTERED BY BMI UPON EXECUTION

BMI
*

THIS AGREEMENT made and entered into on ....,19 .....
between BROADCAST MUSIC, INC., a New York corporation with its principal offices located at 320 West 57th Street.
New York, N.Y. 10019, hereinafter referred to as BMI, and

....
(Legal Name of LICENSEE and Name of Institution)

a college or university with its principal offices located at ....

....

City of .... State .... Zip ....

Tel No. (.......) ....Fice Code Number ....
Area Code

hereinafter referred to as LICENSEE;

WITNESSETH:

WHEREAS, BMI has entered into agreements with various writers, publishers and other organizations, whereby public performance rights to various musical compositions which have vested in and/or are controlled by said writers, publishers and organizations have been either assigned, tranferred and/or granted to BMI; and

WHEREAS, BMI is empowered to license the public performances of those musical compositions contained in its repertoire on a non-exclusive basis; and

WHEREAS, LICENSEE is an institution of higher education generally referred to as a college or university and desires the right to publicly perform those musical compositions as BMI may, during the period hereof, have the right to license;

WHEREAS, BMI and LICENSEE desire to enter into an agreement on an experimental and nonprejudical basis which shall apply for the term of this Agreement only and shall not be binding upon or prejudicial to any position taken by either of the parties for any period subsequent to the termination of this Agreement;

NOW, THEREFORE, the parties hereto mutually agree as follows:

1. DEFINITIONS

(a) "LICENSEE" as used herein shall include the named institution and any of its constituent bodies, agencies, or organizations which within the specific context to which this license is to apply maintain a substantial nexus to the named institution and/or over which the named institution has control or authority.

(b) "Premises" shall include LICENSEE'S campus(es) and any site located off LICENSEE'S campus(es) which has been engaged for use by an organization referred to in Paragraph 1(a). However, in the event LICENSEE has a pecuniary interest in an establishment or property for investment purposes which is not directly related to LICENSEE'S educational purposes at which establishment or property musical compositions are being performed publicly, it is specifically understood and agreed to by LICENSEE that this Agreement shall not apply to such other establishment or property.

(c) "Full-time students" as used herein shall be the sum of (i) all full-time undergraduate and graduate students and (ii) one-third of all part-time undergraduate and graduate students. If during the term of this Agreement, the method of converting part-time students to a full-time equivalency as indicated in subsection (ii) of this Paragraph 1(c) is

PLEASE COMPLETE SHADED AREAS ONLY

1

changed from the Integrated Postsecondary Education Data System (IPEDS) or any superseding Survey conducted annually by the Department of Education, such different method of conversion shall be deemed substituted in said subsection (ii) as of the effective Fall academic term.

(d) "Term" shall mean the period commencing July 1, 1987 and ending June 30, 1992. "First Contract Year" shall mean the period commencing July 1, 1987 and ending June 30, 1988. "Second Contract Year" shall mean the period commencing July 1, 1988 and ending June 30, 1989. "Third Contract Year" shall mean the period commencing July 1, 1989 and ending June 30, 1990. "Fourth Contract Year" shall mean the period commencing July 1, 1990 and ending June 30, 1991. "Fifth Contract Year" shall mean the period commencing July 1, 1991 and ending June 30, 1992.

(e) "Musical attractions" shall mean concerts, stage shows, variety shows, symphonies, recitals, chamber music and other similar performances presented by or under commitment to LICENSEE.

(f) "Campus radio broadcasting station" shall be limited to a radio broadcasting station whose gross income derived from the sale of air time is less than $10,000 annually.

(g) "CPI adjustment" shall mean the difference in the Consumer Price Index (National, All Items), as determined by the United States Department of Labor, between July, 1987 and July of the specified contract year.

2. BMI hereby grants to LICENSEE for the term of this Agreement a non-exclusive license to perform or cause the public performance at LICENSEE'S premises, including, but not limited to, campus radio broadcasting stations, all of the musical works (including, but not limited to, when performed as part of musical attractions) presented by or under commitment to LICENSEE to which BMI shall have the right to grant public performance licenses. This license does not extend to performances of music via any form of televised transmission, whether over-the-air broadcast, cable, satellite or otherwise. This license also does not include dramatic rights, the right to publicly perform dramatico-musical works in whole or in substantial part, the right to present individual works in a dramatic setting or the right to perform the music licensed hereunder in any other context which may constitute an exercise of the "grand rights" therein. This license is not assignable, and no rights other than those mentioned are included in this license.

3. In consideration of the license granted herein, LICENSEE agrees to pay BMI the following license fees:

(a) LICENSEE shall pay BMI for each contract year for all uses of music, including, but not limited to, campus radio broadcasting stations, the "Per Student Fee" set forth in Schedule "A" which is included and made a part of this Agreement. This fee will be based upon the number of full time students as defined in Paragraph 1(c) which are reported in accordance with Paragraph 3(b). If LICENSEE operates campus radio broadcasting stations as defined in this Agreement, the call letters are _____.
                                                               ATTACH LIST IF MORE SPACE REQUIRED

(b) For the First Contract Year, the number of full-time students as defined in Paragraph 1(c) shall be reported for the Fall 1987 academic term upon execution of this Agreement. The Per Student Fee due BMI pursuant to this Agreement for the First Contract Year shall be paid by LICENSEE to BMI on or before April 15, 1988.

LICENSEE represents that for the Fall 1987 academic term:

(i) The number of full-time undergraduate students is . . . . _____ ⎫
                                                                                                                                         ⎪
(ii) The number of full-time graduate students is . . . . _____ ⎬ ADD
                                                                                                                                         ⎪
(iii) The number of part-time undergraduate and graduate students is _____ which when divided by three (3) equals a full-time equivalency of . . . . _____ ⎭

(iv) The total number of "full-time students" is therefore . . . . _____
                                                                                                                                    TOTAL
which when multiplied by the Schedule A fee for the First Contract Year of 13¢ equals . . . .$ _____
and that amount, or $109, whichever is greater, is the fee due BMI by LICENSEE for the First Contract Year.

On or before November 1, 1988, November 1, 1989, November 1, 1990 and November 1, 1991, LICENSEE shall report to BMI, on forms to be supplied by BMI, the number of full-time students as defined in Paragraph 1(c) for the Fall academic term of the contract year, which will establish the Per Student Fee for the Second, Third, Fourth and Fifth Contract Years in accordance with Schedule A. The Per Student Fee due BMI pursuant to this Agreement for the Second, Third, Fourth and Fifth Contract Years shall be paid by LICENSEE to BMI on or before the 20th day of January 1989, 1990, 1991 and 1992.

4. All campus radio broadcasting stations licensed pursuant to this Agreement shall, upon written request from BMI made on not less than two (2) weeks notice specifying the prospective period to be covered by the request, agree to furnish BMI weekly lists of each station's performances of all musical works, indicating the compositions performed by title and composer or by such other convenient method as may be designated by BMI, but such lists need not be furnished for more than two (2) weeks for each contract year of the term of this Agreement.

5. BMI, upon giving reasonable notice to LICENSEE in writing, shall have the right to examine the books and records of account of LICENSEE which pertain solely to this Agreement and which may be necessary to verify any statements rendered and accountings made hereunder.

6. The parties hereto reserve all rights and privileges accorded pursuant to the Copyright Act of 1976, effective January 1, 1978.

7. In the event that BMI, at any time during the term of this Agreement, shall, for the same class and category as that of LICENSEE, issue licenses granting rights similar to those in this Agreement on a more favorable basis, BMI shall, for the balance of the term, offer LICENSEE a comparable agreement. The election restrictions contained in Paragraph 11 of this Agreement shall not apply to any offer and acceptance pursuant to this paragraph.

8. BMI agrees to indemnify, save harmless and defend LICENSEE, its officers and employees, from and against any and all claims, demands or suits that may be made or brought against them or any of them with respect to the performance of any material licensed under this Agreement. Such indemnity shall be limited to works which are licensed by BMI at the time of LICENSEE'S performances, and to works which are, pursuant to a written request by LICENSEE, specifically represented in writing by an Officer of BMI in answer to said written request by LICENSEE, to be licensed by BMI at the time of LICENSEE'S performance. LICENSEE agrees to give BMI immediate notice of any such claim, demand or suit, to deliver to BMI any papers pertaining thereto, and to cooperate with BMI with respect thereto, and BMI shall have full charge of the defense of any such claim, demand or suit.

9. Upon any breach or default of the terms and conditions of this Agreement, BMI may, at its sole option, cancel this Agreement with not less than sixty (60) days notice in writing to LICENSEE. The right to cancel shall be in addition to any and all other remedies which BMI may have. No waiver by BMI of full performance of this Agreement by LICENSEE in any one or more instances shall be deemed a waiver of the right to require full and complete performance of this Agreement thereafter or of the right to cancel this Agreement in accordance with the terms of this paragraph. In the event of such cancellation, BMI agrees to refund to LICENSEE any unearned license fees paid in advance to BMI by LICENSEE.

10. In the event LICENSEE ceases to operate as an institution of higher education, or where LICENSEE ceases the public performance of music licensed by BMI, LICENSEE may cancel this Agreement upon giving sixty (60) days notice in writing to BMI. The right to cancel shall be in addition to any and all other remedies which LICENSEE may have. In the event of such cancellation, BMI agrees to refund to LICENSEE any unearned license fees paid in advance to BMI by LICENSEE.

11. LICENSEE may at the beginning of a contract year and upon giving sixty (60) days written notice to BMI, elect to enter into and execute the College/University Two Tier License offered by BMI, and BMI shall comply with such election. This election may be exercised by LICENSEE only once during the term of this Agreement. If LICENSEE so elects, it is understood that no refund will be due LICENSEE from BMI for license fees.

12. All cancellation and election notices, if any, shall be given in writing by United States *certified* mail sent to either party at the address set forth above. Each party agrees to inform the other, in writing, of any change of address.

13. (a) All disputes of any kind, nature or description arising in connection with the terms and conditions of this Agreement shall be submitted to the American Arbitration Association in New York, New York for arbitration under its then prevailing rules, the arbitrator(s) to be selected as follows: Each of the parties hereto shall, by written notice to the other, have the right to appoint one arbitrator. If, within ten (l0) days following the giving of such notice by one party, the

other shall not, by written notice, appoint another arbitrator, the first arbitrator shall be the sole arbitrator. If two arbitrators are so appointed, they shall appoint a third arbitrator. If ten (l0) days elapse after the appointment of the second arbitrator and the two arbitrators are unable to agree upon the third arbitrator, then either party may, in writing, request the American Arbitration Association to appoint the third arbitrator. The award made in the arbitration shall be binding and conclusive on the parties and judgment may be, but need not be, entered into any court having jurisdiction. Such award shall include the fixing of the costs, expenses and attorneys' fees of arbitration, which shall be borne by the unsuccessful party.

(b) In the event LICENSEE elects to waive the terms set forth in Paragraph 13(a), LICENSEE must cross out Paragraph 13(a) *and* initial the space provided to the left of Paragraph 13(a).

14. This Agreement constitutes the entire understanding between the parties with respect to the subject matter hereof and shall not be binding until signed by both parties. This Agreement cannot be waived or added to or modified orally and no waiver, addition or modification shall be valid unless in writing and signed by the parties.

IN WITNESS WHEREOF, this Agreement has been executed in duplicate originals by the duly authorized representatives of BMI and LICENSEE all as of the date above written.

BROADCAST MUSIC, INC.

. . . .
LICENSEE (Legal Name)

By . . . .   By . . . .
            (Signature)   (Signature)

. . . .
        (Print name of signer)   (Print name of signer)

. . . .
            (Title of signer)   (Title of signer)

PLEASE COMPLETE SHADED AREA ONLY

SCHEDULE A
LICENSEE shall pay to BMI the following Per Student Fee:

CONTRACT YEAR	LICENSE FEE
FIRST (7/1/87-6/30/88)	Thirteen Cents (13¢) per full-time student or $109, whichever is greater.
SECOND (7/1/88-6/30/89)	Thirteen Cents (13¢) plus the CPI adjustment to July, 1988 per full-time student or $109 plus the CPI adjustment to July, 1988, whichever is greater.
THIRD (7/1/89-6/30/90)	Thirteen Cents (13¢) plus the CPI adjustment to July, 1989 per full-time student or $109 plus the CPI adjustment to July, 1989, whichever is greater.
FOURTH (7/1/90-6/30/91)	Thirteen Cents (13¢) plus the CPI adjustment to July, 1990 per full-time student or $109 plus the CPI adjustment to July, 1990, whichever is greater. *= 14 9¢*
FIFTH (7/1/91-6/30/92)	Thirteen Cents (13¢) plus the CPI adjustment to July, 1991 per full-time student or $109 plus the CPI adjustment to July, 1991, whichever is greater.

All license fees based upon the number of full-time students shall be computed to the nearest tenth of a cent and all minimums to the nearest cent.

4

FORM 15.11

BMI EDUCATIONAL INSTITUTION LICENSE (TWO TIER)

C/U—Two Tier-88
57/59

DATE WILL BE ENTERED BY BMI UPON EXECUTION

THIS AGREEMENT made and entered into on . . . . , 19 . . . . . .
between BROADCAST MUSIC, INC., a New York corporation with its principal offices located at 320 West 57th Street, New York, N.Y. 10019,
hereinafter referred to as BMI, and

. . . .

(Legal Name of LICENSEE and Name of Institution)

a college or university with its principal offices located at . . . .

. . . .

City of . . . . State . . . . .Zip . . . .

Tel No. (. . . . .) . . . . .Fice Code Number . . . .
Area Code

hereinafter referred to as LICENSEE;

W I T N E S S E T H:

WHEREAS, BMI has entered into agreements with various writers, publishers and other organizations, whereby public performance rights to various musical compositions which have vested in and/or are controlled by said writers, publishers and organizations have been either assigned, transferred and/or granted to BMI; and

WHEREAS, BMI is empowered to license the public performances of those musical compositions contained in its repertoire on a non-exclusive basis; and

WHEREAS, LICENSEE is an institution of higher education generally referred to as a college or university and desires the right to publicly perform those musical compositions as BMI may, during the period hereof, have the right to license;

WHEREAS, BMI and LICENSEE desire to enter into an agreement on an experimental and nonprejudicial basis which shall apply for the term of this Agreement only and shall not be binding upon or prejudicial to any position taken by either of the parties for any period subsequent to the termination of this Agreement;

NOW, THEREFORE, the parties hereto mutually agree as follows:

1. DEFINITIONS

(a) "LICENSEE" as used herein shall include the named institution and any of its constituent bodies, agencies, or organizations which within the specific context to which this license is to apply maintain a substantial nexus to the named institution and/or over which the named institution has control or authority.

(b) "Premises" shall include LICENSEE'S campus(es) and any site located off LICENSEE'S campus(es) which has been engaged for use by an organization referred to in Paragraph 1(a). However, in the event LICENSEE has a pecuniary interest in an establishment or property for investment purposes which is not directly related to LICENSEE'S educational purposes at which establishment or property musical compositions are being performed publicly, it is specifically understood and agreed to by LICENSEE that this Agreement shall not apply to such other establishment or property.

(c) "Full-time students" as used herein shall be the sum of (i) all full-time undergraduate and graduate students and (ii) one-third of all part-time undergraduate and graduate students. If during the term of this Agreement, the method of converting part-time students to a full-time equivalency as indicated in subsection (ii) of this Paragraph 1(c) is changed from the Integrated Postsecondary Education Data System (IPEDS) or any superseding Survey conducted annually by the Department of Education, such different method of conversion shall be deemed substituted in said subsection (ii) as of the effective Fall academic term.

(d) "Term" shall mean the period commencing July 1, 1987 and ending June 30, 1992. "First Contract Year" shall mean the period commencing July 1, 1987 and ending June 30, 1988. "Second Contract Year" shall mean the period commencing July 1, 1988 and ending June 30, 1989. "Third Contract Year" shall mean the period commencing July 1, 1989 and ending June 30, 1990. "Fourth Contract Year" shall mean the period commencing July 1, 1990 and ending June 30, 1991. "Fifth Contract Year" shall mean the period commencing July 1, 1991 and ending June 30, 1992.

(e) "Theaters" shall include, but not be limited to, concert halls, theaters, auditoriums, amphitheaters, stadiums and similar places of performance, whether enclosed or not.

(f) "Musical attractions" shall mean concerts, stage shows, variety shows, symphonies, recitals, chamber music and other similar performances presented by or under commitment to LICENSEE.

(g) "Campus radio broadcasting station" shall be limited to a radio broadcasting station whose gross income derived from the sale of air time is less than $10,000 annually.

PLEASE COMPLETE SHADED AREAS ONLY

(h) "CPI adjustment" shall mean the difference in the Consumer Price Index (National, All Items), as determined by the United States Department of Labor, between July, 1987 and July of the specified contract year.

(i) Seating Capacity" shall mean the total number of seats permanently affixed in any theater where a musical attraction is performed plus any temporary seats added within the theater for a particular performance. Should a musical attraction be performed at a theater where the seating capactiy has been altered to accommodate a particular musical attraction, or if the total number of seats made available for a particular musical attraction shall be less than that of the seating capacity of said theater, then in those instances, seating capacity shall mean the total number of seats made available for that particular performance. If a site does not have permanent seating, "seating capacity" shall be interpreted to mean the number of persons attending a particular performance.

(j) "Entertainment Costs" shall be deemed to mean the total monies expended for a musical attraction by LICENSEE or LICENSEE'S authorized representatives and shall be limited to main attractions and supporting acts and all monies (including the cost of room, board and transportation) paid to performers, supporting musicians, booking agents and agents of the performers.

2. BMI hereby grants to LICENSEE for the term of this Agreement a non-exclusive license to perform or cause the public performance at LICENSEE'S premises, including, but not limited to, campus radio broadcasting stations, all of the musical works (including, but not limited to, when performed as part of musical attractions) presented by or under commitment to LICENSEE to which BMI shall have the right to grant public performance licenses. This license does not extend to performances of music via any form of televised transmission, whether over-the-air broadcast, cable, satellite or otherwise. This license also does not include dramatic rights, the right to publicly perform dramatico-musical works in whole or in substantial part, the right to present individual works in a dramatic setting or the right to perform the music licensed hereunder in any other context which may constitute an exercise of the "grand rights" therein. This license is not assignable, and no rights other than those mentioned are included in this license.

3. In consideration of the license granted herein, LICENSEE agrees to pay BMI the following license fees:

(a) Except for those uses referred to in Paragraph 3(c), LICENSEE shall pay BMI for each contract year for all other uses of music, including, but not limited to, campus radio broadcasting stations, the "Per Student Fee" set forth in Schedule "A" which is included and made a part of this Agreement. This fee will be based upon the number of full time students as defined in Paragraph 1(c) which are reported in accordance with Paragraph 3(b). If LICENSEE operates campus radio broadcasting stations as defined in this Agreement, the call letters are _____
ATTACH LIST IF MORE SPACE REQUIRED

(b) For the First Contract Year, the number of full-time students as defined in Paragraph 1(c) shall be reported for the Fall 1987 academic term upon execution of this Agreement. The Per Student Fee due BMI pursuant to this Agreement for the First Contract Year shall be paid by LICENSEE to BMI on or before April 15, 1988.

LICENSEE represents that for the Fall 1987 academic term:

(i) The number of full-time undergraduate students is .... _____

(ii) The number of full-time graduate students is .... _____

(iii) The number of part-time undergraduate and graduate students is _____ which when divided by three (3) equals a full-time equivalency of .... _____   ADD

(iv) The total number of "full-time students" is therefore .... _____
TOTAL

which when multiplied by the Schedule A fee for the First Contract Year of 11¢ equals .... $ _____

and that amount, or $84.00, whichever is greater, is the fee due BMI by LICENSEE for the First Contract Year.

On or before November 1, 1988, November 1, 1989, November 1, 1990 and November 1, 1991, LICENSEE shall report to BMI, on forms to be supplied by BMI, the number of full-time students as defined in Paragraph 1(c) for the Fall academic term of the contract year, which will establish the Per Student Fee for the Second, Third, Fourth and Fifth Contract Years in accordance with Schedule A. The Per Student Fee due BMI pursuant to this Agreement for the Second, Third, Fourth and Fifth Contract Years shall be paid by LICENSEE to BMI on or before the 20th day of January 1989, 1990, 1991 and 1992.

(c) LICENSEE agrees to pay BMI, in addition to the Per Student Fee, a fee for each performance of a musical attraction computed on the basis of Schedule "B" included in and made a part of this Agreement. Payment for musical attractions occurring between July 1, 1987 and March 31, 1988 shall be made to BMI by April 15, 1988. Payment for musical attractions occurring on or after April 1, 1988 shall be made to BMI by the tenth (10th) day following the end of the calendar quarter in which such attractions occurred. LICENSEE shall furnish BMI (on forms to be supplied by BMI), at such times as it makes payment of license fees pursuant to this paragraph, with a statement signed by an officer, auditor, or authorized official of LICENSEE covering performances of musical attractions occurring during the calendar quarter for which payment is being made. Such statement shall include the name of each musical attraction, the dates of each musical attraction, the number of performances each day, the theater at which the performance took place, the seating capacity at the theater, the highest stated ticket price for a regularly-scheduled performance, and copies of the programs when available. A statement shall be furnished to BMI by LICENSEE for each calendar quarter regardless of whether or not any musical attractions occurred during that quarter.

(d) No fee shall be due from LICENSEE for musical attractions performed at LICENSEE'S premises which are presented by an outside promoter, where said outside promoter has actually paid a license fee to BMI. Proof of payment by an outside promoter must be furnished by LICENSEE to BMI at the next following reporting date. Should BMI determine that it has not received payment for said musical attraction from such outside promoter, BMI will notify LICENSEE and LICENSEE will be obligated for payment of same.

(e) In the event LICENSEE does not submit to BMI the report(s) as required in Paragraph 3(c), and where BMI advises LICENSEE in writing and where LICENSEE fails to submit said report(s) and payment, where applicable, to BMI within forty-five (45) days of such notification, then LICENSEE will be obligated to pay BMI from the date of such notification to the end of the term of this Agreement the following Per Student Fees:

2   PLEASE COMPLETE SHADED AREAS ONLY

Thirteen (13¢) cents per full-time student for the First Contract Year (minimum fee $109);

Thirteen (13¢) cents plus the CPI adjustment to July, 1988 per full-time student or $109 plus the CPI adjustment to July, 1988, whichever is greater, for the Second Contract Year;

Thirteen (13¢) cents plus the CPI adjustment to July, 1989 per full-time student or $109 plus the CPI adjustment to July, 1989, whichever is greater, for the Third Contract Year;

Thirteen (13¢) cents plus the CPI adjustment to July, 1990 per full-time student or $109 plus the CPI adjustment to July, 1990, whichever is greater, for the Fourth Contract Year;

Thirteen (13¢) cents plus the CPI adjustment to July, 1991 per full-time student or $109 plus the CPI adjustment to July, 1991, whichever is greater, for the Fifth Contract Year.

All license fees based upon the number of full time students shall be computed to the nearest tenth of a cent and all minimums to the nearest cent. LICENSEE automatically waives any right of election pursuant to Paragraph 11. LICENSEE shall continue to be obligated to BMI for fees due BMI pursuant to Schedule B until the date of said notification.

4. All campus radio broadcasting stations licensed pursuant to this Agreement shall, upon written request from BMI made on not less than two (2) weeks notice specifying the prospective period to be covered by the request, agree to furnish BMI weekly lists of each station's performances of all musical works, indicating the compositions performed by title and composer or by such other convenient method as may be designated by BMI, but such lists need not be furnished for more than two (2) weeks for each contract year of the term of this Agreement.

5. BMI, upon giving reasonable notice to LICENSEE in writing, shall have the right to examine the books and records of account of LICENSEE which pertain solely to this Agreement and which may be necessary to verify any statements rendered and accountings made hereunder.

6. The parties hereto reserve all rights and privileges accorded pursuant to the Copyright Act of 1976, effective January 1, 1978.

7. In the event that BMI, at any time during the term of this Agreement, shall, for the same class and category as that of LICENSEE, issue licenses granting rights similar to those in this Agreement on a more favorable basis, BMI shall, for the balance of the term, offer LICENSEE a comparable agreement. The election restrictions contained in Paragraph 11 of this Agreement shall not apply to any offer and acceptance pursuant to this paragraph.

8. BMI agrees to indemnify, save harmless and defend LICENSEE, its officers and employees, from and against any and all claims, demands or suits that may be made or brought against them or any of them with respect to the performance of any material licensed under this Agreement. Such indemnity shall be limited to works which are licensed by BMI at the time of LICENSEE'S performances, and to works which are, pursuant to a written request by LICENSEE, specifically represented in writing by an Officer of BMI in answer to said written request by LICENSEE, to be licensed by BMI at the time of LICENSEE'S performance. LICENSEE agrees to give BMI immediate notice of any such claim, demand or suit, to deliver to BMI any papers pertaining thereto, and to cooperate with BMI with respect thereto, and BMI shall have full charge of the defense of any such claim, demand or suit.

9. Upon any breach or default of the terms and conditions of this Agreement, BMI may, at its sole option, cancel this agreement with not less than sixty (60) days notice in writing to LICENSEE. The right to cancel shall be in addition to any and all other remedies which BMI may have. No waiver by BMI of full performance of this Agreement by LICENSEE in any one or more instances shall be deemed a waiver of the right to require full and complete performance of this Agreement thereafter or of the right to cancel this Agreement in accordance with the terms of this paragraph. In the event of such cancellation, BMI agrees to refund to LICENSEE any unearned license fees paid in advance to BMI by LICENSEE.

10. In the event LICENSEE ceases to operate as an institution of higher education, or where LICENSEE ceases the public performance of music licensed by BMI, LICENSEE may cancel this Agreement upon giving sixty (60) days notice in writing to BMI. The right to cancel shall be in addition to any and all other remedies which LICENSEE may have. In the event of such cancellation, BMI agrees to refund to LICENSEE any unearned license fees paid in advance to BMI by LICENSEE.

11. Unless waived by LICENSEE pursuant to Paragraph 3(e), LICENSEE may at the beginning of a contract year and upon giving sixty (60) days written notice to BMI, elect to enter into and execute the College/University One Tier License offered by BMI, and BMI shall comply with such election. This election may be exercised by LICENSEE only once during the term of this Agreement. If LICENSEE so elects, it is understood that no refund will be due LICENSEE from BMI for license fees. Notwithstanding such election, LICENSEE will continue to be obligated to BMI for fees due BMI for musical attractions which were not reported and/or paid for by LICENSEE during the existence of this Agreement, and BMI retains its rights pursuant to Paragraph 3.

12. All cancellation and election notices, if any, shall be given in writing by United States *certified* mail sent to either party at the address set forth above. Each party agrees to inform the other, in writing, of any change of address.

13. (a) All disputes of any kind, nature or description arising in connection with the terms and conditions of this Agreement shall be submitted to the American Arbitration Association in New York, New York for arbitration under its then prevailing rules, the arbitrator(s) to be selected as follows: Each of the parties hereto shall, by written notice to the other, have the right to appoint one arbitrator. If, within ten (lO) days following the giving of such notice by one party, the other shall not, by written notice, appoint another arbitrator, the first arbitrator shall be the sole arbitrator. If two arbitrators are so appointed, they shall appoint a third arbitrator. If ten (lO) days elapse after the appointment of the second arbitrator and the two arbitrators are unable to agree upon the third arbitrator, then either party may, in writing, request the American Arbitration Association to appoint the third arbitrator. The award made in the arbitration shall be binding and conclusive on the parties and judgment may be, but need not be, entered into any court having jurisdiction. Such award shall include the fixing of the costs, expenses and attorneys' fees of arbitration, which shall be borne by the unsuccessful party.

(b) In the event LICENSEE elects to waive the terms set forth in Paragraph 13(a), LICENSEE must cross out Paragraph 13(a) *and* initial the space provided to the left of Paragraph 13(a).

14. This Agreement constitutes the entire understanding between the parties with respect to the subject matter hereof and shall not be binding until signed by both parties. This Agreement cannot be waived or added to or modified orally and no waiver, addition or modification shall be valid unless in writing and signed by the parties.

3

IN WITNESS WHEREOF, this Agreement has been executed in duplicate originals by the duly authorized representatives of BMI and LICENSEE all as of the date above written.

BROADCAST MUSIC, INC.

....
LICENSEE (Legal Name)

By ....

(Signature)

By ....

(Signature)

....

(Print name of signer)

....

(Print name of signer)

....

(Title of signer)

....

(Title of signer)

PLEASE COMPLETE SHADED AREA ONLY

SCHEDULE A

LICENSEE shall pay to BMI the following Per Student Fee:

CONTRACT YEAR	LICENSE FEE
FIRST (7/1/87-6/30/88)	Eleven Cents (11¢) per full-time student or $84.00, whichever is greater.
SECOND (7/1/88-6/30/89)	Thirteen Cents (13¢) plus the CPI adjustment to July, 1988 minus two (2) cents per full-time student, or $84.00 plus the CPI adjustment to July, 1988, whichever is greater.
THIRD (7/1/89-6/30/90)	Thirteen Cents (13¢) plus the CPI adjustment to July, 1989 minus two (2) cents per full-time student, or $84.00 plus the CPI adjustment to July, 1989, whichever is greater.
FOURTH (7/1/90-6/30/91)	Thirteen Cents (13¢) plus the CPI adjustment to July, 1990 minus two (2) cents per full-time student, or $84.00 plus the CPI adjustment to July, 1990, whichever is greater.
FIFTH (7/1/91-6/30/92)	Thirteen Cents (13¢) plus the CPI adjustment to July, 1991 minus two (2) cents per full-time student, or $84.00 plus the CPI adjustment to July, 1991, whichever is greater.

All license fees based upon the number of full-time students shall be computed to the nearest tenth of a cent and all minimums to the nearest cent.

SCHEDULE B

If the entertainment costs of a musical attraction total $1,500 or more, LICENSEE shall pay to BMI the following fee:

Schedule of Rates

C L A S S	SEATING CAPACITY OF FACILITY	USE HIGHEST STATED ADMISSION PRICE CHARGED FOR A REGULARLY-SCHEDULED PERFORMANCE					
		$0.00 to $3.99	$4.00 to $7.99	$8.00 to $11.99	$12.00 to $15.99	$16.00 to $19.99	$20.00 and over
1	Up to 1,500	$ 20	$ 30	$ 50	$ 60	$ 75	$100
2	1,501 to 2,500	$ 30	$ 40	$ 60	$ 75	$ 90	$120
3	2,501 to 5,000	$ 45	$ 55	$ 80	$100	$120	$150
4	5,001 to 7,500	$ 60	$ 75	$110	$140	$160	$200
5	7,501 to 10,000	$ 80	$100	$150	$180	$200	$250
6	10,001 to 15,000	$125	$140	$175	$200	$230	$280
7	15,001 to 20,000	$175	$190	$220	$250	$280	$330
8	20,001 to 25,000	$210	$230	$250	$270	$310	$370
9	25,001 to 40,000	$230	$250	$275	$310	$360	$410
10	40,001 and over	$320	$340	$360	$380	$410	$460

Where a musical attraction is believed to be comprised entirely of musical compositions for which BMI shall not have the right to grant public performance licenses, LICENSEE may, at its option, submit a schedule including writer and publisher information, for all those musical compositions performed at said musical attraction, and in those instances, after review by BMI, where all of the musical compositions performed at said musical attraction are ones to which BMI does not have the right to grant public performance licenses, no fee shall be due and payable to BMI. In the event no schedule is submitted to BMI, LICENSEE must pay the applicable fee for said musical attraction pursuant to Schedule "B".

FORM 15.12

BMI SINGLE RADIO STATION BLANKET LICENSE

BROADCAST MUSIC, INC.

RADIO—87
BLANKET

SINGLE STATION RADIO BLANKET LICENSE
SHORT METHOD OPTION OR LONG METHOD OPTION

AGREEMENT made at New York, New York, on this _____ day of _____ 19 ___ , between BROADCAST MUSIC, INC., a corporation organized under the laws of the State of New York (hereinafter BMI) with principal offices at 320 West 57th Street, New York, N.Y. 10019 and _____

_____

(Legal Name of LICENSEE)

PLEASE CHECK APPROPRIATE BOX AND COMPLETE

☐ A corporation organized under the laws of the State of_____

☐ A partnership consisting of _____

_____

☐ An individual residing at _____

(hereinafter LICENSEE) with offices presently located at _____

(Street Address)

City _____ State _____ Zip _____ Telephone No. (____) _____

Area Code

and operating the radio broadcasting station presently located at _____

(Street Address)

City _____ State _____ Zip _____ Telephone No. (____) _____

Area Code

and presently designated by the call letters_____ ☐ AM or ☐ FM ____ and assigned frequency_____

(Check Appropriate Box)

1. The Term of this agreement commences as of _____ and ends on December 31, 1991, unless earlier terminated as hereinafter provided. It is further agreed that the terms and conditions of the Single Station License Agreement, as previously amended and executed by BMI and LICENSEE (which had a stated expiration date of December 31, 1985), shall be extended to December 31, 1986. As of January 1, 1987 the terms and conditions of this agreement shall take effect.

2. A. *SHORT METHOD OPTION:*

The fee under the Short Method Option will be calculated as follows:

Net Revenue*
  Less:
    (1) Net Revenue from Political Broadcasting
      and
    (2) Revenue from Licensed Networks
  Equals:
Adjusted Net Revenue* (Amount Subject to BMI Fee*):
  Apply rate of 1.39% if Net Revenue is
    $150,000 or greater
  Apply rate of 1.20% if Net Revenue is
    less than $150,000
  Equals:
License Fee

B. *LONG METHOD OPTION:*

The fee under the Long Method Option will be calculated as follows:

Net Revenue*
  Less:
    (1) Net Revenue from Political Broadcasting
      and
    (2) Revenue from Licensed Networks
  Equals:
Adjusted Net Revenue*
  Less amount by which sum of the following exceeds 15% of Adjusted Net Revenue:
    (1) Net Talent Fees Allowed
    (2) News Ticker and News Audio Service
    (3) Remote Lines
    (4) Broadcast Rights
  Equals:
Amount Subject to BMI Fee*:
  Apply rate of 1.39% if Net Revenue is
    $150,000 or greater
  Apply rate of 1.20% if Net Revenue is
    less than $150,000
  Equals:
License Fee

*DEFINED IN PARAGRAPH 3.
PLEASE COMPLETE WHITE AREA ONLY

In either case the minimum fee shall be $360 per calendar year. In the event that this agreement shall not, during any year, be in effect for the full year, the minimum fee for such year shall be proportionately reduced.

3.   *Definitions:*

A. **"Radio broadcasting"** shall mean aural broadcasting in all of its forms.

B. **"Local program"** shall mean any radio program, including a "cooperative program," broadcast by a station other than a "network program." For the purposes of this agreement, sports, special events and other programs furnished by networks not licensed by BMI, as well as any program originating from a station which holds a BMI Single Station Radio Blanket License, shall be deemed to be "local programs."

C. **"Co-operative program"** shall mean any program furnished by a network to the station under an agreement permitting the station to broadcast such program on a sustaining basis or on a commercial basis under the sponsorship of a local, regional or national advertiser contracting directly with the station or its representative for the incorporation of the commercial credits of such advertiser into such program, as broadcast by the station.

D. **"Network program"** shall mean any radio program simultaneously broadcast by any means by any network licensed as a network by BMI. "Network program" shall include "rebroadcasts," "delayed broadcasts" and "repeat broadcasts" of a network program as those terms are now understood in the broadcasting industry, even though non-simultaneous. Payments made to the originating network by an affiliated station in connection with such program may not be deducted. LICENSEE shall report all billings and/or cash received from the network. "Billing(s)" as used in this agreement shall exclude the non-cash portion of transactions such as trade and barter sales with respect to a station reporting on a billing basis as defined in Paragraph 3.E.(1).

(1) Any program furnished by a network which is not licensed as a network by BMI shall be deemed to be a local program. With respect to any such program:

(a) LICENSEE shall report all billings and/or cash received from the furnishing network.

(b) LICENSEE may deduct amounts paid to the furnishing network for (i) the use of interconnecting facilities necessary to broadcast the program from outside the station's studios (not more than the amount actually paid to a utility company for such), and (ii) broadcast rights (not more than the amount actually paid to or for the original holder of the broadcast rights for the program).

(2) Any program which originates from a station which holds a BMI Single Station Radio Blanket License shall be deemed to be a local program. With respect to any such program:

(a) The originating station shall report all billings and/or cash received from or on behalf of (1) the sponsors of any such program, and (2) affiliated stations. The following deductions shall be allowed against such income:

(i) The actual payments made for the use of transmission facilities necessary to broadcast the program from outside the station's studios, but not more than the amount actually paid to the utility company for such:

(ii) The actual payments made for broadcast rights, but not more than the amount actually paid to or for the original holder of them; and

(iii) The actual payments made by the originating station to its affiliates in connection with such program.

(b) The affiliated station shall include all billings and/or cash received from the originating station in connection with such program or from or on behalf of sponsors of cooperative announcements. If payments are made to the originating station by the affiliated station in connection with such program, the affiliated station may deduct such payments.

E. **"Net Revenue"** shall mean:

(1) When reporting on a "Billing Basis" (see Paragraph 5.B.), all billings (standard accrual method) charged to or on behalf of sponsors and donors, but excluding non-cash billings applicable to transactions such as trade and barter sales, for the use of the broadcasting facilities of the station from:

(a) local programs (including programs furnished by a network not licensed as a network by BMI and programs originating from another station which holds a BMI Single Station License agreement);

(b) network programs;

(c) co-operative programs;

2

(d) contributions or donations; and

(e) the cash portion of billings attributed to "time brokers" or providers of "program services" in "barter" arrangements by such parties that have no direct or indirect managerial ownership or connection with LICENSEE, *reduced by,*

    (i)   bad debts written off or rebates paid,

    (ii)   rate card discounts (cash, quantity and/or frequency actually allowed), and

    (iii)   agency commissions incurred (not to exceed 15%).

(2) When reporting on a "Cash Receipts Basis" (see Paragraph 5.B.), all cash payments made by or on behalf of sponsors (net of agency commissions incurred not to exceed 15%) and donors for the use of the radio broadcasting facilities of the station in the areas indicated in Paragraph 3.E.(1)(a) through (e), above.

F.   **"Adjusted Net Revenue"** shall mean Net Revenue less any sums received from networks licensed by BMI with respect to network programs (but only with respect to that portion of the sums received from the network attributable to such network program announcements which are related to network programs and are carried by the station) and sums received for the broadcasting of local political programs.

G.   **"Amount Subject to BMI Fee"** shall mean Adjusted Net Revenue (Short Method Option) or, at the option of LICENSEE, Adjusted Net Revenue less the total of the following itemized deductions to the extent they exceed 15% of Adjusted Net Revenue (Long Method Option):

(1) Net Talent Fees Allowed. All compensation in excess of the Total Yearly Amount set forth below actually paid by the station to personnel acting as (i) master of ceremonies or disk jockey on musical programs, (ii) vocalist or instrumentalist engaged for a special program, (iii) featured newscaster or news commentator, (iv) featured sportscaster, (v) master of ceremonies on an entertainment program or (vi) announcer. If such person(s) has a 40% or more ownership interest in the station, this deduction shall not be allowed. If such person(s) holds a managerial capacity at the station and spends less than 100% of his or her time performing any of the duties enumerated in this Paragraph 3.G.(1), the total compensation amount shall be reduced in proportion to the amount of time spent on said duties.

Station's Annual Adjusted Net Revenue	Total Yearly Amount
Less than $50,000	$ 5,200
$50,000 to $149,999	15,600
$150,000 to $299,999	23,400
$300,000 to $499,999	35,100
$500,000 to $749,999	39,000
$750,000 to $999,999	45,500
$1,000,000 and over	52,000

The names and compensation must be indicated separately on the Annual Statement supplied by BMI.

If the Annual Statement covers less than a full calendar year, Adjusted Net Revenue must be annualized and the corresponding Total Yearly Amount must be prorated over the reporting period.

(2) News Ticker Service and Audio News Service. LICENSEE may deduct the actual payment made by it to an independent supplier of news service (e.g., AP, UPI), whether for ticker or audio service. These costs must be in connection with general news services and must be paid to an independent supplier of news service.

(3) The actual cost incurred by the station for a specific local commercial program: (i) payments to the telephone company or like transmission utility for remote pick-up necessary to broadcast such program from outside the station's studios; and (ii) rights for broadcasting a sports or other event but not to exceed the amount actually paid to or for the original holder of the broadcast rights for the program.

4.   BMI hereby grants to LICENSEE, for the term hereof, a non-exclusive license to perform, by radio broadcasting on LICENSEE's local programs by the station, non-dramatic performances of all musical works, the right to grant public performance rights which BMI may, during the term hereof, own or control.

A.   The rights granted hereby shall not include the right to perform more than thirty (30) minutes of a full-length dramatic or dramatico-musical work (or a substantial part of a short dramatic or dramatico-musical work) such as an opera, operetta, musical show or ballet, but this exclusion shall not apply to such performances from (1) a score originally written for and performed as part of a radio program or (2) the original cast, sound track or similar album of a dramatic or dramatico-musical work other than an opera.

B. The performances licensed hereunder may originate at any place, whether or not such place is licensed to publicly perform the musical works licensed hereunder, and regardless of the manner, means or methods of such origination. Nothing in this agreement shall be deemed to grant a license to anyone authorizing any public performance in such other place of any such composition.

C. BMI will, upon specific reasonable written request made by LICENSEE, indicate whether a number of specific musical compositions listed by LICENSEE are licensed by BMI. LICENSEE shall provide title, writer/composer and publisher of each musical composition requested to be identified.

5.   A. Commencing on or before April 1, 1988, and on or before April 1 of each year thereafter, LICENSEE shall render Annual Statements to BMI, on forms supplied by BMI, covering the period of the preceding calendar year with respect to billings and/or cash receipts for the use of the facilities of the station for the broadcasting of local programs. If LICENSEE reports via the Long Method Option, it must show all deductions in order to arrive at Amount Subject to BMI Fee as herein provided. In the event that LICENSEE shall fail to make payment or render any Annual Statement under this agreement, when and as due, BMI may, in addition to any and all other remedies which it has at law or in equity, terminate this license upon thirty (30) days' notice in writing, and this license shall thereupon so terminate at the end of such period unless said default shall previously have been cured. The right to cancel shall be in addition to any and all other remedies which BMI may have. No waiver by BMI of full performance of this agreement by LICENSEE in any one or more instances shall be deemed a waiver of the right to require full and complete performance of this agreement thereafter or of the right to cancel this agreement in accordance with the terms of this Paragraph.

B. (1) In the event that LICENSEE was previously licensed for the station by BMI under the Single Station License Agreement which had a stated expiration date of December 31, 1985, and:

(a) If LICENSEE has never submitted an Annual Statement to BMI, LICENSEE shall report for the Term of this agreement on a Billing Basis, or

(b) If LICENSEE has submitted to BMI its 1986 Annual Statement, LICENSEE shall report for the Term of this agreement on the same basis (Billing or Cash Receipts) as that used in its 1986 Annual Statement; provided, however, that, if LICENSEE reported on a Cash Receipts Basis for 1986, LICENSEE may report for the Term of this agreement on a Billing Basis, but only after paying any fees owed BMI for receipts accrued in 1986 but not reported to BMI and after receiving written permission from BMI. However, nothing herein shall be interpreted to permit LICENSEE to change the basis of reporting retroactively, or

(c) If LICENSEE has not submitted to BMI its 1986 Annual Statement, LICENSEE shall report for the Term of this agreement on the same basis (Billing or Cash Receipts) as that used in its last Annual Statement submitted to BMI.

(2) If LICENSEE has never been licensed for the station by BMI prior to January 1, 1987, LICENSEE may report for 1987 on either a Billing or Cash Receipts basis and shall continue to report on that basis for the remainder of the Term of this agreement.

(3) All billings made to the termination of this agreement with respect to local radio broadcasts made during the Term hereof shall be accounted for by LICENSEE as and when such billings are made by LICENSEE.

C. If any Annual Statement is not received by BMI within sixty (60) days of the due date, LICENSEE will be required to use the Short Method Option for such statement.

D. (1) If an AM and FM station in the same market are under common ownership, LICENSEE will be governed as follows:

(a) If LICENSEE files a joint Annual Statement for 1987 for said AM/FM stations, LICENSEE must continue to file Annual Statements on a combined basis for the duration of this agreement. If one of the stations is sold after the initial Annual Statement has been filed by LICENSEE, no other station may be substituted in place of the station sold. Under no circumstances may a combined Annual Statement be filed with BMI where the AM/FM stations are in separate markets.

(b) If LICENSEE files separate Annual Statements for 1987 for the AM/FM stations, LICENSEE must continue to file separate statements for said AM/FM stations for the duration of this agreement.

(c) If LICENSEE's AM/FM stations are simulcast during 80% or more of their broadcast day, LICENSEE shall file a joint Annual Statement for said AM/FM stations.

(2) If commonly owned AM and FM stations are in different markets, LICENSEE shall file separate Annual Statements for the Term of this agreement.

E. For each month during the Term hereof LICENSEE shall, on or before the first day of the following month, pay to BMI a sum equal to one twelfth of the annual fee payable hereunder for the preceding calendar year, plus 8%; provided, however, that if, as and when any Annual Statement required to be supplied to BMI by LICENSEE pursuant to this Paragraph 5 is not received when due, all subsequent monthly payments due hereunder shall be increased by an amount equal to 24% thereof, and such increase shall remain in effect up to and including the month in which any such overdue statement is finally received by BMI. Notwithstanding any of the foregoing, in any calendar year of the term hereof, as of the month when BMI receives the statement required to be supplied by Paragraph 5.A. hereof applicable to any immediately prior year, any adjustment required by a discrepancy between prior billings and monthly payments actually due in accordance with this Paragraph 5.E. shall, at BMI's option, be prorated over the remaining monthly payments due during that calendar year.

F. If the annual license fee for any calendar year of the Term hereof exceeds the monthly installments applicable to such year's fee, LICENSEE shall pay any such excess to BMI at the time the Annual Statement is due. If the amount paid by LICENSEE for said calendar year exceeds the annual license fee due for said year, LICENSEE will be entitled to a credit of the overage paid; provided, that if the overage paid is greater than three times the monthly payments required by Paragraph 5.E. for said calendar year, BMI shall, within thirty (30) days of receipt of written request of LICENSEE, refund the excess payment.

G. BMI may impose a late payment charge of 1% per month from the date the payment was due on any monthly or annual payment that is received by BMI more than one month after the date payment was due.

H. (1) BMI shall have the right by its duly authorized representatives, during customary business hours, on notice in writing of not less than ten (10) business days, to examine the books and records of account of LICENSEE only to such extent as may be necessary to verify any Annual Statements required by this agreement. All data and information coming to BMI's attention as a result of any such examination of LICENSEE's books and records shall be held completely and entirely confidential and shall not be used by BMI other than in connection with its administration of this license.

(2) The period for which BMI may audit pursuant to Paragraph 5.H.(1) hereof shall be limited to two (2) calendar years preceding the year in which the audit is made; provided, that if an audit is postponed at the request of LICENSEE, and BMI grants such postponement, BMI shall have the right to audit for the period commencing with the second calendar year preceding the year in which notification of intention to audit was first given by BMI to LICENSEE.

I. The period for which LICENSEE may amend any Annual Statement submitted pursuant to this agreement shall be limited to two (2) calendar years following the year in which such statement was originally due pursuant to Paragraph 5.A. LICENSEE shall have the right to amend any portion of a previously submitted statement and the right to correct computational or reporting errors. Once LICENSEE submits an Annual Statement to BMI pursuant to this agreement, LICENSEE may amend said statement only one time. If LICENSEE amends a statement pursuant to this provision, the time for BMI to audit said statement will be two (2) years after the filing of said amended statement by LICENSEE.

6. BMI agrees to indemnify, save and hold harmless and to defend LICENSEE, its advertisers and their advertising agencies, and its and their officers, employees and artists, from and against all claims, demands and suits that may be made or brought against them or any of them with respect to the performance under this agreement of any material licensed hereunder, provided that this indemnity shall not apply to broadcasts of any musical work performed by LICENSEE after written request from BMI to LICENSEE that LICENSEE refrain from performance thereof. LICENSEE agrees to give BMI immediate notice of any such claim, demand or suit, and agrees immediately to deliver to BMI all papers pertaining thereto. BMI shall have full charge of the defense of any such claim, demand or suit, and LICENSEE shall cooperate fully with BMI therein.

7. This license shall be non-assignable except to the person, firm or corporation acquiring the Federal Communications Commission license of the station, and upon assignment to such station and upon acceptance in form approved by BMI of the application of LICENSEE hereunder, LICENSEE shall be relieved of future liability under this agreement as long as all statements have been filed by LICENSEE and all fees due BMI under this agreement have been paid to BMI.

8. LICENSEE, upon written request from BMI made on not less than one (1) week's notice specifying the period to be covered, agrees to furnish to BMI lists of LICENSEE's performances of all musical works, indicating the compositions performed by title and composer or by such other convenient method as may be designated by BMI, but such lists need not be furnished for more than one (1) week of each year of the Term.

9. In the event that the Federal Communications Commission revokes or fails to renew the broadcasting license of LICENSEE, or in the event that the governmental rules and regulations applicable to the station are suspended or amended so as to forbid the broadcasting of commercial programs by LICENSEE, LICENSEE may notify BMI thereof, and BMI, within ten (10) days of the receipt of such notice shall, by written notice to LICENSEE, at BMI's option, either terminate or suspend this license and all payments and services hereunder for the period that such condition continues. In the event that BMI elects to suspend this license, such suspension shall not continue for longer than six (6) months, and this license shall automatically terminate at the end of six (6) months' suspension. In the event that the condition giving rise to the suspension shall continue for less than six (6) months, BMI at its option, and on written notice to LICENSEE, may reinstate this license at any time within thirty (30) days after the cessation of such condition.

10. In the event that any law now or hereafter enacted of the state, or political subdivision thereof, in which the station and/or LICENSEE is located shall result in major interference with BMI's operations or in the refusal of a substantial number of radio stations therein to enter into license agreements with BMI or to make payments to BMI, BMI shall have the right at any time to terminate this agreement on no less than sixty (60) days' written notice to LICENSEE.

11. All disputes of any kind, nature or description arising in connection with the terms and conditions of this agreement shall be submitted to the American Arbitration Association in the City and State of New York for arbitration under its then prevailing rules, the arbitrator(s) to be selected as follows: Each of the parties hereto shall by written notice to the other have the right to appoint one arbitrator. If, within ten (10) days following the giving of such notice by one party, the other shall not, by written notice, appoint another arbitrator, the first arbitrator shall be the sole arbitrator. If two arbitrators are so appointed, they shall appoint a third arbitrator. If ten (10) days elapse after the appointment of the second arbitrator and the two arbitrators are unable to agree upon the third arbitrator, then either party may, in writing, request the American Arbitration Association to appoint the third arbitrator. The award made in the arbitration shall be binding and conclusive on the parties and judgment may be, but need not be, entered in any court having jurisdiction. Such award shall include the fixing of the costs, expenses and reasonable attorney's fees of arbitration, which shall be borne by the unsuccessful party.

12. Any notice required or permitted to be given under this agreement shall be in writing and shall be deemed duly given when sent by ordinary first-class U.S. mail to the party for whom it is intended, at its address hereinabove stated, or any other address which either party hereto may from time to time designate for such purpose, and when such notice is so mailed, it shall be deemed given upon the mailing thereof. Any such notice sent to BMI shall be to the attention of the Licensing Department. Any such notice sent to LICENSEE shall be to the attention of the person signing this agreement on behalf of LICENSEE or such other person as LICENSEE may advise BMI in writing.

13. On written notice to LICENSEE, BMI may, effective with such notice, withdraw from the license granted hereunder any musical work as to which any legal action has been instituted or a claim made that BMI does not have the right to license the performing rights in such work or that such work infringes another composition.

14. This agreement shall enure to the benefit of and shall be binding upon the parties and their respective successors and assigns, but no assignment shall relieve the parties of their respective obligations under this agreement.

15. This agreement constitutes the entire understanding between the parties, shall not be binding until signed by both parties and cannot be waived or added to or modified orally, and no waiver, addition or modification shall be valid unless in writing and signed by the parties. This agreement, its validity, construction and effect shall be governed by the laws of the State of New York. The fact that any provisions herein are found to be void or unenforceable by a court of competent jurisdiction shall in no way affect the validity or enforceability of any other provisions.

BROADCAST MUSIC, INC.

LICENSEE (Legal Name)

By _____
(Signature)

By _____
(Signature)

_____
(Print Name of Signer)

_____
(Print Name of Signer)

_____
(Title of Signer)

_____
(Title of Signer)

PLEASE COMPLETE WHITE AREA ONLY

6

FORM 15.13

BMI SINGLE RADIO STATION PER PROGRAM LICENSE

BMI   **BROADCAST MUSIC, INC.**   RADIO-87/PP

SINGLE STATION RADIO PER PROGRAM LICENSE

AGREEMENT, made at New York, N.Y., on this _____ day of _____ , 19 ___ , between BROADCAST MUSIC, INC., a corporation organized under the laws of the State of New York (hereinafter called BMI) with principal offices at 320 West 57th Street, New York, N.Y. 10019 and

_____
(Legal Name of LICENSEE)

☐ A corporation organized under the laws of the State of _____

☐ A partnership consisting of_____

**PLEASE CHECK
APPROPRIATE BOX
AND COMPLETE**

☐ An individual residing at _____

(hereinafter called LICENSEE) with offices located at _____
_____
(Street Address)

City _____ State _____ Zip _____ Telephone No. (_____)
                                                                          Area Code

and operating the radio broadcasting station presently located at _____
_____
(Street Address)

City _____ State _____ Zip _____ Telephone No. (_____) _____
                                               ☐ AM or   Area Code
and presently designated by the call letters_____ ☐ FM _____ and assigned frequency_____
                                               (Check Appropriate Box)

W I T N E S S E T H:

1.   As used in this agreement:

(a) **"Term"** shall mean the period commencing on _____ and ending on December 31, 1991 unless earlier terminated as hereinafter provided. **This agreement may not be entered into retroactively.** It is further agreed that the terms and conditions of the Single Station Blanket License Agreement, as previously amended and executed by BMI and LICENSEE (which had a stated expiration date of December 31, 1985), shall be extended to December 31, 1986. It is further agreed that for the period January 1, 1987 to June 30, 1987, if LICENSEE was licensed at the time of execution of this license under the Single Station License with a stated expiration date of December 31, 1985, the provisions of the Single Station License Agreement with a stated expiration date of December 31, 1991 shall apply. If LICENSEE was previously licensed under the Single Station Per Program License, that agreement shall apply for said six (6) month period.

(b) **"Radio broadcasting"** shall mean aural broadcasting in all of its forms.

(c) **"Programming period"** shall mean a fifteen (15) minute period of broadcasting commencing on the hour and at fifteen (15), thirty (30) and forty-five (45) minutes past the hour without regard to whether such period contains one or more programs or announcements.

(d) **"Network program"** shall mean any radio program simultaneously broadcast by any means by any network licensed as a network by BMI. "Network program" shall include "rebroadcasts," "delayed broadcasts" and "repeat broadcasts" of a network program as those terms are understood in the broadcasting industry, even though non-simultaneous. Payments made to the originating network by an affiliated station in connection with such program may not be deducted. LICENSEE shall report all billings to the network. "Billings" as used in this agreement shall exclude the non-cash portion of transactions such as trade and barter sales.

(1) Any program furnished by a network which is not licensed as a network by BMI shall be deemed to be a "local program". With respect to any such program:

(a) LICENSEE shall report all billings to the furnishing network.

(b) LICENSEE may deduct amounts paid to the furnishing network for (i) the use of interconnecting facilities necessary to broadcast the program from outside LICENSEE's studios (not more than the amount actually paid to a utility company for such), and (ii) broadcast rights (not more than the amount actually paid to or for the original holder of the broadcast rights for the program).

(2) Any program which originates from a station which holds a BMI Single Station Radio Blanket License shall be deemed to be a local program. With respect to any such program:

(a) The originating station shall report all billings to or on behalf of (1) the sponsors of any such program, and (2) affiliated stations. The following deductions shall be allowed against such income:

(i) The actual payments made for the use of transmission facilities necessary to broadcast the program from outside LICENSEE's studios, but not more than the amount actually paid to the utility company for such;

(ii) The actual payments made for broadcast rights, but not more than the amount actually paid to or for the original holder of them; and

PLEASE COMPLETE SHADED AREA ONLY

(iii) The actual payments made by the originating station to its affiliates in connection with such program.

(b) The affiliated station shall include all billings to the originating station in connection with such program or from or on behalf of sponsors of cooperative announcements. If payments are made to the originating station by the affiliated station in connection with such program, the affiliated station may deduct such payments.

(e) **"Local program"** shall mean any radio program, including a "co-operative program", broadcast by the station, other than a "network program". For the purposes of this agreement, sports, special events and other programs furnished by networks not licensed by BMI, as well as any program originating from a station which holds a BMI Single Station Radio Blanket License, shall be deemed to be "local programs".

(f) **"Co-operative program"** shall mean any program furnished by the network to the station under an agreement permitting the station to broadcast such program on a sustaining basis or on a commercial basis under the sponsorship of a local, regional or national advertiser contracting directly with the station or its representative for the incorporation of the commercial credits of such advertiser into such program, as broadcast by the station.

(g) **"Background for an announcement"** shall mean mood, atmosphere or thematic music performed as background to an otherwise non-musical commercial, public service, or station promotional announcement not exceeding sixty (60) seconds in length.

(h) **"Jingle"** shall mean an advertising, promotional or public service announcement containing musical material (with or without lyrics) where the musical material was originally written for advertising, promotional or public service announcement purposes, or a musical work, originally written for other purposes, with the lyrics changed for advertising, promotional or public service announcement purposes, not exceeding sixty (60) seconds in length and used with the permission of the interested writer or publisher affiliated with BMI.

(i) **"Incidental use"** shall mean music used as themes or signatures; bridges, cue or background music aggregating less than two and one-half minutes in duration; public domain music in arrangements controlled by BMI on which BMI pays no royalties; and music which is used only incidentally to the broadcast of an actual public event or sports event.

(j) **"Net Revenue"** shall mean all billings (standard accrual method) charged to or on behalf of sponsors and donors, but excluding non-cash billings applicable to trade and barter sales, for the use of the broadcasting facilities of the station, from:

(1) local programs (including programs furnished by a network not licensed as a network by BMI and programs originating from another station which holds a BMI license agreement);

(2) network programs;

(3) co-operative programs;

(4) contributions or donations; and

(5) the cash portion of billings attributed to "time brokers" or providers of "program services" in "barter" arrangements by such parties that have no direct or indirect managerial ownership or connection with LICENSEE,

reduced by,

(i) bad debts written off or rebates paid, and (ii) rate card discounts (cash, quantity and/or frequency actually allowed). *No agency commissions may be deducted.*

(k) **"Adjusted Net Revenue"** shall mean Net Revenue less any sums received from networks licensed by BMI with respect to network programs (but only with respect to that portion of the sums received from the network attributable to such network program announcements which are related to network programs and are carried by the station) and sums received for the broadcasting of local political programs.

(l) **"Weighted programming period"** shall mean the applicable weight set forth below for the corresponding time period:

	Time Period	Applicable Weight
Weekdays:	Midnight to 6:00 A.M.	.25
	6:00 A.M. to 10:00 A.M.	1.00
	10:00 A.M. to 3:00 P.M.	.50
	3:00 P.M. to 7.00 P.M.	.75
	7:00 P.M. to Midnight	.50
Weekends:	Saturdays and Sundays	.25

(m) **"Compensable weighted programming periods"** shall mean the total of the weighted programming periods which contain local programming that include the performance of any portion of a musical work licensed by BMI, other than as "background for an announcement", a "jingle", or for "incidental use".

(n) **"Revenue per weighted programming period"** shall mean Adjusted Net Revenue for the full calendar year divided by the total number of the weighted programming periods in the full calendar year.

(o) **"Amount Subject to BMI Fee"** shall mean revenue per weighted programming period multiplied by the compensable weighted programming periods in the full calendar year.

2. BMI hereby grants to LICENSEE, for the term hereof, a non-exclusive license to perform, by radio broadcasting on LICENSEE's local programs by the Station, all musical works, the right to grant public performance licenses which BMI may, during the term hereof, own or control.

(a) The rights granted hereby shall not include the right to perform more than thirty (30) minutes of a full-length dramatic or dramatico-musical work (or a substantial part of a short dramatic or dramatico-musical work) such as an opera, operetta, musical show or ballet, but this exclusion shall not apply to such performances from (1) a score originally written for and performed as part of a radio program or (2) the original cast, sound track or similar album of a dramatic or dramatico-musical work other than an opera.

(b) The performances licensed hereunder may originate at any place, whether or not such place is licensed to publicly perform the musical works licensed hereunder, and regardless of the manner, means or methods of such origination. Nothing in this agreement shall be deemed to grant a license to anyone authorizing any public performance in such other place of any such composition.

(c) BMI will, upon specific reasonable written request made by LICENSEE, indicate whether a number of specific musical compositions listed by LICENSEE are licensed by BMI. LICENSEE shall provide the title and the writer/composer and publisher of each musical composition requested to be identified.

3. (a) LICENSE agrees to pay to BMI for each year of the term of this agreement as a license fee hereunder:

(i) 4% (3.5% if Net Revenue is under **$150,000**) of Amount Subject to BMI Fee

plus

(ii) Forty-eight (48) times the station's highest one-minute card rate (regardless of its frequency of use) in effect during any portion of the month; provided, however, that in the event the Station shall have a rate for any period of one minute or less which is greater than the Station's highest one-minute card rate, such higher rate shall be used in computing this fee.

(iii) In no event shall the license fee be less than the amount specified in Paragraph 3(a)(ii) above.

2

(b) For the period July 1, 1987 through December 31, 1987, LICENSEE shall, on or before the first day of each month, pay to BMI an estimated monthly fee computed as follows:

(i) if LICENSEE was previously licensed under the BMI Single Station Per Program License Agreement, in effect through June 30, 1987, an amount equal to the average monthly license fee due for the period January 1, 1987 through June 30, 1987, or four (4) times the Station's current highest one-minute card rate, whichever is higher;

(ii) if LICENSEE was previously licensed under the BMI Single Station License, four (4) times the Station's current highest one-minute card rate plus the license fee provided for in Paragraph 3(a)(i), annualized, applied to the Station's estimated revenue per weighted programming period for 1987 multiplied by the total number of compensable weighted programming periods as determined by the first Monthly Music Report required for 1987. LICENSEE shall furnish BMI with a good faith estimate of its Adjusted Net Revenue for the year 1987 and the revenue per weighted programming period shall be computed by dividing the estimated revenue by the total weighted programming periods for 1987.

(iii) if LICENSEE was not previously licensed for the Station, or if LICENSEE was previously licensed under a BMI Limited Use License, four (4) times the Station's current highest one-minute card rate.

(c) Beginning January 1, 1988 and for all succeeding years of the term of this license, for each month during the term hereof, LICENSEE shall pay to BMI an estimated monthly fee equal to one-twelfth of the actual annual fee for the immediately preceding year, plus 8% of the fee due pursuant to Paragraph 3(a)(i). If the Station was not licensed by BMI during the preceding year, LICENSEE shall furnish BMI with a good faith estimate in writing of its Adjusted Net Revenue for the year being paid and the revenue per weighted programming period shall be computed by dividing the estimated revenue by the Station's total estimated weighted programming periods in the year. At such time as LICENSEE files its Annual Financial Report pursuant to Paragraph 5, LICENSEE's estimated fee shall be adjusted to reflect the actual fee due for such year, which shall become the estimated fee for the year subsequent to the year of the report. The actual fee due for 1987 shall be annualized for the purposes of this Paragraph 3(c).

(d) If the actual annual license fee for any calendar year of the term hereof exceeds the total of the estimated monthly installments for such year's fee, LICENSEE shall pay any such excess to BMI within thirty (30) days of written notification by BMI. If the total of the estimated monthly installments charged to LICENSEE for said calendar year exceeds the actual annual license fee due for said year, LICENSEE will be entitled to a credit of the overage paid or, on written request, a refund, provided that its account is not otherwise in arrears.

(e) LICENSEE agrees that it will not offset or withhold from current payments any amounts due for a preceding year.

(f) LICENSEE agrees that it will not assert any claim or counter-claim for a refund of any amount for any period prior to two (2) years before the then current year of the term of this license.

4. **MONTHLY MUSIC REPORTS:**

(a) LICENSEE agrees to furnish to BMI, within twenty (20) days after the end of each month during the term of this agreement, a full, true, complete and accurate report, on forms furnished by BMI, of the following information with respect to any and all programming periods during the month which have any musical content, except as provided in Paragraph 4(b): The full title of each musical work, the date and time of performance, the name(s) of the writer-composer(s) and publisher(s) as shown on the record or tape label or sheet music and, in the case of a recorded work, the name and label of the manufacturer of the recording. This requirement shall apply to all local programming periods, regardless of their origination.

(b) LICENSEE shall submit a monthly music report, even if no music was used during a month (in which case only the requested identifying and rate card information need be completed), but shall not be required to include the information set forth in Paragraph 4(a) as as to (i) programming periods for which the rate of payment set forth in Paragraph 3(a) is conceded by LICENSEE to be due; (ii) network programming; (iii) incidental use or use as musical commercials, including "background music" or a "jingle" as defined in Paragraph 1 herein; (iv) political programming and (v) local programs cleared at the source. Every programming period which contains music (other than a programming period in which the only music is incidental or part of commercials) shall be listed on the report, even if the music falls into one of the exempt categories enumerated in this Paragraph 4(b)(i), (ii), (iv) and (v). In those cases, however, the category of exemption shall be indicated on the report form, listing the name of the network in the case of a network program and the name of the party from whom clearance was obtained in the case of a local program cleared at the source. It shall be presumed that any programming period for which a complete music report is not furnished by LICENSEE contains BMI music. Anything to the contrary herein notwithstanding, this license shall not extend to or include compositions wholly unreported in such music reports.

5. **ANNUAL FINANCIAL REPORTS:**

(a) On or before the first day of April in each year commencing 1988, LICENSEE shall send to BMI a report of the license fee due for the preceding calendar year. Each such report shall be made by fully completing the Annual Financial Report, a copy of which is attached to and made a part of this agreement.

(b) The Annual Financial Report shall be made on a billing basis. All billings made subsequent to the termination of this agreement with respect to local radio broadcasts made during the term of the agreement shall be accounted for by LICENSEE as if made prior to termination or expiration.

6. **LOGGING REPORTS:**

LICENSEE, upon written request from BMI made on not less than one (1) week's notice specifying the period to be covered by the lists, agrees to furnish to BMI (upon forms to be supplied by BMI) a list of LICENSEE's performances of all musical works, indicating the compositions performed by title and composer or by such other convenient method as may be designated by BMI, but such lists need not be furnished for more than one (1) week of each year of the term.

7. (a) BMI shall have the right by its duly authorized representative(s), during customary business hours, on notice in writing of not less than ten (10) business days, to examine the books and records of account of LICENSEE only to such extent as may be necessary to verify any reports required by this agreement. All data and information coming to BMI's attention as a result of any such examination of LICENSEE's books and records shall be held completely and entirely confidential and shall not be used by BMI other than in connection with administration of this license.

(b) The period for which BMI may audit pursuant to Paragraph 7(a) shall be limited to two (2) calendar years preceding the year in which the audit is made; provided, that if an audit is postponed at the request of LICENSEE, and BMI grants such postponement, BMI shall have the right to audit for the period commencing with the second calendar year preceding the year in which notification of intention to audit was first given by BMI to LICENSEE.

(c) The period for which LICENSEE may amend any Annual Financial Report submitted pursuant to this agreement shall be limited to two (2) calendar years following the year in which such report was originally due pursuant to Paragraph 5. LICENSEE shall have the right to amend any portion of a previously submitted report and the right to correct computational or reporting errors. Once LICENSEE submits a report to BMI pursuant to this agreement, LICENSEE may amend said report only one time. If LICENSEE amends a report pursuant to this provision, the time for BMI to object to or contest said report will be two (2) years after the filing of said amended report by LICENSEE.

8. LICENSEE agrees to furnish to BMI at the time of the signing hereof the document prepared for its advertisers indicating its current card rate as contemplated by Paragraph 3(a)(ii) hereof and thereafter as and when revised, within thirty (30) days thereof.

9.   In the event that LICENSEE shall fail to render any report or statement required hereunder, when and as due, BMI may in addition to any other remedies available to it in this agreement, calculate the estimated amounts payable as hereinafter provided.

10.   BMI agrees to indemnify, save and hold harmless and to defend LICENSEE, its advertisers and their advertising agencies, and its and their officers, employees and artists, from and against all claims, demands and suits that may be made or brought against them or any of them with respect to the performance of any material licensed hereunder, provided that this indemnity shall not apply to broadcasts of any musical work performed by LICENSEE after written request from BMI to LICENSEE that LICENSEE refrain from performance thereof. LICENSEE agrees to give BMI immediate notice of any such claim, demand or suit, and agrees immediately to deliver to BMI all papers pertaining thereto. BMI shall have full charge of the defense of any such claim, demand or suit, and LICENSEE shall cooperate fully with BMI therein.

11.   This license shall be non-assignable except to the person, firm or corporation acquiring the Federal Communications Commission license of the station, and upon assignment to such Station and upon acceptance in form approved by BMI of the application of LICENSEE hereunder, the LICENSEE shall be relieved of future liability under this agreement, provided such assignee executes a new license agreement.

12.   In the event that LICENSEE shall fail to make any payment or render any report or statement under this agreement, when and as due, BMI shall notify LICENSEE in writing of the delinquency and provide at least an additional thirty (30) days within which LICENSEE may submit the payment or report or statement without penalty. If the payment, report or statement is not submitted within the extension period, BMI may, at its option: (a) terminate this license or (b) convert this license to a BMI Single Station Radio Blanket License, effective as of the beginning of the month in which the report or statement was due and for up to a period of one (1) year from that date, after which time LICENSEE shall automatically revert to this license, unless LICENSEE otherwise requests in writing. If BMI chooses not to terminate or convert this license, all subsequent monthly payments due hereunder shall be increased by an amount equal to the legal rate of interest in New York State, and such increase shall remain in effect up to and including the month in which any overdue statement is finally received by BMI. The right to cancel or convert shall be in addition to any and all other remedies which BMI may have. No waiver by BMI of full performance of this agreement by LICENSEE in any one or more instances shall be deemed a waiver of the right to require full and complete performance of this agreement thereafter or of the right to cancel this agreement in accordance with the terms of this Paragraph.

13.   BMI may impose a late payment charge of 1% per month from the date the payment was due on any monthly or annual payment that is received by BMI more than one month after the date payment was due.

14.   In the event that any law now or hereafter enacted of the state, or political subdivision thereof, in which the station and/or LICENSEE is located shall result in major interference with BMI's operations or in the refusal of a substantial number of radio stations therein to enter into license agreements with BMI or to make payments to BMI, BMI shall have the right at any time to terminate this agreement on no less than sixty (60) days' written notice to LICENSEE.

15.   Attached hereto is a form of a Single Station Radio Blanket License. LICENSEE may substitute BMI's then current blanket license (which shall not be substantially different from the attached form) in lieu of this license, provided that LICENSEE has furnished to BMI all reports which are due under this license:

      (a)   Effective as of January 1 in any year, provided notice shall have been given by LICENSEE to BMI not later than thirty (30) days after the fee under this license agreement for the preceding year has been established;

      (b)   Effective as of the first day of the month following the month in which the station has a substantive change of format, provided notice shall have been given by LICENSEE to BMI not later than thirty (30) days after change of format. Notwithstanding anything to the contrary contained herein, upon change of ownership, a new owner shall have a choice of blanket or "per program" license with respect to the period of its ownership, provided such new owner executes a new license agreement. Nothing herein shall be interpreted to relieve LICENSEE of its obligations hereunder.

16.   Wholly-owned AM and FM stations shall report and pay separately, and be treated for all purposes as separate stations.

17.   All disputes of any kind, nature or description arising in connection with the terms and conditions of this agreement shall be submitted to the American Arbitration Association in the City and State of New York for arbitration under its then prevailing rules, the arbitrator(s) to be selected as follows: Each of the parties shall, by written notice to the other, have the right to appoint one arbitrator. If, within ten (10) days following the giving of such notice by one party, the other shall not, by written notice, appoint another arbitrator, the first arbitrator shall be the sole arbitrator. If two arbitrators are so appointed, they shall appoint a third arbitrator. If ten (10) days elapse after the appointment of the second arbitrator and the two arbitrators are unable to agree upon the third arbitrator, then either party may, in writing, request the American Arbitration Association to appoint the third arbitrator. The award made in the arbitration shall be binding and conclusive on the parties and judgment may be, but need not be, entered in any court having jurisdiction. Such award shall include the fixing of the costs, expenses and attorney's fees of arbitration, which shall be borne by the unsuccessful party.

18.   On written notice to LICENSEE, BMI may, effective with such notice, withdraw from the license granted hereunder any musical work as to which any legal action has been instituted or a claim made that BMI does not have the right to license the performing rights in such work or that such work infringes another composition.

19.   This agreement shall enure to the benefit of and shall be binding upon both parties and their respective successors and assigns, but no assignment shall relieve the parties of their respective obligations under this agreement.

20.   Any notice required or permitted to be given under this agreement shall be in writing and shall be deemed duly given when sent by ordinary first-class U.S. mail to the party for whom it is intended, at its address hereinabove stated, or any other address which either party hereto may from time to time designate for such purpose, and when such notice is so mailed, it shall be deemed given upon the mailing thereof. Any such notice sent to BMI shall be to the attention of the Licensing Department. Any such notice sent to LICENSEE shall be to the attention of the person signing this agreement on behalf of LICENSEE or such other person as LICENSEE may advise BMI in writing.

21.   This agreement constitutes the entire understanding between the parties, shall not be binding until signed by both parties and cannot be waived or added to or modified orally, and no waiver, addition or modification shall be valid unless in writing and signed by the parties. This agreement, its validity, construction and effect shall be governed by the laws of the State of New York. The fact that any provisions herein are found to be void or unenforceable by a court of competent jurisdiction shall in no way affect the validity or enforceability of any other provisions.

BROADCAST MUSIC, INC.

                                                           LICENSEE (Legal Name)

By _____   By _____

            (Signature)   **(Signature)**

_____   _____

      (Print name of signer)   **(Print name of signer)**

_____   4   _____

       (Title of signer)   **(Title of signer)**

                                          PLEASE COMPLETE SHADED AREA ONLY

FORM 15.14

ASCAP GENERAL LICENSE
(FOR RESTAURANTS, TAVERNS,
NIGHTCLUBS AND SIMILAR ESTABLISHMENTS)

GENERAL LICENSE AGREEMENT—RESTAURANTS, TAVERNS, NIGHTCLUBS, AND SIMILAR ESTABLISHMENTS

Agreement between AMERICAN SOCIETY OF COMPOSERS, AUTHORS AND PUBLISHERS ("SOCIETY"), located at

and
("LICENSEE"), located at   as follows:

1. Grant and Term of License

(a) SOCIETY grants and LICENSEE accepts for a term of one year, commencing   , and continuing thereafter for additional terms of one year each unless terminated by either party as hereinafter provided, a license to perform publicly at

("the premises"), and not elsewhere, non-dramatic renditions of the separate musical compositions now or hereafter during the term hereof in the repertory of SOCIETY, and of which SOCIETY shall have the right to license such performing rights.

(b) This agreement shall enure to the benefit of and shall be binding upon the parties hereto and their respective successors and assigns, but no assignment shall relieve the parties hereto of their respective obligations hereunder as to performances rendered, acts done and obligations incurred prior to the effective date of the assignment.

(c) Either party may, on or before thirty days prior to the end of the initial term or any renewal term, give notice of termination to the other. If such notice is given the agreement shall terminate on the last day of such initial or renewal term.

2. Limitations on License

(a) This license is not assignable or transferable by operation of law or otherwise, except as provided in paragraph "1(b)" hereof, and is limited to the LICENSEE and to the premises.

(b) This license does not authorize the broadcasting, telecasting or transmission by wire or otherwise, of renditions of musical compositions in SOCIETY'S repertory to persons outside of the premises.

(c) This license does not authorize any performance by means of a coin-operated phonorecord player (jukebox) otherwise covered by the compulsory license provisions of 17 U.S.C. §116.

(d) This license is limited to non-dramatic performances, and does not authorize any dramatic performances. For purposes of this agreement, a dramatic performance shall include, but not be limited to, the following:

    (i)   performance of a "dramatico-musical work" (as hereinafter defined) in its entirety;

    (ii) performance of one or more musical compositions from a "dramatico-musical work" (as hereinafter defined) accompanied by dialogue, pantomime, dance, stage action, or visual representation of the work from which the music is taken;

(iii) performance of one or more musical compositions as part of a story or plot, whether accompanied or unaccompanied by dialogue, pantomime, dance, stage, action, or visual representation;

(iv) performance of a concert version of a "dramatico-musical work" (as hereinafter defined).

The term "dramatico-musical work" as used in this agreement, shall include, but not be limited to, a musical comedy, oratorio, choral work, opera, play with music, revue, or ballet.

3. License Fee

(a) In consideration of the license granted herein, LICENSEE agrees to pay SOCIETY the applicable license fee set forth in the rate schedule printed below and made part hereof, based on "LICENSEE'S Operating Policy" (as hereinafter defined), payable quarterly in advance on January 1, April 1, July 1 and October 1 of each year. The term "LICENSEE'S Operating Policy," as used in this agreement, shall be deemed to mean all of the factors which determine the license fee applicable to the premises under said rate schedule.

(b) LICENSEE warrants that the Statement of LICENSEE'S Operating Policy on the reverse side of this agreement is true and correct.

(c) Said license fee is   Dollars ($)
annually, based on the facts set forth in said Statement of LICENSEE'S Operating Policy.

4. Changes in Licensee's Operating Policy

(a) LICENSEE agrees to give SOCIETY thirty days prior notice of any change in LICENSEE'S Operating Policy. For purposes of this agreement, a change in LICENSEE'S Operating Policy shall be one in effect for no less than thirty days.

(b) Upon any such change in LICENSEE'S Operating Policy resulting in an increase in the license fee, based on the annexed rate schedule, LICENSEE shall pay said increased license fee, effective as of the initial date of such change, whether or not notice of such change has been given pursuant to paragraph 4(a) of this agreement.

(c) Upon any such change in LICENSEE'S Operating Policy resulting in a reduction of the license fee, based on the annexed rate schedule, LICENSEE shall be entitled to such reduction, effective as of the initial date of such change, and to a *pro rata* credit for any unearned license fees paid in advance, provided LICENSEE has given SOCIETY thirty days prior notice of such change. If LICENSEE fails to give such prior notice, any such reduction and credit shall be effective thirty days after LICENSEE gives notice of such change.

(d) In the event of any such change in LICENSEE'S Operating Policy, LICENSEE shall furnish a current Statement of LICENSEE'S Operating Policy and shall certify that it is true and correct.

(e) If LICENSEE discontinues the performance of music at the premises, LICENSEE or SOCIETY may terminate this agreement upon thirty days prior notice, the termination to be effective at the end of such thirty day period. In the event of such termination, SOCIETY shall refund to LICENSEE a *pro rata* share of any unearned license fees paid in advance. For purposes of this agreement, a discontinuance of music shall be one in effect for no less than thirty days.

5. Breach or Default

Upon any breach or default by LICENSEE of any term or condition herein contained, SOCIETY may terminate this license by giving LICENSEE thirty days notice to cure such breach or default, and in the event that such breach or default has not been cured within said thirty days, this license shall terminate on the expiration of such thirty-day period without further notice from SOCIETY. In the event of such termination, SOCIETY shall refund to LICENSEE any unearned license fees paid in advance.

6. Interference in Society's Operations

In the event of:

(a) any major interference with the operations of SOCIETY in the state, territory, dependency, possession or political subdivision in which LICENSEE is located, by reason of any law of such state, territory, dependency, possession or political subdivision; or

(b) any substantial increase in the cost to the SOCIETY of operating in such state, territory, dependency, possession or political subdivision, by reason of any law of such state, territory, dependency, possession or political subdivision, which is applicable to the licensing of performing rights,

SOCIETY shall have the right to terminate this agreement forthwith by written notice and shall refund to LICENSEE any unearned license fees paid in advance.

7. Notices

All notices required or permitted hereunder shall be given in writing by certified United States mail sent to either party at the address stated above. Each party agrees to inform the other of any change of address.

IN WITNESS WHEREOF, this agreement has been duly executed by SOCIETY and LICENSEE this   day of
         , 19

AMERICAN SOCIETY OF COMPOSERS,
AUTHORS AND PUBLISHERS

_____
LICENSEE

By _____

By _____
           DISTRICT MANAGER

_____
Title

(Fill In capacity in which signed:
(a) If corporation, state corporate office held; (b) If partnership, write word "partner" under signature of signing partner; (c) If individual owner, write "individual owner" under signature.)

FORM 15.15

ASCAP HOTELS AND MOTELS LICENSE

HOTELS AND MOTELS

Memorandum of Agreement between AMERICAN SOCIETY OF COMPOSERS. AUTHORS AND PUBLISHERS (hereinafter styled "SOCIETY") and

(hereinafter styled "LICENSEE"), as follows:

1. SOCIETY grants and LICENSEE accepts for a period commencing as of January 1, 1989 and ending December 31, 1993 a license to perform publicly by means of live entertainment or mechanical music (as defined in paragraph 2), and by no other means, at or in any part or section of the hotel or motel known as

(hereinafter called "the premises"), and not elsewhere, non-dramatic renditions of the separate musical compositions copyrighted or composed by members of SOCIETY and of which SOCIETY shall have the right to license the performing rights.

2. This license is limited strictly to the premises. The license fee herein provided to be paid is based upon the performance of such non-dramatic renditions by live entertainment or mechanical means (as hereinafter defined) for the entertainment solely of such persons who may be present on or in the premises, and does not authorize the broadcasting. telecasting or transmission by wire or otherwise, of such performances or renditions to persons outside of the premises, and the same is hereby strictly prohibited unless consent of SOCIETY in writing first be had therefor by LICENSEE or by the person responsible for such broadcasting, telecasting or transmission; nor does this license authorize performances emanating from any point outside the premises or transmitted by any means to the premises in the form of background music services, wired music or in any other form or manner (except as specified herein), it being expressly understood, however, that if SOCIETY grants a license to such outside source authorizing it to supply its service to, and for reproduction or rendition at the premises, LICENSEE shall be authorized to render performances by such means at the premises without further payment to the SOCIETY therefor; nor does it authorize performance as part of an industrial or trade show, exposition or business presentation at the premises.

The term "mechanical music" as used in this Agreement shall mean music which is reproduced at the premises by means other than by live musicians who are performing at the premises, including, but not limited to, audio record or audio tape players. coin-operated phonorecord players (jukeboxes) (other than jukeboxes otherwise covered by the compulsory license provisions of 17 U.S.C. § 116), videotape players, performances in public rooms or guests' private rooms at the premises by means of pay or cable television, motion pictures, videotapes, or any similar means or method (whether transmitted by satellite or otherwise to the premises), or the reception and communication at the premises of radio or television transmissions which originate outside the premises, all subject to the limitations set forth herein.

3. This license shall not extend to or be deemed to include:

(a) Oratorios, choral, operatic or dramatico-musical works (including plays with music, revues and ballets) in their entirety, or songs or other excerpts from operas or musical plays accompanied either by words, pantomime, dance, or visual representation of the work from which the music is taken; but fragments or instrumental selections from such works may be instrumentally rendered without words, dialogue, costume, accompanying dramatic action or scenic accessory, and unaccompanied by any stage action or visual representation (by motion picture or otherwise) of the work of which such music forms a part.

(b) Any work (or part thereof) whereof the stage presentation and singing rights are reserved.

4. SOCIETY reserves the right at any time to withdraw from its repertory and from operation of this license any musical work as to which any suit has been brought or threatened on a claim that such composition infringes a composition not contained in SOCIETY'S repertory, or on a claim SOCIETY does not have the right to license the performing right in such composition.

5. LICENSEE agrees, upon demand in writing of SOCIETY, upon forms supplied by SOCIETY, whenever requested, to furnish a list of all music rendered at the premises hereby licensed, showing the title of each composition, and the publisher thereof.

6. In consideration of the license herein granted LICENSEE agrees to pay to SOCIETY for each contract year during the term of this Agreement the amount for such year set opposite the figure representing the expenditure for all entertainment at the premises during such contract year, as printed below in Schedule I (hereinafter called "the applicable annual rate"), unless mechanical music only is furnished at the premises. If mechanical music only is furnished at the premises and there is no "live" entertainment in any contract year, LICENSEE agrees to pay to SOCIETY the applicable amount printed below in Schedule II. If in any calendar year there should be both "live" entertainment and mechanical music, LICENSEE agrees to pay to SOCIETY in addition to the applicable annual rate in Schedule I, the applicable additional annual rate printed below in Schedule III. The rate paid for all mechanical music uses under Schedule II or III shall be the highest rate applicable to any such use.

The expenditure for all "live" entertainment at the premises for the current contract year of this Agreement is hereby estimated at $ in accordance with the provisions for estimating "Annual Expenditure for All Entertainment at the Premises" as printed below in Schedule I. For each of the succeeding years of this Agreement such annual expenditure for all entertainment at the premises shall be estimated on the basis of the expenditure for all entertainment at the premises for the previous contract year (or part thereof, if LICENSEE operated only part of such previous contract year, in which case such annual expenditure shall be prorated). Within twenty (20) days after the end of each contract year (or part thereof if LICENSEE operated only part of such contract year) during the term of this Agreement an adjustment shall be made on the basis of the expenditure for all entertainment at the premises for such contract year (or such part thereof on a prorated basis).

The total license fee for the first calendar year of this Agreement is estimated at $, based on a license fee under Schedule I of $ and a license fee under Schedule II or III of $.

The term "expenditure for all entertainment at the Premises" as used in this Agreement shall be deemed to include all payments made (whether in money or in any other form) by LICENSEE for all entertainment at the premises, excluding any service in connection with entertainment rendered by the regularly employed staff of LICENSEE, but including the compensation paid to any persons whose services are especially and exclusively engaged for the presentation of any such entertainment.

Where any arrangement either by contract or otherwise exists between LICENSEE and any entity or person presenting entertainment at the premises, which arrangement or contract shall provide that as the consideration or any part thereof, certain or any accommodations or services are to be made available for its or his use, then in such case, the extent of such accommodations or services shall be clearly defined and the reasonable value thereof regarded as an expenditure by LICENSEE for such entertainment and reported to SOCIETY as expended during each contract year in which such entertainment is presented, provided that if LICENSEE and SOCIETY shall fail to agree as to the reasonable value of such accommodations or services the same shall be fixed at a sum equal to one-half of the prevailing rate charged to the guests of the premises for such accommodations or services.

7. (a) LICENSEE shall, on or before the 20th day of January, and on or before the first day of April, July and October of each contract year during the term of this Agreement, pay to SOCIETY a sum equal to one-fourth (¼th) of the annual sum payable hereunder. The payment made on or before the 20th day of January of each contract year during the term of this Agreement shall be accompanied by a statement, on forms to be supplied by SOCIETY, showing (a) the expenditure for all entertainment at the premises for the preceding contract year; (b) if there was mechanical music but no "live" entertainment, said statement shall show: number of guest rooms, whether there is dancing to the mechanical music, a cover, minimum or admission charge to any of the rooms in which mechanical music is furnished, and whether a show or act is presented; or (c) if there were both "live" entertainment and mechanical music, said statement shall show the information described in both (a) and (b) of this paragraph. If LICENSEE operated only part of a contract year, LICENSEE shall furnish such statement to SOCIETY within twenty (20) days after the end of such part of such contract year.

(b) In the event LICENSEE shall be delinquent in the payment of license fees due under Subparagraph "(a)" hereof by forty-five (45) days or more, LICENSEE shall pay a finance charge on the license fees due of 1½% per month, or the maximum rate permitted by law, whichever is lesser, from the date such license fees should have been paid pursuant to Subparagraph "(a)" hereof.

8. (a) SOCIETY shall have the right to require such reasonable data or information relating to the annual expenditure for all entertainment at the premises as provided by this Agreement, in addition to that furnished under Paragraph "7" of this Agreement, as may be deemed necessary in order to ascertain the annual expenditure for all entertainment at the premises, as provided by this Agreement. SOCIETY shall have the further right, by its duly authorized representatives, at any time during customary business hours, to examine the books and records of account of LICENSEE only to such extent as may be necessary to verify such statement or statements as may be rendered pursuant to this Agreement. SOCIETY shall consider all data and information coming to its attention as the result of any such examination of books and records as completely and entirely confidential.

(b) The period for which the SOCIETY may audit pursuant to this Agreement shall be limited to three calendar years preceding the year in which the audit is made; provided, however, that if an audit is postponed at the request of LICENSEE, SOCIETY shall have the right to audit for the period commencing with the third calendar year preceding the year in which notification of intention to audit was first given by SOCIETY to LICENSEE; and provided further, that in the event such audit reveals a deficiency, then such audit may cover the additional preceding three calendar years. This three or six year limitation (as the case may be) shall not apply if LICENSEE fails or refuses after written notice from SOCIETY to produce the books and records necessary to verify any report or statement of accounting required pursuant to this Agreement. Nothing herein shall restrict SOCIETY'S right to audit under previous license agreements, for all periods covered by said agreements, subject to a total of three or six years (as the case may be) for all audits under all said license agreements.

(c) In the event any such audit shows LICENSEE to have underpaid the license fees due SOCIETY by 5% or more, LICENSEE shall pay a finance charge on the license fees shown due of 1½% per month, or the maximum rate permitted by law, whichever is lesser, from the date(s) the license fees should have been paid pursuant to this Agreement.

(d) In the event any such audit shows LICENSEE to have underpaid the license fees due SOCIETY by less than 5%, LICENSEE shall pay a finance charge on the license fees shown due of 1½% per month, or the maximum rate permitted by law, whichever is lesser, from the date SOCIETY demands payment of such amount.

9. Upon any breach or default by LICENSEE of any term or condition herein contained, SOCIETY may terminate this license by giving LICENSEE thirty days notice to cure such breach or default, and in the event that such breach or default has not been cured within said thirty days, this license shall terminate on the expiration of such thirty day period without further notice from SOCIETY. In the event of such termination, SOCIETY shall refund to LICENSEE any unearned license fees paid in advance.

10. In the event that LICENSEE shall discontinue the use of music at the premises before the expiration of any contract year during the term of this Agreement, LICENSEE shall give immediate written notice thereof to SOCIETY and,

within twenty (20) days after the date of such discontinuance, an adjustment shall be made on the following basis for the part of such contract year preceding such discontinuance:

(a) If the music so discontinued is "live" entertainment only, the adjustment shall be computed on the basis of the expenditure for all entertainment at the premises for such part of the contract year preceding such discontinuance as set forth in Schedule I.

(b) If the music so discontinued is mechanical music only, the adjustment shall be computed on the basis of the applicable annual rate set forth in Schedule II, reduced pro rata on the basis of the number of months in which music was performed.

(c) If the music so discontinued is both "live" and mechanical, the adjustment shall be computed on the basis of the expenditure for all entertainment at the premises for such part of the contract year preceding such discontinuance as set forth in Schedule I in addition to the applicable additional annual rate set forth in Schedule III, reduced pro rata on the basis of the number of months in which music was performed.

After such adjustment has been made, LICENSEE shall not be obligated to make further payments to SOCIETY hereunder until such time as LICENSEE shall resume the use of music at the premises during the term of this Agreement. In the event of such resumption by means of "live" entertainment only, LICENSEE shall estimate its expenditure for all entertainment at the premises for the contract year or part thereof in which the use of music is resumed on the basis of the expenditure for all entertainment at the premises during the first full month of operation after such resumption multiplied by 12 or such lesser number of months remaining in such contract year. Within twenty (20) days after the end of such contract year an adjustment shall be made on the basis of the expenditure for all entertainment at the premises for such contract year or part thereof as provided in Paragraph "6" of this Agreement. In the event of such resumption by means of mechanical music only, LICENSEE shall pay the annual amount provided in Schedule II, on the dates specified in Paragraph "7" of this Agreement, reduced pro rata on the basis of the number of months in which no music was performed. In the event of such resumption by means of both "live" entertainment and mechanical music, LICENSEE shall (a) estimate its expenditure for all entertainment at the premises for the contract year or part thereof in which the use of music is resumed on the basis of the expenditure for all entertainment at the premises during the first full month of operation after such resumption multiplied by 12 or such lesser number of months remaining in such contract year and within twenty (20) days after the end of such contract year an adjustment shall be made on the basis of the expenditure for all entertainment at the premises for such contract year or part thereof as provided in Paragraph "6" of this Agreement and (b) pay the additional annual rate provided in Schedule III on the dates specified in Paragraph "7" of this Agreement reduced pro rata on the basis of the number of months in which no music was performed.

11. This Agreement shall enure to the benefit of and shall be binding upon the parties hereto and their respective successors and assigns, but no assignment shall relieve the parties hereto of their respective obligations hereunder.

12. If LICENSEE shall cease to operate the premises, whether by reason of the sale or lease of the premises, or otherwise, then upon said date, this Agreement and the obligation of LICENSEE to make payments to SOCIETY hereunder shall terminate, provided, however, that LICENSEE shall give immediate written notice thereof to SOCIETY setting forth the manner of cessation, and the LICENSEE shall continue to be liable to SOCIETY for the pro rata amount of the then current contract year's payment for the period until said date.

IN WITNESS WHEREOF, this Agreement has been duly subscribed and sealed by SOCIETY and LICENSEE this _____ day of _____ , 19 _____

AMERICAN SOCIETY OF COMPOSERS,
    AUTHORS AND PUBLISHERS   LICENSEE _____

By _____   By _____

                (Title)   (Title)

RATE SCHEDULE—HOTELS AND MOTELS

—If live music *only* is presented, use Schedule I.

—If mechanical music *only* is presented, use Schedule II.

—If *both* live and mechanical music are presented, use Schedules I *and* III.

SCHEDULE I

For "live" entertainment, the sum to be paid by LICENSEE to SOCIETY for each calendar year during the term of this Agreement shall be the amount in the right-hand column below which corresponds to the "Annual Expenditure for all Entertainment at the Premises" during the then current calendar year as shown in the following Schedule:

Annual Expenditure for All Entertainment at the Premises		Annual Rate for Calendar Year				
		1989	1990	1991	1992	1993
Less than	$ 2,000.00	$ 110	$ 113	$ 117	$ 120	$ 125
$ 2,000.00 to	4,999.99	154	159	163	168	175
5,000.00 to	9,999.99	231	238	245	252	263
10,000.00 to	14,999.99	303	312	321	331	344
15,000.00 to	24,999.99	457	471	485	499	519
25,000.00 to	34,999.99	605	623	642	661	688
35,000.00 to	49,999.99	754	777	800	824	857
50,000.00 to	64,999.99	902	929	957	986	1,025
65,000.00 to	79,999.99	1,139	1,173	1,208	1,245	1,294
80,000.00 to	99,999.99	1,518	1,564	1,610	1,659	1,725
100,000.00 to	119,999.99	1,898	1,955	2,014	2,074	2,157
120,000.00 to	139,999.99	2,277	2,345	2,416	2,488	2,588
140,000.00 to	159,999.99	2,657	2,737	2,819	2,903	3,020
160,000.00 to	179,999.99	3,036	3,127	3,221	3,318	3,450
180,000.00 to	199,999.99	3,416	3,518	3,624	3,733	3,882
200,000.00 to	249,999.99	3,795	3,909	4,026	4,147	4,313
250,000.00 to	299,999.99	4,180	4,305	4,435	4,568	4,750
300,000.00 to	349,999.99	4,554	4,691	4,831	4,976	5,175
350,000.00 to	399,999.99	5,060	5,212	5,368	5,529	5,750
400,000.00 to	449,999.99	5,313	5,472	5,637	5,806	6,038
450,000.00 to	499,999.99	5,693	5,864	6,040	6,221	6,470
500,000.00 to	599,999.99	6,050	6,232	6,418	6,611	6,875
600,000.00 to	749,999.99	6,600	6,798	7,002	7,212	7,500
750,000.00 to	999,999.99	7,700	7,931	8,169	8,414	8,751
1,000,000.00 to	1,499,999.99	8,800	9,064	9,336	9,616	10,001
1,500,000.00 to	1,999,999.99	9,900	10,197	10,503	10,818	11,251
2,000,000.00 to	2,999,999.99	11,000	11,330	11,670	12,020	12,501
3,000,000.00 to	3,999,999.99	12,100	12,463	12,837	13,222	13,751
4,000,000.00 to	4,999,999.99	14,300	14,729	15,171	15,626	16,251
5,000,000.00 to	5,999,999.99	15,950	16,429	16,921	17,429	18,126
6,000,000.00 to	6,999,999.99	19,800	20,394	21,006	21,636	22,501
7,000,000.00 and over		19,800	20,394	21,006	23,500	23,500

Method of Estimating "Annual Expenditure for All Entertainment at the Premises" (as defined in Paragraph "6") for the First Calendar Year (or Part Thereof) of this Agreement:

I. If LICENSEE has operated with a policy of music for the full calendar year prior to the commencement date of the Agreement, LICENSEE shall estimate its expenditure for all entertainment at the premises for the first calendar year (or part thereof) of this Agreement on the basis of the expenditure for all entertainment at the premises during such full calendar year prior to the commencement date of this Agreement.

II. If LICENSEE has operated with a policy of music less than a full calendar year prior to the commencement date of this Agreement, LICENSEE shall estimate its expenditure for all entertainment at the premises for the first calendar year (or part thereof) of this Agreement at a sum equal to the average monthly expenditure for all entertainment at the premises during the period of operation prior to the commencement date of this Agreement times the number of months of LICENSEE's operation during said first calendar year or part thereof.

III. If LICENSEE has not operated with a policy of music for any period prior to the commencement date of this Agreement, LICENSEE shall estimate its expenditure for all entertainment at the premises for the first calendar year (or part thereof) of this Agreement on the basis of the expenditure for all entertainment at the premises during the first full month of operation times the number of months of LICENSEE's operation during said first calendar year of part thereof.

SCHEDULE II

MECHANICAL MUSIC ONLY

A. No Dancing; No Cover, Minimum or Admission Charge; and No Show or Acts*

No. of Rooms	Annual Rate for Calendar Years				
	1989	1990	1991	1992	1993
1-300	$168	$175	$182	$190	$199
Over 300	232	241	251	261	274

B. One of: 1) Dancing; 2) Cover, Minimum or Admission Charge; or 3) Show or Acts*

No. of Rooms	Annual Rate for Calendar Years				
	1989	1990	1991	1992	1993
1-100	$225	$234	$243	$253	$266
101-300	309	321	334	347	364
301-500	468	487	506	526	552
Over 500	618	642	668	695	730

C. Two of: 1) Dancing; 2) Cover, Minimum or Admission Charge; or 3) Show or Acts*

No. of Rooms	Annual Rate for Calendar Years				
	1989	1990	1991	1992	1993
1-100	$309	$321	$ 334	$ 347	$ 364
101-300	468	487	506	526	552
301-500	693	720	749	779	818
Over 500	926	963	1,002	1,042	1,094

D. With Dancing, Cover, Minimum or Admission Charge, and Show or Acts*

No. of Rooms	Annual Rate for Calendar Years				
	1989	1990	1991	1992	1993
1-100	$ 514	$ 534	$ 556	$ 578	$ 607
101-300	794	825	858	893	938
301-500	1,066	1,109	1,153	1,199	1,259
Over 500	1,328	1,381	1,436	1,494	1,569

E. With Audio-Visual Works

If audio-visual performances of mechanical music (such as the use of a large-screen projection television or performances in guests' private rooms at the premises by means of pay or cable television, motion pictures, videotapes, or any similar means or method) are given, use the applicable category above and add 50%; such uses do not include performances by means of a single receiving apparatus of a kind commonly used in private homes, unless a direct charge is made to see the transmission or the transmission thus received is further transmitted to the public. Such uses include only performances for which a license is required by the United States Copyright Law.

*"Show or Acts" shall include use of a disc jockey or video jockey.

SCHEDULE III

MECHANICAL MUSIC AND LIVE MUSIC

A. No Dancing; No Cover, Minimum or Admission Charge; and No Show or Acts*

No. of Rooms	Annual Rate for Calendar Years				
	1989	1990	1991	1992	1993
1-300	$ 99	$103	$107	$111	$117
Over 300	140	146	152	158	166

B. One of: 1) Dancing; 2) Cover, Minimum or Admission Charge; or 3) Show or Acts*

No. of Rooms	Annual Rate for Calendar Years				
	1989	1990	1991	1992	1993
1-100	$133	$138	$144	$150	$158
101-300	187	195	202	211	221
301-500	243	253	263	274	288
Over 500	318	331	344	358	376

C. Two of: 1) Dancing; 2) Cover, Minimum or Admission Charge; or 3) Show or Acts*

No. of Rooms	Annual Rate for Calendar Years				
	1989	1990	1991	1992	1993
1-100	$187	$195	$202	$211	$221
101-300	243	253	263	274	288
301-500	346	360	375	390	409
Over 500	505	526	547	569	597

D. With Dancing, Cover, Minimum or Admission Charge, and Show or Acts*

No. of Rooms	Annual Rate for Calendar Years				
	1989	1990	1991	1992	1993
1-100	$ 514	$ 534	$ 556	$ 578	$ 607
101-300	794	825	858	893	938
301-500	1,066	1,109	1,153	1,199	1,259
Over 500	1,328	1,381	1,436	1,494	1,569

E. With Audio-Visual Works

If audio-visual performances of mechanical music (such as the use of a large-screen projection television or performances in guests' private rooms at the premises by means of pay or cable television, motion pictures, videotapes, or any similar means or method) are given, use the applicable category above and add 50%; such uses do not include performances by means of a single receiving apparatus of a kind commonly used in private homes, unless a direct charge is made to see the transmission or the transmission thus received is further transmitted to the public. Such uses include only performances for which a license is required by the United States Copyright Law.

*"Show or Acts" shall include use of a disc jockey or video jockey.

FORM 15.16

ASCAP DANCING SCHOOLS LICENSE

DANCING SCHOOLS

Agreement between AMERICAN SOCIETY OF COMPOSERS, AUTHORS AND PUBLISHERS ("SOCIETY"), located at

and
("LICENSEE"), located at   as follows:

1. Grant and Term of License

(a) SOCIETY grants and LICENSEE accepts for a term of one year, commencing
and continuing thereafter for additional terms of one year each unless terminated by either party as hereinafter provided, a license to perform publicly at any place where LICENSEE gives dance instruction, ("the premises"), and not elsewhere, non-dramatic renditions of the separate musical compositions now or hereafter during the term hereof in the repertory of SOCIETY, and of which SOCIETY shall have the right to license such performing rights.

(b) This agreement shall enure to the benefit of and shall be binding upon the parties hereto and their respective successors and assigns, but no assignment shall relieve the parties hereto of their respective obligations hereunder as to performances rendered, acts done and obligations incurred prior to the effective date of the assignment.

(c) Either party may, on or before thirty days prior to the end of the initial term or any renewal term, give notice of termination to the other. If such notice is given this agreement shall terminate on the last day of such initial or renewal term.

2. Limitations on License

(a) This license is not assignable or transferable by operation of law or otherwise, except as provided in paragraph "1(b)" hereof, and is limited to the LICENSEE and to the premises.

(b) This license does not authorize the broadcasting, telecasting or transmission by wire or otherwise, of renditions of musical compositions in SOCIETY'S repertory to persons outside of the premises.

(c) This license does not authorize any performance by means of a coin-operated phonorecord player (jukebox) otherwise covered by the compulsory license provisions of 17 U.S.C. §116.

(d) This license is limited to non-dramatic performances, and does not authorize any dramatic performances. For purposes of this agreement, a dramatic performance shall include, but not be limited to, the following:

(i) performance of a "dramatico-musical work" (as hereinafter defined) in its entirety;

(ii) performance of one or more musical compositions from a "dramatico-musical work" (as hereinafter defined) accompanied by dialogue, pantomime, dance, stage action, or visual representation of the work from which the music is taken;

(iii) performance of one or more musical compositions as part of a story or plot, whether accompanied or unaccompanied by dialogue, pantomime, dance, stage action, or visual representation;

(iv) performance of a concert version of a "dramatico-musical work" (as hereinafter defined).

The term "dramatico-musical work" as used in this agreement, shall include, but not be limited to, a musical comedy, opera, play with music, revue, or ballet.

(e) This license is limited to performances occurring in the course of and simultaneously with dance instruction given by LICENSEE and does not authorize any performance, at any place where LICENSEE gives such instruction, which is not rendered in the course of and simultaneously with such instruction, except that this license shall extend to performances at one dance recital by LICENSEE'S students per calendar year.

3. License Fee

(a) In consideration of the license granted herein, LICENSEE agrees to pay SOCIETY the applicable license fee set forth in the rate schedule annexed hereto and made a part hereof, subject to adjustment as set forth below, payable annually in advance by January 15 of each year.

(b) Said license fee shall be adjusted annually, in an amount equal to the percentage increase or decrease in the United States Consumer Price Index (all items) published by the United States Government, United States Department of Labor, Bureau of Labor Statistics, between said index in October, 1981 and in October of the year preceding the year for which the adjustment is made. SOCIETY will promptly inform LICENSEE of the amount of each such adjustment.

(c) Each such payment shall be accompanied by LICENSEE'S written statement, on forms supplied free of charge by SOCIETY, setting forth the average number of students per week and the type of dance instruction given during the previous year, which statement shall be certified by LICENSEE as true and correct.

4. Breach or Default

Upon any breach or default by LICENSEE of any term or condition herein contained, SOCIETY may terminate this license by giving LICENSEE thirty days notice to cure such breach or default, and in the event that such breach or default has not been cured within said thirty days, this license shall terminate on the expiration of such thirty-day period without further notice from SOCIETY. In the event of such termination, SOCIETY shall refund to LICENSEE any unearned license fees paid in advance.

5. Interference in Society's Operations

In the event of:

(a) any major interference with the operations of SOCIETY in the state, territory, dependency, possession or political subdivision in which LICENSEE is located, by reason of any law of such state, territory, dependency, possession or political subdivision; or

(b) any substantial increase in the cost to the SOCIETY of operating in such state, territory, dependency, possession or political subdivision, by reason of any law of such state, territory, dependency, possession or political subdivision, which is applicable to the licensing of performing rights,

SOCIETY shall have the right to terminate this agreement forthwith by written notice and shall refund to LICENSEE any unearned license fees paid in advance.

6. Notices

All notices required or permitted hereunder shall be given in writing by certified United States mail sent to either party at the address stated above. Each party agrees to inform the other of any change of address.

IN WITNESS WHEREOF, this agreement has been duly executed by SOCIETY and LICENSEE this

day of _____ , 19____

AMERICAN SOCIETY OF COMPOSERS,
AUTHORS AND PUBLISHERS

_____
LICENSEE

By _____
   DISTRICT MANAGER

By _____

_____
TITLE

(Fill in capacity in which signed:
(a) If corporation, state corporate office held; (b) If partnership, write word "partner" under signature of signing partner; (c) if individual owner, write "individual owner" under signature.)

1991

RATE SCHEDULE – DANCING SCHOOLS

ANNUAL LICENSE FEE

TYPE OF DANCE INSTRUCTION	AVERAGE NUMBER OF STUDENTS PER WEEK****			
	Not More Than 75	Not More Than 150	Not More Than 300	301 and Over
BALLROOM*	$75.67	$151.32	$226.99	$302.65
COMBINATION**	56.74	113.49	170.25	226.99
BALLET***	37.83	75.67	113.49	151.32

*Includes licensees teaching *any* ballroom, social, or round dancing, including any currently popular dance.

**Includes licensees teaching jazz, classical, ballet, tap, modern ballet, acrobatic, gymnastic, square, folk, ethnic, baton, aerobics and "slimnastics".

***Includes licensees teaching ballet *only*.

****Students taking up to 5 hours of instruction per week shall be counted as 1 student per week; students taking 5 or more hours of instruction per week shall be counted as 2 students per week.

FORM 15.17

ASCAP CONCERT AND RECITALS LICENSE (BLANKET)

**CONCERTS AND RECITALS–
BLANKET LICENSE AGREEMENT**

Agreement between AMERICAN SOCIETY OF COMPOSERS. AUTHORS AND PUBLISHERS ("SOCIETY"), located at

and
("LICENSEE"), located at

as follows:

1. Grant and Term of License

(a) SOCIETY grants and LICENSEE accepts for a term of one year commencing
, and continuing thereafter for additional terms of one year each unless terminated by either party as hereinafter provided, a license to perform publicly at concerts or recitals in the United States presented by or under the auspices of LICENSEE, and not elsewhere, nondramatic renditions of the separate musical compositions now or hereafter during the term hereof in the repertory of SOCIETY. and of which SOCIETY shall have the right to license such performing rights.

(b) This agreement shall enure to the benefit of and shall be binding upon the parties hereto and their respective successors and assigns, but no assignment shall relieve the parties hereto of their respective obligations hereunder as to performances rendered, acts done and obligations incurred prior to the effective date of the assignment.

(c) Either party may, on or before thirty days prior to the end of the initial term or any renewal term, give notice of termination to the other. If such notice is given the agreement shall terminate on the last day of such initial or renewal term.

2. Limitations on License

(a) This license is not assignable or transferable by operation of law, devolution or otherwise, except as provided in Paragraph "1(b)" hereof, and is strictly limited to the LICENSEE and to the premises where each concert or recital is presented.

(b) This license does not authorize the broadcasting or telecasting or transmission by wire or other-wise, of renditions of musical compositions in SOCIETY's repertory to persons outside of the premises where each concert or recital shall be presented.

(c) This license is limited to nondramatic performances, and does not authorize any dramatic performances. For purposes of this agreement, a dramatic performance shall include, but not be limited to, the following:

(i) performance of a "dramatico-musical work" (as hereinafter defined) in its entirety;

(ii) performance of one or more musical compositions from a "dramatico-musical work" (as hereinafter defined) accompanied by dialogue, pantomime, dance, stage action, or visual representation of the work from which the music is taken;

(iii) performance of one or more musical compositions as part of a story or plot, whether accompanied or unaccompanied by dialogue, pantomime, dance, stage action, or visual representation;

(iv) performance of a concert version of a "dramatico-musical work" (as hereinafter defined).

The term "dramatico-musical work" as used in this agreement, shall include, but not be limited to, a musical comedy, opera, play with music, revue, or ballet.

(d) This license does not authorize the performance of any special orchestral arrangements or transcriptions of any musical composition in the repertory of SOCIETY, unless such arrangements or transcriptions have been copyrighted by members of SOCIETY or foreign societies which have granted SOCIETY the right to license such performances.

(e) SOCIETY reserves the right at any time to restrict the first American performance of any composition in its repertory and further reserves the right at any time to withdraw from its repertory and from operation of this license, any musical work as to which any suit has been brought or threatened on a claim that such composition infringes a composition not contained in SOCIETY's repertory, or on a claim that SOCIETY does not have the right to license the performing rights in such composition.

3. Notice of Concerts or Recitals

LICENSEE agrees to give SOCIETY written notice of each concert or recital it will present, on forms supplied free of charge by SOCIETY, at least thirty days in advance of such presentation. Such notification shall include the date, name of attraction(s) appearing, name, location and seating capacity of the premises, and highest price of admission (exclusive of tax) for each concert or recital.

4. License Fees

(a) In consideration of the license granted herein, LICENSEE agrees to pay SOCIETY the applicable license fee for each concert or recital presented based on SOCIETY'S current rate schedule, a copy of which is annexed hereto and made a part hereof, payable thirty days in advance of each concert or recital presented.

(b) LICENSEE agrees to furnish to SOCIETY, where available, at the same time payment of license fees is made pursuant to Paragraph "4(a)" of this agreement, a program containing a list of all musical works, including encores, performed by LICENSEE in each of its concerts and recitals.

5. Breach or Default

Upon any breach or default by LICENSEE of any term or condition herein contained, SOCIETY may terminate this license by giving LICENSEE thirty days notice to cure such breach or default, and in the event that such breach or default has not been cured within said thirty days, this license shall terminate on the expiration of such thirty-day period without further notice from SOCIETY. In the event of such termination, SOCIETY shall refund to LICENSEE any unearned license fees paid in advance.

6. Interference in Society's Operations

In the event of:

(a) any major interference with the operations of SOCIETY in the state, territory, dependency, possession or political subdivision in which LICENSEE is located, by reason of any law of such state, territory, dependency, possession or political subdivision; or

(b) any substantial increase in the cost to the SOCIETY of operating in such state, territory, dependency, possession or political subdivision, by reason of any law of such state, territory, dependency, possession or political subdivision, which is applicable to the licensing of performing rights,

SOCIETY shall have the right to terminate this agreement forthwith by written notice.

7. **Notices**

All notices required or permitted hereunder shall be given in writing by certified United States mail sent to either party at the address stated above. Each party agrees to inform the other of any change of address.

IN WITNESS WHEREOF, this agreement has been duly executed by SOCIETY and LICENSEE this day of   , 19   .

AMERICAN SOCIETY OF COMPOSERS,
AUTHORS AND PUBLISHERS

_____
LICENSEE

BY _____   BY _____

_____
TITLE

(Fill in capacity in which signed:
(a) If corporation, state corporate office held; (b) If partnership, write word "partner" under signature of signing partner; (c) If individual owner, write "individual owner" under signature.)

BLANKET CONCERT AND RECITAL LICENSE RATE SCHEDULE

SEATING CAPACITY*	$0.00 to $3.00	$3.01 to $6.00	$6.01 to $9.00	$9.01 to $12.00	$12.01 to $15.00	$15.01 to $18.00	$18.01 to $21.00	$21.01 to $25.00	$25.01 to $30.00	over $30.00
0 - 250	7	14	23	35	47	60	75	90	105	125
251 - 500	11	18	27	39	52	65	80	95	110	130
501 - 750	15	22	31	44	57	70	85	100	115	135
751 - 1,000	19	26	36	51	66	80	97	115	130	155
1,001 - 1,500	24	33	44	60	75	90	110	130	150	175
1,501 - 2,000	29	41	53	70	85	100	125	150	175	205
2,001 - 3,000	35	47	59	77	92	112	137	165	190	225
3,001 - 4,000	41	53	65	85	100	125	150	180	210	250
4,001 - 5,500	53	65	80	100	125	150	180	210	240	280
5,501 - 7,500	65	80	100	125	150	180	210	240	270	310
7,501 - 10,000	80	100	125	150	180	210	240	270	300	340
10,001 - 15,000	100	125	150	180	210	240	270	300	330	370
15,001 - 20,000	125	150	180	210	240	270	300	330	360	400
20,001 - 25,000	150	180	210	240	270	300	330	360	390	440
25,001 - 30,000	180	210	240	270	300	330	360	400	440	490
30,001 - 40,000	210	240	270	300	330	360	410	450	490	540
40,001 - 50,000	250	280	310	340	370	410	450	500	540	590
50,001 - 60,000	290	320	350	380	410	450	500	550	590	650
over 60,000	350	380	410	440	470	510	550	600	650	725

(Header spanning columns: TICKET PRICE)

DISCOUNTS:

1. Twenty-Five or more Concerts or Recitals: A discount of 20% may be deducted from the above fees for payment for each concert or recital in excess of twenty-five performed by LICENSEE during a contract year.

2. Advance Payment for One Hundred or more Concerts or Recitals: A discount of 5% may be deducted from the above fees for payment in advance by LICENSEE to SOCIETY for one hundred or more separate concerts or recitals.

*Where a concert or recital occurs at a location whose total seating capacity has been altered to accomodate a particular performance, the term "seating capacity" shall mean the total number of seats made available for that particular performance.

FORM 15.18

ASCAP CONCERT AND RECITALS LICENSE
(PER CONCERT)

CONCERTS AND RECITALS–
PER CONCERT LICENSE AGREEMENT

Agreement between AMERICAN SOCIETY OF COMPOSERS. AUTHORS AND PUBLISHERS ("SOCIETY"), located at

and
("LICENSEE"), located at

as follows:

1. Grant and Term of License

(a) SOCIETY grants and LICENSEE accepts for a term of one year commencing
, and continuing thereafter for additional terms of one year each unless terminated by either party as hereinafter provided, a license to perform publicly at concerts or recitals in the United States presented by or under the auspices of LICENSEE, and not elsewhere, nondramatic renditions of the separate musical compositions now or hereafter during the term hereof in the repertory of SOCIETY, and of which SOCIETY shall have the right to license such performing rights.

(b) This agreement shall enure to the benefit of and shall be binding upon the parties hereto and their respective successors and assigns, but no assignment shall relieve the parties hereto of their respective obligations hereunder as to performances rendered, acts done and obligations incurred prior to the effective date of the assignment.

(c) Either party may, on or before thirty days prior to the end of the initial term or any renewal term, give notice of termination to the other. If such notice is given the agreement shall terminate on the last day of such initial or renewal term.

2. Limitations on License

(a) This license is not assignable or transferable by operation of law, devolution or otherwise, except as provided in Paragraph "1(b)" hereof, and is strictly limited to the LICENSEE and to the premises where each concert or recital is presented.

(b) This license does not authorize the broadcasting or telecasting or transmission by wire or otherwise, of renditions of musical compositions in SOCIETY's repertory to persons outside of the premises.

(c) This license is limited to nondramatic performances, and does not authorize any dramatic performances. For purposes of this agreement, a dramatic performance shall include, but not be limited to, the following:

(i) performance of a "dramatico-musical work" (as hereinafter defined) in its entirety;

(ii) performance of one or more musical compositions from a "dramatico-musical work" (as hereinafter defined) accompanied by dialogue, pantomime, dance, stage action, or visual representation of the work from which the music is taken;

(iii) performance of one or more musical compositions as part of a story or plot, whether accompanied or unaccompanied by dialogue, pantomime, dance, stage action, or visual representation;

(iv) performance of a concert version of a "dramatico-musical work" (as hereinafter defined). The term "dramatico-musical work" as used in this agreement, shall include, but not be limited to, a musical comedy, opera, play with music, revue, or ballet.

(d) This license does not authorize the performance of any special orchestral arrangements or transcriptions of any musical composition in the repertory of SOCIETY, unless such arrangements or transcriptions have been copyrighted by members of SOCIETY or foreign societies which have granted SOCIETY the right to license such performances.

(e) SOCIETY reserves the right at any time to restrict the first American performance of any composition in its repertory and further reserves the right at any time to withdraw from its repertory and from operation of this license, any musical work as to which any suit has been brought or threatened on a claim that such composition infringes a composition not contained in SOCIETY'S repertory, or on a claim that SOCIETY does not have the right to license the performing rights in such composition.

3. License Fees

In consideration of the license granted herein, LICENSEE agrees to pay SOCIETY the applicable license fee set forth in the rate schedule annexed hereto and made a part hereof, for each concert or recital at which a nondramatic performance of any copyrighted musical composition in the SOCIETY's repertory occurs.

4. Reports of Concerts and Payment of License Fees

(a) At least one week prior to the presentation of any concert or recital by LICENSEE, LICENSEE shall submit to SOCIETY:

(i) Written notice of such concert or recital, on forms supplied free of charge by SOCIETY, including the date and place of such concert or recital, name of the artists or performers appearing, seating capacity, and highest price of admission exclusive of tax; and

(ii) Payment of any license fee required by and set forth in Paragraph "3" hereof.

(b) Within one week after the presentation of any concert or recital licensed hereunder, LICENSEE shall submit to SOCIETY a program containing a list of all musical works, including encores, performed at such concert or recital.

5. Breach or Default

Upon any breach or default by LICENSEE of any term or condition herein contained, SOCIETY may terminate this license by giving LICENSEE thirty days notice to cure such breach or default, and in the event that such breach or default has not been cured within said thirty days, this license shall terminate on the expiration of such thirty-day period without further notice from SOCIETY.

6. Failure to Report Concerts or Recitals and Pay License Fees

In the event LICENSEE presents any concert or recital during the course of which any copyrighted musical composition in SOCIETY'S repertory is performed, and LICENSEE fails to report such concert or recital and pay license fees to SOCIETY as required by Paragraph "4" hereof, this license shall not extend to such concert or recital and such performances shall be deemed to be infringements of the respective copyrights unless such performances have been licensed by SOCIETY'S member(s) in interest. Such failure to report and pay license fees shall be a breach and default under this agreement pursuant to Paragraph "5" hereof.

7. Interference in Society's Operations

In the event of:

(a) any major interference with the operations of SOCIETY in the state, territory, dependency, possession or political subdivision in which LICENSEE is located, by reason of any law of such state, territory, dependency, possession or political subdivision; or

(b) any substantial increase in the cost to the SOCIETY of operating in such state, territory, dependency, possession or political subdivision, by reason of any law of such state, territory, dependency, possession or political subdivision, which is applicable to the licensing of performing rights.

SOCIETY shall have the right to terminate this agreement forthwith by written notice.

8. Notices

All notices required or permitted hereunder shall be given in writing by certified United States mail sent to either party at the address stated above. Each party agrees to inform the other of any change of address.

IN WITNESS WHEREOF, this agreement has been duly executed by SOCIETY and LICENSEE this
          day of   , 19   .

AMERICAN SOCIETY OF COMPOSERS,
AUTHORS AND PUBLISHERS

_____
                                    LICENSEE

BY _____   BY _____

_____
                                    TITLE

(Fill in capacity in which signed:
(a) If corporation, state corporate office held; (b) If
partnership, write word "partner" under signature of signing
partner; (c) If individual owner, write "individual owner"
under signature.)

PER CONCERT LICENSE RATE SCHEDULE

SEATING CAPACITY*	TICKET PRICE									
	$0.00 to $3.00	$3.01 to $6.00	$6.01 to $9.00	$9.01 to $12.00	$12.01 to $15.00	$15.01 to $18.00	$18.01 to $21.00	$21.01 to $25.00	$25.01 to $30.00	over $30.0
0 - 250	11	21	35	53	71	90	113	135	158	188
251 - 500	17	27	41	59	78	98	120	143	165	195
501 - 750	23	33	47	66	86	105	128	150	173	203
751 - 1,000	29	39	54	77	99	120	146	173	195	233
1,001 - 1,500	36	50	66	90	113	135	165	195	225	263
1,501 - 2,000	44	62	80	105	128	150	188	225	263	308
2,001 - 3,000	53	71	89	116	138	168	206	248	285	338
3,001 - 4,000	62	80	98	128	150	188	225	270	315	375
4,001 - 5,500	80	98	120	150	188	225	270	315	360	420
5,501 - 7,500	98	120	150	188	225	270	315	360	405	465
7,501 - 10,000	120	150	188	225	270	315	360	405	450	510
10,001 - 15,000	150	188	225	270	315	360	405	450	495	555
15,001 - 20,000	188	225	270	315	360	405	450	495	540	600
20,001 - 25,000	225	270	315	360	405	450	495	540	585	660
25,001 - 30,000	270	315	360	405	450	495	540	600	660	735
30,001 - 40,000	315	360	405	450	495	540	615	675	735	810
40,001 - 50,000	375	420	465	510	555	615	675	750	810	885
50,001 - 60,000	435	480	525	570	615	675	750	825	885	975
over 60,000	525	570	615	660	705	765	825	900	975	1088

*Where a concert or recital occurs at a location whose total seating capacity has been altered to accomodate a particular performance, the term "seating capacity" shall mean the total number of seats made available for that particular performance.

FORM 15.19

ASCAP CIRCUS LICENSE

Agreement between AMERICAN SOCIETY OF COMPOSERS, AUTHORS AND PUBLISHERS ("SOCIETY"),
located at
and
("LICENSEE"), located at   as follows:

1. Grant and Term of License

(a) SOCIETY grants and LICENSEE accepts for a term of one year, commencing   ,
and continuing thereafter for additional terms of one year each unless terminated by either party as hereinafter
provided, a license to perform publicly at presentations of LICENSEE'S circus, at each of the locations where
such presentations shall be offered ("the premises"), and not elsewhere, non-dramatic renditions of the separate
musical compositions now or hereafter during the term hereof in the repertory of SOCIETY, and of which SOCI-
ETY shall have the right to license such performing rights.

(b) Either party may, on or before thirty days prior to the end of the initial term or any renewal term, give
notice of termination to the other. If such notice is given the agreement shall terminate on the last day of such
initial or renewal term.

2. Limitations on License

(a) This license is not assignable or transferable by operation of law or otherwise, and is limited to the
LICENSEE and to the premises.

(b) This license does not authorize the broadcasting, telecasting or transmission by wire or otherwise, of renditions of musical compositions in SOCIETY'S repertory to persons outside of the premises.

(c) This license is limited to non-dramatic performances, and does not authorize any dramatic performances.
For purposes of this agreement, a dramatic performance shall include, but not be limited to, the following:

(i) performance of a "dramatico-musical work" (as hereinafter defined) in its entirety;

(ii) performance of one or more musical compositions from a "dramatico-musical work" (as hereinafter
defined) accompanied by dialogue, pantomime, dance, stage action, or visual representation of the work
from which the music is taken;

(iii) performance of one or more musical compositions as part of a story or plot, whether accompanied
or unaccompanied by dialogue, pantomime, dance, stage action, or visual representation;

(iv) performance of a concert version of a "dramatico-musical work" (as hereinafter defined).

The term "dramatico-musical work" as used in this agreement, shall include, but not be limited to, a musical
comedy, oratorio, choral work, opera, play with music, revue, or ballet.

3. License Fee

(a) In consideration of the license granted herein, LICENSEE agrees to pay SOCIETY the applicable license
fee set forth in the rate schedule printed on the reverse and made a part hereof for each presentation at each
of the premises, payable for the preceding quarter on January 1, April 1, July 1 and October 1 of each year.

(b) Payments shall be accompanied by a schedule of presentations during the preceding quarter, indicating
the date, location and seating capacity of each presentation, on forms to be supplied free of charge by SOCIETY.

4. Audit

SOCIETY shall have the right, by its duly authorized representative, at any time during customary business hours, to examine the records of LICENSEE, but only to such extent as may be necessary to verify schedules
of presentations and payments based thereon. SOCIETY shall consider all data and information coming to its
attention as the result of such examination as completely and entirely confidential.

5. Breach or Default

Upon any breach or default by LICENSEE of any term or condition herein contained, SOCIETY may terminate this license by giving LICENSEE thirty days notice to cure such breach or default, and in the event that
such breach or default has not been cured within said thirty days, this license shall terminate on the expiration
of such thirty-day period without further notice from SOCIETY. In the event of such termination, SOCIETY shall
refund to LICENSEE any unearned license fees paid in advance.

6. Notices

All notices required or permitted hereunder shall be given in writing by certified United States mail sent to either party at the address stated above. Each party agrees to inform the other of any change of address.

IN WITNESS WHEREOF, this agreement has been duly executed by SOCIETY and LICENSEE this   day of   , 19   .

AMERICAN SOCIETY OF COMPOSERS,
AUTHORS AND PUBLISHERS

LICENSEE

By_____
            DISTRICT MANAGER

By_____

TITLE

(Fill in capacity in which signed:
(a) If corporation, state corporate office held;
(b) If partnership, write word "partner" under signature of signing partner.
(c) If individual owner, write "individual owner" under signature.)

RATE SCHEDULE

Seating Capacity	Rate Per Presentation
0 to 500	$ 2.50
501 to 1,500	$ 5.00
1,501 to 2,500	$ 7.50
2,501 to 3,500	$10.00
3,501 to 4,500	$15.00
4,501 to 5,500	$22.50
5,501 to 6,500	$30.00
6,501 to 7,500	$40.00
7,501 and Over	$50.00

DISCOUNT:

A discount of 20% may be deducted from the above fees for payment for each presentation in excess of twenty-five presented by LICENSEE during the contract year or renewal term.

FORM 15.20

ASCAP SYMPHONY ORCHESTRAS WHICH HAVE ANNUAL TOTAL EXPENSES OF $250,000 OR MORE LICENSE

LICENSE AGREEMENT—SYMPHONY ORCHESTRAS WHICH
HAVE ANNUAL TOTAL EXPENSES OF $250,000 OR MORE

Agreement made between AMERICAN SOCIETY OF COMPOSERS, AUTHORS AND PUBLISHERS ("SOCIETY"), located at One Lincoln Plaza, New York, New York 10023 and

("LICENSEE"), located at   as follows:

1. (a) SOCIETY grants and LICENSEE accepts for a term of three years, commencing October 1, 1990 and ending September 30, 1993, and continuing thereafter for additional terms of one year each unless terminated by either party as hereinafter provided, a license to perform publicly in concerts given by

("orchestra") at

and at other auditoriums in which orchestra shall give performances while on tour (the "premises"), non-dramatic renditions of the separate musical compositions including symphonic and other concert works heretofore copyrighted or composed by members of SOCIETY and now or hereafter during the term hereof in the repertory of SOCIETY, or hereafter during the term hereof copyrighted or composed by members of SOCIETY, or of which SOCIETY shall have the right to license such performing rights.

(b) This license is not assignable nor transferable by operation of law, devolution or otherwise, and is limited strictly to the LICENSEE and to the premises. The license fee herein provided to be paid is based upon the performance of such non-dramatic renditions for the entertainment solely of such persons as may be physically present on or in the premises described, and does not authorize the radio or television broadcasting, or transmission by wire or otherwise, of such performances or renditions to persons outside of such premises, and no license is hereby granted for any such radio or television broadcasting or transmission.

(c) Either party may, on notice given six months prior to the end of the initial or any renewal term, terminate this license effective on the following September 30.

2. (a) This license is limited to performances given in the United States, its territories and possessions, and in any other place not within the territorial jurisdiction of another performing right society to which SOCIETY has granted the right to license public performances of works in SOCIETY's repertory.

(b) This license is limited to symphony orchestras which have annual total expenses of $250,000 or more.

(c) This license shall not extend to or be deemed to include: (i) operatic or dramatico-musical works (including plays with music, revues and ballets) as such, in whole or in part, or songs or other excerpts from operas or musical plays accompanied either by pantomime, dance or visual representation of the work from which the music is taken; but fragments or instrumental selections from such works may be instrumentally rendered without dialogue, costume, accompanying dramatic action or scenic accessory, and unaccompanied by any stage action or visual representation of the work of which such music forms a part; or (ii) the right to perform any special orchestral arrangements or transcriptions of the musical compositions licensed hereunder unless such arrangements or transcriptions have been copyrighted by members of SOCIETY or by members of foreign societies which have granted to SOCIETY the right to license such performances.

3. SOCIETY reserves the right at any time to restrict the first American performance of any composition in its repertory and further reserves the right at any time to withdraw from its repertory and from operation of this license any musical work as to which any suit has been brought or threatened based on a claim that such composition infringes a composition not contained in SOCIETY's repertory, or on a claim that SOCIETY does not have the right to license the performing rights in such composition.

4. LICENSEE agrees to furnish to SOCIETY each month a program containing a list of all musical compositions performed by LICENSEE in each of the performances by the orchestra at the premises during the previous month, including all encores.

5. (a) The term "Adjusted Box Office" as used in this Agreement shall mean all gross box office receipts from concerts and concert fees for all concerts, excluding income from concerts benefiting the orchestra, such as pension fund concerts. Gross receipts shall in no event include income from program advertising, concessions, or recording or radio or television broadcasting activities. Gross receipts from "run-out" concerts and tours shall be adjusted by deducting transportation and per diem costs incurred in connection therewith; but in no event shall such deductible costs for any such concert or tour exceed the gross receipts thereof.

(b) The term "Season" as used in this Agreement shall mean the twelve-month period commencing October 1 of each calendar year and ending on the next September 30.

6. (a) In consideration of the license herein granted, LICENSEE agrees to pay SOCIETY the following license fees:

    (i) On or before April 26, 1991 a sum equal to 0.95% (.0095) of the Adjusted Box Office for the 1989/1990 Season; and

    (ii) On October 1, 1991 and each succeeding October 1 during the term hereof, a sum equal to 0.95% (.0095) of the Adjusted Box Office for the preceding Season.

(b) LICENSEE shall submit a report to SOCIETY simultaneously with each payment specified in subparagraph "6(a)," on forms supplied free of charge by SOCIETY, and certified by LICENSEE, showing the total Adjusted Box Office for the preceding Season.

(c) In the event LICENSEE shall be more than three months delinquent in payment of licensee fees due on or after October 1, 1991 hereunder, LICENSEE shall pay a finance charge on the license fees due of 1% per month, or the maximum rate permitted by law, whichever is less, from the date such license fees were due.

7. (a) SOCIETY shall have the right to require from LICENSEE such reasonable data or information in addition to that furnished by LICENSEE under subparagraph "6(b)" of this Agreement as may be deemed necessary in order to ascertain the Adjusted Box Office, as provided by this Agreement. SOCIETY shall have the further right, by its duly authorized representatives, at any time during customary business hours, to examine the books and records of account of LICENSEE only to such extent as may be necessary to verify such statement or statements as may be required by this Agreement. SOCIETY shall consider all data and information coming to its attention as the result of any such examination of books and records as completely and entirely confidential.

(b) The period for which SOCIETY may audit pursuant to this Agreement shall be limited to three Seasons preceding the Season in which the audit is made provided, however, that if an audit is postponed at the request of LICENSEE, SOCIETY shall have the right to audit for the period commencing with the third Season preceding the Season in which notification of intention to audit was first given by SOCIETY to LICENSEE. This three Season limitation shall not apply if LICENSEE fails or refuses after written notice from SOCIETY to produce the books and records necessary to verify any report or statement of accounting rendered pursuant to this Agreement. Nothing herein shall restrict SOCIETY's right to audit under previous license agreements, for a limit of three Seasons for all such license agreements provided, however, that SOCIETY's right to audit shall not extend to any Season preceding the 1987/1988 Season.

(c) In the event any such audit shows LICENSEE to have underpaid the license fees due SOCIETY by 5% or less, LICENSEE shall pay a finance charge on the additional license fees due at the rate of 1% per month, or at the maximum rate permitted by law, whichever is less, from the date SOCIETY demands payment of such amount.

(d) In the event any such audit shows LICENSEE to have underpaid the license fees due SOCIETY by more than 5%, LICENSEE shall pay a finance charge on the additional license fees due at the rate of 1% per month, or at the maximum rate permitted by law, whichever is less, from the date(s) the license fees were due.

8. Upon any breach or default by either party of any term or condition contained herein, the other party may terminate this license by giving the party in default thirty days' notice to cure such breach or default; and in the event that such breach or default has not been cured within said thirty days, this license shall terminate on the expiration of such thirty-day period without further notice. In the event of such termination, SOCIETY shall refund to LICENSEE any unearned license fees paid in advance.

9. In the event of:

(a) Any major interference with the operations of SOCIETY in the state, territory, dependency, possession or political subdivision in which LICENSEE is located, by reason of any law of such state, territory, dependency, possession or political subdivision; or

(b) Any substantial increase in the cost to SOCIETY of operating in such state, territory, dependency, possession or political subdivision, by reason of any law of such state, territory, dependency, possession or political subdivision, which is applicable to the licensing of performing rights,

SOCIETY shall have the right to terminate this Agreement forthwith by written notice and, in the event of such termination, shall refund to LICENSEE any unearned license fees paid in advance.

10. (a) SOCIETY agrees to indemnify, save and hold LICENSEE, its artists and the proprietors of the premises, harmless, and defend LICENSEE, its artists and the proprietors of said premises from and against any claim, demand or suit that may be made or brought against them or any of them with respect to performances given by LICENSEE during the term hereof in accordance with this license, of "cleared composition(s)" (as hereinafter defined), or of any musical compositions heretofore copyrighted or composed by members of SOCIETY and now or hereafter during the term hereof in SOCIETY's repertory or hereafter during the term hereof copyrighted or composed by present members of SOCIETY or by future members of SOCIETY so long as such present or future members remain members of SOCIETY. In the event of the service upon LICENSEE of any notice, process, paper or pleading under which a claim, demand or action is made or begun against LICENSEE on account of any such matter as is hereinabove referred to, LICENSEE shall promptly give SOCIETY written notice thereof and simultaneously therewith deliver to SOCIETY any such notice, process, paper or pleading, or a copy thereof, and SOCIETY at its own expense shall have sole charge of the defense of any such action or proceeding. LICENSEE, however, shall have the right to engage counsel of its own, at its own expense, who may participate in the defense of any such action or proceeding and with whom counsel for SOCIETY shall cooperate. LICENSEE shall cooperate with SOCIETY in every way in the defense of any such action or proceeding, and in any appeals that may be taken from any judgments or orders entered therein, and shall execute all pleadings, bonds, or other instruments, but at the sole expense of SOCIETY, that may be required in order properly to defend and resist any such action or proceeding, and prosecute any appeals taken therein.

(b) In the event of the service upon LICENSEE of any notice, process, paper or pleading under which a claim, demand, or action is made, or begun against LICENSEE on account of the rendition by LICENSEE of any musical composition (other than a "cleared composition(s)") contained in SOCIETY's repertory but not heretofore or hereafter during the term hereof copyrighted or composed by members of SOCIETY, SOCIETY agrees at the request of LICENSEE to cooperate with and assist LICENSEE in the defense of any such action or proceeding, and in any appeals that LICENSEE may elect to take from any judgments or orders entered therein.

(c) This Paragraph "10" shall not apply to performances of any works that may be restricted under Paragraph "3" if such performances occur after the date of notice of restriction or withdrawal given in accordance with Paragraph "11."

(d) The term "cleared composition(s)" as used in this Agreement shall mean any musical composition which SOCIETY shall have notified LICENSEE is a composition with respect to which SOCIETY is willing to indemnify LICENSEE, provided that SOCIETY may limit such indemnity to a specific program of LICENSEE for which a clearance shall have been given by SOCIETY.

11. All notices required or permitted hereunder shall be given in writing by certified United States mail sent to either party at the address given above. Each party agrees to inform the other of any change of address.

IN WITNESS WHEREOF, this Agreement has been duly executed by SOCIETY and LICENSEE

this _____ day of _____, 19 _____.

AMERICAN SOCIETY OF COMPOSERS,
AUTHORS AND PUBLISHERS

_____
LICENSEE

By_____   By_____

_____
TITLE

(Rev. 91)

List 15.1

Major Overseas Performance Rights Societies

A.P.R.A.   Australian Performing Right Association Ltd.
Australia - New Zealand
    P. O. Box 567
    1A Eden St.
    Crows Nest NSW 2065
    AUSTRALIA

P.R.S.   The Performing Right Society Ltd.
United Kingdom and Northern Ireland
    29-33 Berners Street
    London WIP 4AA
    ENGLAND

S.A.C.E.M.   Societe des Auteurs, Compositeurs et Editeurs
de Musique
France
    225 Avenue Charles de Gaulle
    92521 Nevilly-Sur-Seine
    FRANCE

G.E.M.A.   Gesellschaft fur Musikalische Auftuhrungs
und Mechanische Vervielfaltigungsnechte
Germany
    Rosenheimer Strasse II
    8000 Munich 80
    GERMANY

C.A.P.A.C.   Composers Authors & Publishers Assn of
Canada Ltd.
Canada
    1240 Bay St.
    Toronto, Ontario M5R 2C2
    CANADA

Major Overseas Performance Rights Societies (*cont'd*)

S.I.A.E.   Societa Italiano degli Autori ed Editor:
             Italy
                 Viale della Letteratura 30
                 00144 Rome
                 ITALY

J.A.S.R.A.C. Japanese Society for Rights of Authors,
              Composers & Publishers
              Japan
                  1-7-13 Nishishimbashi
                  Minato-Ku,
                  Tokyo 105
                  JAPAN

S.G.A.E.   Sociedad General de Autores de Espana
             Spain
                 Fernando V1
                 28004 Madrid 4
                 SPAIN

S.T.I.M.   Foreningen Svenska Tonsattares
             Internationella Musikbyra
             Sweden
                 Sandhamsgatan 79
                 102-54 Stockholm
                 SWEDEN

B.U.M.A.   Het Bureau voor Muziek-Auteursrecht
             Netherlands
                 Professor E. M. Meyersiaan 3
                 1183 Av Amstelveen
                 P. O. Box 725 (ZIP 1183 AS)
                 NETHERLANDS

Major Overseas Performance Rights Societies (*cont'd*)

S.A.B.A.M.   Societe Belge des Auteurs
               Compositeurs et Editeurs
               Belgium
                   75-77 Rue d'Arlon
                   1040 Brussels
                   BELGIUM

S.A.M.R.O.   South African Music Rights Organisation
               South Africa
               P. O. Box 9292
               Johannesburg 2000
               SAMBRO House
                   73 Juta Street
                   Braamfonstein 2001,
                   SOUTH AFRICA

CHAPTER 16

THE GRAND RIGHTS CONTROVERSY

SUMMARY

OVERVIEW OF THEATRICAL MUSICAL PRODUCTIONS

1. Non-Musical Play With Incidental Music
2. Play With Music
3. Musical Revue
4. Dramatico-Musical Work

LEGAL BACKGROUND

1. Copyright
2. Licensing By theatrical Production Companies and theatrical Agencies
3. Licensing By Performance Rights Societies
4. Licensing By Music Publishers

DISTINGUISHING BETWEEN DRAMATIC RIGHTS, NONDRAMATIC RIGHTS AND GRAND RIGHTS

1. Dramatic Performance Defined
2. Nondramatic Performance Defined
3. Grand Rights Defined

GRAND PERFORMANCE DISTINGUISHED FROM DRAMATIC PERFORMANCE

ANALYSIS OF VARIOUS DRAMATIC AND NONDRAMATIC USES OF MUSIC

1. Performance Rights Societies
2. Performance License Provisions
3. Eight Examples of Performances of Music
   A. A non-dramatic rendition of a musical composition, that was not originally part of any opera, operetta, musical comedy, play or like production, on stage in a theatre, nightclub, cabaret, concert hall, or like establishment
   B. A dramatic rendition of a musical composition, that was not originally part of an opera, operetta,

735

musical comedy, play or like production, on stage
in a theatre, nightclub, cabaret, concert hall
or like establishment

C. A non-dramatic rendition of a musical composition
that was originally part of an opera, operetta,
musical comedy, play' or like production, on stage
in a theatre, nightclub, cabaret, concert hall, or
like establishment

D. A dramatic rendition of a musical composition,
that was originally part of an opera, operetta,
musical comedy, play or like production, on stage
in a nightclub, cabaret, concert hall, or
like establishment

E. A non-dramatic rendition of a musical composition,
that was not originally part of an opera, operetta,
musical comedy, play or like production, in a
television program, motion picture, videogram
or like work

F. A dramatic rendition of a musical composition, that
was not originally part of an opera, operetta, musical
comedy, play or like production, in a television
program, motion picture, videogram or like work

G. A non-dramatic rendition of a musical composition,
that was originally part of an opera, operetta,
musical comedy, play or like production, in a
television program, motion picture, videogram
or like work

H. A dramatic rendition of a musical composition, that
was originally part of an opera, operetta, musical
comedy, play or like production, in a television
program, motion picture, videogram or like work

RECENT COURT CASES

1. Frank Music Corp. v. MGM Grand Hotel
2. Gershwin v. the Whole Thing Co.

GRAND RIGHT IN A PERSON'S LIFE STORY?

BROADCAST OF AN ENTIRE ALBUM

1. Operas
2. Musical Plays
3. Other Albums

DRAMATIC ADAPTATION RIGHTS

1. Legal Background
2. Popular Songs
3. Show Tunes
4. Music Videos
5. Separate Adaptation License Required
6. Dramatic Adaptation Right is not a Grand Right

DETERMINING WHO HAS THE RIGHT TO LICENSE THESE USES

1. Non-dramatic Performances
2. Dramatic Performances
3. Dramatic Adaptations
4. Grand Performances

LICENSING CONSIDERATIONS

1. Considerations in Granting and Clearing Dramatic Performance Licenses
2. Considerations in Granting and Clearing Adaptation Licenses
3. Considerations in Granting and Clearing Grand Performances

SUMMARY

FORMS

CHAPTER **16**

THE GRAND RIGHTS
CONTROVERSY

As noted in the preceding chapter, performance rights societies only provide licenses to render performances of music that are *nondramatic*. They do not grant licenses to render dramatic performances. This chapter will explore the distinction between dramatic and nondramatic performances and will suggest a framework for answering the question, from whom, if not the performance rights society, must one seek permission to render a *dramatic* performance of a musical composition? This chapter will also provide examples of dramatic and nondramatic uses and will analyze the type of license appropriate for each use.

A considerable amount of confusion among music publishers, songwriters, musical playwrights, producers, and their legal representatives has clouded the licensing of dramatic performances of music on stage, television and motion pictures. Much of this confusion stems from a misunderstanding of the rights involved and, in particular, the frequent misuse of the term, *grand rights*.

Before proceeding with our discussion of the meaning of dramatic, nondramatic, and grand rights, it will be useful to first survey the various ways music may be used in theatrical productions.

OVERVIEW OF THEATRICAL MUSICAL PRODUCTIONS

By theatrical production, we mean a production created for the living stage which contains some literary or visual elements going beyond the mere physical appearance and rendition of music by singers and musicians. It should be noted that the kinds of theatrical productions described below should not be confused with the type of *venue* (e.g., nightclub, cabaret, concert hall, legitimate theatre, etc.) at which these productions may be performed. Each kind of theatrical performance described below may be performed at any of the various kinds of venues.

The theatrical productions in which music may be used can be classified into four categories:

1. Non-Musical Play with Incidental Music

A *non-musical play with incidental music* is what the term implies. The music is usually contracted for after the play is written and is not considered part of the play. An example might be Shakespeare's *Hamlet* with music performed merely incidentally to the play.

2. Play with Music

Play with music is the term reserved for a play that is essentially non-musical, but contains music, with or without lyrics. The music may be integral to the play, used to create atmosphere, indicate the time when the action is taking place, or assist in evoking a mood or the expression of the mood or desires of a character in the play, but it does not have the effect of carrying the action ahead to the extent it does in a dramatico-musical work.

3. Musical Revue

A *musical revue* is a stage presentation of skillfully arranged, separate musical numbers. Years ago, revues, such as Ziegfeld's *Follies,* Earl Carroll's *Vanities*, and George White's *Scandals*, contained a variety of acts, including singing, dancing, sketches, comedy bits, blackouts, and specialty performances of individuals, animal acts, and, of course, chorus girls. Today, revues usually consist entirely of musical numbers, with some sketches or improvisation. A recent example of a musical revue is *Ain't Misbehavin'*.

4. Dramatico-musical work

A *dramatico-musical work* is a theatrical work in which the music is integral to the story told by the book in the sense that the music is used to carry the action of the story forward. Examples include operas, operettas, ballet, and musical plays. An *opera*—once commonly referred to as a *grand opera*—is a play with virtually the entire text of its book, or libretto, set to music or sung, with no or few spoken words. An *operetta* is the same as an opera except that a significant portion of the text of the book is spoken, rather than sung. A *ballet* is an elaborate dramatic dance set to music, often choreographed to render a narrative story. The *musical play*, or musical comedy, the modern successor to the operetta, is a play with music and lyrics that are used to carry forward the action of the story or book of the play, the text of which is rendered in spoken form. Musical plays were once commonly called, *grand musical plays*, but today they are more commonly called simply, *musicals*.

LEGAL BACKGROUND

1. Copyright

The copyright law identifies several categories of works of authorship, including literary works, dramatic works, musical works, choreographic works, pictorial works, sculptural works, and audiovisual works. A book, for example, is considered a *literary work*. A play is considered a *dramatic work*. A song, of course, is a *musical work*. *Plays with music* are considered dramatic works. *Musical revues* may be considered dramatic works, or merely compilations of musical works accompanied by incidental, literary material (e.g., monologue, dialogue, or narration). *Non-musical plays with incidental music*, as we have defined that term, are literary works accompanied by separate musical works.

Wherever the literary contribution to a work is separate from the musical contribution to a work, such as the literary and musical contributions to a non-musical play with incidental music, the copyright in the literary contribution is separate from the copyright in the musical contribution. By contrast, a *dramatico-musical work*, such as an opera or a musical play, is a work whose music is an integral part of the literary material, the music often carrying forward the action of the story. Although a copyright in each contribution to a dramatico-musical work (e.g., literary work, music, lyrics) may be claimed separately, a copyright in the dramatico-musical work as a whole may also be claimed as a single work. For example, the playwright, lyricist, and composer of a musical play can claim a copyright in the musical play in its entirety (including literary material, music and lyrics), with each owning an undivided one-third interest in the copyright in the entire dramatico-musical work.

The owner of the copyright in a book, play, or song has the exclusive right of performance in the book, play, or song. In other words, public performances of these works requires the permission of the copyright owner. Likewise, the owner of a dramatico-musical work, as a single work comprised of music, lyrics and libretto, has the exclusive right of performance in the dramatico-musical work, and the public performance of an opera, musical play, or other dramatico-musical work requires the permission of the copyright owner of the opera or play.

2. Licensing by Theatrical Production Companies and Theatrical Agencies

Public performances of operas, musical plays, and other dramatico-musical works, or portions of such works, at theatres, concert halls, and schools, are licensed by the copyright owners of such works, usually the play's producer or theatrical production company, but sometimes the playwrites themselves. These producers, companies, or playwrights are often represented by agencies specializing in the licensing of dramatico-musical works on their behalf. These agencies include the Tams-Witmark Music Library, Inc., and Samuel French in New York.[1]

3. Licensing By Performance Rights Societies

As noted in the preceding chapter, performance rights societies only license those uses over which they have the authority or right to license. Performance rights societies do not receive any rights from theatrical production companies to license dramatico-musical works (e.g., works which comprise words, music, libretto, scenery, costumes, etc.). Further, performance rights societies receive from their music publisher and song-writer members the right to license only *nondramatic* renditions of their musical compositions, not *dramatic* renditions. Accordingly, performance

---

[1] Samuel French, Inc., 25 West 45th Street, New York, NY 10036, Phone: 1-212-582-4700; Tams-Witmark Music Library, Inc., 560 Lexington Avenue, New York, NY 10022, Phone: 800-221-7196, Fax: 212-688-3232.

licenses issued by the societies to radio and television stations, nightclubs, concert halls, and like establishments, permit the rendition of performances of music in only a manner that is *nondramatic* in nature and do not permit any performances of plays, musicals and other dramatico-musical works.

4. Licensing by Music Publishers

As noted above, theatrical producers, playwrights, or their agencies have the right to license performances of dramatico-musical works; performance rights societies have the right to license nondramatic performances of music in their repertoire (but they have no right to license dramatic performances and no right to license dramatico-musical works). The right to license *all other uses* of music is vested solely in the copyright owner of the music, usually a music publisher. For example, the owner of the copyright in a musical composition that was not originally part of a dramatico-musical work has the exclusive right to license *dramatic* performances of that musical composition. Nondramatic performances of that composition are licensed by the performance rights society to which a license to sublicense nondramatic performances has been granted. In some cases, a music publisher may require the consent of the songwriter to issue certain kinds of licenses, such as licenses to permit the dramatic performance of the composition, but the right to license these uses is vested exclusively in the copyright owner.

DISTINGUISHING BETWEEN DRAMATIC RIGHTS, NONDRAMATIC RIGHTS AND GRAND RIGHTS

As the preceding sections suggest, the question of whether a particular performance is a dramatic performance, a nondramatic performance, or a performance of a dramatico-musical work is an important one, because its answer will determine who among the theatrical producers, music publishers, and songwriters have the right to license the use for which clearance is being sought. It is the question to which we now turn: the distinction between dramatic uses, nondramatic uses, and uses of dramatico-musical works—and the rights which form the basis for licensing such uses: dramatic performance rights, nondramatic performance rights, and grand rights, respectively.

1. Dramatic Performance Defined

The essence of a dramatic performance is drama. The term *drama* implies the telling of a story or the involvement of human conflict. Accordingly, the term *dramatic performance* has been defined as a performance of a musical composition that is woven into and carries forward a definite plot and its accompanying action. Examples of dramatic performances are provided and discussed below.

2. Nondramatic Performance Defined

Conversely, a *nondramatic performance* is a performance of a musical composition that is not woven into or does not carry forward a definite plot and its accompanying action. The mere singing of a song with its lyrics on stage and the broadcasting of a recording of a song on the radio would each constitute a nondramatic performance.

3. Grand Rights Defined

A *grand right* is the exclusive right to license the reproduction, adaptation, performance or other use of a dramatico-musical work, or what was once known as a "grand opera" or "grand musical play." It is a right in all the contributions of the musical play *as a single work*. It is not a right in just the music or in any single song or other literary, musical or other contribution to the play. The subject of the grand right is a collective work comprised of words, music, choreography, the *book* (i.e., the plot, story or libretto), setting, scenery, costumes, and other visual representations. There is no grand right in any of the individual songs in the collective, grand musical play; as we have explained, the copyright in the grand play, including the accompanying music, is quite distinct from the copyrights in the individual compositions that comprise it.

GRAND PERFORMANCE DISTINGUISHED FROM DRAMATIC PERFORMANCE

Accordingly, a *grand performance* is the performance of a grand opera, grand musical play, or other dramatico-musical work, or a substantial, recognizable portion of it. This is not the same as a *dramatic performance* of an individual composition, which is a rendition of a song (regardless of whether the song was originally part of a dramatico-musical work) that is woven into and carries forward a definite plot and its accompanying action.

The fact that there is a distinction between a *dramatic performance* and a *grand performance* may come as a surprise to many publishers and attorneys who have come to understand the terms as synonymous. Many understand the term grand performance to mean any dramatic performance of any musical composition and that all other performances are non-dramatic, or *small performances.*[2] A careful analysis of the rights involved clearly show that this is clearly not a proper usage of the terms.

ANALYSIS OF VARIOUS DRAMATIC AND NONDRAMATIC USES OF MUSIC

To illustrate what a grand right is, it is most useful to first examine what it is not. This section will explore the differences among dramatic, non-dramatic, and grand performances by analyzing several examples of performances of music.

1. Performance Rights Societies

As noted in Chapter 15, songwriters and copyright owners grant to performance rights societies a license to sublicense the rendition of public performances of their musical works. These grants are limited solely to the rendition of performances in a *nondramatic* manner and solely to performances of their *music.* Songwriters and copyright owners do not grant to performance rights societies any right to perform music in a dramatic manner and do not grant to the societies any rights in their literary works, plays, operas, ballets, choreographic works, and other types of works of authorship. For example, in the agreement between

---

[2] See, for example, 3 Nimmer *On Copyright,* Sec. 10.10[E] (1991). To borrow a phrase Nimmer has used with reference to a decision of Judge Friendly: Nimmer is plainly wrong and (as Judge Learned Hand paraphrasing Horace, once said of a decision by Justice Oliver Wendel Holmes), "for once Homer nodded." *Cf.,* 1 Nimmer *On Copyright,* Sec. 307 [307][A][2] (1991).

ASCAP and its writer and publisher members, the member may grant to ASCAP nondramatic performance rights in the separate compositions that may form part of a musical play authored by the songwriter member and owned by the publisher member, but the right to perform the musical play itself is reserved to the members. [3]

Because the performance rights societies have no authority to grant licenses with respect to rights reserved by their members, blanket performance licenses issued by the societies to radio and television stations, nightclubs, concert halls, and like establishments, are careful to permit the rendition of only *nondramatic* performances of music. They do not permit *dramatic* performances and do not permit any performances of plays, musicals and other dramatico-musical works.

These limitations in the scope of licenses issued by performance rights societies are set forth in the nondramatic license forms issued to radio and television stations, nightclubs, concert halls, and other licensees. The specific language used in the several forms of performance license agreements, however, varies considerably. We will review the following three representative provisions and then apply them to specific examples of musical renditions to determine the nature of the use in each example.

2. Performance License Provisions

The current ASCAP general license agreement for restaurants, taverns, nightclubs, and similar establishments states:

This license is limited to nondramatic performances, and does not authorize any dramatic performances. For purposes of this agree-

___

[3] The ASCAP Agreement between the society and its publisher and writers states: The rights hereby granted shall include:

. . .

(b) The non-exclusive right of public performance of the separate numbers, songs, fragments or arrangements, melodies or selections forming part or parts of musical plays and dramatico-musical compositions, the Owner [i.e., writer or publisher] reserving and excepting from this grant the right of performance of musical plays and dramatico-musical compositions on the legitimate stage.

. . .

(d) The non-exclusive right of public performance by television broadcasting; provided, however, that:

ment, a dramatic performance shall include, but not be limited to, the following:

(i) performance of a "dramatico-musical work" (as hereinafter defined) in its entirety;

(ii) performance of one or more musical compositions from a "dramatico-musical work" (as hereinafter defined) accompanied by dialogue, pantomime, dance, stage action, or visual representation of the work from which the music is taken;

(iii) performance of one or more musical compositions as part of a story or plot, whether accompanied or unaccompanied by dialogue, pantomime, dance, stage action, or visual representation;

(i) This grant does not extend to or include the right to license the public performance by television broadcasting or otherwise of any rendition or performance of (a) any opera, operetta, musical comedy, play or like production, as (whether or not such opera, operetta, musical comedy, play or like production was presented on the stage or motion picture form) in a manner which recreates the performance of such composition with substantially such distinctive scenery or costume as was used in the presentation of such opera, operetta, musical comedy, play or like production (whether or not such opera, operetta, musical comedy, play or like production was presented on the stage or in motion picture form): provided, however, that the rights hereby granted shall be deemed to include a grant of right to license non-dramatic performances of compositions by television broadcasting of a motion picture containing such composition if the right in such motion picture other than those granted hereby have been obtained from the parties in interest.

(e) The Owner may at any time and from time to time, in good faith, restrict the radio or television broadcasting of compositions from musical comedies, operas, operettas and motion pictures, or any other composition being excessively broadcast, only for the purpose of preventing harmful effect upon such musical comedies, operas, operettas, motion pictures, or compositions . . .

The BMI Agreement with the Writer states:

5. (a) The rights granted to us [hereunder] shall not include the right to perform or license the performance of more than one song or aria from an opera, operetta, or musical comedy or more than five minutes from a ballet if such performance is accompanied by the dramatic action, costumes or scenery of that opera, operetta, musical comedy or ballet.

(b) You, together with the publisher and your collaborators, if any, of a work, shall have the right jointly, by written notice to us, to exclude from the grant made [hereunder] performances of more than thirty (30) minutes' duration of a work which is an opera, operetta or musical comedy, but this right shall not apply to a work which is the score of a film originally produced for exhibition in motion picture theaters when performed as incorporated in such film, or which is a score originally written for a radio or television program when performed as incorporated in such program.

(iv) performance of a concert version of a "dramatico-musical work" (as hereinafter defined).

The term "dramatico-musical work" as used in this agreement, shall include, but not be limited to, a musical comedy, oratorio, choral work, opera, play with music, revue, or ballet.

The BMI general license agreement for restaurants, taverns, night-clubs, and similar establishments states:

[This] license shall not include dramatic rights, the right to perform dramatico-musical works in whole or in substantial part, the right to present individual works in a dramatic setting or the right to use the music licensed hereunder in any other context which may constitute an exercise of the 'grand rights' therein.

The ASCAP license agreement under which television stations are licensed to perform music within ASCAP's repertoire contains the following definition of dramatic performance:

[A] dramatic performance shall mean a performance of the musical composition on a television program in which there is a definite plot depicted by action and where the performance of the musical composition is woven into and carries forward the plot and its accompanying action. The use of dialogue to establish a mere program format or the use of any non-dramatic device merely to introduce a performance of a composition shall not be deemed to make such performance dramatic.

3. Eight Examples of Performances of Music

The performance license provisions set forth in the preceding section appear to be a function of one or more of the following circumstances: (a) Whether the nature of the performance is dramatic or nondramatic; (b) Whether the musical composition was originally part of a dramatico-musical work; and (c) Whether the performance is rendered on stage or broadcast on television.

We have formulated from the above circumstances eight examples of performances of music helpful to a discussion of the scope of these performance licenses. We will analyze each of them to determine what type of license is appropriate in each case and then determine who is vested with the right to grant the license for the particular use. Finally we will discuss the considerations used in establishing the terms of such licenses.

A. A non-dramatic *rendition of a musical composition, that* was not *originally part of any opera, operetta, musical comedy, play or like production, on stage in a* theatre, nightclub, cabaret, concert hall, or like establishment

Suppose Frank Sinatra sang the song, *Yesterday* (Lennon/McCartney), as part of his popular nightclub act at a Las Vegas resort hotel. His performance would fall within none of the four categories of dramatic performances set forth in the ASCAP general license. The song originated from a single release or record album recorded by *The Beatles* in the late 1960's. Because it did not originate from any opera, operetta, musical comedy, play, ballet, or like production, only subparagraph (iii) of the ASCAP definition might apply:

(iii) performance of one or more musical compositions as part of a story or plot, whether accompanied or unaccompanied by dialogue, pantomime, dance, stage action, or visual representation;

Mr. Sinatra's act is composed of a series of vocal renditions of songs performed on stage with the aid of a microphone backed up by a swing orchestra, with no other significant visual representations— that is, no costume or stage props other than a well-cut tuxedo and an occasional glass of *Jack Daniels*—and as part of no story or plot, other than monologue or dialogue incidental to the introduction and performance of the song. This performance, while quite entertaining, would clearly be considered *non-dramatic*.

Because the performance of *Yesterday* is non-dramatic, the performance is covered by the hotel's blanket license with the performance rights society. No further permission for the use would be required.

B. A dramatic *rendition of a musical composition, that* was not *originally part of an opera, operetta, musical comedy, play or like production, on stage in a* theatre, nightclub, cabaret, concert hall, or like establishment

Suppose the same song, *Yesterday*, was performed by the pop star, Madonna, as part of an elaborate performance that contained significant visual representations, making use of costume, settings, scenery, props, and other visual allusions to, for example, ancient Rome. Again, since the song is not a dramatico-musical work nor was it originally part of one, only the following category of the definition of dramatic performance in the ASCAP license might apply:

> (iii) performance of one or more musical compositions as part of a story or plot, whether accompanied or unaccompanied by dialogue, pantomime, dance, stage action, or visual representation;

Though the performance is accompanied by significant visual representations, it is not being rendered "as part of a story or plot," under the facts in this example. It is merely being performed by an artist in costume in front of scenery—no story or plot accompanies the presentation. It appears, therefore, that this performance would not be considered a dramatic rendition under the definition of dramatic performance set forth in the ASCAP license.

At this point, we will turn to the BMI general license (applying these facts as though the song were in the BMI repertoire):

> [This] license shall not include dramatic rights, . . . the right to present individual works in a dramatic setting or the right to use the music licensed hereunder in any other context which may constitute an exercise of the 'grand rights' therein.

The phrase, "This license shall not include dramatic rights," is unfortunate. As noted in Chapter 2, a *license* is not a *right*—a right is a claim of ownership that allows you to exclude someone from doing something with respect to the subject of your property; a license is a permission or privilege to do something with respect to another's property that you would not otherwise have the privilege to do without the license. What the phrase beginning, "This license shall not include dramatic rights . . .," probably means is, "This license does not include permission to render performances of music that are dramatic or to present individual songs in a dramatic setting. . ."

This still leaves us with the question whether this performance would be considered a *dramatic* performance or a presentation of the song *in a dramatic setting*. If not, then Madonna's performance in this example, like Mr. Sinatra's performance in the preceding example, would be covered by the hotel's BMI license, and no separate license would be required.

For help in determining whether a performance is dramatic or presented in a dramatic setting, most people look to the standard set forth in the definition of dramatic performance contained in the ASCAP television license, which states: a performance of a musical composition on a television program is dramatic if "the musical composition is woven into and carries forward [a definite] plot and its accompanying action."

Interestingly enough, the ASCAP general license is not precisely consistent with this language (saying instead, "performance of one or more compositions *as part of* a story or plot") and the BMI general license does not explicitly use language relating to stories or plots at all. Nevertheless, it is believed that the definition of dramatic performance that appears in the television performance license of ASCAP is most helpful in analyzing whether a performance is dramatic or nondramatic. This is the case regardless of where the performance may be rendered, even though the definition would appear by its terms to be limited to dramatic performances rendered *on television*.

A little history may shed some light on the origin of this useful definition. It is said to have been written by Oscar Hammerstein II in the 1940's. Mr. Hammerstein was concerned that television, a newly emerging medium at that time, would have the potential of competing with and reducing receipts of live theatrical performances of musical plays. It is not difficult to understand why Mr. Hammerstein suggested this particular language. Musical compositions in successful musical plays are not just incorporated randomly between acts in the play; good musical playwrights consciously make use of songs to *carry forward the action* of the play and the best use of music in a musical play is made when a composition is used to underscore a major turning point in the plot, such as a personal discovery of a principal character.[4]

---

[4] See, Frankel, *Writing the Broadway Musical* at p.29 (Drama Book Specialists, New York 1977).

The "woven into and carry forward the plot" language in Mr. Hammerstein's definition, however, seems to do more than protect the economic interests of owners of dramatico-musical works. As incorporated into the ASCAP license, it is not limited to compositions that were originally part of musical plays, operas and like productions; it appears to apply to other songs, as well, including songs such as, *Yesterday*, which were not originally part of dramatico-musical works. Nevertheless, there is still good reason why publishers and writers of non-show music reserve the right to license dramatic performances from performance rights societies.

The main concern of a performing rights society is administering the collection and payment of sums generated by the performances of compositions. While the value of certain performances are given greater weight than others (e.g., a use of a composition in a television commercial might be given more performance credits than the use of the same song as background music in a situation comedy), the importance of the song in relation to the intended use is not taken into consideration in compensating publishers and writers. A use of a particular song in a dramatic rendition (i.e., woven into and carrying forward a plot) is generally more important to the intended use than mere nondramatic renditions.

Though the differences in credits given for various kinds of performances are relatively small, the differences in the license fee charged for dramatic uses of compositions, as opposed to nondramatic uses, may vary greatly. They may vary greatly because the importance of the song in relation to the intended use varies greatly, depending, for example, upon how closely the music is woven into a dramatic plot. The more a song is woven into a plot, the more important it is to the use. The more important the song is in relation to the use desired, the higher the fee that can be commanded for the use.

Songwriters and music publishers reserve the right to issue dramatic performance licenses from their performing rights societies, because they are in a better position than the societies to determine the value of the musical composition in relation to its intended dramatic use and to price the license accordingly. Performing rights societies, who merely survey performances to roughly measure how often the songs in their repertory are performed, are not in the best position to perform this analysis. How a publisher determines the value of a license of a dramatic performance varies from song to song, and from use to use, but the publishers and writers are in a better position to reflect upon such factors and determine the value of the dramatic uses of their musical works. Thus, writers and publishers have more to gain by reserving the rights to grant licenses for the dramatic use of their music, rather than giving the performance rights society such rights.

Determining when a musical composition performed on a television program is "woven into and carries forward the plot and its accompanying action" must obviously be done on a case by case basis. Reasonable minds may differ as to whether the facts presented would lead to a conclusion that any performance is dramatic or non-dramatic. However, even though neither the general performance licenses of ASCAP or BMI mention it specifically, the standard proposed by Oscar Hammerstein II for determining the nature of performances rendered on television programs appears to be the best standard for determining whether any particular performance is dramatic or nondramatic.

If, in our example, Madonna's performance of the song, *Yesterday* were preceded or followed by a dialogue performed on stage to establish the format of the act, or if a non-dramatic device were used merely to introduce her performance of the song, the performance would remain non-dramatic, even if accompanied by significant visual representations, such as costumes and scenery of ancient Rome. However, any variation of facts might change the outcome. If Madonna's act carried a definite plot depicted by action and the performance of the song is woven into and carries forward the plot and its accompanying action, the performance would be dramatic. For example, the performance would probably be dramatic if her act was to some extent based upon the story of *Anthony and Cleopatra* and the song *Yesterday* was woven into the act at a certain point to carry forward the idea that all [her] troubles seemed so far away.

Assuming that the performance were deemed dramatic, then, because the performance is not covered by the ASCAP or BMI licenses (which cover only non-dramatic performances), a dramatic performance license would be required before Madonna could proceed with the performance.

From whom would such a license be cleared? The license for the dramatic performance is not covered by the hotel's blanket performance license and is not available separately from the performance rights societies. The hotel, Madonna, or the producer of her act, would require permission from the copyright owner of the song, which in most cases is the music publisher.

Some would suggest that the license to perform the song dramatically or in a dramatic setting must be cleared by the songwriter, because, they say, "a dramatic performance is an exercise of a grand right" and "grand rights are reserved to songwriters." However, because the song in this example was not originally part of a dramatico-musical work, *no grand right* is involved, and permission would be required from the copyright owner (i.e., the music publisher, not the songwriter).

C. A non-dramatic *rendition of a musical composition that* was *originally part of an opera, operetta, musical comedy, play or like production, on stage in a* theatre, nightclub, cabaret, concert hall, or like establishment

An example of this use may be found in a true story and court trial in which I testified as a witness in early 1948.[5] The copyright owner of *The Student Prince* sued the owner of a cabaret in New York City called *The Harem* (formerly known as *The Latin Quarter*, owned, incidentally, at that time by Lou Walters, the father of newscaster Barbara Walters) for infringement based upon performances at the club of a medley of songs from *The Student Prince*. The nightclub owner claimed the performance was licensed under the club's standard blanket license from ASCAP. The court ruled, correctly in our view, that the performance was covered by the ASCAP license and that the medley did not infringe the musical play, *The Student Prince*. This decision has been criticized as too narrowly construing the scope of the term dramatic performance.[6] A close review of the facts reveals this criticism is misplaced.

The medley of songs from *The Student Prince* was performed by the choral group, *Ben Yost and his Royal Guardsmen*, which was the ninth act in a ten act nightclub show entitled, "The One Thousand and Second Night." The show was not connected by a story line or

---

[5] *April Productions, Inc. v. Strand Enterprises, Inc.*, 221 F.2d 292 (2d Cir. 1955)

[6] 3 Nimmer *On Copyright*, Sec. 10.10[E] n.44 (1991) (stating that, "This decision, if followed, could mean the virtual extinction of dramatic (or grand) performing rights with respect to noninstrumental musical compositions.")

plot and the medley was just one of the numbers performed by the *Royal Guardsmen*, a small part of their act. The stage had no scenery and the act was performed in front of the nightclub stage curtain. The *Royal Guardsmen* did wear costumes—white outfits with fanciful short, red formal jackets. Nevertheless, neither the costumes nor the visual presentation bore any resemblance to the distinctive scenery or costume used in the presentation of the musical play, *The Student Prince*. Finally, the medley was truly a medley; no song from *The Student Prince* was sung in its entirety. I can confirm this because I worked for Ben Yost at the time and I personally arranged the medley that was the subject of this lawsuit. I testified before the Judge in the case that the medley comprised mostly the refrains of songs from the show connected by transitions that I composed.

The court was faced with the task of interpreting an older form of the ASCAP license for performances in nightclubs. The form, which the court was not reticent to criticize (saying, "the form of the license is such that almost nothing is sure"), granted to *The Harem* nightclub permission to render non-dramatic performances of ASCAP music. The court determined that the language granting permission to render "non-dramatic" renditions can best be construed in light of the other provisions of the license which describe what is not included in the license. One of those provisions prohibited the performance of compositions with "words, dialogue, costume accompanying dramatic action or scenery accessory" that was "of the work from which the music was taken." The court observed that the form "on the one hand, describes the performance right granted as 'non-dramatic' but, on the other, in substance authorizes their exercise with 'words, dialogue, costume accompanying dramatic action or scenery accessory'" (as long as such elements were not of the work from which the music was taken). In other words, the ASCAP license permitted the rendition of musical compositions with costume, scenery, dialogue, dramatic actions, and other visual representations without their getting into the "dramatic" class. After closely examining the facts in the case, the court concluded that the performance was non-dramatic. None of the costumes, scenery, dialogue or other visual representations present when the medley was performed bore any resemblance to those used in the presentation of the musical play, *The Student Prince*. Even if *The Harem* put on a dramatic performance, the court said, the selections from *The Student Prince* were not part of it.

If the court had before it the modern ASCAP nightclub perform-ance license to construe, the result would have been no different. The performance of the medley falls within none of the four categories that comprise the definition of a dramatic performance: the performance of a medley of songs from *The Student Prince* is not (i) a performance of *the musical play* itself; (ii) the performance of one or more musical compositions from *The Student Prince* accompanied by dialogue, pan-tomime, dance, stage action, or visual representation *of the work from which the music is taken*; (iii) the performance of one or more musical compositions *as part of a story or plot*, whether accompanied or unac-companied by dialogue, pantomime, dance, stage action, or visual rep-resentation; or (iv) the performance of *a concert version of* the musical play, *The Student Prince*.

Note that even the modern ASCAP license contemplates that a performance of a song originally from a dramatico-musical work may be non-dramatic, even though the performance is accompanied by dia-logue, pantomime, dance, stage action, or visual representation, as long as such elements are not *of the work from which the music is taken*.

Applying the facts of this case to the modern BMI general license, the same result would be reached. The BMI license does not provide permission to perform dramatico-musical works, in whole or in sub-stantial part. The performance of a medley of songs from a musical play should not be construed as the performance of a substantial part of the musical play, unless something more is present that substantially evokes the drama inherent in the musical play. That something may be costumes, scenery, or other visual representations from the musical play or some dialogue from the play, other than that which may be part of the lyrics of the songs.

The BMI general license also states that permission does not in-clude, "the right to present individual works in a dramatic setting." Arguably, the medley from *The Student Prince* could be considered to have been presented in a dramatic setting, if the entire evening's performance at *The Harem* were considered a dramatic performance. But the court specifically held, and correctly, that the worst that could be said about the performance is that the medley was sung in an intermis-sion between the acts of a dramatic performance, and that such a rendition was non-dramatic within the meaning of the ASCAP license. A contrary holding would have the effect of rendering any simple stand-up performance of a song by an act in a variety show a dramatic performance merely because the variety show includes other acts which render dramatic performances.

Arguably, the medley could be considered to have been presented in a dramatic setting if the singers were in costume and the stage contained scenery. But the mere presence of costumes, scenery, or other visual representations should not by themselves render a setting dramatic. Something more must be present: something in the nature of drama. As noted above, the term *drama* implies the acting out or telling of a story, or the involvement of human conflict. For a setting to be dramatic, therefore, the song must either be (i) interwoven into a plot or story, or (ii) the lyrics of the song are rendered with the presence of costumes, scenery, and visual representations from the musical play for which the song was originally written. Either of these, or perhaps other elements, such as dialogue from the musical play, would more strongly evoke the drama of the musical play than the mere performance of the lyrics or an instrumental arrangement.

Accordingly, the performance of a medley of selections from *The Student Prince*, with little more than some fanciful costumes unrelated to the musical play, was not a rendition in a dramatic setting nor a performance of the musical in whole or in substantial part. It was, therefore, a non-dramatic rendition.

D. A dramatic *rendition of a musical composition, that was originally part of an opera, operetta, musical comedy, play or like production, on stage in a* night-club, cabaret, concert hall, or like establishment

A concert performance of a substantial number of songs from the rock opera, *Jesus Christ Superstar* is an example of a performance of music that was originally part of an opera or musical play that was held by a court to be dramatic.[7]

Timothy Rice wrote the opera's libretto and Andrew Lloyd Webber composed the score of the opera's overture and 23 songs which depict the last seven days in the life of Jesus. The Robert Stigwood Group, the

---

[7] *Robert Stigwood Group Limited v. Sperber*, 457 F.2d 50 (2d Cir. 1972).

owner of the exclusive right to make stage and dramatic presentations of the rock opera, brought a lawsuit against a theatrical touring company which produced a series of live stage performances that included 20 of the 23 musical compositions from the opera, all but one of which was rendered in identical sequence as in the original opera. As in the opera, the singers enter and exit, maintaining specific roles and occasionally making gestures, and preserving the story line of the original production. The theatrical company contended that its presentation was a *non-dramatic* performance of the compositions in *Jesus Christ Superstar* which could be performed under the theatre's license from ASCAP. Stigwood took the position that it was a dramatic performance of the songs which was not covered by the ASCAP license.

The court correctly concluded that the production was an infringement on Stigwood's rights in the opera *Jesus Christ Superstar*. However, even though the court pointed out that separate copyright registrations were obtained for the opera as a dramatico-musical work as a whole and for each of the individual musical compositions as musical works, it failed in its analysis to recognize the import of the distinction between the copyright in the opera and the copyrights in the individual compositions.

As a result, the court unnecessarily wrestled with the distinction between dramatic and non-dramatic performances of the songs, when, in fact, it was not dealing with the issue of whether the performances of the songs were done in a dramatic fashion, but with the issue of whether the performance was an infringement of the rights in the dramatico-musical work, *Jesus Christ Superstar*. In other words, the court held that the performance of the songs was *dramatic*, rather than holding that the performance constituted a *grand performance* of the grand opera, *Jesus Christ Superstar*.

To its credit, the court recognized that it was "inescapable that the *story* of the last seven days in the life of Christ is portrayed in the [defendant's] performances substantially as in Superstar." We add emphasis to the word "*story*," because the subject of the infringement was a performance of the dramatico-musical work, including its story or libretto, which is a substantial part of the dramatico-musical work. The lack of costumes or scenery did not prevent the story from being infringed. The rendition of 20 of the 23 songs in virtually the same order as they appeared in the opera, with or without costumes or scenery from the opera, is essentially a performance of the story. It should not make a difference that none of the costumes or scenery used in this performance was from the original opera presentation.

This case can be distinguished from *The Student Prince* case. In the latter, only a medley of a selection of songs from the musical was performed in a short act that was part of a variety show. For the performance of the medley to have been dramatic, something more than the rendition of the medley was required to make the performance tantamount to a performance of the musical play itself, or a substantial part of it—something like dialogue, costumes, scenery, or visual representations from the musical itself. In the *Superstar* case, the play was an opera in which most of the dialogue was comprised in the lyrics. By performing 20 of the 23 songs in order, you, in effect, render a performance of the opera, if not in whole, surely, in substantial part. No costumes, scenery or other visual representations from the original opera need be present under these circumstances to evoke *Superstar's* drama, which was substantially comprised in the lyrics of the 20 songs selected for the performance.

Although ASCAP licensed the non-dramatic performance of the individual musical compositions, ASCAP had no right to license the story, or any performance of the music that includes a substantial performance of the grand opera. The rights in the grand opera were infringed in this case. Since the ASCAP license did not permit this performance, a license would be required from Stigwood, the owners of the exclusive rights to present the opera. Note that even if the music publishing rights to the musical compositions were granted by Stigwood to an independent music publishing company, a license to perform the opera would still be required from Stigwood, not the music publishing company. This is because the rights in the play are separate from the rights in the music, and the music publishing company would have no right to grant a license for this grand performance, unless it were given rights to the play, or some other authorization from the play's owner to do so.

E.   A non-dramatic *rendition of a musical composition, that* was not *originally part of an opera, operetta, musical comedy, play or like production, in a* **television program, motion picture, videogram or like work**

As previously noted, the ASCAP license agreement under which television stations are licensed to perform music within ASCAP's repertoire contains a definition of dramatic performance that boils down to this: a performance of a musical composition on a television program is dramatic if the musical composition is woven into and carries forward a definite plot and its accompanying action. Determining when a musical composition performed on a television program is "woven into and carries forward the plot and its accompanying action" must be done on a case-by-case basis.

Taking the example of Frank Sinatra's singing the song *Yesterday* in his nightclub act, if we were to record Mr. Sinatra's performance on videotape and televise it, the answer to our question would be no different: the performance would not be considered dramatic. It would not be dramatic under the ASCAP license, because there is no definite plot or accompanying action into which the music can be woven or be used to carry forward. Nor would the performance be dramatic under the BMI license, inasmuch as the setting of Frank Sinatra's act would not be considered *dramatic*, in the absence of some plot and accompanying action.

Similarly, a song performed by a singer on a television variety show, such as the *Ed Sullivan Show*, would not be considered dramatic, even though portions of the variety show may contain scenes of a dramatic nature. This would be similar to the facts of *The Student Prince* case, discussed above, where the medley of songs from *The Student Prince* performed by a singing group was not deemed to be a dramatic performance, even though several other acts presented during the course of the evening at *The Harem* nightclub may have been of a dramatic nature.

Certainly, the performance of a musical composition by a band, such as the NBC band on the *Tonight Show*, is not a dramatic performance. Nor would the use of theme music over the main titles of a situation comedy, or the use of background music in a made-for-TV-movie, be considered a dramatic performance. The use of music under those circumstances could not be considered woven into and carrying forward the plot of the dramatic or comedic action.

Perhaps the music played in the background of a breathtaking car chase in a crime drama program might help carry forward the accompanying action, but it would hardly be considered woven into the plot, as nearly any action music could be substituted. The definition of dramatic performance requires, as it should, that the music be both *carrying forward* a definite plot *and* be *woven into* the plot and its accompanying action. Music that accompanies dramatic action just to vicariously enhance the action would not be considered a dramatic use.

F.   A dramatic *rendition of a musical composition, that* was not *originally part of an opera, operetta, musical comedy, play or like production, in a* television program, motion picture, videogram or like work

As we have suggested, the standard used by the ASCAP definition of dramatic performances on television programs—whether the music is woven into and carries forwared a definite plot and its accompanying action—is useful for determining whether performances are dramatic, or whether the performances are rendered on television, on stage, in motion pictures, or elsewhere.

Thus, the analysis of the example of Madonna's singing the song Yesterday in her nightclub act would be the same, whether the act was performed live, broadcast on television, or filmed for theatrical exhibition.

It may be asked whether a rock music "video" containing an audio performance of a song and a theatrical portrayal of the lyrics on screen is a dramatic performance of the song. If the song carries forward a definite plot and is woven into the plot and its accompanying action, then the performance would be dramatic. This might be the case if the story is an allegory which the lyrics help carry forward. If the story had nothing to do with the lyrics, or if there were no story, merely some special effects or the band performing on a stage, then the use would be merely a non-dramatic performance. Finally, if the story presented on the screen is actually a derivative work of the lyrics, then the use would be a *dramatic adaptation* of the lyrics, about which more is said later in this chapter.

G.   A non-dramatic *rendition of a musical composition, that* was *originally part of any opera, operetta, musical comedy, play or like production, in a* television program, motion picture, videogram or like work

It was sometime in the early 1960's, while working at Leo Feist, Inc. music publishing company, when I received a call requesting clearance to use the song, *If I Only Had a Heart* from the MGM film production, *The Wizard of Oz*, which was originally performed by Judy Garland, playing Dorothy, and Ray Bolger, as the Scarecrow. The producers of *The Gary Moore Show* wished to use the song as part of a dance number on the show, which was to be broadcast over the CBS television network. Naturally, I issued the appropriate synchronization license for the use. Unknown to the Gary Moore people or us at Leo Feist, CBS-TV had purchased the exclusive right to broadcast the motion picture, *The Wizard of Oz*, during the Christmas holiday that particular year.

A few days later, during a rehearsal of *The Gary Moore Show*, someone at CBS noticed that dancing girls were wearing scarecrow costumes somewhat similar to those worn by Ray Bolger in the motion picture. When the clearance department and legal staff of CBS heard about it, they raised hell, claiming that their grand rights in the motion picture would be infringed by the dance routine to be performed on *The Gary Moore Show* (infringed by their own network!).

As noted, the ASCAP license agreement under which television stations are licensed to perform music within ASCAP's repertoire contains the following definition of dramatic performance: a performance of a musical composition on a television program is dramatic if the musical composition is woven into and carries forward a definite plot and its accompanying action. It is clear that the mere performance on a variety television program of a single song by a group of dancers in costume does not carry forward a definite plot or story and accompanying action. Thus, the performance is not a dramatic performance.

However, there is another provision in the television license that squarely governs this situation: The ASCAP television license, by its terms,

> does not extend to or include the public performances by television broadcasting or otherwise of any rendition or performance of . . . any composition from any opera, operetta, musical comedy, play *or like production* (whether or not such opera, operetta, musical comedy, play *or like production* was presented on the stage or in motion picture form) in a manner which recreates the performance of such composition with substantially such distinctive scenery or costume as was used in the presentation of such opera, operetta, musical comedy, play *or like production* (whether or not such opera, operetta, musical comedy, play or like production was presented on the stage or in motion picture form). (emphasis added)

The musical motion picture production *The Wizard of Oz* would certainly be considered a production that would fall within the scope of the above provision. Further, the performance of the song, *If I Only Had a Heart* from the film, *The Wizard of Oz*, with scarecrow costumes by several dancers would probably be considered a manner which recreates the performance of the song, though not precisely, with substantially such distinctive costume as was used in the motion picture. Accordingly, the proposed performance would probably have constituted a grand performance in violation of CBS's exclusive rights to televise the motion picture.

To avoid the problem, the producers of *The Gary Moore Show* cleverly changed the routine: Instead of wearing the scarecrow costumes, the dancers performed the routine in their rehearsal clothes. Stories about the incident appeared in the entertainment sections of many newspapers across the country and, needless to say, the show enjoyed one of the best ratings that week.

The above incident carries several lessons for both licensors and licensees. The lesson for music copyright owners is that it is not your responsibility to guarantee that the licensee has all the rights he needs to effect the desired performance. It is the producer's responsibility to make sure he obtains a license to effect a grand performance, if that is what he will need. The producer is in a better position than you are to know just how he will be rendering the performance, and, thus, whether the performance would infringe a grand right, or some other right, such as the laws of defamation or invasion of privacy. All you can provide for the producer is the license to do what you have the right to stop him from doing, such as synchronizing the song in an audiovisual work. By the same token, you should never warrant to a producer that you are giving him all the rights he needs to render the performance, as you can only license that over which you have the right to grant. If the producer renders a grand performance, he is going beyond the license you provide and is engaging in an area for which you have no responsibility.

The lesson for the person who needs to clear licenses is that it is your responsibility to clear all permissions that you require to proceed. Failure to do so will expose you to a claim for copyright infringement or some other violation of the law. Sometimes problems can be avoided by telling the music publisher precisely how you intend to use the music, and the publisher might be able to advise you that you require a license from another party to effect your use. But the copyright owner cannot guarantee that the license granted covers all the permissions that you'll require for your use, and it is not his responsibility to do so. Of course, sometimes you just can't predict a problem, in the same way that the publisher and producers didn't know that CBS acquired exclusive rights to broadcast the motion picture *The Wizard of Oz.*

In the case of *The Gary Moore Show*, the network executives probably over-reacted. The music and scarecrow costumes were going to be performed in the television studio without any scenery or background that could be associated with the film. At best, the use of the song promoted the later broadcast of the full-length motion picture on CBS. At worst, they would be in competition with themselves. If, however, it had been another network that acquired the exclusive rights, the situation could have gotten a lot worse for the producer.

Finally, what should be noted by both licensors and licensees, is that while the performance of the song in scarecrow costumes would have been a *non-dramatic performance* (because the routine, as rendered on the *The Gary Moore Show*, would not have carried forward a definite plot and its accompanying action), it was still a performance that was not covered by the ASCAP television license. It is a *grand performance* of a song from a grand musical work, the motion picture, *The Wizard of Oz.* If the reader has followed this chapter through this point, it should have started to become apparent that a *dramatic performance* is not the same as a *grand performance*. Attempts at simplifying the complex subject of grand rights have led to a misuse of certain important terms. For example, the terms *small performing rights* and *grand performing rights* have been, but should not be, equated with the terms *non-dramatic performing rights* and *dramatic performing rights*, respectively. We will revisit this point later in the chapter.

H. A dramatic *rendition of a musical composition, that was originally part of an opera, operetta, musical comedy, play or like production, in a* television program, motion picture, videogram or like work

In a popular television series about the school life of a group of high school students, one episode called for the students to perform portions of the play, *The Music Man.* The producers soon learned that television synchronization licenses to record the songs from the musical in the television program and the ASCAP licenses of the television stations to perform the songs were not going to be sufficient to clear the use, as the rendition of portions of the musical play constituted a grand performance of the musical, which required the additional permission of the owners of the musical play. Permission from the owners of the *The Music Man* was required, not because the performance was dramatic, but because a use was being made of a substantial part of the musical, and permission was required to perform portions of the musical.

Many years ago, a special television program called *The Helen Morgan Story* was broadcast on the program *Playhouse '90* over the CBS Television network. Helen Morgan was a popular entertainer in the 1920's and 1930's who became known for her singing of melancholy ballads and her gimmick of sitting on top of a piano while singing. Her most memorable role included starring in the Broadway musical, *Show Boat* (1928). Over the years, she became identified with several of the songs from the musical *Showboat*, especially the song *Bill*, which became her theme song. *The Helen Morgan Story* was the story of the entertainer's life, as told by Helen Morgan, sitting on a piano with her legs crossed. The only song featured in the program was her theme song, *Bill*.

What made the performance so unusual was that the song was the only song used in the program and was played throughout the program at various tempos, depending upon the period of the entertainer's life being presented. For example, while Morgan was describing a tranquil period of her life, the song was performed *adagio*; while she was describing a tempestuous period of her life, the song was performed *allegro*. The owners of the song sued CBS, claiming that the use was dramatic, and therefore outside the scope of the ASCAP performance license. The case was settled, but the issue as to whether CBS actually required an additional license is still an interesting one.

If the song *Bill* was performed with dialogue, costumes, scenery or other visual representations from the musical *Showboat*, then the performance would clearly have been a grand performance of the musical, *Showboat* (or a substantial part of it), which would have required permission from the owners of the show. This, however, was clearly not the case in *The Helen Morgan Story* television program. At most, she may have sung the song at a point in the show where she was describing the events surrounding her Broadway experiences, but this would not be a performance of the musical play *Showboat*, without some material from the show, such as dialogue, costume, or scenery, in addition to the rendition of the lyrics of the song.

If the song was "interwoven and carrying forward a definite plot and its accompanying action," the performance would be *dramatic*, requiring a license from the copyright owner of the song, because the ASCAP license for non-dramatic performance would not cover the use. Sometimes the answer to the question of whether a performance carries foward a definite plot is, "I know it when I see it," and the answer in this case may require an actual viewing of the program. If the lyrics of the song *Bill* somehow carried forward the story, then it is more likely that the use was dramatic. For example, if there were an actual person named Bill who played a part in Helen Morgan's life, and the song *Bill* carried forward some action concerning Helen Morgan and the real-life person named Bill, then it could be said the song carried forward the story. If the use of the music was merely instrumental, or if the lyrics of the song *Bill* had no relation to any events in her life, then it is more likely that the song did not carry forward the story.

Even assuming the song did "carry forward" Helen Morgan's telling of the story of her life, the question remains, does a life story have a *plot,* as that term is used in the ASCAP license, or otherwise used in determining whether a performance is dramatic? There is a public policy, grounded in the First Amendment to the U.S. Constitution, favoring the free dissemination of ideas, which, among other things, affords creators of biographical and other historical works a higher degree of flexibility in incorporating into their works the works of others than is afforded creators of purely fictional works. Nevertheless, biographies when presented in television programs and motion pictures, other than pure documentary programs, tend to contain a substantial amount of fictional material. Called *docu-dramas,*[8] these programs, while purporting to be biographies, often contain more fiction than fact, and are created more for their entertainment value than for their value as a contribution to historical knowledge.

In light of the foregoing considerations, it is believed that a performance of a song that carries forward the "plot" and accompanying action

---

[8] See, generally, Lionel S. Sobel, *The Trials and Tribulations of Producing Docu-Dramas*, 5/3 Entertainment Law Reporter 3 (August, 1983).

in a docu-drama would more likely constitute a dramatic use; a performance of a song that carries forward a life story in a pure documentary would be less likely to constitute dramatic use. The question whether *The Helen Morgan Story* would be considered more of the nature of a docu-drama or of the nature of a documentary, and whether the use of the song *Bill* in the *The Helen Morgan Story* was a dramatic or non-dramatic performance, we will leave for historians and legal scholars to ponder.

RECENT COURT CASES

1. Frank Music Corp. v. MGM Grand Hotel

Probably the first court to recognize, at least implicitly, the distinction between a *dramatic performance* of individual songs and the exercise of a grand right, or *grand performance* of a play or musical, is the Ninth Circuit Court of Appeals in a case involving a harem of a different sort.[9]

In 1974, the MGM Grand Hotel in Las Vegas, Nevada, produced a musical revue called, *Hallelujah Hollywood* in the hotel's lavish Ziegfeld Theatre. The show featured ten acts of singing, dancing, and variety performances. Of the ten acts, four were labeled as "tributes" to MGM motion pictures of the past and one was a tribute to the *Ziegfeld Follies*. The remaining acts were variety numbers, which included performances by a live tiger, a juggler, and the magicians, Siegfried and Roy. Act IV of *Hallelujah Hollywood* was entitled *Kismet*, which became the subject of the lawsuit.

The original version of *Kismet* was a dramatic play, written by Edward Knoblock in 1911, which entered the public domain in 1967. In 1952, Edwin Lester acquired the right to produce a musical stage production of the dramatic play *Kismet*. In 1953, Lester hired Luther David and Charles Lederer to write the libretto and Robert Wright and George Forrest to write the music and lyrics for the dramatico-musical adaptation. In 1953, Lederer and Davis copyrighted their dramatico-musical play *Kismet*, and Wright and Forrest assigned to Frank Music Corpora-

---

[9] *Frank Music Corp. v. Metro-Goldwyn-Mayer, Inc.*, 772 F.2d 505 (9th Cir. 1985).

tion the right to copyright all portions of the musical score written for the musical. Frank Music subsequently obtained copyrights for the entire score and for each of the songs in the score. In 1954, Lederer, Wright and Forrest entered into a license agreement with MGM, Inc. granting it the rights to produce a musical motion picture based on their dramatico-musical play. MGM released its motion picture version of *Kismet*, starring Howard Keel and Ann Blyth, in 1955.

The story presented in the MGM film and in the dramatico-musical play is essentially the same as that told in Knoblock's dramatic play. *Kismet* is the tale of a day in the life of a poetic begger named Hajj and his daugher, Marsinah. The story is set in ancient Baghdad, with major scenes in the streets of Baghdad, the Wazir's palace, an enchanted garden, and the Wazir's harem.

Act IV of *Hallelujah Hollywood* presented at the MGM Grand Hotel, entitled *Kismet*, was billed as a tribute to the MGM movie of that name. Comprised of four scenes, the *Kismet* act was eleven and one-half minutes in length. It was set in ancient Baghdad, as was the dramatico-musical play, and the characters were called by the same or similar names as those used in the musical play. Five songs were taken in whole or in part from the musical. No dialogue was spoken during the act, and, in all, it contained 6 minutes of music taken directly from the musical play, and the songs were performed by singers identified as characters from the musical play, dressed in costumes designed to recreate *Kismet*. The performance made use of locale, settings, scenery, props, and dance style music of the type used in the musical play, *Kismet*.

Within a few months after the premier of *Hallelujah Hollywood*, the MGM Grand was informed that it was infringing the *Kismet* musical play. MGM Grand responded that it believed its use of the music from the musical play was covered by its performance license from ASCAP.

The case went to court and the lower court held that the *Kismet* performances at the MGM Grand constituted copyright infringements, because the performance was outside the scope of the ASCAP license. The court addressed two clauses of the ASCAP license: (i) the clause that limits the performances by MGM Grand to "non-dramatic" renditions, and (ii) the clause that excludes from the license "dramatico-musical works, or songs [accompanied by] visual representations of the work from which the music is taken." The lower court ruled that, while the performances were non-dramatic, they were outside the scope of the

latter clause of the ASCAP license, because they contained visual representations from the musical play. (The court of appeals agreed with the
result reached by the lower court, but stated that there was no need to
consider whether Act IV was dramatic or non-dramatic, because the
clause excluding the performance of dramatico-musical work was sufficiently determinative).

Both the lower court and the court of appeals seemed to recognize
that the issue in the case was not whether the performance of the
individual songs was dramatic in nature, but whether the hotel had a
license to present a portion of the dramatico-musical play. In other
words, whether the play producer's *grand right* in the play was
infringed. In this case, the court ruled that the grand right was infringed,
even though the performance may have been nondramatic! So much
for the idea that grand performances are the equivalent of dramatic
performances.

2. Gershwin v. The Whole Thing Co.

A more complex example of a stage performance of music that was
claimed to be unauthorized was the musical revue entitled, *Let's Call the
Whole Thing Gershwin.*[10]

The revue, created in 1978, consisted of theatrical performances of
approximately forty songs, written entirely or largely by George and Ira
Gershwin, and performed by a cast of eight actors and actresses wearing
a variety of costumes and rendering some original dance routines and
dance skits. The revue used some scenery such as photographs of the
Gershwins and a limited amount of dialogue describing the Gershwins,
their music, and the circumstances in which their works were created.
The revue included an identifiable character, Ira Gershwin, who appears
as a man struggling to write lyrics for brother George's music.

After deciding to produce the revue, the producer sought to obtain
licenses from certain music publishers. Having obtained "living stage"
licenses from the music publishers, the producer then proceeded on the
assumption that a license from Mr. Gershwin was not required. When
Mr. Gershwin's attorneys became aware of the fact that the producer was

---

[10] *Gershwin v. The Whole Thing Co.*, 208 U.S.P.Q. (C.D. Cal., 1980).

to stage the revue, they informed the producer that a license was required from Mr. Gershwin because, they asserted, the music publishers did not possess sufficient rights of copyright for the dramatic stage production of the revue and because Mr. Gershwin's "right of publicity" would be invaded by the contemplated production. The producer asserted that its living stage licenses from the music publishers were sufficient and a license from Mr. Gershwin was not required.

After some negotiation, the parties entered into a settlement agreement which enabled the producer to stage the revue without a lawsuit. Nevertheless, after the production opened, a lawsuit ensued over the extent of the rights granted under that agreement. The court granted a preliminary injunction halting the performance of the play beyond a certain date and ordered that the producer not engage in any further agreements for future presentations of the play beyond that date nor present the revue at any location other than at the theatre at which the revue was then being presented.

The legal question explored here is whether, in addition to the license the producer had received from the music publishing companies, a license from the Gershwins was required to produce the revue. Though that question was not specifically resolved by the court, the court's opinion is notable, because it is one of the few cases that attempts to define the term, *grand rights*.

What makes the analysis of this case so complex is the fact that, though some of the songs performed in the revue were originally part of a Gershwin musical or opera, such as *Lady be Good*, and *Porgy and Bess*, others were not, such as the instrumental work, *Concerto in F*.

With respect to the compositions that were not originally part of a Gershwin musical play, the producer received all the licenses it needed under a living stage license that it received from the music publishers to use these songs in a musical revue on stage. Any non-dramatic renditions of the songs were covered by the theatre's performance licenses from ASCAP and BMI; any dramatic renditions (and any non-dramatic renditions, to the extent the theatre was not licensed by the appropriate performance rights societies) were covered by the living stage licenses obtained from the music publishers.

With respect to the compositions that were originally part of a Gershwin musical, the producer only needed a license to the extent the performance would constitute an infringement of the musical or opera in which the songs originally appeared—that is, whether they are performed "in a manner which recreates the performance of such composition with substantially such distinctive scenery or costume *as was used in the presentation of* such opera, operetta, musical comedy, play or like production." To the extent the performances were not used in such manner, the producer could rely on the living stage license that it received from the music publishers.

It would not matter if the performers in the revue were wearing *any* kind of costumes or if the scenery used was *any* kind of scenery. The producer could avoid infringing the *grand right* in the grand operas and grand musical plays as long as the costumes were not from the operas and musicals and the scenery and other visual presentations from the Gershwin musicals and operas. In other words, the libretto, scenery and costumes of the original Gershwin shows form the basis of the *grand rights* the Gershwins have in those shows, not any new plot or unrelated scenery or costumes that may have been created for the revue.

Having seen the musical revue in question, we do not believe that any of the performances in *Let's Call the Whole Thing Gershwin* amounted to a performance that was substantially similar to any of the Gershwin musicals, or any substantial portion of them, in which certain songs in the revue were originally a part. The revue was a series of musical compositions interwoven into an original story that had no resemblance to any of the original musical plays in which the songs originally appeared. The only resemblance was in the fact that the performances in the revue, like some of the songs in the original plays, were rendered live on stage, but the producer already obtained the right to make such living stage performances of the music.

Accordingly, no grand right was invaded, and if the producer would have prevailed on the theory that the libretto was a constitutionally protected biographical work, then, assuming there was nothing in the agreement between the music publishers and the Gershwins reserving to the Gershwins living stage rights to their compositions, the living stage licenses the producer received from the music publishers would have been sufficient to permit performances of the revue and no further rights from the Gershwins were necessary.

We said the case was interesting for the definition it offered for the term *grand rights*:

There are two basic tests to determine whether grand rights are required. Grand Rights are required if (1) a song is used to tell a story .
. . or (2) a song is performed with dialogue, scenery or costumes.

The errors in this over-simplified statement of the definition of
grand rights should be obvious at this point, and it is hoped that courts
would pass over it in favor of a more precise analysis, such as that
rendered in the MGM Grand case discussed previously.

GRAND RIGHT IN A PERSON'S LIFE STORY?

It may be recalled that one of the grounds that Ira Gershwin, by his
attorneys, asserted to prevent the further performances of *Let's Call the
Whole Thing Gershwin* is that the play infringed the right of publicity of
George and Ira Gershwin. The *right of publicity* is the exclusive right a
person has to exploit his or her name, likeness or photograph for commercial or advertising purposes.

A substantial body of law has evolved over the scope of one's right
of publicity, including whether such a right survives a person's death and
inures to the benefit of his estate. Over the past 50 years, the exclusive
right of a person to commercially exploit his name and likeness has
evolved through a number of court decisions, involving a number of well
known celebrities, including Groucho Marx, Elvis Presley, and Nancy
Sinatra. Initially, the courts recognized this commercial right as part of
a person's *right to privacy*; later they began to separately identify a
person's *right of publicity* and some states have since enacted legislation
specifically governing the scope and duration of this right.[11]

A complete discussion of the right of publicity is beyond the scope
of this book. Suffice it to say, however, that if you are seeking to clear
permission to use a musical composition and you also desire to use the
name, likeness or photograph of the songwriter or artist who wrote or
recorded the work, you may be required to obtain a separate clearance
for that use directly from the songwriter or artist.

The Gershwin case presented some interesting issues that have not
been completely decided by the courts. One intriguing issue is the extent

---

[11] See, generally, J.T. McCarthy, *The Rights of Publicity and Privacy* (1987).

to which the right of publicity allows a person to control the use of biographical information about himself. Gershwin claimed that the use of the pictorial and biographical material about him, including the use of the name "Gershwin" in the title of the revue, *Let's Call the Whole Thing Gershwin*, required his permission. The use of such materials, his attorneys asserted, infringed upon Gershwin's right of publicity. In effect, Gershwin was seeking to establish a form of *grand right* in his life story.

As previously noted, the courts have recognized a strong public policy interest in the free dissemination of ideas and information, a policy which finds its basis in the guarantee of free speech in the First Amendment of the U.S. Constitution. For this reason, public figures may not assert a *right of publicity* to prevent the publication of "unauthorized" biographies. It is possible, therefore, that the libretto of *Let's Call the Whole Thing Gershwin* would be deemed primarily biographical in nature and therefore, Gershwin's right of publicity would not have been an effective bar to allowing this information to be used as part of performances of the revue.

The line, however, between a person's name and likeness in a biographical work, the use of which does not require a license, and a person's name and likeness for commercial merchandising purposes, which does require a license, is not always an easy one to draw. Television or motion picture *docu-dramas*, which are based on biographical material, have been challenged as merchandising uses which require permission, on the basis that the fictional "pillow talk" dramatized in these productions does not even pretend to be historical fact, and is created not for historical or general interest, but merely for their entertainment value as fiction.

The issues relating to the right of publicity are complex, and your use of materials concerning celebrities or other public figures may also require a consideration of the law of libel and right of privacy. Accordingly, when treading this ground, you should seek counsel of an attorney experienced in these areas.

BROADCAST OF AN ENTIRE ALBUM

1. Operas

The *Jesus Christ Superstar* case discussed above—involving the stage performance of 20 of the 23 musical compositions from the opera, all but one rendered in identical sequence as in the original opera—raises another interesting question: Does a radio broadcast of an entire cast album of an opera involve more than the mere non-dramatic performance of the musical compositions in the opera? In other words, would an unauthorized broadcast of an entire cast album of an opera constitute an infringement of the opera? The outcome of the *Jesus Christ Superstar* case suggests that the answer is yes.[12] The radio broadcast of an entire cast album of a grand opera would constitute a *grand performance* of the opera, requiring the permission of the owner of the *grand rights* in the opera. To be a grand performance, however, the broadcast would have to be of a substantial number of the songs in the opera in substantially the sequence that they appear in the opera.

2. Musical Plays

A different result may be reached if the broadcast were of an album of a musical play, rather than of an opera. It may be recalled that an *opera* is a play with virtually the entire text of its book, or libretto, set to music or sung, with no or few spoken words. By contrast, a *musical play* is a play with music and lyrics with the text of the book rendered in spoken form. Cast albums of musical plays rarely include all of the spoken text of the book. Accordingly, the broadcast of a cast album of a musical play is less likely to be deemed a grand performance of the musical play than the broadcast of a recording of an opera, because two important parts of the work —the visual presentation and the book—are absent from the performance. A recording of an opera, broadcast in its entirety, includes every element of the opera, except the visual presentation.

Nevertheless, while the broadcast of the cast album of a musical play will not ususally constitute an infringement of the musical play, it may be an infringement of another copyright, which is discussed in the following section.

---

[12] In fact, the court specifically suggested an affirmative answer to this question, but partly on the wrong basis: "Indeed, radio performances of operas are considered dramatic, because the story is told by the music and lyrics." 457 F.2d at 55 (1972).

3. Other Albums

Owners of cast album recordings of musical plays, and, for that matter, owners of all other kinds of record albums—including pop, jazz, and rock recordings—may have an independent ground upon which to enforce an exclusive right to broadcast entire record albums. It has long been the position of the recording industry that the unauthorized broadcast of an entire record album, or substantially all of a record album, with no or few commercial interruptions, constitutes an infringement of copyright. The copyright that provides the basis of such infringement is the copyright in the *compilation* of the songs included on the album.

Under the copyright law, a *compilation* is "a work formed by the collection and assembling of preexisting materials or of data that are selected, coordinated, or arranged in such a way that the resulting work as a whole constitutes an original work of authorship."[13] If the selection and sequential ordering of the recordings on a record album can be considered an original work of authorship, then the unauthorized public performance of the compilation, as a work separate and apart from the recordings that comprise the compilation, would constitute copyright infringement. Some record companies have filed copyight registrations to claim *compilation copyrights* in their selection and arrangement of recordings on the record albums they publish.

Though a compilation copyright in a record album, as a whole, is not a *grand right*, it is akin to a grand right, and a performance of an entire record album, or substantially all of a record album, and is akin to a grand performance of a grand opera or grand musical play.

DRAMATIC ADAPTATION RIGHTS

1. Legal Background

The copyright law grants to the owner of copyright certain exclusive rights in a musical composition, among which, we have noted, are the exclusive right to make copies of the song (called the *reproduction right*), the exclusive right to perform the song (the *performance right*),

---

[13] 17 U.S.C. Sec. 101.

and the exclusive right to prepare derivative works of the song (often referred to as the *adaptation right*).

A copyright owner of a song may exercise his reproduction right by granting a license to allow another to reproduce the song in printed form (by a "print license") or on a record album (by a "mechanical license"). The copyright owner may exercise his performance right by allowing the rendition of the song in a nightclub or by broadcast on live television or radio. Both the reproduction right and the performance right involve the use of the musical composition verbatim —that is, the exercise of these rights involves permission to use the song word-for-word, note-for-note. By contrast, the *adaptation right* involves preparation of a different version of the song or the preparation of another work that is in some way derived from the song. A work that is derived from another work is called a *derivative work*. A copyright owner's exclusive right to prepare adaptations, or derivative works, is a most important right, because it defines the scope of the copyright protection. The copyright law contains a fairly precise definition of the term derivative work:

> A 'derivative work' is a work based upon one or more preexisting works, such as a translation, musical arrangement, dramatization, fictionalization, motion picture version, sound recording, art reproduction, abridgment, condensation, or any other form in which a work may be recast, transformed, or adapted.

Thus, when the music copyright owner commissions the translation of the lyrics of a song into a foreign language or the arrangement of the music for certain instruments, such as a big band arrangement, he is exercising his adaptation right—permitting the preparation of an adaptation or derivative work of the song.

2. Popular Songs

A music copyright owner is also exercising his adaptation right when he allows another to make a dramatization, or dramatic adaptation, of the lyrics of a song. For example, the screenplay and motion picture entitled, *Ode to Billie Joe* was a dramatic adaptation of the song of the same title written and performed by country singer, Bobbie Gentry. Similarly, the 1970's television series *Harper Valley, P.T.A.* was a dramatic adaptation of the lyrics of the song of the same name, written by Tom Hall and originally recorded by country singer Jeannie C. Riley.

The script of a motion picture that is derived from the lyrics of a song would be a "derivative" work of the song. The exclusive right *to prepare derivative works* is a right under copyright completely distinct from the right *to perform a work publicly*. While the singing of the song *Ode to Billie Joe* during the motion picture of that title is a *performance* and its licensing an exercise of the performance right in the song, the creation of the motion picture itself, which is *a dramatic adaptation* of the song, is an exercise of the adaptation right, not the performance right, in the song.

Therefore, neither the creation of the motion picture *Ode to Billie Joe* nor the script from which it is derived is a "performance" of the song. The performance of the movie involves a performance of the song only to the extent the song, as recorded in the soundtrack, is rendered during the performance of the movie. Thus, if one were to make a movie based upon the lyrics of a song—a dramatization or motion picture version of the song—without permission from the copyright owner of the song, the movie maker would be liable not for an unauthorized performance, but for violating the copyright owner's right to make derivative works of the song, that is, the copyright owner's dramatic adaptation right. The right of reproduction in the song would be violated if, and only if, a recording of the song were made part of the motion picture soundtrack without a license; the performance right in the song would be violated only if the soundtrack were performed in theatres without a license. The dramatization of the lyrics involves a separate exclusive right under the copyright —the adaptation right.

3. Show Tunes

Suppose a producer wished to prepare a short movie dramatization of the song *Tea for Two*, a song that was originally part of the Broadway musical, *No, No Nanette*. This movie might be a short love story about a young couple having tea together while discussing their desire to have a boy for her and a girl for him. As long as the movie dramatization of the lyrics did not use any elements of the show, *No, No Nanette*—such as dialogue, costumes, scenery or other visual representations from the musical—the grand rights in the musical would not be infringed. Accordingly, while the producer of the movie would require permission of the copyright owner of the song (i.e., the music publisher) to make the dramatic adaptation, no permission from the owners of the show *No No Nanette* would be required for this use. Of course, if the song *Tea for Two* were to be performed in the movie, either on screen or as background music, or if any of the lyrics were to be quoted as part of the dialogue in the action, then a sychronization license would also be required.

4. Music Videos

It may be interesting to note that some "new music" videos seen on television networks such as MTV may represent examples of dramatic adaptations. Though in many of these video programs, the featured musicians are seen performing the song on a stage or in the streets, some videos depict the performing artists visually portraying or acting out the story of the lyrics. If the visual scenario of the video is a direct dramatization of the song's lyrics, it would be considered a dramatic adaptation, or derivative work, of the song, the making of which, as we have said, requires separate permission from the song's copyright owner. If the artists are acting out a story, but the story is not the story told by the lyrics, the video would not be considered a derivative work, or dramatic adaptation of the song; however, if the song is otherwise interwoven into and carries forward some definite plot, the song is being performed dramatically, and the rendition of a dramatic performance also requires permission from the song's copyright owner.

5. Separate Adaptation License Required

Whether or not a song was originally published as part of a dramatico-musical work, the performance licenses issued by performance rights societies would not cover the adaptation of the song *Ode to Billie Joe* or the song *Tea For Two* into a motion picture, or the song *Harper Valley P.T.A.* into a television series—not by virtue of the dramatic nature of the use, but by virtue of the fact that the uses are not performances. Since performance rights societies only license performances, and not the preparation of derivative works, performance licenses would not authorize the use.

Further, standard synchronization licenses permitting the producer to make reproductions of a recording of the song in timed-relation with audiovisual programs, such as motion pictures, television shows, and music videos, would not include permission to create a dramatic adaptation of the lyrics of the song. In fact, some carefully drafted synchronization licenses specifically exclude such uses by reference.

Accordingly, wherever a license to dramatize a lyric is desired, a separate license under the copyright owner's exclusive adaptation right will be required. Producers should not think they are acquiring such a right by merely obtaining a synchronization license or a performance license.

6. Dramatic Adaptation Right is not a Grand Right

Dramatic adaptations of song lyrics have often been mistakenly associated with the concept of the grand right. As we have stated, the grand right is a performance right—a right in grand operas and musical plays, not in individual songs. Furthermore, the grand right is a right of *performance*. A *dramatic adaptation* is a derivative work of the lyrics of a song, whether or not the song was originally part of a musical play. A derivative work is a *work*— a new version of a song—not a *performance* of the song. Accordingly, the script and motion picture *Ode to Billie Joe*, for example, does *not* involve the exercise of a *grand right*. It is a new work, not a performance (and not a performance of a part of a grand opera or musical play).

DETERMINING WHO HAS THE RIGHT TO LICENSE THESE USES

The party who has the right to license a particular use of music depends upon (1) the proper identification of the rights on the basis of which licenses can be cleared for the use, and (2) the provisions of the contracts governing those rights among those who have an interest (i.e., copyright or contractual) in the music.

Despite the widespread confusion on the subject, it is important to correctly draw a distinction among small dramatic performances, small non-dramatic performances, grand performances, and dramatic adaptations. A proper distinction among these rights is often critical to determining what rights need to be cleared in order to render a dramatic or theatrical performance and who—among the performance rights societies, the songwriters, the playwrights, the music publishers, and the theatrical producers—has the right to license such uses.

1. Non-dramatic Performances

Under their respective agreements with performance rights societies, writers and publishers grant to the performance rights societies a license to sublicense the rendition of non-dramatic performances.

If a song is being performed on a radio station, television station, or in a nightclub, concert hall, or other establishment licensed by the performance rights society, and the use is within the scope of the performance license, then no further license is required to render the performance. A use is outside of the performance license if the performance is dramatic, if the performance is a grand performance of a dramatico-musical work, or if the performance infringes upon any number of other rights of individuals, such as, for example, the right of publicity, the right of privacy, or the right not to be defamed.

The performance rights society has no right to grant licenses for uses that are outside the scope of their standard performance licenses and, accordingly, clearance to make any other use requires permission of some other person or organization who owns the right involved.

2. Dramatic Performances

A *dramatic performance* of an individual composition is a rendition of a song that is woven into and carries forward a definite plot and its accompanying action, regardless of whether the song was originally part of a dramatico-musical work.

Under most standard music publishing agreements, the songwriter grants to the music publisher the undivided copyright in the song. The grant includes a grant of all exclusive rights, including the exclusive right to grant dramatic performance licenses. The only licenses that the songwriter is authorized to grant are those that are specifically reserved to the songwriter in the music publishing contract. The exclusive right to license dramatic performances is not typically among the rights reserved to the writer. The only right typically reserved to the writer is the right to receive the writer's share of performance royalties directly from the writer's performance rights society (e.g., ASCAP or BMI), a right which the writer receives from his performance rights society when he becomes a member. Since the rights the writer retains are limited to the right to grant licenses for non-dramatic performances, the rights to grant licenses to dramatic performances are vested in the music publisher under the broad grant of rights typically made in standard songwriter contracts. Consequently, with respect to most songs that were not originally part of musical plays or other dramatico-musical works, it is the music publisher who is exclusively entitled to grant permission for dramatic performances of the song.

Some songwriter contracts, however, require that the publisher obtain the writer's consent before granting dramatic performance licenses. Such a requirement appears in the standard form contract recommended by the Songwriter's Guild (formerly AGAC). The Songwriter's Guild agreement does not empower the writer to grant dramatic performance licenses; only the publisher has the power to grant such licenses, but the issuance of such licenses requires the consent of the songwriter.

Unless the agreement between the writer and his publisher specifically reserves to the writer the right to license dramatic performances of the composition, or reserves for the writer a right of approval over such dramatic uses, the publisher has the sole right, as between the parties, to license such rights.

3. Dramatic Adaptations

As stated above, songwriters typically grant their undivided interest in the copyright in the song to their music publishers, reserving only the rights related to collecting the writer's share of performance fees for the rendition of non-dramatic performances, which the writer receives from his performance right society. All other rights reside with the music publisher, subject, of course, to the payment of royalties to the writer arising from revenues associated with the exercise of the rights assigned to the music publisher. Thus, the music publisher is typically vested with the exclusive right to license dramatizations, or dramatic adaptations, and other derivative works.

Unless the songwriter's contract provided otherwise, the music publisher would have the sole right as between the songwriter and the music publisher to license dramatic adaptations of the writer's lyrics in any manner and by any means. It will be recalled that a dramatization is a derivative work, not a type of performance. Even if a songwriter contract specifically reserves to the writer the right to license dramatic performances, or reserves to the songwriter the right of consent to the publisher's granting of dramatic performances, this has no affect on the publisher's exclusive right to prepare or license the preparation by others of derivative works, such as dramatizations of lyrics.

Some music publishing agreements provide that the publisher's right to license dramatizations is subject to the consent of the song-writer. Again, such a provision would not give the writer the right to grant dramatic performance licenses; the publisher has the sole power to grant such licenses, but the issuance of such licenses requires the consent of the songwriter.

4. Grand Performances

As we have said, the *grand right* is the exclusive right to license the reproduction, adaptation, performance or other use of a dramatico-musical work, or what was once known as a "grand opera" or "grand musical play." It is a *right in the play, not in the music*, although the play may include music. The *grand right* rests with the owner of the play, not in the owner of the individual compositions in the play.

Accordingly, if you intend to clear a license to render a *grand performance* of a musical play, or a substantial, recognizable portion of the play, then you require permission from the owner of the musical play. If you intend to clear a license to render a *dramatic performance* of an individual composition, which is a rendition of a song (regardless of whether the song was originally part of a dramatico-musical work) that is woven into and carries forward a definite plot and its accompanying action, then you will require permission from the copyright owner of the song, usually a music publisher.

LICENSING CONSIDERATIONS

1. Considerations in Granting and Clearing Dramatic Performance Licenses

A producer who desires to render a performance of music that is interwoven into and carries forward a definite plot and its accompanying action should take care to obtain the additional licenses necessary to effect the desired use. If the use was properly disclosed at the time the producer seeks a synchronization license, an alert music publisher will recognize that a dramatic performance license will also be required for the use.

Because of the infinite variety of ways a song may be dramatically rendered in another work, there are no special standards for determining just how a music copyright owner might arrive at a fee in exchange for permitting the performance. However, copyright owners might use the same considerations for approaching grants of dramatic performance licenses as the considerations they might use relating to the licensing of reproductions of their musical compositions in similar works. These considerations are discussed in Chapters 5 (Basic Considerations), 9 (Synchronization Licenses), 10 (Videogram Licenses), and 14 (Licenses for Computer Software, Multi-Media Programs, and New Media Products). By the same token, the producer might use the considerations for clearing licenses set forth in those same chapters.

The parties should analyze the use carefully to be sure the use does not fall within the scope of what might be considered a dramatic adaptation, some licensing considerations for which are discussed briefly below.

2. Considerations in Granting and Clearing Adaptation Licenses

When a music copyright owner is asked to consider granting a license allowing another to prepare a dramatic adaptation of a song's lyrics (e.g., a motion picture adaptation of the lyrics of *Ode to Billie Joe* or a television adaptation of the lyrics of *Harper Valley P.T.A.*), the copyright owner should immediately do the following: view the lyrics as a literary work.

The considerations for licensing an audiovisual adaptation of a song lyric should be viewed much the same way an author of a novel would consider the licensing of a motion picture or television adaptation of his work. There are many issues the music copyright owner should thought-fully consider, including the negotiation of payments for options that expire if the adaptation is not made within specified periods of time, the disposition of rights and revenues in the event that other adaptations or new versions are made subsequent to the release of the first (e.g, sequels, "pre-quels," remakes, spin-offs, and the like), profit participations, writers credit for the songwriters, and other terms that are customarily negotiated in literary rights contracts. Producers of motion pictures and television programs are generally quite familiar with the issues relating to literary rights acquisitions.

A further analysis of the issues that should be considered in connection with these deals is beyond the scope of this book. The music copyright owner should consider obtaining the special assistance of a literary agent or an attorney who specializes in representing authors who frequently license their literary works for dramatic adaptations.

3.   Considerations in Granting and Clearing Grand Performances

The considerations in granting and clearing the right to perform musical plays, operas, and other dramatico-musical works in their entirety are beyond the scope of this book. Nevertheless, a few important comments relating to the licensing of *portions of* dramatico-musical works is in order.

When play producers and their agents are asked to consider granting a license to use a small portion of their works, such as a few moments of a musical play in a television program or multi-media work, they might use the same considerations in approaching such grants as those concerning the licensing of reproductions of music compositions set forth in Chapters 5 (Basic Considerations), 9 (Synchronization Licenses), 10 (Videogram Licenses), and 14 (Licenses for Computer Software, Multi-Media Programs, and New Media Devices).

An owner of a musical plays who has granted to a music publisher the music publishing rights in and to the individual musical compositions in the play should keep in mind that his right to license reproductions and performances of the musical play is limited to the dramatico-musical play itself and does not extend to the individual songs themselves. Musical play owners, or their agents, may grant, for example, grand performances of the play. This may include a performance of one or more musical compositions from the play, but only to the extent the performance contains elements taken directly from the musical play (e.g., dialogue, pantomine, dance, stage action, costumes, scenery, or other visual representations). If the performance of the music does not contain any such element taken from the musical play, then the right of performance is not controlled by the owner of the musical play, even if the performance contains other dramatic or visual elements. Where the performance of the music does not contain dramatic elements from the musical play, then, unless there are provisions to the contrary in any agreement between the play owners and the music publisher, *the right of performance is controled by the owner of the music publishing rights.* In other words, the music publisher has the sole right to license non-dramatic performances through its performance rights society and dramatic performances directly, provided the performance does not contain any elements from the play that would render the performance a grand performance (the latter of which would require permission from the owner of the play).

SUMMARY

As noted in Chapter 2, words that refer to completely different concepts should not be confused or used indiscriminately. Greater precision in the use of terms of art will promote clarity of thought and avoid costly legal disputes. It is important to correctly draw distinctions among grand rights, dramatic rights, and dramatic adaption rights, so that all parties concerned can properly determine who has the right to license the proposed use.

It is not the music publisher's responsibility to guarantee that the person seeking to clear a license has all the rights he needs to effect the desired performance. It is the producer's responsibility to make sure he obtains a license to effect a grand performance, if that is what he will need. The producer is in a better position than the publisher to know just how the performance will be rendered, and, thus, whether the performance would infringe a grand right, or some other right, such as the laws of defamation or invasion of privacy. All the music publisher can do is provide the producer with the license to do what the publisher would otherwise have the right to stop the producer from doing, such as synchronizing the song in an audiovisual work. It is not the practice of music publishers to represent or warrant that they are providing all the rights the producer requires to render the performance. If the producer intends to render a grand performance, or a performance that infringes on another's right of publicity, invades someone's privacy, or defames someone's reputation, it is the producer's responsibility to properly clear all permissions that he requires to proceed with the performance.

Sometimes the producer can avoid problems by telling the music publisher precisely how he intends to use the music. The publisher might be able to provide additional information about other licenses the producer may require to effect the use, but the music publisher cannot be expected to guarantee that the license it grants covers all the permissions that are required for the use.

APPENDIX TO CHAPTER 16
THE GRAND RIGHTS CONTROVERSY

FORMS

FORM 16.1

License to Perform Music
in a Live Stage Production

January 1, 1995

RE: LIVING STAGE LICENSE

Dear [Producer]:

We hereby grant you, your associates, licensees and assigns the non-exclusive license to perform the musical composition:

in the living stage performance of your production:

by the original company, subject to the following terms and conditions:

1.   This license is non-exclusive and is deemed to have commenced upon the first preview performance.

2.   The territory covered by this license is:

3.   The extent of use shall be as follows:

4.   As consideration for this license, you agree to pay a fee of:

    a)   A royalty rate of _____ Percent (_____ %) of the gross receipts pro-rated amongst all copyrighted songs used, but never less than:

        On- Broadway (500 seats or more) Per Song, Per Week:

        Off-Broadway (499 seats or less): Per Song, Per Week:

    b)   Twenty-Five Dollars ($25.00) per week or Five-Dollars ($5.00) per performance, whichever is greater, for amateur and stock productions and "off-off" Broadway (200 seats or less) performances.

   c)   Production Use: (First class legitimate stage production). In the event any one song controlled by Big Music Publishing Corp. is used exclusively in a production number lasting over five (5) minutes in length, a fee of Two-Hundred-Fifty-Dollars ($250.00) per week will be required, separate and in addition to the fee covering the licensed use of the same song.

5.   This license shall automatically terminate in the event of your failure to pay us the weekly license fee as and when due, or in the event that the first preview performance does not take place within six (6) months from the date of this license.

6.   You agree that prior to the opening of each road-company of players performing in said production incorporating the musical composition licensed hereunder, you will notify us thereof and upon our receipt of such notice, such additional company of players shall be encompassed by this license and subject to its terms and conditions.

7.   No warranty or representation is made in connection with this license except that we warrant we have the right to issue this license subject to the terms and conditions hereof. In any event the total liability under such warranty is limited to the amounts paid by you hereunder.

8.   All programs shall indicate the names of the writers of the composition and shall clearly indicate the use is by permission of BIG MUSIC PUBLISHING CORP.

9.   For each New York City and Los Angeles performance of the Show, you shall cause two (2) adjoining "house" seats in the first ten (10) rows of the center section of the orchestra to be held available at the box office, for us and our designee to purchase, at the box office price. Such tickets shall be so held until 6:00 P.M.

of the day prior to the performance for evening performances and 12:00 noon of the day prior to the performance of matinees.

10.   In the event you license the production for presentation in motion pictures, radio, television, original cast album or any other audio/visual format, any such license shall not include a license to use the Composition in connection therewith, it being understood and agreed that we reserve all such rights. Nevertheless, we agree to negotiate in good faith with any licensee or potential licensee of the Show in respect of the appropriate synchronization, recording and/or performance licenses for the Composition. All Royalties, license fees or other compensation derived by us in connection with any such licenses which may be entered into by us and all royalties and other monies received from uses of the Composition in accordance with any such licenses, including mechanical royalties, sums derived from performing rights societies, etc. shall, as between us, be our sole property and you shall not be entitled to share in any such sums. Similarly, we shall not be entitled to share in any such licensing of your rights for presentation of the Show in such media.

11.   One year after the initial performance of your production, we shall have the continuing right to terminate the rights granted to you herein by giving written notice of our intention to terminate at least ninety (90) days prior to the termination date.

12.   You agree to maintain accurate books and records in connection with said production, which books and records shall, upon reasonable notice, be available for examination by our representatives during the term of this agreement and for a period of two (2) years therefrom.

13.   All rights not specifically granted herein are reserved to and by us.

BIG MUSIC PUBLISHING CORP.

AGREED AND ACCEPTED:

By _____

By _____

FORM 16.2

LICENSE TO PERFORM MUSIC IN A LIVE STAGE PERFORMANCE OF CHOREOGRAPHY

January 1, 1995

RE: CHOREOGRAPHY LICENSE

Gentlemen:

1. We hereby grant you a non-exclusive license to create chore-ography for use in conjunction with the following musical composi-tions and to use said choreography subject to the terms and conditions herein contained:

2. You agree to pay us a royalty of $5.00 per song for each performance containing a performance of any of said choreogra-phy during the term of this license.

3. The term of this license shall be one year from the date of first performance which shall be _____.

4. The territory of this license is limited to the United States and Canada.

5. You shall not have a license to print, copy, arrange or adapt any of said musical compositions or a license to record on phono-graph records, tape, film or any other form of record any of said musical compositions, without further permission.

6. You agree that on all programs and advertising matter and announcements a note will appear as follows under the title of each of said musical compositions:

   Music Used for Choreography by Permission of Big Music Publishing Corp.

7.   You shall account to us at the end of each month during the term hereof in which performances are given, giving us a detailed statement as to the place and the number of performances and pay to us at the same time the royalties provided for in this agreement.

8.   The rights granted herein are personal to you and may not be assigned or sub-licensed.

9.   All other rights in said musical compositions are reserved to us.

If the foregoing correctly sets forth our understanding, kindly sign and return a copy of this letter.

Yours sincerely,   Agreed and Accepted:

By: _____   By: _____

FORM 16.3

COLLABORATION AGREEMENT AMONG
WRITERS OF A MUSICAL PLAY

COLLABORATION AGREEMENT

AGREEMENT made this   day of January   , 1995,
between

(hereinafter "   ") and

                              (hereinafter "   ").

WHEREAS,   and   are
collaborating in the writing of a dramatic-musical play presently
entitled "   " (the "Play"), and

WHEREAS, the parties desire to define their rights and
responsibilities with respect to the Play.

NOW, THEREFORE, in consideration of the mutual covenants
herein contained, it is agreed as follows:

1.   The parties hereto shall undertake jointly to write the
Play, it being understood that   shall be
the bookwriter and lyricist and
shall be the composer.

2.   Each of the parties hereto shall undertake to copyright
the material written by him.

3.   (a)   Except as specifically set forth in Paragraph 3(b)
hereof, all receipts and income from the Play, or from any and all
rights therein, shall be divided as follows:

To   %

To   %

(b)   The authors' share of publishing income from the musical compositions used in the Play shall be divided as follows:

To   %

To   %.

The parties hereto agree that the music publisher for the musical compositions in the Play will be   . Notwithstanding anything contained herein to the contrary, the parties hereto agree that   will be entitled to receive 100% of the music publisher's share of music publishing income.

4.   It is the intention of the parties that the Play shall initially be presented as a first-class Broadway production in New York City.   shall use his best efforts to arrange for a first-class Broadway production of the Play.
        shall have the right to arrange for a first-class Broadway production of the Play; however,   agrees to obtain prior approval of any such efforts on his part, in order to avoid confusion or duplication of efforts. Each of the parties hereto agree to keep the other fully informed of the progress of all negotiations with respect thereto, but the final decision should vest with   .

5.   (a)   After the Play is completed, if deems it necessary to engage another writer or writers to make changes in the Play, he shall have the right so to do. Such new writer or writers shall only be chosen with   consent. In such event, the percentage compensation payable to the new writer or writers shall be borne by   . If there is a dispute with respect to the amount thereof, it shall be resolved in accordance with the provisions of Paragraph 13 hereof.

(b)   In the event of the disability or death of   , the parties hereto agree that any new writer or writers engaged to make changes in the Play will be entitled to receive percentage compensation payable from   share. The parties hereto agree that the difference between the new writer(s)' percentage compensation and   original royalty shall be payable to   heirs. In the event of the death or disability of   shall have the sole approval regarding any new writer or writers engaged to make changes in the Play.

6.   (a)   Except as specifically set forth in Schedule A, annexed hereto and made a part of this Agreement, represents and warrants that his contributions to the book and lyrics of the Play will be wholly original with him and that he is and will be the sole author thereof, and that no incident therein or part thereof is taken from, based upon or adapted from any other literary material, dramatic work, motion picture or other work of any kind, nature or description not in the public domain.
                              agrees to obtain all necessary clearances for any of the materials listed in Schedule A.

(b)   represents and warrants that his contributions to the music of the Play are and will be wholly original and he is and will be the sole composer thereof and no part thereof is or will be taken from, based upon or adapted from any other musical composition or other work of any kind, nature or description not in the public domain.

7.   The parties hereto agree that all rights in and to any music and lyrics which shall be deleted from the Play prior to the official opening performance of the first class Broadway production of the Play in New York City, shall revert to the respective parties hereto for their use free from any claim by the other; provided, however, that shall not have any right to use or authorize the use of any such lyrics which shall:

(i)   refer to any character in the Play by the same name as the character in the Play, if the name is sufficiently distinctive to identify with the Play, or

(ii) depict or portray an important situation which is contained in the Play; or

(iii) contain any of the distinctive dialogue or distinctive phrases from the Play; or

(iv) have as their title the name of any character in or to the title of the Play if such name is sufficiently distinctive to identify with the Play.

8.   All artistic approvals regarding the Play shall be exercised by the mutual decision of
and   ; provided, however, that alterations and omissions from, or additions to, the book and/or lyrics of the Play shall be subject to
                          approval; and alterations in and omissions from, or additions to, the book and/or lyrics of the Play shall be subject to   approval.

9.   Each of the parties hereto agree that they shall each incur their own expenses in connection with the Play and will not look to the other for payment or reimbursement of such expenses.

10.   hereby irrevocably appoints   as his sole and exclusive agent with respect to this Agreement and authorizes and directs

and/or any other third party to make all payments due or to become due to him hereunder to and in the name of said agent and to accept the receipt of said payments. In consideration of services rendered and to be rendered by said agent,   agrees that   is entitled to receive and maintain as his commission 10% of all such monies due and owing to him hereto, except with respect to amateur rights his commission shall be 20%. As of the date of this contract,   is not represented by an agent; however, he shall be free to select an agent to represent him and in such event all payments due shall be paid to such designated agent.

11. Authors' billing shall be substantially as follows:

Books and Lyrics   Music

    by   by

Both of the aforesaid names shall be in the same size, type, color, prominence and boldness, and whenever one name appears, the other shall appear. In the event a new writer or writers is brought in pursuant to Paragraph 5 (a) above, the parties agree to adjust the aforesaid billing accordingly. In the event a new writer or writers is brought in pursuant to Paragraph 5 (b) above,
shall adjust the billing accordingly.

12. The term of this agreement shall be coextensive with life of the copyright, and any renewals of said copyright in and to the book, music and lyrics of the Play.

13. In the event of any dispute arising out of or under this agreement or concerning the Play, or should any differences arise between the parties concerning any dealings between them or as to any of their rights hereunder (whether pursuant to Paragraph 3 and 11 hereof, or otherwise,) such dispute or differences shall be submitted to arbitration by a single arbitrator in New York under the Rules then obtaining of the American Arbitration Association, and the decision of such arbitrator shall be final and binding upon the parties hereto.

14. The terms and conditions of this agreement shall be binding upon and inure to the benefit of the executors, administrators, and assigns of the parties hereto. This agreement may not be modified orally, and shall be construed in accordance with the laws of the State of New York.

IN WITNESS WHEREOF, we have hereunto set our hands and seals the day and year first above written.

_____

_____

THE DIGITAL SAMPLING CONTROVERSY

SUMMARY

TECHNICAL BACKGROUND

RECENT RECORDING PRACTICES

LEGAL BACKGROUND

1. Multiple Copyright Infringement
   - A. Infringement of the Music
     - (a) Clearly Infringing Samples
     - (b) Clearly Non-Infringing Samples
   - B. Infringement of the Sound Recording
2. No Fair Use
3. Permission Required

CONSIDERATIONS IN GRANTING AND CLEARING LICENSES FOR DIGITAL SAMPLES

1. Music Licensing
   - A. Applicability of Compulsory License Provision
   - B. Alternatives Available to the Music Copyright Owner
     - (a) Do Nothing
     - (b) Refuse to License
     - (c) Grant a Mechanical License for a One-Time Flat Fee
     - (d) Grant a Mechanical License for a Royalty
     - (e) Grant a Mechanical License for a Royalty and Take a Share in a Percentage of the Performance Royalties of the New Composition
     - (f) Seek a Co-Ownership Interest in the New Composition
     - (g) Seek an Assignment of the Copyright in the New Composition
2. Sound Recording Licensing
   - A. Flat Fee Licenses
   - B. Royalties

3. Where Sampling Artist's Additional Musical Material
   is Owned By Another

CONCLUSION

FORMS

THE DIGITAL SAMPLING CONTROVERSY

A cold chill raced across the face of the recording industry when a Federal District Court in New York invoked the Seventh Commandment[1] in a lawsuit filed by British recording artist and songwriter Gilbert O'Sullivan against the rap music recording artist Biz Markie and his record company Cold Chillin' Records, after Markie included in his rap album entitled, *I Need a Haircut*, a *digital sample* of three words and their accompanying music taken from the popular recording of O'Sullivan's hit song *Alone Again (Naturally)*.[2] Markie's album might as well have been entitled *I Need a Lawyer*, as the court proceeded to enjoin all sales of the album and specifically referred the matter to the United States Attorney for consideration of prosecution under the provisions of federal law that make such infringements criminal acts subject to fines and imprisonment.[3]

This chapter will sketch the technical and legal background of digital sampling and will outline some of the practices currently emerging in connection with the licensing of and settlement of disputes about sampling activities.

TECHNICAL BACKGROUND

The term *digital sampling*, or *sampling*, refers to the recording of a sound, or a portion of a previously existing sound recording, with the aid of a device that can store the recording in binary form in the memory of

---

[1] *"Thou shalt not steal,"* Exodus, Chapter 20: Verse 15.

[2] *Grand Upright Music Limited v. Warner Bros. Records, Inc.*, No. 91 Civ. 9648 (S.D.N.Y. Dec. 16, 1991).

[3] 17 U.S.C. Sec. 506(a) and 18 U.S.C. Sec. 2319.

a computer. Sampling was made possible by the emergence of digital sound and computer technology developed in the 1960's and 1970's and has been made practical in the 1980's and 1990's by the widespread availability of inexpensive sampling-capable digital synthesizers and personal computers.

In scientific terms, music is a series of sound waves that emanate from a musical instrument (e.g., violin, vocal chords). These waves cause *analogous* vibrations on the human eardrum which are then transmitted to the human brain and, by act of Providence, perceived by the human mind. Sound waves may be recorded in tangible media, such as a phonograph record or tape recorder, by various technological means. These recordings may be made in *analog* form—analogously reflecting the vibrations of the analog sound waves, such as the grooves of a vinyl phonograph record—or in *digital* form, recorded on tape or on compact disk.

An analog performance, or a recording of an analog performance, may be converted to digital form with the aid of a device that converts the analog sound waves into a *digital code*. This is accomplished by breaking down the sound waves into small bits of information that are represented in the form of the binary numbering system (i.e., numbers comprised of solely 0's and 1's). This is the numbering system, or *machine language*, which forms the basis of modern computing.

Digital sampling can be viewed as the "high tech" equivalent of several non-digital or physical sampling techniques, such as scratching and needledropping. The term *scratching* refers to the process of making or recording the sounds produced by turning back and forth a vinyl record while the needle is still in the grooves. The term *needledropping*, also referred to as *looping*, refers to the process of taking a portion of a magnetic tape recording, joining together the beginning and the ending of the selected portion of the tape to form a continuous loop, and playing the loop so that the selected portion of the recording is played over and over. What distinguishes scratching and needledropping, on the one hand, from digital sampling, on the other, is what amounts to the proverbial Pandora's Box of sampling: the digital, binary or machine language of computers.

The significance of the digital format is this: any information that can be stored in a computer in digital form may be readily displayed, modified, copied, or transmitted to an extremely exacting degree of flexibility. Recording artists today have access to a sophisticated array of equipment capable of manipulating digitized sound recordings. For example, using a triggering instrument, such as an electronic keyboard or specially modified set of drums, guitar or reed instrument, an artist may replay sampled sounds at their original pitch (i.e., vibrations per second) or any other pitch desired. The artist can increase or decrease the speed at which the sampled sound is rendered, add new sounds, eliminate sounds, add echo effects, and, by reversing the sequence of the digital information, can even play the notes backwards. The waveform of a sampled sound may even be displayed on a computer screen and modifications may be made in the waveform to more precisely change the characteristics of the sound it produces.

Sounds may be sampled from live performances or recorded sources such as magnetic tapes and compact disks. An artist can sample his own voice, the sounds made by an individual instrument, or the crescendo of an entire orchestra. Because digital samples can be stored for future use, they may easily be distributed on standard computer floppy disks, allowing artists to create and distribute libraries of sampled sounds for reuse by others. The question to which we now turn is whether we can find Hope at the bottom of this Pandora's Box.

RECENT RECORDING PRACTICES

If sampling were performed solely by amateur musicians or computer hobbyists intending only to perform their sampled recordings privately in their own homes, there would be no controversy. Digital sampling has become, however, an attractive practice among young professional recording artists and their producers.

Sampled recordings merged with original material affords the professional recording artist or producer a way to more economically complete the task of producing pop records within tight recording budgets. For many artists, it is easier to select the "right" sound than to produce it from scratch, and using samples of existing recordings obviates the need to employ the talents of live musicians who could otherwise, albeit at greater expense, produce the desired performance or sound mix. Theoretically, a song can be composed entirely by the mere combination of sampled elements of existing recordings.

Though artists will use samples to save money and time, a more common and compelling reason why sampling is often employed stems from a desire to use the distinctive sound of a successful song or recording artist for the express purpose of giving sampling artist's original work a familiar element that listeners will quickly recognize.

LEGAL BACKGROUND

It has been the practice of many artists to engage in sampling under the assumption that sampling is not a copyright infringement, believing that the act of sampling is somehow a *fair use* of copyright. As discussed below, this assumption is invalid, as now confirmed by at least one court.[4]

1. Multiple Copyright Infringement

Unauthorized sampling may be an infringement of both (i) the sound recording from which the sample is taken and (ii) the song underlying the sampled recording. As noted in Chapter 1, the copyright in a sound recording is completely separate from the copyright in the underlying song featured in the sound recording, and the underlying song should not be overlooked when considering the use of a sound recording.

It has been suggested that the standards for infringement of copyright for sound recordings and musical works may be different.[5] The standards for determining infringement by sampling for each will be discussed in the following sections.

A. Infringement of the Music

In general, to prove copyright infringement, a person must show that he owns a copyright in the work and that the alleged infringer has copied it.[6] The question whether a valid copyright subsists in a song or a sound

---

[4] *Grand Upright Music,* supra.

[5] *See,* Broussard, *Current and Suggested Business Practices for the Licensing of Digital Samples,* 11 Loyola Entertainment Law Journal 479, 484 (1991). The authors acknowledge that the following section contains a number of ideas *sampled* from the foregoing thoughtful law review article.

[6] *See generally,* 3 *Nimmer On Copyright,* Sec. 13 (1991).

recording will rarely be at issue in a sampling case;[7] this leaves the issue of whether the work was copied: To prove that his work was *copied* a person must show that the alleged infringer had *access* to the work and that the work and the allegedly infringing work are *substantially similar.* Whether the alleged infringer had *access* to the work will also rarely be at issue in a sampling case, as access will either be admitted or easily proven. The extent of similarity which constitutes a *substantial* and hence infringing similarity has presented difficulties that have long challenged courts engaged in deciding these cases and lawyers engaged in advising their clients on the extent to which a particular use is legally permissible under the law.

Courts have approached the issue of substantial similarity in a variety of ways. Some courts have broken the question down into two parts: (1) whether the work was physically copied and (2) whether the copying was illicit or improper. In the case of sampling, whether the work was physically copied will either be admitted or an easy matter of proof. But proof of physical copying will not end the inquiry. A determination must still be made as to whether the copying was illicit or improper, or, in other words, whether the extent of similarity is sufficiently *substantial* to constitute infringement.

In making this determination, courts will inquire whether the portion copied was a *qualitatively substantial* portion of the work from which it was taken.[8] Courts will find infringement where the quality of the portion taken was "the whole meritorious part of the song,"[9] "so much of what is pleasing to the ears of lay listeners,"[10] "that portion of the [copied work] upon which its popular appeal, and hence, its commercial

---

[7] It is assumed that the musical work, or portion thereof, in question, is copyrightable subject matter. In other words, it is not (i) unoriginal, (ii) merely an idea, procedure, process, system, method of operation, concept, principle, or discovery, (iii) one of only a limited number of ways to express the idea underlying the expression, (iv) dictated by concerns for efficiency, (v) dictated by factors external to the work (such as factors dictated by the market or other works with which it was designed to interact), (vi) in the public domain, (vii) or not a work of authorship or copyrightable subject matter for other reasons.

[8] *M. Witmark & Sons v. Pastime Amusement Co.*, 298 F. 470 (E.D.S.C. 1924), *aff'd*, 2 F.2d 1020 (4th Cir. 1924).

[9] *Northern Music Corp. v. King Record Distrib. Co.*, 105 F.Supp. 393, 397 (S.D.N.Y. 1952).

[10] *Arnstein v. Porter*, 154 F.2d 464, 473, *aff'd on reh'g*, 158 F.2d 795 (2d Cir. 1946).

success, depends,"[11] or "the very part that makes [the copied work] popular and valuable."[12]

In determining what kinds of short portions of musical compositions are qualitatively substantial and hence protectable by copyright law, it will be useful to divide the universe of potential samples into those tending to be clearly infringing and those tending to be noninfringing, recognizing, however, that there will always be those cases in that "gray area" in which the parties may find themselves subject to the most precisely applicable standard ever developed by the courts, "I know it when I see it."[13]

(a) Clearly Infringing Samples

The chorus is often the heart of a song. Because of its brevity, repetitiveness, and frequent placement at the end of the song, the chorus tends to be the most memorable part of the song. In many cases, it would not be difficult for a court to find that the chorus is the very part that makes the song "popular and valuable." Accordingly, should a digital sample be made of a recognizable portion of a chorus, its unauthorized use is likely to be held infringing.

Other phrases of a musical composition that are distinctive and memorable are likely to be deemed qualitatively substantial parts of the song. This may include any phrase that is repeated often in a composition or placed at the beginning or ending of the song.

Even a very short phrase from a musical composition could be infringed by the use of a sample of that phrase if the sampled phrase is repeated through substantial portions of the sampler's new work. For example, if the digital sample contains six notes from a song which repeats those six notes fifteen times, and the digital sample of the six notes is repeated ten times in the sampler's new work, then the sampler has taken sixty notes, not six. In such a case, the sampler's work is more likely to be held substantially similar to the copied work and the un-

---

[11] *Robertson v. Batten, Barton, Durstine & Osborne, Inc.*, 146 F.Supp. 795, 798 (S.D. Cal. 1956).

[12] *Johns & Johns Printing Co. v. Paull-Pioneer Music Corp.*, 102 F.2d 282, 283 (8th Cir. 1939).

[13] *Jacobellis v. Ohio*, 378 U.S. 184 (1964).

authorized distribution of the sampler's new work would constitute copyright infringement.

Finally, the unauthorized use of any sample which is clearly identifiable as having been taken from another copyrighted composition or which an average person would immediately associate with another copyrighted composition is likely to be held an infringement.

(b) Clearly Non-Infringing Samples

Because there is only a limited number of ways in which a short number of musical notes may be expressed, copyright protection does not subsist in exceedingly short phrases of music. Clearly, a single musical note is not protectable by copyright. For the same reason, a two-note phrase is not protectable, and the same is probably true for a three-note phrase. The more notes that are appropriated, the more likely the appropriation will constitute an infringement, but where will the courts draw the line on the use of extremely short phrases?

The smallest appropriation from a musical composition ever held to be infringing was a phrase consisting of six notes.[14] In that case, the two songs before the court were "considerably different, both in theme and execution, except as to [the] phrase, *'I hear you calling me.'* " This phrase, and the music accompanying the words, in both compositions, were "practically identical" and the court held that the use of the phrase was a copyright infringement, because the phrase, despite its brevity, had what "causes audiences to listen, applaud, and buy copies in the corridor on the way out of the theatre."

Nevertheless, samplers should take note[15] of a more recent case in which a court determined that the use of a four-note phrase, together with two of the words accompanying those notes, would have been sufficient to constitute infringement. In *Elsmere Music, Inc. v. NBC,*[16] the song *I Love New York* became the basis of the parody composition, *I Love Sodom,* performed by the "not-ready-for-prime-time-players" on NBC's *Saturday Night Live* television program. In both compositions, the four-note phrase was continually repeated and was referred

---

[14] *Boosey v. Empire Music Co., Inc.,* 224 F.646 (S.D.N.Y. 1915).

[15] Pun intended.

[16] *Elsmere Music, Inc. v. NBC,* 482 F.Supp. 741 (S.D.N.Y. 1980), *aff'd* 623 F.2d (2d Cir. 1980).

to by the court as "the heart of the composition." The court concluded that the use did not constitute infringement, because it was part of a satire, permissible under the doctrine of *fair use* (discussed below). However, the court stated that the taking was of a "substantial nature," "easily recognizable," and "capable of rising to the level of a copyright infringement."

Accordingly, while the sampling of a single note or a phrase of two notes would appear not to be an infringement of a musical composition, the sampling of four notes may be the *sine qua non* of permissible song sampling, at least where the sample includes two of the words accompanying the music. Thus, a single shout rendered by a singer, two chords, or three notes from a nonessential bass line would probably not be qualitatively substantial parts of musical compositions, and therefore not protectable. Commercially insignificant phrases and commonly used phrases would also fall outside the scope of protection.

As noted below, however, sound recordings may be afforded significantly stronger protection than the underlying music, meaning that an infringement of a sound recording may still be found in a sample that appropriates elements that would not constitute an infringement of the underlying musical composition.

B. *Infringement of the Sound Recording*

No known court decisions are available at this time to help determine the extent to which samples may be made of copyrighted recordings without the permission of their owners. Certain provisions of the copyright law, however, do suggest that broader protection against unauthorized sampling may be available for owners of sound recordings than for the owners of musical compositions that may be embodied in those sound recordings.

For example, the Copyright Act states that, "The exclusive rights of the owner of copyright in a sound recording . . . do not extend to the making or duplication of another sound recording that consists *entirely* of an independent fixation of other sounds, even though such sounds imitate or simulate those in the copyrighted sound recording" (emphasis added).[17] By using the words "*entirely* of an independent fixation" in

---

[17] 17 U.S.C. Sec. 114(b).

referring to sound recordings which may imitate or simulate the sounds of another, Congress may have intended that a recording containing *any* sounds of another recording would constitute infringement. Thus, it would appear that any unauthorized use of a digital sample taken from another's copyrighted recording would be an infringement of the copyrighted recording.

In fact, the copyright law specifically provides that the owner of copyright in a sound recording has the exclusive right to prepare derivative works "in which the actual sounds fixed in the sound recording are rearranged, remixed, or otherwise altered in sequence or quality." A recording that embodies samples taken from the sound recording of another is by definition "rearranged, remixed, or otherwise altered in sequence or quality."

It has been suggested that the strong protection implied by the foregoing provisions could be mitigated by a judicially applied standard which permits some degree of *de minimus* copying or copying where the sampled portion of the resulting work is not substantially similar to the copied work.[18] For example, a court could determine that the taking of a millisecond of sound from another's copyrighted recording, or the taking of a more extensive portion that has been modified to the point of being completely unrecognizable or impossible to associate with the copied recording, does not constitute infringement. It is believed, however, that the courts should take what appears to be a rare opportunity to follow a "bright line" rule specifically mandated by Congress. This would result in a substantial reduction of litigation costs and uncertainty attending disputes over sampling infringement of sound recordings and would promote a faster resolution of these disputes.

While the question as to whether an unauthorized use of a digital sample infringes a musical composition may require a full substantial similarity analysis, the question as to whether the use of a sample constitutes infringement of a sound recording could end upon a determination that the sampler physically copied the copyrighted sound recording of another. If the sampler physically copied any portion of another's copyrighted sound recording, then infringement should be

---

[18] Broussard, *Current and Suggested Business Practices for the Licensing of Digital Samples*, at 492, see supra.

found. If the sampler did not physically copy, then there could be no infringement (even if the resulting recording substantially simulates or imitates the original recording).

Even if the courts choose to apply a de minimus standard, or a substantial similarity analysis, the courts are likely to find infringing those samples of recordings that appropriate the style of an artist's performance. This would include any part of the performance that is unique or sufficiently distinctive or identifiable with the artist. Examples may include the distinctive "whoa" of Michael Jackson, shriek of James Brown, snare of Phil Collins, etc.—anything that might be considered a *signature sound* of an artist. None of these would be considered copyrightable as musical compositions, but would clearly be protectable under the copyright of a sound recording.

2. No Fair Use

The doctrine of *fair use* of copyright will not justify sampling for most purposes. In particular, the unauthorized use of the typical digital sample made for the purpose of giving the sampling artist's work a familiar element from another artist's distinctive sound would clearly not be considered a fair use of the copyrighted composition or sound recording from which the sample was taken.

The doctrine of fair use is generally limited to several specific kinds of circumstances defined in the copyright law,[19] such as criticism, news reporting, teaching, or research. Fair use has also been recognized for works created for the purposes of parody and satire, on the basis that society benefits from the social and literary commentary contributed by these kinds of works.[20] The copyright law lists the following four factors to be used by the courts in determining whether the use made of a work in any particular case is a fair use:

(1)   the purpose and character of the use, including whether such use is of a commercial nature or is for nonprofit educational purposes;

(2)   the nature of the copyrighted work;

---

[19] 17 U.S.C. Sec. 107.

[20] *See*, 3 *Nimmer On Copyright*, Sec. 13.05[C] (1991).

(3) the amount and substantiality of the portion used in relation to the copyrighted work as a whole; and

(4) the effect of the use upon the potential market for or value of the copyrighted work.

The application of the first factor would militate against a finding of fair use in a digital sample case, because the purpose and character of the sampler's recording is generally commercial, rather than nonprofit. In applying the second factor, the courts give greater flexibility to those desiring to use portions of informational works, such as compilations of facts or data. Being that musical compositions and sound recordings of musical compositions are purely creative or imaginative works, the second factor is also likely to weigh heavily against a finding of fair use for samplings of those works. The third factor would imply that if the material that was sampled was slight and was not qualitatively substantial, the application of the factor could support a finding of fair use. Of course, all samples that are deemed to have taken a qualitatively substantial part of an existing musical work under a substantial similarity analysis would fail to meet this criterion. Thus, this factor might only apply to *de minimus* use of sound recordings. The fourth factor has been interpreted as including a consideration of whether the use would have a detrimental effect if the practice were widespread. Further, the U.S. Supreme Court has held that "if the defendant's work adversely affects the value of *any of the rights* in the copyrighted work . . . the use is not fair" (emphasis added).[21] One of the rights an owner has in a copyrighted work is the exclusive right to make derivative works. Since the sampling would adversely affect the potential market for similar derivative uses of the song or recording, the fourth factor would not support a finding of fair use.

As demonstrated by the *Elsmere Music* case discussed above, the use of music may be a fair use if the use is for the purpose of parody or satire. The courts have determined that parody and satire are works that should be encouraged and their creation would often not be possible without the doctrine of fair use. However, fair use will apply to samples

---

[21] *Harper & Row v. Nation Enters.*, 471 U.S. 539, 568 (1985).

taken and used for the purposes of parody or satire only if "the parody has neither the intent nor the effect of fulfilling the demand for the original, and where the parodist does not appropriate a greater amount of the original work than is necessary to 'recall or conjure up' the object of his satire."[22] While a single performance of a composition using a sample for the purpose of parody might meet this requirement, a commercial recording of the performance is not likely to pass fair-use muster. It should be clear that unless the sample is being used for some form of criticism, news reporting, teaching, research, parody, satire, or some non-profit use, the doctrine of fair use is not likely to provide a valid defense to copyright infringement.

3. Permission Required

Record companies have tended to be quite tolerant of other record companies whose artists engage in the sampling of their recordings. This tolerance has afforded each record company the informal privilege of tolerating the sampling practices of their own recording artists and producers under contract. As more and more artists become outraged by the sampling of their works, record companies should begin to become less sanguine about these practices.

Music publishers and songwriters, however, have taken a much dimmer view of sampling practices. At least one prominent music publisher has begun reviewing new recordings to listen for samples that may infringe their copyrights. It also should be noted that Gilbert O'Sullivan's record company was not a plaintiff in the songwriter's action against Biz Markie and Markie's record company. Mr. O'Sullivan filed the lawsuit through his own music publishing company, taking on the expense of the litigation himself. As his lawyer explained in a recent music trade magazine, "This case was not brought by some megacompany . . . This case was brought by a solitary artistic person who did not like the idea that somebody was using the song that *he* wrote and the recording that *he* made without his permission. . . . He could have made a deal early on. But that wasn't what he wanted. What he wanted was the recording that he did not like off the market, and that is what he got. If you are a creator, shouldn't that be your right?"

---

[22] *Berlin v. E.C. Publications, Inc.*, 329 F.2d 57 (2d Cir. 1964).

With music publishers searching for authorized samples and filing lawsuits, a recording artist can no longer assume that no one will notice his use of a sample. Nor should the artist assume that he will be absolved of liability as long as an average lay person would not recognize his use of an authorized sample. While it is true the courts have found infringement where the quality of the portion taken was "so much of what is pleasing to the ears of lay listeners" and will often rely on the ears of lay juries to determine whether an average person would clearly identify a sample as having been taken from another song, it is still quite possible that a court could hold a sampler's work an infringement even where an association of the sample with the copied composition is only noticeable by experts or others with trained or sophisticated perceptions. Samplers would therefore be advised to seek permission of the copyright owners even if it is believed that an association could be made only by an expert or that the association is only mildly noticeable. If the sampler knows he physically copied another song or recording, he should seek permission.

Artists intending to use samples from another's copyrighted recording would be strongly advised to maintain a record of the samples used in their recordings and obtain permission from the copyright owners before any distribution takes place. Once the sample is used in a recording that has been distributed to the public, the bargaining leverage of the copyright owner of the composition or recording from which the sample was taken increases significantly.

Finally, samplers seeking the proper clearance should not overlook the fact that two copyrights may be involved in each particular sample. Copyrights in sound recordings are generally owned by the record companies that financed or distributed them, and songs are owned by music publishers. These are rarely the same entities.

CONSIDERATIONS IN GRANTING AND CLEARING LICENSES FOR DIGITAL SAMPLES

This section sketches the considerations in granting and clearing licenses for the use of portions of copyrighted musical compositions and recordings by digital sampling.

1. Music Licensing

When a sampling artist wishes to make copies of a recording containing the sampled musical composition of another, permission will be required from the copyright owner of the musical composition. The permission, if granted without further conditions, will normally be in the form of a mechanical license.

A. *Applicability of Compulsory License Provision*

The use of a sample containing the copyrighted song of another will not, however, be subject to the compulsory license provision of the copyright law.[23] As noted in Chapter 7, Congress specifically recognized the legitimate interests of songwriters who might wish to prevent their musical works from being "perverted, distorted, or travestied."[24] Accordingly, the compulsory license provision provides, "A compulsory license includes the privilege of making a musical arrangement of the work to the extent necessary to conform it to the style or manner of interpretation of the performance involved, but the arrangement shall not change the basic melody or fundamental character of the work . . . except with the express consent of the copyright owner."[25] No doubt most recorded samples will be deemed arrangements that change the fundamental character of the musical works from which they were taken.

Because mechanical licenses for song samples are not subject to the compulsory license provision, the fees and other terms of licenses to make and distribute samples containing copyrighted compositions may be freely negotiated. Even if the compulsory license statute should apply with respect to a given sample—i.e., the sample recording does not change the basic melody or fundamental character of the song—the consequences of a sampling artist not complying with the express terms of the compulsory license provision will have the same effect. It has been the common practice of many sample artists to release their recordings before seeking to obtain the proper mechanical license. The compulsory license provision provides that any person who wishes to obtain a

---

[23] 17 U.S.C. Sec. 115.

[24] House Report of the Copyright Act of 1976, No. 94-1476, at page 109 (September 3, 1976).

[25] 17 U.S.C. Sec. 115 (a) (2).

compulsory license shall, before or within 30 days after making, and before distributing any copies of the work, serve notice of intention to do so on the copyright owner. Once a recording containing the musical work of another is distributed without compliance with the compulsory license provision and without the consent of the copyright owner, a compulsory license is no longer available, and the copyright owner is free to negotiate the terms of the mechanical license without regard to the restrictions set forth in the compulsory license provision.

B. Alternatives Available to the Music Copyright Owner

When a copyright owner is faced with the circumstances of an artist having included a portion of his musical composition in an otherwise original song, the alternatives available to the copyright owner are: (a) do nothing, (b) refuse to license, (c) grant a mechanical license for a one-time flat fee, (d) grant a mechanical license for a royalty, (e) grant a mechanical license for a royalty and take a share in a percentage of the performance royalties of the new composition containing the sample, (f) seek a co-ownership interest in the new composition, or (g) seek an assignment of the copyright in the new composition.

Which of these alternatives the copyright owner chooses will depend upon the circumstances, including the circumstances under which the sampling came to his attention, the value of the song, the importance of the song in relation to its intended use, the leverage he perceives he has over the sampling artist, and the fortitude that may be required to justify his position.

The ability of the music copyright owner to demand a license for the use of a sample containing a portion of his musical composition will depend upon whether the sampling artist's unauthorized use of the sample would constitute an infringement of the copyrighted music. As noted above, in determining whether an unauthorized use of the sample would constitute an infringement of a music copyright, courts will inquire whether the portion copied was a *qualitatively substantial* portion of the work from which it was taken. If it is determined that the portion copied was *qualitatively substantial,* then the inquiry turns to *how* substantial. At this point, the music copyright owner would turn to basic considerations of music licensing, including the value of the song sampled, the importance of the sample in relation to its intended use, and the scope of the use. The outcome of an analysis of these factors will result in a perception about the leverage the copyright owner has over the sampling artist in bargaining for a license.

Other factors affecting the copyright owner's leverage include the circumstances under which the sampling came to his attention. For example, if the sampling artist attempts to obtain permission for the use before releasing the recording, then the availability of other samples containing substitute music will preserve for the sampling artist the ability to walk away from the negotiations. If, however, the recording containing the sample is already on the market when the music copyright owner is engaging in his analysis, the result of the *Grand Upright* case should impress upon both parties the significantly higher bargaining leverage of the copyright owner.

A copyright owner's leverage in bargaining with the sampling artist will influence his fortitude or willingness to take the actions required, up to and including the filing of a lawsuit, to justify his choice among the following alternatives, including the structure of any deal, or the amount of any license fee, to which he may settle upon.

(a) Do Nothing

When a music copyright owner discovers that an artist has made and distributed recordings containing a sampled portion of his copyrighted composition, he may choose to do nothing. This would only be likely in one or more of the following circumstances: the material sampled was not a qualitatively substantial part of the copyright owner's song, the similarity between the owner's musical work and the sampling artist's work was so slight as to render the similarity unrecognizable by the listening public or even a trained ear, or the sampling was so slight that it may be difficult to prove that the similarity of compositions was the result of sampling at all. In any of these circumstances, the copyright owner may decide it is just not worth the trouble to take any further action, if, in fact, he had any action he could take.

If, however, the sampling artist's new composition has become a hit and is receiving a significant amount of airplay and record sales, or if it is merely included in a record album that has become a top seller, it may be worth the trouble for the copyright owner to take steps to enforce his rights under the appropriate circumstances.

(b) Refuse to License

Should the music copyright owner be approached by a sampling artist seeking permission to make and distribute recordings containing a sampled portion of the owner's composition, the copyright owner may refuse to grant a license. This may be a sampling artist's worst nightmare. To repeat the statement made by Gilbert O'Sullivan's attorney, O'Sullivan "could have made a deal early on. But that wasn't what he wanted. What he wanted was the recording that he did not like off the market, and that is what he got."

It has been suggested that Congress consider a compulsory license scheme for the licensing of digital samples similar to the regime currently in place for recordings under Section 115 of the copyright law.[26] This suggestion, however, unreasonably ignores the rights of the creative artist's right not to have his work "perverted, distorted, or travestied," a right which Congress has enacted into law by the express terms of Section 115(a)(2). This section compels music copyright owners to grant licenses for other recordings, but only after the copyright owner already has once permitted the public distribution of recordings of the composition (in audio form only—licensing the work for inclusion in motion picture soundtracks and other audiovisual works would not be considered a distribution for the purpose of this provision). Until that first distribution is made, if ever, the law respects the right of the copyright owner to refuse to permit the distribution of recordings of his copyrighted composition. And, even after such recordings are first distributed, the law compels the copyright owner to license only those recordings which have arrangements that do not change the basic melody or the fundamental character of the owner's musical composition.

Nevertheless, unless the copyright owner has a compelling reason not to license, he should consider licensing his music in sampled recordings. A reasonable reason to refuse to license may be that the recording in which the sample is intended to be used contains indecent,

---

[26] Note, *A New Spin on Music Sampling: A Case of Fair Play,* 105 Harvard Law Review 726, 742 (1992).

racist, or other opprobrious language. Another reason to refuse to
license may be that the sampler's work uses the owner's composition
in a way that mutilates the composition or otherwise offends the
creative sensitivities of the songwriter. Even if the songwriter does
not have a contractual right of consent over such uses, a music publisher
should avoid licensing music in a sampled recording if that action
would harm his business or personal relationship with the songwriter.
Leaving aside such circumstances, a music copyright owner should
not view sampling as a form of stealing, but as a new market in which
to derive revenue for the songs in his catalog.

(c) Grant a Mechanical License for a One-Time Flat Fee

If the copyright owner who discovers the unauthorized use of his
musical composition in a sampled recording decides to do something
about it, such as write a letter demanding that the sampling artist's record
company cease and desist distribution of the offending recording, the
response he receives will depend upon whether the sampling artist or
record company perceives that the recording constitutes an infringement
of copyright in the owner's musical composition. An indignant reply from
the artist's attorney telling the copyright owner, in a more or less dignified
manner, to go away, should require no explanation as to the artist's
perception of the use or evaluation of the copyright owner's position.

If the copyright owner's position is, under the circumstances, a weak
one, the parties may wish to settle upon the issuance of a mechanical
license in exchange for a one-time flat fee. Even if the copyright
owner's perception of his case is stronger than the record company's
perception of it, the copyright owner may still be unwilling to bear the
expense of taking the matter to court, and may accept such an arrangement. The artist or record company may be willing to pay some amount
on a flat fee basis, even where it is felt the music copyright owner's
position is weak, to avoid the costs and risks associated with any
litigation that would be necessary to defend their position.

A form effecting this kind of flat fee arrangement is set forth as Form
17.1 at the end of this chapter.[27]

---

[27] The forms relating to sampling at the end of this chapter are courtesy of Martin Cohen,
Esq. and Ira B. Selsky, Esq. of Los Angeles, California.

On occasion, a copyright owner may be asked to grant such a license on a *gratis* basis—that is, without charge. Music copyright owners, once persuaded to issue a license, will generally charge at least some nominal fee sufficient to cover the administrative costs of issuing the license. This may range from $25 to $50.

(d) Grant a Mechanical License for a Royalty

If, in light of all the circumstances regarding the qualitative substantiality of the music sampled and the importance of its contribution to the recording in which it is used, the sampling artist is persuaded that the copyright owner has a strong position and the fortitude to support that position with legal action, the parties may negotiate a more substantial arrangement.

A straightforward arrangement under which sampled music may be licensed is the issuance of a mechanical license in exchange for a royalty based upon the number of copies of the recording distributed. The royalty in these arrangements is usually a function of the *statutory rate* set forth in the compulsory license provision in the copyright law, as modified from time to time by the Copyright Royalty Tribunal. The sampling artist, however, would take the position that it is unfair for his record company to pay the full statutory rate, because the amount of material sampled from the copyright owner's work represents only a small part of the original musical work in which it is embodied. A copyright owner might therefore be persuaded to accept half of the statutory rate or less, and, in fact, this has become the standard practice. The percentage is typically set between 10% to 50%, with the prevailing rate in average sampling cases being about 30% of statutory.

(e) Grant a Mechanical License for Royalty and Take a Share in a Percentage of the Performance Royalties of the New Composition

Nevertheless, the foregoing arrangement may still not be satisfactory to the copyright owner, who would understandably assert that he should not only receive a portion of the mechanical royalty for copies made and distributed of the recording, but should also share a portion of the performance royalties resulting from the broadcast of the music on radio and television and other public performances.

The most common arrangement under which sampled music is licensed are deals in which the copyright owner grants a mechanical license at some percentage below the statutory rate and the sampling artist agrees that the copyright owner is entitled to receive some percentage of the performance royalties payable by performance rights societies. Even where a significantly substantial amount of the copyright owner's music is sampled, the copyright owner may be willing to accept a mechanical royalty at lower than the statutory rate in exchange for a significant share of the performance royalties, because the latter often represents a greater source of income than mechanical royalties.

A form effecting this kind of sample licensing arrangement is set forth as Form 17.2 at the end of this chapter.

A special problem arises where the sampling artist does not own the composition containing the sampled song. For example, a sampling artist may include a sample of a song in a recording of a song owned by another copyright owner, adding no original material of his own. Under these circumstances, the solution described in this section will not work, because the sampling artist would be entitled to no performance royalties with which to share with the copyright owner. This problem is revisited below.

The solution may also be unsatisfactory to the copyright owner for another reason: mechanical and performance royalties are not the only sources of music publishing revenue. The copyright owner would want an arrangement that assures that he receives a fair share of all sources of subsidiary revenue derived from the composition containing his copyrighted music, including revenue from commercial advertising, motion picture and television synchronization and other licenses. Form 17.2 attempts to address this problem by making all licenses other than mechanical and performance licenses subject to the further permission of the copyright owner. However, the copyright owner might not be convinced that this sufficiently secures his interest in the additional revenue and the sampling artist may feel no assurance that the copyright owner will seek only a fair portion of the additional revenue.

(f) Seek a Co-ownership Interest in the New Composition

Where the sampling artist can be persuaded that the copyright owner has a very strong position and the fortitude to support that position with legal action, the parties may negotiate an arrangement that satisfies the copyright owner's desire to share in all sources of subsidiary revenue derived from the new composition.

The most elegant way to assure that the copyright owner and the sampling artist each receive the proper share of all music publishing income derived from the exploitation of the new composition is for the parties to enter into a co-publishing agreement. Under this arrangement, the copyright owner is granted a co-ownership interest in the new composition containing the sampled material. This has become a fairly common solution to the sampling problem.

Under this arrangement, the percentage of the undivided copyright in the new composition granted to the copyright owner of the sampled material would reflect the qualitative substantiality of the music sampled and the importance of its contribution to the new work as a whole.

When these deals are struck, copyright owners commonly acquire a 25% to 50% co-ownership interest in the new composition. Exclusive administration rights are generally left to the sampling artist's music publisher, who is often more experienced in exploiting music in the same genre of new composition. However, this point is open to negotiation.

Three forms each effecting this kind of licensing arrangement are set forth as Form 17.3, 17.4 and 17.5 at the end of this chapter. Form 17.4 is a short-form agreement that allows each owner to grant mechanical license to others, subject to accounting to the other co-owner of its share of the revenues, but neither may license other uses unless the other has failed to object after receiving notice. Form 17.3, a short-form letter agreement, requires each party to obtain the consent of the other prior to issuing licenses for each of their respective shares. Form 17.5, the long-form, entitles each co-owner to administer its own respective share. None of these solutions seems desirable. The problems arising from ownership of copyrights split in this manner is discussed at length in Chapter 18.

(g) Seek an Assignment of the Copyright in the New Composition

If the copyright owner feels he has the leverage and all the fortitude and money necessary to engage in litigation, then he may insist on nothing less than a complete ownership interest in the new composition.

An extreme position such as this may be justified in cases where the sampled recording adds little original material to the owner's copyrighted song. This may be the case where the new composition is merely a modern arrangement of the song, the instrumental portion of the composition with modified or new lyrics, or the song's lyrics sung to a newly composed music.

In such cases, the music copyright owner could seek to enjoin the sampling artist from collecting any music publishing income in connection with the recording and collect damages for copyright infringement. The result of such a lawsuit could be severe and the sampling artist or its recording company could choose to quickly settle the claim by just assigning all right in the work over to the copyright owner.

2. Sound Recording Licensing

When a sampling artist wishes to make copies of a recording containing the sampled sound recording of another, permission will be required from the copyright owner of the sound recording. The permission, if granted without further conditions, will normally be in the form of a *master use license*.

The alternatives available to the owner of a sound recording faced with an artist having included a portion of his sound recording in an otherwise original sound recording are quite similar to those of the owner of the copyright in the underlying music. Those alternatives need not be repeated here, but a few important differences between practices in sound recording and music licenses for sampling will be pointed out in the context of licenses for sampled recordings.

A. Flat Fee Licenses

As noted, the owner of the sound recording may often have a much stronger case for infringement than the owner of the music underlying the recording, but record companies, who generally own the recordings, are more tolerant of sampling, because they know that artists in their own repertoire frequently engage in similar practices. Thus, it might not always be in the best interests of recording companies to do anything that would unreasonably restrain customary practices or help establish legal case law that supports strong protection against the use of sound recordings or musical compositions in digital samples.

Record companies therefore typically accept one-time flat fee payments for the use of samples from their recordings. Where the sampling is insubstantial or virtually unrecognizable, a record company may grant a license on a gratis or nominal fee basis. Examples of licenses to use a recording sample on a flat fee basis are set forth as Forms 17.6 and 17.7 at the end of this chapter.

B. Royalties

Where the sampling is substantial or recognizable, or if the success of the sampler's recording can clearly be attributed to the distinctive features of the sampled recording, a record company may demand a royalty. In fact, a record company may actually be under an obligation, albeit an implied one, under its recording contract with the recording artist who created the original recording, to use good faith efforts to generate income from sampled uses of the recording. Royalty rates for samples of sound recordings typically range from $\frac{1}{2}$ cent to 5 cents per unit, with advances typically starting at about $5,000. An example of a license to use a recording sample on a royalty basis is set forth as Form 17.8 at the end of this chapter. The record company should review its contract with the artist to determine whether any consent is required prior to issuing such a license.

3. Where Sampling Artist's Additional Musical Material is Owned by Another

As previously noted, a special problem may arise where the sampling artist does not own the composition containing the sampled song. For example, a sampling artist may include a sample of a song in a recording of a song owned by another copyright owner, adding no original material of his own.

If the sampling artist does not own, or claim to own, the new musical composition embodied in his original recording, a co-ownership agreement may be the only solution to a serious sampling problem the artist has created for the several copyright owners affected. In such circumstances, the owners of the two musical compositions used in the unauthorized creation of the new work will need to work out a co-ownership arrangement among themselves. This may be a difficult negotiation, because it would seem that none of the parties involved would have any particular leverage over any of the others. Yet, if the resulting composition became a hit or was included in a hit album, the parties involved would have a great incentive to reach a co-ownership arrangement clarifying where lucrative mechanical royalties, performance royalties, and royalties from subsidiary uses should be paid.

Worse yet, where the work of one party was copied in virtually its entirety and that party is already receiving a mechanical royalty at full statutory rate and all the performance credits, negotiations for a fair share of royalties attempted by a party whose work was subjected to only a small sampling would seem most difficult. The party who is already receiving full royalties—one who has done no wrongdoing—would appear to have little incentive to negotiate, except to avoid the expense of a lawsuit or to maintain good relations with another member of a small industry.

The National Music Publishers' Association (NMPA) offers its services to help mediate or arbitrate disputes between members and can provide a forum with knowledgeable industry veterans to help resolve the dispute in a quick, fair, amicable, and inexpensive way.[28] Music publishers faced with a situation such as that described above should seriously consider inquiring with the NMPA or a similar organization about how they may help the parties resolve such a matter.

CONCLUSION

It has been the practice of sampling artists to sample under the assumption that sampling is not an infringement or with the knowledge that their activity was illegal, but thought their sampling would not be discovered. With music publishers listening carefully for samples containing their copyrighted works, artists can no longer assume their activity will not be noticed. An artist who has incorporated in his recording a digital sample from a song or sound recording of another is likely to be held to have infringed two copyrights—that in a sound

---

[28] National Music Publishers' Association, 205 East 42nd Street, New York, N.Y. 10017, Phone: 212-370-5330.

recording and that in the song embodied in the recording. The first federal judge to have issued a ruling on the issue of such infringement enjoined all sales of the recording and took the unusual step of referring the matter to the U.S. Attorney's office for criminal prosecution. Thus, it is now clear that sampling is illegal and will be dealt with seriously by the law.

A sampler is therefore strongly advised to seek permission wherever he knows he physically copied the sounds of another song. Careful records should be maintained of all samples used during the creation of a recording so that the appropriate permissions can be cleared. Permission should always be cleared *before* any distribution of the recording takes place. By following these procedures, a sampling artist may avoid the substantial risks and consequences of violating the legitimate rights of other songwriters and artists.

APPENDIX TO CHAPTER 17
THE DIGITAL SAMPLING CONTROVERSY

FORMS

FORM 17.1

LETTER IN LIEU OF MECHANICAL LICENSE FOR USE OF DIGITAL SAMPLE FROM A MUSICAL COMPOSITION FOR A FLAT FEE

January 1, 1995

Hollywood, California

Gentlemen:

Reference is hereby made to (a) the musical composition entitled
"   " (the "Composition"), written by
                 (the "Writer"), and (b) the master recording entitled "   "
embodying the performances of   (the "Master").
The following shall confirm your and our agreement with respect to
us embodying portions of the Composition in the Master.

     1.   You hereby grant to us, our licensees, and our assignees, a worldwide license, in perpetuity, to embody in the Master such portions of the Composition as are embodied in that certain demonstration recording of the Master previously delivered to you, the receipt of which you hereby acknowledge, and to exploit solely the Master. We hereby acknowledge and agree that all rights not expressly granted herein are reserved, and that our sole rights hereunder shall be to embody the Composition in, and exploit, the Master.

     2.   We shall pay to you, promptly after the full execution of this agreement, the sum of One Thousand Dollars ($1,000), which sum shall constitute the full and final consideration payable to you in connection with the rights granted by you hereunder, and we shall have no obligation to pay to you or any third party any mechanical royalties, fees, or other sums in connection with our exercise of the rights granted by you hereunder.

3.   You hereby acknowledge and agree that neither you nor the Writer shall have any right, title or interest in or to the Master or the musical composition embodied therein, including, without limitation, any copyright, administration rights, or rights in or to any portion of any income derived therefrom.

4.   You hereby warrant and represent that (a) you control the worldwide right of administration to the Composition, and (b) you have the full right, power and authority to enter into this contract and to grant all of the rights granted by you hereunder. You hereby agree to indemnify us and hold us harmless from any and all losses, expenses, liabilities and damages (including reasonable attorney's fees) arising out of or connected with any claim, demand or action by any third party in respect of a breach by you of your warranties, representations or agreements hereunder, and which is reduced to final judgment or settled with your consent. You agree to reimburse us on demand for any payment made with respect to any losses, expenses, liabilities or damages to which the foregoing indemnity applies. We shall advise you promptly of any such claim, demand or action upon our receipt of notice thereof. You shall have the right, at your sole cost and expense, to participate in the defense of any such claim, demand, or action. You shall have the right, at your election, and at your sole cost and expense, to wholly assume the defense of such claim, demand or action.

If the foregoing accurately reflects your and our understanding and agreement, then please sign this letter where indicated below.

Sincerely,

By: _____

ACCEPTED AND AGREED TO:

By: _____

FORM 17.2

SIDE LETTER FOR USE OF DIGITAL SAMPLE FROM A MUSICAL COMPOSITION—TO BE USED IN CONJUNCTION WITH MECHANICAL LICENSE (SEE FORMS 7.1, 7.2, AND 7.3)

January 1, 1995

RE: (the "Composition")

Dear

In response to your letter dated December 1, 1994, we agree to the reduced mechanical rate of 37.50% of the statutory rate for use of the Composition in   recording of
                              (the "Recording").

Our agreement to grant this reduced rate is expressly conditioned upon the following:

1.   The attached mechanical license shall be executed and returned to us within thirty days of your receipt hereof.

2.   All releases of the Recording shall contain the following label copy: contains portions of   BIG MUSIC CORP. [ASCAP/BMI] Used by Permission.

3.   Recordings shall be cleared with [ASCAP/BMI] and such clearance shall state that the Recording contains an interpolation of the Composition and credit that composition with 50.00% of performance royalties. Within thirty days of your receipt hereof you shall supply us with writer and publisher information sufficient for us to prepare said clearances.

4.   In the event that the Recording is registered for copyright, the Composition shall be identified in space six of the PA

application as a pre-existing work. A copy of said copyright registration shall be sent to us.

5. With respect to territories outside of the United States in which we control a portion of the Composition, you shall cause the publishing designee of the Recording to allow our foreign subpublishers in each respective territory to claim 50.00% of income derived in each respective territory, from the Recording.

6. This agreement is binding only for that percentage of the Composition which is administered by us.

No rights are granted hereunder other than those expressly stated. In the event that you or any third party desires to use the Recording containing portions of the Composition, for any purpose other than that stated herein, the licensor must obtain a license from us for use of the Composition. However we agree to negotiate such licenses on an arms length basis and will not unreasonably deny any such licenses.

Failure to sign this agreement or comply with any of the provisions contained herein shall result in our withdrawal of the reduced mechanical rate or, in some cases, our withdrawal of permission to use the Composition as you have requested.

Sincerely yours,

Agreed to:

By:

Title:

FORM 17.3

LETTER AGREEMENT FOR CO-OWNERSHIP OF MUSICAL COMPOSITION CONTAINING A DIGITAL SAMPLE FROM ANOTHER MUSICAL COMPOSITION

January 1, 1995

Re: _____ (the "Song")

Gentlemen:

This will confirm the agreement between you and Big Music Publishing Co., Inc. ("Big Music") concerning the above-titled Song.

You hereby acknowledge that the Song has incorporated a portion of the musical composition entitled "_____" (the "Original Work") written by   (the "Original Writer"), and owned by_____.

New words and music were written for the Song by _____ _____and _____(the "New Writers").

The Song has been recorded by (the "Artist").

Based upon the foregoing, the parties agree as follows:

1.   The Song will be co-owned by _____ (50%), _____ (25%) and _____ (25%). The writers of the Song will be listed as _____ (50%), _____ (25%) and _____ (25%). The foregoing shall apply to all label copy prepared after the full execution hereof and to the copyright registration form. If the Song has already been registered for copyright in the U.S. Copyright Office, the parties will execute and file appropriate corrections and/or assignments of copyright. In addition, the parties will advise AS-CAP, BMI, the Harry Fox Agency, and all applicable record companies of the terms of this agreement.

2.   Big Music and you will each administer and issue mechanical and other licenses for its/your respective share of the Song worldwide. Neither Big Music nor you shall have the right to license the entire Song for any purpose without the prior written consent of the other. Big Music and you will collect its/your respective share of the Song and will pay its/your own writer(s) and its/your own expenses in connection with the Song.

3.   Neither you nor the New Writers shall have or claim any ownership, income or other interest in the Original Work.

4.   You warrant that you have the right to enter into this agreement and that the New Writers' contribution to the Song is original and does not infringe on the rights of any third party. You will defend and indemnify Big Music from and against any third party claims made in connection with the Song.

5.   It is the intention of the parties that a more formal agreement, i.e., a "co-administration agreement," may be entered into at a later date, but until such agreement is executed, the terms and conditions of this letter agreement shall apply.

Sincerely,

AGREED TO AND ACCEPTED:

By: _____   By: _____

By: _____

FORM 17.4

SHORT FORM LICENSING AND CO-PUBLISHING AGREEMENT FOR A MUSICAL COMPOSITION CONTAINING SAMPLED MATERIAL TAKEN FROM ANOTHER MUSICAL COMPOSITION

LICENSING AND CO-PUBLISHING AGREEMENT

1. **DEFINITIONS**

    In this Agreement, the following definitions shall apply:

    1.1 *XXX:* XXX Music (ASCAP)

    1.2 *YYY:* YYY Music (BMI)

    1.3 *Publisher:* XXX on behalf of itself and YYY, *i. e.,* XXX and YYY, collectively

    1.4 *Licensee:* ZZZ Music (ASCAP)

    1.5 *Writers:* [Writer #1], [Writer #2], [Writer #3], [Writer #4], [Writer #5], and [Writer #6]

    1.6 *Composition:* the derivative musical work entitled "_____," written by the Writers identified above

    1.7 *ASCAP:* American Society of Composers, Authors and Publishers

    1.8 *BMI:* Broadcast Music, Inc.

    1.9 *Derivative Work, Musical Work:* the definitions of these terms are those specified in the Copyright Act of 1976, 17 U.S.C. Section 101

2.   **GRANT OF RIGHTS**

Publisher and Licensee shall jointly own in perpetuity and in the shares indicated in Exhibit A, the entire right, title and interest in the Composition throughout the world, including without limitation, the copyrights (and any renewals or extensions thereto). Publisher and Licensee expressly understand and agree that all rights now and hereafter existing under such copyrights shall be exercised and licensed exclusively by each party as to its own share.

2.1   The performing rights societies of the Composition shall be ASCAP and BMI. Publisher and Licensee irrevocably authorize and instruct each society to divide and pay all publishers' fees and credits of the Compositions for the United States and Canada in the shares indicated in Exhibit A directly to Publisher and Licensee, and neither shall be obliged to account to the other for any part thereof. Notwithstanding anything to the contrary, ASCAP and BMI shall pay the full writers' share directly to the Writers in the shares indicated in Exhibit A.

2.2   Either Publisher or Licensee may issue nonexclusive licenses in respect of the mechanical rights to the Composition in the United States and Canada of the Compositions, provided that the licensees under such licenses shall divide and pay all net license fees directly to Publisher and Licensee in accordance with the shares indicated in Exhibit A.

2.3   As to all licenses other than the mechanical rights licenses referred to above, Publisher and Licensee shall notify each other of any license requests either receives. Either party may grant a license as described in said paragraph if it sends notice by registered or certified mail to the other party notifying it of the terms of a request for a license and the recipient fails to communicate the nonacceptance of the license within 7 days after the notice was sent. Notices will be sent to the last address available to ASCAP or BMI.

2.4   Publisher and Licensee shall license the foreign sub-publishing rights of the Composition in the shares indicated in Exhibit A and neither party shall claim the interest of the other.

2.5   In cases of income derived from the Composition from sources not specified above, all licensees, including printed music licensees and synchronization licensees, shall pay Publisher and Licensee royalties in the shares indicated in Exhibit A. From such royalties Publisher shall bear responsibility of paying writers' royalties to [Writer #1], [Writer #2], and [Writer #3]. From such royalties Licensee shall bear responsibility of paying writers' royalties to [Writer #4], [Writer #5], and [Writer #6].

2.6   Both Publisher and Licensee agree to pay over to the other any moneys in excess of their respective share received from any source within fifteen (15) days of receipt.

3.   TERM

The foregoing shall be effective during the full term of all copyrights of the Compositions. This Agreement is made and entered into as of January 1, 1995.

XXX MUSIC, on behalf of itself   ZZZ MUSIC
   and YYY MUSIC   (LICENSEE)
(PUBLISHER)

_____   _____
By: An Authorized Signature   By: An Authorized Signature

EXHIBIT A

SONG NAME: "_____"

WRITERS:

Names	Percentage Share
[Writer #1]	60.00%
[Writer #2]	5.00%
[Writer #3]	5.00%
[Writer #4]	10.00%
[Writer #5]	10.00%
[Writer #6]	10.00%

PUBLISHERS:

Names	Percentage Share
XXX Music (BMI)	75.00%
YYY Music (ASCAP)	15.00%
ZZZ Music (BMI)	10.00%

Form 17.5

Long Form Licensing and Co-Publishing Agreement for A Musical Composition Containing Sampled Material taken from Another Musical Composition

LICENSING AND CO-PUBLISHING AGREEMENT

1. **DEFINITIONS**

   In this Agreement, the following definitions shall apply:

   1.1 *XXX:* XXX Music (ASCAP)

   1.2 *YYY:* YYY Music (BMI)

   1.3 *Publisher:* XXX on behalf of itself and YYY, *i. e.,* XXX and YYY, collectively

   1.4 *Licensee:* ZZZ Music (ASCAP)

   1.5 *Writers:* [Writer #1], [Writer #2], [Writer #3], [Writer #4], [Writer #5], and [Writer #6]

   1.6 *Composition:* the musical work entitled "_____ _____," and registered in the Copyright Office as _____ .

   1.7 *Existing Material:* original musical or lyrical material (or both) in the Composition authored by _____ _____ written by [Writer #1], [Writer #2], and [Writer #3].

   1.8 *New Material:* original musical or lyrical material (or both) authored by [Writer #4], [Writer #5], and [Writer #6], incorporated in the new composition.

1.9   *New Composition:* the derivative work which is the subject of this Agreement, which will incorporate New Material and Existing Material; *i.e.,* the derivative work entitled "_____"

1.10   *ASCAP:* American Society of Composers, Authors and Publishers.

1.11   *BMI:* Broadcast Music, Inc.

1.12   *Copy, Derivative Work, Musical Work:* the definitions of these terms are those specified in the Copyright Act of 1976, 17 U.S.C., Section 101.

2.   **RECITALS**

2.1   Publisher owns and administers all interest in the copyright in and to the Composition.

2.2   Licensee has engaged [Writer #4], [Writer #5], and [Writer #6] to add the New Material to the Existing Material in order to create the New Composition.

3.   **GRANT OF RIGHTS**

Publisher and Licensee shall jointly own in perpetuity and in the shares indicated in Exhibit A, the entire right, title and interest in the New Composition throughout the world, including without limitation, the copyrights (and any renewals or extensions thereto). Publisher and Licensee expressly understand and agree that all rights now and hereafter existing under such copyrights shall be exercised and licensed exclusively by each party as to its own share.

3.1   Publisher grants to Licensee a worldwide perpetual license to use Existing Material solely for purposes of combining Existing Material with New Material in connection with the creation of the New Composition.

3.2   Except as specified in below, Publisher expressly reserves and retains for its sole benefit all rights in or to the Composition not specifically granted to Licensee. Without limiting the generality of the preceding sentence, Licensee and Publisher expressly understand and agree that the sole rights Licensee acquires under this agreement are the right to use the Existing Material in connection with the creation of the New Composition, and to exploit Existing Material only as incorporated in the New Composition only by means of the exploitation of the New Composition substantially in its entirety.

3.3   Licensee shall not acquire any right to use the likenesses, pictures or biographical materials concerning [Writer #1], [Writer #2], and [Writer #3] in connection with any uses of the New Composition without Publisher's prior written consent, which may be withheld at Publisher's sole discretion.

3.4   All right, title and interest throughout the universe in and to the New Composition, including, without limitation, the worldwide copyright in the New Composition, and all renewals and extensions of copyright, shall be owned in the following shares by Publisher and Licensee:

    3.4.1   Licensee shall own an undivided seventy-five percent (75 %) share of all right, title and interest in and to the New Composition (Licensee's "Respective Share"); and

    3.4.2   Publisher shall own an undivided twenty-five percent (25 %) share of all right, title and interest in and to the New Composition (Licensee's "Respective Share").

    The shares of the New Composition belonging to each party comprising Licensee and Publisher are listed in Appendix A. The shares of the Composition belonging to each party comprising Publisher are listed in Appendix B.

3.5   The copyright in and to the New Composition shall be registered in the Copyright Office of the United States Library of Congress in both Licensee's and Publisher's names, in conformity with Licensee's and Publisher's Respective Shares. Publisher shall effect such registration in the New Composition and the recordation of this license. If the copyright in the New Composition has ever been registered other than in conformity with this Agreement, Licensee and Publisher shall simultaneously with the execution of this Agreement exchange such assignments of the appropriate interest in the copyright as may be necessary to confirm their ownership in and to the New Composition in the records of the Copyright Office of the United States Library of Congress.

4.   ADMINISTRATION

4.1   Subject to the terms and conditions of this Agreement, Licensee and Publisher each shall have the right to administer its own Respective Share in the New Composition throughout the universe during the full term of worldwide copyright, including all renewals and extensions.

4.2   The performing rights societies of the Composition shall be ASCAP and BMI. Publisher and Licensee irrevocably authorize and instruct each society to divide and pay all publishers' fees and credits of the Compositions for the United States and Canada in the shares indicated in Exhibit A directly to Publisher and Licensee, and neither shall be obliged to account to the other for any part thereof. Notwithstanding anything to the contrary, ASCAP and BMI shall pay the full writers' share directly to the Writers in the shares indicated in Exhibit A.

4.3 Publisher and Licensee shall license the foreign sub-publishing rights of the Composition in the shares indicated in Exhibit A and neither party shall claim the interest of the other.

4.4 Licensee and Publisher each shall have the right, throughout the universe to enter into nonexclusive licenses and agreements with respect to the exploitation of mechanical reproduction rights, performing rights and print rights solely with respect to its Respective Share in the New Composition. Licenses with respect to all other uses of the New Composition including, without limitation, so-called synchronization licenses, shall be issued only with both Licensee's and Publisher's prior written approval. Licensee and Publisher must notify any third party seeking a license from either of them in respect of the New Composition of the need to obtain a license from the other.

4.5 Licensee acknowledges and agrees that Publisher's Respective Share of the Composition shall under no circumstances be subject to or affected by any so-called "controlled composition" clause contained in any agreement pertaining to the services of any recording artist who is also a Writer.

4.6 Publisher shall in all instances be entitled to issue licenses for mechanical reproduction of its Respective Share of the Composition in the United States and Canada upon the terms and conditions of a standard Harry Fox Agency or CMRRA license and otherwise throughout the world upon the most favorable terms then currently accorded to publishers of musical works in each country throughout the world.

Publisher agrees to issue a license to _____
for mechanical reproduction of its Respective Share
of the New Composition in accordance with this
paragraph.

4.7   Publisher and its agents and designees shall be
        entitled to receive and collect directly Publisher's
        Respective Share of gross income (as that term is
        hereinafter defined) derived from the New Composi-
        tion, and Publisher shall pay to [Writer #1], [Writer
        #2], and [Writer #3] any and all royalties and other
        consideration to which they are entitled in respect of
        any and all uses of the New Composition.

4.8   Licensee and its agents and designees shall be
        entitled to receive and collect directly Publisher's
        Respective Share of Gross Income derived from the
        Composition, and Licensee shall pay to [Writer #4],
        [Writer #5], and [Writer #6] and any and all other
        parties entitled to receive any royalty or other com-
        pensation in connection with the creation of the New
        Composition any and all royalties and other consid-
        eration to which they are entitled in respect of any
        and all uses of the New Composition.

4.9   *Gross Income* is defined as any and all revenue,
        income and sums, including, without limitation, me-
        chanical royalties, synchronization fees, printing in-
        come, and the "publisher's share" of public
        performance fees, earned in respect of the repro-
        duction and other exploitation of the New Composi-
        tion throughout the United States. For purposes of
        this Agreement, each party's Respective Share of
        Gross Income derived from the New Composition
        shall equal that party's Respective Share of all right,
        title and interest in and to the New Composition set
        forth above.

4.10   Both Publisher and Licensee agree to pay over to the other any moneys in excess of their respective share received from any source within fifteen (15) days of receipt.

5.   REPRESENTATIONS AND WARRANTIES

5.1   Licensee and Publisher hereby warrant and represent that each is affiliated with either ASCAP or BMI. Small performing rights in Licensee's and Publisher's Respective Share of the New Composition shall, to the extent permitted by law, be assigned to and licensed by ASCAP. Licensee and Publisher authorize and direct ASCAP and BMI to collect and receive, in shares corresponding to Licensee's and Publisher's Respective Share, all moneys earned from the public performance of the New Composition in the United States and Canada. ASCAP and BMI shall pay directly to each of Licensee and Publisher, their Respective Share of the so-called "publisher's share" of the aggregate fees derived from the public performance of the New Composition in the United States and Canada.

5.2   Licensee hereby warrants and represents that it is entitled to enter into this agreement, that it is empowered to convey to and confer upon Publisher all of the rights and benefits conveyed by it hereunder; that the New Material is new and original, capable of copyright, and does not infringe upon the rights of any person, firm or corporation, including, without limitation, copyrights, contract rights, or any rights of privacy; and that the New Material is not obscene or defamatory.

5.3   In addition to any warranties Licensee makes to Publisher, Licensee assigns to Publisher the benefits of any warranties or representations which it has obtained or shall obtain under any other agreements it has or will enter, including, without limitation, songwriter's contracts, regarding the New Material and agrees that, without limiting Publisher's right to proceed directly against Licensee in connection with any claim against Publisher that is inconsistent with any warranty or representation made by Licensee hereunder or the generality of the terms and provisions of the indemnity provisions below, Publisher may proceed directly against the maker of any warranty or representation to Licensee in connection with the creation of the New Material or the New Composition, including, without limitation, [Writer #4], [Writer #5], and [Writer #6]. Publisher warrants that it is the sole administrator of the worldwide perpetual rights in and to the existing material, and has the right to grant the rights granted hereunder.

5.4   Licensee and Publisher each shall have the right to prosecute, defend, settle and compromise all suits and actions respecting the New Composition and generally to do and perform all things necessary concerning the same and protect the copyrights therein to prevent and restrain the infringement of copyright or any other rights, but solely with respect to that party's Respective Share in the New Composition. Notwithstanding the foregoing, however, in the event the foregoing actions or proceedings shall involve the rights of both parties, the party instituting any such action or proceeding shall give the other an opportunity to join in such action or proceeding. If the other party shall decline to join in such action or proceeding involving its interest in the New Composition, the party bringing such action shall have the sole right to proceed with respect to its own interest and shall have the right to settle or compromise any such action or proceeding with respect to the entire New Composition. If the interests of a non-joining party shall be represented by the party proceeding with any action with respect to the New Composition any recovery of any moneys as a result of a judgment, settlement or otherwise shall be divided between the parties in proportion to their Respective Shares of the New Composition after first deducting the expenses of obtaining said moneys, including attorney's fees, costs and expenses. Any judgment against an indemnitee and any settlement by an indemnitee of any claim or action against it respecting the New Composition, together with costs and expenses, including counsel fees, shall be covered by the applicable indemnity provisions or Paragraph 11 below.

5.5 Each party hereto hereby indemnifies, saves and holds the other(s), its assigns and licensees, harmless from any and all liability, claims, demands, loss and damage (including reasonable counsel fees and court costs) resulting from any breach of any of the warranties, representations or agreements made by the indemnitor which shall be reduced to a final nonappealable adverse judgment. Each party hereto shall give the other(s) written notice of any claim or action covered by said indemnity, and the other(s) shall have the right, at its election, to furnish, at its expense, counsel to defend against such claim or action.

6. NOTICES

6.1 Licensee's Address:

6.2 Publisher's Address:

6.3 Licensee's and Publisher's respective addresses for all purposes in this Agreement shall be as set forth on above, until written notice of a different address is received by the party notified of that different address.

6.4   All notices shall be in writing and shall either be sent by registered or certified mail (return receipt requested), postage prepaid, or by telegraph, all charges prepaid. The date of mailing or of deposit in a telegraph office, whichever shall be first, shall be deemed the date of service.

6.5   A courtesy copy of notices to hereunder shall be sent to:

7.   INTEGRATION

7.1   This Agreement shall not be deemed to give any right or remedy to any third party whatsoever unless said right or remedy is specifically granted to such third party by the terms of this Agreement.

7.2   Licensee and Publisher shall execute any further documents including, without limitation, assignments of copyright, and perform any other actions necessary to effectuate the terms and provisions of this agreement fully.

7.3   This agreement sets forth the entire understanding between Licensee and Publisher, and cannot be changed, modified or canceled except by an instrument signed by the party sought to be bound.

7.4   This Agreement shall not be binding upon either Licensee or Publisher until duly executed by Licensee and Publisher. Nothing herein contained shall constitute a partnership between or a joint venture between Licensee and Publisher. Neither party shall hold itself out contrary to the terms of this paragraph, and neither party shall become liable for any obligation, act or omission of the other party contrary to the provisions hereof. If any provision of this agreement shall be declared invalid, same shall not affect the validity of the remaining provisions hereof. No waiver of any provision of this agreement or of any default hereunder shall affect the waiving party's rights thereafter to enforce such provision or default, whether or not similar.

8.   RESOLUTION OF DISPUTES/CHOICE OF LAW

8.1   This agreement shall be governed by and construed under the laws of the State of California applicable to agreements wholly performed therein. All disputes between the parties arising hereunder or otherwise involving the New Composition shall be subject solely to the jurisdiction of the state and federal courts sitting within the State of California, and Licensee hereby submits to the personal jurisdiction of those courts for all purposes contemplated by this agreement.

8.2   In the event of any action, suit or proceeding arising from or based on this agreement brought by either party hereto against the other, the prevailing party shall be entitled to recover from the other party its attorneys' fees in connection therewith, in addition to all other costs of the prevailing party in connection with that action, suit or proceeding.

9.   TERM

The foregoing shall be effective during the full term of all copyrights of the Compositions. This Agreement is made and entered into as of April 9, 1992.

[Signature blocks & exhibits omitted.]

FORM 17.6

SHORT FORM MASTER LICENSE FOR USE OF
SOUND RECORDING SAMPLE ON FLAT FEE BASIS

January 1, 1995

Re: "   "(the "Recording")

Gentlemen:

The following will set forth the agreement between you and us concerning the Recording.

You have claimed that the Recording has incorporated portions of your master-recording entitled "   "
(the "Master") performed by
(the "Artist"), and produced by
("Producer").

1.   You hereby grant to us the non-exclusive, worldwide and perpetual right, but not the obligation, to use the Master in and as part of the Recording and all "phonorecords" with the exploitation, advertising, publicity, and promotion of such Recording and phonorecords in all media, markets, and/or formats now or here-after known.

2.   If the Master is included in any such phonorecords re-leased under our authority, we shall pay to you the sum of Two Thousand Dollars ($2,000) within two (2) weeks after the initial release of the first phonorecord embodying the Master, but not later than February 1, 1995, or this agreement will be deemed null and void.

3.   Definitions of terms used in this agreement:

(a) "phonorecord" means any device, at any speed on any material, now or hereafter known, used for the reproduction of sound or sound accompanied by visual images.

4. You warrant and represent that: (a) you have the right to enter into this agreement and grant to us the rights to use the Master as herein provided; and (b) you shall be solely responsible for obtaining and paying for any and all requisite consents to this agreement by Artist, Producer, and any other persons who rendered services in connection with the recording and production of the Master and any other person(s), firm(s), or corporation(s) whose consent(s) may be required in respect of the rights granted to us with respect to the Master hereunder.

5. Each party will indemnify, save and hold the other (and its respective agents, directors, officers, successors, licensees and assigns) harmless from and against any and all damages, costs liabilities, losses and expenses (including reasonable attorneys' fees) arising out of or connected with any third party claim, demand or action inconsistent with any of the warranties, representations or covenants made by the indemnitor in this agreement which results in a final adverse judgment, arbitration award or settlement with the consent of the indemnitor (not to be unreasonably withheld). The indemnified parties agree to give the indemnitor notice of any action to which the foregoing indemnity applies, and the indemnitor may participate in the defense of same, at its expense, through counsel of its choosing.

6. This agreement constitutes the entire agreement between you and us (all prior negotiations, correspondence and agreements whether oral or written being merged herein) and shall be construed in accordance with the laws of the State of California. Any dispute or disagreement with respect to this agreement shall be submitted to the Courts of the State of California or the Federal Courts within the State of California, which courts shall have the exclusive jurisdiction thereof. This agreement shall inure to the benefit of you, us and our respective successors, licensees, assigns, associate, affiliated and subsidiary companies. This

agreement may not be modified except by an instrument in writing signed by both parties. A waiver of any breach of any party in any one instance shall not constitute a waiver of any subsequent breach, whether or not similar.

If the foregoing represents your understanding and agreement, please sign and return a copy of this agreement.

Very truly yours,

By: _____

ACCEPTED AND AGREED:

By: _____

FORM 17.7

LONG FORM MASTER LICENSE FOR USE OF
SOUND RECORDING SAMPLE ON FLAT FEE BASIS

SAMPLING LICENSE

Agreement made as of the 1st day of January, 1995 by and between   ,
a division of   , at
("Licensor") and   , c/o
        , at
        ("Licensee").

1.   TERM

1.01.   The term of this agreement (the "Term") will begin on the date hereof and shall continue in perpetuity.

2.   DEFINITIONS

2.01.   "Master", "Master Recording": The recording(s) of sound, by any method and on any substance or material, intended for reproduction in the form of Phonograph Records, or otherwise.

2.02.   "Records", "Phonograph Records": Any device now or hereafter known, on or by which sound may be recorded and reproduced, which is manufactured or distributed primarily for home and/or consumer and/or juke box use and/or use on or in means of transportation.

2.03.   "Retail List Price": Intentionally Deleted.

2.04.   "Person": Any individual, corporation, partnership, association, or other business entity, or the legal successors or representative of any of the foregoing.

2.05.   "Territory": The World

3.   RIGHTS GRANTED TO LICENSEE

3.01.   Licensor hereby grants Licensee, during the Term hereof and in the Territory, the non-exclusive right to manufacture Records embodying the Master Recording entitled _____ as performed by _____ (the "Product") embodying portions of _____'s Master Recording licensed hereunder entitled _____ (the "Master") as performed by _____ _____ (the "Artist"), and to distribute and sell the Product and Records embodying the Product directly to consumers via mail order and retail.

3.02.   Licensee shall submit to Licensor two (2) copies of each Record embodying the Product.

3.03.   Prior to exercising any of the rights granted to it hereunder, Licensee, or its designee, shall obtain, from the owners of the copyrights in the compositions performed in the Master, all licenses which may be required for the use of those compositions in Records embodying the Product to be marketed by Licensee, or its designee, and shall become a first party to each of the applicable Phonograph Record Manufacturers' Agreements with the American Federation of Musicians, or the successor agreement then in effect.

4.   THIRD PARTY PAYMENTS

4.01.   Licensor shall pay all royalties due by reason of Licensee's sale or licensing of Records embodying the Product, under Licensor's agreements covering the services of record producers and/or performing artists and/or Licensor's acquisition of the Master.

4.02.   (a)   Except as specifically stated otherwise herein Licensee, or its designee, shall make all payments required in connection with the manufacture, sale, licensing or distribution in the Territory of Records embodying the Product hereunder including, without limitation, all royalties and other payments to owners of copyrights in musical compositions, the Music Performance Trust Fund and Special Payments Fund, and any other required unions and union funds. Licensee, or its designee, will comply with the applicable rules and regulations covering any use of the Master by Licensee and/or by Persons deriving rights from Licensee in connection with the manufacture and sale of Records embodying the Product or otherwise.

(b)   Licensee shall pay, or cause to be paid, directly to the proper parties, all sales taxes (as fixed by law), if any, for Records embodying the Product manufactured and sold hereunder, and, to the extent that Licensor may be additionally liable therefor as a result of sales of such Records embodying the Product, all payments to the AFTRA Pension and Welfare Fund.

5.   LICENSOR'S PROPERTY

5.01.   Licensor's copyright and other property or other rights, both statutory and common law, in the Master and tapes thereof, and the performances embodied therein, as well as all other rights in them not specifically herein granted by Licensor, shall be and remain the property of Licensor.

6.   COPYRIGHT NOTICE: CREDIT

6.01.   Each Record embodying the Product will bear a sound recording copyright notice identical to the notice used by Licensor for initial United States release of the Master concerned, or such other notice as Licensor shall require, together with the name of the copyright proprietor as indicated by Licensor; this obligation shall extend to any other form of notice which may in the future be deemed necessary in order to protect Licensor's sound recording copyrights under future legislation which may be passed anywhere throughout the Territory during the Term hereof.

6.02.   All record jackets produced hereunder in connection with   Records comprising the Product shall contain a credit line as follows:

(TITLE) BY (ARTIST) UNDER LICENSE FROM

Such credit line will appear in the liner notes on record jackets and tape containers. The Artist whose performances are embodied in the Master licensed hereunder shall likewise be given a credit in reasonable size type.

7.   PAYMENTS TO LICENSOR

7.01   Licensee shall pay Licensor a non-returnable payment in the amount of ONE THOUSAND FIVE HUNDRED DOLLARS ($1,500.00) payable upon Licensee's execution hereof.

8.   TERMINATION: Intentionally Deleted.

9.   ASSIGNMENT

9.01   Licensor and Licensee (after written notice to Licensor) may, at its election, assign this agreement or any of its rights hereunder.

10.   WARRANTIES

10.01.   Licensor warrants and represents that it has the full right, power and authority to enter into this agreement and to grant the rights herein granted to Licensee. Also, Licensor has the authority to grant the rights regarding the Artist and Producer, and that Licensee is not required to obtain any other consents as to the Master.

10.02.   Licensee warrants and represents the following:

(a)   Licensee has the full right, power and authority to enter into this agreement and to fully perform its obligations hereunder.

(b)   Licensee shall not license, sell or otherwise dispose of or distribute the Product, or Records embodying the Product, hereunder except pursuant to the terms of this agreement, and shall not assign any of Licensee's rights hereunder.

(c)   In the event Licensee fails to pay any mechanical copyright and/or union fund payments due, Licensor shall have the option of making said payments, including settling any disputes with respect thereto, and demanding reimbursement therefor from Licensee (and Licensee shall make such reimbursement) and a material breach of this agreement shall be deemed to have occured.

10.03.   Licensor and Licensee each agree to indemnify and hold the other harmless from any and all liability, claims, demands, loss and reasonable legal fees and expenses of the indemnified party in connection therewith arising out of any failure by the indemnifying party with regard to the representations and warranties made by the indemnifying party herein. It is of the essence of this indemnification that the indemnifying party shall have the rights, at its own cost and expense, to participate in the defense thereof.

11. NOTICES

11.01.   All notices and payments required to be given to Licensor hereunder shall be sent to Licensor at its address first mentioned herein, and all notices to Licensee shall be sent to Licensee at its address first mentioned herein, or such other address as each party respectively may hereafter designate by notice in writing to the other. All notices and payments shall be sent by registered or certified mail, return receipt requested, and the day of mailing of any such notice shall be deemed the date of the giving thereof (except notices of change of address, the date of which shall be the date of receipt by the receiving party). All notices to Licensor shall be served upon Licensor to the attention of the Vice President,   , with a copy to the Vice President, Legal Affairs.

12.   GENERAL PROVISIONS

12.01.   This agreement sets forth the entire under-standing between the parties and may not be modified or amended except by an instrument in writing signed by both parties hereto.

12.02.   It is understood and agreed that in the perform-ance of this agreement Licensee is acting as an independent contractor and shall not be, act, or represent itself as the em-ployee, agent or representative of Licensor and shall not have the right, power, or authority to bind Licensor or make any contract or other agreement or assume or create any obligation or liability, express or implied, on behalf of Licensor. Neither the making of this agreement nor the performance of any of the provisions hereof shall be construed to constitute Licensee the agent or legal representative of Licensor for any purpose, nor shall this agree-ment be deemed to establish a joint venture or partnership be-tween the parties hereto.

12.03.   This agreement is entered into in the State of New York, and shall be construed in accordance with the laws of the said state applicable to contracts to be performed wholly therein. Both Licensor and Licensee agree that any controversy arising under this agreement shall be adjudicated under the jurisdiction of a competent court in the City of New York.

12.04.   The failure of any party at any time to insist upon strict performance of any condition, promise, agreement or understanding set forth herein shall not be construed as waiver or relinquishment of the rights to insist upon strict per-formance of the same condition, promise, agreement or under-standing at a future time.

12.05.   Licensee agrees that the Master licensed hereunder, and Licensor's copyrights and all other rights of property in such Master are unique and valuable assets of Licensor, the loss of which, or the use of which in any way other than as provided for herein, cannot be replaced or compensated for adequately in monetary terms, and Licensee agrees that in the event of any use of the Master other than as provided for herein, Licensor shall be entitled to injunctive relief in addition to all other rights and remedies to which it is entitled to enforce the provisions hereof.

By: _____   By: _____

                                   By: _____

                    (Exhibit A Omitted)

FORM 17.8

LONG FORM MASTER LICENSE FOR USE OF
SOUND RECORDING SAMPLE ON ROYALTY BASIS

AGREEMENT

This will confirm the following agreement dated Jaunary 1, 1995, made by
and between
(hereinafter, "Owner") and _____ (hereinafter, "Licensee").

1. Owner grants to licensee the nonexclusive right and license to use a portion of the Master set forth on Exhibit "A" hereto (the "Master"), as embodied in the tape approved by Owner, with no greater usage of the Master than is contained on the approved tape, in the manufacture, distribution, and sale of records, cassettes, and compact discs of the album entitled "_____" ("Album") embodying the recording "_____" as sampled in "_____" (the "Recording") as performed by _____ ("Artist"). Licensee shall additionally have the right to manufacture, distribute, and sell or authorize the manufacture, distribution, and sale of Single Records, Long Play Singles, CD Singles, or Cassette Singles ("Singles").

2.   The term of this agreement shall be for perpetuity commencing on the date hereof. Contemporaneously with the execution of this agreement, Licensee shall deliver to Owner its check in the amount of SEVEN THOUSAND FIVE HUNDRED DOLLARS ($7,500.00), which sum shall constitute a nonrefundable advance against, and be fully recoupable from any royalties payable by Licensee to Owner as a result of the sale by Licensee of Albums and Singles during the term of this agreement.

3. (a) For all rights and license granted hereunder, Licensee agrees to pay Owner a basic royalty as follows: (i) two cents ($.02) per Master on one hundred percent (100%) of Albums, and (ii) one cent ($.01) per Master on one hundred percent (100%) of Singles, sold and not returned for Distribution through normal retail channels in the United States ("basic U. S. rate"), and, on all other sales, including, but not limited to, foreign, budget, mid-price, record club, PX, mail order, and premium records, and flat fee or flat royalty licenses. Owner's royalties will be computed in the same manner (i. e. , the manner in which so-called "free goods," returns, and reserves are calculated) as the Artist's royalties are computed. Licensee shall send Owner a copy of the relevant provisions immediately upon execution of this agreement by Licensee.

(b) Licensee shall additionally have the right to include the Recording in Compilation albums or Greatest Hits albums released by Licensee, provided Owner receives the royalty specified in subparagraph 3(a)(i), and/or Licensee may license the Recording to third parties for compilation packages, and/or Licensee may sell through Record Clubs and X's, provided Owner receives the royalty specified in subparagraph 3(a)(ii).

(c) Licensee may manufacture and distribute a video embodying the Recording for promotional purposes. Should Licensee manufacture and/or distribute any such video for commercial purposes, Licensee shall pay Owner a royalty of five percent (5%) of the wholesale price, prorated by the number of royalty bearing masters on the video.

(d) Licensee may license the Recording for non-phonograph record purposes (such as film and television), provided Licensee pays Owner a royalty of ten percent (10%) of the net receipts received by licensee, including any and all advances.

(e) Licensee agrees to pay and to be solely responsible for all third party payments that may be due, other than royalties due the artist and producers on the Master, pursuant to the use of the Master on the Recording.

(f)   Licensee shall compute royalties payable to hereunder as of June 30th and December 31st of each year for the preceding six (6) month period, and Licensee shall pay such royalties before or on the succeeding September 30th and March 31st, respectively, and each such payment shall be accompanied by an itemized statement of the computation thereof. Statements shall be rendered, whether or not any sums are due Owner.

(g)   All royalty statements rendered by Licensee shall be binding upon Owner and not subject to any objection by for any reason unless specific objection in writing, stating the basis thereof, is given to Licensee within two (2) years from the date rendered. Owner shall be barred from maintaining or instituting an action or proceeding based upon or relating to any statement unless such action or proceeding is commenced within one (1) year after receipt by Licensee of the written objection. Owner shall have the right to inspect and make abstracts of the books and records of Licensee, its subsidiaries, and affiliates, wherein the same may be, insofar as they relate to this agreement. Such inspection, at Owner's sole expense, shall be made during normal business hours of normal business days and is limited to a period of two (2) years from the date of the applicable statement.

4.   (a)   Licensee agrees to obtain all copyright licenses from the music publishers for the compositions on the Masters listed in Exhibit "A" hereto. Licensee will pay all copyright fees to music publishers with respect to said Masters and shall indemnify and hold Owner harmless with respect to all such fees.

(b)   Licensee agrees that, with respect to the Album jacket and/or any enclosures therein, Owner shall receive the courtesy credit specified in Exhibit "A" hereto in connection with the use of the Master licensed hereunder. Notwithstanding the foregoing, Licensee's inadvertent failure to give such credit shall not be deemed a breach, provided that licensee prospectively cures on all future runs.

5. Owner shall be responsible for and shall pay any Artist's royalties which may become owing in connection with licensee's use of the Masters hereunder.

6.   (a)   Licensee shall not license the Master for use as a premium record or in any other record, except as otherwise provided herein.

(b)   Licensee agrees that it will not sublicense or convey any rights under this agreement not expressly authorized herein. Licensee hereby agrees that it will manufacture or cause the manufacture of, distribute or cause the distribution of, and sell or cause the sale of Recordings covered by this agreement, only to the extent of the rights and license granted by this agreement.

7.   (a)   Licensee represents and warrants that it has the right to enter into this agreement and to make the commitments it makes herein. Licensee agrees to indemnify and hold Owner harmless of and from any and all cost and expense (including, but not limited to, reasonable attorneys' fees), loss, claim, liability, or obligation arising out of:

(i)   Any breach by Licensee of the representations, warranties, and covenants made by it herein; and/or

(ii)   The use on the Album by Licensee of any non-masters or any other claim based on or related to the use of said non-masters.

8. Owner represents and warrants that it has the right to enter into this agreement and to make the commitments it makes herein. Licensee accepts this license without any other warranty or representation by or recourse against Owner.

9.   The rights and license granted to Licensee hereunder are for the territory of the World.

10.   The Master hereunder and all copyrights and rights in and to such Master shall remain the sole and exclusive property of Owner, subject to the right of Licensee to make reproductions pursuant to the terms of this agreement.

11.   Licensee represents and warrants that Licensee's Distributor,   ("   "), is, and intends to remain, a signatory to the then-current American Federation of Musicians (AFM) Phonograph Record Labor Agreement, the Special Payments Fund Agreement, and Phonograph Record Trust Agreement, the American Federation of Television and Radio Artists (AFTRA) National Code of Fair Practice for Phonograph Recordings, and any other union agreement having jurisdiction in the premises. Licensee acknowledges that the license granted hereunder is given in reliance thereon.

12.   Licensee shall deliver two (2) copies of each recorded compact disc and tape configuration authorized under the terms of this agreement. Said Recordings shall be shipped to the attention of Vice President, Business and Legal Affairs, at the address set forth above. Owner reserves the right to determine the quality of the manufactured products and, if it is below 's comparable product standards, Owner shall so advise Licensee. Upon receipt of such a notice of quality deficiency, Licensee shall take immediate steps to improve the quality of its manufactured product so that it shall meet Owner's normal commercial standards.

13.   All notices, statements, and payments which Licensee may be required or desire to serve upon Owner may be served upon Owner by depositing same, postage prepaid, in any mail box, chute, or other receptacle authorized by the United States Postal Service, for mail addressed to Owner at the address set forth above, Attention: Vice President, Business and Legal Affairs, or at such other address as Owner may from time to time designate by written notice to Licensee. The date of service of any notice,

statement, or payment so deposited shall be the date of deposit except for notices of changes of address, which shall be effective upon receipt. All notices which Owner may be required or desire to serve upon Licensee may be served upon Licensee by depositing same, postage prepaid, in any mail box, chute, or other receptacle authorized by the United States Postal Service, for mail addressed to Licensee at the address set forth above, Attention: or at such other address as licensee may from time to time designate by written notice to   . The date of service of any notice so deposited shall be the date of deposit. All payments made hereunder shall be payable to Owner, and shall be forwarded directly to the attention of Vice President, Business and Legal Affairs, at the address listed above.

14.   This agreement shall become effective only when executed by an authorized agent of Owner and an authorized signer on behalf of Licensee. It shall be deemed to have been made in the State of California, and its validity, construction, breach, performance, and operation shall be governed by the laws of the State of California applicable to agreements made in and to be performed in California.

15. Owner may assign this agreement to any parent, subsidiary, or affiliate entity, or any entity which acquires substantially all of Owner's stock or assets, or acquires Owner by way of merger, consolidation, or other reorganization.

16.   In addition to any other rights of termination which Owner may have, Owner shall have the right to terminate this agreement and all of the Licensee's rights hereunder in the event (a) Licensee shall breach any material provision of this agreement; and/or (b) Licensee shall assign or attempt to assign this agreement or any of its rights hereunder to any assignees, whether for the benefit of creditors or otherwise, or make or attempt to make any compromises with creditors.

17.   In the event that any agreement oral or written, between Licensee and any third party with respect to the licensing of said thirty party's master recordings in connection with the Album shall provide for royalty terms and/or for an advance more favorable than provided herein with respect to the Masters being licensed hereunder, Owner shall have the benefit of such more favorable terms from the first record sold.

18.   It is not presently contemplated that a video of the Recording shall be produced by Artist or the label distributing the Recording. However, Artist hereby agrees that, if a video of the Recording is produced, Artist shall use his best efforts to cause his record label to include the Recording in the music video.

19.   Artist shall cause his record label to include the Recording as the B-side of a single record subsequent to the first single record released from the Album. This provision is material to the full performance by Artist and the rights granted to Artist under this agreement.

20.   Attached hereto as Exhibit "B," incorporated herein by its reference, is a direction to pay authorizing Record Company to be paid direct all compensation due under paragraphs 2 and 3 of the Agreement dated January 1, 1995. Artist hereby agrees to cause Owner to make all payments required under the Agreement direct to _____.

IN WITNESS WHEREOF, the parties hereto have executed this agreement on the day and year first above written.

By: _____   _____

EXHIBIT "A"

TO AGREEMENT BETWEEN

AND

<u>**ARTIST**</u>   <u>**TITLE**</u>

COURTESY CREDIT: COURTESY OF

EXHIBIT "B"

January 1, 1995

Gentlemen:

    1.   Reference is made to an agreement dated as of January 1, 1995 entered into among   and me [   ] regarding, among other things, my services as a recording artist, as amended (the "Agreement") All terms defined in the Agreement shall have the same meanings below.

I hereby request. and irrevocably authorize you to make payments to   ("Licensor") with respect to Licensor's licensing of the sample of the Master Recording of the musical composition entitled "   " as performed by (the "Sample") for use in the musical composition entitled "   " as performed by me (the "Master") , on my behalf, as follows:

    (a)   An advance of Seventy-five Hundred Dollars ($7,500.00). This advance will be recoupable by you from all moneys becoming payable to Licensor hereunder. To the extent not so recouped, such advance may be recouped by you from any moneys becoming payable to me, but all amounts so recouped from moneys payable to me shall be credited to my royalty account if subsequently recouped from moneys payable to Licensor. Such advance shall be included as a recording cost item in the recording budget applicable to the Recordings under the Agreement.

    (b)   A royalty (the "License Royalty") of:

    (1)   With respect to USNRC Net Sales of Phonograph Records embodying the Sample as embodied in the Master at a basic rate of two cents (2cts) per unit, instead of the rates fixed in paragraph 9.01 of the Agreement.

(2)   With respect to sales for distribution outside the United States, sales through mail order, sales through Club Operations, sales of Budget, Mid-priced or Premium Records, and flat fee or flat royalty licenses, the License Royalty will be one cent (1 ct) instead of the two cents (2 cts) provided in the preceding sentence.

(3)   The License Royalty will not be payable until you have recouped the Seventy-five Hundred Dollars ($7,500.00) Advance payable pursuant to paragraph 1(a) above. After such recoupment, the License Royalty will be computed and paid prospectively (i. e. , on all such records sold after recoupment).

2.   Your compliance with this authorization will constitute an accommodation to me alone, and nothing herein shall constitute Licensor a beneficiary of or party to this instrument or any other agreement between you and me. All payments hereunder will constitute payment to me and you will have no liability by reason of any erroneous payment you may make or failure to comply with this authorization. I will indemnify and hold you harmless against any claims asserted against you and any damages, losses or expenses incurred by you by reason of any such payment or otherwise in connection herewith.

3.   All moneys becoming payable under this authorization shall be remitted to   , but shall be sent to me, c/o   , and shall be accompanied by statements with respect to such payments.

Licensor's federal tax I. D. number is _____ .

Very truly yours,

_____

THE SPLIT COPYRIGHT SYNDROME

SUMMARY

THE SPLIT COPYRIGHT SYNDROME

A*split copyright* is a copyright owned by two or more people (i.e., one in which two or more persons own an undivided interest). As noted in Chapter 1, control of a copyright by more than one person may pose one of the most frustrating barriers to clearing licenses —locating and obtaining permission from each of the several owners of the copyright. This chapter sketches the chaos that can result from co-ownership of copyright and suggests to copyright co-owners a solution that should enhance the value of their copyright and simplify the task of persons seeking to clear permission for the use of copyrighted compositions.

UNDIVIDED CO-OWNERSHIP OF COPYRIGHT

As the reader may recall from Chapter 2, when a composer and lyricist collaborate in the writing of a song, a copyright is said to *subsist* in the composer and lyricist the moment they fix the song on paper or recording tape. From that moment, the composer and lyricist co-own the *undivided* interest in the entire copyright of the song. The co-owners of a copyright are much like tenants in common of real property. Each author automatically acquires an undivided ownership interest in the *entire* work.

Unless they agree otherwise, the composer and lyricist each acquire a 50% undivided interest in the entire work and they share equally in the revenues generated by the song. Where there are three writers, each will have a 33 1/3% undivided interest in the entire work, and so forth. The writers may, however, agree to another division. For example, where one writer's contribution involved words and music and the other's involved only the words, the two may agree to a 75/25% division.

The reader may further recall from Chapter 3 that copyrights, and exclusive rights under copyright, may be transferred from one person to another. The composer in the above example, may sell to another his 50% undivided interest in the copyright. If he does so, he will then own no part of the copyright and the person to whom the assignment is made, the "assignee," will become the owner of that 50% undivided interest in the copyright. This is typically the effect of a standard music publishing contract between a composer and a music publisher—in exchange for granting his 50% undivided interest in the copyright to the music publisher, the composer is given contractual rights under which he receives the benefits of the publisher's administration services, including the administration of the copyright, the promotion of the song, the collection of revenues from licensing the use of the song, and payment of royalties to the composer, representing the composer's share of such revenues.

In short, when a songwriter signs a standard music publishing contract, he is generally agreeing to assign to the music publisher all of his undivided interest in his song. In some cases, however, the composer assigns only one-half of his undivided interest in the song to the music publisher, with the composer retaining the other half personally or in a separate sole proprietorship music publishing company established for the purpose of holding that interest. In the example of our composer, who started out only owning 50% of the song (his lyricist collaborator owning the other 50%), if the composer should assign half of his 50% undivided interest to a music publisher, then the composer and his music publisher would each own a 25% undivided interest in the copyright, leaving the lyricist, of course, with his 50% undivided interest, which he may retain or assign to the same, or another, music publisher.

In the above example, concerning one song written by two collaborators, as many as four music publishing companies may claim to have an undivided interest in the whole copyright in the song—i.e., the two respective commercial music publishers normally used by the composer and lyricist and the two respective sole proprietorship music publishing companies operated by the composer and lyricist or their respective attorneys, agents, or business managers.

Co-ownership of copyright can also result from a variety of other circumstances. Copyright ownership may be split by a statutory termination of a prior grant of copyright. When a grant of copyright is terminated under the 35 year termination rule[1] or the 19 year termination rule[2] (discussed in Chapter 4), the copyright reverts to the author or authors of the work, or to other persons owning the termination interests, such as a deceased author's surviving spouse or children. Each author or other person to which an undivided interest in the copyright reverts under a statutory termination is in a position to make a further grant of his or her interest to another, such as a music publisher of that person's choosing. Each may choose to grant the reverted rights to a different music publisher or choose to administer those rights himself. A similar split may occur where the renewal rights of a co-writer, discussed in Chapter 4, are assigned to a different publisher than the publisher of the rights of another co-writer.

The provisions of U.S. copyright law concerning termination of grants and renewal rights in no way affects rights arising under any foreign laws. Laws of certain countries provide similar statutory mechanisms that may cause a split copyright. For example, under the British copyright law, all rights under copyright revert to an author's heirs upon the twenty-fifth anniversary of the author's death. Thus, a split copyright results when the British reversionary rights of a co-writer are assigned to a different publisher than the publisher of the rights of another co-writer.

Finally, a division by percentage of ownership between writers is not the only way a copyright may be split. A copyright also may be split by territory. For example, one publisher may own the rights to a composition for the United States and several others may own rights for the rest of the world.

THE PROBLEM—AN ILLUSTRATIVE EXAMPLE

Let us consider an example in which the five members of a rock band collaborated in the writing of a song. Suppose that, upon formation of the band, they had agreed that each contributor would own an equal share of the copyright in any songs composed in collaboration. Thus, in

---

[1] 17 U.S.C. Sec. 203.

[2] 17 U.S.C. Sec. 304(c).

this example, each writer owns a 20% interest in the undivided copyright in the composition.

The first member had previously established his own publishing company, to which he promptly assigned his entire 20% undivided interest.

The second member had previously signed an exclusive songwriter's contract with a major music publisher, and, under that contract, was obligated to assign his entire 20% undivided interest to the publisher.

The third had also previously signed an exclusive songwriter's agreement, but his deal was a "Participation Deal," under which he agreed to assign only half of any undivided interest in any songs he wrote during the term of the contract; this resulted in his assigning half of his 20%, or 10% of the undivided interest in the copyright to his music publisher, and retaining 10% which he assigned to his own publishing company, which the publisher agreed to administer for him for a 15% administration fee.

The fourth member had also signed an exclusive songwriter's agreement, but with a publisher affiliated with the record company with which the band had signed, and his deal was a "Co-Publishing" deal, under which he too agreed to assign only half of any undivided interest in any songs he wrote during the term of the contract; this resulted in his assigning a 10% undivided interest in the copyright to his music publisher, but still retaining the other 10%, which he assigned to his own publishing company. His own music publishing company is run by his attorney and under his co-publishing contract with the record company affiliate, the writer retained the sole right to administer his half of his interest in the copyright. In exchange for a large advance against royalties, this fourth member promptly assigned the foreign rights in his 10% undivided interest to a major European music publishing company.

The fifth member didn't know anything about copyright, but was satisfied that the other members placed his name on the copyright registration form and took no further action, except to send a letter to ASCAP requesting a membership application form.

After several years, the song was becoming recognized as a standard hit and motion picture producers began to seek worldwide synchronization licenses and advertisers began offering large sums for permission to use the song in national television commercials. The band, of course, has long since broken up. One member died of a drug overdose, leaving a widow and two children, and another committed suicide over the frustration of determining his music rights, leaving no heirs but the Chase Manhattan Bank as the executor of his estate.

THE MUSIC CLEARANCE INDUSTRY
—A PARTIAL SOLUTION

The foregoing is an example of what might be called the "Split Copyright Syndrome," and it is not as far-fetched as it might initially appear. The Split Copyright Syndrome has spawned a new industry: music clearance companies. As noted and discussed in Chapter 1, music *clearance* is the process of (1) ascertaining whether a musical composition is protected by copyright, (2) if it is protected, determining who owns the copyright, or, more important, who has the right to administer its licensing, and (3) obtaining permission for the proposed use. Responding to the complexities posed by an increasing number of split copyrights, several entrepreneurs have established companies that specialize in performing the task of music clearance on behalf of motion picture producers, television producers, advertising agencies, and virtually anyone seeking to clear a license for the use of music.

For any clearance projects involving multiple music compositions or new technologies, such as multi-media works, the services of a professional clearance firm is highly recommended.

The Clearing House, Ltd. is one such firm that specializes in representing producers of television programs and motion pictures and others in clearing the use of copyrighted music by its clients. Ronald H. Gertz, Esq., a lawyer and the chief executive officer of Clearing House, Ltd. makes his living on the chaos resulting from the split copyright problem. In his commentary entitled, *Hung Up on Splintered Rights*, which appeared in a January, 1984, issue of *Billboard* magazine, Mr. Gertz artfully described the problem of split copyrights. The article is so instructive that we have obtained his permission to reprint it here in its entirety:

Everyone has heard variations of the oft recycled joke about the three biggest lies in Hollywood. The first two usually are, "The Mercedes is paid for" and "The check is in the mail." The third always seems to be rooted in social comment, like "It's only a cold sore."

My vote for lie number three is, "Don't worry, I control the rights." Accordingly, I am treating all publishers who say that as though they have some bizarre social disease, until proven otherwise.

Behind lie number three are the issues of terminated rights, reversionary rights, split copyrights and separate administration. These concepts and practices have a tendency to fragment the bundle of rights we call a song into a number of separately controlled pieces, creating havoc for anyone wishing to license its use.

The problems engendered apply in any licensing situation, whether the song is to be performed on a television show or the lyrics are to be reprinted on T-shirts.

Terminations and reversions aren't the only way that compositions get split up into little pieces. It happens as a result of legitimate collaboration. It happens when six members of a musical group co-write a song with each member keeping his own publishing and administration.

It also happens when an artist, as an inducement to record a song, takes a percentage of the copyright and administers his or her own share. I've seen situations like the latter with shares as small as 6 1/4%. At that rate, the income generated doesn't even pay the fees of the attorney handling the administration.

When a song is divided into several parts, whether by percentages, territories or both, the result is invariably chaos. How does one locate all the owners? Which owner has the right to give a license to a potential user? What happens when all the owners can't agree on a price for their respective shares?

At what point will an owner, relying on joint ownership rules, tire of the game and license the whole song without regard to the feelings of his co-owners? Will that owner ever account to the other parties? Will he first deduct the cost of traveling to Hollywood to complete the negotiation?

Can the potential music user trust the publisher who says, "Don't worry, I control the rights?"

I have always believed that the basic rule in the music publishing business is to get songs performed. Performances mean royalties and royalties make people happy. But a split copyright, for whatever reason, frequently means fewer performances and less royalties.

While most publishers approach the administration of their catalogs in a professional manner, a growing number fail to grasp the practical and business issues presented. The inability to contact these publishers by phone or letter, and their own lack of knowledge about what causes royalties to be generated, will frequently result in a composition being deleted from a program.

Perhaps a recent experience in attempting to license a song in a two-hour television variety special will serve to illustrate the problem. I squared off against a composition which was to be used as a vocal bridge for about 30 seconds during the course of a 10-song production number. The rights to the song were divided into four separate interests. One publisher controlled the rights in all territories of the world, excluding the United States. The other three publishers each owned 33 1/3% of the U.S. rights.

Publisher number one demanded a laughably high license fee. Number two referred us to his agent, who wouldn't do anything until all the others agreed. Number three, an obvious disciple of Newton Minnow, didn't want his part of the song to contribute to television's vast wasteland, and wouldn't grant permission. Number four was on vacation and could not be reached.

When I told the producer that we could not obtain the rights he needed within his time frame, his musical director came up with a substitute song that, as fate would have it, was divided into only three parts. The owners were willing to grant a license, but each wanted a full license fee for his fractional interest.

When I told the producer that his second choice was going to be the most expensive song in the show, he decided to find a new clearance company. I'm sure that in his mind, with production costs mounting and the minutes ticking by, the most logical thing to do in the face of the message was to kill the messenger.

Since Old Testament prophets frequently suffered the same fate, I didn't feel so bad. But I lost a client, and the publishers lost their respective share of about $5,000 income over the network and syndicated runs. Although the mutuality of loss also softened the blow, I have the hollow feeling that the publishers I dealt with didn't care, and that is what I find so disturbing.

It is clear to me that fragmentation of rights will make it harder and harder for television and film producers to use certain songs. When that occurs, the royalties generated by those songs will begin to decrease. The widows and the publishers will wake up one morning to the startling revelation that "the checks are no longer in the mail."

The solution might be as simple as letting the party with the greatest percentage have the administration rights. That way each party would take his share of the total fee rather than require a user to negotiate a separate dollar amount for each share.

In conclusion, all is again well in Hollywood, the Mercedes is on a lease, and my producer friend is back in the fold. He read the first draft of this commentary and now realizes what the problem really was. His next project is going to be a star-studded musical salute to Stephen "Public Domain" Foster.

LEGAL BACKGROUND

The general rule governing the right of a co-owner to grant non-exclusive licenses for use of the work is this: Unless co-owners have a contract among them which states otherwise, a co-owner can grant a license for the use of the song without the consent of the co-owners, as long as the licensing co-owner accounts and pays to the others their share of the license fee collected.[3]

However, this rule is not entirely settled by law. Courts have held that one co-owner may not unilaterally grant a license that will effectively destroy the value of the copyright. Just what kinds of licenses

---

[3] See generally, 1 Nimmer *On Copyright*, Sec. 6.10.

would be construed as having destroyed the value of the copyright is not clear. Further, and perhaps more important, the above rule is not followed in many countries around the world. In the United Kingdom, France, and many other countries, the rule is: a license is not valid unless all co-owners consent to it.

Relying solely on the U.S. rule, persons seeking to clear permission should feel comfortable in accepting a license offered by only one of several co-owners, provided that the territory of the license is limited to the United States and that the licensee has no reason to believe that there exists an agreement among the co-owners restricting the granting of licenses by the other co-owners. The licensee might also rely on a written warranty from the licensing co-owner that the latter has the right to grant the license without the consent of any of the co-owners.

The practical problem faced by producers of works that include music licensed from one co-owner is the risk that another co-owner will later make an objection. The consequences of having an ineffectual license are great: the producer risks having the distribution of his entire work enjoined by a court. A more important practical problem stems from the fact that advances in worldwide telecommunications are making the economies of countries increasingly interdependent. As a result, licensees are increasingly demanding that the territories of music licenses be made worldwide. If the territory of the license is worldwide, the producer must insist upon receiving the written permission from *all* of the co-owners of the song.

TIP ON CLEARING LICENSES FROM MULTIPLE CO-OWNERS

When you are seeking to clear a license that requires permission from more than one owner, you should condition any obligation to pay license fees to any one co-owner upon your obtaining the necessary license from all the other co-owners. Thus, if you cannot obtain the consent of all other co-owners of the composition, it would then be clear that you have no obligation to pay the negotiated fee to the co-owners from whom you were able to obtain a license, provided, of course, that you make no use of the song.

Alternatively, you may negotiate all the necessary licenses from the various co-owners and then sign them all at once. The problem is that you may find, as co-owners have an opportunity to confer with each other, one or more may have a change of mind and you may find yourself in an endless circle of negotiation. It would be better to get each co-owner to sign an agreement when the fire is hot, and condition your obligations to pay upon your obtaining the consent of the other co-owners.

COPYRIGHT ADMINISTRATION

It is ironic that the most common cause of lost licensing opportunities is the inexperienced co-owner, or the co-owner's attorney, manager or publisher representative, who, in insisting upon a fee that is far higher than any reasonable fee that should be charged for the license, loses the licensing opportunity entirely, not just for him or his client, but for all co-owners—indeed, for the song itself.

It has been the experience of both music clearance firms and professional publishers that too many songwriters who own their own publishing companies turn over absolute control of their publishing activities to an inexperienced or inappropriate representative, often an attorney. Many of these writers do not keep track of what their own attorney is doing. In some cases, the writer fails to realize that, as much as an attorney can be valued for providing legal advice and drafting contracts, the basic business skills of managing the copyright of a song is an entirely different matter. How many times have we seen, where a copyright is split, that a poor co-writer is losing thousands of dollars of revenue due to one co-writer's stubborn lawyer? And when years after a song was a hit, when the songwriter is old and gray and wonders why the licensing revenue for that song has been reduced to a trickle in his retirement years, it may never have occurred to him that the reason for his circumstances is that his attorneys and managers have over the years either asked for exorbitant fees for synchronization licenses or withheld licenses under the assumption that his client didn't want the song used.

It is therefore strongly recommended that the administration of copyright should either be exercised directly by the writer or turned over to a professional music publisher who can make the delicate judgments required to keep their copyrights returning revenues well into the writer's retirement.

CURING THE SPLIT COPYRIGHT SYNDROME

1. Compulsory License

As noted in Chapter 7, one of the benefits of the provision of the copyright law that compels owners to issue mechanical licenses is that it appears to be an effective solution to the split copyright syndrome insofar as it facilitates the clearing of licenses to use music in sound recordings that are not accompanied by audiovisual works. Split copyright does not become an issue when all the co-owners are required to accept no more than the statutory rate. Further, when the person seeking to clear a mechanical license cannot identify or locate the owner of the copyright, the compulsory license provision provides a safe harbor: if the public records of the Copyright Office do not identify the copyright owner and include an address at which notice under the provision can be served, it is sufficient to file the required notice with the Copyright Office.[4] By properly following the procedure and paying the statutory rate set forth in the compulsory license provision, a person seeking to clear permission will be assured a license without taking any risk of liability for copyright infringement.

It has been suggested that a compulsory license provision may be an effective solution to the split copyright problem with respect to the use of music in certain recordings that are accompanied by audiovisual works, or multi-media works. It remains to be seen whether this solution will ever receive legislative attention.

2. Exclusive Administration Rights

The only non-legislative solution that seems to solve the problem at its roots is one which leaves the exclusive right to administer the copyright to just one of the co-owners of the copyright or to an

---

[4] 17 U.S.C. Sec. 115(b)(1).

independent third party who has an incentive and the appropriate resources to maximize the value of the copyright for all concerned. An economist would view the problem of split copyright as one which unnecessarily increases the transaction costs of deriving income from the copyright. Clearly, transaction costs would be reduced if only one person owned or controlled the administration of the copyright.[5] Where only one person controls the administration of a copyright, the person seeking to clear a license for use of the copyrighted material would need only locate and negotiate with that one person—the sole copyright owner or administrator could make the appropriate decisions without requiring the consent of the co-owners. The risk that one of the co-owners, or their representatives or heirs, will impede the income potential of the copyright will be significantly reduced.

3. Co-Publishing Agreement

Control over the administration of the copyright by one co-owner or an independent third party does not require the other co-owners to transfer their ownership interest in the copyright. As noted above, co-owners of copyright can always enter into an agreement that specifically governs their respective rights to grant licenses. This is usually done in the form of a Co-Publishing Agreement, which is an agreement governing the respective administration rights of co-owners of copyright. An example of a Co-Publishing Agreement that vests in one of the parties the exclusive right to issue non-exclusive licenses for the use of the music they co-own is set forth as Form 18.1 at the end of this chapter.

If a co-owner has certain sensitivities about the licensing of his or her music, then appropriate safeguards can be built into the Co-Publishing Agreement providing that his consent be obtained where the permission being requested broaches that area of sensitivity. For example, a co-owner may grant exclusive administration rights to another co-owner, but still require that his or her consent be obtained to permit any change in the lyrics or harmonic structure of the music, to issue any

---

[5] Landes and Posner, *An Economic Analysis of Copyright Law*, 18 Journal of Legal Studies 325 (1989).

mechanical license at less than the prevailing statutory rate, to authorize the use of the title of the song as the title of a play, film or TV program, to authorize the dramatization of the song, to authorize the synchronization of the song in a motion picture, television program, or videogram bearing a rating of "X" or its equivalent, or authorize the use of the song in any political advertisement.

After a decision is made among the co-owners to grant exclusive administration rights, what still remains is the question of who among the co-owners should be given control of the exclusive administration rights. The co-owners can each grant their respective administration rights to the one co-owner who has shown the greatest amount of business acumen or interest in spending the time required to manage the copyright. If it is not readily apparent who among the co-owners would be best for this job, perhaps, as Ron Gertz has suggested, the solution is as simple as letting the party with the greatest percentage have the administration rights.

4. Administration Agreement

Should the co-owners fail to reach an agreement on an effective co-publishing arrangement, they could still effect exclusive control of administration rights in one party by turning to one independent, professional music publisher to administer the copyright on their behalf. Under this arrangement, each writer can maintain his own publishing company and his share of the publishing revenues, but each would agree to grant to a professional music publisher the exclusive right to administer those rights, without restriction, or subject only to restrictions on licensing uses over which one or more of the co-owners may be particularly sensitive. Many music publishers will agree to administer the copyrights owned by others for an administration fee—usually 10–15% of net revenues—without taking an ownership interest in the copyright of the song. An example of a music publishing Administration Agreement is set forth as Form 18.3 at the end of this chapter.

Granting administration rights to an independent music publisher may be the only solution that assures each of the co-owners that the copyright will be administered with each of their interests in mind. The only key decision that would remain is choosing the right music publisher. The risks of that decision can be alleviated in part by carefully negotiating an arrangement with the publisher to assure that the administration rights would revert to the co-owners should the music publisher fail to meet certain performance levels.

Granting administration rights to a professional music publisher may, in fact, be the best solution for the co-owners. Because of its access to vast amounts of information regarding the standard terms and conditions and going rates and practices in licensing music, the professional music publisher is in a better position than most others in maximizing the value of the musical composition.

CONCLUSION

Each of the foregoing alternatives is almost always superior to the state of split copyright and will tend to better maximize the value of the copyright. The reduced transaction costs of having only one person control the administration rights will surely increase net income to the copyright owners. More important, however, is the direct effect on the value of the copyright. The more co-owners of a song there are, the more difficult it is to obtain the consent of all of the owners, and the result will be fewer licenses granted. Fewer licenses will lead to fewer performances; with fewer performances, the song will begin to lose its share of the mind of the listening public, resulting in even fewer performances and fewer requests for licenses. The ultimate result will be a lower income stream for the copyright owners, equating to a reduced copyright value. In cases of three or more co-owners, the solution of a single administrator of all rights should always be superior than each co-owner maintaining control over his or her share of a split copyright.

In the absence of a single administrator solution, it is hoped that a co-owner of copyright who insists upon full control of the administration of his or her co-ownership interest will at least recognize the benefits of maintaining a long-term outlook when considering what fees to charge for permission to use his or her music.

APPENDIX FOR CHAPTER 18
THE SPLIT COPYRIGHT SYNDROME

FORMS

CIRCULARS

FORM 18.1

CO-PUBLISHING AGREEMENT
WITH EXCLUSIVE ADMINISTRATION
RIGHTS GRANTED TO ONE CO-OWNER

CO-PUBLISHING AGREEMENT

THIS AGREEMENT made this   day of   1995, by and between   (hereinafter referred to as "Company") and   (hereinafter referred to as "Participant")

WITNESSETH:

WHEREAS, it is the intention of Company and Participant that they shall jointly own, in equal shares, the musical compositions (hereinafter collectively referred to as the "Composition") listed or described below, so that fifty percent (50%) of the entire worldwide right, title and interest, including the copyright, the right to copyright and the renewal right, in and to the Composition shall be owned by Company and fifty percent (50%) thereof shall be owned by Participant:

WHEREAS, the Composition has been or shall be registered for copyright in the names of Company and Participant in the Copyright Office of the United States of America;

NOW, THEREFORE, for good and valuable consideration the receipt of which is hereby acknowledged by each party hereto, it is agreed as follows:

1.   Company and Participant shall jointly own the Composition, in equal shares, including all of the worldwide right, title and interest, including the copyrights, the right to copyright and the renewal rights, therein and thereto.

2.   The Composition shall be registered for copyright by Company in the names of Company and Participant in the office of

the Register of Copyrights of the United States of America and Company shall take all reasonable measures to protect the copyright in the Composition in those territories which are signatories to the Universal Copyright Convention. If the Composition has heretofore been registered for copyright in the name of Participant, Participant shall simultaneously herewith deliver to Company an assignment of a one-half interest therein, in form acceptable to Company.

3.   Company shall have the sole and exclusive right to administer and exploit the Composition, to print, publish, sell, use and license the use of the Composition throughout the world, and to execute in its own name any and all licenses and agreements affecting or respecting the Composition, including but not limited to licenses for mechanical reproduction, public performance, synchronization uses, subpublication, merchandising, and advertising and to assign or license such rights to others. This statement of exclusive rights is only in clarification and amplification of the rights of Company hereunder and not in limitation thereof.

4.   Company shall be entitled to receive and collect and shall receive and collect all gross receipts derived from the Composition. "Gross receipts," as used herein, shall mean any and all revenue, income and sums derived from the Composition from any and all sources whatsoever.

5.   Company shall pay to Participant fifty percent (50%) of the net income actually received and derived by Company from the Composition. "Net income," as used herein, shall mean the gross receipts derived by Company from the Composition, less the following:

(a)   A sum equal to ten percent (10%) of the Gross Receipts as an administration charge for overhead.

(b)   Royalties and other sums which are paid by Company to the composers and writers of the Composition pursuant to the provisions of the songwriter's agreements between Participant and such composers and writers (a copy of which is attached hereto as Exhibit "A") or which, at Company's election, are paid by Company to Participant, in trust, for payment over by Participant to such composers and writers pursuant to the provisions of said songwriter's agreements;

(c)   Collection or other fees customarily and actually charged by

or any other collection agent which may be used by Company;

(d)   Actual, out-of-pocket administrative and exploitation expenses of Company with respect to the Composition for registration fees, advertising and promotion expenses directly related to the Composition, the costs of transcribing for lead sheets, and the costs of producing demonstration records;

(e)   Attorneys' fees directly related to the defense of claims respecting the Composition, if any, actually paid by Company;

(f)   The costs of printing, engraving, arranging and editing printed editions of the Composition incurred by Company.

6.   The performing rights in the Composition, to the extent permitted by law, shall be assigned to and licensed by The American Society of Composers, Authors and Publishers (ASCAP). ASCAP shall be and hereby is authorized to collect and receive all moneys earned from the public performance of the composition and to pay directly to Company one hundred percent (100%) of the amount allocated by ASCAP as the publisher's share of public performance fees.

7.   Mechanical royalties for the Composition for the United States and Canada shall be collectible by The Harry Fox Agency or any other collection agent which may be designated by Company, provided however, that Company shall, in the case of any record company affiliated with Company, issue the mechanical licenses

directly to said record company at the then current statutory rate and collect mechanical royalties directly therefrom in which case there shall be no collection fee as referred to in paragraph 5(c).

8.   Statements as to moneys payable hereunder shall be sent by Company to Participant semiannually within ninety (90) days after the end of each semiannual calendar period. Statements shall be accompanied by appropriate payments. Participant shall be deemed to have consented to all royalty statements and other accounts rendered by Company to Participant, and said statements and other accounts shall be binding upon Participant and not subject to any objection for any reason, unless specific objection in writing, setting forth the basis thereof, is given by Participant to Company within two (2) years from the date rendered. Participant or a certified public accountant in its behalf may, at reasonable intervals, examine the books of Company pertaining to the Composition during Company's usual business hours and upon reasonable notice. Said books relating to activities and receipts during any accounting period may only be examined as aforesaid during the two (2) year period following service by Company of the statement for said accounting period only during Company's normal business hours and upon ten days' written notice.

9.   Each party hereto shall give the other the equal benefits of any warranties or representations which it obtained or shall obtain under any agreements affecting the Composition.

10.   Company shall have the sole right to prosecute, defend, settle and compromise all suits, claims, and actions respecting the composition, and generally to do and perform all things necessary concerning the same and the copyrights therein, to prevent and restrain the infringement of copyrights or other rights with respect to the Composition. In the event of the recovery by Company of any moneys as a result of a judgment or settlement, such moneys, less an amount equal to the expense of obtaining said moneys, including counsel fees, shall be deemed additional gross receipts hereunder. Participant shall have the right to provide counsel for itself, but at its own expense, to assist in any such manner. Company will

not settle any claim respecting the Composition without Participant's consent, which consent shall not be unreasonably withheld.

11.   The rights of the parties hereto in and to the Composition shall extend for the term of the copyright of the Composition and of any derivative copyrights therein in the United States of America and throughout the rest of the world and for the terms of any renewals or extensions thereof in the United States of America and throughout the rest of the world.

12.   This agreement sets forth the entire understanding between the parties, and cannot be changed, modified or canceled except by an instrument signed by the party sought to be bound. This agreement shall be governed by and construed under the laws of the State of California applicable to agreements wholly performed therein.

13.   Participant hereby warrants and represents that it has the right to enter into this agreement and to grant to Company all of the rights granted herein, and that the exercise by Company of any and all of the rights granted to Company in this agreement will not violate or infringe upon any common law or statutory rights of any person, firm or corporation, including, without limitation, contractual rights, copyrights and rights of privacy. The rights granted herein are free and clear of any claims, demands, liens or encumbrances. Participant agrees to and does hereby indemnify, save and hold Company, its assigns, licensees, and its and their directors, officers, shareholders, agents and employees harmless from any and all liabilities, claims, demands, loss and damage (including attorneys' fees and court costs) arising out of or connected with any claim by a third party which is inconsistent with any of the Warranties, representations, covenants, or agreements made by Participant herein and Participant agrees to reimburse Company, on demand, for any payment made by Company at any time after the date hereof with respect to any liability or claim to which the foregoing indemnity applies. Pending the determination of any such claim, Company may withhold payment of royalties or other moneys hereunder, provided that all amounts so withheld are reason-

ably related to the amount of said claim and the estimated attorneys' fees in connection therewith, and provided further that Participant shall have the right to post a bond in an amount reasonably satisfactory to Company by a bonding company reasonably satisfactory to Company, in which events Company shall not withhold payments as aforesaid.

14. All notices, statements or other documents which either party shall be required or shall desire to give to the other hereunder must be in writing and shall be given by the parties hereto only in one of the following ways: (1) by personal delivery; or (2) by addressing them as indicated below, and by depositing them postage prepaid, in the United States mail, airmail if the address is outside of the state in which such notice is deposited; or (3) by delivering them toll prepaid to a telegraph or cable company. If so delivered, mailed, telegraphed or cabled, each such notice, statement or other document shall, except as herein expressly provided, be conclusively deemed to have been given when personally delivered or on the date of delivery to the telegraph or cable company or 24 hours after the date of mailing, as the case may be. The addresses of the parties shall be those of which the other party actually receives written notice and until further notice are:

       "Company"   "Participant"

A copy of all notices to Participant hereunder shall be sent to:

15. This agreement shall not be deemed to give any right or remedy to any third party whatsoever unless said right or remedy is specifically granted to such third party by the terms hereof.

16. The parties hereto shall execute any further documents including, without limitation, assignments of copyrights, and do all acts necessary to fully effectuate the terms and provisions of this agreement.

17. Company may enter into subpublishing agreements with, or assign, or license any of its rights hereunder to, one or more

other person, firms, or corporations for any one or more countries of the world. In the event Company enters into a subpublishing or administration agreement for any country of the world with a company affiliated with or otherwise related to Company, such agreement shall be deemed to have been made with an independent third party—provided, that no foreign subpublishing agreement respecting the Composition shall be on terms less favorable to Company than what is commonly referred to in the music publishing industry and a 75/25/10 division of royalties and a 50/50/10 division with respect to so-called foreign cover records. Participant acknowledges that Company has the right to administer and publish compositions other than the Composition.

IN WITNESS WHEREOF, the parties have executed this agreement the day and year above set forth.

By _____   By _____

FORM 18.2

ALTERNATIVE CO-PUBLISHING AGREEMENT WITH
EXCLUSIVE ADMINISTRATION RIGHTS
GRANTED TO ONE CO-OWNER,
SUBJECT TO CERTAIN RESTRICTIONS

Dated:

INDEPENDENT MUSIC PUBLISHING COMPANY
Attn:
1234 Main Street
San Jose, California 95000

Re: Co-Publishing and Exclusive Administration Agreement

Gentlemen:

The following, when signed by you and by us, will constitute the terms and conditions of the exclusive co-publishing (i.e., "participation") agreement between you and us.

   1.   Scope of Agreement:

      1.1.   Subject to those requirements and/or restrictions set forth in subparagraph 1.2., below, you and we will each own an undivided 50% share of the copyright in, and we will have exclusive worldwide life-of-copyright administration of, your interest in the songs (and all derivative works based thereon) listed on the attached Schedule "A" (referred to below as the "Subject Compositions").

      1.2.   Although it is intended that we and our foreign subsidiaries, affiliates and licensees have the fullest possible rights to administer and exploit the Subject Compositions, to utilize your name and likeness in connection therewith and to execute PA forms (and other routine copyright documents) in your name and on your behalf as your attorney-in-fact (which appointment is coupled with an interest and is therefore irrevocable), neither we nor they shall do any of the following without your prior written consent in each instance (which consent, unless expressly provided otherwise, shall not be unreasonably withheld by you):

        1.2.1. Authorize any change in the English-language title and/or lyric of any Subject Composition, alter the harmonic structure of any Subject Composition, or alter the melody of any Subject Composition (except insubstantial changes necessary to accommodate the syllabic requirements of foreign languages);

        1.2.2. Issue a mechanical license for the use of any Subject Composition at less than the prevailing statutory or society rate, except in connection with those types of uses for which reduced-rate licenses are customarily granted in the country in question;

        1.2.3. Authorize the use of the title of any Subject Composition as the title of a play, film or TV program, or authorize the dramatization of any Subject Composition;

        1.2.4. Authorize the synchronization of any Subject Composition in (A) a film or TV program bearing a rating of "X" or the equivalent, or (B) any political advertisement.

    2. <u>Collection and Division of Income:</u>

        2.1. Subject to any rights and/or remedies which may be available to us in the event of a material breach of this agreement on your part is not cured as provided in par. 6.3., below, we will be entitled to collect (and shall employ best efforts consistent with our reasonable business judgment to collect) all writer/publisher income (except the writer's share of public performances collected by societies and any other amount normally paid directly to songwriters by a disbursing agent) generated by the Subject Compositions (including pre-Term earnings).

2.1.1. (A) Net Income from Subject Compositions shall be divided 50% to us, 50% to you.

(B) As used herein, "Net Income" shall mean all amounts received by us, or credited to our account in reduction of an advance, from licensees and performing and mechanical rights societies ("Gross Receipts") after deduction of writer royalties as per the annexed Schedule "B" and (1) actual and reasonable out-of-pocket collection costs (including local subpublisher fees or income shares) (2) out-of-pocket copyright registration costs, (3) costs of lead sheets, and (4) demo costs (approved by both parties in writing) to the extent not recouped from writer royalties.

2.1.2. For the purposes of this paragraph, Gross Receipts on printed materials sold (and paid for) shall be deemed to be:

2.1.2. (A) Outside of the U.S. and Canada 12.5% of the marked or suggested retail list price (or the price deemed to be the local equivalent, in any country in which there are no marked or suggested retail list prices) ("list") (prorated in the case of mixed folios and other editions not consisting entirely of Subject Compositions); and

(B) In the U.S. and Canada, 20% of list on piano/vocal sheet music, 12 1/2% of list on folios other than "fake books" or "educational editions", 10% of list on "fake books" and "educational editions" (prorated in either event in the case of mixed folios and other mixed editions), on copies sold and paid for.

(C) In the case of amounts received from third-party print licensees your co-publisher's share shall be 25% while the writer's share shall be 50%.

(D) Print royalties are subject to proration where only part of the composition is a Subject Composition.

      2.1.3.   Gross Receipts received from our affiliates and licensees outside of the U.S. and Canada shall be deemed to be 80% of mechanical income from original records, 60% of mechanical income from Cover Records, 60% of the publisher's share of public performance income, and 80% of other categories of income (other than print).

3.   Accounting and Payment:

      3.1.   We will account to you (and make payment where appropriate) within 60 days following the end of each semi-annual calendar period. However, if the amount due for a specific statement is less than $50., payment may be deferred until the aggregate amount due to you exceeds $50.

      3.2.   We will only be required to account and pay with respect to amounts actually received by us in the U.S. (or credited to our account in reduction of a previous advance received by us in the U.S.).

      3.2.1.   You (or a certified public accountant on your behalf) shall have the right to audit our books and records as to each statement for a period of 2 years after such statement is received (or deemed received as provided below). Legal action with respect to a specific accounting statement or the accounting period to which such statement relates shall be barred if not commenced in a court of competent jurisdiction within 3 years after such statement is received (or deemed received as provided below).

      3.2.2.   For the purposes of calculating such time periods, you shall be deemed to have received a statement when due unless we receive notice of nonreceipt from you (in the manner prescribed in paragraph 7, below) within 30 days thereafter. However, your failure to give such notice shall not affect your right to receive such statement (and, if applicable, your royalty and/or net income payment) after such thirty-day period.

3.3.   In "blocked currency" situations, we shall not be re-quired to pay you until the blockage shall have been removed, but if requested to do so, we shall deposit blocked currency royalties in the local currency in a depository of your choice. The exchange rates used by third parties in accounting to us shall be used by us in accountings hereunder.

3.4.   All payments hereunder shall be subject to all applica-ble taxation statutes, regulations and treaties.

4.   Warranties and Representations:

4.1.   By your signature below, you warrant and repre-sent (1) that you have the right to grant the rights granted to us hereunder, (2) that the Subject Composition does not infringe any third party's rights or violate any applicable criminal statute, includ-ing but not limited to such third party's copyright, trademark, service mark, or right of privacy or publicity, (3) that the Subject Composition is not defamatory and (4) that your music publishing designee will affiliate with ASCAP, BMI or another recognized performing rights society to which the writers of the Subject Compositions are affiliated, and you will immediately advise us of said affiliation.

4.1.1.   Except as set forth in the annexed Schedule "C", neither you nor your music publishing designee, nor anyone acting on your and/or your music publishing designee's behalf or deriving rights from or through you or your music publishing designee (A) has received or will receive an advance, loan or other payment from a performing rights society, record company or other third party which is or may be recoupable from (or otherwise subject to offset against) moneys which would other-wise be collectible by us hereunder, (B) is presently subject to any so-called "controlled compositions" clause under a recording agreement or (C) is presently subject to any provision of a record-ing agreement which would allow a record company to charge any amount against mechanical royalties.

4.1.2. Notwithstanding the foregoing, in the event that any record company to whom you (or an entity furnishing your services) are or may hereafter be under contract charges any advance(s) or other amount(s) against mechanical royalties earned by the Subject Compositions from recordings made under such recording agreement or reduces the amount of mechanical royalties otherwise due to you because the mechanical royalties payable with respect to "outside material" embodied in your recordings causes aggregate mechanical royalties to exceed the per-record maximum rate(s) prescribed in the controlled compositions clause of your recording agreement, then, in addition to any other rights and remedies available to us, we shall be entitled to (A) send a letter of direction in your name advising your record company of the terms of this paragraph 4 and instructing such record company (upon recoupment from record and/or video royalties of any portion(s) of the advance(s) or other amount(s) so charged) to re-credit us directly to the same extent (not to exceed the total amount originally recouped from or charged against mechanical royalties) and (B) reimburse ourselves from any and all moneys (including your writer/publisher royalties) earned hereunder, for any amount charged against mechanical royalties, except to the extent later recovered through the re-crediting process.

4.1.3. In the event of a breach of this paragraph 4.1., we shall (in addition to any other remedies available to us) be entitled to reimburse ourselves from moneys otherwise becoming due to you or your music publishing designee hereunder to the extent that moneys are not collectable by us by reason thereof.

5. Indemnities; Cure of Breaches:

5.1. Each party will indemnify the other against any loss or damage (including court costs and reasonable attorneys' fees) due to a breach of this agreement by that party which results in a judgment against the other party or which is settled with the other party's prior written consent (not to be unreasonably withheld). In addition, your indemnity shall extend to the "deductible" under our errors-and-omissions policy without regard to judgment or settlement. Each party is entitled to be notified of any action against the other brought with respect to any Subject Composition, and to participate in the defense thereof by counsel of its choice, at its sole cost and expense. In the event that one of us refuses to approve a settlement which the other party considers reasonable, the party refusing its consent shall assume the further defense of the subject claim, action or proceeding.

5.2.   If a claim is made against us, we may withhold a reasonable amount from moneys due or to become due to you, but we will refund it (together with interest on the amount released at the regular savings and loan passbook interest rate prevailing in Los Angeles from time to time during the period of withholding) if (and to the extent that) suit is not brought with respect to that sum within 1 year thereafter, and we won't withhold moneys hereunder if (and to the extent that) you provide us with a satisfactory commercial surety bond.

5.3.   Neither party will be deemed in breach unless the other party gives notice and the notified party fails to cure within 30 days after receiving notice; *provided*, that if the alleged breach is of such a nature that it cannot be completely cured within 30 days, the notified party will not be deemed to be in breach if the notified party commences the curing of the alleged breach within such thirty-day period and proceeds to complete the curing thereof with due diligence within a reasonable time thereafter. However, either party shall have the right to seek injunctive relief to prevent a threatened breach of this agreement by the other party. All payments required to be made by us hereunder shall be subject to any rights and/or remedies which may otherwise be available to us in the event of a breach of this agreement on your part not cured in the manner prescribed above, and to any withholding which may be required by the rules and regulations of any taxing jurisdiction having authority.

6. <u>Notices</u>: Notices shall be sent by certified (return receipt requested) or registered mail or telex to you and us (to the attention

of our Vice President of Legal and Business Affairs) at the above addresses or any other addresses the parties designate by notice in like manner. Statements (and payments, if applicable) shall be sent by ordinary mail. If the party's consent is required, it shall not be unreasonably withheld (unless expressly provided otherwise herein) and shall be deemed given unless the notified party gives notice of nonconsent within 15 days after receipt of notice requesting consent.

7. <u>Law and Forum</u>: This Agreement has been entered into in, and is to be interpreted in accordance with the laws of the State of California. All actions or proceedings seeking the interpretation and/or enforcement of this Agreement shall be brought only in the State or Federal Courts located in Los Angeles County, all parties hereby submitting themselves to the jurisdiction of such courts for such purpose.

Very truly yours,

BIG MUSIC PUBLISHING CORP.

By: _____

AGREED AND ACCEPTED:

INDEPENDENT MUSIC PUBLISHING COMPANY

By: _____
    Fed. I.D.#:
    Soc. Sec. #:

SCHEDULE "A"

Titles	Composers/%	% Controlled
I LOVE YOU	Cameron Composer (1/2)100% Larry Lyrics (1/2)	

SCHEDULE "B"

WRITER ROYALTIES

(1)   U.S. and Canada:
Print: (all on net paid sales):

Piano/vocal sheet: 7 cents

Folios (other than "fake books" or "educational editions"): 12 1/2% of wholesale (prorated in the case of "mixed" folios to reflect number of royalty-bearing compositions);

"Fake books" and "educational editions": 10% of wholesale (subject to same pro-ration);

(2)   Mechanical Royalties: 50% of gross receipts

(3)   Performance Royalties: if collected directly by us and not through a society: 50% of gross receipts

(4)   Foreign Income: 50% of gross receipts

(5)   Other Income: 50% of gross receipts; provided, that Writer shall not be entitled to receive any portion of any amount received by us from a source which pays writer an equivalent amount directly (including but not limited to distributions from a performing rights society and direct payments of portions of any blank tape tax or

charge which may be enacted by Congress if writers and publishers are paid separately).

(6)　Demo Costs: To the extent approved by both parties in writing in advance, we shall pay for the cost of making demonstration records of the Subject Compositions. One-half (1/2) of a pro rata share corresponding to Writer's percentage of the Subject Compositions of such total costs shall be deemed additional advances to Writer hereunder.

Above royalties to be prorated where only part of the subject composition is subject to this agreement.

SCHEDULE "C"

(Pursuant to subparagraph 4.1.1., if applicable.)

SCHEDULE "D"

Date: January 1, 1995

American Society of Composers,
Authors & Publishers
One Lincoln Plaza
New York, N.Y. 10023

Gentlemen:

You are hereby authorized and directed to pay to our administrator, Big Music Publishing Corp. ("Administrator"), at 1000 Sunset Boulevard, Hollywood, California 90069, and we hereby assign
to Administrator, all moneys payable from and after the date hereof
(regardless of when earned) as our share of the publisher's public
performance royalties with respect to the compositions described
below:

<u>COMPOSITION</u>   <u>COMPOSERS</u>

Copies of all statements shall be sent to Administrator and to
us.

The foregoing authorization and direction shall remain in full
force and effect until modified or terminated by both the undersigned and Administrator.

Very truly yours,

INDEPENDENT MUSIC
PUBLISHING COMPANY

By: _____

FORM 18.3

ADMINISTRATION AGREEMENT

MUSIC PUBLISHING ADMINISTRATION AGREEMENT

AGREEMENT made as of the   day of   , 19 , between

          , a New York corporation (hereinafter referred to as "Publisher", whose address is

and   , a New York corporation (hereinafter referred to as "Administrator"), whose address is

IN CONSIDERATION of the mutual covenants and promises hereinafter set forth, it is hereby agreed by the parties hereto as follows;

1.   Publisher hereby designates Administrator and Administrator hereby accepts such designation and undertakes to act as the sole selling agent and business supervisor of Publisher throughout the world.

2.   Administrator shall provide all necessary administrative management services and supervisory facilities for Publisher and agrees to take all necessary and proper steps to protect the copyrights owned by Publisher. Such services, facilities and protective measures shall be comparable, at least to the best facilities, services and protective measures provided by Administrator to any other company for which Administrator shall also be acting during the term hereof in the same capacity as it agrees herein to act for Publisher. Such services and facilities shall include rent, procurement of supplies, selling, invoicing dispatching, shipping, bookkeeping, and collection of accounts, local telephone service and all other services not hereinafter specifically excepted. For all such services and personnel, Administrator shall be authorized to retain   percent (%) of the gross income received by or on behalf of Publisher from all sources during the term of this agreement (the "Administration Fee").

3.   Publisher will pay the salaries of any employees (subject to written approval by Publisher) employed by and for Publisher exclusively for the exploitation of its catalogue. Administrator agrees, nevertheless, to advance for the account of Publisher all sums required for the defraying of the costs and expenses with respect thereto.

4.   With respect to all compositions owned or controlled by Publisher, Publisher will pay the following:

(a)   All expenses for the purchase of music paper and other inventory, printing engraving, autographing, orchestrating, authors' royalties, advertising in trade periodicals, disc jockey records and other trade publicity;

(b)   Costs of any authorized special arrangements required by Publisher for the exploitation of its catalogue;

(c)   All accounting and legal fees incurred solely with respect to the compositions;

(d)   Any fees required to be paid to   for the collection of mechanical and synchronization fees due to Publisher by reason of licenses issued by
but in no event shall such fees exceed five percent (5%) of mechanical license fees and ten percent (10%) of synchronization license fees without first having obtained the consent of Publisher. No expenses other than those referred to above shall be charged to Publisher without the consent of Publisher. Administrator agrees to advance for the account of Publisher all sums required for the defraying of the costs and expenses with respect thereto.

5.   Advances made by Administrator pursuant to paragraphs 3 and 4 of this agreement, and any additional advances made by Administrator which Administrator agrees to advance to or for the account of Publisher when and if necessary, for the purpose of conducting the music business of Publisher, will be repaid to Administrator from the gross income received by or on

behalf of Publisher from all sources, after first deducting the Administration Fee.

6.   After deduction of its administration fee and all costs and expenses which it is permitted to charge against gross income pursuant to the terms of this agreement (including all advances properly made), Administrator shall pay or cause the payment to Publisher of the entire net income earned by or with respect to each musical composition presently in the Publisher's catalogue or which may during the term of this agreement be acquired by Publisher.

7.   Administrator agrees to render semi-annual financial statements prepared by a Certified Public Accountant to the stockholders of Publisher, no later than ninety (90) days following the termination of each semi-annual accounting period.

8.   This agreement shall commence on the date hereof and shall continue for   ( ) years. Thereafter, this agreement shall continue from year to year unless terminated upon ninety (90) days' written notice delivered by either party to the other.

9.   This agreement shall be construed in accordance with the laws of the State of New York applicable to agreements wholly to be performed therein. The invalidity or unenforceability of any provision hereof shall in no way affect the validity or enforceability of any other provisions of this agreement.

10.   This agreement contains the entire understanding between the parties hereto and all of its terms and conditions shall be binding upon and shall inure to the benefit of the respective parties hereto and their respective successors and assigns. No subsequent modification or waiver shall be valid or binding unless reduced to written form and signed by the party or parties sought to be charged.

Publisher

By: _____

Administrator

By: _____

CIRCULAR 18.1

U.S. COPYRIGHT OFFICE CIRCULAR R22 "HOW TO INVESTIGATE THE COPYRIGHT STATUS OF A WORK"

How to Investigate the Copyright Status of a Work

IN GENERAL

Methods of Approaching a Copyright Investigation

There are several ways to investigate whether a work is under copyright protection and, if so, the facts of the copyright. These are the main ones:

1. Examine a copy of the work (or, if the work is a sound recording, examine the disk, tape cartridge, or cassette in which the recorded sound is fixed, or the album cover, sleeve, or container in which the recording is sold) for such elements as a copyright notice, place and date of publication, author and publisher (for additional information, see p. 6, "Copyright Notice");

2. Make a search of the Copyright Office catalogs and other records; or

3. Have the Copyright Office make a search for you.

A Few Words of Caution About Copyright Investigations

Copyright investigations often involve more than one of these methods. Even if you follow all three approaches, the results may not be completely conclusive. Moreover, as explained in this circular, the changes brought about under the Copyright Act of 1976 and the Berne Convention Implementation Act of 1988 must be considered when investigating the copyright status of a work.

This circular offers some practical guidance on what to look for if you are making a copyright investigation. It is important to realize, however, that this circular contains only general information, and that there are a number of exceptions to the principles outlined here. In many cases it is important to consult a copyright attorney before reaching any conclusions regarding the copyright status of a work.

HOW TO SEARCH
COPYRIGHT OFFICE CATALOGS AND RECORDS

Catalog of Copyright Entries

The Copyright Office publishes the *Catalog of Copyright Entries (CCE)*, which is divided into parts according to the classes of works registered. The present categories include: "Nondramatic Literary Works," "Performing Arts," "Motion Pictures and Filmstrips," "Sound Recordings," "Serials and Periodicals," "Visual Arts," "Maps," and "Renewals." Effective with the Fourth Series, Volume 2, 1979 Catalogs, the CCE has been issued in microfiche form only; previously, each part of the *Catalog* was issued at regular intervals in book form. Each CCE segment covers all registrations made during a particular period of time. Renewals made for any class during a particular period can be found in Part 8, "Renewals."

Before 1978, the catalog parts reflected the classes that existed at that time. Renewals for a particular class are found in the back section of the catalog for the class of work renewed (for example, renewal registrations for music made in 1976 appear in the last section of the music catalog for 1976).

A number of libraries throughout the United States maintain copies of the *Catalog,* and this may provide a good starting point if you wish to make a search yourself. There are some cases, however, in which a search of the *Catalog* alone will not be sufficient to provide the needed information. For example:

- Since the *Catalog* does not include entries for assignments or other recorded documents, it cannot be used for searches involving the ownership of rights.

- There is usually a time lag of a year or more before the part of the **Catalog** covering a particular registration is published.

- The *Catalog* entry contains the essential facts concerning a registration, but it is not a verbatim transcript of the registration record.

Individual Searches of Copyright Records

The Copyright Office is located in the Library of Congress James Madison Memorial Building, 101 Independence Ave., S.E., Washington, D.C.

Most records of the Copyright Office are open to public inspection and searching from 8:30 a.m. to 5 p.m. Monday through Friday (except legal holidays). The various records freely available to the public include an extensive card catalog, an automated catalog containing records from 1978 forward, record books, and microfilm records of assignments and related documents. Other records, including correspondence files and deposit copies, are not open to the public for searching. However, they may be inspected upon request and payment of a $20-per hour search fee.

If you wish to do your own searching in the Copyright Office files open to the public, you will be given assistance in locating the records you need and in learning searching procedures. If the Copyright Office staff actually makes the search for you, a search fee must be charged. The search will not be done while you wait.

SEARCHING BY THE COPYRIGHT OFFICE

In General

Upon request, the Copyright Office staff will search its records at the statutory rate of $20 for each hour or fraction of an hour consumed. Based on the information you furnish, we will provide an estimate of the total search fee. If you decide to have the Office staff conduct the search, you should send the estimated amount with your request. The Office will then proceed with the search and send you a typewritten report or, if you prefer, an oral report by telephone. If you request an oral report, please provide a telephone number where you can be reached during normal business hours (8:30 a.m.-5 p.m. Eastern time).

Search reports can be certified on request, for an extra fee of $20. Certified searches are most frequently requested to meet the evidentiary requirements of litigation.

Your request, and any other correspondence, should be addressed to:

Reference and Bibliography Section, LM-451
Copyright Office
Library of Congress Washington, D.C. 20559
(202) 707-6850

What the Fee Does Not Cover

Note that the search fee does *not* include the cost of additional certificates, photocopies of deposits, or copies of other Office records. For information concerning these services, request Circular 6.

Information Needed

The more detailed information you can furnish with your request, the less time-consuming and expensive the search will be. Please provide as much of the following information as possible:

• The title of the work, with any possible variants;

• The names of the authors, including possible pseudonyms;

• The name of the probable copyright owner, which may be the publisher or producer;

• The approximate year when the work was published or registered;

• The type of work involved (book, play, musical composition, sound recording, photograph, etc.);

- For a work originally published as a part of a periodical or collection, the title of that publication and any other information, such as the volume or issue number, to help identify it;

- Motion pictures are often based on other works such as books or serialized contributions to periodicals or other composite works. If you desire a search for an underlying work or for music from a motion picture, you must specifically request such a search. You must also identify the underlying works and music and furnish the specific titles, authors, and approximate dates of these works; and

- The registration number or any other copyright data.

Searches Involving Assignments and Other Documents Affecting Copyright Ownership

The Copyright Office staff will also, for the standard hourly search fee, search its indexes covering the records of assignments and other recorded documents concerning ownership of copyrights. The reports of searches in these cases will state the facts shown in the Office's indexes of the recorded documents, but will offer no interpretation of the content of the documents or their legal effect.

LIMITATIONS ON SEARCHES

In determining whether or not to have a search made, you should keep the following points in mind:

No Special Lists

The Copyright Office does not maintain any listings of works by subject, or any lists of works that are in the public domain.

Contributions

Individual works, such as stories, poems, articles, or musical compositions that were published as contributions to a copyrighted periodical or collection, are usually not listed separately by title in our records.

No Comparisons

The Copyright Office does not search or compare copies of works to determine questions of possible infringement or to determine how much two or more versions of a work have in common.

Titles and Names Not Copyrightable

Copyright does not protect names and titles, and our records list many different works identified by the same or similar titles. Some brand names, trade names, slogans, and phrases may be entitled to protection under the general rules of law relating to unfair competition, or to registration under the provisions of the trademark laws. Questions about the trademark laws should be addressed to the Commissioner of Patents and Trademarks, Washington, D.C. 20231. Possible protection of names and titles under common law principles of unfair competition is a question of state law.

No Legal Advice

The Copyright Office cannot express any opinion as to the legal significance or effect of the facts included in a search report.

SOME WORDS OF CAUTION

Searches Not Always Conclusive

Searches of the Copyright Office catalogs and records are useful in helping to determine the copyright status of a work, but they cannot be regarded as conclusive in all cases. The complete absence of any information about a work in the office records does not mean that the work is unprotected. The following are examples of cases in which information about a particular work may be incomplete or lacking entirely in the Copyright Office:

- Before 1978, unpublished works were entitled to protection at common law without the need of registration.

- Works published with notice prior to 1978 may be registered at **any** time within the first 28-year term; to obtain renewal protection, however, the claimant must register and renew such work by the end of the 28th year.

- For works that came under copyright protection after 1978, registration may be made at any time during the term of protection; it is not generally required as a condition of copyright protection (there are, however, certain definite advantages to registration; please call or write for Circular 1, "Copyright Basics").

- Since searches are ordinarily limited to registrations that have already been cataloged, a search report may not cover recent registrations for which catalog records are not yet available.

- The information in the search request may not have been complete or specific enough to identify the work.

- The work may have been registered under a different title or as part of a larger work.

Protection in Foreign Countries

Even if you conclude that a work is in the public domain in the United States, this does not necessarily mean that you are free to use it in other countries. Every nation has its own laws governing the length and scope of copyright protection, and these are applicable to uses of the work within that nation's borders. Thus, the expiration or loss of copyright protection in the United States may still leave the work fully protected against unauthorized use in other countries.

OTHER CIRCULARS

For further information, request Circulars 15, "Renewal of Copyright,"15a. "Duration of Copyright,"15t, "Extension of Copyright Terms," and 6, "Obtaining Copies of Copyright Office Records and Deposits," from:

Publications Section, LM-455
Copyright Office Library of Congress
Washington, D.C. 20559
OR

You may call (202) 707-9100 at any time, day or night, to leave a request for forms or circulars as a recorded message on the Forms HOTLINE. Requests made on the HOTLINE number are filled and mailed promptly.

IMPACT OF COPYRIGHT ACT ON COPYRIGHT INVESTIGATIONS

On October 19, 1976, the President signed into law a complete revision of the copyright law of the United States (Title 17 of the United States Code). Most provisions of this statute came into force on January 1,1978, superseding the previous copyright act of 1909, and made significant changes in the copyright law. Other significant changes resulted from the Berne Convention Implementation Act of 1988, which took effect March 1, 1989. If you need more information about the provisions of either law, write or call the Copyright Office. For information about the Berne Law, request Circular 93. Printed information about the 1976 law is available only through the Superintendent of Documents, U.S. Government Printing Office, Washington, D.C. 20402-9325 for $3.75: request stock number 030-002-00168-3. You may order by telephone from the order desk by calling (202) 783-3238. To order via fax machine please call (202) 275-0019.

For copyright investigations, the following are some of the main points to consider about the impact of the Copyright Act of 1976 and the Berne Convention Implementation Act of 1988:

A Changed System of Copyright Formalities

Some of the most sweeping changes under the 1976 Act involve copyright formalities; that is, the procedural requirements for securing and maintaining full copyright protection. The old system of formalities involved copyright notice, deposit and registration, recordation of transfers and licenses of copyright ownership, and United States manufacture, among other things. In general, while retaining formalities, the 1976 law reduced the chances of mistakes, softened the consequences of errors and omissions, and allowed for the correction of errors.

The Berne Convention Implementation Act of 1988 reduced formalities, most notably making the addition of the previously mandatory copyright notice optional. It should be noted that the amended notice requirements are not retroactive.

Automatic Copyright

Under the present copyright law, copyright exists in original works of authorship created and fixed in any tangible medium of expression, now known or later developed, from which they can be perceived, reproduced, or otherwise communicated, either directly, or indirectly with the aid of a machine or device. In other words, copyright is an incident of creative authorship not dependent on statutory formalities. Thus, registration with the Copyright Office generally is not required, but there are certain advantages that arise from a timely registration. For further information on the advantages of registration, write or call the Copyright Office and request Circular 1, "Copyright Basics."

Copyright Notice

Both the 1909 and the 1976 copyright acts require a notice of copyright on published works. For most works, a copyright notice consists of the symbol ©, the word "Copyright," or the abbreviation "Copr. ," together with the name of the owner of copyright and the year of first publication; for example :" ©Joan Crane 1987" or "Copyright 1987 by Abraham Adams."

For sound recordings published on or after February 15, 1972, a copyright notice might read" ℗1987 XYZ Records, Inc." (See page 8 for more information about sound recordings.)

For mask works a copyright notice might read" Ⓜ SDR Industries." (Request Circular 100 for more information.)

The 1976 law prescribes that all visually perceptible published copies of a work, or published phonerecords of a sound recording, shall bear a proper copyright notice. This applies to such works published before March 1,1989. After March 1,1989, notice of copyright on these works is optional. Adding the notice, however, is strongly encouraged and, if litigation involving the copyright occurs, certain advantages exist for adding the notice.

The requirement for the notice under the 1976 law applied equally whether the work was published in the United States or elsewhere by authority of the copyright owner. Compliance with the statutory notice requirements was the responsibility of the copyright owner. Unauthorized publication without the copyright notice, or with a defective notice, does not affect the validity of the copyright in the work.

Advance permission from, or registration with, the Copyright Office is not required before placing a copyright notice on copies of the work, or on phonorecords of a sound recording. Moreover, for works first published on or after January 1,1978 through February 28, 1989, omission of the required notice, or use of a defective notice, did not result in forfeiture or outright loss of copyright protection. Certain omissions of, or defects in the notice of copyright, however, may lead to loss of copyright protection if certain steps are not taken to correct or cure the omissions or defects. The Copyright Office has issued a final regulation (37 CFR 201.20) which suggests various acceptable positions for the notice of copyright. For further information, write to the Copyright Office and request Circular 3,"Copyright Notice".

Works Already in the Public Domain

Neither the 1976 Act nor the Berne Convention Implementation Act of 1988 restores protection to works that fell into the public domain before the passage of the laws. If copyright in a particular work has been lost, the work is permanently in the public domain in this country, and neither law will revive protection. Under the copyright law in effect prior to January 1, 1978, copyright could be lost in several situations: the most common were publication without the required copyright notice, expiration of the first 28-year copyright term without renewal, or final expiration of the second copyright term.

Scope of Exclusive Rights Under Copyright

The present law has changed and enlarged in some cases, the scope of the copyright owner's rights as against users of a work. The new rights apply to all uses of a work subject to protection by copyright after January 1, 1978, regardless of when the work was created.

DURATION OF COPYRIGHT PROTECTION

Works Originally Copyrighted On or After January 1, 1978

A work that is created and fixed in tangible form for the first time on or after January 1,1978, is automatically protected from the moment of its creation, and is ordinarily given a term enduring for the author's life, plus an additional 50 years after the author's death. In the case of "a joint work prepared by two or more authors who did not work for hire," the term lasts for 50 years after the last surviving author's death. For works made for hire, and for anonymous and pseudonymous works (unless the author's identity is revealed in the Copyright Office records), the duration of copyright will be 75 years from publication or 100 years from creation, whichever is less.

Works created before the 1976 law came into effect, but neither published nor registered for copyright before January 1, 1978, have been automatically brought under the statute and are now given Federal copyright protection. The duration of copyright in these works will generally be computed in the same way as for new works: the life-plus-50 or 75/100-year terms will apply. However, all works in this category are guaranteed at least 25 years of statutory protection.

Works Copyrighted Before January 1, 1978

Under the law in effect before 1978, copyright was secured either on the date a work was published with notice of copyright, or on the date of registration if the work was registered in unpublished form. In either case, copyright endured for a first term of 28 years from the date on which it was secured. During the last (28th) year of the first term, the copyright was eligible for renewal. The new copyright law has extended the renewal term from 28 to 47 years for copyrights in existence on January 1, 1978. However, the copyright still must be renewed in the 28th calendar year to receive the 47-year period of added protection. For more detailed information on the copyright term, write or call the Copyright Office and request Circulars 15a and 15t.

WORKS FIRST PUBLISHED BEFORE 1978: THE COPYRIGHT NOTICE

General Information About the Copyright Notice

In investigating the copyright status of works first published before January 1, 1978, the most important thing to look for is the notice of copyright. As a general rule under the previous law, copyright protection was lost permanently if the notice was omitted from the first authorized published edition of a work, or if it appeared in the wrong form or position. The form and position of the copyright notice for various types of works were specified in the copyright statute. Some courts were liberal in overlooking relatively minor departures from the statutory requirements, but a basic failure to comply with the notice provisions forfeited copyright protection and put the work into the public domain in this country.

Absence of Copyright Notice

For works first published before 1978, the complete absence of a copyright notice from a published copy generally indicates that the work is not protected by copyright. For works first published before March 1, 1989, the copyright notice is mandatory. Some works may contain a notice, others may not. The absence of a notice in March 1, 1989 and later works does not necessarily indicate that the work is in the public domain.

Unpublished Works. No notice of copyright was required on the copies of any unpublished work. The concept of "publication" is very technical, and it was possible for a number of copies lacking a copyright notice to be reproduced and distributed without affecting copyright protection.

Foreign Editions. Under certain circumstances, the law exempted copies of a copyrighted work from the notice requirements if they were first published outside the United States. Some copies of these foreign editions could find their way into the United States without impairing the copyright.

Accidental Omission. The 1909 statute preserved copyright protection if the notice was omitted by accident or mistake from a "particular copy or copies."

Unauthorized Publication. A valid copyright was not secured if someone deleted the notice and/or published the work without authorization from the copyright owner.

Sound Recordings. Reproductions of sound recordings usually contain two different types of creative works: the underlying musical. dramatic, or literary work that is being performed or read, and the fixation of the actual sounds embodying the performance or reading. For protection of the underlying musical or literary work embodied in a recording, it is not necessary that a copyright notice covering this material appear on the phonograph records or tapes in which the recording is reproduced. As noted above, a special notice is required for protection of the recording of a series of musical, spoken, or other sounds which were fixed on or after February 15, 1972. Sound recordings fixed before February 15, 1972, are not eligible for Federal copyright protection. The Sound Recording Act of 1971, the present copyright law, and the Berne Convention Implementation Act of 1988 cannot be applied or be construed to provide any retroactive protection for sound recordings fixed before that date. Such works, however, may be protected by various state laws or doctrines of common law.

The Date in the Copyright Notice

If you find a copyright notice, the date it contains may be important in determining the copyright status of the work. In general, the notice on works published before 1978 must include the year in which copyright was secured by publication (or, if the work was first registered for copyright in unpublished form, the year in which registration was made). There are two main exceptions to this rule.

- For pictorial, graphic, or sculptural works (Classes F through K under the 1909 law) the law permitted omission of the year date in the notice.

- For "new versions" of previously published or copyrighted works, the notice was not usually required to include more than the year of first publication of the new version itself. This is explained further under "Derivative Works" below.

The year in the notice usually (though not always)indicated when the copyright began. It is therefore significant in determining whether a copyright is still in effect; or, if the copyright has not yet run its course, the year date will help in deciding when the copyright is scheduled to expire. For further information about the duration of copyright, request Circular 15a.

In evaluating the meaning of the date in a notice, you should keep the following points in mind:

WORKS PUBLISHED AND COPYRIGHTED BEFORE JANUARY 1. 1978: A work published before January 1, 1978, and copyrighted within the past 75 years may still be protected by copyright in the United States if a valid renewal registration was made during the 28th year of the first term of the copyright. If renewed, and if still valid under the other provisions of the law, the copyright will expire 75 years from the end of the year in which it was first secured.

Therefore. the United States copyright in any work published or copyrighted more than 75 years ago (75 years from January 1st in the present year) has expired by operation of law, and the work has permanently fallen into the public domain in the United States. For example, on January 1, 1991, copyright in works first published or copyrighted before January 1, 1916, will have expired; on January 1, 1992, copyright in works first published or copyrighted before January 1,1917, will have expired.

WORKS FIRST PUBLISHED OR COPYRIGHTED BETWEEN JANUARY 1, 1916, AND DECEMBER 31, 1949, BUT NOT RENEWED: If a work was first published or copyrighted between January 1, 1916, and December 31, 1949, it is important to determine whether the copyright was renewed during the last (28th) year of the first term of the copyright. This can be done by searching the Copyright Office records or catalogs, as explained above. If no renewal registration was made, copyright protection expired permanently on the 28th anniversary of the date it was first secured.

WORKS FIRST PUBLISHED OR COPYRIGHTED BETWEEN JANUARY 1, 1916, AND DECEMBER 31, 1949, AND REGISTERED FOR RENEWAL: When a valid renewal registration was made and copyright in the work was in its second term on December 31,1977, the renewal copyright term was extended under the present act to 47 years. In these cases, copyright will last for a total of 75 years from the end of the year in which copyright was originally secured. Example: Copyright in a work first published in 1919, and renewed in 1947, will expire on December 31 , 1994.

WORKS FIRST PUBLISHED OR COPYRIGHTED BETWEEN JANUARY 1, 1950, AND DECEMBER 31,1977: If a work was in its first 28-year term of copyright protection on January 1, 1978, it must be renewed in a timely fashion to secure the maximum term of copyright protection provided by the present copyright law. If renewal registration is made during the 28th calendar year of its first term, copyright will endure for 75 years from the end of the year copyright was originally secured. If not renewed, the copyright expires at the end of its 28th calendar year.

UNPUBLISHED, UNREGISTERED WORKS: Before 1978, if a work had neither been "published" in the legal sense nor registered in the Copyright Office, it was subject to perpetual protection under the common law. On January 1, 1978, all works of this kind, subject to protection by copyright, were automatically brought under the Federal copyright statute. The duration of these Federal copyrights will vary, but none of them will expire before December 31,2002.

Derivative Works

In examining a copy (or a record, disk, or tape) for copyright information, it is important to determine whether that particular version of the work is an original edition of the work or a "new version." New versions include musical arrangements, adaptations, revised or newly edited editions, translations, dramatizations, abridgments, compilations, and works republished with new matter added. The law provides that derivative works are independently copyrightable and that the copyright in such a work does not affect or extend the protection, if any, in the underlying work. Under the 1909 law, courts have also held that the notice of copyright on a derivative work ordinarily need not include the dates or other information pertaining to the earlier works incorporated in it. This principle is specifically preserved in the present copyright law.

Thus, if the copy (or the record, disk, or tape) constitutes a derivative version of the work, these points should be kept in mind:

- The date in the copyright notice is not necessarily an indication of when copyright in all of the material in the work will expire. Some of the material may already be in the public domain, and some parts of the work may expire sooner than others.

- Even if some of the material in the derivative work is in the public domain and free for use, this does not mean that the "new" material added to it can be used without permission from the owner of copyright in the derivative work. It may be necessary to compare editions to determine what is free to use and what is not.

- Ownership of rights in the material included in a derivative work and in the preexisting work upon which it may be based may differ, and permission obtained from the owners of certain parts of the work may not authorize the use of other parts.

The Name in the Copyright Notice

Under the copyright statute in effect before 1978, the notice was required to include "the name of the copyright proprietor." The present act requires that the notice include "the name of the owner of copyright in the work, or an abbreviation by which the name can be recognized, or a generally known alternative designation of the owner." The name in the notice (sometimes in combination with the other statements on the copy, record, disk, tape, container, or label) often gives persons wishing to use the work the information needed to identify the owner from whom licenses or permission can be sought. In other cases, the name provides a starting point for a search in the Copyright Office records or catalogs, as explained at the beginning in this circular.

In the case of works published before 1978, copyright registration is made in the name of the individual person or the entity identified as the copyright owner in the notice. For works published after 1978, registration is made in the name of the person or entity owning all the rights on the date the registration is made. This may or may not be the name appearing in the notice. In addition to its records of copyright registration, the Copyright Office maintains extensive records of assignments, exclusive licenses, and other documents dealing with copyright ownership.

Ad Interim

Ad interim copyright was a special short-term copyright that applied to certain books and periodicals in the English language, first manufactured and published outside the United States. It was a partial exception to the manufacturing requirements of the previous United States copyright law. Its purpose was to secure temporary United States protection for a work, pending the manufacture of an edition in the United States. The ad interim requirements changed several times over the years, and were subject to a number of exceptions and qualifications.

The manufacturing provisions of the copyright act expired on July 1,1986, and are no longer a part of the copyright law. The transitional and supplementary provisions of the act provide that for any work in which ad interim copyright was subsisting or capable of being secured on December 31, 1977, copyright protection would be extended for a term compatible with the other works in which copyright was subsisting on the effective date of the new act. Consequently, if the work was first published on or after July 1, 1977, and was eligible for ad interim copyright protection, the provisions of the present copyright act will be applicable to the protection of these works. Anyone investigating the copyright status of an English-language book or periodical first published outside the United States before July 1,1977, should check carefully to determine:

- Whether the manufacturing requirements were applicable to the work; and

- If so, whether the ad interim requirements were met.

CHAPTER 19

TYPICAL LICENSE FEES

SUMMARY

PRINT LICENSE FEES

1. Standard Publishing Agreement Between Songwriter and Music Publisher
2. Agreement Between Music Publisher and Independent Print Publisher
3. Printing of Lyrics

MECHANICAL LICENSE FEES

ELECTRICAL TRANSCRIPTION FEES

SYNCHRONIZATION FEES

1. Television Synchronization License Fees
2. Theatrical Motion Picture Synchronization License Fees
3. Non-Theatrical Film Synchronization License Fees
4. Synchronization License for Music Videos

VIDEOGRAM FEES

1. For Motion Picture Videograms
2. For Music Videos
3. Video Yearbooks
4. Corporate Video Synchronization License

COMMERCIAL ADVERTISING LICENSE FEES

1. Television Commercial Synchronization License
2. Radio Commercial Electrical Transcription License
3. Print Advertising

MUSIC BOXES AND COMMERCIAL PRODUCT LICENSE FEES

COMPUTER SOFTWARE, MULTI-MEDIA, AND NEW MEDIA PRODUCT FEES

1. Video Arcade Games

PERFORMANCE LICENSE FEES

LIVING STAGE PERFORMANCE LICENSE FEES

SAMPLING LICENSE FEES

1. Music
2. Sound Recordings Index

MIDI SOFTWARE FEES

CIRCULARS

CIRCULAR 19.1   The ASCAP Survey and Your Royalties

CHAPTER **19**

TYPICAL LICENSE FEES

Having explored the various types of licenses by which permission to use music is granted and the considerations involved in negotiating the terms of those licenses, we need only consider the license fees that are typically charged for the various uses of music. This chapter provides some of the ranges within which license fees have tended to fall at about the time this book was published in the Fall of 1992.

It should be noted that, in many cases, the fee ranges set forth below are based upon some broad generalizations and assumptions. Consequently, these fees do not take into consideration some of the key considerations discussed in this book, including the countervailing factors of (i) the importance of the song in relation to its intended use and (ii) the availability of close substitutes for the song. For example, if a song is needed to merely establish the setting of a scene in the 1940's, the song *As Time Goes By* from the motion picture *Casablanca* might fulfill that need quite well. However, songs such as *Boogie Woogie Bugle Boy* and *I'll Be with You in Apple Blossom Time* (made popular by the Andrews Sisters) may serve that purpose just as well. If the licensor of *As Time Goes By* were to quote too high a license fee, the producer may choose one of the other ready alternatives. If, on the other hand, the song is required for a movie such as Woody Allen's *Play It Again, Sam,* virtually no close substitutes will do, and it is more likely a producer would expect to pay a license fee in the high end of the range, if not above the range, for the use of that song.

Nevertheless, despite the generalizations made and the likelihood that these ranges will, *As Time Goes By,* become obsolescent, the fees stated in this chapter may still be useful for the information they provide about relative values—that is, the fees as they relate in proportion to each other—which is not likely to change significantly over time.

PRINT LICENSE FEES

Presently, publishers are using the following formula for sheet music, folios and other printed items such as orchestrations for dance orchestras, brass bands and vocal arrangements:

1. Standard Publishing Agreement Between Songwriter and Music Publisher

Music publisher typically agrees to pay the songwriter the following amounts:

1. Sheet music: 6 to 10 cents per copy, with the median average being 8 cents per copy.

Where the writer has an unusual amount of leverage, he or she may be able to persuade the publisher to give 10 to 15% percent of publisher's net wholesale price or net revenues from sheet music; the cents-per-copy structure for sheet music has long been considered a "sacred cow" and exceptions are rarely made. Many old publishing contracts provide for rates as low as 2 or 3 cents per copy; the days of 50-cent sheet music went out with high button shoes, and, perhaps in this era of inflation, the percentage royalty structure is more appropriate.

2. Arrangements: 10 to 15 percent of the established wholesale selling price of the item, with 12 1/2 percent being quite common.

3. Folios: 10 to 15 percent of the established wholesale selling price of the item, with 12 1/2 percent being quite common, prorated over the number of copyrighted songs in the folio.

4. Educational and Concert Editions: 10 percent of the established wholesale selling price of the item.

2. Agreement Between Music Publisher and Independent Print Publisher

Print publisher typically agrees to pay the music publisher the following amounts:

1. Sheet music: 35 to 50 cents per copy.

2. Folios: 10% to 15% of suggested retail price prorated over all copyrighted songs used in the folio.

3. Personality Folio: 10% to 15% of suggested retail price prorated over all copyrighted songs used in the folio, plus additional 2 1/2% to

5% for the right to publish photograph, likeness, and biographical material about the artist. Advance against royalty: $150-200.

4. Educational and Concert Editions: 10% of suggested retail price.

3. Printing of Lyrics

1. Books: $25 to $150, plus two copies of the book upon publication, to quote a lyric from a copyrighted song in a novel, textbook, or other works of fiction or non-fiction.

2. Magazine advertising: $2,500 to $5,000 per year.

3. Greeting Cards: 5% of the retail selling price of the item.

4. Record albums: 2 cents per lyric per copy.

5. Promotional albums: Free.

6. Lyric Magazines: $100 per song for 1 year; additional $75 if song reaches Hot 100 song listing in Billboard or Cash Box.

MECHANICAL LICENSE FEES

1. Statutory Rate: As of January 1, 1992, the statutory rate is 6 1/4 cents for recordings up to five minutes in length and, if over 5 minutes, 1.2 cents per minute of playing time. The statutory rate will be adjusted every two years through 1996 according to changes in the Consumer Price Index.

2. Special Rates: 50% to 75% of statutory for budget line records.

ELECTRICAL TRANSCRIPTION FEES

1. Syndicated radio programs: $50 per song, per copy; does not include performance license.

2. Radio Transcriptions (for programming introductions, themes, background music and breaks, etc.): Free. These are usually distributed free of charge to encourage radio stations to use them and thereby generate lucrative performance fees.

3. Background Music Services:

A. Muzak: $12.50 per composition for 3 years; $5.00 for one year; performance license obtained from performance rights society.
B. 3M: statutory rate for mechanical license; 3 cents per copy for performance license.

SYNCHRONIZATION FEES

1. Television Synchronization License Fees

The typical provisions for the use of a song in a television program is as follows:

Term	Territory	Background	Foreground	Special
5 year	worldwide	$750-1,000	$1,000-1,200	$1,500-2,000
life of copyrt	worldwide	$2,000-3,000	$3,000-4,000	$5,000-7,500

The music copyright owner would normally reduce the above fees by 25% if the producer agrees to use the song in every episode of a television series (thereby increasing performance fees significantly).

Use of the title of the song as the title of the television series would warrant an additional $2,500 per episode and for the use of the title of the song as the title of a particular episode of a television program, $1,500 over the above fees. Similarly, use of the music over the closing credits of a television program would merit an additional fee of $500 to $750.

The above fees do not include an additional fee or royalty payable for the distribution of the television program in videocassettes or laser discs for the home video market. See the section regarding Videogram License Fees, below.

2. Theatrical Motion Picture Synchronization License Fees

The typical provisions for the use of a song in a theatrical motion picture are as follows:

Term	Territory	Background	Foreground	Special
life of copyright	worldwide	$12,500-15,000	$20,000-25,000	$25,000-30,000

Use of the title of the song as the title of the motion picture should bring an additional $50,000 to $75,000 over the above fees. Similarly, use of the music over the opening or closing credits would merit an additional fee of $25,000 to $35,000.

The above fees do not include an additional fee or royalty payable for the distribution of the motion picture in videocassettes or laser discs for the home video market. See the section regarding Videogram License Fees, below.

The above fees for theatrical motion picture synchronization includes the license component for performances in movie theaters in the United States. Unless the license specifies the synchronization component and performance component separately, the music publisher usually considers that 1/2 of the stated fee is allocated to performance rights. Public performances in theaters in other countries are subject to local performance fees collected by local performance rights societies.

3. Non-Theatrical Film Synchronization License Fees

The fee for the use of a musical composition in a corporate video to be used for in-house training or trade show convention use ranges from $1,000 to $1,500. The term is generally one to three years.

4. Synchronization License for Music Videos

When a popular song video is to be used on television purely for promotional purposes, a handling fee of $25 is charged. However, you can expect these fees to increase as the broadcast of these videos are becoming less promotional and more for the purpose of pure entertainment. The license does not include the *performance* of the song on television or the distribution of the video in videocassettes or laser disks for the home video market.

VIDEOGRAM FEES

1. For Motion Picture Videograms

The average per unit royalty for each song used in a videocassette, laser disc or other home video device is currently between 7 to 10 cents. The actual per unit royalty would vary according to the considerations set forth above, such as whether the use is background, foreground, or special. An advance against royalties of about $250 is normally requested.

Recently, it has been the practice of motion picture producers to ask for terms that would allow them to buy-out the videogram license for a one-time flat fee payment. While music publishers have resisted this, a producer might typically pay, in addition to the standard synchronization license fee, a flat fee videogram license buy-out of $5,000 to $10,000. Since no public performance fees are collected on performances in the home, publishers will normally make every effort to avoid offering a buy-out provision and may suggest instead an advance that would cover 20,000 or more units, which should be more than sufficient to cover a normal home video release of the motion picture.

With respect to the actual royalty rates, though some uses will warrant better terms than others, the range of rates is generally a narrow one.

2. For Music Videos

No standards have yet emerged in the licensing of music videos for home video distribution. Until that time, synchronization licenses will continue to provide a short-term (perhaps two years) license for a flat fee with additional negotiations at the end of the term.

3. Video Yearbooks

There is a $50 charge for high school; $100 for college, per song.

4. Corporate Videogram Synchronization License

There is a fixing fee of $500; royalty of $.10 per unit; buy-out of royalty about $5,000. Term can be up to five years.

COMMERCIAL ADVERTISING LICENSE FEES

1. Television Commercial Synchronization License

It is difficult to describe what a "typical" fee would be for the use of a song in a television commercial, because terms and conditions for such licenses vary widely. However, with the aid of a few assumptions, a baseline can be formed that might assist in determining the appropriate license fee for other works and uses under other circumstances.

Let us assume you are licensing the standard song, *As Time Goes By*, the song made famous by the classic motion picture, *Casablanca*. The fee for a non-exclusive license for the use of the song for one year in a television commercial for network broadcast in the United States and Canada might be $150,000. If the use were limited to a particular average-sized state, the fee might be $15,000. If the use were limited to a major metropolitan area, such as New York City or Southern California, the fee might be $12,500, and for other medium-sized to large cities, the fee might be $5,000 to $7,500. Use in smaller cities and towns are generally requested for a shorter period of time; in these cases, the fee might be $1,000 per week, but you must be careful that the town is not within the broadcast range of a major city, in which case a higher fee may be warranted.

When licenses of a duration shorter than one year are requested, the above fees can be prorated. For example, during a recent economic recession, advertising agencies began requesting for their clients licenses of six months in length. The quote for such a license may be 60% of what you would normally charge for the same license of one year duration. It is important to limit the duration of these licenses to one year or less. A song that becomes too closely associated with a nationally advertised product could lose its value as a commercial vehicle for other products. If an advertiser wants to continue to use the song for a long term, you can better evaluate what you need to charge by giving yourself an opportunity to reevaluate the fee each year. You lose this flexibility by giving longer term licenses, such as for five or more years. If an advertiser insists on a longer term license, consider providing an option to renew, upon which an additional license fee is to be paid. For the reason just mentioned, you should require a premium for the option itself and you should try to limit the renewal to one option year.

When advertisers request exclusivity, the better policy is to avoid providing it altogether. Nevertheless, if the circumstances require it, and you can be careful to narrowly define the scope of the exclusivity as suggested in Chapter 12, you can demand a premium of as much as 100% of the normal fee for the license. Remember that if you provide exclusivity to a local advertiser, you may have restricted your ability to enter into a more lucrative nationwide license with an advertiser of a competing product. All exclusive licenses, of whatever duration, should be entered into with extreme care.

2. Radio Commercial Electrical Transcription License

Normal nation-wide radio license for one-year term should cost between $35,000 to $50,000.

Short term regional radio broadcasts, not within the broadcast range of major cities, would be $500 per week.

3. Print Advertising

On occasion, an advertising agency, on behalf of its client, would request a quote for the use of a lyric to promote its client's product in magazine and newspaper advertisements. The typical fee for such use in an advertisement would be $5,000 to $10,000, for a term of one year.

MUSIC BOXES AND COMMERCIAL PRODUCT LICENSE FEES

Royalty: 5% of the retail selling price per unit.
Advance: $100-$2,000.
Note: A licensee may take the position that the fee should be governed by the compulsory license provision, because the recordings are not accompanied by an audiovisual work. The statutory rate is likely to be significantly less than a percentage of the retail price. However, most publishers will insist upon some percentage of the suggested retail selling price of the item, and, as a practical matter, the manufacturer can either accept the publisher's terms or attempt to obtain a compulsory license under the copyright statute; however, the administrative burdens of complying with the compulsory license provision may outweigh its advantages and manufacturers often accept the publisher's terms.

COMPUTER SOFTWARE, MULTI-MEDIA, AND NEW MEDIA PRODUCT FEES

Royalty: 5% of the retail selling price per unit.

Proration: When more than one song is used in a particular product, the fee should be pro-rated among all the copyrighted songs, and copyrighted arrangements of public domain songs, used.

Advance: $100-$2,000.

1. Video Arcade Games

For large video arcade games retailing from $1000 to $3000 per unit, a fee of 1/2% to 1% of the retail selling price might be considered. Publisher might accept a maximum per unit royalty of $10 or $15 per unit. Performance rights are not included and it is the responsibility of the arcade to get appropriate performance rights from ASCAP and BMI.

PERFORMANCE LICENSE FEES

Performance license rate schedules may be obtained directly from the performance rights societies:

American Society of Composers, Authors & Publishers (ASCAP)
1 Lincoln Plaza
New York, New York 10023
Phone: 212-595-3050
Fax: 212-724-9064

Broadcast Music, Inc. (BMI)
320 West 57th Street
New York, New York 10019
Phone: 212-586-2000
Fax: 212-246-2163

SESAC, Inc.
156 West 56th St.
New York, NY, 10019
Phone: 212-586-3450
Fax: 212-397-4682

LIVING STAGE PERFORMANCE LICENSE FEES

Fees for a performance of a song in a "revue" or regular Broadway-type show would depend upon the strength of the use and size of the theater.

The royalty rate for a visual vocal performance in an Off-off Broadway theater (99 seats or less) could be $5 a performance.

Off Broadway theater (up to 500 seats) fees could range from $75 to $100 per week. For a major performance of a work over four or five minutes in duration, a special additional fee up to $250 might be in order.

On-Broadway, a good fee would be $150 per eight performance week per song or 5% gross receipts prorated among all copyrighted songs in the play.

Publishers licensing works for the living stage must remember they are not granting a grand performance license, which may only be obtained from the owners of the show.

SAMPLING LICENSE FEES

1. Music

Buy-outs: $1,000 to $5,000.
Mechanical: 10% to 50% of statutory.
Co-ownership: 25% to 50% interest.

2. Sound Recordings

Buy outs: $500 -$5000.
Royalties: 1/2 cent to 3 cents.

MIDI SOFTWARE FEES

Royalty Per Unit: 5% of Retail Selling Price.
Royalty Per Song: 50¢.
Advance: $250.

APPENDIX TO CHAPTER 19
TYPICAL LICENSE FEES

CIRCULARS

CIRCULAR 19.1   The ASCAP Survey and Your Royalties

CIRCULAR 19.1

THE ASCAP SURVEY AND YOUR ROYALTIES

OVERVIEW

ASCAP's survey and distribution system has as its goal the fair and sensible allocation of license fees to the Society's members and the members of foreign societies who license through ASCAP.

ASCAP currently licenses:

- about 900 local commercial television stations
- about 8,500 local commercial radio stations
- three national television networks
- 35 cable program services and the major cable system operators having the majority of cable subscribers
- about 300 non-commercial television broadcasters
- about 1,500 non-commercial radio broadcasters
- hundreds of background music services (including airlines) representing some 200,000 background/ foreground music users
- about 2,000 colleges and universities
- about 2,100 symphony orchestras and concert promoters
- tens of thousands of "general" licensees: bars, restaurants, hotels, ice and roller skating rinks, circuses, theme parks, and veterans and fraternal organizations.

We estimate that there are well over one billion ASCAP-licensed performances each year.

Following the collection of ASCAP's revenues, operating costs are deducted and the remainder is distributed. About 80¢ of every dollar we receive is paid out each year.

Revenues from each group of ASCAP licensees are segregated and distribution of royalties is made on the basis of performances by licensees within each group. Thus, local radio revenues are distributed on the basis of local radio performances; local television revenues on the basis of local television performances, and so on. One exception is in the "serious," or "standard," music field. ASCAP multiplies by five the license fees received for live serious concert performances to increase the fund from which composers and publishers of serious music are paid.

Every performance picked up in ASCAP's survey will generate a certain number of credits, the number varying with the medium in which the performance takes place (e.g., local radio, network television), the type of use (e.g., feature, theme, background, etc.), and, in the case of radio and television, the station weight of the station airing the performance. For network television performances the number of stations carrying the show also affects the credits generated by a performance. The length of the work is not a factor except in the case of background music (i.e., music used as underscoring in films and television programs), certain feature performances of less than 45 seconds on television, and performances of "serious" music, where the duration of a performance, and, in the case of live concerts, instrumentation also affect the number of credits a particular performance will generate.

The dollar value of a performance credit is determined by dividing the total number of ASCAP credits being processed into the total number of dollars available for distribution.

The following table illustrates the ASCAP credit values for the most recent 5-year period:

Survey Year	Publisher Credit Value
1990 (4Q89-3Q90)	$3.33
1989 (4Q88-3Q89)	$3.10
1988 (4Q87-3Q88)	$2.79
1987 (4Q86-3Q87)	$2.78
1986 (4Q85-3Q86)	$2.36

The ASCAP survey is the product of long experience and reflects the views of independent survey experts as well as the United States Government. Our survey is monitored by two Special Distribution Advisers, whose semi-annual reports to a United States District Court are also sent to the members.

The survey may be divided into two components: those performances counted on a census basis, and those included on a sample basis. We take a census, or full count, of all performances on network television and the Home Box Office (HBO) cable service, and of performances of serious music in concert and symphony halls. Also included on a census basis are certain background/foreground music services and a group of non-broadcast, non-concert licensees. ASCAP can do a complete count of the performances on these licensees because the universe to be sampled is relatively small and performance information relatively simple to process. For all other media, we rely on a sample of performances.

THE CENSUS

NETWORK TELEVISION

ASCAP is able to count all network television music performances because there are only three networks; program logs and cue sheets are provided to us by the networks and program producers; and the fees involved are substantial.

In addition to the logs and cue sheets, ASCAP makes audio and video tapes of network television performances to verify the accuracy of information furnished by the networks and program producers.

SYMPHONY AND CONCERT HALLS AND EDUCATIONAL INSTITUTIONS

The census operates here by means of programs submitted to us by symphony orchestras, promoters of serious music concerts, and colleges and universities submit. One exception to this census is for those performances in educational institutions where the artist is paid less than $1,500. These performances are included in the survey on a sample basis.

BACKGROUND/FOREGROUND MUSIC SERVICES

Customusic, Magnetronics, and Tape-Athon are all included on a census basis, using reports submitted to us by these services. ASCAPs survey of performances by Audio Environments, Inc. (AEI) captures a complete count of AEI foreground performances and a sample of AEI background performances. ASCAP has now doubed its sample of performances by two major users, MUZAK and airlines.

GENERAL LICENSEES

ASCAP conducts a census of performances on the two units of Disney on Ice, and the two units of the Ringling Brothers' Circus.

THE SAMPLE

ASCAP finds sampling performances necessary because it is not possible, as a practical and economic matter, to count each of the millions of music performances in the United States. Even if ASCAP could obtain data concerning all music performances, the cost of researching and processing that data would be so prohibitive that we would have little, if anything, left to distribute.

ASCAP's sample is *random, stratified,* and *disproportionate.* A *random* sample is scientific by definition. It is determined solely by mathematical probability and leaves no room for personal discretion. The randomness extends to the time periods of the day, and to the days of the year. Under this system, every performance has a chance of coming into the survey.

Our sample is *stratified* because licensees are classified into groups that have significant common characteristics. This enhances sampling precision. ASCAP's samples are stratified by media (*e.g.,* local radio, local television); by type of community (*e.g.,* metropolitan, rural); by major geographic regions (*e.g.*, New England, Middle Atlantic, Pacific); and by size of the licensee in terms of annual fees to ASCAP (*e.g.*, $1,000 to $10,000; $10,000 to $20,000 and so on).

Thus, rather than draw a random sample for local radio from the entire United States and Puerto Rico, we draw a random sample simultaneously from each of 432 "stratified cells." In other words, we might sample a radio station in a rural area in the $5,000 to $10,000 license fee range. At the same time, we might also be sampling a radio station in the metropolitan Chicago area in the $300,000 to $400,000 license fee range. A similar procedure is followed for the random sample of local TV stations.

Our sample is *disproportionate* because the depth of the sample varies with the amount of the fees paid by licensees within each stratified cell. A station which pays ASCAP $20,000 in license fees is sampled twice as much as a station which pays ASCAP only $10,000. The greater the license fees, the greater the sampling depth. All radio and television stations that pay $10,000 or more per year are included in the sample.

LOCAL RADIO

It is estimated that the local radio stations in the United States broadcast an average of 18 hours per day, or some 53 million hours per year. ASCAP samples 60,000 of these hours each year, including both commercial and college/university stations. This amount, considered statistically representative by our independent survey experts, was reviewed by the Bureau of the Census, U.S. Department of Commerce, and approved by the U.S. Department of Justice.

ASCAP obtains its performance information by taping local radio. Our system of identifying works by means of our taping procedures, has less than a 2% margin of error. Moreover, our taping is carried out with absolute confidentiality. Neither the stations, the ASCAP Board, nor ASCAP management have prior knowledge as to which stations are being taped. Because ASCAP relies on tape recordings of broadcasts, it employs a large staff of specialists in music identification to analyze the tapes and prepare lists of all works performed. Feature works which cannot be identified through the usual process are referred to a special group called "solfeggists" who maintain a file of such works according to the do-re-mi scale. This enables us to credit these performances when the works are identified subsequently.

The completed list of identified works, along with similar lists from other media, are the basic data used to determine royalty distributions.

SEARCHING BY THE COPYRIGHT OFFICE

There are some 900 local television stations in the United States. Our television sample consists of 30,000 hours of local programming. To determine what works are being performed, we use a combination of cue sheets, tapes and the various regional issues of *TV Guide*--a weekly publication containing comprehensive listings of all TV stations and programs in the country.

PUBLIC BROADCASTING SERVICE

We sample 1,530 hours of Public Television per year and 690 hours of National Public Radio. The procedures followed in conducting these surveys are similar to those followed in commercial broadcasting. Fewer hours are sampled because the fees paid are much lower than those paid by commercial broadcasters.

BACKGROUND/FOREGROUND
MUSIC SERVICES

ASCAP receives about 90% of its background/foreground music license fees from MUZAK and AEI. These significant users provide music performance information via computer file delivery compatible with ASCAP's computer system which enables ASCAP to efficiently process these performances.

As indicated above, there are other background music performances that are processed on a complete count (or census) basis.

The airlines provide copies of the program listings in their in-flight magazines.

Sums received from other, unsurveyed, background music licensees are distributed on the basis of feature performances on radio and television.

GENERAL
LICENSING

The majority of our general licensees are not surveyed. This is because surveying the tens of thousands of users would cost more than we could possibly collect. Therefore, following the advice of our independent survey experts, and with the exceptions noted above, we use feature performances on radio and TV as "proxies" for the distribution of the monies received from these users. We believe our extensive survey of radio and television performances fairly reflects the many kinds of music performed by our general licensees.

CABLE

When we speak of cable television we distinguish between "secondary transmissions" and cable originations. They are two different sources of music and two different surveys of performances. Secondary transmissions originate as over-the-air broadcasts that cable systems pick up and retransmit to their subscribers. They are licensed by virtue of a compulsory license provision of the Copyright Act that also sets the fee. The Copyright Royalty Tribunal determines how that fee is to be allocated among the various claimants (including non-music as well as music copyright proprietors). ASCAP's share of these fees is distributed based on a sample of performances by those local television stations which are re-transmitted by cable systems.

Cable originators are not subject to the compulsory license. Fees are arrived at by negotiation or by Court determination. At this time, virtually all program services and most cable systems are licensed by ASCAP but interim license fees set by the Court are being paid only by the services and not yet by the cable systems. Distributions are being made on a census basis for HBO and on a sample basis for the following: American Movie Classics, Arts & Entertainment, Black Entertainment Television, Bravo, Cinemax, CNN, CNN Headline News, Country Music Television, Discovery Channel, The Disney Channel, Family Channel, HBO, Lifetime, The Movie Channel, MTV, The Nashville Network, Nickelodeon, Playboy, Prism, Showtime, Turner Network Television, and USA Network.

Performances on all the foregoing cable program services appear on members' statements under the "Cable" heading.

Index